INTRODUCTION TO FOOD ENGINEERING

Second Edition

FOOD SCIENCE AND TECHNOLOGY

International Series

A complete list of the books in this series appears at the end of the volume.

INTRODUCTION TO
FOOD ENGINEERING

Second Edition

R. Paul Singh

*Department of Agricultural Engineering
and Department of Food Sciences & Technology
University of California
Davis, California*

Dennis R. Heldman

*Food Science / Engineering Unit
University of Missouri
Columbia, Missouri*

ACADEMIC PRESS, INC.

Harcourt Brace & Company

San Diego   New York   Boston

London   Sydney   Tokyo   Toronto

Copyright © 1993, 1984 by ACADEMIC PRESS, INC.
All Rights Reserved.
No part of this publication may be reproduced or transmitted in any form or by any means, electronic or mechanical, including photocopy, recording, or any information storage and retrieval system, without permission in writing from the publisher.

Academic Press, Inc.
1250 Sixth Avenue, San Diego, California 92101-4311

United Kingdom Edition published by
Academic Press Limited
24–28 Oval Road, London NW1 7DX

Library of Congress Cataloging-in-Publication Data

Introduction to food engineering, second edition / edited by R. Paul Singh,
   Dennis R. Heldman.
      p.   cm. –- (Food and science technology)
    Includes index.
    ISBN 0-12-646381-6
    1. Food industry and trade.   I. Singh, R. Paul.   II. Heldman,
Dennis R.   III. Series.
    TP370.P62   1993
    664–dc20   92-42884
                                                                CIP

PRINTED IN THE UNITED STATES OF AMERICA
93 94 95 96 97 98   M M   9 8 7 6 5 4 3 2 1

Contents

CHAPTER 2

Fluid Flow in Food Processing   42

CHAPTER 3

Energy for Food Processing   95

CHAPTER 4

Heat Transfer in Food Processing   129

CHAPTER 5

Thermal Processing   **225**

CHAPTER 6

Aseptic Processing and Packaging   **244**

CHAPTER 7

Refrigeration   259

About the Authors

When coauthors Dr. R. Paul Singh and Dr. Dennis R. Heldman last teamed up in 1984 to create the first edition of this text, they produced a popular and esteemed tome on the engineering concepts and unit operations used in food processing. Each author's expanded list of accomplishments since then is evidence that neither wanted to rest on past accomplishments. This new edition captures much of the work each has done during the last nine years, as well as much of their earlier research. Included here is a brief biography on Dr. Singh and Dr. Heldman.

Singh is a professor of food engineering at the University of California, Davis, where he regularly teaches undergraduate and graduate-level courses on topics in food engineering. In 1988 he received the International Award from the Institute of Food Technologists (IFT), reserved for a member of the Institute who "has made outstanding efforts to promote the international exchange of ideas in the field of food technology." He received the Young Educator Award from the American Society of Agricultural Engineers in 1986. IFT awarded him the Samuel Cate Prescott Award for Research in 1982. He has helped establish food engineering programs in Portugal, Indonesia, and India and has lectured extensively on food engineering topics in 30 different nations in Europe, Asia, and Latin America. Singh has authored, or coauthored, six books and published more than 150 technical papers. His research program at Davis addresses measurement of food properties and study of food processing operations using mathematical simulations.

Heldman is a professor of food process engineering at the University of Missouri, Columbia, where he provides leadership for the Foods, Feeds and Products Cluster of the Food for the Twenty-First Century Program. Before returning to a university post in 1992, Heldman held positions as principal with Weinberg Consulting Group Inc., executive vice president for the National Food Processors Association, and vice president of process research and development with Campbell Soup Company. Until 1984 he had devoted nearly 20 years to teaching and research in food engineering at Michigan State University. Heldman received the DFISA-ASAE Food

Engineering Award in 1981, the Distinguished Alumni Award from the College of Agriculture, Home Economics and Natural Resources at The Ohio State University in 1978, and the Young Researcher's Award from the American Society of Agricultural Engineers in 1974. Heldman is author, coauthor, or editor of ten books, bulletins, or handbooks as well as more than 125 journal articles. He is a Fellow of the Institute of Food Technologists (1981) and the American Society of Agricultural Engineers (1984).

Foreword

Food engineering is frequently the first course in which a food science student is exposed to quantitative examination of the interaction of physical and energy transfer operations with food materials. It is also frequently the first opportunity for the student to apply the "mathematics through calculus" that is required in food science programs. As a result of these two conditions, it is absolutely essential to have a textbook that introduces the concepts in food engineering and requires students to draw on their previous courses in physics and mathematics. A student's introduction to food engineering can be a most traumatic experience, especially if their food chemistry and food biology courses have not stressed quantitative relationships. Although students have had background courses requiring quantitative skills, including chemistry and food microbiology courses, they generally have not been required to exercise and apply those skills. In addition, students frequently enroll in food science because they imagine it to be a more qualitative, ethereal study of the goodness factors of food. They think that quantitative descriptions of momentum, heat, and mass transfer are things that engineers do and that should not concern food scientists. In recognized food science curricula, of course, nothing could be further from the truth.

The study of fluid flow, heat generation and transfer, thermal processing (including aseptic processing and packaging), freezing, evaporation, and drying constitute an introduction to food engineering. In this text, Drs. Singh and Heldman have relied on their many years of teaching food engineering to food science students to present food engineering concepts of these unit operations in a logical progression. Each chapter begins with a description of the application of the particular principle, followed by the quantitative relationships that define the processes. In this way, the student is introduced first to why the topic is important and then to its important elements. Given my 23 years of experience teaching food engineering, I believe this is an excellent way to introduce the student to food engineering.

Food engineering is an essential component of a first-class food science curriculum. It not only introduces the student to food engineering principles so that he or she can interact with colleagues on multimember teams in the food industry, but it also establishes the process of critical thinking and problem solving that is so much in vogue today. Food engineering can be used to reinforce the scientific principles of hypothesis generation and hypothesis testing. In addition, it forces us to think quantitatively about the relationships between cause and effect.

Finally, I want to congratulate Drs. Singh and Heldman on the excellent second edition of *Introduction to Food Engineering* that they have authored. I am extremely proud to have been asked to write the foreword for such an important introductory text. I can think of no one more eminently qualified than Drs. Singh and Heldman to author such a text. They have indeed made a valuable contribution to our profession of food science.

Daryl Lund
Executive Dean
Agriculture and Natural Resources
Rutgers, The State University of New Jersey

Preface

Food engineering has been evolving toward a separate and unique engineering discipline for over 30 years. During this same period of time, the subject of food engineering has become a critical component of the undergraduate curriculum in food science. The concepts and principles of engineering provide the quantitative basis for description and presentation of food processing and related operations required during the manufacturing of consumer food products. The importance of engineering principles is reflected in the unit operations associated with conversion of raw products into safe, high-quality foods.

The standard curriculum in food science, as required by the Institute of Food Technologists, contains six required core courses. The description of the food engineering course is as follows:

> ...lecture and laboratory to study the engineering concepts and unit operations used in food processing. Engineering principles should include materials and energy balances, thermodynamics, fluid flow, heat transfer and mass transfer.

This book responds directly to this description and is presented in a format designed to assist the undergraduate food science major in learning the principles. Presentation of these principles during the third year of the curriculum provides an excellent basis for the fourth year capstone course.

This book covers many of the same subjects as the first edition. The principles of fluid flow, energy, heat transfer, refrigeration, freezing, evaporation, psychrometrics, and dehydration are presented in separate chapters. In addition, new chapters are devoted to thermal processing, aseptic processing, and mass transfer. Emphasis is placed on application of principles through the use of example problems. In order to improve the computer literacy of students, a large number of examples that use spreadsheet programs are included. These spreadsheet programs illustrate deductive reasoning using "what-if" analysis, by examining the influence of input parameters on quantitative results. Key charts and tables are incorporated into the book to provide the student with experience in selection of appropriate input data for problem solutions.

Along with presentation of basic principles, we have incorporated descriptive information on typical equipment used to carry out the unit operations. It is anticipated that these illustrations of equipment will assist the student in understanding the engineering principles. Problems are a key component of most engineering courses. All chapters in this book are followed by a list of problems to be used in testing the student's understanding of the principles presented in the chapter. It should be noted that selected problems with advanced level of difficulty are identified and should be reserved until the student has more experience with information in a given chapter.

We are pleased to have this opportunity to participate in the food science student's introduction to food engineering. The unique blending of principles with applications to food processing is challenging, but it provides insight into the principles as well as the processes. The subjects selected to illustrate the engineering principles also provide an opportunity to demonstrate the relationship of engineering to the chemistry, microbiology, nutrition, and processing of foods.

We express appreciation to many individuals who have contributed to the content of this book. Many helpful suggestions have been received from faculty who have used the first edition in teaching engineering principles to food science majors. These suggestions have provided many ideas to benefit future students. We gratefully acknowledge the assistance provided by Ms. Leigh Ann Empie and Ms. Seema Atwal in typing and proofreading the drafts.

R. Paul Singh
Dennis R. Heldman

CHAPTER 1

Introduction

Physics, chemistry, and mathematics are essential subjects necessary to gain an understanding of principles that govern most of the unit operations commonly found in the food industry. For example, if a food engineer is asked to design a food process that involves heating or cooling, then he (or she) must be well aware of the physical principles that govern heat transfer. The engineer's work is often expected to be quantitative, therefore his or her ability to use mathematics is essential. Foods undergo changes as a result of processing; such changes may be physical, chemical, enzymatic, or microbiological. It is often necessary to know the kinetics of chemical changes that occur during processing. Such quantitative knowledge is a prerequisite to the design and analysis of food processes. It is expected that prior to studying food engineering principles, the student will have taken basic courses in mathematics, chemistry, and physics. In this chapter, we review some selected physical and chemical concepts that are important in food engineering.

1.1   Dimensions

A physical entity, which can be observed and/or measured, is defined qualitatively by a dimension. For example, time, length, area, volume, mass, force, temperature, and energy are all considered dimensions. The quantitative magnitude of a dimension is expressed by a unit. For example, a unit of length may be measured as a meter, a centimeter, or a millimeter.

Primary dimensions, such as length, time, temperature, mass, and force, express a physical entity. Secondary dimensions involve a combination of primary dimensions (e.g., volume is length cubed; velocity is distance divided by time).

It is necessary for equations to be dimensionally consistent. Thus, if the dimension of the left-hand side of an equation is "length," it is necessary that the dimension of the right-hand side also be "length"; otherwise the equation is incorrect. This is a good method to check the accuracy of equations. In solving numerical problems, it is always useful to write units for each of the dimensional quantities within the equations. This practice is helpful to avoid mistakes in calculations.

1.2 Engineering Units

Physical quantities are measured using a wide variety of unit systems. The most common systems include the Imperial (English) system; the centimeter, gram, second (cgs) system; and the meter, kilogram, second (mks) system. The use of these systems, along with myriad symbols to designate units, has often caused considerable confusion. International organizations have attempted to standardize unit systems, symbols, and the quantities. As a result of international agreements, the "Système International d'Unités," or the SI units, have emerged. The SI units consist of seven base units, two supplementary units, and a series of derived units.

1.2.1 Base Units

The SI system is based on a choice of seven well-defined units, which by convention are regarded as dimensionally independent. The definitions of these seven base units are as follows:

(1) Unit of length (meter): The *meter* (m) is the length equal to 1,650,763.73 wavelengths in vacuum of the radiation corresponding to the transition between the levels $2p_{10}$ and $5d_5$ of the krypton-86 atom.

(2) Unit of mass (kilogram): The *kilogram* (kg) is equal to the mass of the international prototype of the kilogram. (The international prototype of the kilogram is a particular cylinder of platinum–iridium alloy, which is preserved in a vault at Sèvres, France, by the International Bureau of Weights and Measures.)

(3) Unit of time (second): The *second* (s) is the duration of 9,192,631,770 periods of radiation corresponding to the transition between the two hyperfine levels of the ground state of the cesium-133 atom.

(4) Unit of electric current (ampere): The *ampere* (A) is the constant current that, if maintained in two straight parallel conductors of infinite length, of negligible circular cross section, and placed 1 m apart in vacuum, would produce between those conductors a force equal to 2×10^{-7} newton/meter of length.

(5) Unit of thermodynamic temperature (kelvin): The *kelvin* (K) is the fraction 1/273.16 of the thermodynamic temperature of the triple point of water.

TABLE 1.1
SI Base Units

Measurable attribute of phenomena or matter	Name	Symbol
Length	meter	m
Mass	kilogram	kg
Time	second	s
Electric current	ampere	A
Thermodynamic temperature	kelvin	K
Amount of substance	mole	mol
Luminous intensity	candela	cd

(6) Unit of amount of substance (mole): The *mole* (mol) is the amount of substance of a system that contains as many elementary entities as there are atoms in 0.012 kg of carbon 12.

(7) Unit of luminous intensity (candela): The *candela* (cd) is the luminous intensity, in the perpendicular direction, of a surface of $1/600,000$ m^2 of a blackbody at the temperature of freezing platinum under a pressure of 101,325 newtons/m^2.

The above base units, along with their symbols, are summarized in Table 1.1.

1.2.2 Derived Units

Derived units are algebraic combinations of base units expressed by means of multiplication and division. Often, for simplicity, derived units carry special names and symbols that may be used to obtain other derived units. Definitions of some commonly used derived units are as follows:

(1) Newton (N): The *newton* is the force that gives to a mass of 1 kg an acceleration of 1 m/s^2.

(2) Joule (J): The *joule* is the work done when due to force of 1 N the point of application is displaced by a distance of 1 m in the direction of the force.

(3) Watt (W): The *watt* is the power that gives rise to the production of energy at the rate of 1 J/s.

(4) Volt (V): The *volt* is the difference of electric potential between two points of a conducting wire carrying a constant current of 1 A, when the power dissipated between these points is equal to 1 W.

(5) Ohm (Ω): The *ohm* is the electric resistance between two points of a conductor when a constant difference of potential of 1 V, applied between these two points, produces in this conductor a current of 1 A, when this conductor is not being the source of any electromotive force.

(6) Coulomb (C): The *coulomb* is the quantity of electricity transported in 1 s by a current of 1 A.

(7) Farad (F): The *farad* is the capacitance of a capacitor between the plates of which there appears a difference of potential of 1 V when it is charged by a quantity of electricity equal to 1 C.

(8) Henry (H): The *henry* is the inductance of a closed circuit in which an electromotive force of 1 V is produced when the electric current in the circuit varies uniformly at a rate of 1 A/s.

TABLE I.2
Examples of SI Derived Units Expressed in Terms of Base Units

Quantity	SI unit	
	Name	Symbol
Area	square meter	m^2
Volume	cubic meter	m^3
Speed, velocity	meter per second	m/s
Acceleration	meter per second squared	m/s^2
Density, mass density	kilogram per cubic meter	kg/m^3
Current density	ampere per square meter	A/m^2
Magnetic field strength	ampere per meter	A/m
Concentration (of amount of substance)	mole per cubic meter	mol/m^3
Specific volume	cubic meter per kilogram	m^3/kg
Luminance	candela per square meter	cd/m^2

TABLE I.3
Examples of SI Derived Units with Special Names

Quantity	SI unit			
	Name	Symbol	Expression in terms of other units	Expression in terms of SI base units
Frequency	hertz	Hz		s^{-1}
Force	newton	N		$m \cdot kg \cdot s^{-2}$
Pressure, stress	pascal	Pa	N/m^2	$m^{-1} \cdot kg \cdot s^{-2}$
Energy, work, quantity of heat	joule	J	$N \cdot m$	$m^2 \cdot kg \cdot s^{-2}$
Power, radiant flux	watt	W	J/s	$m^2 \cdot kg \cdot s^{-3}$
Quantity of electricity, electric charge	coulomb	C		$s \cdot A$
Electric potential, potential difference, electromotive force	volt	V	W/A	$m^2 \cdot kg \cdot s^{-3} \cdot A^{-1}$
Capacitance	farad	F	C/V	$m^{-2} \cdot kg^{-1} \cdot s^4 \cdot A^2$
Electric resistance	ohm	Ω	V/A	$m^2 \cdot kg \cdot s^{-3} \cdot A^{-2}$
Conductance	siemens	S	A/V	$m^{-2} \cdot kg^{-1} \cdot s^3 \cdot A^2$
Celsius temperature	degree Celsius	°C		K
Luminous flux	lumen	lm		$cd \cdot sr$
Illuminance	lux	lx	lm/m^2	$m^{-2} \cdot cd \cdot sr$

TABLE 1.4

Examples of SI Derived Units Expressed by Means of Special Names

Quantity	SI unit		
	Name	Symbol	Expression in terms of SI base units
Dynamic viscosity	pascal second	Pa · s	$m^{-1} \cdot kg \cdot s^{-1}$
Moment of force	newton meter	N · m	$m^2 \cdot kg \cdot s^{-2}$
Surface tension	newton per meter	N/m	$kg \cdot s^{-2}$
Power density, heat flux density, irradiance	watt per square meter	W/m²	$kg \cdot s^{-3}$
Heat capacity, entropy	joule per kelvin	J/K	$m^2 \cdot kg \cdot s^{-2} \cdot K^{-1}$
Specific heat capacity	joule per kilogram kelvin	J/(kg · K)	$m^2 \cdot s^{-2} \cdot K^{-1}$
Specific energy	joule per kilogram	J/kg	$m^2 \cdot s^{-2}$
Thermal conductivity	Watt per meter kelvin	W/(m · K)	$m \cdot kg \cdot s^{-3} \cdot K^{-1}$
Energy density	joule per cubic meter	J/m³	$m^{-1} \cdot kg \cdot s^{-2}$
Electric field strength	volt per meter	V/m	$m \cdot kg \cdot s^{-3} \cdot A^{-1}$
Electric charge density	coulomb per cubic meter	C/m³	$m^{-3} \cdot s \cdot A$
Electric flux density	coulomb per square meter	C/m²	$m^{-2} \cdot s \cdot A$

(9) Weber (Wb): The *weber* is the magnetic flux that, linking a circuit of one turn, produces in it an electromotive force of 1 V as it is reduced to zero at a uniform rate in 1 s.

(10) Lumen (lm): The *lumen* is the luminous flux emitted in a point solid angle of 1 steradian by a uniform point source having an intensity of 1 cd.

In Tables 1.2, 1.3, and 1.4, examples are given of SI derived units expressed in terms of base units, SI derived units with special names, and SI derived units expressed by means of special names, respectively.

1.2.3 Supplementary Units

This class of units contains two purely geometric units, which may be regarded either as base units or as derived units.

(1) Unit of plane angle (radian): The *radian* (rad) is the plane angle between two radii of a circle that cut off on the circumference an arc equal in length to the radius.

(2) Unit of solid angle (steradian): The *steradian* (sr) is the solid angle that, having its vertex in the center of a sphere, cuts off an area of the surface of the sphere equal to that of a square with sides of length equal to the radius of the sphere.

TABLE 1.5
SI Supplementary Units

	SI unit	
Quantity	Name	Symbol
Plane angle	radian	rad
Solid angle	steradian	sr

The supplementary units are summarized in Table 1.5.

EXAMPLE 1.1

Determine the following unit conversions to SI units:

(a) a density value of 60 lb_m/ft^3 to kg/m^3
(b) an energy value of 1.7×10^3 Btu to kJ
(c) an enthalpy value of 2475 Btu/lb_m to kJ/kg
(d) a pressure value of 14.69 psig to kPa
(e) a viscosity value of 20 cp to Pa · s

SOLUTION

We will use conversion factors for each unit separately from Table A.1.2.

(a) Although a composite conversion factor for density, 1 lb_m/ft^3 = 16.0185 kg/m^3, is available in Table A.1.2, we will first convert units of each dimension separately. Since

$$1 \ lb_m = 0.45359 \ kg$$

$$1 \ ft = 0.3048 \ m$$

Thus,

$$\left(60 \ lb_m/ft^3\right)\left(0.45359 \ kg/lb_m\right)\left(\frac{1}{0.3048} \ m/ft\right)^3$$

$$= 961.1 \ kg/m^3$$

An alternative solution involves the direct use of the conversion factor for density,

$$\frac{\left(60 \ lb_m/ft^3\right)\left(16.0185 \ kg/m^3\right)}{\left(1 \ lb_m/ft^3\right)} = 961.1 \ kg/m^3$$

(b) For energy

$$1 \ Btu = 1.055 \ kJ$$

Thus,

$$\frac{\left(1.7 \times 10^3 \ Btu\right)\left(1.055 \ kJ\right)}{\left(1 \ Btu\right)} = 1.8 \times 10^3 \ kJ$$

(c) For enthalpy, the conversion units for each dimension are

$$1 \text{ Btu} = 1.055 \text{ kJ}$$
$$1 \text{ lb}_m = 0.45359 \text{ kg}$$

Thus,

$$(2475 \text{ Btu/lb}_m)(1.055 \text{ kJ/Btu})\left(\frac{1}{0.45359 \text{ kg/lb}_m}\right)$$

$$= 5757 \text{ kJ/kg}$$

Alternately, using the composite conversion factor for enthalpy of

$$1 \text{ Btu/lb}_m = 2.3258 \text{ kJ/kg}$$

$$\frac{(2475 \text{ Btu/lb}_m)(2.3258 \text{ kJ/kg})}{(1 \text{ Btu/lb}_m)} = 5756 \text{ kJ/kg}$$

(d) For pressure

$$\text{psia} = \text{psig} + 14.69$$

The gauge pressure, 14.69 psig, is first converted to the absolute pressure, psia (see Section 1.11 for more discussion on gauge and absolute pressures).

$$14.69 \text{ psig} + 14.69 = 29.38 \text{ psia}$$

The unit conversions for each dimension are

$$1 \text{ lb} = 4.4482 \text{ N}$$
$$1 \text{ in.} = 2.54 \times 10^{-2} \text{ m}$$
$$1 \text{ Pa} = 1 \text{ N/m}^2$$

Thus,

$$(29.28 \text{ lb/in.}^2)(4.4482 \text{ N/lb})\left(\frac{1}{2.54 \times 10^{-2} \text{ m/in.}}\right)^2\left(\frac{1 \text{ Pa}}{1 \text{ N/m}^2}\right)$$

$$= 201877 \text{ Pa}$$
$$= 201.88 \text{ kPa}$$

Alternately, since

$$1 \text{ psia} = 6.895 \text{ kPa}$$

$$\frac{(29.28 \text{ psia})(6.895 \text{ kPa})}{(1 \text{ psia})} = 201.88 \text{ kPa}$$

(e) For viscosity

$$1 \text{ cp} = 10^{-3} \text{ Pa} \cdot \text{s}$$

Thus,

$$\frac{(20 \text{ cp})(10^{-3} \text{ Pa} \cdot \text{s})}{(1 \text{ cp})} = 2 \times 10^{-2} \text{ Pa} \cdot \text{s}$$

EXAMPLE 1.2

Starting with Newton's second law of motion, determine units of force and weight in SI and English units.

SOLUTION

(a) Force

Newton's second law of motion states that force is directly proportional to mass and acceleration. Thus,

$$F \propto ma$$

Using a constant of proportionality k,

$$F = kma$$

where in **SI units**,

$$k = 1 \frac{N}{kg \cdot m/s^2}$$

Thus,

$$F = 1 \left(\frac{N}{kg \ m/s^2} \right)(kg)(m/s^2)$$

$$F = 1 \ N$$

In **English units** the constant k is defined as

$$k = \frac{1}{32.17} \frac{lb_f}{lb_m \ ft/s^2}$$

More commonly, another constant g_c is used where

$$g_c = 1/k = 32.17 \left(\frac{lb_m}{lb_f} \right) \left(\frac{ft}{s^2} \right)$$

Thus

$$F = \frac{ma}{g_c}$$

or

$$F = \frac{1}{32.17} \left(\frac{lb_f}{lb_m \ ft/s^2} \right)(lb_m)(ft/s^2)$$

$$F = \frac{1}{32.17} \ lb_f$$

(b) Weight

Weight W' is the force exerted by the earth's gravitational force on an object. Weight of 1 kg mass can be calculated as

$$W' = kmg$$

$$= \left(1 \frac{N}{kg \ m/s^2} \right)(1 \ kg) \left(9.81 \ \frac{m}{s^2} \right)$$

$$= 9.81 \ N$$

In English units,

$$W' = kmg$$

$$= \frac{1}{32.17} \left(\frac{lb_f}{lb_m \ ft/s^2} \right)(1 \ lb_m)(32.17 \ ft/s^2)$$

$$= 1 \ lb_f$$

1.3 System

A region prescribed in space or a finite quantity of matter is called a system. The system is enclosed by an envelope, which is referred to as a

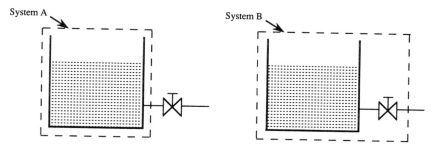

Fig. 1.1 Examples of systems and their boundaries.

boundary. The boundary of a system can be real, such as walls of a tank, or it can be an imaginary surface that encloses the system. For example, in Fig. 1.1, the boundary in system A is along the walls of a storage tank; thus it does not include the pipe and the valve. However, in system B, the boundary envelops the tank, valve, and the pipe. The composition of a system is described by the components present inside the system boundary. A careful description of the system is vital in engineering analysis.

Both open and closed systems are often encountered. In closed systems, the boundary of the system is impervious to any flow of matter. In an open system, heat and/or matter can flow into or out of the system. For example, a system boundary that contains only a small section of the wall is impervious to the flow of matter, and may be considered a closed system. On the other hand, system B in Fig. 1.1 is an open system since both heat and liquid can flow through the system.

1.4 Properties

Properties are those observable characteristics, such as pressure, temperature, or color, that define the equilibrium state of a thermodynamic system. Properties do not depend on how the state of a system is attained: they are only functions of the state of a system. Thus, properties are independent of the process by which a system attained a certain state.

1.4.1 Intensive Properties

Intensive properties do not depend on the mass of a system, such as temperature, pressure, and density.

1.4.2 Extensive Properties

An extensive property depends on the size of the system: for example, mass, length, volume, energy. This definition implies that an extensive property of a system is a sum of respective partial property values of the components of a system.

Three properties, one of which may be mass, are required to uniquely give an extensive property of a single-component system.

The ratio of two extensive properties of a homogeneous system is an intensive property. For example, the ratio of the two extensive properties mass and volume is density, which is an intensive property.

The state of a system is defined by independent properties. Once the properties become fixed, when the state of a system is defined, they are called dependent properties.

1.5 Area

Area is a quantitative measure of a plane or a curved surface. It is defined as the product of two lengths. In the SI system, the unit is square meters (m^2).

Surface area of a food product is required in a number of process calculations. For example, when calculating heat and mass transfer across the surface of a food material, the surface area of the food must be known. Certain physical processes increase the surface area, such as prior to spray drying, a liquid stream is converted to spray droplets, increasing the surface area of the liquid, thus enhancing the drying process. In Table 1.6, surface areas of some typical foods are given. In certain food processing applications, the surface-area-to-volume ratio must be known. For example, in canning of foods, a higher surface-area-to-volume ratio will result in faster heating of the geometrical center of the container, thus minimizing overheating of the product. For this reason, retortable pouches are often considered better than cylindrical cans. Because of their slab shape, the pouches have high surface area per unit volume, thus resulting in a more rapid heating of the slowest heating point when compared with cylindrical cans. Among various geometrical shapes, a sphere has the largest surface-area-to-volume ratio.

TABLE 1.6
Surface Area of Foods

	Mean surface area (cm^2)
Apple, Delicious	140.13
Pear, Bartlett	145.42
Plum, Monarch	35.03
Egg (60 g)	70.5

Source: Mohsenin (1978).

1.6 Density

Density is defined as mass per unit volume with dimensions (mass)/(length)^3. The SI units for density are kg/m^3. Density is an indication of how matter is composed in a body. Materials with more compact molecular arrangement have higher densities. The values of density for various metals and nonmetals are given in Appendix A.3. Density of a given substance may be divided by density of water at the same temperature to obtain specific gravity.

There are three types of densities when dealing with foods, namely solid density, particle density, and bulk density. The values of these different types of densities depend on how the pore spaces present in a food material are considered.

If the pore spaces are disregarded, the solid density of most food particles (Table 1.7) is 1400–1600 kg/m^3, except for high fat or high salt foods (Peleg, 1983).

Particle density accounts for the presence of internal pores in the food particles. This density is defined as a ratio of the actual mass of a particle to its actual volume.

Bulk density is defined as the mass of particles occupied by a unit volume of bed. Typical values of bulk densities for food materials are given in Table 1.8. This measurement accounts for the void space between the particles. The void space in food materials can be described by determining the **porosity**, which is expressed as the volume not occupied by the solid material.

Thus,

$$\text{Porosity} = 1 - \frac{\text{Bulk density}}{\text{Solid density}} \qquad (1.1)$$

The interparticle porosity may be defined as follows:

$$\text{Interparticle porosity} = 1 - \frac{\text{Bulk density}}{\text{Particle density}} \qquad (1.2)$$

TABLE 1.7
Solid Densities of Major Ingredients of Foods

Ingredient	kg/m^3	Ingredient	kg/m^3
Glucose	1560	Fat	900–950
Sucrose	1590	Salt	2160
Starch	1500	Citric acid	1540
Cellulose	1270–1610	Water	1000
Protein (globular)	~ 1400		

Source: Peleg (1983).

TABLE 1.8
Bulk Density of Selected Food Materials

Material	Bulk density (kg/m³)
Beans, cocoa	1073
Beans, soy, whole	800
Coconut, shredded	320–352
Coffee beans, green	673
Coffee, ground	400
Coffee, roasted beans	368
Corn, ear	448
Corn, shelled	720
Milk, whole dried	320
Mustard seed	720
Peanuts, hulled	480–720
Peas, dried	800
Rapeseed	770
Rice, clean	770
Rice, hulls	320
Sugar, granulated	800
Wheat	770

Relationships have been developed to determine density based on experimental data. For example, for skim milk

$$\rho = 1036.6 - 0.146T + 0.0023T^2 - 0.00016T^3 \qquad (1.3)$$

where T is temperature in degrees Celsius.

1.7 Concentration

Concentration is a measure of the amount of substance contained in a unit volume. Concentration may be expressed as weight per unit weight, or weight per unit volume. Normally, concentration is given in percentage when weight per unit weight measurement is used. Thus, a food containing 20% fat will contain 20 g of fat in every 100 g of food. Concentration values are also expressed as mass per unit volume—for example, mass of a solute dissolved in a unit volume of the solution.

Another term used to express concentration is *molarity* or molar concentration. Molarity is the concentration of solution in grams per liter divided by the molecular weight of the solute. To express these units in a dimensionless form, *mole fraction* may be used; this is the ratio of the number of moles of a substance divided by the total number of moles in the system.

Thus, for a solution containing two components, A and B, with number of moles n_A and n_B respectively, the mole fraction of A, X_A, is

$$X_A = \frac{n_A}{n_A + n_B} \qquad (1.4)$$

Concentration is sometimes expressed by **molality**. The molality of a component A in a solution is defined as the amount of a component per unit mass of some other component chosen as the solvent. The SI unit for molality is mole per kilogram.

A relationship between molality, M'_A, and mole fraction, X_A, for a solution of two components, in which the molecular weight of solvent B is M_B, is

$$X_A = \frac{M'_A}{M'_A + \dfrac{1000}{M_B}} \qquad (1.5)$$

Both molality and mole fraction are independent of temperature.

EXAMPLE 1.3

Develop a spreadsheet on a computer to calculate concentration units for a sugar solution. The sugar solution is prepared by dissolving 10 kg of sucrose in 90 kg of water. The density of the solution is 1040 kg/m^3. Determine

    (i) concentration, weight per unit weight
    (ii) concentration, weight per unit volume
  (iii) °Brix
  (iv) molarity
   (v) mole fraction
  (vi) molality
 (vii) Using the spreadsheet, recalculate (i) to (vi) if the (a) sucrose solution contains 20 kg of sucrose in 80 kg of water, and density of the solution is 1083

	A	B
1	Given	
2	Amount of Sucrose	10
3	Amount of water	90
4	Density of solution	1040
5		
6	Volume of solution	=(B2+B3)/B4
7	Concentration w/w	=B2/(B2+B3)
8	Concentration w/v	=B2/B6
9	Brix	=B2/(B2+B3)*100
10	molarity	=B8/342
11	mole fraction	=(B2/342)/(B3/18+B2/342)
12	molality	=(B2*1000)/(B3*342)

Fig. 1.2 Spreadsheet for calculation of sugar solution concentration in Example 1.3.

	A	B	C	D	E
1	Given				Units
2	Amount of Sucrose	10	20	30	kg
3	Amount of water	90	80	70	kg
4	Density of solution	1040	1083	1129	kg/m^3
5					
6	Volume of solution	0.0962	0.0923	0.0886	m^3
7	Concentration w/w	0.1	0.2	0.3	kg solute/kg solution
8	Concentration w/v	104	216.6	338.7	kg solute/m^3 solution
9	Brix	10	20	30	(kg solute/kg solution)*100
10	molarity	0.30	0.63	0.99	mole solute/liter of solution
11	mole fraction	0.0058	0.0130	0.0221	
12	molality	.325	.731	1.253	mole solute/kg solvent

Fig. 1.3 Results of the spreadsheet calculation in Example 1.3.

kg/m^3; (b) sucrose solution contains 30 kg of sucrose in 70 kg of water, and density of the solution is 1129 kg/m^3.

SOLUTION

(1) The spreadsheet is written using EXCEL™, on an Apple Macintosh computer, as shown in Fig. 1.2.

(2) The results from the spreadsheet calculation are shown in Fig. 1.3.

(3) Once the spreadsheet is prepared according to step (1), the given values are easily changed to calculate all other unknowns.

1.8   Moisture Content

Moisture content expresses the amount of water present in a moist sample. Two bases are widely used to express moisture content, namely moisture content wet basis and moisture content dry basis.

Moisture content, wet basis (MC_{wb}), is the amount of water per unit mass of moist (or wet) sample.

Thus,

$$MC_{wb} = \frac{\text{mass of water}}{\text{mass of moist sample}} \qquad (1.6)$$

Moisture content, dry basis (MC_{db}), is the amount of water per unit mass of dry solids (bone dry) present in the sample.

Thus,

$$MC_{db} = \frac{\text{mass of water}}{\text{mass of dry solids}} \qquad (1.7)$$

A relationship between MC_{wb} and MC_{db} may be developed as follows

$$MC_{wb} = \frac{\text{mass of water}}{\text{mass of moist sample}} \qquad (1.8)$$

$$MC_{wb} = \frac{\text{mass of water}}{\text{mass of water} + \text{mass of dry solids}} \qquad (1.9)$$

Divide both numerator and denominator of Eq. (1.9) with mass of dry solids

$$MC_{wb} = \frac{\text{mass of water/mass of dry solids}}{\text{mass of water/mass of dry solids} + 1} \qquad (1.10)$$

$$MC_{wb} = \frac{MC_{db}}{MC_{db} + 1} \qquad (1.11)$$

The above relationship is useful to calculate MC_{wb} when MC_{db} is known. Similarly, if MC_{wb} is known, then MC_{db} may be calculated from the following equation:

$$MC_{db} = \frac{MC_{wb}}{1 - MC_{wb}} \qquad (1.12)$$

The moisture content values in the preceding equations are expressed in fractions. It may be noted that moisture content dry basis may have values greater than 100%, since the amount of water present in a sample may be greater than the amount of dry solids present.

EXAMPLE 1.4

Convert a moisture content of 85% wet basis to moisture content dry basis.

SOLUTION

   (i) $MC_{wb} = 85\%$
   (ii) In fractional notation, $MC_{wb} = 0.85$
   (iii) From equation,

$$MC_{db} = \frac{MC_{wb}}{1 - MC_{wb}}$$

$$= \frac{0.85}{1 - 0.85}$$

$$= 5.67$$

or

$$MC_{db} = 567\%$$

EXAMPLE 1.5

Develop a table of conversions from moisture content wet basis to moisture content dry basis between 0% MC_{wb} to 90% MC_{wb} in steps of 10 percent.

	A	B
1	Moisture Content (wb)	Moisture Content (db)
2	0	=A2/(100-A2)*100
3	10	=A3/(100-A3)*100
4	20	=A4/(100-A4)*100
5	30	=A5/(100-A5)*100
6	40	=A6/(100-A6)*100
7	50	=A7/(100-A7)*100
8	60	=A8/(100-A8)*100
9	70	=A9/(100-A9)*100
10	80	=A10/(100-A10)*100
11	90	=A11/(100-A11)*100

Fig. 1.4 Spreadsheet for converting moisture content wet basis to moisture content dry basis in Example 1.5.

SOLUTION

(i) Since repetitive computations are involved, a spreadsheet is prepared as follows.

(ii) In an EXCEL spreadsheet (Fig. 1.4), enter 0 to 90 in steps of 10 in column A.

(iii) Enter the formula given in Eq. (1.12) in cell B2, modified to account for percent values and following spreadsheet notation,

$$MC_{db} = A2/(100 - A2) * 100$$

(iv) Copy cell B2 into cells B3 to B11.

(v) The output is obtained as shown on the spreadsheet in Fig. 1.5.

(vi) A plot of the values in columns A and B may be obtained using the chart command of EXCEL. This plot (Fig. 1.6) is useful in converting moisture content values from one basis to another.

	A	B
1	Moisture Content (wb)	Moisture Content (db)
2	0	0.00
3	10	11.11
4	20	25.00
5	30	42.86
6	40	66.67
7	50	100.00
8	60	150.00
9	70	233.33
10	80	400.00
11	90	900.00

Fig. 1.5 Results of the spreadsheet calculation in Example 1.5.

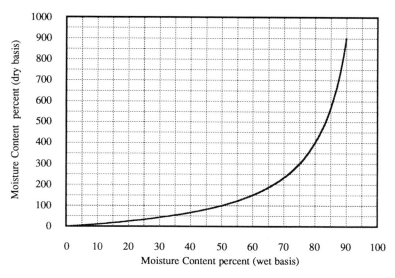

Fig. 1.6 Plot of moisture content wet basis versus moisture content dry basis.

1.9 Equation of State and Perfect Gas Law

The thermodynamic properties of a simple system are established by any two independent properties. A functional relationship between the properties of a system is called an equation of state. Values of two properties of a system help establish the value of the third property.

For a perfect gas, an equation of state is a relationship between pressure, volume, and temperature. The equation may be written as

$$PV' = RT_A \tag{1.13}$$

or

$$P = \rho RT_A \tag{1.14}$$

where P is absolute pressure (Pa), V' is specific volume (m^3/kg), R is the gas constant (m$^3 \cdot$ Pa/kg $\cdot$ K), T_A is absolute temperature (K), and ρ is density (kg/m^3).

At room temperature, real gases such as hydrogen, nitrogen, helium, and oxygen follow the perfect gas law (very closely).

The equation of state for a perfect gas may also be written on a mole basis as

$$PV = mRT_A = (m/M)R_0T_A = nR_0T_A \tag{1.15}$$

where V is the volume (of m kg or n mol), m^3; $R_0 = M \times R$ is the universal gas constant, independent of the nature of a gas, 8314.41 m$^3 \cdot$ Pa/kg $\cdot$ mol K; and M is the molecular weight of the substance.

1.10   Phase Diagram of Water

Water is considered to be a pure substance. It has a homogeneous and invariable chemical composition even though it may undergo a change in phase. Therefore, liquid water, or a mixture of ice and liquid water, and steam, a mixture of liquid water and water vapor, are both pure substances.

When a substance occurs in a liquid state at its saturation temperature and pressure, it is called a **saturated liquid**. If at the saturation pressure, the temperature of the liquid is lowered below the saturation temperature, it is called a **subcooled liquid**. In the case where, at the saturation temperature, a substance exists partly as liquid and partly as vapor, the ratio of the mass of water vapor to the total mass of the substance is expressed as the **quality** of the vapors. For example, if steam has 0.1 kg water and 0.9 kg vapor, the quality of steam is 0.9 divided by 1.0 (which represents the total mass of steam); thus steam quality equals 0.9 or 90%.

When a substance occurs as a vapor at the saturation temperature and pressure, it is called **saturated vapor**. Saturation temperature is the temperature at which vaporization takes place at a given pressure. This pressure is called the **saturation pressure**. Thus, water at 100°C has a saturation pressure of 101.3 kPa. When the temperature of the vapor is greater than the saturation temperature at the existing pressure, it is called **superheated vapor**.

A phase diagram of water, shown in Fig. 1.7, is useful to study pressure–temperature relationships between various phases. This diagram gives the limiting conditions for solid, liquid, and gas (or vapor) phases. At

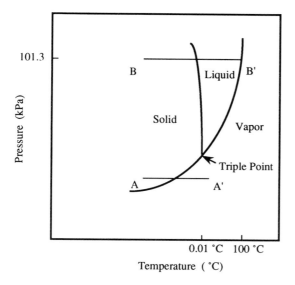

Fig. 1.7   Phase diagram for water.

any location within the areas separated by the curves, the pressure and temperature combination permits only one phase (solid, liquid, or vapor) to exist. Any change in temperature and pressure up to the points on the curves will not change the phase. As shown in Fig. 1.7, the sublimation line separates solid from vapor phase, the fusion line separates solid from liquid phase, and the vaporization line separates liquid phase from vapor phase. The three lines meet at a triple point. The triple point identifies a state in which the three phases—namely, solid, liquid, and vapor—may all be present in equilibrium. The triple point for water is at 0.01°C.

The phase diagram shown in Fig. 1.7 is useful in examining processes conducted at constant pressure with change of phase. For example, line AA′ is a constant-pressure process conducted at a low temperature, where ice sublimates into the vapor phase. There is no liquid phase in this case. Line BB′ represents a heating process at or above atmospheric pressure where initially solid ice melts into the liquid state followed by vaporization of water at a higher temperature.

Phase diagrams are important in studying processes such as extraction, crystallization, distillation, precipitation, and freeze concentration.

1.11 Pressure

The pressure exerted by a system is the force normal to a unit area of the system boundary. The dimensions of pressure are $(mass)(time)^{-2}(length)^{-1}$. In the SI system, the units are N/m^2. This unit is also called a pascal (named after Blaise Pascal[1]). Since the pascal unit is small in magnitude, another unit, bar, is used, where

$$1 \text{ bar} = 10^5 \text{ Pa} = 100 \text{ kPa}$$

The standard atmospheric pressure is defined as the pressure produced by a column of mercury 760 mm high. The standard atmospheric pressure can be expressed using different systems of units, as

$$1 \text{ atm} = 14.696 \text{ lb/in.}^2 = 1.01325 \text{ bar} = 101.325 \text{ kPa} \qquad (1.16)$$

In situations involving fluid flow, pressure is often expressed in terms of **height** or **"head"** of a fluid. The height of a fluid that can be supported by pressure acting on it can be written mathematically as

$$P = \rho g h$$

where P is absolute pressure (Pa), ρ is fluid density (kg/m^3), g is acceleration due to gravity (9.81 m/s^2), and h is height of fluid (m).

---

1. Blaise Pascal (1623–1662), a French philosopher and mathematician, was the founder of modern theory of probabilities. He studied hydrostatic and atmospheric pressure and derived Pascal's law of pressure. He is credited with inventing the first digital computer and the syringe. In addition to studying physical sciences, he became a scholar of religion, and in 1655 he wrote *Les Provinciales*, a defense of Jansenism against the Jesuits.

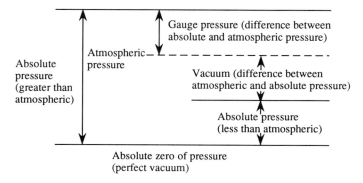

Fig. 1.8 Illustration of the relationships between the terms used to define pressure.

Thus, two atmospheric pressures will support

$$\frac{2 \times (101.325 \times 10^3 \text{ N/m}^2)}{(13546 \text{ kg/m}^3)(9.81 \text{ m/s})} = 1525 \text{ mm of mercury}$$

In expressing units for **vacuum** in the English system, the atmospheric pressure is referred to as 0 inches of mercury. Perfect vacuum is 29.92 inches of mercury. Thus, 15 inches of mercury has a higher pressure than 20 inches of mercury. In the SI system, the convention to express vacuum is opposite to that of the English system. The units are given in pascals. At perfect vacuum, the absolute pressure is 0 Pa (recall that one atmospheric pressure is 101.325 kPa). The relationship between the English system and the SI system for expressing vacuum can be written as

$$\text{Absolute pressure (Pa)} = 3.38638 \times 10^3 (29.92 - I) \qquad (1.17)$$

where I is inches of mercury.

Pressure measured with a pressure gauge is called **gauge pressure**. The gauge pressure can be converted to **absolute pressure** with the following relationship:

$$\text{Absolute pressure} = \text{gauge pressure} + \text{atmospheric pressure}$$

A visual description of these relationships between the various terms used to define pressure is given in Fig. 1.8.

In fluid flow problems, two additional terms are often encountered, namely, static pressure and impact pressure. *Static pressure* is the pressure measured by a device if it is moving with the same velocity as the fluid velocity. *Impact pressure* is force per unit area perpendicular to the direction of flow when the fluid is brought reversibly to rest.

1.12 Enthalpy

Enthalpy is an extensive property, expressed as a sum of internal energy and the product of pressure and specific volume.

$$H = U + PV \qquad\qquad (1.18)$$

where H is enthalpy (kJ/kg), U is internal energy (kJ/kg), P is pressure (kPa), and V is specific volume (m^3/kg).

It should be noted that enthalpy is an energy quantity in special cases only. For example, enthalpy of air in a room is not an energy quantity. This is true because the product of pressure and specific volume in this case is not an energy quantity. The only energy of the air in the room is its internal energy. When a fluid enters or leaves an open system, the product of pressure and specific volume represents flow energy. In this case enthalpy of the fluid represents the sum of internal energy and flow energy.

Enthalpy value is always given relative to a reference state in which the value of enthalpy is arbitrarily selected, usually zero for convenience. For example, steam tables give enthalpy of steam, assuming that at 0°C the enthalpy of saturated liquid is zero.

1.13 Laws of Thermodynamics

First Law of Thermodynamics: The first law of thermodynamics is a statement of the conservation of energy. The law states

> The energy of an isolated system remains constant.

Stated in other words,

> Energy can be neither created nor destroyed but can be transformed from one form to another.

Second Law of Thermodynamics: The second law of thermodynamics is useful in examining the direction of energy transfer or conversion. The following two statements of the second law on the following page are by Rudolf Clausius[2] and Lord Kelvin,[3] respectively.

---

2. Rudolf Clausius (1822–1888), a German mathematical physicist, is credited with making thermodynamics a science. In 1850, he presented a paper that stated the second law of thermodynamics. He developed the theory of the steam engine, and his work on electrolysis formed the basis of the theory of electrolytic dissociation.

3. Lord Kelvin (1824–1907) was a Scottish mathematician, physicist, and engineer. At the age of 22, he was awarded the chair of natural philosophy at the University of Glasgow. He contributed to the development of the law of conservation of energy; absolute temperature scale, which was named after him; electromagnetic theory of light; and mathematical analysis of electricity and magnetism. A prolific writer, he published over 600 scientific papers.

No process is possible whose sole result is the removal of heat from a reservoir (system) at one temperature and the absorption of an equal quantity of heat by a reservoir at a higher temperature.

No process is possible whose sole result is the abstraction of heat from a single reservoir and the performance of an equivalent amount of work.

It is the second law of thermodynamics that helps explain why heat always flows from a hot object to a cold object; why two gases placed in a chamber will mix throughout the chamber, but will not spontaneously separate once mixed; and why it is impossible to construct a machine that will operate continuously while receiving heat from a single reservoir and producing an equivalent amount of work.

1.14 Conservation of Mass

The law of conservation of mass can be expressed mathematically using the following equation:

$$
\begin{array}{l}
\text{Material} \\
\text{input through} \\
\text{the system} \\
\text{boundary}
\end{array}
-
\begin{array}{l}
\text{material} \\
\text{output through} \\
\text{the system} \\
\text{boundary}
\end{array}
+
\begin{array}{l}
\text{material} \\
\text{generation} \\
\text{within the} \\
\text{system} \\
\text{boundary}
\end{array}
-
\begin{array}{l}
\text{material} \\
\text{consumption} \\
\text{within the} \\
\text{system} \\
\text{boundary}
\end{array}
=
\begin{array}{l}
\text{material} \\
\text{accumulation} \\
\text{within the} \\
\text{system} \\
\text{boundary}
\end{array}
\qquad (1.19)
$$

If there is no generation or consumption of material, the above equation reduces to

$$
\begin{array}{l}
\text{Material} \\
\text{input through} \\
\text{the system} \\
\text{boundary}
\end{array}
-
\begin{array}{l}
\text{material} \\
\text{output through} \\
\text{the system} \\
\text{boundary}
\end{array}
=
\begin{array}{l}
\text{material} \\
\text{accumulation} \\
\text{within the} \\
\text{boundary}
\end{array}
\qquad (1.20)
$$

In addition, if under steady-state conditions no accumulation of mass occurs within the system boundary, the following simple relationship holds:

$$
\begin{array}{l}
\text{Material input} \\
\text{through the} \\
\text{system boundary}
\end{array}
=
\begin{array}{l}
\text{material output} \\
\text{through the} \\
\text{system boundary}
\end{array}
\qquad (1.21)
$$

Material balances are useful in evaluating individual pieces of equipment, such as a pump or a homogenizer, as well as overall plant operations consisting of several processing units, for example, a tomato paste manufacturing line as shown in Fig. 1.9. Compositions of raw materials and product streams, waste streams, and by-product streams can be evaluated by using material balances.

The following steps should be useful in conducting the mass balance in an organized manner.

(1) Collect all known data on mass and composition of all inlet and exit streams from the statement of the problem.

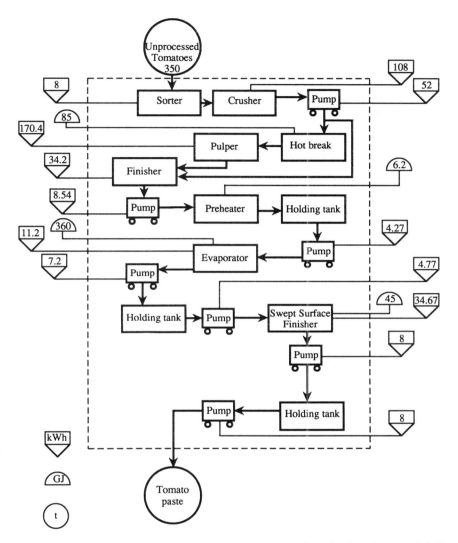

Fig. 1.9 Energy accounting diagram of tomato paste manufacturing based on an eight-hour shift. [From Singh *et al.* (1980).]

(2) Draw a block diagram, indicating the process, with inlet and exit streams properly identified. Draw the system boundary.

(3) Write all available data on the block diagram.

(4) Select a suitable basis (such as mass or time) for calculations. The selection of basis depends on the convenience of computations.

(5) Using Eq. (1.5), write material balances in terms of the selected basis for calculating unknowns. For each unknown, one independent material balance is required.

(6) Solve material balances to determine the unknowns.

The use of material balances is illustrated with the following examples.

EXAMPLE 1.6

In a furnace, 95% of carbon is converted to carbon dioxide and the remainder to carbon monoxide. By material balance, predict the quantities of gases appearing in the flue gases leaving the furnace.

GIVEN

Carbon converted to $CO_2 = 95\%$
Carbon converted to $CO = 5\%$

SOLUTION

(1) Basis is 1 kg of carbon
(2) The combustion equations are

$$C + O_2 = CO_2$$
$$C + \tfrac{1}{2}O_2 = CO$$

(3) From the above equations, 44 kg carbon dioxide is formed by combustion of 12 kg carbon, and 28 kg carbon monoxide is formed by combustion of 12 kg carbon.
(4) Then, the amount of CO_2 produced,

$$\frac{(44 \text{ kg } CO_2)(0.95 \text{ kg C burned})}{12 \text{ kg C burned}} = 3.48 \text{ kg } CO_2$$

(5) Similarly, the amount of CO produced,

$$\frac{(28 \text{ kg } CO_2)(0.05 \text{ kg C burned})}{12 \text{ kg C burned}} = 0.12 \text{ kg CO}$$

(6) Thus, the flue gases contain 3.48 kg CO_2 and 0.12 kg CO for every kilogram of carbon burned.

EXAMPLE 1.7

A wet food product contains 70% water. After drying, it is found that 80% of original water has been removed. Determine (a) mass of water removed per kilogram of wet food and (b) composition of dried food.

GIVEN

Initial water content $= 70\%$
Water removed $= 80\%$ of original water content

SOLUTION

(1) Select basis $= 1$ kg wet food product
(2) Mass of water in inlet stream $= 0.7$ kg
(3) Water removed in drying $= 0.8(0.7) = 0.56$ kg/kg of wet food material
(4) Write material balance on water,

$$\text{Water in dried food} = 0.7(1) - 0.56 = 0.14 \text{ kg}$$

(5) Write balance on solids,

$$0.3(1) = \text{solids in exit stream}$$
$$\text{Solids} = 0.3 \text{ kg}$$

(6) Thus, the dried food contains 0.14 kg water and 0.3 kg solids.

EXAMPLE 1.8

A membrane separation system is used to concentrate total solids (TS) in a liquid food from 10 to 30%. The concentration is accomplished in two stages with the first stage resulting in release of a low-total-solids liquid stream. The second state separates the final concentration product from a low-total-solids stream, which is returned to the first stage. Determine the magnitude of the recycle stream when the recycle contains 2% TS, the waste stream contains 0.5% TS, and the stream between stages 1 and 2 contains 25% TS. The process should produce 100 kg/min of 30% TS.

GIVEN (Fig. 1.10)

Concentration of inlet stream = 10%
Concentration of exit stream = 30%
Concentration of recycle stream = 2%
Concentration of waste stream = 0.5%
Concentration of stream between two stages = 25%
Mass flow rate of exit stream = 100 kg/min

SOLUTION

(1) Select 1 min as a basis.
(2) For the total system

$$F = P + W$$
$$Fx_F = Px_P + Wx_W$$
$$F = 100 + W$$
$$F(0.1) = 100(0.3) + W(0.005)$$

where x is the solids fraction.

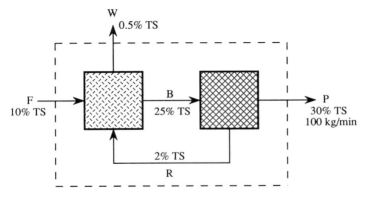

W
0.5% TS

F
10% TS

B
25% TS

P
30% TS
100 kg/min

2% TS

R

Fig. 1.10 A schematic arrangement of equipment described in Example 1.8.

(3) For the first stage

$$F + R = W + B$$
$$Fx_F + Rx_R = Wx_W + Bx_B$$
$$F(0.1) + R(0.02) = W(0.005) + B(0.25)$$

(4) From step (2)

$$(100 + W)(0.1) = 30 + 0.005W$$
$$0.1W - 0.005W = 30 - 10$$
$$0.095W = 20$$
$$W = 210.5 \text{ kg/min}$$
$$F = 310.5 \text{ kg/min}$$

(5) From step (3)

$$310.5 + R = 210.5 + B$$
$$B = 100 + R$$
$$310.5(0.1) + 0.02R = 210.5(0.005) + 0.25B$$
$$31.05 + 0.02R = 1.0525 + 25 + 0.25R$$
$$4.9975 = 0.23R$$
$$R = 21.73 \text{ kg/min}$$

(6) The results indicate that the recycle stream will be flowing at a rate of 21.73 kg/min.

EXAMPLE 1.9

Potato flakes (moisture content = 75% wet basis) are being dried in a concurrent flow drier. The moisture content of the air entering the drier is 0.08 kg of water per 1 kg dry air. The moisture content of air leaving the drier is 0.18 kg water per 1 kg of dry air. The air flow rate in the drier is 100 kg dry air per hour. As shown in Fig. 1.11, 50 kg of wet potato flakes enter the drier per hour. At steady state, calculate the following:

(a) What is the mass flow rate of "dried potatoes"?
(b) What is the moisture content, dry basis, of "dried potatoes" exiting the drier?

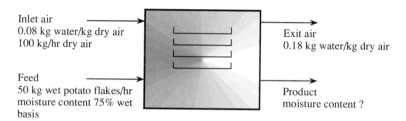

Inlet air
0.08 kg water/kg dry air
100 kg/hr dry air

Exit air
0.18 kg water/kg dry air

Feed
50 kg wet potato flakes/hr
moisture content 75% wet basis

Product
moisture content ?

Fig. 1.11 System diagram for Example 1.9.

GIVEN

Weight of potato flakes entering the drier $F = 50$ kg
Time $= 1$ h

SOLUTION

(1) Basis $= 1$ h
(2) Mass of air entering the drier = mass of dry air + mass of water

$$I = 100 + 100 \times 0.08$$
$$I = 108 \text{ kg}$$

(3) Mass of air leaving the drier = mass of dry air + mass of water

$$E = 100 + 100 \times 0.18$$
$$E = 118 \text{ kg}$$

(4) Total balance on the drier

$$I + F = E + P$$
$$108 + 50 = 118 + P$$
$$P = 40 \text{ kg}$$

(5) Solid balance on the drier

Solid content in feed is calculated from the definition of the wet basis moisture content [Eq. (1.6)], rewriting Eq. (1.6) as

$$1 - \text{MC}_{wb} = 1 - \frac{\text{mass of water}}{\text{mass of moist sample}}$$

or

$$1 - \text{MC}_{wb} = \frac{\text{mass of dry solids}}{\text{mass of moist sample}}$$

or

$$\text{Mass of dry solids} = \text{Mass of moist sample} \, (1 - \text{MC}_{wb})$$

Therefore,

$$\text{Mass of solid content in feed} = F(1 - 0.75)$$

If y is the solid fraction in the product stream P, then solid balance on the drier gives

$$0.25F = y \times P$$
$$y = \frac{0.25 \times 50}{40}$$
$$= 0.3125$$

Thus,

$$\frac{\text{mass of dry solids}}{\text{mass of moist sample}} = 0.3125$$

or

$$1 - \frac{\text{mass of dry solids}}{\text{mass of moist sample}} = 1 - 0.3125$$

Therefore, moisture content in the exit potato stream is

$$1 - 0.3125 = 0.6875 \text{ wet basis}$$

(6) The wet basis moisture content is converted to dry basis moisture content.

$$MC_{db} = \frac{0.6875}{1 - 0.6875}$$

$$MC_{db} = 2.2 \text{ kg water per 1 kg dry solids}$$

(7) The mass flow rate of potatoes exiting the drier is 40 kg at a moisture content of 2.2 kg water per 1 kg dry solids.

EXAMPLE 1.10

An experimental engineered food is being manufactured using five stages, as shown in Fig. 1.12. The feed is 1000 kg/hr. Various streams have been labeled along with the known composition values on the diagram. Note that the

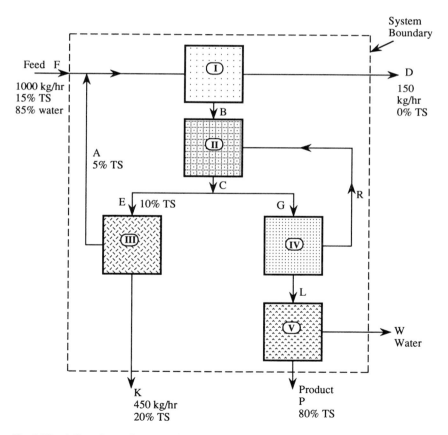

Fig. 1.12 A flow sheet of an experimental food manufacturing system.

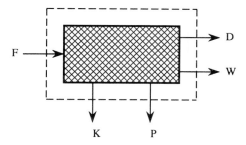

Fig. 1.13 Total system for Example 1.10.

composition of each stream is in terms of solids and water only. Stream C is divided equally into streams E and G. Product P, with 80% solids, is the desired final product. Stream K produces a by-product at the rate of 450 kg/hr with 20% solids. Calculate the following:

(a) Calculate the mass flow rate of product P.
(b) Calculate the mass flow rate of recycle stream A.
(c) Calculate the mass flow rate of recycle stream R.

GIVEN

Feed = 1000 kg/hr
Solid content of P = 80%
Mass rate of stream K = 450 kg/hr
Solids in stream K = 20%

GIVEN

(1) Basis = 1 hr
(2) Consider total system, solid balance (Fig. 1.13).

$$0.15 \times F = 0.2 \times K + 0.8 \times P$$

$$0.15 \times 1000 = 0.2 \times 450 + 0.8 \times P$$

$$150 = 90 + 0.8 \times P$$

$$P = \frac{60}{0.8} = 75 \text{ kg}$$

$$P = 75 \text{ kg}$$

(3) Consider stage III (Fig. 1.14).

Total balance

$$E = A + K; \qquad E = A + 450 \qquad (1)$$

Solid balance

$$0.1E = 0.05A + 0.2K$$

$$0.1E = 0.05A + 0.2 \times 450$$

$$0.1E = 0.05A + 90 \qquad (2)$$

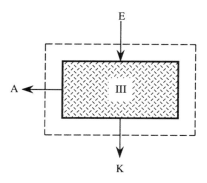

Fig. 1.14   Illustration of stage III of the system in Example 1.10.

Solve preceding Eqs. (1) and (2) simultaneously.

$$E = 1350 \text{ kg}$$

$$A = 900 \text{ kg}$$

(4) Since C is divided equally into E and G,

$$G = 1350 \text{ kg with 10\% solid}$$

(5) For total system, conduct total balance to find W.

$$F = K + P + D + W$$

$$1000 = 450 + 75 + 150 + W$$

$$W = 325 \text{ kg}$$

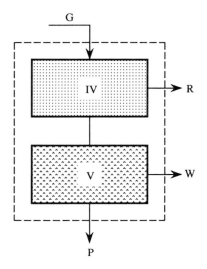

Fig. 1.15   Illustration of stages IV and V of the system in Example 1.10.

(6) Consider stages IV and V together (Fig. 1.15).

$$G = R + W + P$$
$$1350 = R + 325 + 75$$
$$R = 950 \text{ kg}$$

(7) The mass flow rates of streams P, A, and R are 75 kg, 900 kg, and 950 kg, respectively.

1.15 Energy

Energy, a scalar quantity, was first hypothesized as a concept by Newton[4] to express kinetic and potential energies. Energy cannot be observed directly, but using indirect methods it can be recorded and evaluated. The common unit used to express energy is the joule.

Energy E of a system is a property since it is associated mainly with the state of the system. There are two types of energy, external and internal.

External energy is possessed by a system by virtue of its position or velocity. In food processing applications, we are more concerned with the change in energy than the absolute energy values.

The change in energy resulting from moving an object from one location at height h_1 to another location at height h_2 is called **potential energy**, thus

$$\Delta E_{\text{PE}} = mgh_2 - mgh_1 \tag{1.22}$$

where m is mass (kg), g is acceleration due to gravity (m/s^2), and h_1 and h_2 are height (m).

The change in energy in a system caused by changing its velocity from v_1 to v_2 is called **kinetic energy**, or

$$\Delta E_{\text{KE}} = \tfrac{1}{2}m\left(v_2^2 - v_1^2\right) \tag{1.23}$$

Internal energy U of a system is due to the atomic or molecular structure of the system. The various types of internal energy are nuclear, chemical, molecular, and thermal. The change in internal energy of a system is denoted by ΔU.

Thus,

$$\text{Total change in energy } \Delta E = \Delta U + \Delta E_{\text{KE}} + \Delta E_{\text{PE}} \tag{1.24}$$

In food processing applications, we are often concerned with energy crossing the boundaries of a system. For example, in a pumping application, a fluid may be crossing the system boundary. Similarly, heating a

4. Sir Isaac Newton (1643–1727), an English physicist and mathematician, laid the foundation of calculus, discovered the composition of white light, studied mechanics of planetary motion, derived the inverse square law, and in 1687 authored the *Principia*.

liquid food in a vessel, heat is crossing the walls of the vessel that may comprise the system boundary. The energy crossing the system boundaries is called energy in transit. All forms of energy in transit are imbibed in heat or work. It is important to note that heat or work are not properties of the system because, depending on the path taken from initial to final state, the values of heat or work may be different for each path.

Heat Q is energy transferred due to a temperature differential present between the system and its surroundings. By convention, Q is positive when heat is *entering* the system and negative when heat is *leaving* the system.

Heat can be determined if the heat capacity c is known. Thus,

$$Q = \int_{T_1}^{T_2} c \, dT \tag{1.25}$$

If the path for energy transfer is under constant pressure, then

$$Q = \int c_p \, dT \tag{1.26}$$

Under constant volume conditions

$$Q = \int c_v \, dT \tag{1.27}$$

The numerical values of c_p and c_v are similar for solids and liquids; however, they can be considerably different for gases.

1.16 Work

Whenever there is an action on a system other than due to temperature difference, the energy crossing the system boundary is called work. The path between the initial state and the final state must be specified in order to calculate the work done. This means that work done in going from an initial to a final state can have any value depending on the path chosen. Since work cannot be specified from knowing only the state of the system, work is not a property.

A sign convention must be used to express work. Work done *on* the system *by* the surroundings is negative, while work done *by* the system *on* the surroundings is positive. Thus, work will carry a negative sign any time energy crosses the system boundary *into* the system. Some common situations that involve computation of work are given in the following.

Any time an object is moved from one location to another, work is done on the object. This results in a change in potential energy (ΔE_{PE}) of the object as defined by Eq. (1.22). Since work is done on the object, it will carry a negative sign; therefore,

$$W = -\Delta E_{PE} \tag{1.28}$$

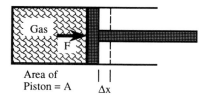

Area of
Piston = A

Δx

Fig. 1.16 Schematic illustration of the expansion of a gas in a cylinder.

When the velocity of an object is increased from v_1 to v_2, there is a corresponding change in the kinetic energy (E_{KE}) of the object; thus,

$$\tfrac{1}{2}mv_2^2 - \tfrac{1}{2}mv_1^2 = \Delta E_{KE} \tag{1.29}$$

Since work is done on the object to raise its velocity, work carries a negative sign

$$W = -\Delta E_{KE} \tag{1.30}$$

Similarly, if there is any friction (f) present in the system, work must be done to overcome it. This can be again expressed as

$$W = -f \tag{1.31}$$

Another situation that involves calculation of work is the expansion of a gas in a cylinder, as shown in Fig. 1.16. Consider a cylinder of an engine, where an expanding gas does work against a moveable piston. The moveable piston has an area A. The pressure on the cylinder is P. The force F exerted by the gas on the piston is

$$F = PA \tag{1.32}$$

Due to the expansion of gas, the piston moves by a distance Δx; then the work done by the gas on the piston is

$$dW = PA\,dx \tag{1.33}$$

or

$$dW = P\,dV \tag{1.34}$$

The total work done by the gas is obtained by integrating Eq. (1.34).

$$W = \int P\,dV \tag{1.35}$$

In case the gas is being compressed in a cylinder, Eq. (1.35) will still hold but ΔV will be negative, indicating that the gas does negative work.
A complete equation for work may be written as

$$W = \int P\,dV - \Delta E_{KE} - \Delta E_{PE} - f \tag{1.36}$$

1.17   Conservation of Energy

The first law of thermodynamics (i.e., "the energy of an isolated system remains constant") is useful in conducting an energy balance. The approach is similar to the mass balance, as presented in Section 1.14. Accordingly, assuming there is no energy generation within the system,

$$
\begin{array}{l}
\text{Energy input} \\
\text{through the} \\
\text{system boundary}
\end{array}
-
\begin{array}{l}
\text{energy output} \\
\text{through the} \\
\text{system boundary}
\end{array}
=
\begin{array}{l}
\text{energy accumulation} \\
\text{within the} \\
\text{system boundary}
\end{array}
\tag{1.37}
$$

The first law of thermodynamics gives a quantitative expression for the principle of energy conservation. According to the first law, the total energy change of a closed system is equal to the heat added to the system minus the work done by the system. Using appropriate signs based on conventions, this can be written mathematically as

$$
\Delta E = Q - W \tag{1.38}
$$

The total energy ΔE of a system is composed of internal thermal energy U, kinetic energy E_{KE}, and potential energy E_{PE}. Thus,

$$
\Delta U + \Delta E_{KE} + \Delta E_{PE} = Q - W \tag{1.39}
$$

Equation (1.36) may be rearranged as,

$$
W + f = \int P\, dV - \Delta E_{KE} - \Delta E_{PE} \tag{1.40}
$$

Eliminating W, ΔE_{KE} and ΔE_{PE} between Eq. (1.39) and Eq. (1.40),

$$
\int P\, dV + \Delta U = Q + f \tag{1.41}
$$

or

$$
\Delta U = Q + f - \int P\, dV \tag{1.42}
$$

From an elementary theorem of calculus, we know that

$$
d(PV) = P\, dV + V\, dP \tag{1.43}
$$

or integrating,

$$
\Delta PV = \int P\, dV + \int V\, dP \tag{1.44}
$$

Thus, we can write

$$
\int P\, dV = \Delta PV - \int V\, dP \tag{1.45}
$$

or substituting Eq. (1.45) into Eq. (1.42)

$$
\Delta U + \Delta PV = Q + f + \int V\, dP \tag{1.46}
$$

Writing Eq. (1.46) in expanded form, noting that Δ for internal energy means final minus initial energy in time, and Δ for other terms means out minus in,

$$U_2 - U_1 + P_2V_2 - P_1V_1 = Q + f + \int V\,dP \tag{1.47}$$

$$(U_2 + P_2V_2) - (U_1 + P_1V_1) = Q + f + \int V\,dP \tag{1.48}$$

In Section 1.12, $U + PV$ was defined as enthalpy, H. Thus,

$$H_2 - H_1 = Q + f + \int V\,dP \tag{1.49}$$

Enthalpy H is widely used in process calculations. Tabulated values of enthalpy are available for many substances, for example, steam, ammonia, food products (see Tables A.4.2, A.6.2, and A.2.7).

For a heating process under constant pressure, friction is absent, and third term on the right-hand side in Eq. (1.49) is zero; thus,

$$H_2 - H_1 = Q \tag{1.50}$$

or

$$\Delta H = Q \tag{1.51}$$

Constant pressure processes are most commonly encountered in food processing applications, thus from Eq. (1.51) change in enthalpy is simply called the **heat content**.

The change in enthalpy ΔH of a system can be determined by actually measuring the change in heat content, Q, for a batch heating process, provided the process occurs at a constant pressure. A calculation procedure may be used to determine the change in enthalpy by using either measured or tabulated properties. We will consider two cases, a process involving sensible heating/cooling, and another process where heating/cooling involves phase change.

1. *Sensible heating at constant pressure.* If the heating process involves an increase in temperature from T_1 to T_2, then,

$$\Delta H = H_2 - H_1 = Q = m\int_{T_1}^{T_2} c_p\,dT \tag{1.52}$$

$$\Delta H = mc_p(T_2 - T_1) \tag{1.53}$$

where c_p is heat capacity (J/kg °C), m is mass, T is temperature and $1, 2$ are initial, final values.

2. *Heating at constant pressure involving phase change.* Heating/cooling processes may occur involving latent heat, where the temperature remains constant while the latent heat is added or removed. For example, when ice is melted, latent heat of fusion is required. Similarly, latent heat of vaporization must be added to water to vaporize it into steam. The latent heat of fusion for water at 0°C is 333.2 kJ/kg. The latent heat of vaporization of

water varies with temperature and pressure. At 100°C, the latent heat of vaporization of water is 2257.06 kJ/kg. The following example illustrates the enthalpy calculations involving latent heats.

EXAMPLE I.II

Five kilograms of ice at −10°C is heated to melt it into water at 0°C; then additional heat is added to vaporize the water into steam. The saturated vapors exit at 100°C. Calculate the different enthalpy values involved in the process. Specific heat of ice is 2.05 kJ/kg K. Specific heat of water is 4.182 kJ/kg K, latent heat of fusion is 333.2 kJ/kg, and latent heat of vaporization at 100°C is 2257.06 kJ/kg.

GIVEN

A plot of temperature versus enthalpy is shown in Fig. 1.17. Note that temperature remains constant in regions that involve latent heat.

SOLUTION

The enthalpy calculations are made separately for each zone in Fig. 1.17.

  (1) Zone A-B

$$\Delta H_{AB} = \Delta Q = m \int_{-10}^{0} c_p \, dT$$

$$= 5(\text{kg}) \times 2.05 \left(\frac{\text{kJ}}{\text{kg}^\circ\text{C}} \right)(0 + 10)^\circ\text{C}$$

$$= 102.5 \frac{\text{kJ}}{\text{kg}}$$

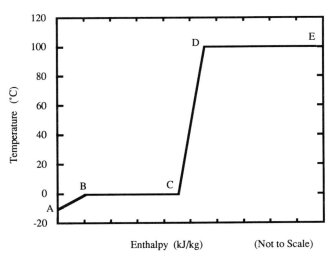

Fig. I.17 A plot of temperature versus enthalpy for melting and vaporization of ice.

(2) Zone B-C

$$\Delta H_{BC} = mH_{latent}$$

$$= 5 \text{ (kg)} \times 333.2\left(\frac{kJ}{kg}\right)$$

$$= 1666 \text{ kJ}$$

(3) Zone C-D

$$\Delta H_{CD} = \Delta Q = m\int_0^{100} c_p \, dT$$

$$= 5(\text{kg}) \times 4.182\left(\frac{kJ}{kg\,°C}\right) \times (100 - 0)(°C)$$

$$= 2091 \text{ kJ}$$

(4) Zone D-E

$$\Delta H_{DE} = mH_{latent}$$

$$= 5(\text{kg}) \times 2257.06\left(\frac{kJ}{kg}\right)$$

$$= 11,285.3 \text{ kJ}$$

(5) Total change in enthalpy

$$\Delta H = \Delta H_{AB} + \Delta H_{BC} + \Delta H_{CD} + \Delta H_{DE}$$
$$= 102.5 + 1666 + 2091 + 11,285.3$$
$$= 15144.8 \text{ kJ}$$

It is evident that almost 70% of the enthalpy is associated with the vaporization process.

EXAMPLE 1.12

A tubular water blancher is being used to process lima beans (Fig. 1.18). The product mass flow rate is 860 kg/hr. It is found that the theoretical energy consumed for the blanching process amounts to 1.19 GJ/hr. The energy lost due to lack of insulation around the blancher is estimated to be 0.24 GJ/hr. If the total energy input to the blancher is 2.71 GJ/hr,

(a) Calculate the energy required to reheat water.
(b) Determine the percent energy associated with each stream.

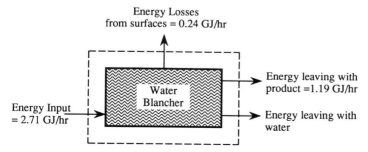

Fig. 1.18 A schematic of a water blancher.

GIVEN

Product mass flow rate = 860 kg/hr
Theoretical energy required by product = 1.19 GJ/hr
Energy lost due to lack of insulation = 0.24 GJ/hr
Energy input to the blancher = 2.71 GJ/hr

APPROACH

We will first write an energy balance and then solve for the unknowns.

SOLUTION

(1) Select 1 hr as a basis.
(2) Energy balance may be written as follows:

Energy input to blancher = energy out with product + energy loss due to lack of insulation + energy out with water

(3) Substituting appropriate values in the energy balance,

$$2.71 = 1.19 + 0.24 + E_W$$

we get

$$E_W = 1.28 \text{ GJ/hr}$$

Thus, the blancher requires $2.71 - 1.28 = 1.43$ GJ/hr to both reheat water and maintain it at conditions necessary to accomplish the blanching process.

(4) The above values can be converted to percentage of total thermal energy input as follows:

$$\text{Energy out with product} = \frac{(1.19)}{2.71}(100) = 43.91\%$$

$$\text{Energy loss due to lack of insulation} = \frac{(0.24)(100)}{2.71} = 8.86\%$$

$$\text{Energy out with water} = \frac{(1.28)(100)}{2.71} = 47.23\%$$

(5) The results indicate that this water blancher operates at about 44% thermal energy efficiency.

EXAMPLE 1.13

Steam is used for peeling of potatoes in a semicontinuous operation. Steam is supplied at the rate of 4 kg per 100 kg of unpeeled potatoes. The unpeeled potatoes enter the system with a temperature of 17°C, and the peeled potatoes leave at 35°C. A waste stream from the system leaves at 60°C. (See Fig. 1.19.) The specific heats of unpeeled potatoes, waste stream, and peeled potatoes are 3.7, 4.2, and 3.5 kJ/kg · K, respectively. If the heat content (assuming 0°C reference temperature) of the steam is 2750 kJ/kg, determine the quantities of the waste stream and the peeled potatoes from the process.

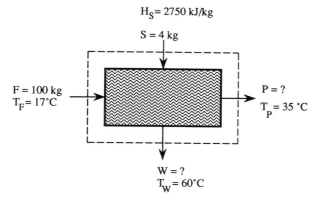

Fig. 1.19 A block diagram showing arrangement of equipment described in Example 1.13.

GIVEN

Mass flow of steam = 4 kg per 100 kg of unpeeled potatoes
Temperature of unpeeled potatoes = 17°C
Temperature of peeled potatoes = 35°C
Temperature of waste stream = 60°C
Specific heat of unpeeled potatoes = 3.7 kJ/kg K
Specific heat of peeled potatoes = 3.5 kJ/kg K
Specific heat of waste stream = 4.2 kJ/kg K
Heat content of steam = 2750 kJ/kg

SOLUTION

(1) Select 100 kg of unpeeled potatoes as a basis.
(2) From mass balance

$$F + S = W + P$$
$$100 + 4 = W + P$$
$$W = 104 - P$$

(3) From energy balance

$$Fc_p(T_F - 0) + SH_s = Wc_p(T_W - 0) + Pc_p(T_P - 0)$$
$$100(3.7)(17) + 4(2750) = W(4.2)(60) + P(3.5)(35)$$
$$6290 + 11000 = 252W + 122.5P$$

(4) From step (3)

$$17290 = 252(104 - P) + 122.5P$$
$$252P - 122.5P = 26208 - 17290 = 8918$$
$$P = 68.87 \text{ kg}$$
$$W = 35.14 \text{ kg}$$

(5) The results show that for every 100 kg of unpeeled potatoes, there will be 68.87 kg of peeled potatoes and 35.14 kg of waste stream in this steam-peeling operation.

___

1.18 Power

Power is defined as rate of doing work, with the dimensions $(mass)(length)^2(time)^{-3}$ and SI units of watts (W). In the English system the commonly used unit for power is horsepower (hp), where 1 hp = 0.7457 kW.

Problems

1.1 The following unit conversions are illustrations of the SI system of units. Convert:

(a) A thermal conductivity value of 0.3 Btu/hr·ft·°F to W/m·°C
(b) A surface heat transfer coefficient value of 105 Btu/hr·ft²· °F to W/m²·°C.
(c) A latent heat of fusion value of 121 Btu/lb$_m$ to J/kg.

1.2 A liquid product with 10% product solids is blended with sugar before being concentrated (removal of water) to obtain a final product with 15% product solids and 15% sugar solids. Determine the quantity of final product obtained from 200 kg of liquid product. How much sugar is required? Compute mass of water removed during concentration.

1.3 A food product is being frozen in a system capable of removing 6000 kJ of thermal energy. The product has a specific heat of 4 kJ/kg ·°C above the freezing temperature of −2°C, the latent heat of fusion equals 275 kJ/kg, and the frozen product has a specific heat of 2.5 kJ/kg ·°C below −2°C. If 10 kg of product enters the system at 10°C, determine the exit temperature of the product.

1.4 A liquid food product is being cooled from 80 to 30°C in an indirect heat exchanger using cold water as a cooling medium. If the product mass flow rate is 1800 kg/hr, determine the water flow rate required to accomplish product cooling if the water is allowed to increase from 10 to 20°C in the heat exchanger. The specific heat of product is 3.8 kJ/kg · K and the value for water is 4.1 kJ/kg · K.

1.5 Milk is flowing through a heat exchanger at a rate of 2000 kg/hr. The heat exchanger supplies 111,600 kJ/hr. The outlet temperature of the product is 95°C. Determine the inlet temperature of the milk. The product specific heat is 3.9 kJ/kg ·°C.

List of Symbols

A area (m^2)

a acceleration (m/s^2)

c specific heat (kJ/kg °C)

c_p specific heat at constant pressure (kJ/kg °C)

c_v specific heat at constant volume (kJ/kg °C)

E energy (kJ/kg)

E_{KE} kinetic energy (kJ/kg)

E_{PE} potential energy (kJ/kg)

F force (N)

f friction energy (kJ/kg)

g acceleration due to gravity (m/s^2)

g_c constant

H enthalpy (kJ)

h height of fluid (m)

H_s enthalpy of steam (kJ/kg)

I constant in Eq. (1.17)

k proportionality constant

M molecular weight

M' molality (mole solute/kg solvent)

m mass (kg)

MC_{db} moisture content, dry basis (kg water/kg dry solids)

MC_{wb} moisture content, wet basis (kg water/kg wet product)

n number of moles

P pressure (Pa)

Q heat (kJ/kg)

R gas constant ($m^3 \cdot Pa/kg \cdot K$)

ρ density (kg/m^3)

R_0 universal gas constant ($8314.41\ m^3 \cdot Pa/kg \cdot mol \cdot K$)

T temperature (°C)

T_A absolute temperature (K)

U internal energy (kJ/kg)

v velocity (m/s)

V' specific volume (m^3/kg)

W work (kJ/kg)

W' Weight (N)

x mass fraction (dimensionless)

X_A mole fraction of A

Bibliography

Earle, R. L. (1983). "Unit Operations in Food Processing," 2nd ed. Pergamon Press, Oxford.

Himmelblau, D. M. (1967). "Basic Principles and Calculations in Chemical Engineering," 2nd ed. Prentice-Hall Englewood Cliffs, New Jersey.

Mohsenin, N. N. (1978). "Physical Properties of Plant and Animal Materials: Structure, Physical Characteristics and Mechanical Properties," 2nd ed. Gordon and Breach Science Publishers, New York.

Peleg, M. (1983). Physical characteristics of food powders. In "Physical Properties of Foods" (M. Peleg and E. B. Bagley, eds.) AVI Publ. Co., Westport, Connecticut.

Singh, R. P., Carroad, P. A., Chinnan, M. S., Rose, W. W., and Jacob, N. L. (1980). Energy accounting in canning tomato products. *J. Food Sci.* **45**, 735–739.

Toledo, R. T. (1991). "Fundamentals of Food Process Engineering," 2nd ed. Van Nostrand Reinhold, New York.

Watson, E. L., and Harper, J. C. (1988). "Elements of Food Engineering," 2nd ed. Van Nostrand Reinhold, New York.

CHAPTER 2

Fluid Flow in Food Processing

In any commercial food processing plant, the movement of liquid products or product ingredients from one location to another becomes an essential operation. Various systems are used for transport of raw or unprocessed components, as well as processed products before packaging. The design of these systems in food processing is unique from most other applications due to the essential needs of sanitation to maintain product quality. In addition, the transport system must be designed to allow for ease and efficiency in cleaning. This section will deal with several aspects of liquid food transport as needed to gain an understanding of the factors considered in design of liquid food transport systems.

2.1 Liquid Transport Systems

A typical liquid transport system will consist of four basic components, as illustrated in Fig. 2.1. The liquid product will be contained in some vessel prior to transport, and a second vessel after the desired transport is achieved. Between the two vessels is the conduit or pipeline for liquid flow. Unless flow can be achieved by gravity, the third primary component is the pump, where mechanical energy is used to enhance product transport. The fourth component of the system is the valve used to control or direct flow. The vessels used in these types of systems may be of any size and configuration.

2.1.1 Pipelines for Processing Plants

The pipelines used for liquid foods and liquid food components have numerous unique features. Probably the most evident feature is the use of stainless steel for construction. This metal provides smoothness, cleanabil-

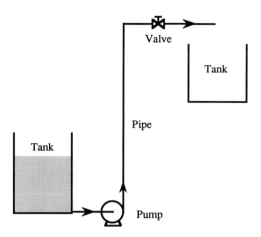

Fig. 2.1 Schematic illustration of a liquid food transport system.

ity, and corrosion prevention. The corrosion resistance of stainless steel is attributed to "passivity": the formation of a surface film on the metal surface when exposed to air. In practice, this surface film must re-form each time after the surface is cleaned. Failure to establish "passivity," or any action resulting in film removal, will create an active site for corrosion. It follows that stainless steel surfaces do require care to maintain corrosion resistance, especially after cleaning. More detailed description of corrosion mechanisms is given by Heldman and Seiberling (1976).

A typical pipeline for liquid food transport contains several essential components. In addition to the straight lengths of pipe, which may vary in diameter from 2 to 10 cm, elbows and tees become essential to changing the direction of product movement. As illustrated in Fig. 2.2, these components or fittings are welded into the pipeline or system and may be used in several different configurations. Another component of the pipeline is the valve used for liquid foods; the most popular is the air-actuated valve illustrated in Fig. 2.3. The popularity of this valve is associated with the ability for remote operation, often based on some type of preset signal.

It is essential that all components of the pipeline system contribute to sanitary handling of the product. The stainless-steel surfaces assure smoothness needed for cleaning and sanitizing. In addition, proper use of the system provides the desired corrosion prevention. Since cleaning of these systems is most often accomplished by in-place cleaning (CIP), design of the system must account for this factor.

2.1.2 Types of Pumps

With the exception of situations where gravity can be used to move liquid product or product components, some type of mechanical energy must be

Fig. 2.2 A typical liquid food processing system, illustrating pipelines and pipeline components. (Courtesy of CREPACO, Inc.)

introduced to overcome the forces opposing transport. The two most popular types of pumps in the food industry are centrifugal and positive displacement. There are variations within each of these types, but the concepts of operation for each type is the same.

a. Centrifugal Pumps

The utilization of centrifugal force to increase the liquid pressure is the basic concept associated with operation of a centrifugal pump. As illustrated schematically in Fig. 2.4a, the pump consists of a motor-driven impeller enclosed in a case. Product enters the pump at the center of impeller rotation and, due to the centrifugal force, moves to the impeller periphery. At this point, the liquid experiences maximum pressure and moves through the exit to the pipeline.

Most sanitary centrifugal pumps, used in the food industry use two-vane impellers (Fig. 2.4b). Impellers with three and four vanes are available and may be used in some applications. Centrifugal pumps are most efficient with low-viscosity liquids when flow rates are high and pressure requirements are moderate. Liquids with high viscosity are difficult to transport with centrifugal pumps, due to higher friction that prevents the attainment of the required liquid velocities.

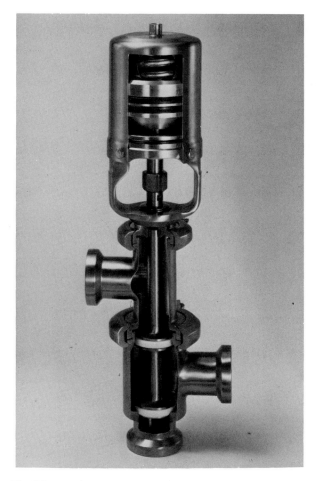

Fig. 2.3   An air-actuated valve for liquid foods. (Courtesy of Cherry-Burrell Corporation.)

Flow rates through a centrifugal pump are controlled by the use of a valve on the discharge pipe. This approach provides an inexpensive means for flow-rate regulation, including complete closure of the discharge valve to stop flow. Since this step will not damage the pump, it is used frequently in liquid food processing operations. Blocking flow from a centrifugal pump for long periods of time is not recommended due to the possibilities of damage to the product. The simple design of the centrifugal pump makes it easily adaptable to in-place cleaning.

b. Positive Displacement Pumps

By application of direct force to a confined liquid, a positive displacement pump produces the pressure required to move the liquid product.

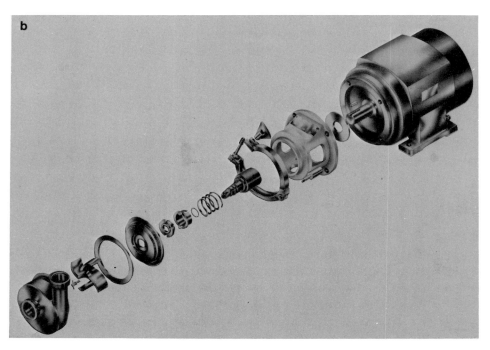

Fig. 2.4 (a) Exterior view of a centrifugal pump. (Courtesy of Cherry-Burrell Corporation.) (b) A centrifugal pump with components. (Courtesy of CREPACO, Inc.)

Fig. 2.5   A positive displacement pump with illustration of internal components. (Courtesy of Tri-Canada, Inc.)

The product movement is directly related to the speed of the moving parts within the pump. Thus the product flow rates are accurately controlled by drive speed to the pump. The mechanism of operation also allows a positive displacement pump to transport liquids with high viscosities.

A **rotary pump** is one type of positive displacement pump and is illustrated in Fig. 2.5. Although there are several types of rotary pumps, the general operating concept involves enclosure of a pocket of liquid between the rotating portion of the pump and the pump housing. The pump delivers a set volume of liquid from the inlet to the pump outlet. Rotary pumps include sliding vane, lobe type, internal gear, and gear type pumps. In most cases, at least one moving part of the rotary pump must be made of a material that will withstand rubbing action occurring within the pump. This is an important feature of the pump design that ensures tight seals. The rotary pump has a capability to reverse the flow direction by reversing the direction of rotor rotation.

The second type of positive displacement pump is the **reciprocating pump**. As suggested by the name, pumping action is achieved by application of force by a piston to a liquid within a cylinder. The liquid moves out of the cylinder through an outlet valve during forward piston movement. Reciprocating pumps usually consist of several cylinder–piston arrangements operating at different cycle positions to ensure more uniform outlet pressures. Most applications are for low-viscosity liquids requiring low flow rates and high pressures.

The **axial flow** type of positive displacement pump is the least used type in the food industry. The pump uses a single-helix rotor and double-helix case to move liquid product in a direction parallel to the axis of rotor rotation. The pump is adaptable to high-viscosity liquids as well as low-viscosity liquids and can be used for slurries or suspensions without damage to pump components or the product.

2.2 Properties of Liquids

The transport of a liquid food by one of the systems described in the previous section is directly related to liquid properties, primarily viscosity and density. These properties will influence the power requirements for liquid transport as well as the flow characteristics within the pipeline. An understanding of the physical meaning associated with these properties is necessary to deal more effectively with the design of a transport system. In addition, an appreciation of the approaches used for measurement of these properties is useful. First, we will consider how materials respond to the application of a force.

2.2.1 Role of Stress in Fluid Flow

Fluid flow takes place when stress is applied on a fluid. Stress is defined as force per unit area. When a force acting on a surface is perpendicular to it, the stress is called **normal stress**. More commonly, normal stress is referred to as **pressure**. When the force acts parallel to the surface, the stress is called **shear stress**, σ. When shear stress is applied to a fluid, the fluid cannot support the shear stress; instead the fluid deforms, or simply stated, it flows.

The influence of shear stress on solids and liquids leads to a broad classification of such materials as plastic, elastic, and fluid.

In the case of an **elastic** solid, when shear stress is applied, there is a proportional finite deformation, and there is no flow of the material. On removal of the applied stress, the solid returns to its original shape.

A **plastic** material, on the other hand, deforms continuously on the application of shear stress; the rate of deformation is proportional to the shear stress. When the shear stress is removed, the object shows some recovery. Examples include Jell-O and some types of soft cheese.

A **fluid** deforms continuously on the application of shear stress. The rate of deformation is proportional to the applied shear stress. There is no recovery; that is, the fluid does not retain or attempt to retain its original shape when the stress is withdrawn.

When normal stress or pressure is applied on a liquid, there is no observed appreciable effect. Thus, liquids are called **incompressible** fluids, whereas gases are **compressible** fluids, since increased pressure results in considerable reduction in volume occupied by a gas.

2.2.2 Density

The density of a liquid is defined as its mass per unit volume and is expressed as kg/m^3 in the SI unit system. In a physical sense, the magnitude of the density is the mass of a quantity of a given liquid occupying a defined unit volume. The most evident factor is that the magnitude of density is influenced by temperature. For example, the density of water decreases consistently with temperature as temperatures exceed 4°C (see Table A.4.1).

Densities of liquids are most often measured by a hand hydrometer. This instrument measures specific gravity: the ratio of the density of the given liquid to the density of water at the same temperature. The instrument is a weighted float attached to a small-diameter stem containing a scale of specific-gravity values. The float will sink into the unknown liquid by an amount proportional to the specific gravity, and the resulting liquid level is read on the stem scale. Care must be taken, when converting specific gravity values to density, to ensure that the value for density of water at the measurement temperature is utilized.

2.2.3 Viscosity

The liquid property that has the most dramatic influence on flow characteristics is viscosity. Viscosity is the liquid property that describes the magnitude of the resistance due to shear forces within the liquid.

As noted in Section 2.2.1, a fluid does not permanently resist distortion; instead, it changes its shape. When subjected to stress, the fluid will continue to deform, that is, it will flow. The velocity of flow increases with increasing stress. Different fluids exhibit different degrees of resistance to the applied stress. The fluid property that denotes the resistance between the internal layers of a fluid to the movement is called **viscosity**. A more quantitative understanding of these viscous forces is developed in the following paragraphs.

Consider that a fluid of interest is contained by two infinitely large (very long and very wide) parallel plates separated by a small distance Δy, as shown in Fig. 2.6. The top plate is subjected to a constant force F. Therefore, the top plate moves in the direction of the applied force, parallel to the bottom plate. The velocity of the top plate is constant at Δu,

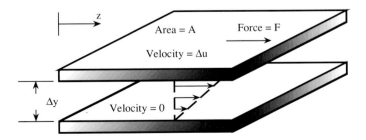

Fig. 2.6 Schematic illustration of velocity profile in liquid as used to define viscosity.

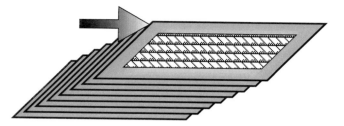

Fig. 2.7 Illustration of drag generated on underlying cards as the top card in a deck is moved. This is analogous to the movement of the top layer of a fluid.

while the bottom plate is stationary. One may visualize that, between the two plates, the fluid consists of several layers, each layer moving in the z direction. The top fluid layer in contact with the top plate is moving at a velocity of Δu; however, the next layer below it moves at a slightly lower velocity, and so on to the bottom-most layer that is in contact with the bottom plate (which is stationary). Thus a layer of liquid tends to drag the adjacent layer immediately below it. This situation is analogous to a deck of cards: If the top card in the deck is moved in the z direction, it drags the card immediately below it, and that card drags the one below it, and so on, as seen in Fig. 2.7.

The velocity profile of different layers is linear with y direction. Based on experimental observations, the magnitude of force F is found to be directly proportional to both velocity Δu and surface area A of the plate, and inversely proportional to the separation between the two plates Δy.

Thus,

$$F \propto A \frac{\Delta u}{\Delta y} \tag{2.1}$$

or

$$\frac{F}{A} = -\mu \frac{\Delta u}{\Delta y} \tag{2.2}$$

where μ is proportionality constant, called the coefficient of viscosity.

The negative sign is introduced since momentum is transferred down the gradient from high to low velocity regions.

If in Eq. (2.2) Δy is allowed to approach zero, then,

$$\sigma = \frac{F}{A} = -\mu \frac{du}{dy} \tag{2.3}$$

Liquids that follow Eq. (2.3) are called Newtonian liquids. Water is a Newtonian liquid; other foods that exhibit Newtonian characteristics include honey, fluid milk, and fruit juices. Some examples of coefficients of viscosity are given in Table 2.1. Properties of non-Newtonian liquids will be discussed later in Section 2.3.4.

TABLE 2.1
The Viscosity of Some Common Materials at Room Temperature

Liquid	Viscosity, approximate (Pa · s)
Air	10^{-5}
Water	10^{-3}
Olive oil	10^{-1}
Glycerol	10^0
Liquid honey	10^1
Golden syrup	10^2
Glass	10^{40}

Shear stress σ is obtained using Eq. (2.3). Since force is expressed by N (newtons) and area by m^2 (meters squared),

$$\sigma = \frac{N}{m^2} = Pa$$

In Eq. (2.3), the term du/dy is called **rate of shear** or **shear rate**. Its units are $1/s$, determined by dividing the change in velocity (m/s) by distance (m).

Therefore, the units of the viscosity coefficient are

$$\mu = \frac{\sigma}{du/dy} = \frac{Pa}{1/s} = Pa \cdot s$$

Other unit systems produce different units for viscosity. The most common is the cgs system, where shear stress is dyn/cm^2 and shear rate is $1/s$, or

$$\mu = \frac{dyn \cdot s}{cm^2} = poise$$

Frequently, viscosity of liquids will be expressed in centipoise (0.01 poise). The viscosity of water is about 1 centipoise at ambient temperatures, whereas the viscosity of honey is 8880 centipoise.

EXAMPLE 2.1

Determine the shear stress for water at ambient temperature when exposed to a shear rate of $100 \ s^{-1}$.

GIVEN

Viscosity of water at ambient temperature = 1 centipoise = 0.01 poise = 0.01 $dyn \cdot s/cm^2$

Conversion to SI units: 1 centipoise = 10^{-3} Pa · s

APPROACH

Use the basic definition of viscosity, Eq. (2.3), to calculate shear stress from the knowledge of viscosity and shear rate.

SOLUTION

(1) For cgs systems

$$\sigma = (0.01 \text{ poise})(100 \text{ s}^{-1}) = 1 \text{ dyn/cm}^2$$

(2) For SI systems

$$\sigma = (10^{-3} \text{ Pa} \cdot \text{s})(100 \text{ s}^{-1}) = 0.1 \text{ Pa}$$

(3) Note: $1 \text{ dyn/cm}^2 = 1 \text{ g/cm} \cdot \text{s}^2 = 0.1 \text{ kg/m} \cdot \text{s}^2 = 0.1 \text{ N/m}^2 = 0.1 \text{ Pa}$

2.3 Measurement of Viscosity

Viscosity of a liquid can be measured using a variety of approaches and methods. The capillary tube and the rotational viscometer are the more common types of instruments used in measuring viscosity of liquids.

2.3.1 Capillary Tube Viscometer

The capillary tube measurement is based on the schematic illustration shown in Fig. 2.8. As shown, the pressure (ΔP) is sufficient to overcome the shear forces within the liquid and produce flow of a given rate. The shear forces are operating on all internal liquid surfaces for the entire length L of tube and distance r from the tube center. The shear stress is force per unit

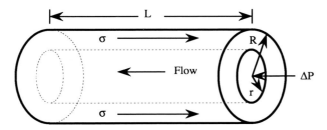

Fig. 2.8   Force balance for a section of capillary tube.

area, where area is the circumferential area; then

$$\sigma = \frac{F}{2\pi rL} \tag{2.4}$$

and the pressure (ΔP) is force per unit area, where area is cross-sectional area. Then

$$\Delta P = \frac{F}{\pi r^2} \tag{2.5}$$

or

$$F = (\pi r^2)\, \Delta P \tag{2.6}$$

Thus

$$\sigma = \frac{\Delta P(\pi r^2)}{2\pi rL} = \frac{\Delta P r}{2L} \tag{2.7}$$

From Eq. (2.7), it is evident that the shear stress σ will increase from a value of zero at the center of the tube to $\Delta PR/2L$ at the tube wall (where $r = R$).

Combining Eq. (2.1) and Eq. (2.7),

$$\frac{\Delta P r}{2L} = -\mu \frac{du}{dr} \tag{2.8}$$

By separating the variables,

$$du = -\frac{\Delta P}{2\mu L} r\, dr \tag{2.9}$$

and by integration from the tube wall R where $u = 0$ to any location r where the local velocity is u,

$$\int_0^u du = -\frac{\Delta P}{2\mu L} \int_R^r r\, dr \tag{2.10}$$

then

$$u = \frac{\Delta P}{4\mu L}(R^2 - r^2) \tag{2.11}$$

Equation (2.11) is an expression for the velocity profile indicating that, for a liquid with viscosity μ, the liquid velocity will be u at location r when a pressure drop ΔP exists across the tube length L.

The cross-sectional area of a shell within the tube (Fig. 2.8) can be expressed as

$$dA = 2\pi r\, dr \tag{2.12}$$

Then the volume of liquid flowing in the shell per unit time (i.e., volumetric flow rate) must be velocity u multiplied by area dA, or

$$d\dot{V} = (u)(2\pi r\, dr) \tag{2.13}$$

By integration from the tube center ($r = 0$) to the tube wall ($r = R$), and substituting for the velocity u from Eq. (2.11),

$$\dot{V} = \int_0^R 2\pi r \frac{\Delta P}{4\mu L} \left[(R^2 - r^2) \right] dr \qquad (2.14)$$

$$\dot{V} = \frac{\pi \Delta P R^4}{8\mu L} \qquad (2.15)$$

Equation (2.15) provides the basis for design and operation of any capillary tube viscometer. For a tube with length L and radius R, measurement of a volumetric flow rate $\dot{V}$ at a pressure ΔP will allow determination of viscosity μ.

$$\mu = \frac{\pi \Delta P R^4}{8 L \dot{V}} \qquad (2.16)$$

Since Eq. (2.16) is derived for a Newtonian fluid, any flow rate–pressure drop combination will give the same viscosity value.

Equation 2.15 is also useful in determining the volumetric flow rate in a circular pipe when the dimensions of the pipe (namely radius and length), viscosity of liquid, and the pressure drop along the pipe are known.

EXAMPLE 2.2

A capillary tube viscometer is being used to measure the viscosity of honey at 30°C. The tube radius is 2.5 cm and the length is 25 cm. The following data have been collected:

ΔP (Pa)	$\dot{V}$ (cm^3/s)
10.0	1.25
12.5	1.55
15.0	1.80
17.5	2.05
20.0	2.55

Determine the viscosity of honey from the data collected.

GIVEN

Data required to compute viscosity values from Eq. (2.16), for example,

$$\Delta P = 12.5 \text{ Pa}$$
$$R = 2.5 \text{ cm} = 0.025 \text{ m}$$
$$L = 25 \text{ cm} = 0.25 \text{ m}$$
$$\dot{V} = 1.55 \text{ cm}^3/\text{s} = 1.55 \times 10^{-6} \text{ m}^3/\text{s}$$

APPROACH

The viscosity for each pressure difference (ΔP) and flow rate ($\dot{V}$) combination can be computed from Eq. (2.16).

SOLUTION

(1) Using Eq. (2.16), a viscosity value can be computed for each ΔP–$\dot{V}$ combination; for example,

$$\mu = \frac{\pi(12.5 \text{ Pa})(0.025 \text{ m})^4}{8(0.25 \text{ m})(1.55 \times 10^{-6} \text{ m}^3/\text{s})} = 4.948 \text{ Pa} \cdot \text{s}$$

(2) By repeating the same calculation at each ΔP–$\dot{V}$ combination, the following information is obtained:

ΔP (Pa)	$\dot{V}$ ($\times 10^{-6}$ m^3/s)	μ (Pa · s)
10	1.25	4.909
12.5	1.55	4.948
15	1.8	5.113
17.5	2.05	5.238
20	2.55	4.812

(3) Although there is some variability in viscosity with pressure (ΔP), there is no indication of a consistent trend, and the best estimate of the viscosity would be the arithmetic mean.

$$\mu = 5.004 \text{ Pa} \cdot \text{s}$$

If we allow the gravitational force to provide the pressure for liquid flow, such as in a glass capillary tube, then a simple variation of the mathematical formulation developed for the capillary tube viscometer is used. By recognizing that

$$\Delta P = \frac{\rho V g}{A} \tag{2.17}$$

or

$$\Delta P = \rho L g \tag{2.18}$$

then Eq. (2.16) becomes

$$\mu = \frac{\pi \rho L g R^4}{8 L \dot{V}} = \frac{\pi \rho g R^4}{8 \dot{V}} \tag{2.19}$$

Since the viscosity measurements will be a function of time for liquid to flow from the capillary tube, then noting that the volume of the cylindrical tube is $V = \pi R^2 L$ and mass = (volume)(density), we get

$$\mu = \frac{\pi \rho g R^4 t}{8 V} = \frac{mgt}{8 \pi L^2} \tag{2.20}$$

Equation (2.20) illustrates that viscosity of a liquid measured by a glass capillary tube will be a function of the liquid mass m in the tube, the acceleration due to gravity ($g = 9.8$ m/s^2), and the tube length L. By measurement of the time for the liquid to drain from the tube, the viscosity can be determined.

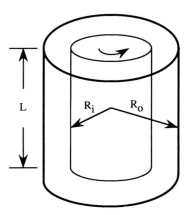

Fig. 2.9   Schematic illustration of coaxial-cylinder rotational viscometer.

2.3.2   Rotational Viscometer

The second type of viscometer is the rotational viscometer illustrated in
Fig. 2.9. This illustration is more specific for a coaxial-cylinder viscometer
with the liquid placed in the space between the inner and outer cylinders.
The measurement involves recording of torque Ω required to turn the
inner cylinder at a given number of revolutions per unit time. To calculate
viscosity from the measurements, the relationships between torque Ω and
shear stress σ, as well as revolutions per unit second N and shear rate γ
must be established.

   It can be shown that the relationship between torque Ω and shear
stress σ will be

$$\Omega = 2\pi r^2 L \sigma \qquad (2.21)$$

where the length L of the cylinder and the radial location r between the
inner and outer cylinder are accounted for. The shear rate γ for a
rotational system becomes a function of angular velocity ω as follows:

$$\gamma = r\frac{d\omega}{dr} \qquad (2.22)$$

By substitution of these relationships into Eq. (2.3),

$$\frac{\Omega}{2\pi L r^2} = -\mu\left(r\frac{d\omega}{dr}\right) \qquad (2.23)$$

   To obtain the desired relationship for viscosity, an integration between
the outer and inner cylinders must be performed.

$$\int_0^{\omega_i} d\omega = -\frac{\Omega}{2\pi\mu L}\int_{R_o}^{R_i} r^{-3}\, dr \qquad (2.24)$$

where the outer cylinder (R_o) is stationary ($\omega = 0$) and the inner cylinder

(R_i) has an angular velocity $\omega = \omega_i$. The integration leads to

$$\omega_i = \frac{\Omega}{4\pi\mu L}\left(\frac{1}{R_i^2} - \frac{1}{R_o^2}\right)$$

(2.25)

and since

$$\omega_i = 2\pi N$$

(2.26)

then

$$\mu = \frac{\Omega}{8\pi^2 NL}\left(\frac{1}{R_i^2} - \frac{1}{R_o^2}\right)$$

(2.27)

Equation (2.27) illustrates that liquid viscosity can be determined using a coaxial-cylinder viscometer with an inner cylinder radius R_i, length L, and outer cylinder radius R_o by measurement of torque Ω at a given N (revolutions per unit second).

A variation of the coaxial-cylinder viscometer is the single-cylinder viscometer. In this device, a single cylinder of radius R_i is immersed in a container with the test sample. Then the outer cylinder radius R_o approaches infinity, and Eq. (2.27) becomes

$$\mu = \frac{\Omega}{8\pi^2 NLR_i^2}$$

(2.28)

Several rotational viscometers operate using the single-cylinder principle, which assumes that the wall of the vessel containing the liquid during measurement has no influence on the shear stresses within the liquid. This may be a relatively good assumption for Newtonian liquids but should be evaluated carefully for each liquid to be measured.

EXAMPLE 2.3

A single-cylinder rotational viscometer with a 1-cm radius and 6-cm length is being used to measure liquid viscosity. The following torque readings were obtained at several values of revolutions per minute (rpm):

N (rpm)	$\Omega(\times 10^{-3}$ N $\cdot$ cm$)$
3	1.2
6	2.3
9	3.7
12	5.0

Compute the viscosity of the liquid based on the information provided.

GIVEN

Equation (2.28) requires the following input data (for example):

$$\Omega = 2.3 \times 10^{-3} \text{ N} \cdot \text{cm} = 2.3 \times 10^{-5} \text{ N} \cdot \text{m}$$
$$N = 6 \text{ rpm} = 0.1 \text{ rev/s}$$
$$L = 6 \text{ cm} = 0.06 \text{ m}$$
$$R_i = 1 \text{ cm} = 0.01 \text{ m}$$

APPROACH

Use Eq. (2.28) to calculate viscosity from each rpm–torque reading combination.

SOLUTION

(1) Using Eq. (2.28) and the given data,

$$\mu = \frac{(2.3 \times 10^{-5} \text{ N} \cdot \text{m})}{8\pi^2(0.1 \text{ rev/s})(0.06 \text{ m})(0.01 \text{ m})^2} = 0.485 \text{ Pa} \cdot \text{s}$$

(2) Using the same approach, values of viscosity are obtained for each N–Ω combination.

N (rev/s)	Ω ($\times 10^{-5}$ N $\cdot$ m)	m (Pa $\cdot$ s)
0.05	1.2	0.507
0.1	2.3	0.485
0.15	3.7	0.521
0.2	5.0	0.528

(3) Since it is assumed that the liquid is Newtonian, the four values can be used to compute an arithmetic mean of

$$\mu = 0.510 \text{ Pa} \cdot \text{s}$$

2.3.3 Influence of Temperature on Viscosity

The magnitude of the viscosity coefficient for a liquid is significantly influenced by temperature. Since temperature is changed dramatically during many processing operations, it is important to obtain appropriate viscosity values for liquids over the range of temperatures encountered during processing. This temperature dependence of viscosity also requires that during measurements of viscosity, extra care must be taken to avoid temperature fluctuations. In the case of water, the temperature sensitivity of viscosity from Table A.4.1 is estimated to be 3%/°C at room temperature. This means that ±1% accuracy in its measurement requires the sample temperature to be maintained within ±0.3°C.

There is considerable evidence that the influence of temperature on viscosity for a liquid food may be described by an Arrhenius-type relationship.

$$\ln \mu = \ln B_A + \frac{E_a}{R_g T_A} \tag{2.29}$$

where B_A is the Arrhenius constant, E_a is an activation energy constant, and R_g is the gas constant. Equation (2.29) can be used to reduce the number of measurements required to describe the influence of temperature on viscosity of a liquid food. If values can be obtained at three or more temperatures within the desired range and the magnitudes of the constants $(B_A$ and $E_a/R_g)$ can be established, the viscosity coefficient at other temperatures within the range can be predicted with reasonable accuracy.

2.3.4 Properties of Non-Newtonian Liquids

The properties of non-Newtonian liquids can be studied by classifying these liquids as time-independent and time-dependent (Fig. 2.10). The **time-independent non-Newtonian** liquids respond immediately with a flow as soon as a small amount of shear stress is applied. Unlike Newtonian liquids, the relationship between shear stress and shear rate is nonlinear, as shown in Fig. 2.11. There are two important types of **time-independent non-Newtonian liquids**, namely, shear-thinning liquids and shear-thickening liquids. The differences between these two types of liquids can be easily understood by considering another commonly used term called apparent viscosity.

An **apparent viscosity** is calculated by using a gross assumption that the non-Newtonian liquid is obeying Newton's law of viscosity [Eq. (2.3)]. Thus, at any selected shear rate, a straight line is drawn from the selected point on the curve to the origin (Fig. 2.12). The slope of this straight line gives a value for the apparent viscosity. It should be evident that using this

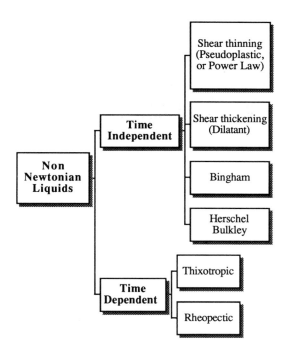

Fig. 2.10 Classification of non-Newtonian liquids.

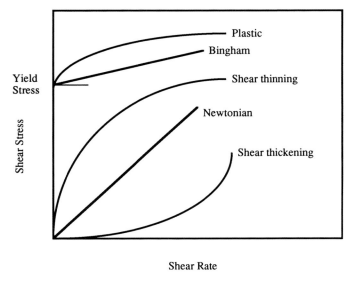

Fig. 2.11   Shear stress–shear rate relationships for Newtonian and non-Newtonian liquids.

method, the value obtained for the apparent viscosity is dependent on the selected shear rate. For a **shear-thinning liquid**, as the shear rate increases, the apparent viscosity decreases; thus the name—shear thinning—is used to describe the behavior of these liquids. It should be noted that apparent viscosity must always be expressed along with the value of shear rate used to calculate it; otherwise, it is meaningless.

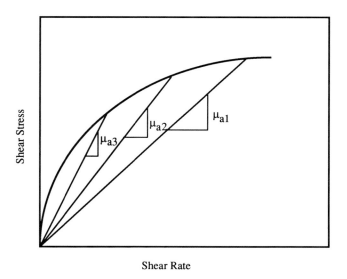

Fig. 2.12   Determination of apparent viscosity from shear stress–shear rate plot.

Shear-thinning liquids are also called **pseudoplastic** or **power law** liquids. Some common examples of shear-thinning liquids are condensed milk, fruit purees, mayonnaise, mustard, and vegetable soups.

If the increase in shear rate results in an increase in the apparent viscosity, then the liquid is called a **shear-thickening liquid** (or sometimes called **dilatant liquid**). Examples of shear-thickening liquids include homogenized peanut butter, 60% suspension of corn starch in water.

Time-dependent non-Newtonian liquids obtain a constant value of apparent viscosity only after a certain finite time has elapsed after the application of shear stress. These types of liquids are also called **thixotropic** materials; examples include certain types of starch pastes. For more discussion of these types of liquids refer to Doublier and Lefebvre (1989).

Another important class of non-Newtonian liquids require the application of **yield stress** prior to any response. For example, certain types of tomato catsup will not flow until a certain yield stress is applied. For these types of liquids, a plot of shear stress against shear rate does not pass through the origin, as shown in Fig. 2.11. After the application of yield stress, the response of these liquids can be similar to a Newtonian liquid; in that case they are called **Bingham liquids**. On the other hand, if the response of the liquid, after the yield stress is applied, is similar to a shear-thinning flow, then they are called **plastic**.

A common mathematical model may be used to express the non-Newtonian characteristics. This model is referred to as **Herschel–Bulkley model** (Herschel and Bulkley, 1926).

$$\sigma = K\left(\frac{du}{dy}\right)^n + \sigma_0 \qquad (2.30)$$

where the values for the different coefficients are given in Table 2.2.

TABLE 2.2
Values of Coefficients in Herschel – Bulkley Fluid Model

Fluid	K	n	σ_0	Typical examples
Herschel–Bulkley	> 0	$0 < n < \infty$	> 0	minced fish paste, raisin paste
Newtonian	> 0	1	0	water, fruit juice, honey, milk, vegetable oil
Shear-thinning (pseudoplastic)	> 0	$0 < n < 1$	0	applesauce, banana puree, orange juice concentrate
Shear-thickening	> 0	$1 < n < \infty$	0	some types of honey, 40% raw corn starch solution
Bingham Plastic	> 0	1	> 0	toothpaste, tomato paste

Source: Steffe (1992).

2.4   Handling Systems for Newtonian Liquids

In a food processing plant, liquid foods are processed in a variety of ways, including heating, cooling, concentrating, or mixing. The movement of these liquid foods from one location to another is mostly achieved by using pumps, although gravity systems are employed when feasible. Depending on the velocity of the liquid and the internal viscous and inertial forces, different types of flow characteristics are obtained. The energy required to pump a liquid would be different under different flow conditions. In this section, we will study quantitative methods to describe the flow characteristics and mathematical expressions that are useful in determining the energy required to transport liquid foods.

2.4.1   Flow Characteristics

The flow of a liquid within a pipe or tube can be characterized in several ways. These flow characteristics have a significant influence on the transport of the liquid and the energy requirements. Flow may be expressed as mass flow rate $\dot{m}$ or volumetric flow rate $\dot{V}$; the respective equations are

$$\text{mass flow rate } \dot{m} = \rho A \bar{u} \tag{2.31}$$

$$\text{volumetric flow rate } \dot{V} = A \bar{u} \tag{2.32}$$

The mass flow rate $\dot{m}$ in kg/s is a function of density ρ, the cross-sectional area A of the pipe or tube, and the mean velocity $\bar{u}$ of the liquid. The use of the bar on symbol $\bar{u}$ indicates that it represents a mean value for velocity. The volumetric flow rate $\dot{V}$ is a product of cross-sectional area A of the pipe and the mean fluid velocity $\bar{u}$. In most cases, transport of liquids in a pipeline will be a steady-state process, such that the mass flow rate at location 1 ($\dot{m}_1$ or $\dot{V}_1$) will equal the mass flow rate at location 2 ($\dot{m}_2$ or $\dot{V}_2$).

EXAMPLE 2.4

Water at 20°C is being pumped through a 4 cm diameter pipe at a rate of 1.5 kg/s. Determine the mean velocity for water in the 4-cm pipe, and determine the new velocity if the tube diameter changes to 8 cm.

GIVEN

> Mass flow rate ($\dot{m}$) = 1.5 kg/s
> Pipe diameter (D) = 4 cm = 0.04 m
> Water density (ρ) = 998.2 kg/m^3, from Table A.4.1

$$A = \frac{\pi D^2}{4} = \pi (0.04)^2 / 4 = 1.257 \times 10^{-3} \text{ m}^2$$

APPROACH

The mean velocity $\bar{u}$ can be computed using Eq. (2.31) with the given data.

SOLUTION

(1) For pipe diameter of 4 cm,

$$\bar{u} = \frac{\dot{m}}{\rho A} = \frac{(1.5 \text{ kg/s})}{(998.2 \text{ kg/m}^3)(1.257 \times 10^{-3} \text{ m}^2)} = 1.195 \text{ m/s}$$

(2) For pipe diameter of 8 cm,

$$\bar{u} = \frac{(1.5 \text{ kg/s})}{(998.2 \text{ kg/m}^3)\left[\pi(0.08 \text{ m})^2/4\right]} = 0.299 \text{ m/s}$$

(3) Based on the above computation, for a constant mass flow rate, a doubling in the diameter of the pipe resulted in the mean velocity decreasing by a factor of 4.

2.4.2 Reynolds Number

Reynolds (1874)[1] studied the flow characteristics of fluids by injecting a dye into a liquid flowing in a pipe. At low liquid velocities, the dye moves in a streamline manner in the axial direction, as shown in Fig. 2.13. However, at higher velocities, the straight parallel lines of fluid flow are disrupted and dye gets dispersed soon after being released into the liquid. The streamline flow is called **laminar** flow and the erratic flow obtained at higher liquid velocities is called **turbulent** flow.

The flow characteristics described for laminar flow are influenced by liquid properties and flow dimensions. As mass-flow rate is increased, the forces of momentum or inertia increase; but these forces are resisted by friction or viscous forces within the flowing liquid. As the opposing forces reach a certain balance, changes in the flow characteristics occur. Based on experiments conducted by Reynolds (1874), it was concluded that the momentum forces are a function of density, tube diameter, and mean velocity. In addition, the friction or viscous forces are a function of liquid viscosity. Based on this analysis, a Reynolds number was defined as the ratio of the inertial forces to the viscous forces.

$$N_{\text{Re}} = \frac{\text{inertial forces}}{\text{viscous forces}} = \frac{\rho D \bar{u}}{\mu} \tag{2.33}$$

1. Osborne Reynolds, (1842–1912) was a British physicist, engineer, and educator. He was appointed the first professor of engineering at Owens College, Manchester, where he retired in the same position in 1905. His major work was in the study of hydrodynamics. He developed a theory of lubrication, studied the condensation process and provided a mathematical foundation (in 1883) to the turbulence phenomenon in fluid flow. His work resulted in important redesign of boilers and condensers, and development of turbines.

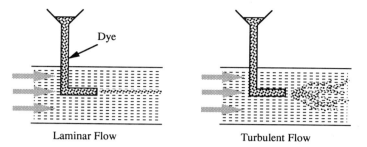

Laminar Flow   Turbulent Flow

Fig. 2.13   Illustration of the types of flow of a liquid at low velocities (left) and high velocities (right).

This unique number is dimensionless and can be used to define the flow characteristics in a tube or pipe.

The Reynolds number provides an appreciation of energy dissipation caused by viscous effects. From Eq. (2.33), when the viscous forces have a dominant effect on energy dissipation, the Reynolds number is small, or flow is in laminar region. As long as the Reynolds number is 2100 or less, the flow characteristics will be laminar or streamline. On the other hand, a Reynolds number greater than 10,000 indicates small influence of viscous forces on energy dissipation, leading to turbulence.

2.4.3   Laminar Flow

At low mass-flow rates, when the flow of liquid within a pipe or tube is streamline or laminar, Eq. (2.11) is used to compute the velocity profile. These calculations reveal that the velocity profile is parabolic and the mean fluid velocity is approximately 0.5 times the maximum velocity at the tube center (Fig. 2.14). This observation is illustrated in the following example.

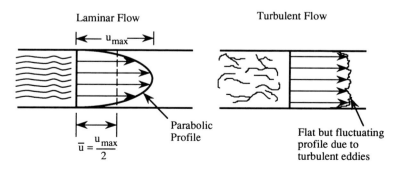

Fig. 2.14   Velocity profile in a liquid flowing under laminar and turbulent conditions.

EXAMPLE 2.5

A fluid is flowing under laminar conditions in a cylindrical pipe of 2 cm diameter. The pressure drop is 11 Pa, the viscosity of the fluid is 5 Pa · s, and the pipe is 10 cm long. Calculate the mean velocity and velocity of fluid at different radial locations in the pipe.

GIVEN

Diameter of pipe = 2 cm
Length of pipe = 10 cm
Pressure drop = 11 Pa
Viscosity = 5 Pa · s

APPROACH

We will use Eq. (2.11) to calculate velocity at different radial locations.

SOLUTION

(1) From Eq. (2.11)

$$u = \frac{\Delta P}{4\mu L}(R^2 - r^2)$$

The velocity is calculated at $r = 0, 0.25, 0.5, 0.75$ and 1 cm.

$r = 0$ cm	$u = 0.055$ cm/s
$r = 0.25$ cm	$u = 0.0516$ cm/s
$r = 0.5$ cm	$u = 0.0413$ cm/s
$r = 0.75$ cm	$u = 0.0241$ cm/s
$r = 1$ cm	$u = 0$ cm/s

(2) The mean velocity is calculated from step 1 as 0.034 m/s; this value is approximately half of the maximum velocity.

2.4.4 Turbulent Flow

As mass flow rate in a tube is increased so that values of the Reynolds number exceed 2100, the flow within the tube becomes erratic and mixing of liquid occurs within the flow cross section (Fig. 2.13). The intensity of this mixing increases as Reynolds number increases from 4000 to 10,000. At higher values of Reynolds number, the turbulence is fully developed, and the velocity profile is relatively flat and the mean velocity is approximately 0.8 times the maximum velocity.

EXAMPLE 2.6

Calculate the minimum mass flow rate required to establish fully developed turbulent flow of a cleaning solution in a 5 cm diameter stainless steel pipe. The cleaning solution has a density of 1050 kg/m³ and a viscosity of 995 × 10^{-6} Pa · s.

GIVEN

Density (ρ) = 1050 kg/m³
Pipe diameter (D) = 5 cm = 0.05 m
Viscosity (μ) = 995 × 10^{-6} Pa · s
Reynolds number (N_{Re}) = 10,000 for fully developed turbulent flow

APPROACH

Using Eq. (2.33) and the information given, compute the minimum velocity required to assure fully developed turbulent flow. The mass flow rate can be computed from Eq. (2.31).

SOLUTION

(1) Using Eq. (2.33),

$$N_{Re} = \frac{\rho D \bar{u}}{\mu} = \frac{(1050 \text{ kg/m}^3)(0.05 \text{ m})(\bar{u})}{(995 \times 10^{-6} \text{ Pa} \cdot \text{s})} = 10,000$$

$$\bar{u} = 0.1895 \text{ m/s}$$

(2) Using Eq. (2.31),

$$\dot{m} = \rho A \bar{u} = (1050 \text{ kg/m}^3)\left[\pi(0.05 \text{ m})^2/4\right](0.1895 \text{ m/s})$$

$$\dot{m} = 0.391 \text{ kg/s}$$

2.4.5 Friction

The forces that must be overcome in order to pump a liquid through a pipe or tube derive from several sources. As we saw in Section 2.2.3, viscous forces are important in liquid flow; these forces occur due to the movement of one layer of liquid over another. The other important class of forces are friction forces resulting from shear stresses at the wall. The friction forces vary with conditions such as Reynolds number and surface roughness. The influence of the friction forces is expressed in the form of a **friction factor** f. The following mathematical development is for laminar flow conditions.

The total force F due to friction is a function of wall surface area A, kinetic energy KE, and the friction factor.

$$F = A\rho(\text{KE})f \qquad (2.34)$$

Kinetic energy represents the energy associated with a flowing liquid and is defined on a per unit mass basis as

$$KE = \bar{u}^2/2 \qquad (2.35)$$

Based on these expressions, the friction factor can be defined as

$$f = \frac{F/A}{\rho(KE)} = \frac{2\sigma_w}{\rho\bar{u}^2} \qquad (2.36)$$

where shear stress at the wall σ_w represents the friction forces F over the wall area A.

We can also write shear stress at the walls, σ_w, from Eq. (2.7) as

$$\sigma_w = \frac{\Delta P_f \, R}{2L} \qquad (2.37)$$

where ΔP_f represents pressure drop due to friction forces.

Shear stress at any location inside the pipe may be written as (from Section 2.3.1)

$$\sigma = \frac{\Delta P_f \, r}{2L} \qquad (2.38)$$

Dividing Eq. (2.38) by Eq. (2.37),

$$\frac{\sigma}{\sigma_w} = \frac{r}{R} \qquad (2.39)$$

or

$$\sigma = \sigma_w \frac{r}{R} \qquad (2.40)$$

Combining Eq. (2.40) with Eq. (2.1), we get

$$\frac{\sigma_w r}{R} = -\mu \frac{du}{dr} \qquad (2.41)$$

Rearranging Eq. (2.41) by separating variables,

$$du = -\frac{\sigma_w r \, dr}{\mu R} \qquad (2.42)$$

and integrating Eq. (2.42) we obtain,

$$\int_{u_{max}}^{0} du = -\frac{\sigma_w}{\mu R} \int_{0}^{R} r \, dr \qquad (2.43)$$

and

$$u_{max} = \frac{\sigma_w R}{2\mu} \qquad (2.44)$$

For laminar flow, maximum velocity $u_{max} = 2\bar{u}$; then

$$\bar{u} = \frac{\sigma_w R}{4\mu} \qquad (2.45)$$

From Eq. (2.36), by rearranging

$$\sigma_{\text{w}} = \frac{\rho \bar{u}^2 f}{2} \tag{2.46}$$

Substituting Eq. (2.46) in Eq. (2.45), and noting that $R = D/2$,

$$\bar{u} = \frac{\rho \bar{u}^2 D f}{16 \mu} \tag{2.47}$$

Thus for laminar flow, rearranging Eq. (2.47)

$$f = \frac{16 \mu}{\rho \bar{u} D} = \frac{16}{N_{\text{Re}}} \tag{2.48}$$

If Eqs. (2.36) and (2.37) are combined directly, then

$$f = \frac{2 \Delta P_{\text{f}} R}{2 L \rho \bar{u}^2} = \frac{2 \Delta P_{\text{f}} D}{\rho 4 L \bar{u}^2} \tag{2.49}$$

or, rearranging,

$$\frac{\Delta P_{\text{f}}}{\rho} = 4 f \left(\frac{\bar{u}^2 L}{2D} \right) \tag{2.50}$$

Equation (2.50) is known as the **Darcy**[2] **equation**, but a more frequently used form is the **Fanning equation**.

$$E_{\text{f}} = \frac{\Delta P_{\text{f}}}{\rho} = 2 f \frac{\bar{u}^2 L}{D} \tag{2.51}$$

This equation is used to compute pressure loss due to friction (ΔP_{f}) in pipes and tubes.

The **Poiseuille**[3] **equation** is obtained by combining Eq. (2.48) and Eq. (2.50)

$$\Delta P_{\text{f}} = \frac{32 \mu \bar{u} L}{D^2} \tag{2.52}$$

The Poiseuille equation may be used to compute pressure loss due to friction directly, when flow is laminar. Note that Eq. (2.52) can be obtained directly from Eq. (2.15) by recognizing the $\dot{V} = A\bar{u} = \pi R^2 \bar{u}$.

As indicated, the friction factor f, also called Fanning friction factor as it appears in Eq. (2.51), can be computed directly from Eq. (2.48) for laminar flow situations. For turbulent flow, the same friction factor is

---

2. Henri-Philibert-Gaspard Darcy (1803–1858), a French hydraulic engineer, was the first person to develop a mathematical formulation of laminar flow of fluids in porous materials. His work laid the foundation for the subject of groundwater hydrology. In Dijon, his native city, he supervised the design and construction of the municipal water supply system. In his work he studied the flow of groundwater through granular material.

3. Jean-Louis-Marie Poiseuille (1799–1869), a French physiologist, studied the flow rate of fluids under laminar condition in circular tubes. The same mathematical expression was also determined by Gotthilf Hagen; therefore the relationship is called the Hagen–Poiseuille equation. Poiseuille also studied the circulation of blood and the flow of fluids in narrow tubes.

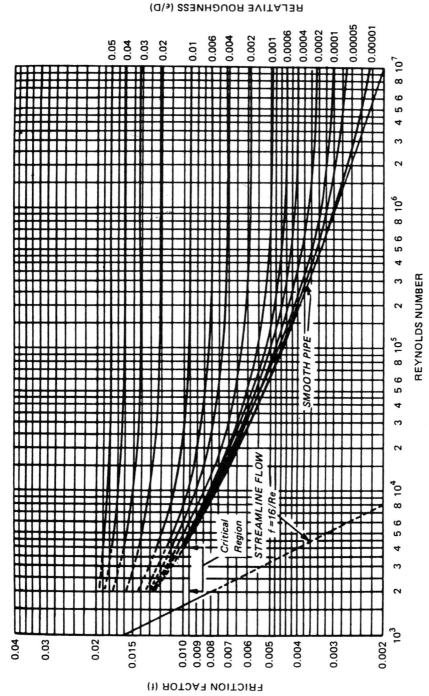

Fig. 2.15 The Moody diagram for the Fanning friction factor. Equivalent roughness for new pipes (ε in meters): cast iron, 259×10^{-6}; drawn tubing, 1.5235×10^{-6}; galvanized iron, 152×10^{-6}; steel or wrought iron, 45.7×10^{-6}. [Based on L. F. Moody (1944). *Trans. ASME* **66**, 671.]

obtained from the **Moody chart** in Fig. 2.15. The Moody chart presents the friction factor as a function of Reynolds number for various magnitudes of relative roughness. At low Reynolds number ($N_{Re} \ll 2100$), the curve is described by Eq. (2.48) and is not influenced by surface roughness ε. In the transition from laminar to turbulent flow or critical region, either set of curves can be utilized. Most often, the friction factor is selected for turbulent flow, since it assures that the pressure loss due to friction will not be underestimated.

Colebrook (1939) suggested an equation as an alternative to the graphical representation of friction factor shown in Fig. 2.15. His equation for calculating friction factor is as follows:

$$\frac{1}{\sqrt{f}} = -4 \log \left[\frac{1}{3.7} \frac{\varepsilon}{D} + \frac{1.255}{N_{Re}\sqrt{f}} \right] \tag{2.53}$$

For fully developed turbulent flow in a rough pipe,

$$\frac{1}{\sqrt{f}} = 4 \log \left(3.7 \frac{D}{\varepsilon} \right) \tag{2.54}$$

Equation (2.53) is solved by trial and error since f appears on both sides of the equation.

EXAMPLE 2.7

Water at 30°C is being pumped through a 30-m section of 2.5-cm diameter steel pipe at a mass flow rate of 2 kg/s. Compute the pressure loss due to friction in the pipe section.

GIVEN

Density (ρ) = 995.7 kg/m^3, from Table A.4.1
Viscosity (μ) = 792.377 × 10^{-6} Pa · s, from Table A.4.1
Length (L) of pipe = 30 m
Diameter (D) of pipe = 2.5 cm = 0.025 m
Mass flow rate ($\dot{m}$) = 2 kg/s

APPROACH

The pressure drop due to friction is computed using Eq. (2.51) with the information given. Equation (2.51) requires knowledge of the friction factor f as obtained from Fig. 2.15. Figure 2.15 can be used as soon as the turbulence (N_{Re}) and relative roughness (ε/D) values have been determined.

SOLUTION

(1) Compute mean velocity $\bar{u}$ from Eq. (2.31).

$$\bar{u} = \frac{(2 \text{ kg/s})}{(995.7 \text{ kg/m}^3)\left[\pi(0.025 \text{ m})^2/4 \right]} = 4.092 \text{ m/s}$$

(2) Compute Reynolds number.

$$N_{\text{Re}} = \frac{(995.7 \text{ kg/m}^3)(0.025 \text{ m})(4.092 \text{ m/s})}{(792.377 \times 10^{-6} \text{ Pa} \cdot \text{s})} = 128,550$$

(3) Using information given and Fig. 2.15, relative roughness can be computed.

$$\varepsilon/D = \frac{45.7 \times 10^{-6} \text{ m}}{0.025 \text{ m}} = 1.828 \times 10^{-3}$$

(4) Using the computed Reynolds number and the computed relative roughness, friction factor f is obtained from Fig. 2.15.

$$f = 0.006$$

(5) Using Eq. (2.51),

$$\frac{\Delta P}{\rho} = 2(0.006)\frac{(4.092 \text{ m/s})^2(30 \text{ m})}{(0.025 \text{ m})} = 241.12 \text{ m}^2/\text{s}^2$$

(6) Note that

$$\frac{\Delta P}{\rho} = 241.12 \text{ m}^2/\text{s}^2 = 241.12 \frac{\text{N} \cdot \text{m}}{\text{kg}} = 241.12 \text{ J/kg}$$

represents the energy consumed due to friction on a per-unit-mass basis.

(7) The pressure loss is calculated as

$$\Delta P = (241.12 \text{ J/kg})(995.7 \text{ kg/m}^3) = 240.08 \times 10^3 \text{ kg/m} \cdot \text{s}^2$$

$$\Delta P = 240.08 \text{ kPa}$$

2.5   Mechanical Energy Balance

The energy requirement for pumping a liquid using pipelines is dependent on a variety of factors. The schematic diagram in Fig. 2.16 illustrates that the energy requirements for the pump is influenced by

- Friction in the straight length of pipe.
- Energy requirements to move the liquid from one level to a higher level.
- Energy required to maintain the desired flow velocity.
- Energy required to overcome any pressure differences between input and output from the pump.
- Friction created by changes in cross-sectional area of flow, pipe fittings, direction change, and any friction imposed by equipment introduced into the transport system.

These factors will be considered individually in this section.

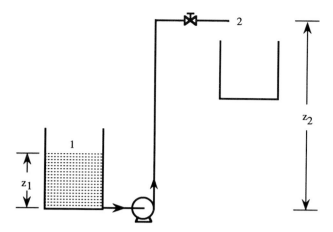

Fig. 2.16 Schematic illustration of pipelines for liquid food.

2.5.1 Potential Energy

The energy required to overcome a change in elevation during liquid
transport is potential energy. The general expression would be

$$\Delta PE = g(Z_2 - Z_1) \tag{2.55}$$

where Z_1, Z_2 are the elevations indicated in Fig. 2.16, and the acceleration
due to gravity (g) converts the elevation to energy units (J/kg). It should
be evident that if the location upstream from the pump is above the
downstream location, the potential energy will assist the pump by reducing
the energy requirement by a corresponding amount.

2.5.2 Kinetic Energy

To change the velocity of a flowing liquid, the pump must increase the
kinetic energy of the liquid. This change can be expressed as

$$\Delta KE = \frac{\bar{u}_2^2 - \bar{u}_1^2}{2\alpha} \tag{2.56}$$

where the change is related to the difference in liquid velocities at two
different locations along the pipeline system, with $\alpha = 0.5$ for laminar flow
and $\alpha = 1.0$ for turbulent flow. In most applications, the velocity at location 1 will be zero and the energy requirement will be the magnitude
required to achieve the desired liquid velocity.

Note that the units of kinetic energy (J/kg) are derived in the same
manner as in step (6) of Example 2.7.

2.5.3 Pressure Energy

In some types of transport systems, the pressure may change from one location to another in the system. Such changes may add to the energy requirement as

$$\frac{\Delta P}{\rho} = \frac{P_2 - P_1}{\rho} \tag{2.57}$$

with the liquid density introduced to assure consistency of energy units (J/kg). Note that liquid density does not change in the type of systems being analyzed.

2.5.4 Friction Energy

In Eq. (2.51), the pressure loss due to friction in a straight length of pipe was presented in the form of the Fanning equation. The friction energy or energy requirement due to friction would be

$$E_f = \frac{\Delta P_f}{\rho} \tag{2.58}$$

and for straight pipe, Eq. (2.51) is used.

Other components of the pipeline system for liquid transport will contribute to energy loss due to friction. A sudden contraction in the cross-section of the pipe can be evaluated as

$$\frac{\Delta P_f}{\rho} = K_f \frac{\bar{u}^2}{2} \tag{2.59}$$

where

$$K_f = 0.4\left(1.25 - D_2^2/D_1^2\right) \qquad \text{at} \quad D_2^2/D_1^2 < 0.715$$

$$K_f = 0.75\left(1 - D_2^2/D_1^2\right) \qquad \text{at} \quad D_2^2/D_1^2 > 0.715$$

In a similar manner, the sudden increase in the cross-section of a pipe will contribute to energy loss due to friction. These losses can be estimated from

$$\frac{\Delta P_f}{\rho} = \frac{\bar{u}_1^2}{2}\left[1 - (A_1/A_2)\right]^2 \tag{2.60}$$

where parameters having a subscript of one are located upstream from the expansion.

All pipe fittings such as elbows, tees, and valves will contribute to energy losses due to friction. The friction contribution from each of these fittings can be expressed as some equivalent length of straight pipe L_e and added to the actual length of pipe in Eq. (2.51). This step is accomplished by using values of L_e/D obtained from Table 2.3. By selecting a value of L_e/D ratio for the appropriate fitting given in the table, the equivalent length is computed using the pipe diameter.

TABLE 2.3
Friction Losses for Standard Fittings

Fitting	L_e/D
Elbow, 90°, square	60
Elbow, 90°, standard	32
Elbow, 90°, medium sweep	26
Elbow, 90°, long sweep	20
Elbow, 45°, standard	15
Tee, used as elbow, entering branch	70
Tee, used as elbow, entering tee run	60
Tee, used as coupling, branch plugged	20
Gate valve, open	7
Gate valve, half open	200
Globe valve, open	300
Angle valve, open	170
Diaphragm valve, open	105

Other processing equipment, such as a heat exchanger that may be installed in the liquid transport system, will usually have some assigned pressure drop due to friction. If not, a value should be obtained by measurement. By dividing the pressure drop value by the liquid density, the appropriate energy units are obtained.

2.5.5 Computation of Pumping Requirements

In Section 1.17, the first law of thermodynamics was expressed as

$$W = \int P\,dV - \Delta\mathrm{KE} - \Delta\mathrm{PE} - f \qquad (2.61)$$

This equation may be rearranged for the transport system described in Fig. 2.16. The energy is supplied by the pump and must be equal to the various forms of energy defined in the previous sections. This equation becomes

$$E_\mathrm{p} = \Delta\mathrm{PE} + \Delta\mathrm{KE} + \frac{\Delta P}{\rho} + E_\mathrm{f} \qquad (2.62)$$

where E_p is energy supplied by the pump and E_f includes all forms of energy loss due to friction. Equation (2.62) can be written in the following form:

$$gZ_1 + \frac{\bar{u}_1^2}{2\alpha} + \frac{P_1}{\rho} + E_\mathrm{p} = gZ_2 + \frac{\bar{u}_2^2}{2\alpha} + \frac{P_2}{\rho} + E_\mathrm{f} \qquad (2.63)$$

with subscripts consistent with locations identified in Fig. 2.16. In this form, Eq. (2.63) is known as the **Bernoulli equation**.

TABLE 2.4
Pipe and Heat-Exchanger Tube Dimensions

Nominal size (in.)	Steel pipe (Schedule 40)		Sanitary pipe		Heat-exchanger tube (18 Gauge)	
	ID in./(m)	OD in./(m)	ID in./(m)	OD in./(m)	ID in./(m)	OD in./(m)
0.5	0.622 (0.01579)[a]	0.840 (0.02134)	—	—	0.402 (0.01021)	0.50 (0.0127)
0.75	0.824 (0.02093)	1.050 (0.02667)			0.652 (0.01656)	0.75 (0.01905)
1	1.049 (0.02644)	1.315 (0.03340)	0.902 (0.02291)	1.00 (0.0254)	0.902 (0.02291)	1.00 (0.0254)
1.5	1.610 (0.04089)	1.900 (0.04826)	1.402 (0.03561)	1.50 (0.0381)	1.402 (0.03561)	1.50 (0.0381)
2.0	2.067 (0.0525)	2.375 (0.06033)	1.870 (0.04749)	2.00 (0.0508)	—	—
2.5	2.469 (0.06271)	2.875 (0.07302)	2.370 (0.06019)	2.5 (0.0635)		
3.0	3.068 (0.07793)	3.500 (0.08890)	2.870 (0.07289)	3.0 (0.0762)	—	—
	4.026 (0.10226)	4.500 (0.11430)	3.834 (0.09739)	4.0 (0.1016)		

Source: Toledo (1991).
[a] Numbers in parentheses represent the dimension in meters.

The power requirements for the pump may be computed by noting that power is rate of doing work; if the mass flow rate $\dot{m}$ is known, then

$$\text{Power} = \dot{m}(E_p) \qquad (2.64)$$

To calculate pump sizes, accurate sizes of pipes being utilized must be incorporated into computations. The information in Table 2.4 provides the type of values needed for this purpose. Note the variations in diameters of steel pipe as compared to sanitary pipe for the same nominal size.

EXAMPLE 2.8

A 20° Brix (20% sucrose by weight) apple juice is being pumped at 27°C from an open tank through a 1-in. nominal diameter sanitary pipe to a second tank at a higher level, illustrated in Fig. 2.16. The mass flow rate is 1 kg/s through 30 m of straight pipe with two 90° standard elbows and one angle valve. The supply tank maintains a liquid level of 3 m, and the apple juice leaves the system at an elevation of 12 m above the floor. Compute the power requirements of the pump.

GIVEN

Product viscosity $(\mu) = 2.1 \times 10^{-3}$ Pa · s, assumed to be same as for water, from Table A.2.4

Product density $(\rho) = 997.1$ kg/m³, estimated from density of water at 25°C

Pipe diameter $(D) = 1$ in. nominal $= 0.02291$ m, from Table 2.4

Mass flow rate $(\dot{m}) = 1$ kg/s

Pipe length $(L) = 30$ m

90° standard elbow friction, $L_e/D = 32$, from Table 2.3

Angle valve friction, $L_e/D = 170$, from Table 2.3.

Liquid level $Z_1 = 3$ m, $Z_2 = 12$ m

APPROACH

Power requirements for the pump can be computed using the mechanical energy balance or the Bernoulli equation after pressure drop due to friction has been computed for each component within the system.

SOLUTION

(1) First, compute mean velocity using mass flow rate equation.

$$\bar{u} = \frac{\dot{m}}{\rho A} = \frac{(1 \text{ kg/s})}{(997.1 \text{ kg/m}^3)\left[\pi(0.02291 \text{ m})^2/4\right]} = 2.433 \text{ m/s}$$

(2) By computation of Reynolds number,

$$N_{\text{Re}} = \frac{(997.1 \text{ kg/m}^3)(0.02291 \text{ m})(2.433 \text{ m/s})}{(2.1 \times 10^{-3} \text{ Pa} \cdot \text{s})}$$

$$= 26{,}465$$

it is established that flow is turbulent.

(3) By using the Bernoulli equation (2.63) and identification of reference points, the following expression is obtained:

$$g(3) + E_p = g(12) + \frac{(2.433)^2}{2} + E_f$$

where reference 1 is at the upper level of the supply tank, $\bar{u}_1 = 0$, and $P_1 = P_2$.

(4) By computing E_f, the power can be determined. Based on $N_{\text{Re}} = 2.6465 \times 10^4$ and smooth pipe, $f = 0.006$ from Fig. 2.15.

(5) The entrance from the tank to the pipeline can be accounted for by Eq. (2.59), where

$$K_f = 0.4(1.25 - 0) \qquad \text{since} \quad D_2^2/D_1^2 = 0$$

$$= 0.5$$

and

$$\frac{\Delta P_f}{\rho} = 0.5\frac{(2.433)^2}{2} = 1.48 \text{ J/kg}$$

(6) The contribution of the elbows and the angle valve to friction is determined by using an L_e/D ratio from Table 2.3. For the standard smooth-fitting elbow, $L_e = 32(0.02291)2 = 1.466$ m. For the angle valve, $L_e/D = 170$ and $L_e = 170(0.02291) = 3.895$ m.

(7) By using the Fanning equation (2.51),

$$\frac{\Delta P_f}{\rho} = 2(0.006)\frac{(2.433)^2}{0.02291}(30 \text{ m} + 1.466 \text{ m} + 3.895 \text{ m})$$

$$= 109.63 \text{ J/kg}$$

(8) Using the expression obtained from the Bernoulli equation,

$$E_p = 9.81(12 - 3) + \frac{(2.433)^2}{2} + (109.63 + 1.48)$$

$$= 202.36 \text{ J/kg}$$

which represents the energy requirement of the pump.

(9) Since power is energy use per unit time,

$$\text{Power} = (202.36 \text{ J/kg})(1 \text{ kg/s}) = 202.36 \text{ J/s}$$

(10) The above answer must be considered theoretical, since delivery of power to the pump may be only 60% efficient; then actual power is

$$\text{Power} = 202.36/0.6 = 337 \text{ W}$$

EXAMPLE 2.9

Develop a spreadsheet using the data given in Example 2.8. Rework the problem using the spreadsheet. Determine the influence on the power requirements of changing the pipe length to 60, 90, 120, and 150 m. Also, determine the influence on the power requirement of changing the pipe diameter to 1.5 in., 2 in., and 2.5 in. nominal diameters.

GIVEN

The conditions are the same as in Example 2.8.

APPROACH

We will develop a spreadsheet using EXCEL™. The mathematical expressions will be the same as those used in Example 2.8. For the friction factor we will obtain the value from Fig. 2.15 and substitute it into the spreadsheet.

SOLUTION

The spreadsheet is developed as shown in Fig. 2.17. All mathematical equations are the same as those used in Example 2.8. The influence of changing length and diameter is seen in the plots. As is evident, for the conditions used in this example, there is a dramatic influence on power requirement when the pipe diameter is decreased from 2.5 in. to 1.5 in.

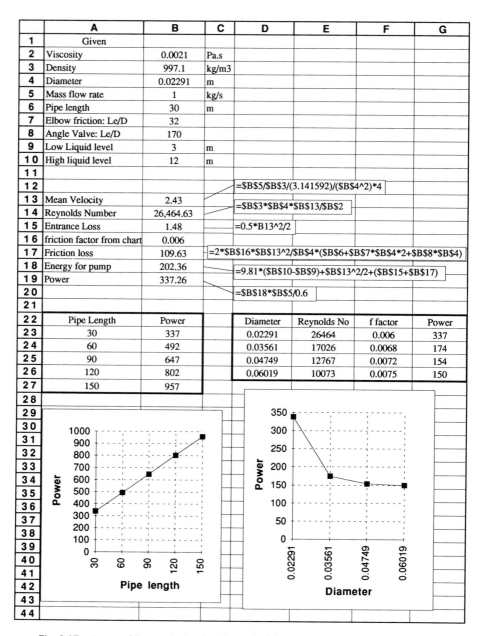

	A	B	C	D	E	F	G
1		Given					
2	Viscosity	0.0021	Pa.s				
3	Density	997.1	kg/m3				
4	Diameter	0.02291	m				
5	Mass flow rate	1	kg/s				
6	Pipe length	30	m				
7	Elbow friction: Le/D	32					
8	Angle Valve: Le/D	170					
9	Low Liquid level	3	m				
10	High liquid level	12	m				
11							
12				=$B$5/$B$3/(3.141592)/($B$4^2)*4			
13	Mean Velocity	2.43					
14	Reynolds Number	26,464.63		=$B$3*$B$4*$B$13/$B$2			
15	Entrance Loss	1.48		=0.5*B13^2/2			
16	friction factor from chart	0.006					
17	Friction loss	109.63		=2*$B$16*$B$13^2/$B$4*($B$6+$B$7*$B$4*2+$B$8*$B$4)			
18	Energy for pump	202.36		=9.81*($B$10-$B$9)+$B$13^2/2+($B$15+$B$17)			
19	Power	337.26					
20				=$B$18*$B$5/0.6			
21							
22	Pipe Length	Power		Diameter	Reynolds No	f factor	Power
23	30	337		0.02291	26464	0.006	337
24	60	492		0.03561	17026	0.0068	174
25	90	647		0.04749	12767	0.0072	154
26	120	802		0.06019	10073	0.0075	150
27	150	957					

Fig. 2.17 A spreadsheet solution for Example 2.9.

2.6 Pump Selection and Performance Evaluation

2.6.1 Characteristic Diagram of Pumps

In designing a liquid transport system, the need for a pump is determined on the basis of flow and pressure requirements. In selecting a pump for a given system, it is imperative that the characteristics of the system are clearly defined. The pump requirements are based on the system characteristics. The following information about the system must be known:

- Flow rate of liquid that is to be pumped, commonly referred to as capacity.
- The required differential pressure, or commonly referred to as head.
- The available net positive suction head (NPSHA). This term is further explained in the following sections.
- The shape of head and capacity curves for the pump.
- The pump speed.
- Characteristics of the liquid.

In a centrifugal pump, the pressure is developed by the rotating impeller. The impeller (Fig. 2.18) imparts a centrifugal force on the liquid entering the center of the impeller; the liquid is then forced through the impeller passageways into the pump casing to the discharge outlet. The pressure developed by a pump is commonly called **head**. Thus the centrifugal force acting on the liquid develops a head. This head varies depending

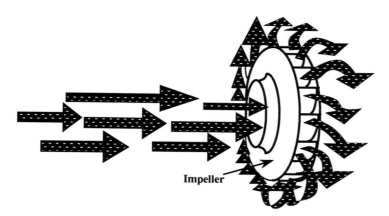

Fig. 2.18 Impeller of a centrifugal pump. [From Lobanoff, V. S., and Ross, R. R. (1985). "Centrifugal Pumps Design and Application." Gulf Publishing Co., Houston.]

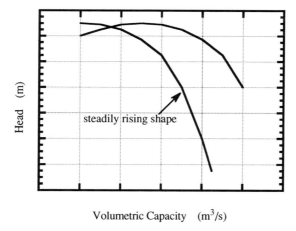

Volumetric Capacity   (m³/s)

Fig. 2.19   Sample curves of head versus capacity.

on the amount of liquid entering the pump. Mathematical analysis of the forces acting on the liquid at the periphery of the impeller gives the relationship between the developed head and the volumetric flow rate. There are a number of different shapes for head–capacity curves; two of these shapes are shown in Fig. 2.19. The steadily rising shape is indicative of a stable centrifugal pump. In this case the head curve rises steadily; that is, the slope of the curve is always negative.

For purposes of evaluating pump performance, the pump manufacturers give **characteristic curves** for their pumps. These curves are graphical plots of head, power consumption, and efficiency with respect to the volumetric flow rate (or capacity). As seen in Fig. 2.20, the developed head decreases with increasing flow rate due to increased frictional losses. The power requirements increase with increasing flow rate. The efficiency increases dramatically at low flow rates; however, at high flow rates, the efficiency reaches a maximum and subsequently drops.

The characteristic curves are useful in rating pumps. The manufacturers typically rate their pumps in terms of capacity and head at peak efficiency. As observed in Figure 2.20, the peak efficiency is 78% at about $3.2 \text{ m}^3/\text{s}$. Above this efficiency, the head decreases with increasing flow rate and the power requirements increase.

2.6.2   Net Positive Suction Head

Another parameter that requires careful attention in pump design is called **net positive suction head (NPSH)**. The NPSH is the difference between the pressure at the pump inlet and the vapor pressure of liquid being

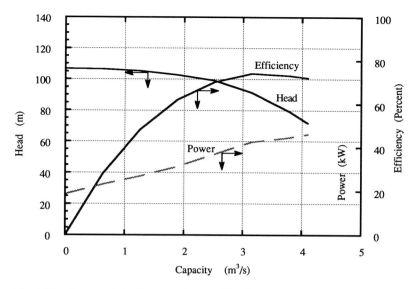

Fig. 2.20 Characteristic diagram of a centrifugal pump.

pumped. This difference is necessary to avoid cavitation. **Cavitation** causes flashing of vapor inside a pump, leading to reduced pump capacity as well as damage to the internal parts.

Two NPSH values are important in pump design, namely **available NPSH** and **required NPSH**.

The required NPSH is a function of the impeller design; its value, determined by testing, is provided by the pump manufacturer. Required NPSH refers to the minimum head required by the pump to maintain stable operation. It is based on a datum elevation usually taken as the center line of the impeller.

The available NPSH is a function of the suction system of the pump. It is calculated in meters of water by using the following formula.

$$\mathrm{NPSH}_A = h_a - h_{vp} - h_s - h_f \tag{2.65}$$

where h_a is absolute pressure (m of water), h_{vp} is vapor pressure of liquid (m of water), h_s is static head of liquid above the center line of the pump (m of water), and h_f is friction losses throughout the suction system (m of water).

2.6.3 Affinity Laws

A set of formulas known as affinity laws govern the performance of the centrifugal pumps at various impeller speeds. These formulas are as follows:

$$\dot{V}_2 = \dot{V}_1(N_2/N_1) \tag{2.66}$$

$$h_2 = h_1(N_2/N_1)^2 \tag{2.67}$$

$$P'_2 = P'_1(N_2/N_1)^3 \tag{2.68}$$

These equations can be used to calculate the effects of changing impeller speed on the performance of a given centrifugal pump. The following example illustrates the use of these formulas.

EXAMPLE 2.10

A centrifugal pump is operating with following conditions:
   volumetric flow rate = 5 m³/s
   total head = 10 m
   power = 2 kW
   impeller speed = 1750 rpm

Calculate the performance of this pump if it is operated at 3500 rpm.

SOLUTION

The ratio of speeds is

$$\frac{N_2}{N_1} = \frac{3500}{1750} = 2$$

Therefore, using Eqs. (2.66), (2.67), (2.68),

$$\dot{V}_2 = 5 \times 2 = 10 \text{ m}^3/\text{s}$$

$$h_2 = 10 \times 2^2 = 40 \text{ m}$$

$$P'_2 = 2 \times 2^3 = 16 \text{ kW}$$

2.7 Flow Measurement

The measurement of flow rate in a liquid transport system is an essential component of the operation. As has been illustrated in the previous sections, knowledge of flow rate and/or liquid velocity is important in design calculations. In addition, periodic measurements during actual operations are required to ensure that system components are performing in an expected manner.

There are several types of flow measurement devices that are inexpensive and lead to direct quantification of the mass flow rate or velocity. These methods include (a) Pitot tube, (b) orifice meter, and (c) venturi tube. For all three of these methods, a portion of the measurement involves pressure

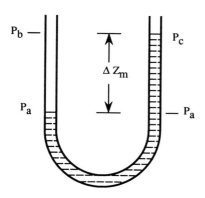

Fig. 2.21 U-tube manometer.

difference. The device most often used for this purpose is a manometer. The U-tube manometer illustrated in Fig. 2.21 will contain a manometer fluid and each arm of the tube will be connected to an appropriate location on the flow measuring device. When a pressure difference ΔP exists between the two arms of the manometer, it will be proportional to the change in height ΔZ of the manometer fluid. This relationship can be derived from Eq. (2.63) by recognizing that work E_p is zero, friction E_f is negligible, and $\bar{u}_1 = \bar{u}_2 = 0$; then

$$\frac{P_1 - P_2}{\rho} = g(Z_2 - Z_1) \qquad (2.69)$$

where the pressure difference $P_1 - P_2$ would be a function of change in height of flowing liquid, $Z_2 - Z_1$. To express the weight difference in terms of manometer liquid, the density ρ_m of the manometer liquid must be accounted for. By analysis of the illustration in Fig. 2.21, the pressures at various locations in the U-tube manometer can be expressed as

$$\frac{P_a - P_b}{\rho} = \frac{P_a - P_c}{\rho_m} = g\,\Delta Z_m \qquad (2.70)$$

and, by eliminating P_a,

$$P_b - P_c = (\rho_m - \rho)g\,\Delta Z_m \qquad (2.71)$$

Then

$$\frac{P_b - P_c}{\rho} = \left(\frac{\rho_m}{\rho} - 1\right)g\,\Delta Z_m \qquad (2.72)$$

which is equivalent to Eq. (2.69). Another approach to present the expression would be

$$Z_2 - Z_1 = \Delta Z_m\left(\frac{\rho_m}{\rho} - 1\right) \qquad (2.73)$$

indicating that change in height $(Z_2 - Z_1)$ in terms of flowing liquid would be equal to the right side of Eq. (2.73) for a manometer fluid with density

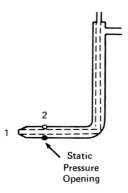

Static
Pressure
Opening

Fig. 2.22   Schematic diagram of a Pitot tube.

$\rho_{\rm m}$. As is evident from these derivations, the manometer fluid must have a higher density than the flowing liquid and must be immiscible in the liquid. In most cases, the flow of liquids will be accomplished using mercury as the manometer fluid.

2.7.1   The Pitot Tube

A schematic of a velocity measurement system called a Pitot[4] tube is presented in Fig. 2.22. As indicated, the system is designed with two small concentric tubes with each tube leading to a separate outlet. The inlet to the inner tube is oriented directly into the fluid flow, while the inlet to the outer tube is through several openings on the circumference of the tube. As designed, the Pitot tube will measure the sum of velocity pressure and static pressure at the entrance to the inner tube and static pressure only at the entrance to the outer tube.

An analysis of the flow characteristics at the entrances to the Pitot tube can be accomplished by using Eq. (2.63). By assigning reference points 1 and 2 to the inner tube and outer tube entrances, respectively, there is no difference in elevation ($Z_1 = Z_2$). In addition, the work $E_{\rm p}$ and friction energy $E_{\rm f}$ terms can be assumed to be negligible between points 1 and 2.

---

4. Henri Pitot (1695–1771) was a French hydraulic engineer who began his career as a mathematician. In 1724, he was elected to the French Academy of Sciences. In Montpellier, he was in charge of constructing an aqueduct that included a 1 km long Romanesque stone arch section. His studies included flow of water in rivers and canals, and he invented a device to measure fluid velocities.

At the entrance to the inner tube (reference point 1), the fluid velocity is zero ($u_1 = 0$). Based on these observations, Eq. (2.63) becomes

$$\frac{P_1}{\rho} = \frac{u_2^2}{2} + \frac{P_2}{\rho} \tag{2.74}$$

or

$$u_2 = C\left[\frac{2(P_1 - P_2)}{\rho}\right]^{1/2} \tag{2.75}$$

Equation (2.75) indicates that the fluid velocity in a stream can be determined using a Pitot tube by measurement of pressure difference $P_1 - P_2$. The density ρ of the fluid must be known, and a tube coefficient C is introduced to account for small influences due to friction. In most situations, $C = 1.0$. Based on this analysis, it should be evident that a Pitot tube will measure fluid velocity at any point where the tube is introduced into the fluid stream.

By introducing Eq. (2.71) into Eq. (2.75),

$$u_2 = C\left[\frac{2g}{\rho}(\rho_m - \rho)\, \Delta Z_m\right]^{1/2} \tag{2.76}$$

the velocity can be measured directly from the change in height of a manometer fluid (ΔZ_m) when the two sides of the U-tube manometer are connected to the two outlets from the Pitot tube. The only other requirements for Eq. (2.76) are knowledge of the fluid densities ρ_m and ρ, acceleration due to gravity (g), and the tube coefficient C.

EXAMPLE 2.11

A Pitot tube is being used to measure maximum velocity for water flow in a pipe. The tube is positioned with inlet to the inner tube along the center axis of the pipe. A U-tube manometer gives a reading of 20 mm Hg. Calculate the velocity of water, assuming a tube coefficient of 1.0. The density of mercury is 13,600 kg/m³.

GIVEN

Manometer reading = 20 mm Hg = 0.02 m Hg
Density (ρ_m) of mercury = 13,600 kg/m³
Density (ρ) of water = 998 kg/m³
Tube coefficient (C) = 1.0

APPROACH

By using Eq. (2.76), the velocity of water can be computed.

SOLUTION

(1) Using Eq. (2.76) with $C = 1$,

$$u_2 = 1.0\left[\frac{2(9.81 \text{ m/s}^2)}{998 \text{ kg/m}^3}(13{,}600 \text{ kg/m}^3 - 998 \text{ kg/m}^3)(0.02 \text{ m})\right]^{1/2}$$

$$u_2 = 2.226 \text{ m/s}$$

2.7.2 The Orifice Meter

By introducing a restriction of known dimensions into flow within a pipe or tube, the relationship between pressure across the restriction and velocity through the restriction can be used to measure fluid flow rate. An orifice meter is a ring introduced into a pipe or tube that reduces the cross-sectional area of tube by a known amount. By attaching pressure taps or transducers at locations upstream and downstream from the orifice, the pressure change can be measured.

The analysis of the flow characteristics in the region near the orifice can be conducted using Eq. (2.63). Reference location 1 will be of sufficient distance upstream that the orifice does not influence flow characteristics. Reference location 2 is just slightly downstream from the orifice, where velocity is the same as within the orifice. Figure 2.23 illustrates the flow stream profile around the orifice meter and the reference locations. The pipe diameter is D_1 and the orifice diameter is D_2. Using Eq. (2.63),

$$\frac{\bar{u}_1^2}{2} + \frac{P_1}{\rho} = \frac{\bar{u}_2^2}{2} + \frac{P_2}{\rho} \tag{2.77}$$

Using the mass-flow Eq. (2.31)

$$\dot{m} = \rho A_1 \bar{u}_1 = \rho A_2 \bar{u}_2$$

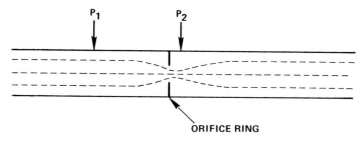

Fig. 2.23 Orifice meter.

and

$$\bar{u}_1 = \frac{A_2}{A_1}\bar{u}_2 = \frac{D_2^2}{D_1^2}\bar{u}_2 \tag{2.78}$$

By combining Eq. (2.77) and (2.78),

$$\frac{\bar{u}_2^2}{2} + \frac{P_2}{\rho} = \left(\frac{D_2}{D_1}\right)^4 \frac{\bar{u}_2^2}{2} + \frac{P_1}{\rho} \tag{2.79}$$

or

$$\bar{u}_2 = C\left[\frac{2(P_1 - P_2)}{\rho\left(1 - (D_2^4/D_1^4)\right)}\right]^{1/2} \tag{2.80}$$

which allows computation of the velocity at location 1 from the pressure difference $P_1 - P_2$ and the diameter of the pipe or tube D_1 and the orifice diameter D_2. By introducing Eq. (2.72), the following relationship is obtained:

$$\bar{u}_2 = C\left\{\frac{2g\left(\frac{\rho_m}{\rho} - 1\right)\Delta Z_m}{\left[1 - (D_2/D_1)^4\right]}\right\}^{1/2} \tag{2.81}$$

which allows computation of average velocity in the fluid stream from the change in manometer fluid height and the density of the manometer fluid.

The magnitude of the orifice coefficient C is a function of exact location of the pressure taps, the Reynolds number, and the ratio of pipe diameter to orifice diameter. At $N_{Re} = 30,000$, the coefficient C will have a value of 0.61, and the magnitude will vary with N_{Re} at lower values. It is recommended that orifice meters be calibrated in known flow conditions to establish the exact values of the orifice coefficient.

2.7.3 The Venturi Meter

To reduce the energy loss due to friction created by an orifice meter, a venturi tube of the type illustrated in Fig. 2.24 can be utilized. An analysis similar to that presented for the orifice meter leads to the following equation:

$$\bar{u}_2 = C\left[\frac{2g\left(\frac{\rho_m}{\rho} - 1\right)\Delta Z_m}{1 - (D_2/D_1)^4}\right]^{1/2} \tag{2.82}$$

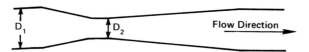

Fig. 2.24 Schematic diagram of a venturi meter.

where the average velocity $\bar{u}_2$ is at reference location 2, where the diameter D_2 is the smallest value for the venturi. The venturi meter requires careful construction to assure proper angles of entrance to and exit from the venturi. The meter requires a significant length of pipe for installation when compared to the orifice meter. In general, the orifice meter is considered to be less costly and simpler to design than the venturi meter.

EXAMPLE 2.12

An orifice meter is being designed to measure steam flow to the specific operation in the food processing plant. The steam has a mass flow rate of approximately 0.1 kg/s in a 7.5 cm diameter (ID) pipe with a pressure of 198.53 kPa. Determine the density of the manometer fluid to be used so that pressure differences can be detected accurately and reasonably. A manometer of less than 1 m height can be considered reasonable.

GIVEN

Mass flow rate ($\dot{m}$) of steam = 0.1 kg/s
Pipe diameter (D_1) = 7.5 cm = 0.075 m
Steam density (ρ) = 1.12 kg/m³ from Table A.4.2 at pressure of 198.53 kPa
Orifice coefficient (C) = 0.61 at N_{Re} = 30,000

APPROACH

To use Eq. (2.81) to compute density of manometer fluid (ρ_m), the orifice diameter D_2 and manometer fluid height ΔZ_m must be assumed.

SOLUTION

(1) By assuming an orifice diameter D_2 of 6 cm or 0.06 m,

$$\bar{u} = \frac{\dot{m}}{\rho A} = \frac{(0.1 \text{ kg/s})}{(1.12 \text{ kg/m}^3)\left[\pi(0.06 \text{ m})^2/4\right]} = 31.578 \text{ m/s}$$

(2) Since the manometer fluid height (ΔZ_m) must be less than 1 m, a value of 0.1 m will be assumed. Using Eq. (2.81),

$$31.578 \text{ m/s} = 0.61\left[\frac{2(9.81 \text{ m/s}^2)\left(\dfrac{\rho_m}{1.12 \text{ kg/m}^3} - 1\right)(0.1 \text{ m})}{1 - (0.06/0.075)^4}\right]^{1/2}$$

$$\rho_m = 904.3 \text{ kg/m}^3$$

(3) The above density could be obtained by using light oil with density of 850 kg/m³.

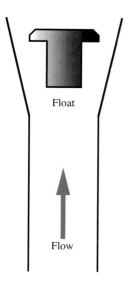

Float

Flow

Fig. 2.25 A variable flow meter.

2.7.4 Variable-Area Meters

The flowmeters considered in the preceding sections, namely orifice and venturi tube, involve a change in flow rate through a constant cross-sectional area that generates a variable pressure drop which is a function of the flow rate. In a variable-area meter, the fluid stream is throttled by a constriction arranged in a manner such that the cross-sectional area is varied. This allows a variation of flow while maintaining a nearly constant pressure drop. The cross-sectional area in these devices is related to the flow rate by proper calibration.

A popular type of variable flow meter is a **rotameter**, shown in Fig. 2.25. In this device, the height of a plummet, also called "bob" or "float," in a tapered tube indicates the flow. The float moves up or down in a vertically mounted tapered tube. The largest diameter of the tube is at the top. The fluid moves up from the bottom and lifts the float. Because of the higher density of the float, the passage remains blocked until the pressure builds up and the buoyant effect of the fluid lifts the float; the fluid then flows between the float and tube wall. As the passage for flow increases, a dynamic equilibrium is established between the position of the float and the pressure difference across the float and the buoyant forces. A scale mounted on the outside of the tube provides a measurement of the vertical displacement of the float from a reference point, the fluid flow in the tube can thus be measured. As the float is raised higher in the tapered tube, a greater area becomes available for the fluid to pass through; this is why this meter is called variable-area flow meter.

The tube material is typically glass, acrylic, or metal. For measuring low flow rates a ball or plumb-bob float shape is used, whereas for high flow capacities and applications that require high accuracy with constant viscosity, a streamlined float shape is used. The float materials commonly used include black glass, red sapphire, stainless steel, and tungsten. The capacities of rotameters are usually given in terms of two standard fluids: water at 20°C and air at 20°C at 101.3 kPa. A proper flow meter can be selected based on the float selection curves and capacity tables supplied by the manufacturers. A single instrument can cover a wide range of flow, up to tenfold; using floats of different densities, ranges up to two-hundredfold are possible. Unlike orifice meters, the rotameter is not sensitive to velocity distribution in the approaching stream. The installation of rotameters requires no straight section of pipe either upstream or downstream.

Industrial rotameters offer excellent repeatability over a wide range of flows. Their standard accuracy is $\pm 2\%$ of full scale with capacities of 6.38×10^{-8} to 1.14×10^{-2} m^3/s of water and 4.7×10^{-7} to 0.34 m^3/s of air at standard temperature and pressure. Rotameters are also available for special requirements such as low volume, and high pressure. These instruments are calibrated when obtained from the manufacturer with a given size and shape bob and for a given bob density for a fluid or specified specific gravity.

2.7.5 Other Measurement Methods

In addition to methods that detect flow due to pressure changes created by a restriction in flow followed by measurement of pressure drop caused by the restriction, several methods have been developed for unique applications in the food industry. These methods vary considerably in operation principles but meet the needs for sanitary design.

The use of volumetric displacement as a flow measurement principle involves the use of a measuring chamber of known volume and containing a rotating motor. As flow is directed through the chamber, the rotor turns and displaces known volume magnitudes. The flow rate is detected by monitoring the number of revolutions of the rotor and accounting for the volume in each revolution.

Several flow measurement methods use ultrasonic frequency as a flow-sensing mechanism. Generally, these methods use the response from a frequency wave directed at the flow as an indication of flow rate. As the flow changes, the frequency changes. The Doppler shift is one method of flow detection; changes in flow rate cause shifts in the wave frequency as the wave passes through the flow.

The use of the vortex created by inserting an object of irregular shape into the flow stream provides an alternate method of flow measurement. Since the vortices move downstream with a frequency that is a function of flow rate, this frequency can be used as an indicator of flow rate. Typically, the frequencies are measured by placing heated thermistors in the vortex stream followed by detection of cooling rates.

The flow rate of a fluid in a tube can be detected by placing a turbine wheel into the flow stream. As flow rate changes, the rotation speed changes in some proportional manner. Detection of rotation is accomplished by using small magnets attached to the rotating part of the turbine. The magnets generate a pulse to be detected by a coil circuit located on the outside tube wall.

Each of the flow measurement methods described have unique features, and their use will be determined by the circumstances of the application. All have been used in various situations in the food industry.

Problems

2.1 A capillary tube is being used to measure the viscosity of a Newtonian liquid. The tube has a 4-cm diameter and a length of 20 cm. Estimate the viscosity coefficient for the liquid if a pressure of 2.5 kPa is required to maintain a flow rate of 1 kg/s. The liquid density is 998 kg/m^3.

2.2 Calculate the viscosity of a fluid that would allow a pressure drop of 35 kPa over a 5-m length of 3.4-in. stainless steel sanitary pipe if the fluid is flowing at 0.12 m^3/hr and has a density of 1010 kg/m^3. Assume laminar flow.

2.3 A 2 cm diameter, 5 cm long capillary-tube viscometer is being used to measure viscosity of a 10-Pa · s liquid food. Determine the pressure required for measurement when a flow rate of 1 kg/min is desired and $\rho = 1000$ kg/m^3.

2.4 Calculate the Reynolds number for 25°C water flow in a 1-in. nominal diameter sanitary pipe at 0.5 kg/s. What are the flow characteristics?

2.5 Sulfuric acid with a density of 1980 kg/m^3 and a viscosity of 26.7 cP is flowing in a 35 mm diameter pipe. If the acid flow rate is 1 m^3/min, what is the pressure loss due to friction for a 30-m length of smooth pipe?

2.6 Compute the mean and maximum velocities for a liquid with a flow rate of 20 liters/min in a 1.5-in. nominal diameter sanitary pipeline. The liquid has a density of 1030 kg/m^3 and viscosity of 50 cP. Is the flow laminar or turbulent?

2.7 Calculate the total equivalent length of 1-in. wrought iron pipe that would produce a pressure drop of 70 kPa due to fluid friction, for a fluid flowing at a rate of 0.05 kg/s, a viscosity of 2 cP, and density of 1000 kg/m^3.

*2.8 A solution of ethanol is pumped to a vessel 25 m above a reference level through a 25-mm inside diameter steel pipe at a rate of 10 m^3/hr. The length of pipe is 30 m and contains two elbows with friction equivalent to 20 diameters each. Compute the power requirements of the pump. Solution properties include density of 975 kg/m^3 and viscosity of 4×10^{-4} Pa · s.

2.9 A capillary-tube viscometer is being selected to measure viscosity of a liquid food. The maximum viscosity to be measured will be 230 cP and the maximum flow rate that can be measured accurately is 0.015 kg/min. If the tube length is 10 cm and a maximum pressure of 25 Pa can be measured, determine the tube diameter to be used. The density of the product is 1000 kg/m^3.

2.10 The flow of a liquid in a 2-in. diameter steel pipe produces a pressure drop due to friction of 72.68 kPa. The length of pipe is 40 m and the mean velocity is 3 m/s. If the density of the liquid is 1000 kg/m^3, then

   (a) Determine the Reynolds number.
   (b) Determine if the flow is laminar or turbulent.
   (c) Compute viscosity of the liquid.
   (d) Estimate the temperature, if the liquid is water.
   (e) Compute the mass flow rate.

*2.11 A single-cylinder rotational viscometer is used to measure a liquid with viscosity of 100 cP using a spindle with 6-cm length and 1-cm radius. At maximum shear rate (rpm = 60), the measurements approach a full-scale reading of 100. Determine the spindle dimensions that will allow the viscometer to measure viscosities up to 10,000 cP at maximum shear rate.

*2.12 A pump is being used to transport a liquid food product (ρ = 1000 kg/m^3, μ = 1.5 cP) from a holding tank to a filling machine at a mass flow rate of 2 kg/s. The liquid level in the holding tank is 10 m above the pump, and the filling machine is 5 m above the pump. There is 100 m of 2-in. nominal diameter sanitary pipeline between the holding tank and the filling machine, with one open globe valve and four medium-sweep 90° elbows in the system. The product is being pumped through a heat exchanger with 100 kPa of pressure drop due to friction before filling. Determine the theoretical power requirement for the pump.

* Indicates an advanced level of difficulty in solving.

List of Symbols

A area (m^2)

α constant: 0.5 for laminar flow, 1.0 for turbulent flow

B_A Arrhenius constant

C coefficient used in flow measurement

D pipe or tube diameter (m)

E energy (J/kg)

ε surface roughness (m)

E_a activation energy (kJ/kg)

E_p energy supplied by the pump (J/kg)

F force (N)

f friction factor

g acceleration due to gravity (m/s^2)

γ rate of shear (1/s)

h pressure head (m)

K_f coefficient used in friction equations for fittings

K consistency coefficient in Eq. (2.30) (Pa · s^n)

KE kinetic energy (J/kg)

L length (m)

L_e equivalent length (m)

μ coefficient of viscosity (Pa · s)

m mass (kg)

$\dot{m}$ mass flow rate (kg/s)

N rotational speed, revolutions per second

N_{Re} Reynolds number

n flow behavior index

P pressure (Pa)

P' power (kW)

PE potential energy (J/kg)

R radius (m)

ρ density (kg/m^3)

r radial coordinate

R_g gas constant (kJ/kg · K)

σ shear stress (Pa)

T temperature (°C)

t time (s)

u liquid velocity (m/s)

$\bar{u}$ mean liquid velocity (m/s)

V volume (m^3)

$\dot{V}$ volumetric flow rate (m^3/s)

ω angular velocity (rad/s)

W_s work (kJ/kg)

y distance coordinate in y direction (m)

Z elevation (m)

z vertical coordinate

Ω torque (N · m)

ΔP pressure drop (Pa)

Subscripts: A, Absolute; f, friction; i, inner; m, manometer; o, outer; w, wall.

Bibliography

Brennan, J. G., Butters, J. R., Cowell, N. D., and Lilly, A. E. V. (1990). "Food Engineering Operations," 3rd ed. Elsevier Science Publishing Co., New York.

Charm, S. E. (1978). "The Fundamentals of Food Engineering," 3rd ed. AVI Publ. Co., Westport, Connecticut.

Colebrook, C. F. (1939). Friction factors for pipe flow. *Inst. Civil Eng.* **11**, 133.

Doublier, J. L., and Lefebvre, J. (1989). Flow properties of fluid food materials. *In* "Food Properties and Computer-Aided Engineering of Food Processing Systems" (R. P. Singh and A. G. Medina, eds.), pp. 245–269. Kluwer Academic Publishers, Dordrecht, The Netherlands.

Earle, R. L. (1983). "Unit Operations in Food Processing," 2nd ed. Pergamon Press, Oxford.

Farrall, A. W. (1976). "Food Engineering Systems," Vol. 1. AVI Publ. Co., Westport, Connecticut.

Farrall, A. W. (1979). "Food Engineering Systems," Vol. 2. AVI Publ. Co., Westport Connecticut.

Heldman, D. R., and Seiberling, D. A. (1976). *In* "Dairy Technology and Engineering" (W. J. Harper and C. W. Hall, eds.) pp. 272–321. AVI Publ. Co., Westport, Connecticut.

Heldman, D. R., and Singh, R. P. (1981). "Food Process Engineering," 2nd ed. AVI Publ. Co., Westport, Connecticut.

Herschel, W. H., and Bulkley, R. (1926). Konsistenzmessungen von gummi-benzollusungen. *Kolloid-Zeitschr.* **39**, 291.

Loncin, M., and Merson, R. L. (1979). "Food Engineering; Principles and Selected Applications." Academic Press, New York.

Reynolds, O. (1874). "Papers on Mechanical and Physical Subjects." The University Press, Cambridge, England.

Slade, F. H. (1967). "Food Processing Plant," Vol. 1. CRC Press, Cleveland, Ohio.

Slade, F. H. (1971). "Food Processing Plant," Vol. 2 CRC Press, Cleveland, Ohio.

Steffe, J. F. (1992). "Rheological Methods in Food Process Engineering." Freeman Press, East Lansing, Michigan.

Toledo, R. T. (1991). "Fundamentals of Food Process Engineering," 2nd ed. Van Nostrand Reinhold, New York.

Watson, E. L., and Harper, J. C. (1988). "Elements of Food Engineering," 2nd ed. Van Nostrand Reinhold, New York.

CHAPTER 3

Energy for Food Processing

The modern food processing plant cannot function without adequate supplies of basic and unique utilities. The use of large quantities of water is not unexpected due to the handling of foods in water and the needs for water as a cleaning medium. Electricity is used as a utility to power many motors and related equipment throughout food processing. Heated air and water are used for a variety of purposes, with energy provided from several fuel sources, including natural gas, coal, or oil. Refrigeration is a much used utility throughout the food industry, with most applications involving conversion of electrical energy into cold air. Steam is a utility similar to refrigeration, in that the availability of the utility is dependent on generating facilities at a location near the point of use.

Within this chapter, three of the utilities used in food processing will be analyzed in some detail. These utilities include (a) generation and utilization of steam, (b) natural gas utilization, and (c) electric power utilization. Water utilization will not be analyzed, except as a part of steam generation, since it is not viewed as a source of energy in most applications. The subject of refrigeration will be described in a separate chapter to adequately reflect the importance of this subject.

3.1 Generation of Steam

Steam represents the vapor state of water and becomes a source of energy when the change-of-state is realized. This energy can be used for increasing the temperature of other substances, such as food products, and results in production of a water condensate as the energy is released. The vapor state of water or steam is produced by addition of energy from a more basic source, such as fuel oil or natural gas, to convert water from a liquid to a vapor state.

This section will first describe typical systems used in the food industry for conversion of water to steam. The thermodynamics of phase change will be discussed and will be used to explain steam tables. The values tabulated in steam tables will be used to illustrate energy requirements for steam generation, as well as availability of energy from steam to use in food processing. The efficient conversion of energy from the source used to generate steam to some food processing application will be emphasized.

3.1.1 Steam Generation Systems

The systems for generation of steam can be divided into two major classifications: (a) fire-tube and (b) water-tube. Both systems are used in the food industry, but water-tube systems are designed for the more modern applications. The steam generation system or boiler is a vessel designed to bring water into contact with a hot surface, as required to convert liquid to vapor. The hot surface is maintained by using hot gases, usually combustion gases from natural gas or other petroleum products. The boiler vessel is designed to contain the steam and to withstand the pressures resulting from the change of state for water.

Fire-tube steam generators (Fig. 3.1) utilize hot gases within tubes surrounded by water to convert the water from liquid to vapor state. The resulting heat transfer causes the desired change of state with the vapors generated contained within the vessel holding the water. A water-tube steam generator (Fig. 3.2) utilizes heat transfer from hot gas surrounding the tubes to the water flowing through the tubes to produce steam. The

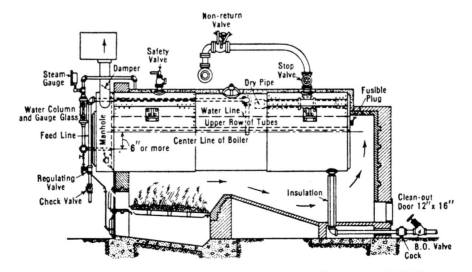

Fig. 3.1 The horizontal return tubular (HRT) fire-tube boiler. [From Farrall (1979.]

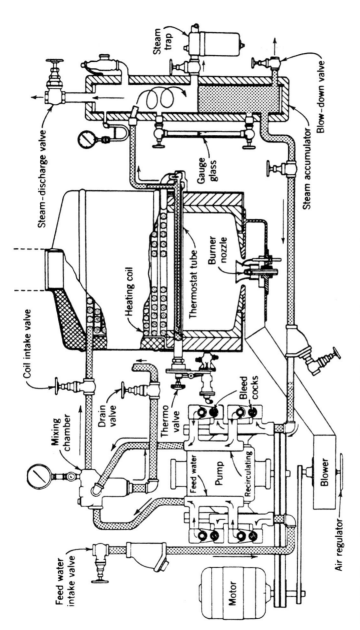

Fig. 3.2 Water-tube steam generator. (Courtesy of Cherry-Burrell Corporation.)

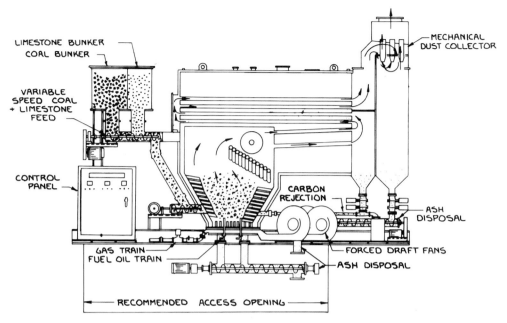

Fig. 3.3 Steam generation system. (Courtesy of Johnson Boiler Company.)

heat transfer in the water-tube system tends to be somewhat more rapid due to the ability to maintain turbulent flow within the liquid flow tube.

Water-tube boilers generally operate with larger capacities and at higher pressures. These systems have greater flexibility and are considered safer to operate than the counterpart fire-tube systems. The safety feature is most closely associated with the change-of-phase occurring within small tubes in a water-tube system as compared to a large vessel with a fire-tube system. The latter system does have an advantage when the load on the system varies considerably with time. Nearly all modern installations in the food industry are the water-tube design.

One of the more recent developments is the utilization of alternate fuels as a source of energy for steam generation. In particular, combustible waste materials from processing operations have become a viable alternative. In many situations, these materials are available in large quantities and may represent a disposal problem.

The steam generation systems do require modifications in design to accommodate different combustion processes, as illustrated in Fig. 3.3. The advantage of these systems is the opportunity to establish cogeneration, as described in Fig. 3.4. This arrangement utilizes steam generated from waste materials to generate electric power, as well as provide steam for processing operations. Depending on the availability of waste materials, significant percentages of electric power demand can be produced from waste materials.

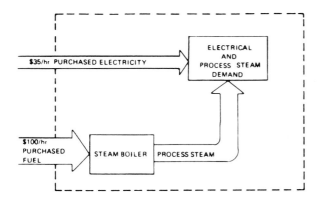

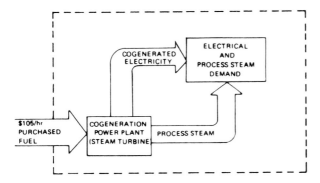

Fig. 3.4   Steam generation system with cogeneration. [From Teixeira (1980).]

3.1.2   Thermodynamics of Phase Change

The conversion of water from a liquid to vapor state can be described in terms of thermodynamic relationships. If the phase change for water is presented as a pressure–enthalpy relationship, it appears as shown in Fig. 3.5. The bell-shaped curve represents the pressure, temperature, and enthalpy relationships of water at its different states. The left-side curve is the saturated liquid curve, whereas the right-side curve is the saturated vapor curve. Inside the bell-shaped curve any location indicates a mixture of liquid and vapor. The region to the right side of the saturated vapor curve indicates superheated vapors. And the region to the left side of the saturated liquid curve indicates subcooled liquid. At atmospheric pressure, the addition of sensible heat increases the heat content of liquid water until it reaches the saturated liquid curve.

As an illustration, consider a process ABCD on Fig. 3.5. Point A represents water at 80°C and 0.1 MPa pressure. The enthalpy content is about 300 kJ/kg of water. As heat is added to the water, the temperature

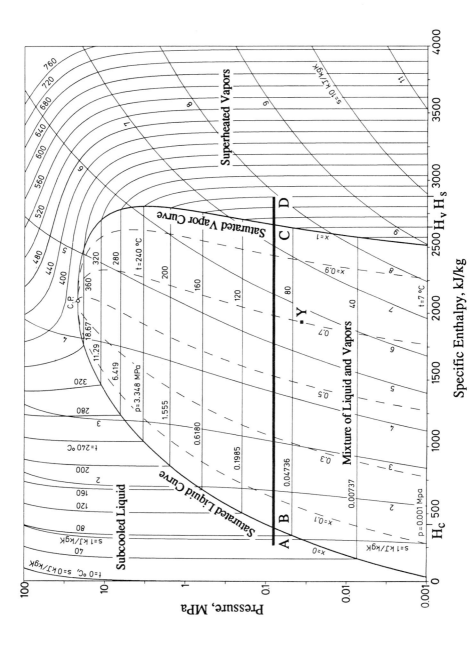

Fig. 3.5 Pressure–enthalpy diagram for steam–water and vapor. [From Straub, U. G., and Scheibner, G. (1984). "Steam Tables in SI Units," 2nd ed. Springer-Verlag, Berlin.]

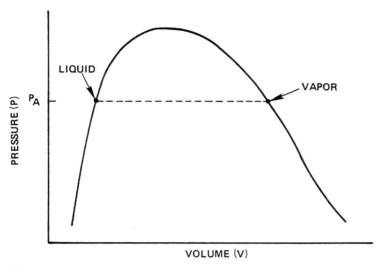

Fig. 3.6 Pressure–volume relationships for liquid and vapor.

increases to 100°C at point B on the saturated liquid curve. The enthalpy content of saturated water at point B is H_c (referring to enthalpy of condensate), which can be read off the chart as 400 kJ/kg. Further addition of thermal energy (in the form of latent heat) causes a phase change. As additional heat is added more liquid water changes to vapor state. At point C, all the water has changed into vapors, thus producing saturated steam at 100°C. The enthalpy of saturated steam at point C is H_v (referring to enthalpy of saturated vapors) or 2650 kJ/kg. Further addition of thermal energy results in superheated steam at the same pressure but higher temperatures. Point D represents superheated steam at 200°C with an enthalpy content H_s (referring to superheated steam) of 2850 kJ/kg. While Fig. 3.5 provides a conceptual understanding of the steam generation processes, steam tables (to be described in the following section) give more accurate values.

By plotting the water phase-change process on pressure–volume coordinates, Fig. 3.6 is obtained. This illustrates that a significant increase in volume occurs during the conversion of water from a liquid to vapor state. In practice, this conversion occurs within a constant-volume vessel, resulting in an increase in pressure as a result of the phase-change process. In a continuous steam generation process, the pressure and corresponding temperature of the steam to be used for processing operations are established by the magnitude of thermal energy added from the fuel source.

The third thermodynamic relationship would be on temperature–entropy coordinates, as illustrated in Fig. 3.7. This relationship indicates that the phase change from liquid to vapor is accompanied by an increase in entropy. Although this thermodynamic property has less practical use

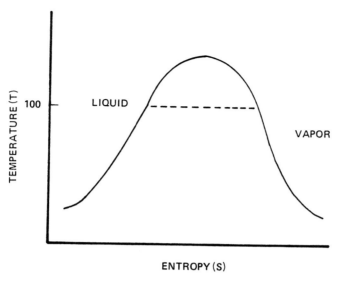

Fig. 3.7 Temperature–entropy relationships for liquid and vapor.

than enthalpy, it has interesting characteristics. For example, the pressure decrease resulting in a temperature decrease (referred to as "flash cooling") is, ideally, an isoentropic or constant entropy process. In a similar manner, the compression of steam from a low to a high pressure is a constant entropy process with a corresponding increase in temperature.

There are numerous terms unique to the subject of steam generation. *Saturated liquid* is the condition when **water** is at equilibrium with its vapor. This condition exists at any pressure and corresponding temperature when the liquid is at the boiling point. *Saturated vapor* is **steam** at equilibrium with liquid water. Likewise, the condition exists at any pressure and temperature at the boiling point. *Superheated vapor* is steam at any pressure and temperature when the heat content is greater than saturated vapor. The conditions existing between saturated liquid and saturated vapor are represented by mixtures of liquid and vapor representing a transition due to phase change. The extent to which the phase change has progressed is defined as *steam quality*. Normally, steam quality is expressed as a percentage indicating the heat content of the vapor–liquid mixture. In Fig. 3.5, point Y indicates a mixture of liquid and vapor. The steam quality of the mixture represented by this point is 0.7 or 70%, meaning 70% of the mixture is vapor and the remaining 30% is in a liquid state. The enthalpy of steam with a steam quality less than 100% is expressed by the following equation:

$$H = H_c + x_s(H_v - H_c) \qquad (3.1)$$

The above equation may be rearranged into the following alternative form:

$$H = (1 - x_s)H_c + x_s H_v \qquad (3.2)$$

The specific volume of steam with a steam quality of x_s can be expressed by

$$V' = (1 - x_s)V_c' + x_s V_v' \qquad (3.3)$$

3.1.3   Steam Tables

In the previous section, we saw the use of diagrams to obtain thermodynamic properties of steam. A more accurate procedure to obtain these values is by using tables (see Tables A.4.2 and A.4.3). Table A.4.2 presents the properties of saturated steam. The properties include specific volume, enthalpy, and entropy, all presented as a function of temperature and pressure. Each property is described in terms of a magnitude for saturated liquid, an additional value for saturated vapor, and a value representing the difference between vapor and liquid. For example, the latent heat of vaporization, as given in Table A.4.2, is the difference between the enthalpy of saturated vapor and saturated liquid.

The properties of superheated steam are presented in Table A.4.3. The specific volume, enthalpy, and entropy are presented at several temperatures above saturation at each pressure. The property values represent the influence of temperature on the magnitude of specific volume, enthalpy, and entropy.

Another procedure to obtain thermodynamic properties of steam is with the use of mathematical equations. These mathematical equations are available in literature. When programmed into a computer, these equations allow determination of enthalpy values. A set of these empirical equations, suggested by Martin (1961) and Steltz and Silvestri (1958) are presented in Example 3.3. This example uses a spreadsheet for the determination of the thermodynamic properties.

EXAMPLE 3.1

Determine the volume and enthalpy of steam at 120°C with 80% quality.

GIVEN (from Table A.4.2)
   Specific volume of liquid (V_c') = 0.0010603 m³/kg
   Specific volume of vapor (V_v') = 0.8919 m³/kg
   Enthalpy of liquid (H_c) = 503.71 kJ/kg
   Enthalpy of vapor (H_v) = 2706.3 kJ/kg

APPROACH

The volume and enthalpy of the 80% quality steam can be determined from the saturation conditions using appropriate proper proportions based on steam quality expressed as a fraction.

SOLUTION

(1) For enthalpy

$$H = H_c + x_s(H_v - H_c) = (1 - x_s)H_c + x_sH_v$$

$$= 0.2(503.7) + 0.8(2706.3)$$

$$= 2265.78 \text{ kJ/kg}$$

(2) For specific volume

$$V' = (1 - x_s)V'_c + x_sV'_v$$

$$= 0.2(0.0010603) + 0.8(0.8919)$$

$$= 0.7137 \text{ m}^3/\text{kg}$$

(3) Note that a small error results from ignoring the volume of saturated liquid.

$$V' = x_sV'_v = 0.8(0.8919) = 0.7135 \text{ m}^3/\text{kg}$$

EXAMPLE 3.2

Fluid milk is being heated from 60 to 115°C at a rate of 500 kg/hr using steam as a heating medium. The heat exchanger being utilized has an efficiency of 85%, and the steam quality will be 90%. The system is designed to allow condensate to be released at 115°C. The mass and volume flow rate of steam required for this process is to be determined.

GIVEN

Product flow rate $(\dot{m})$ = 500 kg/hr
Specific heat of milk (c_p) = 3.86 kJ/kg ·°C (Table A.2.1)
Initial product temperature (T_i) = 60°C
Final product temperature (T_o) = 115°C
Steam quality (x_s) = 90%
Steam temperature (T_s) = 120°C; selected to assure a minimum temperature gradient of 5°C between steam and product

For steam temperature of 120°C, pressure will be 198.55 kPa, and (from Table A.4.2):

$$H_c = 503.71 \text{ kJ/kg} \qquad V'_c = 0.0010603 \text{ m}^3/\text{kg}$$

$$H_v = 2706.3 \text{ kJ/kg} \qquad V'_v = 0.8919 \text{ m}^3/\text{kg}$$

APPROACH

The thermal energy requirements for the product will be used to establish the mass flow rate of steam required. The volumetric flow rate is computed from the mass flow rate and specific volume of steam.

SOLUTION

(1) Thermal energy requirement

$$q = \dot{m}c_p(T_o - T_i) = (500 \text{ kg/hr})(3.86 \text{ kJ/kg})(115° \text{C} - 60° \text{C})$$
$$= 106,150 \text{ kJ/hr}$$

or for 85% heat exchanger efficiency.

$$q = \frac{106,150}{0.85} = 124,882 \text{ kJ/hr}$$

(2) For steam quality of 90%,

$$H = (0.1)503.71 + (0.9)2706.3 = 2486.04 \text{ kJ/kg}$$

(3) The thermal energy content of condensate leaving the heat exchanger will be (the specific heat for water is obtained from Table A.4.1)

$$H_c = (4.228 \text{ kJ/kg°C})(115° \text{C}) = 486 \text{ kJ/kg}$$

(4) Since the thermal energy provided by steam will be

$$q_s = \dot{m}_s(H - H_c)$$

and this magnitude must match the steam requirements, then

$$\dot{m}_s = \frac{124,882 \text{ kJ/hr}}{(2486.04 - 486) \text{ kJ/kg}} = 62.44 \text{ kg/hr}$$

(5) For 90% quality,

$$V' = (0.1)0.0010603 + (0.9)0.8919 = 0.8028 \text{ m}^3/\text{kg}$$

(6) Volumetric flow rate = $(62.35 \text{ kg/hr})(0.8028 \text{ m}^3/\text{kg}) = 50.05 \text{ m}^3/\text{hr}$.
(7) Steam generation system capacity

$$124,882 \text{ kJ/hr} = 34,689 \text{ J/s} = 34,689 \text{ W}$$
$$= 34.7 \text{ kW}$$
$$= 46.5 \text{ hp}$$

EXAMPLE 3.3

Develop a spreadsheet program for predicting enthalpy values of saturated and superheated steam.

APPROACH

We will use the numerical equations given by Martin (1961) and Steltz and Silvestri (1958) to program an EXCEL™ spreadsheet.

SOLUTION

The spreadsheets with equations and a sample calculation for steam at a temperature of 120°C are as shown in Figs. 3.8 and 3.9. The results are given

	A	B
1	Temperature C?	120
2		=B1*1.8+32
3		7.46908269
4		=-0.00750675994
5		-0.0000000046203229
6		-0.001215470111
7		0
8		=B2-705.398
9		=(EXP(8.0728362+B8*(B3+B4*B8+B5*B8^3+B7*B8^4)/(1+B6*B8)/(B2+459.688)))*6.89473
10	Pressure kPa?	=B9
11		=B10*0.1450383
12	Temperature C?	=B1
13		=B12*1.8+32
14		=(B13+459.688)/2.84378159
15		=0.0862139787*B14
16		=LN(B15)
17		=-B16/0.048615207
18		=0.73726439-0.0170952671*B17
19		=0.1286073*B11
20		=LN(B19)
21		=B20/9.07243502
22		=14.3582702+45.4653859*B21
23		=(B15)^2/0.79836127
24		=0.00372999654/B23
25		=186210.0562*B24
26		=EXP(B25+B20-B16+4.3342998)
27		=B26-B19
28		=B24*B27^2
29		=B28^2
30		=3464.3764/B15
31		=-1.279514846*B30
32		=B28*(B31+41.273)
33		=B29*(B15+0.5*B30)
34		=2*(B32+2*B33)
35		=B28*(B30*B28-B31)
36		=18.8131323+B22*B21
37		=B26+2*(B26*B25)
38		=B37*B34/B27+B34-B35-B37
39		-32.179105
40		1.0088084
41		-0.00011516996
42		0.00000048553836
43		-0.00000000073618778
44		9.6350315E-13
45	Vv	=(0.0302749643*(B34-B27+83.47150448*B15)/B19)*0.02832/0.45359
46	Hc	=(B39+B40*B13+B41*B2^2+B42*B2^3+B43*B2^4+B44*B2^5)*2.3258
47	Hv or Hs	=(835.417534-B17+B14+0.04355685*(B32+B23-B27+B38))*2.3258
48	Hevap	=B47-B46

Fig. 3.8 Spreadsheet for predicting enthalpy values of saturated and superheated steam in Example 3.3.

	A	B	C
1	Temperature C?	120	
2		248	For calculations involving saturated vapors: Enter temperature in cell B1, =B9 in cell B10, and =B1 in cell B12
3		7.46908269	
4		-0.00750676	
5		-4.62E-09	
6		-1.22E-03	
7		0	
8		-457.398	
9		198.558129	
10	Pressure kPa?	198.558129	For calculations involving superheated vapors: Enter pressure in cell B10 and temperature in cell B12
11		28.79853348	
12	Temperature C?	120	
13		248	
14		248.8545543	
15		21.45474124	
16		3.065945658	
17		-63.06556831	
18		1.815387125	
19		3.703701635	
20		1.309332761	
21		0.144319883	
22		20.91982938	
23		576.5634419	
24		6.46936E-06	
25		1.204659912	
26		43.91899067	
27		40.21528903	
28		0.010462699	
29		0.000109468	
30		161.4736976	
31		-206.6079934	
32		-1.729850209	
33		0.011186715	
34		-3.414953557	
35		2.179353383	
36		21.83227963	
37		149.7338856	
38		-168.0431145	
39		-3.22E+01	
40		1.0088084	
41		-1.15E-04	
42		4.86E-07	
43		-7.36E-10	
44		9.64E-13	
45	Vv	0.891717572	
46	Hc	503.41	For superheated vapors Hs is given by cell B47
47	Hv or Hs	2705.613646	
48	Hevap	2202.201327	

Fig. 3.9   Sample calculation spreadsheet for Example 3.3.

in cells B45 through B48, as follows:

$$V_v = 0.89 \text{ m}^3/\text{kg}$$
$$H_c = 503.4 \text{ kJ}/\text{kg}$$
$$H_v = 2705.6 \text{ kJ}/\text{kg}$$
$$H_{evap} = 2202.2 \text{ kJ}/\text{kg}$$

3.1.4 Steam Utilization

The capacity of the steam generation system in a food processing plant is established by requirements of the individual operations using steam. The requirements are expressed in two ways: (a) the temperature of steam needed as a heating medium, and (b) the quantity of steam required to supply the demands of the operation. Since the temperature requirement is a function of pressure, this establishes one of the operating conditions of the system. In addition, the steam properties are a function of pressure (and temperature), which in turn influences the quantity of steam utilized.

The steps involved in determining the capacity of a steam generation system include the following. The thermal energy requirements of all operations utilizing steam from a given system are determined. In most situations, those requirements will establish maximum temperature required and therefore the pressure at which the steam generation system must operate. After the operating pressure of the system is established, the properties of steam are known and the thermal energy available from each unit of steam can be determined. This information can then be used to compute quantities of steam required for the process. An important consideration in sizing the pipe connecting the process to the steam generation system is the volume of steam required. Using the quantity of steam required as expressed in mass units, and the specific volume of the steam being used, the volumetric flow rate for steam leading to the process is computed.

The use of steam by various processes in a food processing plant requires a transport system. The steam generation system is connected to the processes using steam by a network of pipelines. The transport system must account for two factors: (a) the resistance to flow of steam to the various locations, and (b) the loss of thermal energy of heat content during transport.

The transport of steam involves many of the considerations presented in Chapter 2. The flow of steam through a processing plant pipeline can be described by factors in the mechanical energy balance equation, Eq. (2.63). In many situations, the steam generation system and the process using the steam will not be at the same elevation, and the first term on each side of the equation must be considered. Since the steam velocity within the steam generation system will be essentially zero, the kinetic energy term on the left side of the equation will be zero, at least in comparison to the same term on the right side of the equation. The pressure terms in Eq. (2.63) are very important, since the left side represents the pressure at the steam generation system while the right side will be the pressure at the point of use. Since no work E_p is being done on the steam during transport, this term is zero; but the energy loss due to friction will be very important. In many situations, the energy loss due to friction can be translated directly into the loss of pressure between the steam generation system and the point of steam use.

EXAMPLE 3.4

Steam is being transported from a steam generation system to a process at the rate of 1 kg/min through a 2-in. (nominal diameter) steel pipe. The distance is 20 m and there are five 90° standard elbows in the pipeline. If the steam is being generated at 143.27 kPa, compute the pressure of the steam at the point of use. The viscosity of steam is 10.335×10^{-6} Pa · s.

GIVEN

Steam flow rate $(\dot{m}_s) = 1$ kg/min
Steam pressure = 143.27 kPa
Pipe diameter $(D) = 2$ inches (nominal) = 0.0525 m
Pipe length $(L) = 20$ m
Fittings include five 90° standard elbows
Steam viscosity $(\mu) = 10.335 \times 10^{-6}$ Pa · s

APPROACH

By using the mechanical energy balance and computation of energy losses due to friction, the pressure losses for the 20-m length of pipe will be determined.

SOLUTION

(1) To use Eq. (2.51), the friction factor f must be determined from the Reynolds number and the relative roughness, for a steam density of 0.8263 kg/m³ obtained at 143.27 kPa.

$$\bar{u} = \frac{(1 \text{ kg/min})(1/60 \text{ min/s})}{(0.8263 \text{ kg/m}^3)\left[\pi(0.0525 \text{ m})^2/4\right]} = 9.32 \text{ m/s}$$

and

$$N_{\text{Re}} = \frac{(0.8263 \text{ kg/m}^3)(0.0525 \text{ m})(9.32 \text{ m/s})}{(10.335 \times 10^{-6} \text{ Pa} \cdot \text{s})} = 39,120$$

(2) For steel pipe (using Fig. 2.15),

$$\frac{\varepsilon}{D} = \frac{45.7 \times 10^{-6} \text{ m}}{0.0525 \text{ m}} = 0.00087$$

(3) The friction factor f is determined from Fig. 2.15.

$$f = 0.0061$$

(4) The energy loss due to friction is computed using Eq. (2.51).

$$\frac{\Delta P}{\rho} = 2(0.0061)\frac{(9.32 \text{ m/s})^2(20 \text{ m})}{(0.0525 \text{ m})} = 403.7 \text{ J/kg}$$

(5) Energy loss due to friction in five standard elbows with

$$L_e/D = 32 \text{ from Table 2.3}$$

and

$$L_e = 32(0.0525)(5) = 8.4 \text{ m}$$

and

$$\frac{\Delta P_f}{\rho} = 2(0.0061)\frac{(9.32 \text{ m/s})^2(8.4 \text{ m})}{(0.0525 \text{ m})} = 169.6 \text{ J/kg}$$

(6) Using the mechanical energy balance, Eq. (2.63), without elevation and work terms and with velocity of zero at steam generation system,

$$\frac{143,270 \text{ Pa}}{0.8263 \text{ kg/m}^3} = \frac{(9.32 \text{ m/s})^2}{2} + \frac{P_2}{\rho} + (403.7 + 169.6)$$

or

$$\frac{P_2}{\rho} = 173,387.4 - 43.4 - 573.3 = 172,770.7 \text{ J/kg}$$

(7) By assuming that steam density has not changed,

$$P_2 = (172,770.7 \text{ J/kg})(0.8263 \text{ kg/m}^3) = 142.76 \text{ kPa}$$

indicating that change in steam pressure due to friction losses during flow is relatively small.

EXAMPLE 3.5

A liquid food with 12% total solids is being heated by steam injection using steam at a pressure of 232.1 kPa. (See Fig. 3.10.) The product enters the heating system at 50°C at a rate of 100 kg/min and is being heated to 120°C. The product specific heat is a function of composition as follows:

$$c_p = c_{pw}(\text{mass fraction H}_2\text{O}) + c_{ps}(\text{mass fraction solid})$$

and the specific heat of product at 12% total solids is 3.936 kJ/kg°C. Determine the quantity and minimum quality of steam to ensure that the product leaving the heating system has 10% total solids.

GIVEN

Product total solids in $(X_A) = 0.12$
Product mass flow rate $(\dot{m}_A) = 100$ kg/min
Product total solids out $(X_B) = 0.1$
Product temperature in $(T_A) = 50°C$

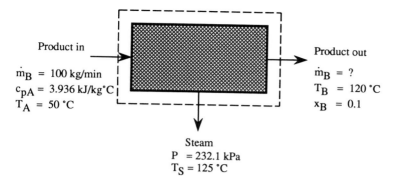

Fig. 3.10 System diagram for Example 3.5.

Product temperature out $(T_B) = 120°C$
Steam pressure $= 232.1$ kPa, $(T_s) = 125°C$
Product specific heat in $(c_{PA}) = 3.936$ kJ/kg $·°C$

APPROACH

(1) Set up mass balance equations.

$$\dot{m}_a + \dot{m}_S = \dot{m}_B$$

$$\dot{m}_A X_A = \dot{m}_B X_B$$

(2) Set up energy balance equation using reference temperature of 0°C.

$$\dot{m}_A c_{PA}(T_A - 0) + \dot{m}_S H_S = \dot{m}_B c_{PB}(T_B - 0)$$

(3) By solving the mass balance equations for $\dot{m}_B$ and $\dot{m}_S$, the enthalpy of steam (H_s) required can be computed.

SOLUTION

(1) Mass and solid balance

$$100 + \dot{m}_s = \dot{m}_B$$

$$100(0.12) + 0 = \dot{m}_B(0.1)$$

$$\dot{m}_B = \frac{12}{0.1} = 120 \text{ kg/min}$$

(2) Then

$$\dot{m}_s = 120 - 100 = 20 \text{ kg/min}$$

(3) From energy balance

$$(100)(3.936)(50 - 0) + (20)H_s = (120)c_{PB}(120 - 0)$$

where

$$c_{PB} = (4.232)(0.9) + c_{PS}(0.1)$$

from

$$3.936 = (4.178)(0.88) + c_{PS}(0.12)$$

$$c_{PS} = 2.161$$

then

$$c_{PB} = 4.025 \text{ kJ/kg°C}$$

(4) Solving for enthalpy (H_s),

$$H_S = \frac{(120)(4.025)(120) - (100)(3.936)(50)}{20}$$

$$H_S = 1914.0 \text{ kJ/kg}$$

(5) From properties of saturated steam for 232.1 kPa,

$$H_c = 524.99 \text{ kJ/kg}$$

$$H_v = 2713.5 \text{ kJ/kg}$$

then

$$\% \text{ Quality} = \frac{1914 - 524.99}{2713.5 - 524.99}(100)$$

$$= 63.5\%$$

(6) Any steam quality above 63.5% will result in higher total solids in heated product.

3.2 Fuel Utilization

The energy requirements for food processing are met in a variety of ways. In general, the traditional energy sources are utilized to generate steam as well as provide for other utilities used in the processing plant. As illustrated in Table 3.1, the energy types include natural gas, electricity, petroleum products, and coal. Although the information presented was collected in 1973 and percentages of natural gas utilization have declined somewhat, it seems evident that food processing has a definite dependence on petroleum products and natural gas.

To use the energy associated with natural gas and petroleum products, they are exposed to a combustion process to release the available energy. The combustion process is a rapid chemical reaction involving fuel components and oxygen. The primary fuel components involved in the reaction include carbon, hydrogen, and sulfur, with the last being an undesirable component. The oxygen for the reaction is provided by air, which must be mixed with fuel in the most efficient manner.

3.2.1 Systems

The burner is the primary component of the system required for combustion of natural gas or petroleum products. Burners are used to produce the hot gases required in steam generation or the heated air for space heating in a building. Burners are designed to introduce fuel and air into the combustion chamber in a manner leading to the more efficient generation of energy.

A typical burner is illustrated by Fig. 3.11, a single circular register burner for both natural gas and oil. The orientation of doors in the air

TABLE 3.1
**Energy Use by Fuel Type for 14 Leading Energy-Using Food
and Kindred Products Industries for 1973**

Industry	Energy use by type of fuel (%)					
	Natural gas	Purchased electricity	Petroleum products	Coal	Other	Total
Meat packing	46	31	14	9	0	100
Prepared animal feeds	52	38	10	< 1	0	100
Wet corn milling	43	14	7	36	0	100
Fluid milk	33	47	17	3	0	100
Beet sugar processing	65	1	5	25	4	100
Malt beverages	38	37	18	7	0	100
Bread and related products	34	28	38	0	0	100
Frozen fruits and vegetables	41	50	5	4	0	100
Soybean oil mills	47	28	9	16	0	100
Canned fruits and vegetables	66	16	15	3	0	100
Cane sugar refining	66	1	33	0	0	100
Sausage and other meat	46	38	15	1	0	100
Animal and marine fats and oils	65	17	17	1	0	100
Manufactured ice	12	85	3	0	0	100

Source: Unger, S. G. (1975). Energy utilization in the leading energy–consuming food processing industries. *Food Technol.* **29**(12), 33–43.

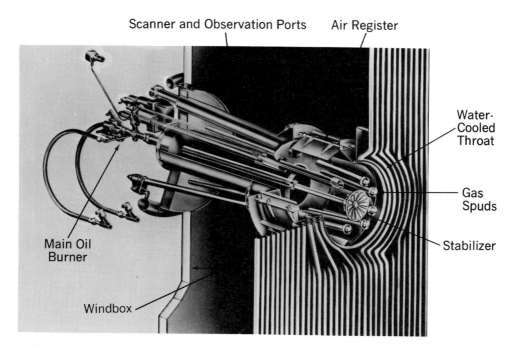

Fig. 3.11 Circular register burner with water-cooled throat for oil and gas firing. [From the Babcock & Wilcox Handbook (1978).]

register provides turbulence needed to create mixing of fuel and air, as well as producing a desirable short flame. Burners are designed to minimize maintenance by keeping exposure of the burner to a minimum and allowing the replacement of vulnerable components while the unit continues to operate.

Safety is a definite concern in operating any system involving combustion. Ignition of a burner should occur at a location close to the burner, even at much higher air flows than required. Safety precautions should apply during starting and stopping of the system, as well as during load changes and variations in fuel.

3.2.2 Mass and Energy Balance Analysis

The combustion process can be described by equations involving the reaction between methane and oxygen as follows:

$$CH_4 + 2\,O_2 + 7.52\,N_2 = CO_2 + 2\,H_2O + 7.52\,N_2 \qquad (3.4)$$

where 3.76 mol N_2 per mol O_2 are included in air for combustion and in the reaction processes. Actual fuel gas will contain 85.3% CH_4 (by volume), and the reaction will appear as follows:

$$0.853\,CH_4 + 0.126\,C_2H_6 + 0.001\,CO_2$$
$$+ 0.017\,N_2 + 0.003\,O_2 + 2.147\,O_2 + 8.073\,N_2$$
$$= 1.106\,CO_2 + 2.084\,H_2O + 8.09\,N_2 \qquad (3.5)$$

where the theoretical balance has been established to indicate that 10.22 m^3 air would be needed for each cubic meter of fuel gas.

In actual combustion reactions, as much as 10% excess air will be provided and the reaction equation will appear as

$$0.853\,CH_4 + 0.126\,C_2H_6 + 0.001\,CO_2$$
$$+ 0.017\,N_2 + 0.003\,O_2 + 2.362\,O_2 + 8.88\,N_2$$
$$= 1.106\,CO_2 + 0.2147\,O_2 + 2.084\,H_2 + 8.897\,N_2 \qquad (3.6)$$

and indicate that the excess air produces excess oxygen and nitrogen in the flue gas from the combustion process. On a dry basis, the composition of the flue gas would be 87.1% nitrogen, 10.8% carbon dioxide, and 2.1% oxygen, where percentages are in volume basis.

The use of excess air is important to assure efficient combustion. Without sufficient oxygen, the reaction will be incomplete, resulting in the production of carbon monoxide (CO) along with associated safety hazards. In addition, the inefficient combustion has nearly 70% less heat released by the reaction. The amount of excess air must be controlled, however, since the air that is not involved in the reaction absorbs heat energy and decreases the amount of heat released by the combustion process.

The heat of combustion for a given reaction is dependent on the mixture of gases within the fuel. For the fuel previously described, the heat of combustion will be approximately 36,750 kJ/m^3. The losses with flue gas can be compared to this value, which would represent the maximum

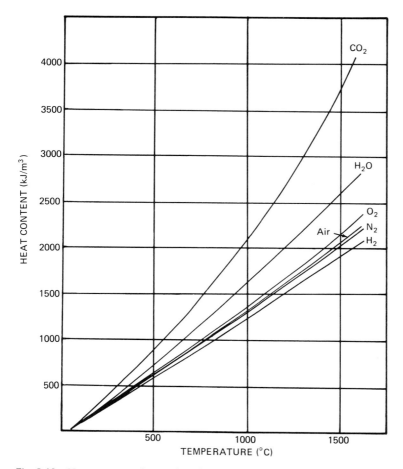

Fig. 3.12 Heat content of gases found in flue products.

achievable from the process. The flue gas losses would be dependent on heat content of each component in the flue gas, and these values are a function of gas temperature, as indicated by Fig. 3.12. Using this information, the energy losses associated with the previously described situation can be estimated (based on 1 m^3 fuel with 370°C flame gas).

$$CO_2 \quad 1.106\,\text{m}^3 \times 652\,\text{kJ/m}^3 = \quad 721.1\,\text{kJ}$$
$$O_2 \quad 0.2147\,\text{m}^3 \times 458\,\text{kJ/m}^3 = \quad 98.3\,\text{kJ}$$
$$H_2O \quad 2.084\,\text{m}^3 \times 522\,\text{kJ/m}^3 = 1087.9\,\text{kJ}$$
$$N_2 \; . \quad 8.897\,\text{m}^3 \times 428\,\text{kJ/m}^3 = 3807.9\,\text{kJ}$$
$$\overline{\quad 5715.2\,\text{kJ}}$$

This estimate indicates that flue gas energy losses are 5715.2 kJ/m^3 of fuel gas used. This represents 15.6% of the total energy available from the combustion process.

3.2.3 Burner Efficiencies

As indicated in Section 3.2.1, one of the primary purposes of the fuel burner is to assure optimum mixing of fuel and air. Without mixing, the combustion process will be incomplete and will produce the same results as insufficient oxygen. The burner is the key component of the combustion system in assuring that minimum amounts of excess air are required to maintain efficient combustion while minimizing the losses of energy in flue gas.

EXAMPLE 3.6

Natural gas is being burned to produce thermal energy required to convert water to steam in a steam generator. The natural gas composition is 85.3% methane, 12.6% ethane, 0.1% carbon dioxide, 1.7% nitrogen, and 0.3% oxygen. An analysis of the flue gas indicates that the composition is 86.8% nitrogen, 10.5% carbon dioxide, and 2.7% oxygen. Determine the amount of excess air being utilized and the percentage of energy loss in the flue gas leaving at 315°C.

GIVEN

> Composition of natural gas
> Composition of flue gas after combustion
> All CO_2 in flue must originate with natural gas: 1.106 m^3 CO_2/m^3 fuel.

APPROACH

The amount of excess air in the reaction can be evaluated by writing the reaction equation in a balanced manner and determining the extra oxygen in the reaction. The energy loss in the flue gas is based on thermal energy content in the flue gas, as determined from Fig. 3.12.

SOLUTION

(1) Based on the flue gas composition and the observation that the reaction must produce 1.106 m^3 CO_2/m^3 fuel,

$$10.5\% \ CO_2 = 1.106 \ m^3$$

$$2.7\% \ O_2 = 0.284 \ m^3$$

$$86.8\% \ N_2 = 9.143 \ m^3$$

(2) The reaction equation becomes

$$0.853 \ CH_4 + 0.126 \ C_2H_6 + 0.001 \ CO_2 + 0.017 \ N_2$$

$$+ \ 0.003 \ O_2 + 2.428 \ O_2 + 9.126 \ N_2$$

$$= 1.106 \ CO_2 + 0.284 \ O_2 + 2.084 \ H_2O + 9.143 \ N_2$$

(3) Based on the analysis presented,

$$\text{Excess air} = \frac{0.284}{2.428 - 0.284} = 13.25\%$$

where the percentage of excess air is reflected in the amount of oxygen in the flue gas as compared to oxygen associated with the air involved in the reaction.

(4) Using the composition of flue gas and the heat content of various components from Fig. 3.12, the following computations are obtained:

$$CO_2 \quad 1.106 \text{ m}^3 \times 577.4 \text{ kJ/m}^3 = 638.6 \text{ kJ}$$

$$O_2 \quad 0.284 \text{ m}^3 \times 409.8 \text{ kJ/m}^3 = 116.4 \text{ kJ}$$

$$H_2O \quad 2.084 \text{ m}^3 \times 465.7 \text{ kJ/m}^3 = 970.5 \text{ kJ}$$

$$N_2 \quad 9.143 \text{ m}^3 \times 372.5 \text{ kJ/m}^3 = 3405.8 \text{ kJ}$$

$$\overline{5131.3 \text{ kJ}}$$

The analysis indicates that 5131.3 kJ are lost with flue gas per cubic meter of fuel used in the process.

(5) Using the heat combustion of 36,750 kJ/m^3 for the fuel, the loss of energy with flue gas represents 14% of the energy available from the fuel.

3.3 Electric Power Utilization

Electric power has become so commonplace in the food industry that modern plants could not operate without this power source. In fact, most plants of significant size have acquired "back-up" electrical power generators to use in case disruptions in the primary supply occur. It is quite evident that electric power represents the most versatile and flexible power source available. In addition, the cost of electric power is very attractive when compared to other sources. In Fig. 3.13, a tomato processing line is shown along with energy requirements to operate each unit operation. As seen in this figure, most of the process equipment require electrical energy for their operation.

3.3.1 Electrical Terms and Units

As in most physical systems, electricity has a unique set of terms and units. These terms and units are entirely different from most physical systems, and it requires careful analysis to relate the terms to applications. This presentation is elementary and is intended to be a brief introduction to the subject. The following terms are essential.

Electricity can be defined as the flow of electrons from atom to atom in an electrical conductor. Most materials can be considered conductors, but will vary in the ability to conduct electricity.

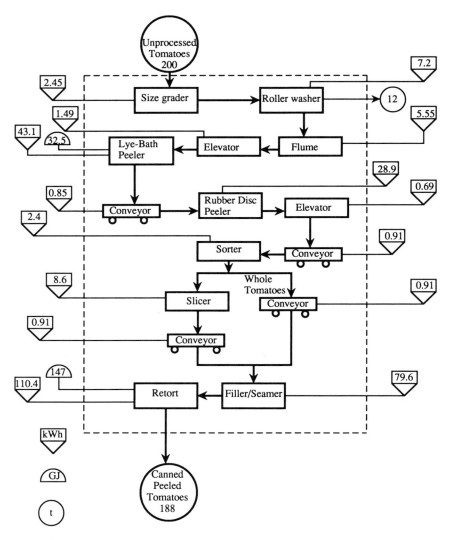

Fig. 3.13 Energy accounting diagram of peeled tomato canning based on an eight-hour shift. [From Singh *et al.* (1980).]

Ampere is the unit used to describe the magnitude of electrical current flowing in a conductor. By definition, 1 ampere (A) is 6.06×10^{18} electrons flowing past a given point per second.

Voltage is defined as the force causing current flow in an electrical circuit. The units for voltage are volts.

Resistance is the term used to describe the characteristics of a conductor that resists current flow. The ohm is the unit of electrical resistance.

Direct current is the type of electrical current flow in a simple electrical circuit. The current flow will occur from a positive to a negative terminal of a voltage generator.

Alternating current describes the type of voltage generated by an AC (alternating current) generator. Measurement of the actual voltage generated would indicate that the magnitude varies with time and a uniform frequency. The voltage ranges from positive to negative values of equal magnitudes. Most electrical service in the United States operates at 60 cycles per second (cps).

Single-phase is the type of electrical current generated by a single set of windings in a generator designed to convert mechanical power to electrical voltage. The rotor in the generator is a magnet that produces magnetic lines as it rotates. These magnetic lines produce a voltage in the iron frame (stator) that holds the windings. The voltage produced becomes the source of alternating current.

Three-phase is the type of electrical current generated by a stator with three sets of windings. Since three AC voltages are generated simultaneously, the voltage can be relatively constant. This type of system has several advantages compared to single-phase electricity.

Watt is the unit used to express electrical power or the rate of work. In a direct current (DC) system, power is the product of voltage and current, while computation of power from an alternating current (AC) system requires use of power factor.

Power factors are ratios of actual power to apparent power from an alternating current system. These factors should be as large as possible to ensure that excessive current is not carried through motors and conductors to achieve power ratings.

Conductors are materials used to transmit electrical energy from source to use. Ratings of conductors are on the basis of resistance to electrical flow.

3.3.2 Ohm's Law

The most basic relationship in electrical power use is Ohm's[1] law, expressed as

$$E_v = IR_E \tag{3.7}$$

where the voltage E_v is equal to the product of current I and resistance R_E. As might be expected, this relationship illustrates that for a given voltage, the current flow in a system will be inversely proportional to the resistance in the conductor.

1. George Simon Ohm (1789–1854). A German physicist, in 1817 he was appointed as a professor of mathematics at the Jesuit College, Cologne. In 1827, he wrote the paper *Die galvanische Kette, mathamatisch bearbeitet* (The Galvanic Circuit Investigated Mathematically), but he remained unrecognized for his contribution. He resigned from his professorship to join Polytechnic School in Nurnberg. Finally, in 1841, he was awarded the Copley medal by the Royal Society of London.

As indicated earlier, the power generated is the product of voltage and current.

$$\text{Power} = E_v I \tag{3.8}$$

or

$$\text{Power} = I^2 R_E \tag{3.9}$$

or

$$\text{Power} = \frac{E_V^2}{R_E} \tag{3.10}$$

These relationships can be applied directly to direct current (DC) systems and to alternating current (AC) with slight modifications.

EXAMPLE 3.7

A 12-volt battery is being used to operate a small DC motor with an internal resistance of 2 ohms. Compute the current flow in the system and the power required to operate the motor.

GIVEN

Battery with voltage E_v = 12 volts
DC motor with resistance R_E = 2 ohms

APPROACH

The current flow in the motor can be computed using Eq. (3.7), and power required can be determined from Eq. (3.8), (3.9), or (3.10).

SOLUTION

(1) Using Eq. (3.7),

$$I = \frac{E_V}{R_E} = \frac{12}{2} = 6 \text{ A}$$

indicating a current flow of 6 A in the system.

(2) The power required can be computed from Eq. (3.10)

$$\text{Power} = \frac{(12)^2}{2} = 72 \text{ W}$$

or 0.072 kW for the motor.

3.3.3 Electric Circuits

The manner in which conductors are used to connect the electric power source to the point of use is the electrical circuit. There are three basic types of circuits, with the series circuit being the simplest. As indicated by Fig. 3.14, this type of circuit is recognized by having the resistances connected in series with the power source. In this type of situation, each resistance would probably represent the points at which the electrical

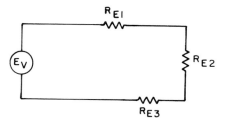

Fig. 3.14 Electrical circuit with resistances in series.

power is used. Often, these points are referred to as electrical loads. Application of Ohm's law to this situation leads to

$$E_v = I(R_{E1} + R_{E2} + R_{E3}) \tag{3.11}$$

indicating that resistances in series are additive. In addition, the voltage is often expressed as the sum of the voltage drop across each resistance in the circuit.

A parallel electrical circuit has the resistance or loads connected in parallel with the power source, as illustrated in Fig. 3.15. When Ohm's law is applied to the parallel circuit, the following relationship applies:

$$E_V = I \bigg/ \left(\frac{1}{R_{E1}} + \frac{1}{R_{E2}} + \frac{1}{R_{E3}} \right) \tag{3.12}$$

with the inverse of each resistance being additive. The most complex basic electrical circuit has a combination of series and parallel resistances, as illustrated in Fig. 3.16. To analyze relationships between voltage and resistances, the combination circuit must be treated in two parts. First, the three resistances (R_{E1}, R_{E2}, R_{E3}) must be resolved as an equivalent R_e.

$$\frac{1}{R_e} = \frac{1}{R_{E1}} + \frac{1}{R_{E2} + R_{E3}} \tag{3.13}$$

Then the circuit can be analyzed by applying Ohm's law in the following manner:

$$E_v = I(R_{E4} + R_e) \tag{3.14}$$

since in the modified circuit, the resistance R_{E4} and R_e are in series.

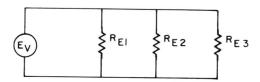

Fig. 3.15 Electrical circuit with resistances in parallel.

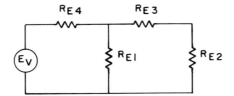

Fig. 3.16 Electrical circuit with resistances in series and parallel.

EXAMPLE 3.8

The four resistances in Fig. 3.16 are $R_{E1} = 25$ ohms, $R_{E2} = 60$ ohms, $R_{E3} = 20$ ohms, $R_{E4} = 20$ ohms. Determine the voltage source E_v required to maintain a voltage drop of 45 volts across the resistance R_{E2}.

GIVEN

Four resistances as identified in Fig. 3.16.
Voltage $(E_{v2}) = 45$ V

APPROACH

The voltage source E_v required can be evaluated by analysis of the circuit in terms of individual components and equivalent resistances.

SOLUTION

(1) By using Ohm's law, the current flow through the resistance R_{E2} will be

$$I_2 = \frac{45}{60} = 0.75 \text{ A}$$

(2) Since the current flow through R_{E3} must be the same as R_{E2}, then

$$E_{V3} = (0.75)(20) = 15 \text{ V}$$

(3) Due to the circuit design, the voltage drop across R_{E1} must be the same as across R_{E2} plus R_{E3}; therefore,

$$E_{V2} + E_{V3} = 45 + 15 = 60 = I_1(25)$$

$$I_1 = \frac{60}{25} = 2.4 \text{ A}$$

(4) The current flow through R_{E4} must be the total for the circuit, or

$$I_4 = 0.75 + 2.4 = 3.15 \text{ A}$$

which is the current drawn from the voltage source E_v as well.

(5) The equivalent resistance for the circuit will be

$$\frac{1}{R_e} = \frac{1}{25} + \frac{1}{60 + 20}$$

$$R_e = 19.05 \text{ ohms}$$

3.3.4 Electric Motors

The basic component of an electric energy utilization system is the electric motor. This component converts electrical energy into mechanical energy to be used in operation of processing systems with moving parts.

The majority of the motors used in food processing operations are alternating current (AC), and functions depend on three basic electrical principles. These principles include the electromagnet, formed by winding insulated wire around a soft iron core. Current flow through the wire produces a magnetic field in the iron core; orientation of the field is dependent on the direction of current flow.

The second electrical principle involved in operation of a motor is electromagnetic induction. This phenomenon occurs when an electric current is induced in a circuit as it moves through a magnetic force field. The induced electric current produces a voltage within the circuit, with magnitude that is a function of the strength of the magnetic field, the speed at which the circuit moves through the field, and the number of conductor circuits in the magnetic field.

The third electrical principle is alternating current. As indicated earlier, this term refers to a current that changes direction of flow in a consistent manner. Normal electric service is 60 cps, indicating that the change in current flow direction occurs 60 times per second.

An electric motor contains a stator: a housing that has two iron cores wound with insulated copper wire. The two cores or windings are located opposite one another, as illustrated in Fig. 3.17, and the leads from the windings connected to a 60-cps alternating current source. With this arrangement, the stator becomes an electromagnet with reversing polarity as the current alternates.

A second component of an electric motor is the rotor: a rotating drum of iron with copper bars. The rotor is placed between the two poles or windings of the stator (Fig. 3.18). The current flow to the stator and the resulting electromagnetic field produces current flow within the copper bars of the rotor. The current flow within the rotor creates magnetic poles, which in turn react with the magnetic field of the stator to cause rotation of the rotor. Due to the 60-cps alternating current to the stator, the rotation

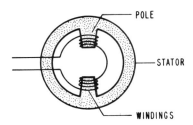

Fig. 3.17 Schematic diagram of a stator. [From Merkel (1983).]

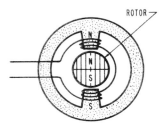

ROTOR

Fig. 3.18   Schematic diagram of a stator with the rotor. [From Merkel (1983).]

of the rotor should be 3600 revolutions per minute (rpm), but it typically operates at 3450 rpm.

Although there are numerous types of electric motors, they operate on these same basic principles. The most popular motor in the food processing plant is the single-phase, alternating current motor. There are different types of single-phase motors; the differences are primarily related to the starting of the motor.

The selection of the proper motor for a given application is of importance when ensuring that efficient conversion of electrical to mechanical energy occurs. The selection process takes into account the type of power supply available, as well as the use of the motor. The type and size of load must be considered, along with the environmental conditions of operation and the available space.

3.3.5   Electrical Controls

The efficient use of electrical energy and the equipment that is operated by this energy source is related to the opportunity for automatic control. Since the operation of processes and equipment in a food processing plant depends on responses to physical parameters, automatic control involves conversion of the physical parameter into an electrical response or signal. Fortunately, these conversions can be achieved rather easily using a variety of electrical transducers.

The control of electrical circuits is accomplished by using several different types of transducers. A magnetic relay utilizes a coil that produces electromagnetism to move a contact mechanically and complete the primary circuit. Thermostats and humidistats are controllers that use some physical change in temperature or humidity to provide the mechanical movement required to complete an electrical circuit. A timing device utilizes movement of the clock mechanism to mechanically bring two points into contact and complete an electrical circuit. Photoelectric controls use a photocell to produce a small current required to bring the points in the primary circuit into contact and allow for current flow. Time-delay relays, pressure switches, and limit switches are other types of controls used to accomplish the same type of electrical power utilization.

3.3.6 Electric Lighting

Another primary use of electric power in food processing plants is to provide illumination of work spaces. Often the efficiency of workers within the plant will be dependent on the availability of proper lighting. The design of a lighting system for a workspace will depend on several factors. The light must be properly distributed within the space, and the light source must be of sufficient size and efficiency. The light source must be properly supported and easily replaced or serviced. Finally, the cost of the entire system will be a factor to consider.

Light can be defined as visually evaluated radiant energy. Light is a small portion of the electromagnetic spectrum and varies in color depending on the wavelength. The intensity of a light at a point location is measured in the unit *lux*: the magnitude of illumination at a distance of one meter from a standard candle. A light source can be expressed in lumens: the amount of light on one square meter of surface when the intensity is one lux.

Two types of light sources are used in food processing plants: the incandescent lamp and the fluorescent lamp. The incandescent lamp uses a tungsten filament as a resistance to current flow. Due to the high electrical resistance of wire, the flow of current through the filament produces a glow and light. These types of lamps will provide efficiencies of approximately 20 lumens per watt.

A fluorescent lamp uses an inductance coil to create a current discharge within the tube. The heat from the discharge causes electrons to be removed from mercury vapor within the tube. The return of the electrons to the shell of mercury vapor causes emission of ultraviolet rays. These rays react with phosphor crystals at the tube surface to produce light. Fluorescent lamps are two to three times more efficient than comparable incandescent lamps. Although there are other factors to consider when comparing incandescent and fluorescent lamps, the efficiency and the longer life of fluorescent lamps are the most important.

One of the basic decisions related to lighting system design is determining the number of light sources required to maintain a desired level of illumination. An expression for illumination can be

$$\text{Illumination} = \frac{(\text{lumens/lamp}) \times \text{CU} \times \text{LLF}}{\text{area/lamp}} \tag{3.15}$$

where CU is the coefficient of utilization and LLF is the light loss factor.

The above equation indicates that the illumination maintained in a given space is a function of the magnitude of the light source and the number of lamps in the space. The coefficient of utilization CU accounts for various factors within the space, such as room size proportions, location of lamps, and workspace light. Light loss factors LLF account for room surface dust, lamp dust, and lamp lumen depreciation.

EXAMPLE 3.9

A work area within a food processing plant is to be maintained at a light intensity of 800 lux. The room is 10 by 25 m, and 500-watt incandescent lamps (10,600 lumens/lamp) are to be utilized. A CU of 0.6 and LLF of 0.8 have been established. Determine the number of lamps required.

GIVEN

> Desired light intensity = 800 lux
> Room size = 10 m by 25 m = 250 m^2
> Lamps are 500 W, or 10,600 lumens/lamp
> Coefficient of utilization CU = 0.6
> Light loss factor LLF = 0.8

APPROACH

Equation (3.15) can be used to determine area/lamp, and the result is combined with given room area to calculate the number of lamps required.

SOLUTION

(1) Equation (3.15) can be used to compute the area per lamp allowed for the desired illumination.

$$\text{Area/lamp} = \frac{10,600 \times 0.6 \times 0.8}{800} = 6.36 \text{ m}^2$$

(2) Based on the above,

$$\text{Number of lamps} = \frac{10 \times 25}{6.36} = 39.3 \quad \text{or} \quad 40$$

Problems

3.1 Compute the energy requirements to convert 50°C water to superheated steam at 170°C when the pressure is 210.82 kPa.

3.2 Determine the quality of steam at 169.06 kPa when 270 kJ/kg of energy are lost from saturated steam. What is the steam temperature?

3.3 Calculate the amount of energy (kJ/kg) required to convert saturated water at 150 kPa to superheated steam at 170°C and at the same pressure.

3.4 Determine the quality of steam at 143.27 kPa after a loss of 270 kJ/kg from the saturated steam conditions. What is the steam temperature?

3.5 A fruit juice is being heated in an indirect heat exchanger using steam as a heating medium. The product flows through the heat exchanger at a rate of 1500 kg/hr and the inlet temperature is 20°C. Determine the quantity of steam required to heat the product to 100°C when only latent heat of vaporization (2200 kJ/kg) is used for heating. The specific heat of the product is 4 kJ/kg ·°C.

*3.6 A pudding mix is being formulated to achieve a total solids content of 20% in the final product. The initial product has a temperature of 60°C and is preheated to 90°C by direct steam injection using saturated steam at 105°C. If there is no additional gain or loss of moisture from the product, what is the total solids content of the initial product?

*3.7 Steam with 80% quality is being used to heat a 40% total solids tomato puree as it flows through a steam injection heater at a rate of 400 kg/hr. The steam is generated at 169.06 kPa and is flowing to the heater at a rate of 50 kg/hr. Assume that the heat exchanger efficiency is 85%. If the specific heat of the product is 3.2 kJ/kg · K, determine the temperature of the product leaving the heater when the initial temperature is 50°C. Determine the total solids content of the product after heating. Assume the specific heat of the puree is not influenced by the heating process.

3.8 Natural gas combustion is being used for steam generation and 5% excess air is incorporated into the combustion. Estimate the composition of the flue gas and compute the percent thermal energy loss if the flue gas temperature is 20°C.

3.9 An electrical circuit includes a voltage source and two resistances (50 and 75 ohm) in parallel. Determine the voltage source required to provide 1.6 amp of current flow through the 75-ohm resistance and compute current flow through the 50-ohm resistance.

*3.10 The manufacturing of pie filling involves blending of concentrated product with liquid sugar and heating by steam injection. The product being manufactured will contain 25% product solids and 15% sugar solids and will be heated to 115°C. The process has input streams of concentrated product with 40% product solids at 40°C and 10 kg/s and liquid sugar with 60% sugar solids at 50°C. Heating is accomplished using steam at 198.53 kPa. The concentrated product entering the process and the final product have specific heats of 3.6 kJ/kg ·°C, whereas the liquid sugar has a

---

*Indicates an advanced level of difficulty in solving.

specific heat of 3.8 kJ/kg · °C. Determine (a) the rate of product manufacturing; (b) the flow rate of liquid sugar into the process; (c) the steam requirements for the process; and (d) the quality of steam required for the process.

List of Symbols

c_p	specific heat (kJ/kg · K)	μ	viscosity (Pa · s)
CU	coefficient of utilization	N_{Re}	Reynolds Number,
D	diameter (m)		dimensionless
ΔP	pressure drop (Pa)	P	pressure (Pa)
ε	surface roughness factor (m)	q	heat transfer rate (kJ/s)
E_v	voltage (volts)	ρ	density
f	friction factor	R_E	electrical resistance (ohms)
H	enthalpy (kJ/kg)	R_e	equivalent electrical
H_{evap}	latent heat of evaporation		resistance (ohms)
	(kJ/kg)	s	entropy (kJ/kg · K)
I	current (amperes)	T	temperature (°C or K)
L	length (m)	u	average fluid velocity (m/s)
L_e	equivalent length (m)	V'	specific volume (m³/kg)
LLF	light loss factor	x_s	steam quality
$\dot{m}$	mass flow rate		

Subscripts: c, liquid/condensate; v, vapor; i, initial; o, outer; s, steam.

Bibliography

Babcock & Wilcox Handbook (1978). "Steam—Its Generation and Use." Babcock & Wilcox Co., New York.

Farrall, A. W. (1979). "Food Engineering Systems." Vol. 2. AVI Publ. Co., Westport, Connecticut.

Gustafson, R. J. (1980). "Fundamentals of Electricity for Agriculture." AVI Publ. Co., Westport, Connecticut.

Martin, T. W. (1961). Improved computer oriented methods for calculation of steam properties. *J. Heat Transfer* **83**, 515–516.

Merkel, J. A. (1983). "Basic Engineering Principles," 2nd ed. AVI Publ. Co., Westport, Connecticut.

Singh, R. P., Carroad, P. A., Chinnan, M. S., Rose W. W., and Jacob, N. L. (1980). Energy accounting in canning tomato products. *J. Food Sci.* **45**, 735–739.

Steltz, W. G., and Silvestri, G. J. (1958). The formulation of steam properties for digital computer application. *Trans. ASME* **80**, 967–973.

Teixeira, A. A. (1980). Cogeneration of electricity in food processing plants. *Agric. Eng.* **61**(1), 26–29.

Watson, E. L., and Harper, J. C. (1988). "Elements of Food Engineering," 2nd ed. Van Nostrand Reinhold, New York.

CHAPTER 4

Heat Transfer in Food Processing

Heating and cooling of foods are the most common processes found in a food processing plant. In the modern industrialized food industry, it is common to find unit operations such as refrigeration, freezing, thermal sterilization, drying, and evaporation. These unit operations involve transfer of heat between a product and some heating or cooling medium. Heating and cooling of food products is necessary for processes that result in preventing microbial and enzymatic degradation. In addition, desired sensorial properties are imparted to foods when they are heated or cooled.

The study of heat transfer is important as it provides a basis on how various food processes operate. In this chapter, we will study various fundamentals of heat transfer and learn how they are related to design and operation of food processing equipment.

In the beginning section of this chapter, we will study heat-exchange equipment. We will observe that there is a wide variety of heat-exchange equipment available for food applications. This description will identify the need to study properties of foods that affect the design and operation of heat exchangers. We will examine various approaches to obtain thermal properties of foods. Following the discussion on thermal properties of foods, we will consider basic modes of heat transfer such as conduction, convection, and radiation. Simple mathematical equations will be developed that will allow prediction of heat transfer in solids as well as liquid foods. These mathematical equations will provide us with sufficient tools to design and evaluate the performance of simple heat exchangers. Next, we will consider more complicated situations arising from heat transfer under unsteady-state conditions, when temperature changes with time. A good understanding of the various concepts presented in this chapter is important, since these concepts will be the basis for topics in the following chapters.

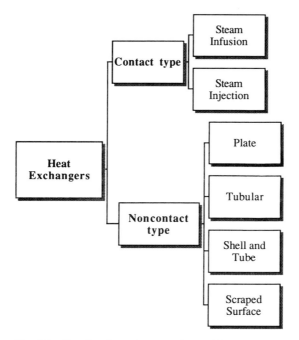

Fig. 4.1   Classification of commonly used heat exchangers.

4.1   Systems for Heating and Cooling Food Products

In a food processing plant, heating and cooling of foods is conducted in equipment called heat exchangers. As shown in Fig. 4.1, heat exchangers can be broadly classified into noncontact type and contact type. As the name implies, in noncontact-type heat exchangers the product and heating or cooling medium are kept physically separated, usually by a thin metal wall. On the other hand in contact-type heat exchangers, there is direct physical contact between the product and the heating or cooling streams.

For example, in a steam-injection system, steam is directly injected into the product to be heated. In a plate heat exchanger, a thin metal plate separates the product stream from the heating or cooling stream while allowing heat transfer to take place without mixing. In the following subsections, some of the commonly used heat exchangers in the food industry will be discussed.

4.1.1   Plate Heat Exchanger

The plate heat exchanger invented more than 60 years ago has found wide application in the dairy and food beverage industry. A schematic of a plate

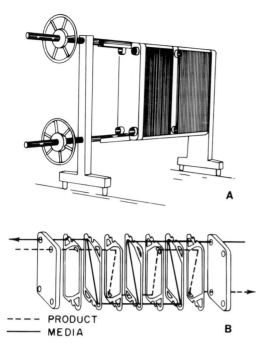

PRODUCT
MEDIA
A

B

Fig. 4.2 (A) Plate heat exchanger; (B) schematic view of fluid flow between plates. (Courtesy of Cherry-Burrell Corporation.)

heat exchanger is shown in Fig. 4.2. This heat exchanger consists of a series of parallel, closely spaced stainless-steel plates pressed in a frame. Gaskets, made of natural or synthetic rubber, seal the plate edges and ports to prevent intermixing of liquids. These gaskets help to direct the heating or cooling and the product streams into the respective alternate gaps. The direction of the product stream versus the heating/cooling stream can be either parallel flow (same direction) or counterflow (opposite direction) to each other. The influence of the direction of flow on the performance of the heat exchanger will be discussed later in Section 4.4.7.

The plates used in the plate heat exchanger are constructed from stainless steel. Special patterns are pressed on the plates to cause increased turbulence in the product stream, thus achieving better heat transfer. An example of such a pattern is a shallow herringbone-ribbed design, as shown in Fig. 4.3.

Plate heat exchangers are suitable for low-viscosity liquid foods (viscosity less than 5 Pa · s). If suspended solids are present, the equivalent diameter of the particulates should be less than 0.3 cm. Larger particulates can bridge across the plate contact points and may "burn on" in the heating section.

In industrial-size plate heat exchangers, product flow rates from 5000 to 20,000 kg/hr are often obtained. When using plate heat exchangers,

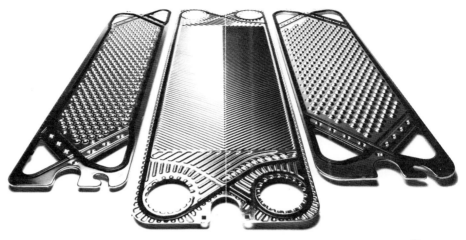

Fig. 4.3 Illustration of patterns pressed on plates used on a plate heat exchanger. (Courtesy of Cherry-Burrell Corporation.)

care should be taken to minimize the deposition of solid food material, such as milk proteins, on the surface of the plates. This deposition, also called "fouling," will decrease the heat transfer rate from the heating medium to the product; in addition, the pressure drop will increase over a period of time. Eventually, the process is stopped and the plates are cleaned. For dairy products, with ultra-high-temperature applications, the process time is often limited to 3 to 4 hr. Plate heat exchangers offer the following advantages:

- The maintenance of these heat exchangers is simple, and they can be easily and quickly dismantled for product surface inspection.
- The plate heat exchangers have a sanitary design for food applications.
- Their capacity can be easily increased by adding more plates to the frame.
- With plate heat exchangers, one can heat or cool product to within 1°C of the adjacent media temperature, with less capital investment than other noncontact-type heat exchangers.
- Plate heat exchangers offer opportunities for energy conservation by regeneration.

As shown in a simple schematic, Fig. 4.4, a liquid food is heated to the pasteurization or other desired temperature in the heating section; the heated fluid then surrenders part of its heat to the incoming raw fluid in the regeneration section. The cold stream is heated to a temperature where it requires little additional energy to bring it up to the desired temperature. For regeneration, additional plates are required; however, the additional capital cost may be quickly recovered by lowered operating costs.

An actual two-way regeneration process is shown in Fig. 4.5 for pasteurizing grape juice. After the "starter" juice has been heated to 88°C, it is

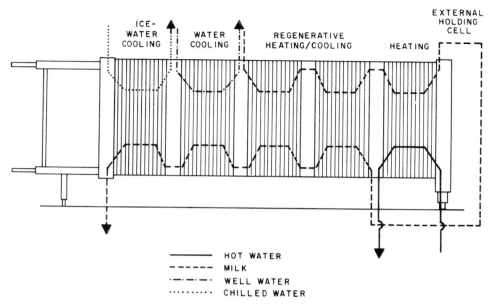

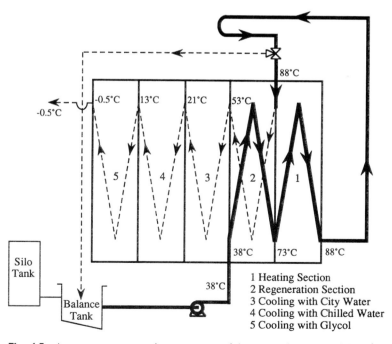

Fig. 4.4 A five-stage plate pasteurizer for processing milk. (Reprinted with permission of Alfa-Laval AB, Tumba, Sweden, and Alfa-Laval, Inc., Fort Lee, New Jersey.)

Fig. 4.5 A two-way regeneration system used in processing grape juice. (Courtesy of APV Equipment, Inc.)

passed through a holding loop and into the regenerative section. In this section, the juice releases its heat to incoming raw juice entering into the exchanger at 38°C. The temperature of raw juice increases to 73°C, while the "starter" juice temperature decreases to 53°C. In this example, the regeneration is [(88 − 38)/(73 − 38)] × 100 or 70%, since the incoming raw juice was heated to 70% of its eventual pasteurization temperature without the use of steam as heating medium. The juice heated to 73°C passes through the heating section, where its temperature is raised to 88°C by using 93°C hot water as heating medium. The heated juice is then pumped to the regeneration section, where it preheats the incoming raw juice, and the cycle continues. The cooling of hot pasteurized juice is accomplished by using city water, chilled water, or recirculated glycol. It should be noted that in the above example, less heat has to be removed from the pasteurized juice, thus decreasing the cooling load by the regeneration process.

4.1.2 Tubular Heat Exchanger

The simplest noncontact-type heat exchanger is a double-pipe heat exchanger. This heat exchanger consists of a pipe located concentrically inside another pipe. The two fluid streams flow in the annular space and the inner pipe, respectively.

The streams may flow in the same direction (parallel flow) or in the opposite direction (counterflow). Figure 4.6 is a schematic of a counterflow double-pipe heat exchanger.

A slight variation of a double-pipe heat exchanger is a triple-tube heat exchanger, shown in Fig. 4.7. In this type of heat exchanger, product flows in the inner annular space, whereas the heating/cooling medium flows in the inner tube and outer annular space. The innermost tube may contain specially designed obstructions to create turbulence and better heat transfer. Some specific industrial applications of triple-tube heat exchangers include heating single-strength orange juice from 4 to 93°C and then

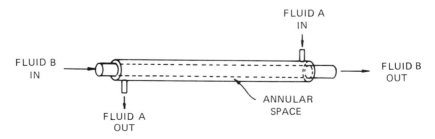

Fig. 4.6 Schematic illustration of a tubular heat exchanger.

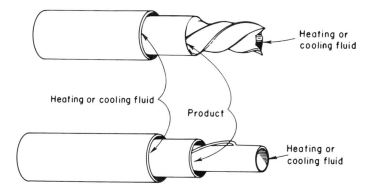

Fig. 4.7 Schematic illustration of a triple-tube heat exchanger. (Courtesy of Paul Mueller Co.)

cooling to 4°C; cooling cottage cheese wash water from 46 to 18°C with chilled water; and cooling ice cream mix from 12 to 0.5°C with ammonia.

Another common type of heat exchanger used in the food industry is a shell-and-tube heat exchanger for such applications as heating liquid foods in evaporation systems. As shown in Fig. 4.8, one of the fluid streams flows inside the tube while the other fluid stream is pumped over the tubes through the shell. Maintaining the fluid stream in the shell side to flow over the tubes, rather than parallel to the tubes, allows higher rates of heat transfer. Baffles located in the shell side allow the cross-flow pattern. One or more tube passes can be accomplished, depending on the design. The shell-and-tube heat exchanger shown in Fig. 4.8 is a two-tube pass arrangement, since the stream inside the tube moves first in one direction in the upper section and then in the opposite direction in the lower section.

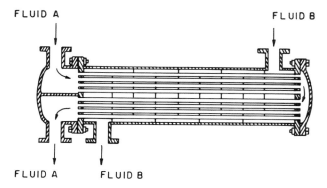

Fig. 4.8 A shell-and-tube heat exchanger with one shell pass and two tube passes.

4.1.3 Scraped-Surface Heat Exchanger

In conventional types of tubular heat exchangers, heat transfer to a fluid stream is affected by hydraulic drag and heat resistance due to film buildup or "fouling" on the tube wall. This heat resistance can be minimized if the inside surface is continuously scraped by some mechanical means. The scraping action allows rapid heat transfer to a relatively small product volume. A scraped-surface heat exchanger, used in food processing, is shown schematically in Fig. 4.9.

The food contact areas of a scraped-surface cylinder are fabricated from stainless steel (type 316), pure nickel, hard chromium-plated nickel, or other corrosion-resistant material. The inside rotor contains blades that are covered with plastic laminate or molded plastic (Fig. 4.9). The rotor speed varies between 150 and 500 rpm. Although higher rotation speed allows better heat transfer, it may affect the quality of the processed product by possible maceration. Thus, the rotor speed and the annular space between the rotor and the cylinder are carefully selected for the product being processed.

As seen in Fig. 4.9, the cylinder containing the product and the rotor is enclosed in an outside jacket. The heating/cooling medium is supplied to

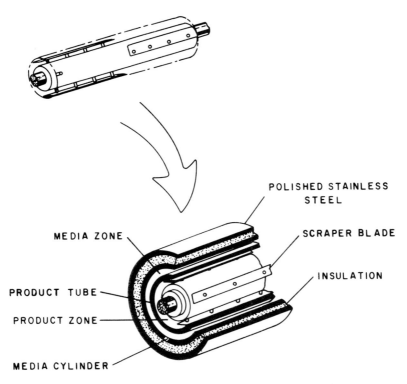

Fig. 4.9 A scraped-surface heat exchanger with a cutaway section illustrating various components. (Courtesy of Cherry-Burrell Corporation.)

this outside jacket. Commonly used media include steam, hot water, brine, or a refrigerant such as Freon. Typical temperatures used for processing products in scraped-surface heat exchangers range from −35 to 190°C.

The constant blending action accomplished in the scraped-surface heat exchanger is often desirable to enhance the uniformity of product flavor, color, aroma, and textural characteristics. In the food process industry, the applications of scraped-surface heat exchangers include heating, pasteurizing, sterilizing, whipping, gelling, emulsifying, plasticizing, and crystallizing. Liquids with a wide range of viscosities that can be pumped are processed in these heat exchangers; examples include fruit juices, soups, citrus concentrate, peanut butter, baked beans, tomato paste, and pie fillings.

4.1.4 Steam-Infusion Heat Exchanger

A steam-infusion heat exchanger provides a direct contact between steam and the product. As shown in Fig. 4.10, product in liquid state is pumped to the top of the heat exchanger and then allowed to flow in thin sheets in the heating chamber. The viscosity of the liquid determines the size of the spreaders. Products containing particulates, such as diced vegetables, meat chunks, rice, can be handled by specially designed spreaders. High rates of heat transfer are achieved when steam contacts tiny droplets of the food. The temperature of the product rises very rapidly due to steam condensation. The heated products with condensed steam are released from the chamber at the bottom. A specific amount of liquid is retained in the bottom of the chamber to achieve desired cooking.

The temperature difference of the product between the inlet and the outlet to the heating chamber may be as low as 5.5°C, such as for deodorizing milk (76.7–82.2°C), or as high as 96.7°C, such as for sterilizing puddings for aseptic packaging (48.9–145.6°C).

The water added to the product due to steam condensation is sometimes desirable, particularly if the overall process requires addition of water. Otherwise, the added water of condensation can be "flashed off" by pumping the heated liquid into a vacuum cooling system. The amount of water added due to condensation can be computed by measuring the temperature of the product fed to the heat exchanger and the temperature of the product discharged from the vacuum cooler.

This type of heat exchanger has applications in cooking and/or sterilizing a wide variety of products, such as concentrated soups, chocolate, processed cheese, ice cream mixes, puddings, fruit pie fillings, and milk.

4.1.5 Epilogue

In the preceding subsections, several types of commonly used heat exchangers have been discussed. It should be evident that a basic understand-

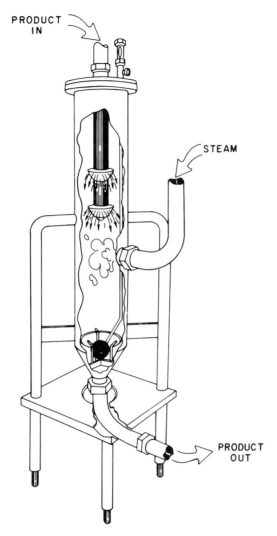

PRODUCT
IN

STEAM

PRODUCT
OUT

Fig. 4.10 A steam-infusion heat exchanger. (Courtesy of CREPACO, Inc.)

ing of the mechanisms of heat transfer, both in the equipment material and
in foods, is necessary before the heat exchange equipment can be designed
or evaluated. A wide variety of food products is processed using heat
exchangers. These products offer unique and often complex problems
related to heat transfer. In the following sections a quantitative description
will be developed emphasizing the following:

(1) *Thermal properties*. Properties such as specific heat, thermal conductivity and thermal diffusivity of food and equipment materials (such as
metals) play an important role in determining the rate of heat transfer.

(2) *Mode of heat transfer.* A mathematical description of the actual mode of heat transfer, such as conduction, convection, and/or radiation is necessary to determine quantities, such as total amount of heat transferred from heating or cooling medium to the product.

(3) *Steady-state and unsteady-state heat transfer.* Calculation procedures are needed to examine both the unsteady-state and steady-state phases of heat transfer.

The analytical treatment will be developed for cases involving simple heat transfer. For more complex treatment of heat transfer, such as for non-Newtonian liquids, the textbook by Heldman and Singh (1981) is recommended.

4.2   Thermal Properties of Foods

4.2.1   Specific Heat

Specific heat is the quantity of heat that is gained or lost by a unit weight of product to accomplish a desired change in temperature, without a change in state.

$$c_P = \frac{Q}{M(\Delta T)} \qquad (4.1)$$

where Q is heat gained or lost (kJ), M is mass (kg), ΔT is temperature change in the material (°C), and c_P is specific heat (kJ/kg · °C).

Specific heat of a product is influenced by the product components, moisture content, temperature, and pressure. The specific heat increases as the product moisture content increases. The specific heat of a gas at constant pressure c_P is greater than its specific heat at constant volume, c_v. In most food processing applications, specific heat at constant pressure c_P is used since pressure is generally kept constant.

For processes where a change of state takes place, such as freezing, an apparent specific heat is used. Apparent specific heat incorporates the heat involved in the change of state in addition to the sensible heat.

Values of specific heat for a variety of foods and nonfood materials obtained by experimental procedures by various researchers are given in Tables A.2.1, A.3.1, and A.3.2. Specific heat can also be predicted using either of the following two empirical equations.

For meat products with moisture in the range of 26 to 100% moisture content and fruit juices with moisture content greater than 50%, Dickerson (1969) proposed the following expression:

$$c_P = 1.675 + 0.025w \qquad (4.2)$$

where w is water content (%).

TABLE 4.1
Composition Values of Selected Foods

Food	Water (%)	Protein (%)	Fat (%)	Carbohydrate (%)	Ash (%)
Apples, fresh	84.4	0.2	0.6	14.5	0.3
Applesauce	88.5	0.2	0.2	10.8	0.6
Asparagus	91.7	2.5	0.2	5.0	0.6
Beans, lima	67.5	8.4	0.5	22.1	1.5
Beef, hamburger, raw	68.3	20.7	10.0	0.0	1.0
Bread, white	35.8	8.7	3.2	50.4	1.9
Butter	15.5	0.6	81.0	0.4	2.5
Cod	81.2	17.6	0.3	0.0	1.2
Corn, sweet, raw	72.7	3.5	1.0	22.1	0.7
Cream, Half-and-Half	79.7	3.2	11.7	4.6	0.6
Eggs	73.7	12.9	11.5	0.9	1.0
Garlic	61.3	6.2	0.2	30.8	1.5
Lettuce, Iceburg	95.5	0.9	0.1	2.9	0.6
Milk, whole	87.4	3.5	3.5	4.9	0.7
Orange juice	88.3	0.7	0.2	10.4	0.4
Peaches	89.1	0.6	0.1	9.7	0.5
Peanuts, raw	5.6	26.0	47.5	18.6	2.3
Peas, raw	78.0	6.3	0.4	14.4	0.9
Pineapple, raw	85.3	0.4	0.2	13.7	0.4
Potatoes, raw	79.8	2.1	0.1	17.1	0.9
Rice, white	12.0	6.7	0.4	80.4	0.5
Spinach	90.7	3.2	0.3	4.3	1.5
Tomatoes	93.5	1.1	0.2	4.7	0.5
Turkey	64.2	20.1	14.7	0.0	1.0
Turnips	91.5	1.0	0.2	6.6	0.7
Yoghurt, (whole milk)	88.0	3.0	3.4	4.9	0.7

For products whose composition is known, the following equation may be used:

$$c_p = 1.424m_c + 1.549m_p + 1.675m_f + 0.837m_a + 4.187m_m \quad (4.3)$$

where m is mass fraction; the subscripts are c, carbohydrate; p, protein; f, fat; a, ash; and m, moisture. The units for specific heat are kJ/kg $\cdot$ °C. These units are equivalent to kJ/kg $\cdot$ K, since 1° temperature change is the same in Celsius or kelvin scale.

The food composition values may be obtained from *Agriculture Handbook No. 8* (Watt and Merrill, 1975). Some composition values of selected foods are given in Table 4.1.

EXAMPLE 4.1

Predict the specific heat for a model food with following composition: carbohydrate 40%, protein 20%, fat 10%, ash 5%, moisture 25%.

GIVEN

$$m_c = 0.40 \qquad m_p = 0.2 \qquad m_f = 0.1 \qquad m_a = 0.05 \qquad m_m = 0.25.$$

APPROACH

Since product composition is given, Eq. (4.3) will be used to calculate specific heat.

SOLUTION

(1) Using Eq. (4.3),

$$c_p = (1.424)(0.4) + (1.549)(0.2) + (1.675)(0.1)$$
$$+ (0.837)(0.05) + (4.187)(0.25)$$
$$= 2.14 \text{ kJ/kg} \cdot °C$$

(2) The specific heat for the model food is estimated to be 2.14 kJ/kg · °C.

4.2.2 Thermal Conductivity

Thermal conductivity of a product gives in quantitative terms the rate of heat that will be conducted through a unit thickness of the material if a unit temperature gradient exists across that thickness.

In SI units, thermal conductivity is

$$k = \frac{J}{s \cdot m \cdot °C} = \frac{W}{m \cdot °C} \tag{4.4}$$

The variability in magnitude of thermal conductivity of different commonly encountered materials can be appreciated by observing the following values of thermal conductivity:

Metals: 50–400 W/m · °C
Alloys: 10–120 W/m · °C
Water: 0.597 W/m · °C (at 20°C)
Air: 0.0251 W/m · °C (at 20°C)
Insulating materials: 0.035–0.173 W/m · °C

Thermal conductivity of most high-moisture foods have values closer to the thermal conductivity of water. Values of thermal conductivity of a number of foods and nonfood materials, obtained experimentally, are given in Tables A.2.2, A.3.1, and A.3.2. In addition to the tabulated values, the following regression equations developed by Sweat (1974, 1975) may be used.

For fruits and vegetables with water content greater than 60%,

$$k = 0.148 + 0.00493w \tag{4.5}$$

where k is thermal conductivity (W/m · °C) and w is water content, (%).

For meats, temperature 0–60°C, water content 60–80%, wet basis,

$$k = 0.08 + 0.0052w \qquad (4.6)$$

Another empirical equation that was developed by Sweat (1986) by fitting a set of 430 data points for solid and liquid foods is as follows,

$$k = 0.25m_c + 0.155m_p + 0.16m_f + 0.135m_a + 0.58m_m \qquad (4.7)$$

For this additive model, the food composition values may be obtained from *Agriculture Handbook No. 8* (Watt and Merrill, 1975). Composition values of selected foods are given in Table 4.1.

The above equations predict thermal conductivity of foods within 15% of experimental values. Thermal conductivity is commonly expressed as W/m · °C. These units are equivalent to W/m · K or J/s · m · K.

EXAMPLE 4.2

Predict thermal conductivity of beef roll that contains 60.1% moisture.

GIVEN

Product: beef
Moisture content: 60.1%

APPROACH

We will use Eq. (4.6), which is recommended for meats.

SOLUTION

(1) $k = 0.080 + (0.0052)(60.1)$
    $= 0.393 \text{ W/m} \cdot °C$
(2) The thermal conductivity of beef roll is predicted to be 0.393 W/m · °C.

4.3 Modes of Heat Transfer

4.3.1 Conductive Heat Transfer

Conduction is the mode of heat transfer in which the transfer of energy takes place at a molecular scale. As molecules attain thermal energy, they vibrate at their respective locations. The amplitude of vibration increases with higher thermal energy level. These vibrations are transmitted from one molecule to another without actual translatory motion of the molecules.

Another theory on mechanism of conduction states that conduction occurs at molecular level due to the drift of electrons. These free electrons are prevalent in metals, and they carry both thermal and electrical energy.

It is for this reason that good conductors of electricity are also good conductors of thermal energy (e.g., silver, copper).

It is important to note that in conductive heat transfer, there is no physical movement of the material. Conduction is the common mode of heat transfer in heating/cooling of opaque solid media.

If a temperature gradient exists in a body, heat transfer will take place from the high-temperature region to the low-temperature region. The heat flux is proportional to the temperature gradient. Thus,

$$\frac{q_x}{A} \propto \frac{dT}{dx} \tag{4.8}$$

or by inserting the constant of proportionality,

$$q_x = -kA\frac{dT}{dx} \tag{4.9}$$

where q_x is rate of heat flow in x direction by conduction (W); k is thermal conductivity (W/m · °C); A is area (normal to x direction) through which heat flows (m^2); T is temperature (°C); and x is length, a variable (m).

The above rate equation describes conductive heat transfer through a system. This equation is also Fourier's law for heat conduction, after Joseph Fourier, a French mathematical physicist.

The negative sign in Eq. (4.9) indicates that heat will flow from higher temperature to lower temperature, thus satisfying the second law of thermodynamics. As shown in Fig. 4.11, the gradient dT/dx is negative since temperature decreases with increasing values of x. Heat transfer always occurs from a higher temperature to a lower temperature. In Eq. (4.9), a negative sign is used to obtain a positive value for heat flow.

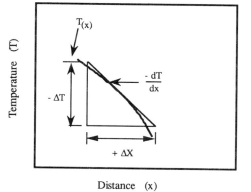

Fig. 4.11   Sign convention for conductive heat flow.

EXAMPLE 4.3

One face of a stainless-steel plate 1 cm thick is maintained at 110°C, while the other face is at 90°C (Fig. 4.12). Assuming steady-state conditions, calculate the rate of heat flux through the plate. The thermal conductivity of stainless steel is 17 W/m · °C.

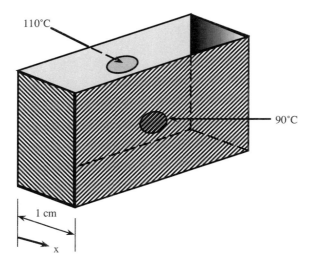

Fig. 4.12 Heat flow in a plate.

GIVEN

Thickness of plate = 1 cm = 0.01 m
Temperature of one face = 110°C
Temperature of other face = 90°C
Thermal conductivity of stainless steel = 17 W/m · °C

APPROACH

For steady-state heat transfer in rectangular coordinates we will use Eq. (4.9) to compute heat flux.

SOLUTION

(1) From Eq. (4.9)

$$\frac{q}{A} = -\frac{(17 \text{ W/m} \cdot °C)(110°C - 90°C)}{(0 \text{ m} - 0.01 \text{ m})}$$

$$= 34{,}000 \text{ W/m}^2$$

(2) Heat flux is calculated to be 34,000 W/m². A positive sign is obtained for the heat flux, as heat flows "downhill" from 110 to 90°C.

4.3.2 Convective Heat Transfer

When a fluid flows over a solid body such as inside a pipe, heat exchange will occur between the solid and the fluid, whenever there is a temperature difference between the two. The heat exchange occurs due to convective heat transfer. Heating/cooling of gases and liquids are common examples of fluid streams that exchange heat with solid surfaces by convection. Depending on whether the flow of the fluid is artificially induced or natural, there are two types of convective heat transfer: forced convection and free (also called natural) convection. Forced convection involves use of some mechanical means, such as a pump or a fan, to induce the movement of the fluid. In contrast, free convection occurs due to density differences caused by temperature gradients within the system. Both these mechanisms may cause either laminar or turbulent flow of the fluid.

Heat transfer from a heated flat plate exposed to a fluid is examined in Fig. 4.13. The surface temperature of the plate is T_p , and the temperature of the fluid is T_∞. The velocity of the fluid reduces to zero at the surface of the plate due to the viscous action. Thus, the heat transfer in the boundary layer, where velocity is zero, must occur due to conduction. Away from the wall, heat transfer to the fluid is due to convection. In practice, it is difficult to determine the thickness of the boundary layer. The rate of heat transfer is expressed by Newton's law of cooling, which accounts for the overall effect of convection.

$$q = hA(T_p - T_\infty) \tag{4.10}$$

In this equation, the rate of heat transfer q is expressed as a function of the overall temperature gradient $(T_p - T_\infty)$. The area is A (m^2) and h is the convective heat-transfer coefficient (sometimes called surface heat-transfer coefficient), expressed as W/m$^2 \cdot °$C.

Equation (4.10) can also be viewed as the definition of the convective heat-transfer coefficient. Some approximate values of h are given in Table 4.2. A high value of h reflects a high rate of heat transfer. Forced

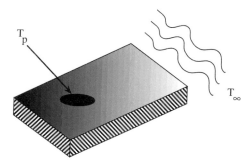

Fig. 4.13 Convective heat loss from a flat plate.

TABLE 4.2
Some Approximate Values of Convective Heat-Transfer Coefficient

Fluid	Convective heat-transfer coefficient (W/m$^2 \cdot$ K)
Air	
Free convection	5–25
Forced convection	10–200
Water	
Free convection	20–100
Forced convection	50–10,000
Boiling water	3,000–100,000
Condensing water vapor	5,000–100,000

convection offers a higher value of h than free convection. For example, blowing air on the surface of a mug containing coffee allows the coffee to cool faster.

EXAMPLE 4.4

The rate of heat flux from a metal plate is 1000 W/m^2. The surface temperature of the plate is 120°C, and ambient temperature is 20°C. (See Fig. 4.14.) Estimate the convective heat-transfer coefficient.

GIVEN

Plate surface temperature = 120°C
Ambient temperature = 20°C
Rate of heat flux q/A = 1000 W/m^2

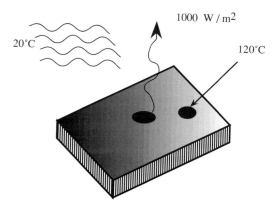

Fig. 4.14 Convective heat loss from a plate.

APPROACH

Since rate of heat flux is known, we will estimate the convective heat transfer coefficient directly from Newton's law of cooling, Eq. (4.10).

SOLUTION

(1) From Eq. (4.10)

$$h = \frac{1000 \text{ W/m}^2}{120°C - 20°C}$$

$$= 10 \text{ W/m}^2 \cdot °C$$

(2) The convective heat-transfer coefficient is found to be 10 W/m² ·°C.

4.3.3 Radiative Heat Transfer

Radiative heat transfer occurs between two surfaces by the emission and later absorption of electromagnetic radiation. In contrast to conduction and convection, radiation requires no physical medium for its propagation; it can even occur in perfect vacuum.

Energy radiated (or emitted) from a surface is proportional to the absolute temperature raised to the fourth power and surface characteristics. More specifically, the heat flux from a surface is expressed by the following equation:

$$\frac{q}{A} = \sigma \varepsilon T_A^4 \qquad (4.11)$$

where σ is the Stefan–Boltzmann[1] constant, equal to 5.669×10^{-8} W/m² · K⁴. The emissivity ε describes the extent to which a surface is similar to a blackbody. For blackbody, the value of emissivity is 1. Values of emissivity for several surfaces are given in Table 4.3. Note that increasing temperature results in decreasing wavelength.

1. Josef Stefan (1835–1893). An Austrian physicist, he began his academic career at the University of Vienna as a lecturer. In 1866, he was appointed director of the Physical Institute. Using empirical approaches, he derived the law describing radiant energy from blackbodies. Five years later, another Austrian, Ludwig Boltzmann, provided the thermodynamical basis of what is now known as the Stefan–Boltzmann law.

TABLE 4.3
Emissivity of Various Surfaces

Material	Wavelength and average temperatures				
	9.3 μm 38°C	5.4 μm 260°C	3.6 μm 540°C	1.8 μm 1370°C	0.6 μm Solar
Metals					
Aluminum					
Polished	0.04	0.05	0.08	0.19	~ 0.3
Oxidized	0.11	0.12	0.18		
24-ST weathered	0.4	0.32	0.27		
Surface roofing	0.22				
Anodized (at 1000°F)	0.94	0.42	0.60	0.34	
Brass					
Polished	0.10	0.10			
Oxidized	0.61				
Chromium, polished	0.08	0.17	0.26	0.40	0.49
Copper					
Polished	0.04	0.05	0.18	0.17	
Oxidized	0.87	0.83	0.77		
Iron					
Polished	0.06	0.08	0.13	0.25	0.45
Cast, oxidized	0.63	0.66	0.76		
Galvanized, new	0.23	–	–	0.42	0.66
Galvanized, dirty	0.28	–	–	0.90	0.89
Steel plate, rough	0.94	0.97	0.98		
Oxide	0.96	–	0.85	–	0.74
Magnesium	0.07	0.13	0.18	0.24	0.30
Silver, polished	0.01	0.02	0.03	–	0.11
Stainless steel					
18-8, polished	0.15	0.18	0.22		
18-8, weathered	0.85	0.85	0.85		
Steel tube					
Oxidized	–	0.80			
Tungsten filament	0.03	–	–	~ 0.18	0.36[a]
Zinc					
Polished	0.02	0.03	0.04	0.06	0.46
Galvanized sheet	~ 0.25				
Building and insulating materials					
Asphalt	0.93	–	0.9	–	0.93
Brick					
Red	0.93	–	–	–	0.7
Fire clay	0.9	–	~ 0.7	~ 0.75	
Silica	0.9	–	~ 0.75	0.84	
Magnesite refractory	0.9	–	–	~ 0.4	
Enamel, white	0.9				
Paper, white	0.95	–	0.82	0.25	0.28
Plaster	0.91				
Roofing board	0.93				
Enameled steel, white	–	–	–	0.65	0.47
Paints					
Aluminized lacquer	0.65	0.65			
Lacquer, black	0.96	0.98			
Lampblack paint	0.96	0.97	–	0.97	0.97

Table 4.3 (*Continued*)

	Wavelength and average temperatures				
Material	9.3 μm 38°C	5.4 μm 260°C	3.6 μm 540°C	1.8 μm 1370°C	0.6 μm Solar
Red paint	0.96	–	–	–	0.74
Yellow paint	0.95	–	0.5	–	0.30
Oil paints (all colors)	~ 0.94	~ 0.9			
White (ZnO)	0.95	–	0.91	–	0.18
Miscellaneous					
Ice	~ 0.97[b]				
Water	~ 0.96				
Carbon, T-carbon, 0.9% ash	0.82	0.80	0.79		
Wood	~ 0.93				
Glass	0.90	–	–	–	(Low)

Source: Adapted from Kreith (1973). Copyright © 1973 by Harper and Row Publishers, Inc. Reprinted by permission of the publisher.
[a]At 3315°C.
[b]At 0°C.

EXAMPLE 4.5

Calculate the rate of heat energy emitted by 100 m² of a polished iron surface (emissivity = 0.06). The temperature of the surface is 37°C.

GIVEN

Emissivity ε = 0.06
Area A = 100 m²
Temperature = 37°C = 310 K

APPROACH

We will use the Stefan–Boltzmann law, Eq. (4.11), to calculate the rate of heat transfer due to radiation.

SOLUTION

(1) From Eq. (4.11)

$$q = (5.669 \times 10^{-8} \text{ W/m}^2 \cdot \text{K}^4)(0.06)(100 \text{ m}^2)(310 \text{ K})^4$$
$$= 3141 \text{ W}$$

(2) The total energy emitted by the polished iron surface is 3141 watts.

4.4 Applications of Steady-State Heat Transfer

In this section, several applications of steady-state heat transfer will be considered. In steady-state heat transfer the temperature in a system remains constant with time; however, it may vary with location.

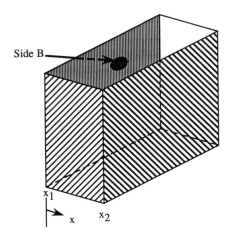

Side B

x_1

x x_2

Fig. 4.15 Heat conduction in a slab.

4.4.1 Conductive Heat Transfer in a Rectangular Slab

Consider a slab of constant cross-sectional area as shown in Figure 4.15. The temperature on side B is known. We will develop an equation that will be useful to determine temperature at any location inside the slab under steady-state conditions.

This problem is solved by first writing Fourier's law,

$$q_x = -kA\frac{dT}{dx} \tag{4.12}$$

The boundary conditions are

$$x = x_1 \qquad T = T_1$$

$$x = x_2 \qquad T = T_2 \tag{4.13}$$

Separating variables in Eq. (4.12), we get

$$\frac{q_x}{A}\,dx = -k\,dT \tag{4.14}$$

Integrating and substituting limits, we have

$$\int_{x_1}^{x}\frac{q_x}{A}\,dx = -\int_{T_1}^{T}k\,dT \tag{4.15}$$

where T is temperature at location x, and both are variable.

Since q_x and A are independent of x, and k is assumed to be independent of T, Eq. (4.15) can be rearranged to give

$$\frac{q_x}{A}\int_{x_1}^{x}dx = -k\int_{T_1}^{T}dT \tag{4.16}$$

Finally, integrating the above equation, we get

$$\frac{q_x}{A}(x - x_1) = -k(T - T_1) \tag{4.17}$$

or

$$T = T_1 - \frac{q_x}{kA}(x - x_1) \tag{4.18}$$

Equation (4.18) can be used to calculate temperature at any location in a flat slab.

EXAMPLE 4.6

For the metal plate in Example 4.3, calculate temperature at 0.5 cm from the 110°C-temperature face (see Fig. 4.16).

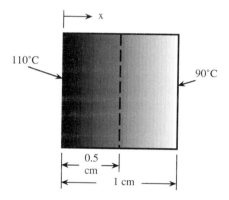

Fig. 4.16 Conductive heat transfer in a plate.

GIVEN

See Example 4.3.
Location at which temperature desired = 0.5 cm = 0.005 m
Heat flux q/A = 34,000 W/m²

APPROACH

We will use Eq. (4.18) to calculate temperature at the midplane.

SOLUTION

(1) From Eq. (4.18)

$$T = 110°C - \frac{(34{,}000 \text{ W/m}^2)(0.005 \text{ m} - 0 \text{ m})}{(17 \text{ W/m} \cdot °C)}$$

$$T = 110 - 10 = 100°C$$

(2) The temperature at the midplane is 100°C. This temperature was expected, since the thermal conductivity is constant, and temperature profile will be linear.

4.4.2 Conductive Heat Transfer through a Tubular Pipe

Consider a long hollow cylinder of inner radius r_i, outer radius r_o, and length L, as shown in Fig. 4.17. Let the inside wall temperature be T_i and outside wall temperature be T_o. It is desired to calculate the rate of heat transfer along the radial direction in this pipe. Assume thermal conductivity of the metal remains constant with temperature.

The Fourier law in cylindrical coordinates may be written as

$$q_r = -kA\frac{dT}{dr} \tag{4.19}$$

where q_r is the rate of heat transfer in the radial direction.

Substituting for circumferential area,

$$q_r = -k(2\pi rL)\frac{dT}{dr} \tag{4.20}$$

The boundary conditions are

$$T = T_i \quad \text{at} \quad r = r_i$$

$$T = T_o \quad \text{at} \quad r = r_o \tag{4.21}$$

Integrating Eq. (4.20), we get

$$\frac{q_r}{2\pi L}\int_{r_i}^{r_o}\frac{dr}{r} = -k\int_{T_i}^{T_o}dT \tag{4.22}$$

It should be noted that in cylindrical coordinates the circumferential area varies in the radial direction (in contrast to constant area in the flat slab we considered in Section 4.4.1).

Equation (4.22) gives

$$\frac{q_r}{2\pi L}\ln r\Big|_{r_i}^{r_o} = -kT\Big|_{T_i}^{T_o} \tag{4.23}$$

$$q_r = \frac{2\pi Lk(T_i - T_o)}{\ln(r_o/r_i)} \tag{4.24}$$

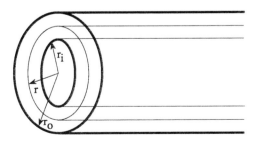

Fig. 4.17 Conductive heat transfer in a hollow cylindrical object.

EXAMPLE 4.7

A 2 cm thick steel pipe (thermal conductivity = 43 W/m · °C) with 6-cm inside diameter is being used to convey steam from a boiler to process equipment for a distance of 40 m. The inside pipe surface temperature is 115°C, and the outside pipe surface temperature is 90°C (see Fig. 4.18). Under steady-state conditions, calculate the total heat loss to the surrounding.

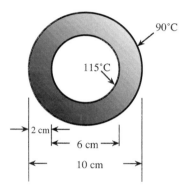

Fig. 4.18   Heat conduction in a metal pipe.

GIVEN

Thickness of pipe = 2 cm = 0.02 m
Inside diameter = 6 cm = 0.06 m
Thermal conductivity k = 43 W/m · °C
Length L = 40 m
Inside temperature T_i = 115°C
Outside temperature T_o = 90°C

APPROACH

Heat loss is to be determined using the two surface temperatures of the pipe. We will use Eq. (4.24) to compute rate of heat transfer due to conduction.

SOLUTION

(1) Using Eq. (4.24)

$$q = \frac{2\pi(40 \text{ m})(43 \text{ W/m} \cdot °\text{C})(115°\text{C} - 90°\text{C})}{\ln(0.05/0.03)}$$

$$= 528,903 \text{ W}$$

(2) The total heat loss from the pipe is 528,903 watts.

4.4.3 Heat Conduction in Multilayered Systems

a. Composite Rectangular Wall (in Series)

Let us consider heat transfer through a composite wall made of several materials of different thermal conductivities and thicknesses. All materials are arranged in series, as shown in Fig. 4.19. An example is a wall of a cold storage, constructed of different layers of materials and insulation.

From Fourier's law,

$$q = -kA\frac{dT}{dx}$$

This may be rewritten as

$$\Delta T = -\frac{q\,\Delta x}{kA} \tag{4.25}$$

Thus, for materials B, C, and D, we have

$$\Delta T_B = -\frac{q\,\Delta x_B}{k_B A} \qquad \Delta T_C = -\frac{q\,\Delta x_C}{k_C A} \qquad \Delta T_D = -\frac{q\,\Delta x_D}{k_D A} \tag{4.26}$$

From Fig. 4.19,

$$\Delta T = T_1 - T_2$$
$$= \Delta T_B + \Delta T_C + \Delta T_D \tag{4.27}$$

From Eqs. (4.25), (4.26), and (4.27),

$$T_1 - T_2 = -\left(\frac{q\,\Delta x_B}{k_B A} + \frac{q\,\Delta x_C}{k_C A} + \frac{q\,\Delta x_D}{k_D A}\right) \tag{4.28}$$

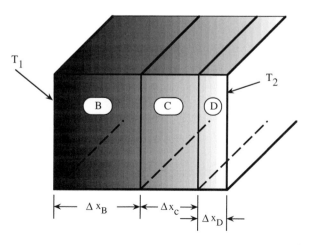

Fig. 4.19 Conductive heat transfer in a composite rectangular wall.

The preceding equation may be arranged to give

$$T_1 - T_2 = -\frac{q}{A}\left(\frac{\Delta x_B}{k_B} + \frac{\Delta x_C}{k_C} + \frac{\Delta x_D}{k_D}\right) \qquad (4.29)$$

where $(\Delta x_B/k_B) + (\Delta x_C/k_C) + (\Delta x_D/k_D)$ is the composite thermal resistance offered by the wall.

EXAMPLE 4.8

A cold storage wall (3 m × 6 m) is constructed of 15 cm thick concrete (thermal conductivity = 1.37 W/m · °C). Insulation must be provided to maintain a heat transfer rate through the wall at or below 500 W (see Fig. 4.20). If the thermal conductivity of the insulation is 0.04 W/m · °C, compute the required thickness of insulation. The outside surface temperature of the wall is 38°C and the inside wall temperature is 5°C.

GIVEN

Wall dimensions = 3 m × 6 m
Thickness of concrete wall = 15 cm = 0.15 m
$k_{concrete}$ = 1.37 W/m · °C
Maximum heat gain permitted, q = 500 W
$k_{insulation}$ = 0.04 W/m · °C
Outer wall temperature = 38°C
Inside wall (concrete/insulation) temperature = 5°C

APPROACH

Addition of insulation to a concrete wall indicates that this problem involves conduction in a multilayered composite wall. We will use Eq. (4.29).

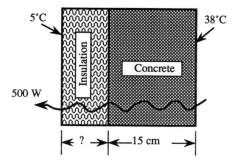

Fig. 4.20 Conductive heat transfer in a concrete wall with insulation.

SOLUTION

(1) From Eq. (4.29)

$$5°C - 38°C = -\left[\frac{(500\text{ W})(0.15\text{ m})}{(1.37\text{ W/m}\cdot°C)(18\text{ m}^2)} + \frac{(500\text{ W})(\Delta x\text{ m})}{(0.04\text{ W/m}\cdot°C)(18\text{ m}^2)}\right]$$

$$\Delta x = 0.043\text{ m}$$

(2) An insulation with a thickness of 4.3 cm will ensure that heat loss from the wall will remain below 500 W. This thickness of insulation allows a 91% reduction in heat loss.

---

b. Composite Cylindrical Tube (in Series)

Figure 4.21 shows a composite cylindrical tube made of two layers. The rate of heat transfer in this composite tube may be calculated as follows.

In Section 4.4.2 we found that rate of heat transfer through a single-wall cylinder is

$$q_r = \frac{2\pi Lk(T_i - T_o)}{\ln(r_o/r_i)}$$

Let us define a logarithmic mean area A_{lm} such that

$$q_r = kA_{lm}\frac{(T_i - T_o)}{(r_o - r_i)} \tag{4.30}$$

where

$$A_{lm} = 2\pi L\frac{(r_o - r_i)}{\ln(r_o/r_i)} \tag{4.31}$$

Thus, Eq. (4.30) may be rewritten as

$$(T_i - T_o) = \frac{(r_o - r_i)q_r}{kA_{lm}} \tag{4.32}$$

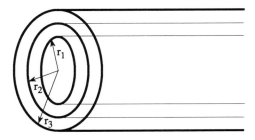

Fig. 4.21   Conductive heat transfer in concentric cylindrical pipes.

Rewriting the above equation for both layers gives

$$(T_1 - T_2) = \frac{(r_2 - r_1)q_r}{(kA_{lm})_{12}}$$ (4.33)

$$(T_2 - T_3) = \frac{(r_3 - r_2)q_r}{(kA_{lm})_{23}}$$ (4.34)

Adding Eqs. (4.33) and (4.34) yields

$$T_1 - T_2 + T_2 - T_3 = \left[\frac{r_2 - r_1}{(kA_{lm})_{12}} + \frac{r_3 - r_2}{(kA_{lm})_{23}} \right] q_r$$ (4.35)

$$q_r = \frac{T_1 - T_3}{\left(\dfrac{\Delta r}{kA_{lm}} \right)_{12} + \left(\dfrac{\Delta r}{kA_{lm}} \right)_{23}}$$ (4.36)

EXAMPLE 4.9

A stainless-steel pipe (thermal conductivity = 17 W/m · °C) is being used to convey heated oil (see Fig. 4.22). The inside surface temperature is 130°C. The pipe is 2 cm thick with an inside diameter of 8 cm. The pipe is insulated with 0.04 m thick insulation (thermal conductivity = 0.035 W/m · °C). The outer insulation temperature is 25°C. Calculate the temperature of interface between steel and insulation. Assume steady-state conditions.

GIVEN

Thickness of pipe = 2 cm = 0.02 m
Inside diameter = 8 cm = 0.08 m
k_{steel} = 17 W/m · °C
Thickness of insulation = 0.04 m
$k_{insulation}$ = 0.035 W/m · °C
Inside pipe surface temperature = 130°C

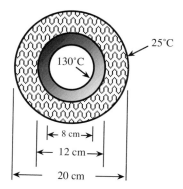

Fig. 4.22 Conductive heat transfer in a pipe with insulation.

Outside insulation surface temperature = 25°C
Pipe length = 1 m (assumed)

APPROACH

Since this problem deals with heat conduction in a multilayer cylinder, we will use Eq. (4.36). First, we will calculate log-mean areas to be used in Eq. (4.36). After calculating steady-state heat flow, the temperature at the interface will be determined by Eq. (4.34).

SOLUTION

(1) Assume pipe length = 1 m.
(2) Calculating the log-mean areas from Eq. (4.31),

$$(A_{lm})_{12} = (2\pi)(1 \text{ m}) \left[\frac{0.06 \text{ m} - 0.04 \text{ m}}{\ln\left(\frac{0.06}{0.04}\right)} \right] = 0.31 \text{ m}^2$$

$$(A_{lm})_{23} = (2\pi)(1 \text{ m}) \left[\frac{0.1 \text{ m} - 0.06 \text{ m}}{\ln\left(\frac{0.1}{0.06}\right)} \right] = 0.492 \text{ m}^2$$

(3) From Eq. (4.36)

$$q = \frac{(130°C - 25°C)}{\dfrac{(0.06 \text{ m} - 0.04 \text{ m})}{(17 \text{ W/m} \cdot °C)(0.31 \text{ m}^2)} + \dfrac{(0.1 \text{ m} - 0.06 \text{ m})}{(0.035 \text{ W/m} \cdot °C)(0.492 \text{ m}^2)}}$$

$$= 45.1 \text{ W}$$

(4) Using Eq. (4.34)

$$T_2 = 130°C - \frac{(0.06 \text{ m} - 0.04 \text{ m})(45.1 \text{ W})}{(17 \text{ W/m} \cdot °C)(0.31 \text{ m}^2)} = 129.8°C$$

(5) The interfacial temperature is 129.8°C. Interfacial temperature between the surface and insulation must be known to ensure structural integrity of the insulation at that temperature. In this example it is observed that the temperature drop across the stainless-steel wall is only 0.2°C. This was expected, since stainless steel has high thermal conductivity.

EXAMPLE 4.10

A stainless-steel pipe (thermal conductivity 15 W/m · K) is being used to transport heated oil at 125°C (see Fig. 4.23). The inside surface temperature of the pipe is 120°C. The pipe has an inside diameter of 5 cm and is 1 cm thick. Insulation is necessary to keep the heat loss from the oil below 25 W/m length of the pipe. Due to space limitations, only 5 cm thick insulation can be provided. The outside surface temperature of the insulation must be above 20°C (the dewpoint temperature of surrounding air) to avoid condensation of water on the surface of insulation. Calculate the thermal conductivity of insulation that will result in minimum heat loss while avoiding water condensation on its surface.

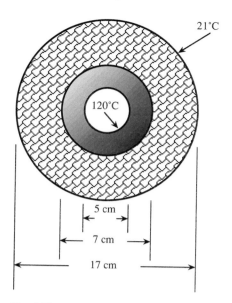

Fig. 4.23 Cross-sectional view of a pipe with insulation.

GIVEN

Thermal conductivity of steel = 15 W/m · K
Temperature of oil = 125°C
Inside pipe surface temperature = 120°C
Inside diameter = 0.05 m
Pipe thickness = 0.01 m
Heat loss permitted in 1 m length of pipe = 25 W
Insulation thickness = 0.05 m
Outside surface temperature > 20°C = 21°C (assumed)

APPROACH

We will use Eq. (4.36) to calculate the unknown thermal conductivity of the insulation.

SOLUTION

(1) Equation (4.36) is

$$q = \frac{T_1 - T_3}{\left(\dfrac{\Delta r}{kA_{lm}}\right)_{12} + \left(\dfrac{\Delta r}{kA_{lm}}\right)_{23}}$$

(2) The log-mean areas are calculated per meter length of the pipe as follows:

$$(A_{lm})_{12} = 2\pi L \frac{r_2 - r_1}{\ln(r_2/r_1)}$$

$$= 2\pi(1\text{ m})\left[\frac{0.035\text{ m} - 0.025\text{ m}}{\ln(0.035/0.025)}\right] = 0.1867\text{ m}^2$$

and

$$(A_{lm})_{23} = 2\pi L \frac{r_3 - r_2}{\ln(r_3/r_2)}$$

$$= 2\pi(1 \text{ m})\left[\frac{0.085 \text{ m} - 0.035 \text{ m}}{\ln(0.085/0.035)}\right] = 0.3541 \text{ m}^2$$

(3) From step 1

$$25 = \frac{(120°C - 21°C)}{\dfrac{0.01 \text{ m}}{(15 \text{ W/m} \cdot °C)(0.1867 \text{ m}^2)} + \dfrac{0.05 \text{ m}}{(k \text{ W/m} \cdot °C)(0.03541 \text{ m}^2)}}$$

or

$$0.0036 + \frac{0.05}{k \times 0.3541} = 3.96$$

(4) Solving, $k = 0.0357$ W/m $\cdot$ °C.

(5) An insulation with a thermal conductivity of 0.0357 W/m $\cdot$ °C will ensure no condensation on its outer surface.

4.4.4 Estimation of Convective Heat-Transfer Coefficient

The convective heat-transfer coefficient h is predicted from empirical correlations. The coefficient is influenced by such parameters as type and velocity of the fluid, physical properties of the fluid, the temperature difference, and the geometrical shape of the physical system under consideration. Dimensional analysis is used to develop empirical correlations that allow estimation of h.

The empirical correlations useful in predicting h are presented in the following sections for both forced and free convection. Physical systems most commonly encountered in convective heat transfer in food processing are discussed. All correlations apply to Newtonian fluids only. For expressions for non-Newtonian fluids, the textbook by Heldman and Singh (1981) is recommended.

a. Forced Convection

In forced convection, the fluid is forced to move over an object by external mechanical means, such as an electric fan, pump, or a stirrer (Fig. 4.24). The general correlation involves the dimensionless numbers

$$N_{Nu} = f(N_{Re}, N_{Pr}) \tag{4.37}$$

where N_{Nu} is Nusselt number $= hD/k$; h is convective heat-transfer coefficient (W/m$^2 \cdot$ °C); D is characteristic dimension (m); k is thermal conductivity of fluid (W/m $\cdot$ °C); N_{Re} is Reynolds number $= \rho \bar{u} D/\mu$; ρ is density of fluid (kg/m^3); $\bar{u}$ is velocity of fluid (m/s); D is diameter (m); μ is

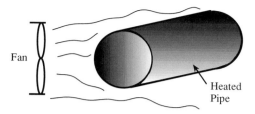

Fig. 4.24 Forced convective heat loss from a heated pipe.

viscosity (Pa · s); N_{Pr} is Prandtl number $= \mu c_p/k$; c_p is specific heat (kJ/kg · °C); and f stands for "function of."

Laminar Flow in Pipes For Reynolds number less than 2100 and flow in a horizontal pipe, the following equations may be used:

For $\left(N_{Re} \times N_{Pr} \times \dfrac{D}{L} \right) < 100$,

$$N_{Nu} = 3.66 + \frac{0.085\left(N_{Re} \times N_{Pr} \times \dfrac{D}{L} \right)}{1 + 0.045\left(N_{Re} \times N_{Pr} \times \dfrac{D}{L} \right)^{0.66}}\left(\frac{\mu_b}{\mu_w} \right)^{0.14}$$

(4.38)

For $\left(N_{Re} \times N_{Pr} \times \dfrac{D}{L} \right) > 100$,

$$N_{Nu} = 1.86\left(N_{Re} \times N_{Pr} \times \frac{D}{L} \right)^{0.33}\left(\frac{\mu_b}{\mu_w} \right)^{0.14}$$

(4.39)

All physical properties are evaluated at the bulk fluid temperature except μ_w, which is evaluated at the surface temperature of the wall.

EXAMPLE 4.11

Water flowing at a rate of 0.02 kg/s is heated from 20 to 60°C in a horizontal pipe (inside diameter = 2.5 cm). The inside pipe surface temperature is 90°C. (See Fig. 4.25.) Estimate the convective heat-transfer coefficient if the pipe is 1 m long.

GIVEN

Water flow rate = 0.02 kg/s
Inlet temperature = 20°C
Exit temperature = 60°C
Inside diameter = 2.5 cm = 0.025 m
Inside pipe surface temperature = 90°C
Length of pipe = 1 m

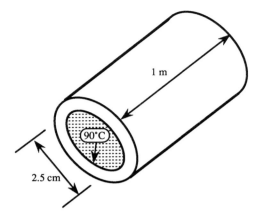

Fig. 4.25 Convective heat transfer inside a pipe.

APPROACH

Since water is flowing due to some external means, the problem indicates forced convective heat transfer. We will first determine if the flow is laminar by calculating Reynolds number. If the Reynolds number is less than 2100, we will compute $(N_{Re} \times N_{Pr} \times D/L)$ to select either Eq. (4.38) or (4.39) to calculate the Nusselt number. From Nusselt number we will calculate the h value.

SOLUTION

(1) Physical properties of water are needed to calculate Reynolds number. All physical properties except μ_w must be evaluated at average bulk fluid temperature, $(20 + 60)/2 = 40°C$. From Table A.4.1 at $40°C$,

Density $\rho = 992.2 \text{ kg/m}^3$
Specific heat $c_p = 4.175 \text{ kJ/kg} \cdot °C$
Thermal conductivity $k = 0.633 \text{ W/m} \cdot °C$
Viscosity (absolute) $\mu = 658.026 \times 10^{-6} \text{ Pa} \cdot \text{s}$
Prandtl number $N_{Pr} = 4.3$

Thus,

$$N_{Re} = \frac{\rho \bar{u} D}{\mu} = \frac{4\dot{m}}{\pi \mu D}$$

$$= \frac{(4)(0.02 \text{ kg/s})}{(\pi)(658.026 \times 10^{-6} \text{ Pa} \cdot \text{s})(0.025 \text{ m})} = 1547.9$$

Note that $1 \text{ Pa} = 1 \text{ kg/m} \cdot \text{s}^2$. Since the Reynolds number is less than 2100, the flow is laminar.

(2) To select the appropriate equation for the Nusselt number, compute the product of

$$\left(N_{Re} \times N_{Pr} \times \frac{D}{L} \right) = (1547.9)(4.3)(0.025) = 166.4$$

(3) Therefore, we select Eq. (4.39), and using $\mu_w = 308.909 \times 10^{-6}$ Pa · s at 90°C,

$$N_{Nu} = 1.86(166.4)^{0.33}\left(\frac{658.026 \times 10^{-6}}{308.909 \times 10^{-6}}\right)^{0.14}$$

$$= 11.2$$

(4) The convective heat-transfer coefficient can be obtained from the Nusselt number.

$$h = \frac{N_{Nu}k}{D} = \frac{(11.2)(0.633 \text{ W/m} \cdot {}^\circ\text{C})}{(0.025 \text{ m})}$$

$$= 284 \text{ W/m}^2 \cdot {}^\circ\text{C}$$

(5) The convective heat-transfer coefficient is estimated to be 284 W/m² · °C.

Transition Flow in Pipes For Reynolds numbers between 2,100 and 10,000, simple empirical correlations are available. Figure 4.26 may be used to estimate convective heat transfer coefficient.

Turbulent Flow in Pipes The following equation may be used for Reynolds numbers greater than 10,000:

$$N_{Nu} = 0.023N_{Re}^{0.8} \times N_{Pr}^{0.33} \times \left(\frac{\mu_b}{\mu_w}\right)^{0.14} \tag{4.40}$$

The fluid properties, except μ_w, are evaluated at the mean bulk fluid temperature. If the bulk fluid temperature varies from inlet to exit of the pipe, the average of two values must be used.

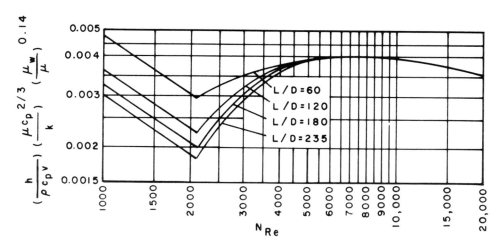

Fig. 4.26 A plot to determine convective heat-transfer coefficient for flow in pipes. [From Perry and Chilton (1973). Reproduced with permission of the publisher.]

EXAMPLE 4.12

If the rate of water flow in Example 4.11 is raised to 0.2 kg/s from 0.02 kg/s while all other conditions are kept the same, calculate the new convective heat-transfer coefficient.

GIVEN

See Example 4.11.
New mass flow rate of water = 0.2 kg/s

APPROACH

We will calculate the Reynolds number to find whether the flow is turbulent. If the flow is turbulent, we will use Eq. (4.40) to compute the Nusselt number. The surface heat-transfer coefficient will be computed from the Nusselt number.

SOLUTION

(1) First, we compute the Reynolds number using some of the properties obtained in Example 4.11.

$$N_{Re} = \frac{(4)(0.2 \text{ kg/s})}{(\pi)(658.026 \times 10^{-6} \text{ Pa} \cdot \text{s})(0.025 \text{ m})} = 15{,}479$$

Thus, flow is turbulent.

(2) For turbulent flow, we select Eq. (4.40).

$$N_{Nu} = (0.023)(15479)^{0.8}(4.3)^{0.33}\left(\frac{658.026 \times 10^{-6}}{308.909 \times 10^{-6}}\right)^{0.14}$$

$$= 93$$

(3) The convective heat transfer can be computed as

$$h = \frac{N_{Nu}k}{D} = \frac{(93)(0.633 \text{ W/m} \cdot \text{°C})}{(0.025 \text{ m})}$$

$$= 2355 \text{ W/m}^2 \cdot \text{°C}$$

(4) The convective heat-transfer coefficient for turbulent flow is estimated to be 2355 W/m$^2 \cdot$°C. This value is more than 10 times higher than the value of h for laminar flow calculated in Example 4.11.

EXAMPLE 4.13

What is the expected percent increase in convective heat-transfer coefficient if the velocity of a fluid is doubled while all other related parameters are kept the same for turbulent flow in a pipe?

APPROACH

We will use Eq. (4.40) to solve this problem.

SOLUTION

(1) For turbulent flow in a pipe,

$$N_{\text{Nu}} = 0.023 N_{\text{Re}}^{0.8} \times N_{\text{Pr}}^{0.33} \times \left(\frac{\mu_b}{\mu_w}\right)^{0.14}$$

We can rewrite the above equation as

$$N_{\text{Nu}_1} = f(v_1)^{0.8}$$

$$N_{\text{Nu}_2} = f(v_2)^{0.8}$$

$$\frac{N_{\text{Nu}_2}}{N_{\text{Nu}_1}} = \left(\frac{v_2}{v_1}\right)^{0.8}$$

(2) Since $v_2 = 2v_1$,

$$\frac{N_{\text{Nu}_2}}{N_{\text{Nu}_1}} = (2)^{0.8} = 1.74$$

$$N_{\text{Nu}_2} = 1.74 N_{\text{Nu}_1}$$

(3) The above expression implies that $h_2 = 1.74 h_1$. Thus,

$$\% \text{ Increase} = \frac{1.74 h_1 - h_1}{h_1} \times 100 = 74\%$$

(4) As expected, velocity has a considerable effect on the convective heat-transfer coefficient.

Convection in Noncircular Ducts For noncircular ducts, an equivalent diameter D_e is used.

$$D_e = \frac{4 \times \text{free area}}{\text{wetted perimeter}} \tag{4.41}$$

Flow Past Immersed Objects In several applications, the fluid may flow past certain immersed objects. For these cases, the heat transfer depends on the geometrical shape of the body, the relative position of the body, proximity of other bodies, flow rate, and fluid properties.

For a flow past single spheres, when the single sphere may be heated or cooled, the following equation will apply:

$$N_{\text{Nu}} = 2 + 0.60 N_{\text{Re}}^{0.5} \times N_{\text{Pr}}^{1/3} \quad \text{for} \quad \begin{cases} 1 < N_{\text{Re}} < 70,000 \\ 0.6 < N_{\text{Pr}} < 400 \end{cases} \tag{4.42}$$

The fluid properties are evaluated at the film temperature T_f where

$$T_f = \frac{T_{\text{wall}} + T_{\text{medium}}}{2}$$

For heat transfer in flow past other immersed objects, such as cylinders and plates, correlations are available in Perry and Chilton (1973).

EXAMPLE 4.14

Calculate convective heat-transfer coefficient when air at 90°C is passed through a deep bed of green peas. Assume surface temperature of a pea to be 30°C. The diameter of each pea is 0.5 cm. The velocity of air through the bed is 0.3 m/s.

GIVEN

Diameter of a pea = 0.005 m
Temperature of air = 90°C
Temperature of a pea = 30°C
Velocity of air = 0.3 m/s

APPROACH

Since the air flows around a spherically immersed object (green pea), we will estimate N_{Nu} from Eq. (4.42). The Nusselt number will give us the value for h.

SOLUTION

(1) The properties of air are evaluated at T_f, where

$$T_f = \frac{T_{wall} + T_{medium}}{2} = \frac{30 + 90}{2} = 60°C$$

From Table A.4.4,

$$\rho = 1.025 \text{ kg/m}^3$$
$$c_p = 1.017 \text{ kJ/kg} \cdot °C$$
$$k = 0.0279 \text{ W/m} \cdot °C$$
$$\mu = 19.907 \times 10^{-6} \text{ Pa} \cdot s$$
$$N_{Pr} = 0.71$$

(2) The Reynolds number is computed as

$$N_{Re} = \frac{(1.025 \text{ kg/m}^3)(0.3 \text{ m/s})(0.005 \text{ m})}{(19.907 \times 10^{-6} \text{ Pa} \cdot s)}$$

$$= 77.2$$

(3) From Eq. (4.42),

$$N_{Nu} = 2 + 0.6(77.2)^{0.5}(0.71)^{0.33}$$

$$= 6.71$$

(4) Thus

$$h = \frac{6.71(0.0279 \text{ W/m} \cdot °C)}{(0.005 \text{ m})} = 37 \text{ W/m}^2 \cdot °C$$

(5) The convective heat-transfer coefficient is 37 W/m² · °C.

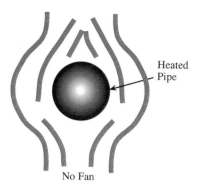

Fig. 4.27 Free convective heat loss from a heated pipe.

b. Free Convection

Free convection occurs due to density differences in fluids as they come into contact with a heated surface (Fig. 4.27). The low density of fluid at a higher temperature causes buoyancy forces, and as a result, heated fluid moves upward and colder fluid takes its place.

Empirical expressions useful in predicting convective heat-transfer coefficients are of the following form

$$N_{Nu} = \frac{hD}{k} = a(N_{Gr}N_{Pr})^m \qquad (4.43)$$

where a and m are constants; N_{Gr} is the Grashof number, $(D^3\rho^2 g\beta\,\Delta T)/\mu^2$;

TABLE 4.4
Value of a and m for Eq. (4.43)

Configuration	$N_{Gr}N_{Pr}$[a]	a	m
Vertical surfaces	$< 10^4$	1.36	1/5
D = vertical dimension < 1 m	$10^4 < N_{Gr}N_{Pr} < 10^9$	0.59	1/4
	$> 10^9$	0.13	1/3
Horizontal cylinder	$< 10^{-5}$	0.49	0
D = diameter < 20 cm	$10^{-5} < N_{Gr}N_{Pr} < 10^{-3}$	0.71	1/25
	$10^{-3} < N_{Gr}N_{Pr} < 1$	1.09	1/10
	$1 < N_{Gr}N_{Pr} < 10^4$	1.09	1/5
	$10^4 < N_{Gr}N_{Pr} < 10^9$	0.53	1/4
	$> 10^9$	0.13	1/3
Horizontal flat surface	$10^5 < N_{Gr}N_{Pr} < 2 \times 10^7$ (FU)	0.54	1/4
	$2 \times 10^7 < N_{Gr}N_{Pr} < 3 \times 10^{10}$(FU)	0.14	1/3
	$3 \times 10^5 < N_{Gr}N_{Pr} < 3 \times 10^{10}$ (FD)	0.27	1/4

Source: Adapted from Perry and Chilton (1973). Reproduced with permission of the publisher.
[a]FU is facing upward; FD is facing downward.

D is characteristic dimension (m); ρ is density (kg/m^3); g is acceleration due to gravity (9.80665 m/s^2); β is coefficient of volumetric expansion (K^{-1}); ΔT is temperature difference between wall and the surrounding bulk (°C); and μ is viscosity (Pa · s). All physical properties are evaluated at the film temperature, $T_f = (T_w + T_b)/2$.

Table 4.4 gives various constants that may be used in Eq. (4.43) for natural convection from vertical plates and cylinders, and from horizontal cylinders and plates.

EXAMPLE 4.15

Estimate the convective heat-transfer coefficient for convective heat loss from a horizontal 10 cm diameter steam pipe. The surface temperature of the uninsulated pipe is 130°C, and the air temperature is 30°C (see Fig. 4.28).

GIVEN

> Diameter of pipe = 10 cm = 0.1 m
> Pipe surface temperature $T_w = 130°C$
> Ambient temperature $T_b = 30°C$

APPROACH

Since no mechanical means of moving air are indicated, heat loss from the horizontal pipe is by free convection. After finding the property values of air at film temperature, we will calculate the Grashof number. The product of the Grashof number and Prandtl number will allow determination of a and m parameters from Table 4.4; these parameters will be used in Eq. (4.43). We will then compute the surface heat-transfer coefficient from the Nusselt number.

SOLUTION

(1) Since no mechanical means of moving the air are indicated, heat loss is by free convection.

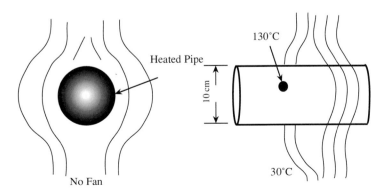

Fig. 4.28 Convective heat loss from a horizontal pipe.

(2) The film temperature is obtained as

$$T_f = \frac{T_w + T_b}{2} = \frac{130 + 30}{2} = 80°C$$

(3) The properties of air at 80°C are obtained from Table A.4.4.

$$\rho = 0.968 \text{ kg/m}^3$$

$$\beta = 2.83 \times 10^{-3} \text{ K}^{-1}$$

$$c_p = 1.019 \text{ kJ/kg} \cdot °C$$

$$k = 0.0293 \text{ W/m} \cdot °C$$

$$\mu = 20.79 \times 10^{-6} \text{ N} \cdot \text{s/m}^2$$

$$N_{Pr} = 0.71$$

$$g = 9.81 \text{ m/s}^2$$

(4) We calculate the product of N_{Gr} and N_{Pr} to select a and m values from Table 4.3.

$$N_{Gr} = \frac{D^3 \rho^2 g \beta \, \Delta T}{\mu^2}$$

$$= \frac{(0.1 \text{ m})^3 (0.968 \text{ kg/m}^3)^2 (9.81 \text{ m/s}^2)(2.83 \times 10^{-3} \text{ K}^{-1})(130°C - 30°C)}{(20.79 \times 10^{-6} \text{ N} \cdot \text{s/m}^2)^2}$$

$$= 6.019 \times 10^6$$

(Note that $1N = \text{kg} \cdot \text{m/s}^2$.) Thus,

$$N_{Gr} \times N_{Pr} = (6.019 \times 10^6)(0.71) = 4.27 \times 10^6$$

(5) For $N_{Gr} N_{Pr} = 4.27 \times 10^6$, from Table 4.4, the parameter $a = 0.53$ and $m = 1/4$.

(6) From Eq. (4.43),

$$N_{Nu} = 0.53(4.27 \times 10^6)^{1/4} = 24.1$$

(7) Thus,

$$h = \frac{(24.1)(0.0293 \text{ W/m} \cdot °C)}{(0.1 \text{ m})} = 7 \text{ W/m}^2 \cdot °C$$

4.4.5 Estimation of Overall Heat-Transfer Coefficient

In many heating/cooling applications, conductive and convective heat transfer may occur simultaneously. An example shown in Fig. 4.29 involves heat transfer across a pipe that carries a fluid at a different temperature than the temperature on the outside of the pipe.

Assuming the temperature of the fluid inside is higher than outside ($T_i > T_\infty$), heat flows from inside to outside. The heat flow will occur through three layers of resistance determined by the convective heat

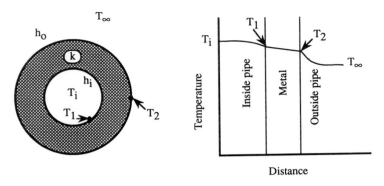

Fig. 4.29 Combined conductive and convective heat transfer.

transfer inside, conductive heat transfer in the metal, and the convective heat transfer outside. An overall expression for heat transfer may be written as

$$q = U_i A_i (T_i - T_\infty) \qquad (4.44)$$

where A_i is the inside area of the pipe and U_i is the overall heat-transfer coefficient based on the inside area. In addition, the rate of heat transfer through individual layers is

$$q = h_i A_i (T_i - T_1) \qquad (4.45)$$

$$q = k A_m \frac{(T_1 - T_2)}{(r_2 - r_1)} \qquad (4.46)$$

and

$$q = h_o A_o (T_2 - T_\infty) \qquad (4.47)$$

Thus,

$$\frac{q}{h_i A_i} = T_i - T_1 \qquad (4.48)$$

$$\frac{q(r_2 - r_1)}{k A_{lm}} = T_1 - T_2 \qquad (4.49)$$

$$\frac{q}{h_o A_o} = T_2 - T_\infty \qquad (4.50)$$

and from Eq. (4.44),

$$\frac{q}{U_i A_i} = T_i - T_\infty \qquad (4.51)$$

Adding Eqs. (4.48), (4.49), and (4.50), and equating to Eq. (4.51),

$$\frac{q}{U_i A_i} = \frac{q}{h_i A_i} + \frac{q(r_2 - r_1)}{k A_{lm}} + \frac{q}{h_o A_o} \qquad (4.52)$$

or

$$\frac{1}{U_i A_i} = \frac{1}{h_i A_i} + \frac{(r_2 - r_1)}{k A_{lm}} + \frac{1}{h_o A_o} \qquad (4.53)$$

The above expression allows determination of the overall heat-transfer coefficient. The selection of area to calculate the overall heat transfer is quite arbitrary. For example, if U_o is selected as the overall heat-transfer coefficient based on outside area of the pipe, then Eq. (4.44) will be modified to

$$q = U_o A_o (T_i - T_\infty) \qquad (4.54)$$

The final calculated value of rate of heat transfer remains the same regardless of the area chosen for the analysis, as will be shown in the following example.

EXAMPLE 4.16

A 2.5-cm inside diameter pipe is being used to convey a liquid food at 80°C. (See Fig. 4.30.) The inside convective heat-transfer coefficient is 10 W/m² · °C. The pipe (0.5 cm thick) is made of steel (thermal conductivity = 43 W/m · °C). The outside ambient temperature is 20°C. The outside convective heat-transfer coefficient is 100 W/m² · °C. Calculate the overall heat transfer coefficient and the heat loss from 1-m length of the pipe.

GIVEN

       Inside diameter of pipe = 0.025 m
       Bulk temperature of liquid food = 80°C
       Inside convective heat-transfer coefficient = 10 W/m² · °C
       Outside convective heat-transfer coefficient = 100 W/m² · °C
       k_{steel} = 43 W/m · °C
       Outside ambient temperature = 20°C

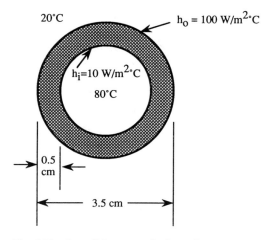

Fig. 4.30 Overall heat transfer in a pipe.

APPROACH

The overall heat-transfer coefficient can be computed by using a basis of either the inside area of the pipe or the outside area of the pipe. We will use Eq. (4.53) to find U_i and then use a modification of Eq. (4.53) to find U_o. We will prove that the computed rate of heat flow will remain the same regardless of whether U_i or U_o is selected.

SOLUTION

(1) Calculate the overall heat-transfer coefficient based on inside area.

$$\frac{1}{U_i A_i} = \frac{1}{h_i A_i} + \frac{(r_o - r_i)}{k A_{\mathrm{lm}}} + \frac{1}{h_o A_o}$$

(2) By canceling area terms and noting that $A_i = 2\pi r_i L$,

$$\frac{1}{U_i} = \frac{1}{h_i} + \frac{(r_o - r_i) r_i}{k r_{\mathrm{lm}}} + \frac{r_i}{h_o r_o}$$

(3)

$$r_{\mathrm{lm}} = \frac{r_o - r_i}{\ln(r_o/r_i)} = \frac{0.0175 \text{ m} - 0.0125 \text{ m}}{\ln\left(\dfrac{0.0175}{0.0125}\right)} = 0.01486 \text{ m}$$

(4) Substituting,

$$\frac{1}{U_i} = \frac{1}{\left(10 \text{ W/m}^2 \cdot {}^\circ\text{C}\right)} + \frac{(0.0175 \text{ m} - 0.0125 \text{ m})0.0125 \text{ m}}{(43 \text{ W/m} \cdot {}^\circ\text{C})(0.01486 \text{ m})}$$

$$+ \frac{0.0125 \text{ m}}{\left(100 \text{ W/m}^2 \cdot {}^\circ\text{C}\right)(0.0175 \text{ m})}$$

$$= 0.1 + 0.0001 + 0.00714 = 0.10724 \text{ m}^2 \cdot {}^\circ\text{C/W}$$

Thus, $U_i = 9.32$ W/m$^2 \cdot {}^\circ$C.

(5) Heat loss

$$q = U_i A_i (80 - 20)$$

$$= \left(9.32 \text{ W/m}^2 \cdot {}^\circ\text{C}\right)(2\pi)(1 \text{ m})(0.0125 \text{ m})(60^\circ\text{C})$$

$$= 43.9 \text{ W}$$

(6) Overall heat-transfer coefficient based on outside area may be computed as

$$\frac{1}{U_o A_o} = \frac{1}{h_i A_i} + \frac{(r_o - r_i) r_o}{k A_{\mathrm{lm}}} + \frac{1}{h_o A_o}$$

(7)

$$\frac{1}{U_o} = \frac{r_o}{h_i r_i} + \frac{(r_o - r_i) r_o}{k r_{\mathrm{lm}}} + \frac{1}{h_o}$$

$$= \frac{0.0175 \text{ m}}{\left(10 \text{ W/m}^2 \cdot {}^\circ\text{C}\right)(0.0125 \text{ m})} + \frac{(0.0175 \text{ m} - 0.0125 \text{ m})0.0175 \text{ m}}{(43 \text{ W/m} \cdot {}^\circ\text{C})(0.01486 \text{ m})}$$

$$+ \frac{1}{100 \text{ W/m}^2 \cdot {}^\circ\text{C}}$$

$$= 0.14 + 0.00014 + 0.01$$

$$= 0.1501 \text{ m}^2 \cdot {}^\circ\text{C/W}$$

$$U_o = 6.66 \text{ W/m}^2 \cdot {}^\circ\text{C}$$

(8) Heat loss

$$q = U_o A_o (80 - 20)$$

$$= (6.66 \text{ W/m}^2 \cdot {}^\circ\text{C})(2\pi)(0.0175 \text{ m}^2)(60{}^\circ\text{C})$$

$$= 43.9 \text{ W}$$

(9) As expected, the total heat loss remains the same regardless of which area was selected for computing overall heat-transfer coefficient.

(10) It should be noted from steps (4) and (7) that the resistance offered by the metal wall is considerably smaller than the resistance offered in the convective layers.

4.4.6 Role of Insulation in Reducing Heat Loss from Process Equipment

Food processing equipment is often insulated to minimize the rate of heat transfer from it to the surroundings. If no insulation is provided, heat loss from the external surfaces of the process equipment can occur by all three modes of heat transfer, that is, conduction, convection, and radiation. Heat loss by conduction mode through air will be small because air is a poor conductor of heat ($k_{air} = 0.0258$ W/m °C at 30°C). Radiative heat losses are proportional to the fourth power of the difference between the equipment's surface temperature and the ambient temperature. This loss will be small if the difference in temperatures is small; however, it can be considerable with increased temperature differences. The major loss of heat will be due to convection, since convective currents will be easily set up if there is a temperature difference between the body and the surroundings. Insulation is necessary to decrease the rate of heat transfer between an object and the surroundings. The insulation material selected for this purpose must have a low thermal conductivity and an ability to decrease convective currents.

Materials used for insulation include cork, magnesia, glass, and wool. Asbestos was used extensively in the past for its insulating properties; however, asbestos fibers have been shown to cause cancer and, therefore, it is not used any more. Prefabricated sections of magnesia and other insulating materials can be easily applied to pipes, and removed when necessary.

The reduction in heat loss by the addition of insulation can be calculated by using the methods presented in the preceding sections.

a. Mean Critical Thickness of Insulation

We know that the rate of heat loss from a pipe is described by Eq. (4.10), or

$$q = hA(T_p - T_\infty)$$

Equation (4.10) suggests that if the area A is increased, the rate of heat loss q will increase. When insulation is added to a pipe, obviously, the outside surface area of the pipe will increase. This would indicate an increased rate of heat transfer (countering the purpose of installing insulation). The insulation material has a low thermal conductivity, thus it reduces the conductive heat transfer and as a result lowers the temperature difference between the outer surface temperature of the insulation and the surrounding bulk fluid temperature. This contradiction indicates that there must be a critical thickness of insulation. The thickness of insulation must be greater than the critical thickness, so that the rate of heat loss is reduced as desired. A criterion for critical thickness of insulation can be determined as follows.

Consider an insulation layer of thermal conductivity k in the form of a hollow cylinder of length L, as shown in Fig. 4.17. The inside radius of this hollow cylinder is r_i and the outside radius is r_o. The inside surface temperature is T_i and the outside surface temperature is T_o. The outside convective heat transfer coefficient is h_o. The surrounding bulk fluid temperature is T_b. Then the rate of heat transfer through the insulation layer and the convective boundary layer offering heat resistance is

$$q = \frac{T_i - T_b}{\dfrac{1}{2\pi Lk} \ln \dfrac{r_o}{r_i} + \dfrac{1}{2\pi r_o Lh_o}} \tag{4.55}$$

In Eq. (4.55), as the outside radius r_o increases, then in the denominator, the first term increases but the second term decreases. Thus, there must be a critical radius r_c that will allow maximum rate of heat transfer q. The critical radius r_c can be obtained by differentiating Eq. (4.55) and setting the resulting equation equal to zero. Thus,

$$\frac{dq}{dr_o} = -\frac{2\pi kL(T_i - T_b)}{[\ln(r_o/r_i) + k/h_o r_o]^2}\left(\frac{1}{r_o} - \frac{k}{h_o r_o^2}\right) = 0 \tag{4.56}$$

In Eq. (4.56) T_i, T_b, k, L, r_o, r_i are constant terms; therefore,

$$\left(\frac{1}{r_o} - \frac{k}{h_o r_o^2}\right) = 0 \tag{4.57}$$

When the outside radius becomes equal to the critical radius, or $r_o = r_c$, we get

$$r_c = \frac{k}{h_o} \tag{4.58}$$

Equation (4.58) is useful in calculating the thickness of the critical insulation. If the outer radius, with insulation, is less than the critical radius as calculated from Eq. (4.58), then heat loss will increase due to increased surface area. The increase in heat transfer will continue to occur until the outer radius becomes equal to the critical radius. Further increase in the outer radius will then result in decreased heat loss. The following example illustrates the concept of critical thickness of insulation.

EXAMPLE 4.17

A stainless-steel steel pipe has the following dimensions: inside diameter = 2.5 cm and outside diameter = 4.5 cm. The outside pipe surface temperature is 120°C. The pipe will be covered with an insulation material. Two types of insulating materials are available with the following thermal conductivities: material A, k_A = 0.1 W/m°C; material B, k_B = 0.5 W/m°C.

(a) The outside convective heat transfer coefficient is 5.68 W/m² °C. Using a spreadsheet, develop plots of the ratio of rate of heat loss of insulated pipe to rate of heat loss with bare pipe (q-insulated/q-bare) versus radius of insulating materials. Using the q-insulated/q-bare plots or values from the spreadsheet, determine the critical radius of insulation.

(b) If the convective heat transfer coefficient is increased to 10 W/m² °C, then using q-insulated/q-bare plots or values from the spreadsheet, determine the critical radius of insulation and the radius of insulation that must be exceeded to accomplish a decrease in the rate of heat flux from the bare pipe.

GIVEN

Inside radius of insulation = 1.25 cm
Outside radius of pipe = 2.25 cm
Thermal conductivity k_A = 0.1 W/m°C
Thermal conductivity k_B = 0.5 W/m°C
Convective heat transfer coefficient (part a) = 5.68 W/m² °C
Convective heat transfer coefficient (part b) = 10 W/m² °C

APPROACH

Since the outside radius of the pipe is 2.25 cm, the inside radius of the insulation will be 2.25 cm. Since several repeated calculations are involved we will program a spreadsheet to solve this problem. (See Figs. 4.31 and 4.32.)

SOLUTION

(1) When no insulation is provided, then for a metal pipe with an outside radius of r_2,

$$q_{bare} = 2\pi r_2 L h_o(T_s - T_b)$$

	A	B	C	D	E
1	r2	2.25		r3	q-insulated/q-bare
2	k	0.1		2.25	=(D2/$B$1)*(1/(1+(D2*$B$3/$B$2/100)*LN(D2/$B$1)))
3	h	5.68		3.25	=(D3/$B$1)*(1/(1+(D3*$B$3/$B$2/100)*LN(D3/$B$1)))
4	k/h	=B2/B3*100		4.25	=(D4/$B$1)*(1/(1+(D4*$B$3/$B$2/100)*LN(D4/$B$1)))
5				5.25	=(D5/$B$1)*(1/(1+(D5*$B$3/$B$2/100)*LN(D5/$B$1)))
6	r2	2.25		6.25	=(D6/$B$1)*(1/(1+(D6*$B$3/$B$2/100)*LN(D6/$B$1)))
7	k	0.5		7.25	=(D7/$B$1)*(1/(1+(D7*$B$3/$B$2/100)*LN(D7/$B$1)))
8	h	5.68		8.25	=(D8/$B$1)*(1/(1+(D8*$B$3/$B$2/100)*LN(D8/$B$1)))
9	k/h	=B7/B8*100		9.25	=(D9/$B$1)*(1/(1+(D9*$B$3/$B$2/100)*LN(D9/$B$1)))
10				10.25	=(D10/$B$1)*(1/(1+(D10*$B$3/$B$2/100)*LN(D10/$B$1)

Fig. 4.31 Spreadsheet of equations for solving Example 4.17.

	A	B	C	D	E	F	G	H
1	ri	2.25			q-insulated/q-bare	q-insulated/q-bare	q-insulated/q-bare	q-insulated/q-bare
2	k	0.1		2.25	1.000	1.000	1.000	1.000
3	h	5.68		3.25	0.860	1.272	0.658	1.166
4	k/h	1.76056		4.25	0.745	1.445	0.510	1.226
5				5.25	0.662	1.550	0.428	1.235
6	ri	2.25		6.25	0.600	1.610	0.376	1.220
7	k	0.5		7.25	0.554	1.641	0.340	1.195
8	h	5.68		8.25	0.517	1.653	0.313	1.166
9	k/h	8.80282		9.25	0.488	1.654	0.292	1.137
10				10.25	0.464	1.647	0.275	1.109
11	ri	2.25		11.25	0.443	1.636	0.262	1.082
12	k	0.1		12.25	0.426	1.621	0.250	1.057
13	h	10		13.25	0.411	1.605	0.240	1.033
14	k/h	1		14.25	0.397	1.588	0.232	1.012
15				15.25	0.386	1.571	0.225	0.991
16	ri	2.25		16.25	0.375	1.553	0.218	0.973
17	k	0.5		17.25	0.366	1.536	0.212	0.955
18	h	10		27.25	0.306	1.389	0.176	0.830
19	k/h	5		37.25	0.274	1.286	0.157	0.756
20				47.25	0.254	1.211	0.145	0.705
21				57.25	0.239	1.154	0.137	0.669
22				67.25	0.229	1.109	0.130	0.640
23				77.25	0.220	1.072	0.125	0.617
24				87.25	0.213	1.041	0.121	0.598
25				97.25	0.207	1.014	0.118	0.582
26				107.25	0.202	0.991	0.115	0.568
27				117.25	0.197	0.971	0.112	0.556
28				127.25	0.193	0.953	0.110	0.545
29				137.25	0.190	0.937	0.108	0.536
30				147.25	0.187	0.923	0.106	0.527

Fig. 4.32 Spreadsheet of the solution to Example 4.17.

(2) The rate of heat transfer from an insulated pipe, where the annular insulating shell has an inside radius of r_2 and an outer radius of r_3,

$$q_{\text{insulated}} = 2\pi r_3 L h_o \frac{(T_s - T_b)}{1 + (r_3 h_o/k)\ln r_3/r_2}$$

(3) Then,

$$\frac{q_{\text{insulated}}}{q_{\text{bare}}} = \frac{r_3}{r_2}\left(\frac{1}{1 + \dfrac{r_3 h_o}{k}\ln \dfrac{r_3}{r_2}}\right)$$

(4) The equation derived in step (3) is entered in cell E2. Note k/h is multiplied by 100 to obtain the value for critical radius in centimeters. Cell D2 contains the outer radius for insulation, r_3. Using Data Series command (for EXCEL™), a series is set up for r_3 increasing from 2.25 cm to 17.25 cm in 1-cm increments, and from 17.25 cm to 147.25 cm in 10-cm increments. The cell E2 is copied in cells E3 : E30. Similar procedure is used to set up columns F, G, and H. The values obtained for q-insulated/q-bare are plotted against r_3.

(5) It is evident from Fig. 4.33 and tabulated results in the spreadsheet, that when the critical radius is less than r_3, insulation results in decrease of rate

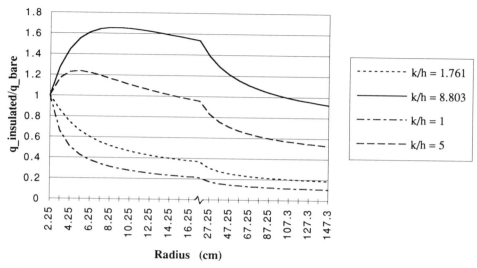

Fig. 4.33 Plot of the ratio of rate of heat loss of insulated pipe to rate of heat loss with bare pipe versus the radius of insulating materials.

of heat loss; for example, in the first case, the critical radius calculated as 1.761 cm is less than 2.25 cm, the outer radius of insulation. The ratio q-insulated/q-bare decreases continually. In the second case, the critical radius is 8.803 cm; since it is more than 2.25 cm, the ratio q-insulated/q-bare increases. This indicates that an increased rate of heat loss will occur with added thickness of insulation; this heat loss reaches a maximum value when the outer radius of insulation is 8.803 cm. Adding more thickness of insulation decreases the q-insulated/q-bare ratio. The rate of heat loss from insulated pipe decreases below that of bare pipe only when the outside radius exceeds 103.3 cm. Similar results are seen in cases 3 and 4.

4.4.7 Design of a Tubular Heat Exchanger

A major objective in designing a tubular heat exchanger is to determine the required heat-transfer area for a given application. We will use the following assumptions:

1. Heat transfer is under steady-state conditions.
2. The overall heat-transfer coefficient is constant throughout the length of pipe.
3. There is no axial conduction of heat in the metal pipe.
4. The heat exchanger is well insulated. There is negligible heat loss to the surroundings.

Heat transfer from one fluid to another can be described by the following expression:

$$dq = U_i (\Delta T)_{\text{overall}} dA_i \qquad (4.59)$$

where U_i is the overall heat transfer coefficient based on the inside area of the inner pipe. The term $(\Delta T)_{\text{overall}}$ is the difference between the bulk temperatures of the hot and the cold fluids.

An energy balance for the double-pipe heat exchanger, shown in Fig. 4.34, is given by

$$dq = \dot{m}_c c_{pc} dT_c = \dot{m}_h c_{ph} dT_h = U_i (T_h - T_c) dA_i \qquad (4.60)$$

For temperature plots shown in Fig. 4.34, the slope of the ΔT line gives

$$\frac{d\,\Delta T}{dq} = \frac{\Delta T_2 - \Delta T_1}{q} \qquad (4.61)$$

or

$$\frac{1}{U_i \Delta T}\left(\frac{d\,\Delta T}{dA_i}\right) = \frac{\Delta T_2 - \Delta T_1}{q} \qquad (4.62)$$

Integrating,

$$\frac{1}{U_i}\int_{\Delta T_1}^{\Delta T_2}\frac{d\,\Delta T}{\Delta T} = \frac{(\Delta T_2 - \Delta T_1)}{q}\int_0^{A_i} dA_i \qquad (4.63)$$

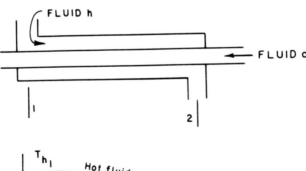

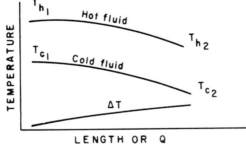

Fig. 4.34 Temperature profile in a tubular heat exchanger.

Thus,

$$q = U_i A_i \frac{(\Delta T_2 - \Delta T_1)}{\ln(\Delta T_2 / \Delta T_1)} \tag{4.64}$$

where

$$\frac{\Delta T_2 - \Delta T_1}{\ln(\Delta T_2 / \Delta T_1)} \equiv \text{log mean temperature difference} \tag{4.65}$$

Equation (4.64) was derived for the counterflow heat exchanger. The same expression can be obtained for a parallel-flow configuration.

EXAMPLE 4.18

A liquid food (specific heat = 4.0 kJ/kg · °C) flows in the inner pipe of a double-pipe heat exchanger. The liquid food enters the heat exchanger at 20°C and exits at 60°C (See Fig. 4.35). The flow rate of the liquid food is 0.5 kg/s. In the annular section, hot water at 90°C enters the heat exchanger and flows countercurrently at a flow rate of 1 kg/s. The average specific heat of water is 4.18 kJ/kg · °C. Assume steady-state conditions.

(1) Calculate the exit temperature of water.
(2) Calculate log-mean temperature difference.
(3) If the average overall heat transfer coefficient is 2000 W/m² · °C and the diameter of the inner pipe is 5 cm, calculate the length of the heat exchanger.
(4) Repeat the above calculations for a parallel-flow configuration.

GIVEN

Liquid food:
Inlet temperature = 20°C
Exit temperature = 60°C
Specific heat = 4.0 kJ/kg · °C
Flow rate = 0.5 kg/s

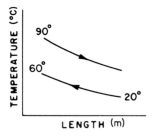

Fig. 4.35 Temperature plots for a counterflow heat exchanger.

Water:
  Inlet temperature = 90°C
  Specific heat = 4.18 kJ/kg · °C
  Flow rate = 1.0 kg/s

Heat exchanger:
  Diameter of inner pipe = 5 cm
  Flow = countercurrent

APPROACH

We will first calculate the exit temperature of hot water by using a simple heat balance equation. Then we will compute log-mean temperature difference. The length of the heat exchanger will be determined from Eq. (4.64). The solution will be repeated for parallel-flow configuration to obtain a new value for log-mean temperature difference and length of the heat exchanger.

SOLUTION

(1) Using a simple heat balance,

$$q = \dot{m}_c c_{pc} \Delta T_c = \dot{m}_h c_{ph} \Delta T_h$$
$$= (0.5 \text{ kg/s})(4 \text{ kJ/kg} \cdot °C)(60°C - 20°C)$$
$$= (1 \text{ kg/s})(4.18 \text{ kJ/kg} \cdot °C)(90°C - T_e °C)$$
$$T_e = 70.9°C$$

(2) The exit temperature of water is 70.9°C.

(3) From Eq. (4.65),

$$(\Delta T)_{lm} = \frac{\Delta(T)_1 - \Delta(T)_2}{\ln\left[\dfrac{\Delta(T)_1}{\Delta(T)_2}\right]} = \frac{(70.9 - 20) - (90 - 60)}{\ln\left(\dfrac{50.9}{.30}\right)} = 39.5°C$$

(4) The log-mean temperature difference is 39.5°C.

(5) From Eq. (4.64),

$$q = UA(\Delta T)_{lm} = U\pi D_i L(\Delta T)_{lm}$$

where q, from step (1), is

$$q = (0.5 \text{ kg/s})(4 \text{ kJ/kg} \cdot °C)(60°C - 20°C) = 80 \text{ kJ/s}$$

Thus,

$$L = \frac{(80 \text{ kJ/s})(1000 \text{ J/kJ})}{(\pi)(0.05 \text{ m})(39.5°C)(2000 \text{ W/m}^2 \cdot °C)} = 6.45 \text{ m}$$

(6) The length of the heat exchanger, when operated countercurrently, is 6.5 m.

(7) For parallel-flow operation, the system diagram will be as shown in Fig. 4.36.

(8) Assuming that for parallel flow the exit temperature will be same as for counterflow, $T_e = 70.9°C$.

(9) Log-mean temperature difference is calculated from Eq. (4.65).

$$(\Delta T)_{lm} = \frac{(90 - 20) - (70.9 - 60)}{\ln\left(\dfrac{90 - 20}{70.9 - 60}\right)} = 31.8°C$$

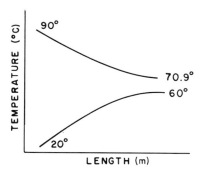

Fig. 4.36   Temperature plots for a parallel-flow heat exchanger.

(10) The log-mean temperature difference for parallel flow is 31.8°C, about 8°C less than that for the countercurrent flow arrangement.

(11) The length can be computed as in step (5).

$$L = \frac{(80 \text{ kJ/s})(1000 \text{ J/kJ})}{(\pi)(0.05 \text{ m})(31.8°\text{C})(2000 \text{ W/m}^2 \cdot °\text{C})} = 8 \text{ m}$$

(12) The length of the heat exchanger, when operated as parallel flow, is 8 m. This length of heat exchanger is longer by 1.55 m to obtain the same exit temperature of hot-water stream as for the counterflow arrangement.

EXAMPLE 4.19

Steam with 90% quality, at a pressure of 143.27 kPa, is condensing in the outer annular space of a 5-m-long double-pipe heat exchanger (see Fig. 4.37). Liquid food is flowing at a rate of 0.5 kg/s in the inner pipe. The inner pipe has an inside diameter of 5 cm. The specific heat of the liquid food is 3.9 kJ/kg · °C.

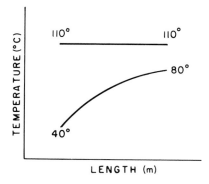

Fig. 4.37   Temperature plots for a double-pipe heat exchanger.

The inlet temperature of the liquid food is 40°C and the exit temperature is 80°C.

(a) Calculate the average overall heat-transfer coefficient.
(b) If the resistance to conductive heat transfer caused by the inner steel pipe is negligible, and the convective heat-transfer coefficient on the steam side is very large (approaches infinity), estimate the convective heat-transfer coefficient for the liquid food in the inside pipe.

GIVEN

Steam pressure = 143.27 kPa
Length = 5 m
Flow rate of liquid = 0.5 kg/s
Inside diameter = 0.05 m
Specific heat = 3.9 kJ/kg · °C
Product inlet temperature = 40°C
Product exit temperature = 80°C

APPROACH

We will obtain steam temperature from Table A.4.2. We also note that steam quality has no effect on the steam condensation temperature. We will calculate the heat required to raise the liquid food temperature from 40 to 80°C. Next, we will calculate log-mean temperature difference. Then we will obtain the overall heat-transfer coefficient by equating the heat gain of the liquid food and heat transfer across the pipe wall, from steam to the liquid food.

SOLUTION

Part (a)

(1) From steam table (Table A.4.2), steam temperature = 110°C.
(2)

$$q = \dot{m}c_p \, \Delta T$$
$$= (0.5 \text{ kg/s})(3.9 \text{ kJ/kg} \cdot °C)(1000 \text{ J/kJ})(80°C - 40°C)$$
$$= 78,000 \text{ J/s}$$

(3)

$$q = UA(\Delta T)_{lm} = \dot{m}c_p \, \Delta T$$

$$(\Delta T)_{lm} = \frac{(110 - 40) - (110 - 80)}{\ln\left(\dfrac{110 - 40}{110 - 80}\right)} = 47.2°C$$

and

$$A = \pi(0.05)(5) = 0.785 \text{ m}^2$$

(4)

$$U = \frac{\dot{m}c_p \, \Delta T}{A(\Delta T)_{lm}} = \frac{(78,000 \text{ J/s})}{(0.785 \text{ m}^2)(47.2°C)} = 2105 \text{ W/m}^2 \cdot °C$$

(5) Overall heat-transfer coefficient = 2105 W/m² · °C

Part (b)

The overall heat-transfer equation may be written as follows:

$$\frac{1}{U_i A_i} = \frac{1}{h_i A_i} + \frac{\Delta r}{k A_{lm}} + \frac{1}{h_o A_o}$$

The second term on the right-hand side of the above equation is zero, since the resistance offered by steel to conductive heat transfer is considered negligible. Likewise, the third term is zero, because the convective heat-transfer coefficient is very large. Therefore,

$$U_i = h_i$$

or

$$h_i = 2105 \text{ W/m}^2 \cdot {}^\circ\text{C}$$

4.4.8 Importance of Surface Characteristics in Radiative Heat Transfer

All materials in the universe emit radiation of an electromagnetic nature based on their surface temperature. At temperature of 0° K the emission of radiation ceases. The characteristics of the radiation are also dependent on temperature. As temperature increases the wavelength decreases, for example, radiation emitted by the sun is shortwave compared to the longwave radiation emitted by the surface of a coffee mug.

When radiation of a given wavelength, as shown in Fig. 4.38, is incident on an object, the following expression holds true:

$$\phi + \chi + \psi = 1 \tag{4.66}$$

where ϕ is absorptivity, χ is reflectivity, and ψ is transmissivity.

As shown in Fig. 4.38, some of the incident radiation is reflected, some transmitted, and some absorbed. The absorbed radiation will result in increase of temperature.

To compare the absorption of radiation for different materials, an ideal reference called a blackbody is used. For a blackbody, the absorptivity value is 1.0. It should be noted that nothing in the universe is a true blackbody; even lampblack has $\phi = 0.99$ and $\chi = 0.01$. Regardless, blackbody is a useful concept for comparing radiative properties of different materials.

The absolute magnitudes of ϕ, χ, and ψ depend on the nature of the incident radiation. Thus, a brick wall of a house is opaque to visible light but transparent to radio waves.

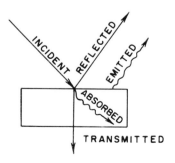

TRANSMITTED

Fig. 4.38 Radiant energy incident on a semiopaque object.

The difference between energy radiated and energy reflected must be clearly distinguished. These are quite different terms. A material, depending on its surface absorptivity value, will reflect some of the incident radiation. In addition, based on its own temperature it will emit radiation, as shown in Fig. 4.38. The amount of radiation emitted can be computed from Eq. (4.11).

Kirchoff's law states that the emissivity of a body is equal to its absorptivity for the same wavelength. Thus, mathematically,

$$\varepsilon = \phi \tag{4.67}$$

The use of this identity is discussed in the following example.

EXAMPLE 4.20

Compare the selection of white paint versus black paint for painting the rooftop of a warehouse. The objective is to allow minimum heat gain from the sun during summer.

GIVEN

White paint from Table 4.3:

$$\varepsilon_{\text{shortwave}} = 0.18$$
$$\varepsilon_{\text{longwave}} = 0.95$$

Black paint from Table 4.3:

$$\varepsilon_{\text{shortwave}} = 0.97$$
$$\varepsilon_{\text{longwave}} = 0.96$$

APPROACH

From the emissivity values, we will examine the use of white or black paint for both short- and longwave radiation.

SOLUTION

(1) White paint: $\varepsilon_{\text{shortwave}} = 0.18$, so $\chi_{\text{shortwave}} = 1 - 0.18$, assuming $\psi = 0$, and thus $\chi_{\text{shortwave}} = 0.82$. Thus, of the total shortwave radiation incident on rooftop, 18% is absorbed and 82% reflected.

(2) White paint, $\varepsilon_{\text{longwave}} = 0.95$. The white-painted surface, in terms of longwave radiation, emits 95% of radiation emitted by a blackbody.

(3) Black paint: $\varepsilon_{\text{shortwave}} = 0.97$, therefore $\phi_{\text{shortwave}} = 0.97$. Thus, of the total shortwave radiation incident on rooftop, 97% of radiation incident on it is absorbed and 3% is reflected.

(4) Black paint: $\varepsilon_{\text{longwave}} = 0.96$. The black-painted surface, in terms of longwave radiation, emits 96% of radiation emitted by a blackbody.

(5) White paint should be selected, as it absorbs only 18% shortwave (solar) radiation compared to 97% by black paint. Both black paint and white paint are similar in emitting longwave radiation to the surroundings.

4.4.9   Radiative Heat Transfer between Two Objects

The transfer of heat by radiation between two surfaces is dependent on the emissivity of the radiating surface and the absorptivity of that same surface. The expression normally used to describe this type of heat transfer is as follows:

$$q_{1-2} = A\sigma\left(\varepsilon_1 T_{A1}^4 - \phi_{1-2} T_{A2}^4\right) \qquad (4.68)$$

where ε_1 is the emissivity of the radiating surface at temperature T_{A1} and ϕ_{1-2} is the absorptivity of the surface for radiation emitted at temperature T_{A2}.

Although the basic expression describing radiative heat transfer are given by Eqs. (4.11) and (4.68), one of the important factors that requires attention is the shape of the object. The shape factor accounts for the fraction of the radiation emitted by the high-temperature surface that is not absorbed by the low-temperature surface. For example, Eq. (4.68) assumes that all radiation emitted at temperature T_{A1} is absorbed by the surface at temperature T_{A2}. If both the surfaces are blackbodies, then the expression describing heat transfer and incorporating the shape factor would be as follows:

$$q_{1-2} = \sigma F_{1-2} A_1\left(T_{A1}^4 - T_{A2}^4\right) \qquad (4.69)$$

where F_{1-2} is the shape factor, and it physically represents the fraction of the total radiation leaving the surface A_1 that is intercepted by the surface A_2. The values of shape factors have been tabulated and presented in the form of curves of the type shown in Figs. 4.39 and 4.40. In the first case, the shape factors deal only with adjacent rectangles, which are in perpendicular planes. Figure 4.40 can be utilized for various shapes, including disks, squares, and rectangles.

Equation (4.69) does not account for nonblackbodies, and Eq. (4.11) does not account for the shape factor; therefore, an expression that combines the two must be used. Such an expression would be

$$q_{1-2} = \sigma A_1 \zeta_{1-2}\left(T_{A1}^4 - T_{A2}^4\right) \qquad (4.70)$$

where the ζ_{1-2} factor accounts for both shape and emissivity. This factor can be evaluated by the following expression:

$$\zeta_{1-2} = \cfrac{1}{\cfrac{1}{F_{1-2}} + \left(\cfrac{1}{\varepsilon_1} - 1\right) + \cfrac{A_1}{A_2}\left(\cfrac{1}{\varepsilon_2} - 1\right)} \qquad (4.71)$$

Equations (4.70) and (4.71) can be used to compute the net radiant heat transfer between two gray bodies in the presence of radiating surfaces at uniform temperatures.

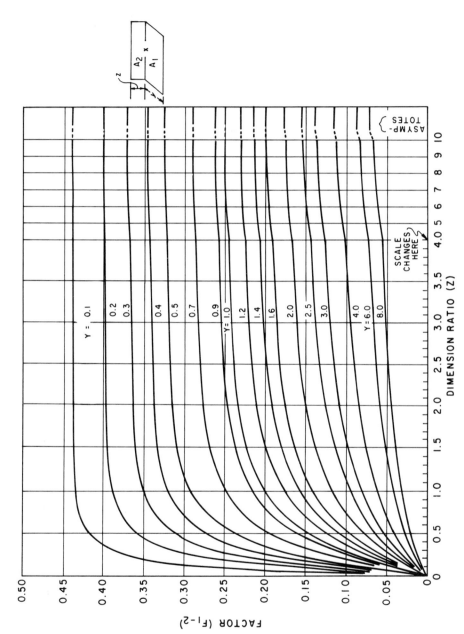

Fig. 4.39 Shape factors for adjacent rectangles in perpendicular planes. Y(dimension ratio) $= y/x$; $Z = z/x$. [Adapted from Hottel (1930).]

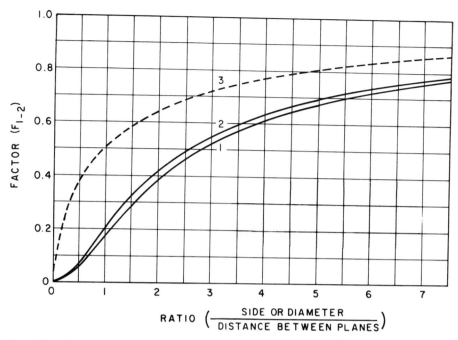

Fig. 4.40 Shape factors for equal and parallel squares, rectangles, and disks. (1) Direct radiation between disks; (2) direct radiation between squares; (3) total radiation between squares or disks connected by nonconducting but reradiating walls. [Adapted from Hottel (1930).]

EXAMPLE 4.21

Compute the radiative heat transfer received by a rectangular product moving through a radiation-type heater. (See Fig. 4.41.) The radiation source is one vertical wall of the heater and is held at a constant temperature of 200°C while the product is moving perpendicular to the radiation source. The product temperature is 80°C with an emissivity of 0.8. The product dimensions are 15 × 20 cm, while the radiation source is 1 × 5 m.

GIVEN

> Temperature of heater = 200°C
> Product temperature = 80°C
> Emissivity of product = 0.8
> Product dimensions = 0.15 m × 0.2 m
> Heater dimensions = 1 m × 5 m

APPROACH

To compute ζ_{1-2} factor from Eq. (4.70) we will use Fig. 4.39, for objects perpendicular to each other, for F_{1-2} value. Then we will use Eq. (4.70) to calculate radiative heat received by the rectangular product.

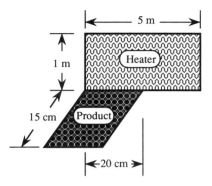

Fig. 4.41 Radiation heater.

SOLUTION

(1) To use Eq. (4.70), the ζ factor must be computed from Eq. (4.71).

$$\zeta_{1-2} = \cfrac{1}{\cfrac{1}{F_{1-2}} + \left(\cfrac{1}{1} - 1\right) + \cfrac{5}{0.03}\left(\cfrac{1}{0.8} - 1\right)}$$

where F_{1-2} must be obtained from Fig. 4.39 for $z/x = 5.0$ and $y/x = 0.75$.

$$F_{1-2} = 0.28$$

Then

$$\zeta_{1-2} = \frac{1}{(3.57 + 0 + 41.67)} = \frac{1}{45.24} = 0.0221$$

(2) From Eq. (4.70),

$$q_{1-2} = \left(5.669 \times 10^{-8} \text{ W/m}^2 \cdot \text{K}^4\right)(0.0221)(5 \text{ m}^2)\left[(473 \text{ K})^4 - (353 \text{ K})^4\right]$$

$$= 216 \text{ W}$$

4.5 Unsteady-State Heat Transfer

Unsteady-state (or transient) heat transfer is that phase of the heating and cooling process when the temperature is changing with time. During this phase, temperature is a function of both location and time. This is in contrast to steady-state heat transfer, when temperature varies only with location. During the initial unsteady-state period, many important reactions in the food may take place. In thermal processes, the unsteady-state phase may even dominate the entire process; for example, in several pasteurization and food sterilization processes unsteady-state period is an important component of the process. Analysis of temperature variations with time during the unsteady-state period is essential in designing such a process.

Fig. 4.42 An infinite cylinder.

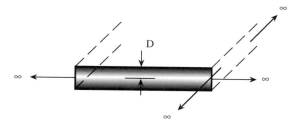

Fig. 4.43 An infinite plate.

Since temperature is a function of two independent variables, time and location, the following partial differential equation is the governing equation for a one-dimensional case:

$$\frac{\partial T}{\partial t} = \frac{k}{\rho c_p}\left(\frac{\partial^2 T}{\partial x^2}\right) \tag{4.72}$$

where T is temperature (°C), t is time (s), and x is location (m). The combination of properties $k/\rho c_p$ is defined as thermal diffusivity, α.

The solution of this governing equation involves the use of advanced mathematics. Myers (1971) gives the complete derivation for various types of boundary-value problems encountered in unsteady-state heat transfer. It is important to note that analytical solution of Eq. (4.72) is possible only for some simplified geometrical shapes such as a sphere, an infinite cylinder, and an infinite slab.

An infinite cylinder refers to a cylinder of finite diameter that is infinitely long along its axis (Fig. 4.42). Similarly, an infinite slab refers to a rectangular slab of one finite dimension (such as thickness), with the other four sides extending to infinity (Fig. 4.43).

4.5.1 Importance of External versus Internal Resistance to Heat Transfer

Consider an object immersed in a fluid (Fig. 4.44). If the fluid is at a temperature different than the initial temperature of the solid, the temperature inside the solid will increase or decrease until it reaches a value in equilibrium with the temperature of the fluid.

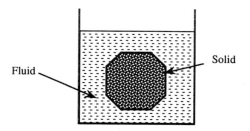

Fig. 4.44 A solid immersed in a fluid experiencing unsteady-state heat transfer.

During the unsteady-state heating period, the temperature inside a solid object (initially at a uniform temperature) will vary with location and time. Assuming the location of interest is at the center of the solid, on immersing the solid in a fluid, the heat transfer from fluid to center of the solid will encounter two resistances: convective resistance in the fluid layer surrounding the solid, and conductive resistance inside the solid. The ratio of the internal resistance to heat transfer in the solid to the external resistance to heat transfer in the fluid is defined as the Biot number N_{Bi}.

$$\frac{\text{Internal resistance to heat transfer}}{\text{External resistance to heat transfer}} = N_{\mathrm{Bi}} \qquad (4.73)$$

or

$$N_{\mathrm{Bi}} = \frac{D/k}{1/h} \qquad (4.74)$$

or

$$N_{\mathrm{Bi}} = \frac{hD}{k} \qquad (4.75)$$

where D is a characteristic dimension.

For Biot numbers greater than 40, there is negligible surface resistance to heat transfer; in other words, the h value is considerably higher than k. For Biot numbers less than 0.1, there is negligible internal resistance to heat transfer, indicating the value of k is much larger than the value of h. Between a Biot number of 0.1 and of 40 there is a finite internal and external resistance to heat transfer. Steam condensing on the surface of a broccoli stem will result in negligible surface resistance to heat transfer. On the other hand, a metal can containing hot tomato paste, being cooled in a stream of cold air, will present finite internal and surface resistance to heat transfer. In the following subsections, the three cases are considered separately.

4.5.2 Negligible Internal Resistance to Heat Transfer ($N_{Bi} < 0.1$)

For a Biot number smaller than 0.1, there is a negligible internal resistance to heat transfer. This condition will occur in heating and cooling of most solid metal objects. Such a condition will not occur with solid foods, since the thermal conductivity of a solid food is relatively small.

Negligible internal resistance to heat transfer also means that the temperature is uniform throughout the interior of the object. This condition is accomplished in objects with high thermal conductivity where heat is transferred instantaneously through the object, thus avoiding temperature gradients with location. Another way to obtain such a condition is a well-stirred liquid food in a container. For this case, there will be no temperature gradient with location, as the product is well mixed.

A mathematical expression to describe heat transfer for negligible internal resistance case may be developed as follows.

Consider an object at low uniform temperature, immersed in a hot fluid at temperature T_a. For unsteady-state period, the heat balance gives

$$q = \rho V c_p \frac{dT}{dt} = hA(T_a - T) \tag{4.76}$$

where T_a is the temperature of the surrounding medium and A is the surface area of the object.

By separating variables,

$$\frac{dT}{(T_a - T)} = \frac{hA\,dt}{\rho c_p V} \tag{4.77}$$

$$-\ln(T_a - T)\big|_{T_i}^{T} = \frac{hA}{\rho c_p V} \int_0^t dt \tag{4.78}$$

$$-\ln\left(\frac{T_a - T}{T_a - T_i}\right) = \frac{hAt}{\rho c_p V} \tag{4.79}$$

$$\frac{T_a - T}{T_a - T_i} = e^{-(hA/\rho c_p V)t} \tag{4.80}$$

The above exponential expression may be used for cases involving heating/cooling with negligible internal resistance to heat transfer.

EXAMPLE 4.22

Calculate the temperature of tomato juice (density = 980 kg/m³) in a steam-jacketed hemispherical kettle after 5 min of heating. (See Fig. 4.45.) The radius of the kettle is 0.5 m. The convective heat-transfer coefficient in the steam jacket is 5000 W/m² · °C. The inside surface temperature of the kettle is 90°C. The initial temperature of tomato juice is 20°C. Assume specific heat of tomato juice is 3.95 kJ/kg · °C.

GIVEN

    Kettle:
        Surface temperature $T_a = 90°C$
        Radius of kettle = 0.5 m

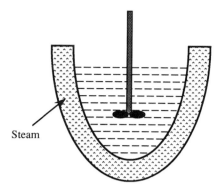

Fig. 4.45 Heating tomato juice in a hemispherical steam-jacketed kettle.

Tomato juice:
  Initial temperature $T_i = 20°C$
  Specific heat $c_p = 3.95$ kJ/kg · °C
  Density $\rho = 980$ kg/m³
Time of heating $t = 5$ min

APPROACH

Since the product is well mixed, there are no temperature gradients inside the vessel, and we have negligible internal resistance to heat transfer. We will use Eq. (4.80) to find the temperature after 5 min.

SOLUTION

(1) We will use Eq. (4.80). First, the inside surface area and volume of the hemispherical kettle is computed.

$$A = 2\pi r^2 = 2\pi(0.5)^2 = 1.57 \text{ m}^2$$

$$V = \tfrac{2}{3}\pi r^3 = \tfrac{2}{3}\pi(0.5)^3 = 0.26 \text{ m}^3$$

(2) Using Eq. (4.80),

$$\frac{90 - T}{90 - 20} = \exp \frac{-(5000 \text{ W/m}^2 \cdot °C)(1.57 \text{ m}^2)(300 \text{ s})}{(980 \text{ kg/m}^3)(3.95 \text{ kJ/kg} \cdot °C)(1000 \text{ J/kJ})(0.26 \text{ m}^3)}$$

$$\frac{90 - T}{90 - 20} = 0.096$$

$$T = 83.3°C$$

(3) The product temperature will rise to 83.3°C in 5 min of heating.

EXAMPLE 4.23

An experiment was conducted to determine surface convective heat-transfer coefficient for peas being frozen in an air-blast freezer. For this purpose, a metal analog of peas was used. The analog was a solid copper ball with a diameter of 1 cm. A small hole was drilled to the center of the copper ball, and a thermocouple junction was located at the center using a high conductivity epoxy. The density of copper is 8954 kg/m^3, and its specific heat is 3830 kJ/kg K. The copper ball (at a uniform initial temperature of 10°C) was hung in the path of air flow (at −40°C) and the center temperature indicated by the thermocouple was recorded. The following table lists the temperatures at one-minute intervals for 14 minutes. Determine the surface heat-transfer coefficient from these data.

Time (s)	Temperature (°C)
0	10.00
60	9.00
120	8.00
180	7.00
240	6.00
300	5.00
360	4.00
420	3.50
480	2.50
540	1.00
600	1.00
660	0.00
720	−2.00
780	−2.00
840	−3.00

GIVEN

Diameter of copper ball $D = 1$ cm
Density of copper $\rho = 8954$ kg/m^3
Specific heat of copper $c_p = 3830$ J/kg K
Initial temperature of copper $T_i = 10$°C
Temperature of cold air $= -40$°C

APPROACH

We will use a modified form of Eq. (4.80) to plot the temperature–time data. If these data are plotted on a semilog paper, we can obtain the h value from the slope. An alternative approach is to use statistical software to develop a correlation and determine the slope.

SOLUTION

(1) Equation 4.80 may be rewritten as follows:

$$\ln(T - T_a) = \ln(T_i - T_a) - \frac{hAt}{\rho c_p V}$$

(2) The tabulated data on temperature time is converted to $\ln(T - T_a)$.

(3) Using a statistical software (e.g., STATVIEW™), a correlation is obtained between t and $\ln(T - T_a)$. The results are

$$\text{slope} = -3.5595 \times 10^{-4} \quad 1/\text{s}$$

(4) Thus,

$$\frac{hA}{\rho c_\mathrm{p} V} = 3.5595 \times 10^{-4}$$

(5) Surface area of sphere, $A = 4\pi r^2$

Volume of sphere, $V = 4\pi r^3/3$

(6) Substituting given and calculated values in the expression in step (4), we get

$$h = 20 \ \mathrm{W/m^2 \, ^\circ C}$$

(7) A pea held in the same place as the copper ball in the blast of air will experience a convective heat-transfer coefficient of 20 W/m² °C.

4.5.3   Finite Internal and Surface Resistance to Heat Transfer (0.1 < N$_{\mathrm{Bi}}$ < 40)

The solutions of Eq. (4.72) for well-defined shapes such as sphere, infinite cylinder, and infinite slab are complicated.

These solutions have been reduced to temperature–time charts, as shown in Figs. 4.46, 4.47, and 4.48. These temperature–time charts introduce a new dimensionless number, called the Fourier[2] number.

$$\text{Fourier number} = N_{\mathrm{Fo}} = \frac{k}{\rho c_\mathrm{p}} \frac{t}{D^2} = \frac{\alpha t}{D^2} \qquad (4.81)$$

where D is a characteristic dimension. The value for D indicates the shortest distance from the surface to the center of the object.

For a sphere, D equals radius of the sphere; for an infinite cylinder, D equals radius of the cylinder; and for an infinite slab, D equals half the thickness of the slab.

The physical significance of the Fourier number can be examined by rearranging Eq. (4.81) as follows:

$$N_{\mathrm{Fo}} = \frac{\alpha t}{D^2} = \frac{k(1/D)D^2}{\rho c_\mathrm{p} D^3/t}$$

$$= \frac{\text{rate of heat conduction across } D \text{ in volume } D^3 \ (\mathrm{W/^\circ C})}{\text{rate of heat storage in volume } D^3 \ (\mathrm{W/^\circ C})}$$

For a given volume element, the Fourier number is a measure of the rate of heat conduction per unit rate of heat storage. Thus, a larger value

---

2. Joseph Baron Fourier (1768–1830) was a French mathematician and highly regarded Egyptologist. In 1798, he accompanied Napoleon to Egypt and conducted extensive research on Egyptian antiques. From 1798 to 1801 he served as a Secretary of Institut d'Egypte in Cairo. His work *Theorie analytique de la chaleur* (The Analytical Theory of Heat) was started in 1807 in Grenoble and was completed in 1822 in Paris. He developed a mathematical basis for the conductive heat transfer in solids.

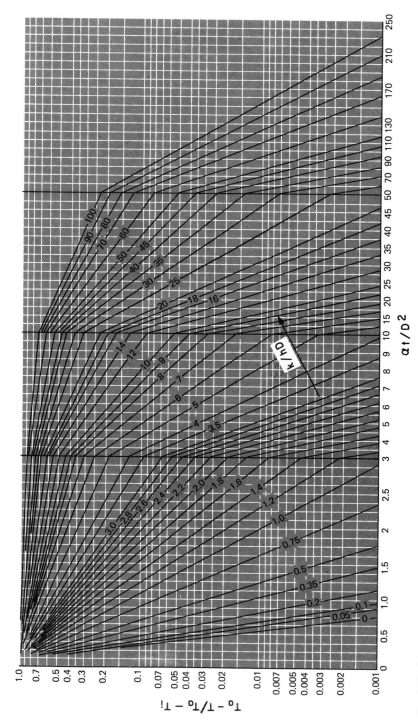

Fig. 4.46 Temperature at geometric center of a sphere of radius D. [From Holman (1990).]

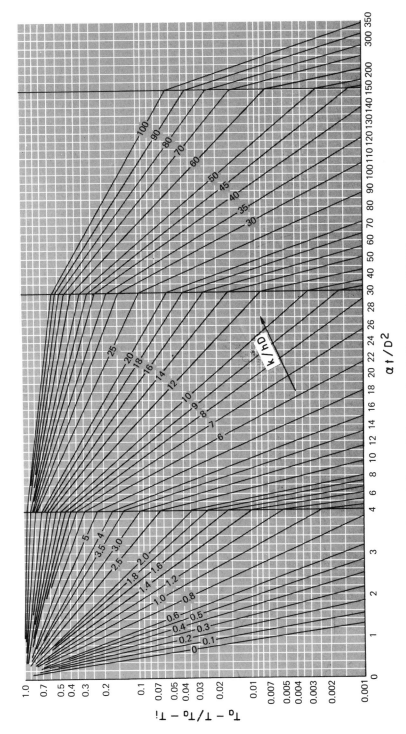

Fig. 4.47 Temperature at the axis of an infinitely long cylinder of radius D. [From Holman (1990).]

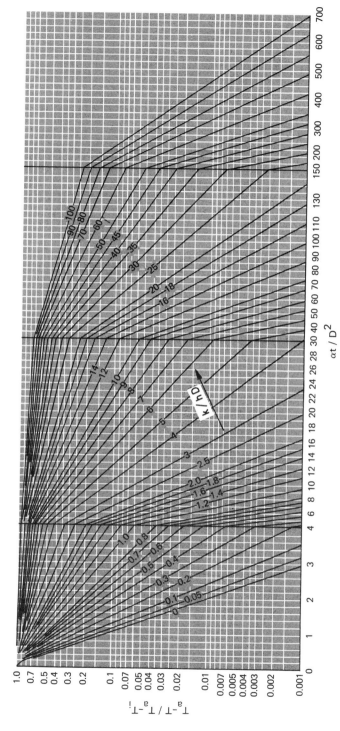

Fig. 4.48 Temperature at the midplane of an infinite slab of thickness $2D$. [From Holman (1990).]

197

of Fourier number indicates deep penetration of heat into the solid in a given period of time.

On the ordinate of the temperature–time chart in Figs. 4.46, 4.47, and 4.48, the temperature ratio

$$\frac{T_a - T}{T_a - T_i}$$

is plotted on a log scale, whereas the Fourier number is plotted on adjoining linear scales on the abscissa. In the above temperature ratio, T is the variable temperature at time t, T_i is the initial temperature, and T_a is the temperature of the surrounding medium. This temperature ratio may be viewed as the unaccomplished rise (or fall) in temperature at a given time. The denominator of this ratio, $T_a - T_i$, is the maximum possible temperature rise (or fall). The numerator, $T_a - T$, is the temperature change at time t.

4.5.4   Negligible Surface Resistance to Heat Transfer ($N_{Bi} > 40$)

For situations where the Biot number is greater than 40, indicating negligible surface resistance to heat transfer, Figs. 4.46, 4.47, and 4.48 may be used. The lines for $k/hD = 0$ represent negligible surface resistance to heat transfer.

4.5.5   Finite Objects

It has been shown mathematically (Myers, 1971) that

$$\left(\frac{T_a - T}{T_a - T_i}\right)_{\substack{\text{finite} \\ \text{cylinder}}} = \left(\frac{T_a - T}{T_a - T_i}\right)_{\substack{\text{infinite} \\ \text{cylinder}}} \left(\frac{T_a - T}{T_a - T_i}\right)_{\substack{\text{infinite} \\ \text{slab}}} \tag{4.82}$$

and

$$\left(\frac{T_a - T}{T_a - T_i}\right)_{\substack{\text{finite} \\ \text{brick shape}}} = \left(\frac{T_a - T}{T_a - T_i}\right)_{\substack{\text{infinite} \\ \text{slab, width}}} \left(\frac{T_a - T}{T_a - T_i}\right)_{\substack{\text{infinite} \\ \text{slab, depth}}}$$

$$\times \left(\frac{T_a - T}{T_a - T_i}\right)_{\substack{\text{infinite} \\ \text{slab, height}}} \tag{4.83}$$

These expressions allow determination of temperature ratios for objects of finite geometry, such as a cylindrical can commonly used in heat sterilization of foods. Although the mathematics to prove Eqs. (4.82) and (4.83) is

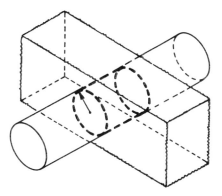

Fig. 4.49 A finite cylinder considered as part of an infinite cylinder and an infinite slab.

beyond the scope of this text, Fig. 4.49 may be studied as a visual aid. The finite cylinder can be visualized as a part of an infinite cylinder and a part of an infinite slab. Heat transfer in a radial direction is similar to heat transfer for an infinite cylinder. Invoking the infinite cylinder shape, we mean that heat transfer to the geometric center is only through the radial direction, while the ends of the cylinder are too far to have any measurable influence on heat transfer. Heat transfer from the two end surfaces is similar to heat transfer for an infinite slab. Considering the finite cylinder to be an infinite slab will account for all the heat transfer from the two ends of the cylindrical can while ignoring heat transfer in the radial direction. This approach allows us to include heat transfer both from the radial direction and the cylinder ends. Similarly, a brick-shaped object can be considered to be constructed from three infinite slabs maintaining width, depth, and height, respectively, as the finite thickness.

4.5.6 Procedures to Use Temperature–Time Charts

The following steps may be used when examining heat transfer in finite objects with the use of temperature–time charts.

Heat transfer to an object of finite cylindrical shape, such as a cylindrical can, requires the use of temperature–time charts for both infinite cylinder and infinite slab. Thus, if the temperature at the geometric center of the finite cylinder is required at a given time, the following steps may be used.

A. For an infinite cylinder:

(1) Calculate the Fourier number, using radius of the cylinder as the characteristic dimension.

(2) Calculate the Biot number, using radius of the cylinder as the characteristic dimension.

(3) Use Fig. 4.47 to find temperature ratio:

$$\left(\frac{T_a - T}{T_a - T_i} \right)_{\text{infinite cylinder}}$$

B. For an infinite slab:

(1) Calculate the Fourier number, using half-height (or half-length) as the characteristic dimension.

(2) Calculate the Biot number, using half-height (or half-length) as characteristic dimension.

(3) Use Fig. 4.48 to determine temperature ratio:

$$\left(\frac{T_a - T}{T_a - T_i} \right)_{\text{infinite slab}}$$

The temperature ratio for a finite cylinder is then calculated from Eq. (4.82). The temperature at the geometric center can be computed if surrounding medium temperature T_a and initial temperature T_i are known.

Steps similar to those above may be used to compute temperature at the geometric center for a finite slab-shaped object (such as a parallelepiped or a cube). In the case of a spherical object, such as an orange, Fig. 4.46 for a sphere is used.

The following examples are given to illustrate the procedures presented in this section.

EXAMPLE 4.24

Estimate the time when the temperature at the geometric center of a 6 cm diameter apple held in a 2°C water stream reaches 3°C. The initial uniform temperature of the apple is 15°C. The convective heat transfer coefficient in water surrounding the apple is 50 W/m² · °C. The properties of the apple are thermal conductivity $k = 0.355$ W/m · °C; specific heat $c_p = 3.6$ kJ/kg · °C; and density $\rho = 820$ kg/m³.

GIVEN

Diameter of apple = 0.06 m
Convective heat-transfer coefficient $h = 50$ W/m² · °C
Temperature of water stream $T_a = 2$°C
Initial temperature of apple $T_i = 15$°C
Final temperature of geometric center $T = 3$°C
Thermal conductivity $k = 0.355$ W/m · °C
Specific heat $c_p = 3.6$ kJ/kg · °C
Density $\rho = 820$ kg/m³

APPROACH

Considering an apple to be a sphere in shape, we will use Fig. 4.46 to find the Fourier number. The time of cooling will be computed from Eq. (4.81).

SOLUTION

(1) From given temperatures, we first calculate the temperature ratio.

$$\left(\frac{T_a - T}{T_a - T_i}\right) = \frac{2 - 3}{2 - 15} = 0.077$$

(2) The Biot number is computed as

$$N_{Bi} = \frac{hD}{k} = \frac{\left(50 \text{ W/m}^2 \cdot {}^\circ\text{C}\right)\left(0.03 \text{ m}\right)}{\left(0.355 \text{ W/m} \cdot {}^\circ\text{C}\right)} = 4.23$$

Thus,

$$1/N_{Bi} = 0.237$$

(3) From Fig. 4.46, for a temperature ratio of 0.077 and $(1/N_{Bi})$ of 0.237, the Fourier number can be read as

$$N_{Fo} = 0.5$$

(4) The time is calculated from the Fourier number.

$$\frac{k}{\rho c_P}\frac{t}{D^2} = 0.5$$

$$t = \frac{\left(0.5\right)\left(820 \text{ kg/m}^3\right)\left(3.6 \text{ kJ/kg} \cdot {}^\circ\text{C}\right)\left(0.03 \text{ m}\right)^2\left(1000 \text{ J/kJ}\right)}{\left(0.355 \text{ W/m} \cdot {}^\circ\text{C}\right)}$$

$$= 3742 \text{ s}$$

$$= 1.04 \text{ hr}$$

EXAMPLE 4.25

Estimate the temperature at the geometric center of a food product contained in a 303 × 406 can exposed to boiling water at 100°C for 30 min. The product is assumed to heat and cool by conduction. The initial uniform temperature of the product is 35°C. The properties of the food are thermal conductivity $k = 0.34$ W/m · °C; specific heat $c_p = 3.5$ kJ/kg · °C; and density $\rho = 900$ kg/m³. The convective heat transfer coefficient for the boiling water is estimated to be 2000 W/m² · °C.

GIVEN

Can dimensions:

$$\text{Diameter} = 3\tfrac{3}{16} \text{ inches} = 0.081 \text{ m}$$

$$\text{Height} = 4\tfrac{7}{16} \text{ inches} = 0.11 \text{ m}$$

Convective heat transfer coefficient $h = 2000 \text{ W/m}^2 \cdot {}^\circ\text{C}$
Temperature of heating media $T_a = 100^\circ\text{C}$
Initial temperature of food $T_i = 35^\circ\text{C}$
Time of heating $= 30 \text{ min} = 1800 \text{ s}$
Properties:

$$k = 0.34 \text{ W/m} \cdot {}^\circ\text{C}$$

$$c_p = 3.5 \text{ kJ/kg} \cdot {}^\circ\text{C}$$

$$\rho = 900 \text{ kg/m}^3$$

APPROACH

Since a finite cylindrical can may be considered a combination of infinite cylinder and infinite slab, we will use time–temperature figures for both these shapes to find respective temperature ratios. The temperature ratio for a finite cylinder will then be calculated from Eq. (4.82).

SOLUTION

(1) First, we estimate temperature ratio for an infinite cylinder.
(2) Biot number $= hD/k$ where D is radius $= 0.081/2 = 0.0405 \text{ m}$

$$N_{Bi} = \frac{(2000 \text{ W/m}^2 \cdot {}^\circ\text{C})(0.0405 \text{ m})}{(0.34 \text{ W/m} \cdot {}^\circ\text{C})} = 238$$

Thus,

$$1/N_{Bi} = 0.004$$

(3) The Fourier number for an infinite cylinder is

$$N_{Fo} = \frac{k}{\rho c_p}\left(\frac{t}{D^2}\right)$$

$$= \frac{(0.34 \text{ W/m} \cdot {}^\circ\text{C})(1800 \text{ s})}{(900 \text{ kg/m}^3)(3.5 \text{ kJ/kg} \cdot {}^\circ\text{C})(1000 \text{ J/kJ})(0.0405 \text{ m})^2}$$

$$= 0.118$$

(4) The temperature ratio can be estimated from Fig. 4.47 for $1/N_{Bi} = 0.004$ and $N_{Fo} = 0.118$ as

$$\left(\frac{T_a - T}{T_a - T_i}\right)_{\text{infinite cylinder}} = 0.8$$

(5) Next, we estimate the temperature ratio for an infinite slab.
(6) Biot number $= hD/k$ where D is half-height $= 0.111/2 = 0.055 \text{ m}$

$$N_{Bi} = \frac{(2000 \text{ W/m}^2 \cdot {}^\circ\text{C})(0.055 \text{ m})}{(0.34 \text{ W/m} \cdot {}^\circ\text{C})} = 323.5$$

Thus,

$$1/N_{\text{Bi}} = 0.003$$

(7) The Fourier number for an infinite slab is

$$N_{\text{Fo}} = \frac{kt}{\rho c_p D^2}$$

$$= \frac{(0.34 \text{ W/m} \cdot {}^\circ\text{C})(1800 \text{ s})}{(900 \text{ kg/m}^3)(3.5 \text{ kJ/kg} \cdot {}^\circ\text{C})(1000 \text{ J/kJ})(0.055 \text{ m})^2}$$

$$= 0.064$$

(8) The temperature ratio can be estimated from Fig. 4.48 for $1/N_{\text{Bi}} = 0.003$ and $N_{\text{Fo}} = 0.064$ as

$$\left(\frac{T_a - T}{T_a - T_i}\right)_{\text{infinite slab}} = 0.99$$

(9) The temperature ratio for a finite cylinder is computed using Eq. (4.82).

$$\left(\frac{T_a - T}{T_a - T_i}\right)_{\text{finite cylinder}} = (0.8)(0.99) = 0.792$$

Therefore,

$$T = T_a - 0.792(T_a - T_i)$$

$$= 100 - 0.792(100 - 35)$$

$$= 48.4{}^\circ\text{C}$$

(10) The temperature at the geometric center of the can after 30 min will be 48.4°C. Note that most of the heat transfers radially; only a small amount of heat transfers axially, since

$$\left(\frac{T_a - T}{T_a - T_i}\right)_{\text{infinite slab}} = 0.99$$

or a value close to 1. If

$$\left(\frac{T_a - T}{T_a - T_i}\right) = 1$$

then $T = T_i$; this means that the temperature at the end of the heating period is still T_i, the initial temperature, indicating no transfer of heat. Conversely, if

$$\left(\frac{T_a - T}{T_a - T_i}\right) = 0$$

then $T_a = T$, indicating that the temperature at the end-of-heating period equals that of the surrounding temperature.

EXAMPLE 4.26

The following solutions of the governing equation for unsteady-state heat transfer [Eq. (4.72)] have been suggested by Whitaker (1977) and Heldman and

Singh (1981). These solutions are for situations involving Biot numbers greater than 40.

Infinite cylinder

$$T = T_a + 2(T_i - T_a) \sum_{n=0}^{\infty} \frac{e^{-\lambda_n^2 \alpha t/D^2} J_0(\lambda_n r/D)}{\lambda_n J_1(\lambda_n)} \quad (4.84)$$

Infinite slab

$$T = T_a + (T_i - T_a) \sum_{n=0}^{\infty} \frac{[2(-1)^n] e^{-\lambda_n^2 \alpha t/D^2}}{\lambda_n} \cos(\lambda_n x/D) \quad (4.85)$$

Sphere

$$T = T_a + (T_a - T_i)\frac{2}{\pi}\left(\frac{D}{r}\right)$$

$$\times \sum_{n=1}^{\infty} \frac{(-1)^{n+1}}{n} e^{(-n^2\pi^2\alpha t/D^2)} \sin(n\pi r/D) \quad (4.86)$$

	B	C	D E	F	G	H	I
2	SPHERE - Negligible Surface Resistance to Heat Transfer						
5	Domain: 0<r<D						
7	Example			Terms of Series	=((-1^(E9+1))/E9*EXP(-		
8	Fourier Number =	0.3		n term_n	E9*E9*PI()*PI()*$C$8)*SIN(E9*PI()*$C$9))		
9	r/D =	0.00001		1 1.62651E-06			
10	Results			2 -2.25721E-10			
11	Temperature Ratio =	0.104		3 8.39653E-17	Steps:		
12				4 -8.37219E-26			
13	=SUM(F9:F38)*2/PI()*(1/$C$9)			5 2.23764E-37	1) Enter numbers 1 through 30 in		
14				6 -1.60306E-51	cells E9 through E38.		
15				7 3.07839E-68			
16				8 -1.58455E-87			
17				9 2.1863E-109	2) Enter formula in cell F9, then		
18				10 -8.0855E-134	copy it into cells F10 to F38.		
19				11 8.0154E-161			
20				12 -2.1299E-190	3) Enter formula in cell C11.		
21				13 1.517E-222			
22				14 -2.8963E-257	4) Enter Fourier Number in cell C8		
23				15 1.4822E-294	and radial location/(Characteristic		
24				16 0	Dimension) in cell C9. For a sphere,		
25				17 0	characteristic dimension is radius.		
26				18 0			
27				19 0			
28				20 0	If temperature ratio is desired at the		
29				21 0	center of the sphere, do not use r=0		
30				22 0	instead use a very small number for		
31				23 0	cell C9.		
32				24 0			
33				25 0			
34				26 0	5) The result is shown in Cell C11.		
35				27 0			
36				28 0			
37				29 0			
38				30 0			

Fig. 4.50 Spreadsheet solution (sphere) for Example 4.26.

Using the above equations, develop spreadsheet programs, and compare the calculated results with the values obtained from charts given in Figs. 4.46, 4.47, and 4.48.

APPROACH

We will use spreadsheet EXCEL and program Eqs. (4.84–4.86). Since these equations involve series solutions, we will consider the first 30 terms of each series, which should be sufficiently accurate for our purposes.

SOLUTION

The spreadsheets written for a sphere, infinite cylinder, and infinite slab are shown in Figures 4.50, 4.51 and 4.52, respectively. These spreadsheets also include results for temperature ratios for arbitrarily selected Fourier numbers. The calculated results for temperature ratios compare favorably with those estimated from Figs. 4.46, 4.47, and 4.48.

INFINITE CYLINDER - Negligible Surface Resistance to Heat Transfe

Domain: 0<r<D

	Example			Terms of Series J0 for -3<C<3					J1 for 3<C<inf	
	Fourier Number=	0.2	n	lambda_n	ArgJ0	J0			J1(lambda_n)	term_n
	r/D =	0	0	2.4048255577	0	1	0.820682791	0.195379932	0.519147809	0.251944131
	Results		1	5.5200781103	0	1	0.802645916	3.23090329	-0.340264805	-0.001200985
	Temperature Ratio= 0.5015		2	8.6537279129	0	1	0.799856138	6.340621261	0.271452299	1.33199E-07
			3	11.7915344391	0	1	0.79895277	9.467043934	-0.232459829	-3.0563E-13
			4	14.9309177086	0	1	0.798552578	12.5997901	0.206546432	1.4036E-20
			5	18.0710639679	0	1	0.798341245	15.73559327	-0.187728803	-1.27219E-29
			6	21.2116366299	0	1	0.798216311	18.87310399	0.173265895	2.25935E-40
			7	24.3524715308	0	1	0.798136399	22.01166454	-0.161701553	-7.82877E-53
			8	27.4934791320	0	1	0.798082224	25.15091632	0.152181217	5.27858E-67
			9	30.6346064684	0	1	0.798043816	28.29064728	-0.144165981	-6.91297E-83

Steps:

1) Enter numbers 0 to 9 in cells E9 to E18

2) Enter coefficients as indicated in cells F9 to F18.

3) Enter formulas for cells G9, H9, I9, J9, K9 and L9, and copy into cells G10 to G18, H10 to H18, I10 to I18, J10 to J18, K10 to K18 and L10 to L18, respectively.

4) Enter formula for cell C11

5) Enter Fourier number in cell C8 and r/(characteristic dimension) in cell C9.

6) Results are shown in cell C11

C11: =2*SUM(L9:L18)

G9: =$C$9*F9

H9: =1-2.2499997*(G9/3)^2+1.2656208*(G9/3)^4-0.3163866*(G9/3)^6+0.0444479*(G9/3)^8-0.0039444*(G9/3)^10+0.00021*(G9/3)^12

I9: =0.79788456+0.00000156*(3/F9)+0.01659667*(3/F9)^2+0.00017105*(3/F9)^3-0.00249511*(3/F9)^4+0.00113653*(3/F9)^5-0.00020033*(3/F9)^6

J9: =F9-2.35619449+0.12499612*(3/F9)+0.0000565*(3/F9)^2-0.00637879*(3/F9)^3+0.00074348*(3/F9)^4+0.00079284*(3/F9)^5-0.00029166*(3/F9)^6

K9: =F9^(-1/2)*I9*COS(J9)

L9: =EXP(-F9*F9*$C$8)*H9/(F9*K9)

Fig. 4.51 Spreadsheet solution (infinite cylinder) for Example 4.26.

	A	B	C	D	E	F	G	H
1								
2		INFINITE SLAB - Negligible Surface Resistance to Heat Transfer						
3								
4								
5		Domain: -D<x<D				=(2*E9+1)/2*PI()		
6								
7		Example					Terms of Series	
8		Fourier Number =	1			n	lambda_n	term_n	=(2*(-1)^E9)*EXP(-F9*F9*$C$8)/F9*COS(F9*$C$9)
9		x/D =	0			0	1.570796327	0.107977045	
10		Results				1	4.71238898	-9.62899E-11	
11		Temperature Ratio =	0.1080			2	7.853981634	4.13498E-28	
12						3	10.99557429	-5.65531E-54	
13						4	14.13716694	2.25317E-88	
14		=SUM(G9:G39)				5	17.27875959	-2.5264E-131	
15						6	20.42035225	7.8374E-183	
16		Steps:				7	23.5619449	-6.6622E-243	
17		1) Enter numbers 0 to 30				8	26.70353756	0	
18		in cells E9 to E39				9	29.84513021	0	
19		2) Enter formula in cell F9				10	32.98672286	0	
20		3) copy formula from cell				11	36.12831552	0	
21		F9 to cells F10 to F39.				12	39.26990817	0	
22		4) Enter formula in cell G9.				13	42.41150082	0	
23		5) copy formula from cell				14	45.55309348	0	
24		G9 to cells G10 to G39.				15	48.69468613	0	
25		6) Enter formula in cell				16	51.83627878	0	
26		C11.				17	54.97787144	0	
27		7) Enter Fourier number in				18	58.11946409	0	
28		cell C8 and x/D in cell C9.				19	61.26105675	0	
29		8) Result is shown in cell				20	64.4026494	0	
30		C11.				21	67.54424205	0	
31						22	70.68583471	0	
32						23	73.82742736	0	
33						24	76.96902001	0	
34						25	80.11061267	0	
35						26	83.25220532	0	
36						27	86.39379797	0	
37						28	89.53539063	0	
38						29	92.67698328	0	
39						30	95.81857593	0	

Fig. 4.52   Spreadsheet solution (infinite slab) for Example 4.26.

4.6   Microwave Heating

Electromagnetic radiation is classified by wavelength or frequency. The electromagnetic spectrum between frequencies of 300 MHz and 300 GHz is represented by microwaves. Since microwaves are used in radar, navigational equipment, and communication equipment, their use is regulated by governmental agencies. In the United States, the Federal Communications Commission (FCC) has set aside two frequencies for industrial, scientific, and medical (ISM) apparatus in the microwave range, namely, 915 ± 13 MHz, and 2450 ± 50 MHz. Similar frequencies are regulated worldwide through the International Telecommunication Union (ITU).

Microwaves have certain similarities to visible light. Microwaves can be focused into beams. They can transmit through hollow tubes. Depending on the dielectric properties of a material, they may be reflected or absorbed by the material. Microwaves may also transmit through materials without any absorption. Packaging materials such as glass, ceramics, and most thermoplastic materials allow microwaves to pass through with little or no absorption. When traveling from one material to another, microwaves may change direction, similar to the bending of light rays when they pass from air to water.

In contrast to conventional heating systems, microwaves penetrate a food and heating extends within the entire food material. The rate of heating is therefore more rapid. It is important to note that microwaves generate heat due to their interactions with the food materials. The microwave radiation itself is nonionizing radiation. It is distinctly different from ionizing radiation such as X rays and gamma rays. When foods are exposed to microwave radiation, no known nonthermal effects are produced in food materials (Mertens and Knorr, 1992; IFT, 1989).

The wavelength, frequency, and velocity of electromagnetic waves are related by the following expression.

$$\lambda = v/f \tag{4.87}$$

where, λ is wavelength in meters; f is frequency in hertz; v is velocity $(300 \times 10^8$ m/s).

Using Eq. (4.87), the wavelengths of the permitted ISM frequencies in the microwave range can be calculated as

$$\lambda_{915} = \frac{3 \times 10^8 \ (\text{m/s})}{915 \times 10^6 \ (1/\text{s})} = 0.328 \ \text{m}$$

and

$$\lambda_{2450} = \frac{3 \times 10^8 \ (\text{m/s})}{2450 \times 10^6 \ (1/\text{s})} = 0.122 \ \text{m}$$

4.6.1   Mechanisms of Microwave Heating

The absorption of microwaves by a dielectric material results in the microwaves giving up their energy to the material, with a consequential rise in temperature. The two important mechanisms that explain heat generation in a material placed in a microwave field are ionic polarization and dipole rotation.

a. Ionic Polarization

When an electrical field is applied to food solutions containing ions, the ions move at an accelerated pace due to their inherent charge. The

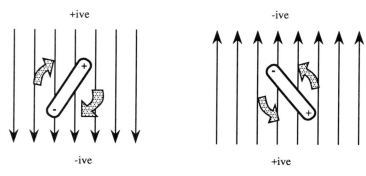

Fig. 4.53 Movement of a dipole in an electrical field. [From Decarau and Peterson (1986).]

resulting collisions between the ions cause the conversion of kinetic energy of the moving ions into thermal energy. A solution with high concentration of ions would have more frequent ionic collisions and therefore exhibit an increase in temperature.

b. Dipole Rotation

Food materials contain polar molecules such as water. These molecules generally have a random orientation. However, when an electric field is applied the molecules orient themselves according to the polarity of the field. In a microwave field, the polarity alternates rapidly (e.g., at the microwave frequency of 2,450 MHz, the polarity changes 2.45 billion cycles per second). The polar molecules rotate to maintain alignment with the rapidly changing polarity (Fig. 4.53). Such rotation of molecules leads to friction with the surrounding medium, and heat is generated. With increasing temperatures, the molecules try to align more rapidly with the applied field. Several factors influence the microwave heating of a material, including the size, shape, state (e.g., water or ice), and properties of the material, and the processing equipment.

4.6.2 Dielectric Properties

In microwave processing we are concerned with the electrical properties of the material being heated. The important electrical properties are the relative dielectric constant ε' and the relative dielectric loss ε''. The term *loss* implies the conversion (or "loss") of electrical energy into heat, and the term *relative* means relative to free space.

The relative dielectric constant ε' expresses the ability of the material to store electrical energy, and the relative dielectric loss ε'' denotes the ability of the material to dissipate the electrical energy. These properties provide an indication of the electrical insulating ability of the material. Foods are in fact very poor insulators; therefore, they generally absorb a large fraction of the energy when placed in a microwave field, resulting in instantaneous heating (Mudgett, 1986). The dielectric loss factor for the material ε'', which expresses the degree to which an externally applied electric field will be converted to heat, is given by

$$\varepsilon'' = \varepsilon' \tan \delta \qquad (4.88)$$

The loss tangent $\tan \delta$ provides an indication of how well the material can be penetrated by an electrical field and how it dissipates electrical energy as heat.

4.6.3 Conversion of Microwave Energy into Heat

The microwave energy in itself is not thermal energy; rather, heating is a consequence of the interactions between microwave energy and a dielectric material. The conversion of the microwave energy to heat can be approximated with the following equation (Decarau and Peterson, 1986; Copson, 1975).

$$P_{\mathrm{D}} = 55.61 \times 10^{-14} E^2 f \varepsilon' \tan \delta \qquad (4.89)$$

where P_{D} is the power dissipation (W/cm^3); E is electrical field strength (V/cm); f is frequency (Hz); ε' is relative dielectric constant, and $\tan \delta$ is the loss tangent.

In Eq. (4.89), the dielectric constant ε' and the loss tangent $\tan \delta$ are the properties of the material, and the electrical field strength E and frequency f represent the energy source. Thus, there is a direct relationship between the material being heated and the microwave system providing the energy for heating. It is evident in Eq. (4.89) that increasing the electrical field strength has a dramatic effect on the power density, since the relationship involves a square term.

The governing heat transfer equation presented earlier in this chapter [Eq. (4.72)] can be modified for use in predicting heat transfer in a material placed in a microwave field. A heat generation term q''' equivalent to the power dissipation obtained from Eq. (4.89) is introduced in Eq. (4.72). Thus for transient heat transfer in an infinite slab, we can obtain the following expression for a one-dimensional case,

$$\frac{\partial^2 T}{\partial x^2} + \frac{q'''}{k} = \frac{\rho c_{\mathrm{p}}}{k} \frac{\partial T}{\partial t} \qquad (4.90)$$

Numerical techniques are used to solve the preceding equation (Mudgett, 1986).

4.6.4 Penetration Depth of Microwaves

The energy transfer between microwaves and the material exposed to the microwave field is influenced by the electrical properties of the material. The distribution of energy within a material is determined by the attenuation factor α'.

The attenuation factor α' is calculated from the values for the loss tangent, relative dielectric constant, and the frequency of the microwave field:

$$\alpha' = \frac{2\pi}{\lambda}\left[\frac{\varepsilon'}{2}\left(\sqrt{1 + \tan^2\delta} - 1\right)\right]^{1/2} \tag{4.91}$$

The penetration of an electrical field can be calculated from the attenuation factor. As shown by von Hippel (1954), the depth Z below the surface of the material at which the electrical field strength is $1/e$ that of the electrical field in the free space is the inverse of the attenuation factor. Thus,

$$Z = \frac{\lambda}{2\pi}\left[\frac{2}{\varepsilon'\left(\sqrt{1 + \tan^2\delta} - 1\right)}\right]^{1/2} \tag{4.92}$$

Noting that frequency and wavelength are inversely related, it is evident from Eq. (4.92) that microwave energy at 915 MHz penetrates more deeply than at 2450 MHz.

In addition to the foregoing description of penetration of a microwave field in a material, the depth of penetration for microwave power is usually described in two different ways. First, the penetration depth is the distance from the surface of a dielectric material where the incident power is decreased to $1/e$ of the incident power. Lambert's expression for power absorption gives,

$$P = P_0 e^{-2\alpha' d} \tag{4.93}$$

where P_0 is the incident power, P is the power at the penetration depth, d is the penetration depth, and α' is the attenuation factor.

If the power is reduced to $1/e$ of the incident power at depth d, we have $P/P_0 = 1/e$. Therefore, from Eq. (4.93), $2\alpha'd = 1$ or $d = 1/2\alpha'$.

The second definition of the penetration depth is stated in terms of half-power depth (i.e., the half-power depth is the distance from the surface of a material where the power is one-half of the incident power). Therefore, at half-power depth $P/P_0 = 1/2$. From Eq. (4.93), $e^{-2\alpha'd} = 1/2$, and solving for d we get $d = 0.347/\alpha'$.

EXAMPLE 4.27

In a paper on microwave properties, Mudgett (1986) provides data on dielectric constants and loss tangents for raw potatoes. For a microwave frequency of

2450 MHz and at 20°C, the dielectric current is 64 and the loss tangent is 0.23. Determine the attenuation factor, the field penetration depth, and the depth below the surface of a potato at which the microwave power is reduced to one-half of the incident power.

APPROACH

We will use Eqs. (4.91) and (4.92) to determine the attenuation factor and the penetration depth for the microwave field, respectively. The distance from the surface of the material at which the power is reduced to one-half of the incident power will be calculated using modifications of Eq. (4.93).

SOLUTION

(1) From Eq. (4.91)

$$\alpha' = \frac{2\pi \times 2450 \times 10^6 (1/s)}{3 \times 10^8 (m/s) \times 100 (cm/m)} \left[\frac{64}{2} \left(\sqrt{1 + (0.23)^2} - 1 \right) \right]^{1/2}$$

$$\alpha' = 0.469 \ (cm^{-1})$$

(2) The penetration depth for the microwave field is the inverse of α' as seen in Eq. (4.92). Therefore,

$$\text{Field penetration depth} = Z = 1/\alpha' = 1/0.469 = 2.13 \ cm$$

(3) To obtain the half-power depth of penetration, we use the modification of Lambert's expression, Eq. (4.93), and solve for d.

$$d = \frac{0.347}{\alpha'} = \frac{0.347}{0.469} = 0.74 \ cm$$

(4) The half-power depth for potatoes at 2450 MHz and 20°C is calculated to be 0.74 cm.

4.6.5 Microwave Oven

A typical microwave oven consists of the following major components (Fig. 4.54):

Power supply   The purpose of the power supply is to draw electrical power from the line and convert it to the high voltage required by the magnetron. The magnetron usually requires several thousand volts of direct current.

Magnetron or power tube   The magnetron is an oscillator capable of converting the power supplied into microwave energy. The magnetron emits high-frequency radiant energy. The polarity of the emitted radiation changes between negative and positive at high frequencies (e.g., 24.5 billion times per second for a magnetron operating at a frequency of 2450 MHz, the most common frequency used for domestic ovens).

Wave guide or transmission section   The wave guide propagates, radiates, or transfers the generated energy from the magnetron to the oven

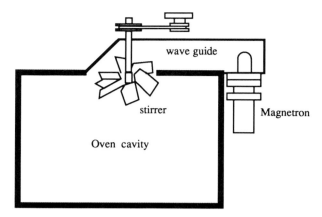

Fig. 4.54 Major components of a microwave oven.

cavity. In a domestic oven, the wave guide is a few centimeters long; whereas in industrial units it can be a few meters long. The energy loss in the wave guide is usually quite small.

Stirrer   The stirrer is usually a fan-shaped distributor which rotates and scatters the transmitted energy throughout the oven. The stirrer disturbs the standing wave patterns, thus allowing better energy distribution in the oven cavity. This is particularly important when heating nonhomogenous materials like foods.

Oven cavity or oven   The oven cavity encloses the food to be heated within the metallic walls. The distributed energy from the stirrer is reflected by the walls and intercepted by the food from many directions with more or less uniform energy density. The energy impinging on the food is absorbed and converted into heat. The size of the oven cavity is influenced by the wavelength. The length of the cavity wall should be greater than one-half the wavelength and should be any multiple of a half-wave in the direction of the wave propagation. The wavelength of 2450 MHz frequency was earlier calculated to be 12.2 cm; therefore, the oven cavity wall must be greater than 6.1 cm. The oven cavity door includes safety controls and seals to retain the microwave energy within the oven during the heating process.

4.6.6 Microwave Heating of Foods

Heating of foods in a microwave field offers several advantages over more conventional methods of heating. The following are some of the important features of microwave heating that merit consideration.

Speed of heating   The speed of heating of a dielectric material is directly proportional to the power output of the microwave system. In industrial units, the typical power output may range from 5 to 100 kW.

Although in the microwave field high speed of heating is attainable, many food applications require good control on how fast the foods are heated. Very high speed heating may not allow desirable physical and biochemical reactions to occur. The speed of heating in a microwave is controlled by controlling the power output. The power required for heating is also proportional to the mass of the product.

Frozen foods   The heating behavior of frozen foods is markedly influenced by the uniquely different dielectric properties of ice and water (Table 4.5). Due to its low dielectric loss factor, ice is more transparent to microwaves than water. Thus, ice does not heat as well as water. Therefore, when using microwaves to temper frozen foods, care is taken to keep the temperature of the frozen food just below the freezing point. If the ice melts, then there can be runaway heating because the water will heat much more rapidly due to the high dielectric loss factor of water.

Shape and density of the material   The shape of the food material is important in obtaining uniformity of heating. Nonuniform shapes result in local heating; similarly, sharp edges and corners cause nonuniform heating.

Food composition   The composition of the food material affects how it heats in the microwave field. The moisture content of food directly affects the amount of microwave absorption. A higher amount of water in a food increases the dielectric loss factor ε''. In the case of foods of low moisture content, the influence of the specific heat on the heating process is more pronounced than that of the dielectric loss factor. Therefore, due to their low specific heat, foods with low moisture content also heat at acceptable rates in microwaves. If the food material is highly porous with a significant amount of air, then due to low thermal conductivity of air the material will act as a good insulator and show good heating rates in microwaves. Another compositional factor that has a marked influence on heating rates in microwaves is the presence of salt. As stated previously, an increased concentration of ions promotes heating in microwaves. Thus, increasing the salt level in foods increases the rate of heating. Although oil has a much lower dielectric loss factor than water, oil has a specific heat less than half that of water. Since a product with high oil content

TABLE 4.5
Dielectric Properties of Water and Ice at 2450 MHz

	Relative dielectric constant, ε'	Relative dielectric loss constant, ε''	Loss tangent, tan δ
Ice	3.2	0.0029	0.0009
Water (at 25°C)	78	12.48	0.16

Source: Schiffman (1986).

will require much less heat to increase in temperature, the influence of specific heat becomes the overriding factor and oil exhibits a much higher rate of heating (Ohlsson, 1983). More details on these and other issues important during the microwave heating of foods are elaborated by Schiffman (1986) and by Decarau (1986).

The industrial applications of microwave processing of foods are mostly for tempering of frozen foods (increasing the temperature of frozen foods to -4 to $-2°C$), such as meat, fish, butter, and berries; for drying of pasta, instant tea, herbs, mushrooms, fish protein, bread crumbs, onions, rice cakes, seaweed, snack foods, and egg yolk; for cooking of bacon, meat patties, and potatoes; for vacuum drying of citrus juices, grains, and seeds; for freeze drying of meat, vegetables, and fruits; for pasteurization and sterilization of prepared foods; for baking of bread and doughnuts; and for roasting of nuts, coffee beans, and cocoa beans (Giese, 1992; Decarau, 1992).

Problems

4.1 Calculate the rate of heat transfer per unit area through a 200 mm thick concrete wall when the temperatures are 20°C and 5°C on the two surfaces, respectively. The thermal conductivity of concrete is 0.935 W/m · °C.

4.2 An experiment was conducted to measure thermal conductivity of a formulated food. The measurement was made by using a large plane plate of the food material, which was 5 mm thick. It was found, under steady-state conditions, that when a temperature difference of 35°C was maintained between the two surfaces of the plate, a heat-transfer rate per unit area of 4700 W/m^2 was measured near the center of either surface. Calculate the thermal conductivity of the product, and list two assumptions used in obtaining the result.

4.3 Estimate the thermal conductivity of applesauce at 35°C. (Water content = 78.8% wet basis.)

4.4 A 10 m long pipe has an inside radius of 70 mm, an outside radius of 80 mm, and is made of stainless steel ($k = 15$ W/m · °C). Its inside surface is held at 150°C, while its outside surface is at 30°C. There is no heat generation, and steady-state conditions hold. Compute the rate at which heat is being transferred across the pipe wall.

4.5 A plane piece of insulation board is used to reduce the heat loss from a hot furnace wall into the room. One surface of the board is at 100°C and the other surface is at 20°C. It is desired to keep the heat loss down to 120 W/m^2 of the insulation board. If the thermal conductivity of the board is 0.05 W/m ·°C, calculate the required thickness of the board.

*4.6 Steam with 80% quality is being used to heat a 40% total solids tomato puree as it flows through a steam injection heater at a rate of 400 kg/hr. The steam is generated at 169.06 kPa and is flowing to the heater at a rate of 50 kg/hr. If the specific heat of the product is 3.2 kJ/kg · K, determine the temperature of the product leaving the heater when the initial temperature is 50°C. Determine the total solids content of the product after heating. Assume the specific heat of the heated puree is 3.5 kJ/kg ·°C.

4.7 Air at 25°C blows over a heated steel plate with its surface maintained at 200°C. The plate is 50 × 40 cm and 2.5 cm thick. The convective heat-transfer coefficient at the top surface is 20 W/m^2 · K. The thermal conductivity of steel is 45 W/m · K. Calculate the heat loss per hour from the top surface of the plate.

4.8 A liquid food is being heated in a tubular heat exchanger. The inside pipe wall temperature is 110°C. The internal diameter of pipe is 30 mm. The product flows at 0.5 kg/s. If the initial temperature of the product is 7°C, compute the convective heat-transfer coefficient. The thermal properties of the product are the following: specific heat = 3.7 kJ/kg ·°C, thermal conductivity = 0.6 W/m ·°C, product viscosity = 500 × 10^{-6} Pa · s, density = 1000 kg/m^3, product viscosity at 110°C = 410 × 10^{-6} Pa · s.

4.9 Compute the convective heat-transfer coefficient for natural convection from a vertical, 100 mm diameter, 0.5 m long, stainless-steel pipe. The surface temperature of the insulated pipe is 145°C, while the air temperature is 40°C.

*4.10 A 30 m long pipe with an external diameter of 75 mm is being used to convey steam at a rate of 1000 kg/hr. The steam pressure is 198.53 kPa. The steam enters the pipe with a dryness fraction of 0.98 and must leave the other end of the pipe with a minimum dryness fraction of 0.95. Insulation with a thermal conductivity of 0.2 W/m · K is available. Determine the minimum thickness of insulation necessary. The outside surface temperature of insulation is assumed to be 25°C. Neglect the conductive resistance of the pipe material and assume no pressure drop across the pipe.

4.11 Estimate the convective heat-transfer coefficient for natural convection from a horizontal steam pipe. The outside surface temperature

---

*Indicates an advanced level of difficulty in solving.

of the insulated pipe is 80°C. The surrounding air temperature is 25°C. The outside diameter of the insulated pipe is 10 cm.

4.12 A vertical cylindrical container is being cooled in ambient air at 25°C with no air circulation. If the initial temperature of the container surface is 100°C, compute the surface heat-transfer coefficient due to natural convection during the initial cooling period. The diameter of the container is 1 m, and it is 2 m high.

4.13 Water at a flow rate of 1 kg/s is flowing in a pipe of internal diameter 5 cm. If the inside pipe surface temperature is 90°C and mean bulk water temperature is 50°C, compute the convective heat-transfer coefficient.

*4.14 A flat wall is exposed to an environmental temperature of 38°C. The wall is covered with a layer of insulation 2.5 cm thick whose thermal conductivity is 1.8 W/m · K, and the temperature of the wall on the inside of the insulation is 320°C. The wall loses heat to the environment by convection. Compute the value of the convection heat-transfer coefficient that must be maintained on the outer surface of the insulation to ensure that the outer surface temperature does not exceed 40°C.

4.15 Steam at 150°C flows inside a pipe that has an inside radius of 50 mm and an outside radius of 55 mm. The convective heat-transfer coefficient between the steam and the inside pipe wall is 2500 W/m^2 · °C. The outside surface of the pipe is exposed to ambient air at 20°C with a convective heat-transfer coefficient of 10 W/m^2 · °C. Assuming steady state and no heat generation, calculate the rate of heat transfer per meter from the steam to the air across the pipe. Assume thermal conductivity of stainless steel is 15 W/m · °C.

4.16 The outside wall of a refrigerated storage room is 10 m long and 3 m high and is constructed with 100-mm concrete block ($k = 0.935$ W/m · °C) and 10 cm of fiber insulation board ($k = 0.048$ W/m · °C). The inside of the room is at -10°C and the convective heat-transfer coefficient is 40 W/m^2 · K, while the outside temperature is 30°C with a convective heat-transfer coefficient of 10 W/m^2 · K on the outside wall surface. Calculate the overall heat-transfer coefficient.

4.17 A walk-in freezer with 4-m width, 6-m length, and 3-m height is being built. The walls and ceiling contain 1.7 mm thick stainless steel ($k = 15$ W/m · °C), 10 cm thick foam insulation ($k = 0.036$ W/m · °C), and some thickness of corkboard ($k = 0.043$ W/m · °C) to be established, and 1.27-cm-thickness wood siding ($k = 0.104$ W/m · °C). The inside of the freezer is maintained at -40°C. Ambient air outside the freezer is at 32°C. The convective heat-transfer coefficient is 5 W/m^2 · K on the wood side of the wall and

2 W/m^2 · K on the steel side. If the outside air has a dew point of 29°C, calculate the thickness of corkboard insulation that would prevent condensation of moisture on the outside wall of the freezer. Calculate the rate of heat transfer through the walls and ceiling of this freezer.

4.18 A liquid food is being conveyed through an uninsulated pipe at 90°C. The product flow rate is 0.25 kg/s and has a density of 1000 kg/m^3, specific heat of 4 kJ/kg · K, viscosity of 8 × 10^{-6} Pa · s, and thermal conductivity of 0.55 W/m · K. Assume the viscosity correction is negligible. The internal pipe diameter is 20 mm with 3-mm thickness made of stainless steel ($k = 15$ W/m · °C). The outside temperature is 15°C. If the outside convective heat transfer coefficient is 18 W/m^2 · K, calculate the steady-state heat loss from the product per unit length of pipe.

4.19 A liquid food is being pumped in a 1 cm thick steel pipe. The inside diameter of the pipe is 5 cm. The bulk temperature of liquid food is 90°C. The inside pipe surface temperature is 80°C. The surface heat transfer coefficient inside the pipe is 15 W/m^2 · K. The pipe has a 2 cm thick insulation. The outside bulk air temperature is 20°C. The surface heat-transfer coefficient on the outside of insulation is 3 W/m^2 · K.

  (a) Calculate the insulation surface temperature exposed to the outside.
  (b) If the pipe length is doubled, how would it influence the insulation surface temperature? Discuss.

4.20 For a metal pipe used to pump tomato paste, the overall heat transfer coefficient based on internal area is 2 W/m^2 · K. The inside diameter of the pipe is 5 cm. The pipe is 2 cm thick. The thermal conductivity of the metal is 20 W/m · K. Calculate the outer convective heat-transfer coefficient. The inside convective heat-transfer coefficient is 5 W/m^2 · K.

4.21 A cold-storage room is maintained at − 18°C. The internal dimensions of the room are 5 m × 5 m × 3 m high. Each wall, ceiling, and floor consists of an inner layer of 2.5 cm thick wood with 7 cm thick insulation and an 11-cm brick layer on the outside. The thermal conductivities of respective materials are wood (0.104 W/m · K), glass fiber (0.04 W/m · K), and brick 0.69 W/m · K. The convective heat-transfer coefficient for wood to still air is 2.5 W/m^2 · K, and from moving air to brick is 4 W/m^2 · K. The outside ambient temperature is 25°C. Determine:

  (a) The overall heat transfer coefficient.
  (b) The temperature of the exposed surfaces.
  (c) The temperatures of the interfaces.

*4.22 Steam at 169.60 kPa is condensed inside a pipe (internal diameter = 7 cm, thickness = 3 mm). The inside and outside convective heat-transfer coefficients are 1000 and 10 W/m² · K, respectively. The thermal conductivity of the pipe is 45 W/m · K. Assume that all thermal resistances are based on the outside diameter of the pipe, and determine the following:

   (a) Percentage resistance offered by the pipe, by the steam, and by the outside.
   (b) The outer surface temperature of the pipe if the temperature of the air surrounding the pipe is 25°C.

4.23 A steel pipe (outside diameter 100 mm) is covered with two layers of insulation. The inside layer, 40 mm thick, has a thermal conductivity of 0.07 W/m · K. The outside layer, 20 mm thick, has a thermal conductivity of 0.15 W/m · K. The pipe is used to convey steam at a pressure of 700 kPa. The outside temperature of insulation is 24°C. If the pipe is 10 m long, determine the following, assuming the resistance to conductive heat transfer in steel pipe and convective resistance on the steam side are negligible:

   (a) The heat loss per hour.
   (b) The interface temperature of insulation.

*4.24 A 1 cm thick steel pipe, 1 m long, with an internal diameter of 5 cm is covered with 4 cm thick insulation. The inside wall temperature of the steel pipe is 100°C. The ambient temperature around the insulated pipe is 20°C. The convective heat-transfer coefficient on the outer insulated surface is 50 W/m² · K. Calculate the temperature at the steel insulation interface. The thermal conductivity of steel is 54 W/m · K, and the thermal conductivity of insulation is 0.04 W/m · K.

*4.25 Saturated refrigerant (Freon, R-12) at −40°C flows through a copper tube of 20 mm inside diameter and wall thickness of 2 mm. The copper tube is covered with 40 mm thick insulation ($k = 0.02$ W/m · K). Determine the heat gain per meter of the pipe. The internal and external convective heat transfer coefficients are 500 and 5 W/m² · K, respectively. The ambient air temperature is 25°C. Compare the amount of refrigerant vaporized per hour per meter length of pipe for insulated versus uninsulated pipe. The latent heat of the refrigerant at −40°C is 1390 kJ/kg.

4.26 In a concurrent-flow tubular heat exchanger, a liquid food, flowing in the inner pipe, is heated from 20 to 40°C. In the outer pipe the heating medium (water) cools from 90 to 50°C. The overall heat-transfer coefficient based on the inside diameter is 2000 W/m² · °C. The inside diameter is 5 cm and length of the heat exchanger is 10 m. The average specific heat of water is 4.181 kJ/kg · °C. Calculate the mass flow rate of water in the outer pipe.

*4.27 A countercurrent heat exchanger is being used to heat a liquid food from 15 to 70°C. The heat exchanger has a 23-mm internal diameter and 10-m length with an overall heat-transfer coefficient, based on the inside area, of 2000 W/m^2 · K. Water, the heating medium, enters the heat exchanger at 95°C, and leaves at 85°C. Determine the flow rates for product and water that will provide the conditions described. Use specific heats of 3.7 kJ/kg · K for product and 4.18 kJ/kg · K for water.

4.28 A 10 m long countercurrent-flow heat exchanger is being used to heat a liquid food from 20 to 80°C. The heating medium is oil, which enters the heat exchanger at 150°C and exits at 60°C. The specific heat of the liquid food is 3.9 kJ/kg · K. The overall heat-transfer coefficient based on the inside area is 1000 W/m^2 · K. The inner diameter of the inside pipe is 7 cm.

  (a) Estimate the flow rate of the liquid food.
  (b) Determine the flow rate of the liquid food if the heat exchanger is operated in a concurrent-flow mode for the same conditions of temperatures at the inlet and exit from the heat exchanger.

4.29 Calculate the radiative heat gain in watts by a loaf of bread at a surface temperature of 100°C. The surrounding oven surface temperature is 1000°C. The total surface area of the bread is 0.15 m^2 and the emissivity of the bread surface is 0.80. Assume the oven is a blackbody radiator.

4.30 It is desired to predict the temperature after 30 min at the geometric center of a cylindrical can containing a model food. The dimensions of the can are 5 cm diameter and 3 cm height. The thermal conductivity of the food is 0.5 W/m · C, specific heat = 3.9 kJ/kg · °C, and density = 950 kg/m^3. There is a negligible surface resistance to heat transfer. The surrounding medium temperature is 100°C and the uniform initial temperature of food is 20°C.

4.31 An 8-m^3 batch of oil with specific heat of 2 kJ/kg · K and density of 850 kg/m^3 is being heated in a steam-jacketed, agitated vessel with 1.5 m^2 of heating surface. The convective heat-transfer coefficient on the oil side is 500 W/m^2 · K, and 10,000 W/m^2 · K on the steam side. If the steam temperature is 130°C and the initial temperature is 20°C, estimate the oil temperature after 10 min.

4.32 Water at 5°C is being used to cool apples from an initial temperature of 20 to 8°C. The water flow over the surface of the apple creates a convective heat transfer coefficient of 10 W/m^2 · K. Assume the apple can be described by a sphere with an 8-cm diameter and the geometric center is to be reduced to 8°C. The apple properties include thermal conductivity of 0.4 W/m · K. Specific heat of 3.8 kJ/kg · K and density of 960 kg/m^3. Determine the time that the apples must be exposed to the water.

4.33 A liquid food with density of 1025 kg/m^3 and specific heat of 3.77 kJ/kg · K is being heated in a can with 8.5 cm diameter and 10.5 cm height. The heating will occur in a retort with temperature at 115°C and convective heat-transfer coefficients of 50 W/m^2 · K on the inside of the can and 5000 W/m^2 · K on the outside surface. Determine the product temperature after 10 min if the initial temperature is 70°C.

*__4.34__ A conduction-cooling food product with density of 1000 kg/m^3, specific heat of 4 kJ/kg · K, and thermal conductivity of 0.4 W/m · K has been heated to 80°C. The cooling of the product in a 10 cm high and 8 cm diameter can is accomplished using cold water with a convective heat-transfer coefficient of 10 W/m^2 · K on the can surface. Determine the water temperature required to reduce the product temperature at geometric center to 50°C in 7 hr. Neglect conductive heat resistance through can wall.

4.35 Cooked mashed potato is cooled on trays in a chilling unit with refrigerated air at 2°C blown over the product surface at high velocity. The depth of product is 30 mm and the initial temperature is 95°C. The product has a thermal conductivity of 0.37 W/m · K, specific heat of 3.7 kJ/kg · K, and density of 1000 kg/m^3. Assuming negligible resistance to heat transfer at the surface, calculate product temperature at the center after 30 min.

4.36 Program Example 4.9 on a spreadsheet. Determine the interfacial temperatures if the following thicknesses of insulation are used: (a) 2 cm; (b) 4 cm; (c) 6 cm; (d) 8 cm; (e) 10 cm.

4.37 A pure copper sphere of radius 1 cm is dropped into an agitated oil bath that has a uniform temperature of 130°C. The initial temperature of the copper sphere is 20°C. Using a spreadsheet predict the internal temperature of the sphere at 5 min intervals until it reaches 130°C for three different convective heat transfer coefficients: 5, 10, and 100 W/m^2 · °C, respectively. Plot your results as temperature versus time.

4.38 Heated water with a bulk temperature of 90°C is being pumped at a rate of 0.1 kg/s in a metal pipe placed horizontally in ambient air. The pipe has an internal diameter of 2.5 cm and it is 1 cm thick. The inside pipe surface temperature is 85°C. The outside surface of the pipe is at 80°C and exposed to the air. The bulk temperature of the air is 20°C.

(a) Determine the convective heat transfer coefficient for water inside the pipe.

(b) Determine the convective heat transfer coefficient for air outside the pipe.

(c) It is desired to double the convective heat transfer coefficient inside the pipe. What operating conditions should be changed? By how much?

4.39 A solid food is being cooled in a cylindrical can of dimensions 12 cm diameter and 3 cm thickness. The cooling medium is cold water at 2°C. The initial temperature of the solid food is 95°C. The convective heat transfer coefficient is 200 W/m² ·°C.

(a) Determine the temperature at the geometric center after 3 hr. The thermal properties of the solid food are $k = 0.36$ W/m·°C, density of 950 kg/m³, and specific heat of 3.9 kJ/kg·°C.

(b) Is it reasonable to assume the cylindrical can to be an infinite cylinder (or an infinite slab)? Why?

4.40 A three-layered composite pipe with an inside diameter of 1 cm has an internal surface temperature of 120°C. The first layer, from the inside to the outside, is 2 cm thick with a thermal conductivity of 15 W/m ·°C, the second layer is 3 cm thick with a thermal conductivity of 0.04 W/m ·°C, the third layer is 1 cm thick and has a thermal conductivity of 164 W/m ·°C. The outside surface temperature of the composite pipe is 60°C.

(a) Determine the rate of heat transfer through the pipe under steady-state conditions.

(b) Can you suggest an approach that will allow you to quickly make an estimate for this problem?

4.41 It is known that raw eggs will become hard when heated to 72°C. To manufacture diced eggs, trays of liquid egg are exposed to steam for cooking.

(a) How long will it take to cook the eggs given the following conditions? The tray dimension is 30 cm long, 30 cm wide, and 2 cm deep. The liquid egg inside the tray is 1 cm deep. The thermal conductivity of liquid egg is 0.45 W/m·°C; density is 800 kg/m³, specific heat is 3.8 kJ/kg·°C; surface convective heat transfer coefficient is 5000 W/m²·°C; and the initial temperature of liquid egg is 2°C. Steam is available at 169.06 kPa. Ignore resistance to heat transfer caused by the metal tray.

(b) What rate of steam flow per tray of liquid egg must be maintained to accomplish the above? The latent heat of vaporization at 169.06 kPa is 2216.5 kJ/kg.

4.42 Determine the time required for the center temperature of a cube to reach 80°C. The cube has a volume of 125 cm³. The thermal conductivity of the material is 0.4 W/m · °C; density is 950 kg/m^3; and specific heat is 3.4 kJ/kg · K. The initial temperature is 20°C. The surrounding temperature is 90°C. The cube is immersed in a fluid that results in a negligible surface resistance to heat transfer.

4.43 A tubular heat exchanger is being used for heating a liquid food from 30°C to 70°C. The temperature of the heating medium decreases from 90° to 60°C.

> (a) Is the flow configuration in the heat exchanger countercurrent or concurrent flow?
> (b) Determine the log mean temperature difference.
> (c) If the heat transfer area is 20 m^2 and the overall heat transfer coefficient is 100 W/m^2·°C, determine the rate of heat transfer from the heating medium to the liquid food.
> (d) What is the flow rate of the liquid food if the specific heat of the liquid is 3.9 kJ/kg·°C? Assume no heat loss to the surroundings.

4.44 What is the flow rate of water in a heat exchanger if it enters the heat exchanger at 20°C and exits at 85°C? The heating medium is oil, where oil enters at 120°C and leaves at 75°C. The overall heat transfer coefficient is 5 W/m^2 · °C. The area of the heat exchanger is 30 m^2.

4.45 A liquid food at 75°C is being conveyed in a steel pipe ($k = 45$ W/m · °C). The pipe has an internal diameter of 2.5 cm and it is 1 cm thick. The overall heat transfer coefficient based on internal diameter is 40 W/m^2 · K. The internal convective heat transfer coefficient is 50 W/m^2 · K. Calculate the external convective heat transfer coefficient.

4.46 Set up Example 4.16 on a spreadsheet. Determine the heat loss from 1 m length of the pipe if the inside diameter of the pipe is (a) 2.5 cm; (b) 3.5 cm; (c) 4.5 cm; (d) 5.5 cm.

List of Symbols

A	area (m^2)	χ	reflectivity, dimensionless
a	constant in Eq. (4.43)	D	diameter or characteristic
α	thermal diffusivity (m^2/s)		dimension (m)
α'	attenuation factor (m^{-1})	D_e	equivalent diameter (m)
β	coefficient of volumetric	d	penetration depth (m)
	expansion	E	electrical field strength
c_p	specific heat at constant		(V/cm)
	pressure (kJ/kg ·°C)	ε	emissivity, dimensionless
c_v	specific heat at constant	ε'	relative dielectric constant,
	volume (kJ/kg ·°C)		dimensionless

ε'' relative dielectric loss constant, dimensionless

F shape factor, dimensionless

f frequency (Hz)

g acceleration due to gravity (m/s^2)

h convective heat transfer coefficient (W/m^2 · K)

k thermal conductivity (W/m ·°C)

L length (m)

λ wavelength (m)

M mass (kg)

m mass fraction, dimensionless

$\dot{m}$ mass flow rate (kg/s)

μ viscosity (Pa · s, N · s/m^2)

N_{Bi} Biot number, dimensionless

N_{Fo} Fourier number, dimensionless

N_{Gr} Grashof number, dimensionless

N_{Nu} Nusselt number, dimensionless

N_{Pr} Prandtl number, dimensionless

N_{Re} Reynolds number, dimensionless

P power at the penetration depth (W)

P_D power dissipation (W/cm^3)

P_0 incident power (W)

ϕ absorptivity, dimensionless

ψ transmissivity, dimensionless

Q heat gained or lost (kJ)

q rate of heat transfer (W)

q''' rate of heat generation (W/m^3)

r radius or variable distance in radial direction (m)

ρ density (kg/m^3)

σ Stefan–Boltzmann constant (5.669×10^{-8} W/m^2 · K^4)

T temperature (°C)

t time (s)

T_A absolute temperature (K)

T_a temperature of surrounding medium (°C)

T_f film temperature (°C)

T_i initial temperature (°C)

T_p plate surface temperature (°C)

T_s surface temperature (°C)

T_∞ temperature of surrounding fluid (°C)

$\tan \delta$ loss tangent, dimensionless

U overall heat transfer coefficient (W/m^2 ·°C)

$\bar{u}$ volume (m^3)

v velocity (m/s)

w water content (%)

x mass fraction, or variable distance in x direction (m)

Z depth (m)

ζ factor to account for shape and emissivity, dimensionless

Subscripts: a, ash; b, bulk; c, carbohydrate; f, fat; i, inside surface; lm, log-mean; m, moisture; o, outside surface; p, protein; r, radial direction; x, x direction, w, at wall.

Bibliography

Brennan, J. G., Butters, J. R., Cowell, N. D., and Lilly, A. E. V. (1990). "Food Engineering Operations", 3rd ed. Elsevier Science Publishing Co., New York.

Copson, D. A. (1975). "Microwave Heating." AVI Publ. Co., Westport, Connecticut.

Coulsen, J. M., and Richardson, J. F. (1978). "Chemical Engineering," Vol. 1, Pergamon Press, Oxford.

Decarau, R. V. (1992). "Microwave Foods: New Product Development." Food and Nutrition Press, Trumbull, Connecticut.

Decarau, R. V., and Peterson, R. A. (1986). "Microwave Processing and Engineering." VCH Publ., Deerfield Beach, Florida.

Dickerson, R. W., Jr. (1969). Thermal properties of foods. In "The Freezing Preservation of Foods," 4th ed., Vol. 2. (D. K. Tressler, W. B. Van Arsdel, and M. J. Copley, eds.), pp. 26–51. AVI Publ. Co., Westport, Connecticut.

Giese, J. (1992). Advances in microwave food processing. Food Tech. 46(9), 118–123.

Heldman, D. R., and Singh, R. P. (1981). "Food Process Engineering," 2nd ed. AVI Publ. Co., Westport, Connecticut.

Holman, J. P. (1990). "Heat Transfer," 7th ed. McGraw-Hill, New York.

Hottel, H. C. (1930). Radiant heat transmission. Mech. Eng. 52(7), 700.

IFT (1989). Microwave food processing. A Scientific Status Summary by the IFT Expert Panel on Food Safety and Nutrition. Food Tech. 43(1), 117–126.

Kreith, F. (1973). "Principles of Heat Transfer." IEP-A Dun-Donnelley Publisher, New York.

Mertens, B., and Knorr, D. (1992). Developments of nonthermal processes for food preservation. Food Tech. 46(5), 124–133.

Mudgett, R. E. (1986). Microwave properties and heating characteristics of foods. Food Tech. 40(6), 84–93.

Myers, G. E. (1971). "Analytical Methods in Conduction Heat Transfer." McGraw-Hill, New York.

Ohlsson, T. (1983). Fundamentals of microwave cooking. Microwave World 4(2), 4.

Perry. R. H., and Chilton, C. H. (1973). "Chemical Engineer's Handbook." McGraw-Hill, New York.

Schiffman, R. F. (1986) Food product development for microwave processing. Food Tech. 40(6), 94–98.

Schneider, P. J. (1963). "Temperature Response Charts." Wiley, New York.

Sweat, V. E. (1974). Experimental values of thermal conductivity of selected fruits and vegetables. J. Food Sci. 39, 1080.

Sweat, V. E. (1975). Modeling thermal conductivity of meats. Trans. Am. Soc. Agric. Eng. 18(1), 564–565, 567, 568.

Sweat, V. E. (1986). Thermal properties of foods. In "Engineering Properties of Foods," (M. A. Rao and S. S. H. Rizvi, eds.), pp. 49–87. Marcel Dekker Inc., New York.

von Hippel, A. R. (1954). "Dielectrics and Waves." MIT Press, Cambridge, Massachusetts.

Whitaker, S. (1977). "Fundamental Principles of Heat Transfer." Krieger Publishing Co., Melbourne, Florida.

CHAPTER 5

Thermal Processing

In the food industry, thermal processing is accepted terminology to describe the heating, holding, and cooling process required to eliminate the potential for a foodborne illness. Pasteurization is one type of thermal processing designed for a specific pathogenic microorganism, but it does not result in a shelf-stable product without refrigeration. Commercial sterilization is the process that leads to shelf-stable products in cans and similar containers. The subject is treated in different ways in standard references such as Ball and Olson (1957), Stumbo (1973), NFPA (1980), and Lopez (1969).

5.1 Decimal Reduction Time *D*

During thermal sterilization of foods, the population of microorganisms present in the food decreases depending on the temperature of the product. The population of vegetative cells, such as *E. coli*, *Salmonella* or *Listeria monocytogenes*, will decrease in a logarithmic manner. The population of microbial spores will decrease according to a similar pattern, but after an initial lag time. A typical plot of microbial population over time is shown in Fig. 5.1. By plotting the same data on semilog ordinates, a straight line is obtained as shown in Fig. 5.2. The slope of the straight line is related directly to the decimal reduction time, *D*.

The decimal reduction time *D* is defined as the time necessary for 90% reduction in the microbial population. When the microbial population is plotted on semilog coordinates, the *D* value is the time required for a one log-cycle reduction in the number of microorganisms. The initial microbial population has no influence on the *D* value since the magnitude is directly related to the slope of the straight line. Exposure of the microbial population to higher temperatures results in a decrease in the *D* value, as shown in Fig. 5.3.

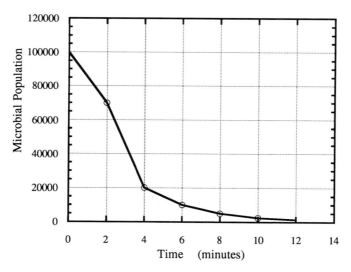

Fig. 5.1 A typical plot of microbial population versus time.

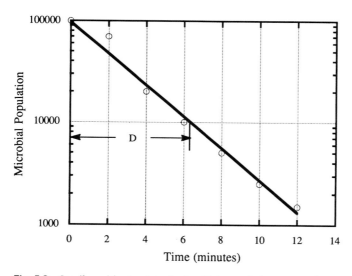

Fig. 5.2 Semilogarithmic plot of microbial population versus time.

Based on the definition of decimal reduction time, the following equation can be used:

$$\log N_0 - \log N = t/D \qquad (5.1)$$

or

$$D = \frac{t}{\log N_0 - \log N} \qquad (5.2)$$

and

$$N/N_0 = 10^{-t/D} \qquad (5.3)$$

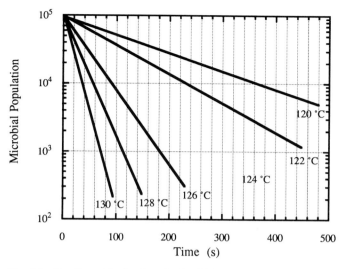

Fig. 5.3 Semilogarithmic plot of microbial population over time for several temperatures.

EXAMPLE 5.1

The following data were obtained from a thermal resistance experiment conducted on a spore suspension at 112°C:

Time (minutes)	Number of survivors
0	10^6
4	1.1×10^5
8	1.2×10^4
12	1.2×10^3

Determine the *D* value of the microorganism.

APPROACH

The microbial population will be plotted on a semilog plot to obtain the slope.

SOLUTION

(1) On a semilog graph paper, plot the number of survivors as a function of time (Fig. 5.4). From the straight line obtained, determine the slope, which gives the *D* value as 4.1 minutes.

(2) Alternatively, this problem can be solved using a spreadsheet by first taking the natural logarithm of the number of survivors and entering the data in a linear regression model. The *D* value of 4.1 minutes is obtained.

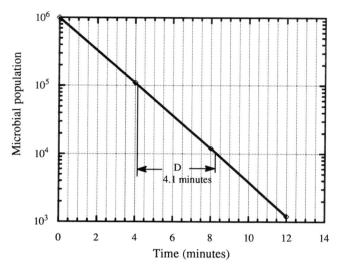

Fig. 5.4 Graphical determination of decimal reduction time D for Example 5.1.

5.2 Thermal Resistance Constant z

The thermal resistance constant z is a unique factor describing thermal resistance of the bacterial spores. It is defined as the increase in temperature necessary to cause 90% reduction in the decimal reduction time D. The D values for different temperatures are plotted on semilog coordi-

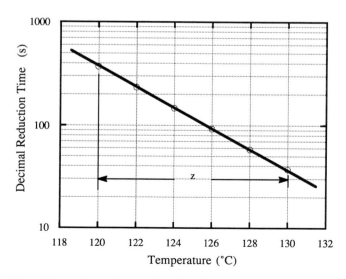

Fig. 5.5 Semilogarithmic plot of decimal reduction time versus temperature, showing a graphical representation of the z value.

nates and the temperature increase for a one log-cycle change in D values represents the z value, as shown in Fig. 5.5. Based on the definition, z can be expressed by the following equation:

$$z = \frac{T_2 - T_1}{\log D_{T_1} - \log D_{T_2}}$$ (5.4)

EXAMPLE 5.2

The decimal reduction times D for a spore suspension were measured at several temperatures, as follows:

Temperature (°C)	D (minutes)
104	27.5
107	14.5
110	7.5
113	4.0
116	2.2

Determine the thermal resistance constant z for the spores.

APPROACH

The D values will be plotted versus temperature on semilog coordinates and the z value is estimated from the slope of the established straight line.

SOLUTION

(1) Using semilog graph paper, the D values are plotted versus temperature (Fig. 5.6).

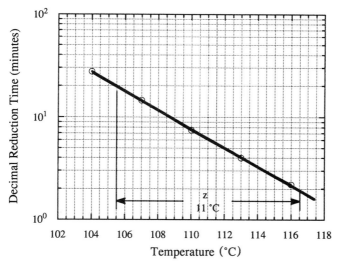

Fig. 5.6 Graphical determination of z value for Example 5.2.

(2) A straight line through the plotted points is established.

(3) Based on the straight-line curve, a temperature increase of 11°C is required for a one log-cycle reduction in the D value.

(4) Based on the above analysis, $z = 11$°C.

(5) Alternately, z can be estimated using a linear regression program to analyze the relationship between logarithm of D values versus temperature. The z value is 11.1°C.

5.3   Thermal Death Time F

The thermal death time F is the time required to cause a stated reduction in a population of microorganisms or spores. This time can be expressed as a multiple of D values. For example, a 99.99% reduction in microbial population is equivalent to four log-cycle reductions or $F = 4D$. Typically, in thermal processing of shelf-stable foods, the value used for thermal death time is $F = 12D$, with the D value for *Clostridium botulinum*.

In food science literature, it is customary to express F with a subscript denoting the temperature and a superscript of the z value for the microorganism being considered. Thus, F_T^z is the thermal death time for a temperature T and a thermal resistance constant z. For reference purposes, a commonly used thermal death time is F_{250}^{18} in the Fahrenheit temperature scale or F_{121}^{10} in the Celsius temperature scale. This reference thermal death time, simply written as F_0, represents the time for a given reduction in population of a microbial spore with a z value of 10°C (or 18° F) at 121°C (or 250°F).

5.4   Spoilage Probability

When considering shelf-stable food products, the thermal process can be designed to eliminate spoilage in addition to microbial safety. The spoilage probability is used to estimate the number of spoiled containers within a total batch of processed product.

From Eq. (5.1), for a total exposure of thermal death time F,

$$\log N_0 - \log N = F/D \qquad (5.5)$$

Then, if r is the number of containers processed, and N_0 is the initial number of spores per container, the total microbial load at the beginning of the process equals rN_0, and

$$\log(rN_0) - \log(rN) = F/D \qquad (5.6)$$

If the goal of a thermal process is to achieve a probability of one microorganism in the entire batch, then

$$\log(rN_0) = F/D \tag{5.7}$$

or

$$rN_0 = 10^{F/D} \tag{5.8}$$

and

$$\frac{1}{r} = \frac{N_0}{10^{F/D}} \tag{5.9}$$

EXAMPLE 5.3

Estimate the spoilage probability of a 50-minute process at 113°C when $D_{113} = 4$ minutes and the initial microbial population is 10^4 per container.

APPROACH

Use Eq. (5.9) to compute spoilage probability.

SOLUTION

1. From Eq. (5.9),

$$\frac{1}{r} = \frac{10^4}{10^{50/4}} = \frac{10^4}{10^{12.5}} = 10^{-8.5}$$

Therefore,

$$r = 10^{8.5} = 10^8 \times 10^{0.5} = 10^8 \times \sqrt{10}$$

$$= 3.16 \times 10^8$$

2. Since $r = 3.16 \times 10^8$, then spoilage of one container in 3.16×10^8 can be expected, or approximately three containers from 10^9 containers processed.

5.5 Relationships between Chemical Kinetics and Thermal Processing Parameters

The kinetics of a chemical reaction is often described by the order of the reaction, and the rate constant can be calculated. Thermal process calculations involve changes in microbial population, and these changes can be described by the same expressions as chemical kinetics. In this section, important relationships between the parameters from chemical kinetics literature and thermal processing of foods will be described.

5.5.1 Decimal Reduction Time D and Rate Constant k

Since the decrease in microbial population generally follows an exponential path, the change should follow first-order kinetics. Therefore,

$$\frac{dN}{dt} = -kN \tag{5.10}$$

By separating variables and integrating from initial population (N_0) at time zero to a final population (N) at time t,

$$\ln \frac{N}{N_0} = -kt \tag{5.11}$$

By changing the logarithmic base from natural to $\log_{10}$ (and simply writing log instead of $\log_{10}$)

$$2.303 \log \frac{N}{N_0} = -kt$$

or

$$\log N - \log N_0 = -\frac{k}{2.303} t \tag{5.12}$$

From Eq. (5.1)

$$\log N_0 - \log N = +t/D$$

and by comparison,

$$k = 2.303/D \tag{5.13}$$

EXAMPLE 5.4

Compute the first-order rate constant corresponding to the decimal reduction time (D) found in Example 5.1.

APPROACH

Use Eq. (5.13) to compute the rate constant. Alternatively, the k value could be obtained directly from the slope of the curve in Fig. 5.4.

SOLUTION

Using Eq. (5.13),

$$k = \frac{2.303}{4.1} = 0.56/\text{minute}$$

5.5.2 Q_{10} and Thermal Resistance Constant z

Q_{10} is often used to describe the effect of temperature on the reaction rate. By definition,

$$Q_{10} = \frac{k_{T_2}}{k_{T_1}} \tag{5.14}$$

where k_{T_1} is the rate constant at temperature $T_1°C$, and k_{T_2} is the rate constant at temperature $T_2°C$ where

$$T_2 = T_1 + 10°C$$

From Eq. (5.13)

$$k_T = 2.303/D_T$$

Thus,

$$Q_{10} = \frac{2.303/D_{T_2}}{2.303/D_{T_1}} = \frac{D_{T_1}}{D_{T_2}} \tag{5.15}$$

From Eq. (5.4)

$$z = \frac{T_2 - T_1}{\log D_{T_1} - \log D_{T_2}}$$

or, for a temperature change $(T_2 - T_1)$ of 10°C,

$$\frac{D_{T_1}}{D_{T_2}} = 10^{10/z} \tag{5.16}$$

Comparing Eqs. (5.15) and (5.16)

$$Q_{10} = 10^{10/z} \tag{5.17}$$

or

$$z = \frac{10}{\log Q_{10}} \tag{5.18}$$

EXAMPLE 5.5

Estimate Q_{10} for the temperature influence on decimal reduction time in Example 5.2.

APPROACH

The most direct approach uses Eq. (5.17) to compute Q_{10} from the thermal resistance (z) obtained in Example 5.2.

SOLUTION

(1) Using Eq. (5.17),

$$Q_{10} = 10^{10/z} = 10^{10/11} = 8.1$$

(2) Note that the thermal resistance (z) must be in degrees Celsius to use Eq. (5.17).

5.5.3 Activation Energy E_a and Thermal Resistance Constant z

In chemical kinetics, the Arrhenius equation is used to describe the influence of temperature on the rate constant. Thus,

$$k = B \exp(-E_a/R_g T_A) \tag{5.19}$$

or

$$\ln k = \ln B - \frac{E_a}{R_g T_A}$$

For a temperature change between T_{A_1} and T_{A_2}

$$\ln k_1 = \ln B - \frac{E_a}{R_g T_{A_1}} \tag{5.20}$$

$$\ln k_2 = \ln B - \frac{E_a}{R_g T_{A_2}} \tag{5.21}$$

Subtracting Eq. (5.20) from (5.21)

$$\ln \frac{k_2}{k_1} = \frac{E_a}{R_g} \left(\frac{1}{T_{A_1}} - \frac{1}{T_{A_2}} \right) \tag{5.22}$$

By changing natural logarithm to $\log_{10}$,

$$\log \frac{k_2}{k_1} = \frac{E_a}{2.303 R_g} \left(\frac{1}{T_{A_1}} - \frac{1}{T_{A_2}} \right) \tag{5.23}$$

Since $k = 2.303/D$

$$\log \frac{k_2}{k_1} = \log \frac{D_1}{D_2} \tag{5.24}$$

From Eq. (5.16),

$$\frac{D_{T_1}}{D_{T_2}} = 10^{(T_2 - T_1)/z}$$

Substituting Eq. (5.24),

$$\log \frac{k_2}{k_1} = \frac{T_2 - T_1}{z}$$

Substituting in Eq. (5.22),

$$\frac{T_2 - T_1}{z} = \frac{E_a}{2.303 R_g} \left(\frac{1}{T_{A_1}} - \frac{1}{T_{A_2}} \right)$$

or

$$E_a = \frac{2.303 R_g}{z} \left(\frac{T_2 - T_1}{\frac{1}{T_{A_1}} - \frac{1}{T_{A_2}}} \right)$$

Since $T_{A_2} - T_{A_1} = T_2 - T_1$, therefore

$$E_a = \frac{2.303 R_g}{z} \left[T_{A_1} \times T_{A_2} \right] \tag{5.25}$$

For a small difference between T_{A_1} and T_{A_2}, and

$$T_{A_1} T_{A_2} = T_{A_1}^2$$

and $R_g = 8.314$ kJ/kg K,

$$E_a = \frac{19.15}{z} T_A^2 \tag{5.26}$$

5.5.4 Q_{10} and Activation Energy E_a

From Eqs. (5.14) and (5.19),

$$Q_{10} = \frac{k_{T+10}}{k_T} = \frac{B \exp\left[-E_a / R_g (T_A + 10) \right]}{B \exp\left[-E_a / R_g T_A \right]}$$

$$\log Q_{10} = \frac{E_a}{2.303 R_g} \left[\frac{10}{T_A (T_A + 10)} \right] \tag{5.27}$$

EXAMPLE 5.6

Estimate the activation energy (E_a) for the temperature influence on microbial death rate illustrated in Example 5.2.

APPROACH

Use Eq. (5.26) to compute E_a from the thermal resistance (z).

SOLUTION

Using Eq. (5.26),

$$E_a = \frac{19.15}{z} T_A^2 = \frac{19.15}{11} (383)^2 = 2.55 \times 10^5 \text{ kJ/kg}$$

Alternately, the activation energy (E_a) can be estimated from a plot of first-order rate constant (k) versus the inverse of absolute temperature $(1/T_A)$ on a semilogarithmic scale. The slope of the straight line equal 30.62×10^3 then.

$$\frac{E_a}{R_g} = 30.62 \times 10^3$$

$$E_a = 30.62 \times 10^3 \times 8.314 = 2.54 \times 10^5 \text{ kJ/kg}$$

5.6   General Method for Process Calculation

The General Method for Process Calculation is based on a classic paper by Bigelow *et al.* (1920). It forms the basis of modern thermal process calculations. A major requirement of the general method is that the thermal death time of the organism considered for the process must be known for all temperatures attained during the process.

The procedure involves development of a sterility curve for the process. This curve is drawn with the ordinate scale equal to the sterilizing rate (F/t), which is equal to the reciprocal of $\log^{-1}[(121 - T)/z]$ or $10^{[(121 - T)/z]}$. This rate is plotted versus time; the area under the curve provides the lethal effect in time units. This method will be described using the following description of a continuous high-temperature, short-time (HTST) processing of liquid foods.

Commercial sterilization of liquid foods can be accomplished by either retort sterilization or in a continuous-flow system using HTST sterilization. The latter requires aseptic packaging of the product to assure the desired results of the process.

The continuous HTST process for either pasteurization or sterilization is unique in that a major portion of the lethality may be accumulated during a holding period at the temperature of the heating medium. The extent to which the heating and cooling portions of the process will contribute to the lethality is dependent on the rates of heating and cooling and, in turn, on the method of heating and cooling. HTST pasteurization systems may utilize plate heat exchangers for both heating and cooling and have relatively long heating and cooling times. Continuous HTST sterilization systems may use a steam injection heating system to accomplish rapid heating of the product and allow "flashing" to less than atmospheric pressure as an approach to cooling the product. The combination of steam-injection heating and flash cooling also stabilizes the water content of the product. If the temperature reduction by flash cooling is equal to the increase in temperature achieved by steam injection, there is essentially no change in the total solids content of the product because the water added as steam is removed by evaporation during the flash cooling.

The objective of the following examples is to describe procedures to be utilized in design of processes for continuous HTST pasteurization or sterilization. The procedures are graphical in nature and will be helpful in illustrating the concept of lethality. Probably the key factor to be illustrated is that product temperatures below the heating-medium temperature may contribute to the process in a significant manner depending on the holding time at a given temperature.

The concept of lethality is utilized to describe the time–temperature influence of a thermal process. In general, lethality expresses the influence of the process in terms of a process equivalent to holding time at a reference temperature. The times utilized in discussion of thermal processes usually are thermal death times, F.

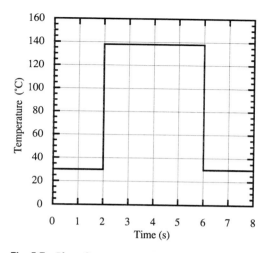

Fig. 5.7 Plot of temperature versus time for the conditions of Example 5.7.

EXAMPLE 5.7

A thermal process is accomplished by instantaneous heating to 138°C followed by a four-second hold and instantaneous cooling. Estimate the lethality at 121°C when the thermal resistance (z) for the microorganism is 8.5°C.

APPROACH

Use Eq. (5.16) modified to express thermal death times and compute lethality. Figure 5.7 shows a plot of temperature with respect to time.

SOLUTION

(1) Using a modified form of Eq. (5.16),

$$\frac{F_{138}}{F_{121}} = 10^{(121-138)/8.5}$$

or

$$F_{121} = (4 \text{ s})10^{(138-121)/8.5} = 4(10^2) = 400 \text{ s}$$

(2) The lethality at 121°C (F_{121}) is 100 times greater than at 138°C (F_{138}), in order to represent equivalent thermal processes.

Under actual situations, the heating and cooling portions of the process will not be instantaneous. These circumstances lead to accumulation of lethality during the heating and cooling steps.

EXAMPLE 5.8

The process in Example 5.7 is modified to allow for a one-second heating step and one-second cooling step in addition to the four second holding component. Estimate the total lethality at 121°C.

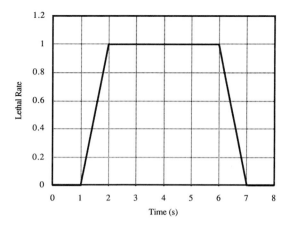

Fig. 5.8   Plot of lethal rate versus time for the conditions of Example 5.8.

APPROACH

The lethality can be estimated by a plot of lethal rate $(10^{(T-138)/8.5})$ versus time, followed by measurement of the area under the curve.

SOLUTION

(1) The lethality for the heating and cooling portions of the process can be estimated by assuming that lethal rate is a linear function of time (Fig. 5.8).

(2) Based on this assumption, the area during the heating process is 0.125 s and for cooling is a similar value.

(3) The lethality at 138°C becomes

$$F_{138} = 0.5 + 4 + 0.5 = 5 \text{ s}$$

(4) At a temperature of 121°C

$$F_{121} = 5 \times 10^{(138-121)/8.5} = 5(10^2) = 500 \text{ s}$$

indicating that heating and cooling add 100 s to the lethality, as compared to the previous example.

Continuous HTST sterilization and pasteurization processes allow direct application of the lethality concept due to the uniform heating of the entire product and the well-defined heating, holding, and cooling segments of the process.

EXAMPLE 5.9

In pilot plant testing of a liquid food subjected to an HTST process, one microorganism survived the heat treatment. Laboratory tests established that

$D_{121} = 1.1$ minute and $z = 11°C$ for the microorganism. The maximum initial count of the microorganism in the food is assumed to be $10^5/g$, and the largest container to be used is 1000 g. A process is desired that will assure that spoilage occurs in less than one container per 10,000. Temperatures at selected points in the process are as follows:

Process	Time	Temperature
	(s)	(°C)
Heating	0.5	104
Heating	1.3	111
Heating	3.4	127
Heating	5.3	135
Heating	6.5	138
Holding	8.3	140
Holding	12.3	140
Cooling	12.9	127
Cooling	14.1	114
Cooling	16.2	106

Calculate the minimum holding time needed to achieve the desired result.

APPROACH

Compute the additional holding time required to achieve the desired spoilage rate.

SOLUTION

(1) Since the desired process will reduce the microbial population to one survivor in 10,000 containers or one microorganism in $10^7/g$, the process must be adequate to reduce the population from $10^5/g$ to one in 10^7 g, or $10^{-7}/g$.

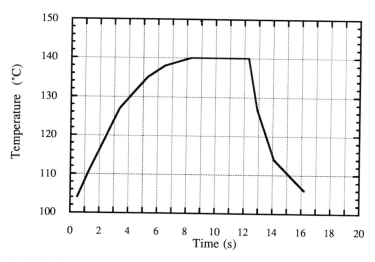

Fig. 5.9   Plot of temperature versus time for the process of Example 5.9.

TABLE 5.1
Lethality Calculations for Example 5.9

Time (s)	Midpoint temperature (°C)	Incremental lethality (s)
0.8	107	0.001
1.8	114.8	0.005
2.8	122.4	0.025
3.8	128.7	0.094
4.8	132.9	0.226
5.8	136.25	0.456
6.8	138.3	0.701
7.8	139.4	0.882
8.8	140	1.000
9.8	140	1.000
10.8	140	1.000
11.8	140	1.000
12.8	129.2	0.104
13.8	117.25	0.008
14.8	111	0.002
15.8	108	0.001
		$\overline{6.505}$

This is equivalent to a reduction of 12 log cycles and the process must be equivalent to $12D_{121}$ or $F_{121} = 12(1.1) = 13.2$ minutes.

(2) To determine the adequacy of the process described, the lethality in terms of equivalent time at 121°C must be determined.

(3) The time–temperature relationship as measured during the process has been plotted in Fig. 5.9. In addition, the midpoint temperatures for one-second intervals throughout the process have been identified as illustrated in Table 5.1. Note that the midpoint temperatures have been chosen so that temperatures fall at the midpoint of each of the four seconds during holding. Since the midpoint of a one-second interval is 0.5 s, the midpoints for the holding period would be $8.3 + 0.5 = 8.8$, and 9.8, 10.8, and 11.8 s. All midpoint temperatures and corresponding times are listed in Table 5.1.

(4) For this situation, the lethality using the temperature at holding as a reference would be computed as

$$\text{Lethal rate} = 10^{(T-140)/z}$$

Since one-second intervals have been chosen, a histogram to illustrate graphical integration used to obtain total lethality can be constructed (Fig. 5.10). The area under the histogram chart is 6.505 s, the same as the total for the lethality column in Table 5.1. The accumulated lethality represents a process of 140°C for 6.505 s.

(5) The computed process is equivalent to

$$F_{121}^{11} = F_{140}^{11} \times 10^{(140-121)/11} = 6.505(53.4) = 347 \text{ s} = 5.79 \text{ minutes}$$

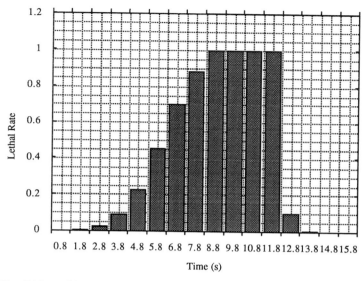

Fig. 5.10 A histogram showing the use of graphical integration to determine total lethality.

(6) Since the desired process is 13.2 minutes, an additional 7.41 minutes of process at 121°C is required.

(7) The additional process can be accomplished by extending the holding time beyond the four seconds. By converting the additional process to an equivalent time at 140°C,

$$F_{140}^{11} = F_{121}^{11} \times 10^{(121-140)/11} = 7.41(0.0187) = 0.139 \text{ minutes} = 8.31 \text{ s}$$

(8) The total holding required to provide the desired process would become

$$4 + 8.31 = 12.31 \text{ s}$$

Problems

5.1 Determine the D value for the microorganism when given the following thermal resistance data for a spore suspension:

Time (minutes)	Number of survivors
0	10^6
15	2.9×10^5
30	8.4×10^4
45	2.4×10^4
60	6.9×10^3

Plot the survivor curve on regular and semilogarithmic coordinates.

5.2 The results of a thermal resistance experiment gave a D value of 7.5 minutes at 110°C. If there were 4.9×10^4 survivors at 10 minutes determine the ratio (N/N_0) for 5, 15, and 20 minutes.

5.3 Determine the z value for a microorganism that has the following decimal reduction times; $D_{110} = 6$ minutes, $D_{116} = 1.5$ minutes, $D_{121} = 0.35$ minutes, and $D_{127} = 0.09$ minutes.

5.4 An F_0 value of 7 minutes provides an acceptable economic spoilage for a given product. Determine the process time at 115°C.

5.5 Determine the Q_{10} value for the thermal process in problem 5.3.

5.6 If the z value of a microorganism is 19°C, compute the Q_{10} value.

5.7 If the z value of a microorganism is 16.5°C and D_{121} is 0.35 minute, what is D_{110}?

5.8 The retention of vitamin B in pork luncheon meat can be described by the following data at 121°C:

Time	% Retention
2.6	95
7.4	90
15.0	80
47.0	50

The z value for vitamin B is 12°C and the F_0 for the spoilage organism is 15 minutes. Determine the process that will provide 99% retention of vitamin B.

5.9 To ensure that *Cl. botulinum* survives in fewer than one of every billion cans processed, a minimum process of $12D$ is used. Compute the maximum allowable population per can that will maintain this spoilage probability.

5.10 The spoilage microorganism for a raw food product has a D value of 5 minutes. Compute the spoilage probability if the initial population per can is 10 and a process equivalent to $F_0 = 3$ minutes is utilized.

List of Symbols

B Arrhenius constant from Eq. (5.19) (1/s)

D decimal reduction time (s)

E_a activation energy (kJ/kg)

F thermal death time (s)

F_0 standard thermal death time at 121°C and $z = 10$°C.

k reaction rate constant (1/t)

N microbial population or component concentration

Q_{10} parameter describing temperature dependence of reaction

r number of containers processed

R_g gas constant (kJ/kg K)

t time (s)
T temperature (°C)

T_A absolute temperature (K)
z thermal resistance factor (°C)

Subscripts: T, temperature; 0, initial; 1, reference; 2, reference.

Superscript: z, thermal resistance reference.

Bibliography

Ball, C. Olin, and Olson, F. C. W. (1957). "Sterilization in Food Technology." McGraw-Hill, New York.

Bigelow, W. D., Bohart, G. S., Richardson, A. C., and Ball, C. O. (1920). Heat penetration in processing canned foods. National Canners Association Bulletin, No. 16L.

Lopez, A. (1969). "A Complete Course in Canning," 9th ed. The Canning Trade, Baltimore, Maryland.

NFPA (1980). "Laboratory Manual for Food Canners and Processors." Vol. 1. AVI Publishing Co., Westport, Connecticut.

Stumbo, C. R. (1973). "Thermobacteriology in Food Processing." Academic Press, New York.

CHAPTER 6

Aseptic Processing and Packaging

During the 1980s, spectacular growth in marketing of aseptic food products occurred in the United States. Aseptic processing of fruit juices and juice drinks in individual-serving containers became common in the market place, followed by other consumer products such as soups, puddings, milk and milk products, and baby foods. In the institutional market, the quality of tomato concentrate and tomato was improved through application of aseptic technology.

Aseptic processing and packaging involves sterilization of the product and the container separately, followed by packaging in a sterile environment (as shown in Fig. 6.1). Packaging involves filling the processed food in sterilized containers and sealing in a steam environment used to maintain aseptic conditions.

Mitchell (1989) has reviewed the history of aseptic processing in the United States. Some of the important developments are summarized in the following paragraph.

It was the pioneering efforts of C. Olin Ball in 1927, that led to the development of the HCF (heat, cool, and fill) process. The procedure involved sterilizing empty containers and food material separately (Ball, 1936). This process is considered to be the forerunner of today's aseptic technology. High costs and operational problems at that time prevented the HCF process from becoming a commercial success. Another method called the Avoset process used sterilized air around the filling area with UV lamps and positive air pressure.

A major development occurred in the late 1940s with the commercialization of the DOLE aseptic process (Martin, 1948). This system used superheated steam to sterilize metal containers and covers, flash heating and cooling of liquid food in a tubular heat exchanger, aseptic filling of cold sterile product into sterile containers followed by sealing of containers in a steam atmosphere. Applications of the DOLE system included processing soups (split-pea soup), specialty sauces, purees, and milk products.

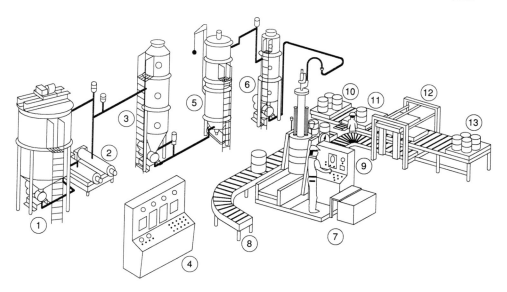

Fig. 6.1 Aseptic processing system: (1) feed tank with pump; (2) scraped surface heaters; (3) steam-pressurized hot-hold vessel with aseptic pump; (4) master process control panel; (5) aseptic scraped surface cooler; (6) nitrogen pressurized cold surge; (7) aseptic low-pressure drum filler; (8) empty drum feed conveyor; (9) uppender; (10) palletized empty drum feed; (11) manual drum depalletizer; (12) semiautomatic drum palletizer; (13) palletized full drum discharge.

In 1958, another milestone was achieved with the development of the commercial aseptic 55-gallon (213 liters) drum filler for tomato paste. Further modifications resulted in the FranRica Drum Filler Systems that are currently used for 1 million drums on an annual basis worldwide. Even larger bulk containers from 55 to 125,000 gallons (213 liters to 484,000 liters) are now aseptically filled (Dixon *et al.*, 1963).

During the 1960s, hydrogen peroxide was approved as a sterilant for the packages by Tetrapak (Sizer, 1982). The vertical form, fill and seal Tetrapak unit (also called Brikpak filler) is now used worldwide. Laminated packaging material is used for desired functional properties such as sealing and as a barrier to oxygen and light.

The bag-in-box concept developed by Scholle Corporation has replaced metal cans in the institutional distribution market. The size of the aseptic bag-in-box ranges from 1 to 500 gallons (4 to 1900 liters). Even larger bulk tanks (up to 40,000 gallon or 155,000 liters) have been sterilized with iodopher solution and filled with tomato and other fruit products.

Use of polymeric containers for aseptic packaging requires that the product temperature during filling be 32°C or less. The package sterility can be obtained by use of hydrogen peroxide (officially accepted by FDA in the United States in February 1981). The residual hydrogen peroxide level must not exceed 0.1 ppm.

Major challenges exist when considering aseptic technology for low-acid products particulates. Since product particles heat by conduction, and the surrounding carrier liquid heats mostly by convection, the heat transfer and flow problems must be fully characterized. In Section 6.2, relevant mathematical expressions will be developed for use in design and evaluation of aseptic processing systems.

6.1 Equipment Components

The primary components of an aseptic processing and packaging system include

- deaerator
- heating and cooling section
- holding tube
- packaging system
- pumps and flow control

6.1.1 Deaerator

Deaeration is an equipment component that exposes the product to a vacuum as part of a continuous flow system. The product must be deaerated to remove oxygen prior to heating to minimize oxidative reactions that may impair the quality of the product during processing as well as during storage.

6.1.2 Heating and Cooling Sections

Heating may be accomplished by using direct heat exchangers such as steam injection and steam infusion heaters. Water added to the product due to steam condensation must be removed during flash cooling. Indirect heating and cooling systems are more commonly used. Heat exchangers for this purpose include tubular, plate, and scraped-surface.

Low-acid liquid foods that contain particles present an extra challenge to the heating and cooling system. Heating, in an indirect type of system, usually results in the carrier liquid being over-processed to ensure adequate processing of the particles. The APV Jupiter system offers an alternative of heating particles and liquid in separate systems, but the system has not achieved commercial acceptance.

The heating section alone is not sufficient to achieve desired lethality for the following reasons:

(1) Liquid foods with high viscosity tend to increase in temperature at a slower rate.

(2) If heat resistant enzymes are present in the food, they may survive a high temperature/short time process.

(3) Particulates heat slower than the surrounding fluid, thus an equilibration time is required to achieve desired lethality at the particle center.

6.1.3   Holding Tube

The holding tube is an important component of the aseptic processing system. Although lethality accumulates in the heating, holding, and cooling sections, FDA will consider only the lethality accumulating in the holding section (Dignan *et al.*, 1989). It follows that the design of the holding tube is crucial to achieve a uniform and sufficient thermal process. Some of the design requirements are

1. The tube must slope upwards at a minimum of 0.25 inch per foot (2.1 cm per meter) to eliminate air pockets and promote drainage following cleaning of the system.
2. The interior surface of the holding tube must be smooth.
3. No product heating can occur along the tube.
4. It must be easy to disassemble the holding tube for inspection purposes.
5. The design must prevent changing the dimensions of the holding tube during assembly.
6. The tube should not be exposed to condensate or cold air draft.
7. The pressure in the tube must be higher than the vapor pressure of the liquid to prevent flashing or boiling of product.
8. There should be appropriate temperature sensors and controller devices at the inlet and exit of the holding tube.

6.1.4   Packaging Systems

Numerous systems can be used to package aseptically processed foods. Differences in systems are primarily related to the size and shape of the package as well as the type of material.

The key component of all packaging systems is the design of the space where product is introduced into the package. This space must be sterilized in a manner that prevents the product from post-processing contamination during package filling.

6.1.5   Pumps and Flow Control

A metering pump, located upstream from the holding tube is used to maintain the required product flow rate. Usually a positive displacement pump is used for this application. Centrifugal pumps are more sensitive to pressure drop and should be used only for CIP applications.

6.2 Mathematical Formulation of an Aseptic Process

Aseptic processing involves primarily liquid foods, such as juices, drinks, and soups, and some liquid foods containing particulates, such as meat balls in gravy or fruit in a carrier liquid. Thermal process calculations for aseptic processing are complicated since these problems involve solution of simultaneous momentum and heat transfer. Additional complexity results due to the non-Newtonian flow characteristics of the carrier liquids. When particulates are present in the liquid, the slowest heating location will be at the center of the largest particulate, therefore heat transfer into the particulate must be calculated. Depending on the inertial and viscous forces, a portion of the fluid may move faster than that remaining in a tube, leading to a distribution of residence times. Mathematical models that incorporate these issues are useful in developing process requirements and in design of the processing equipment.

The mathematical formulation of an aseptic process for a liquid product containing particulates involves description of rate processes that include heating and cooling of the fluid; heat transfer to the food particulates; flow behavior of the fluid and the particulates; and the residence times of the product within the heating, holding, and cooling sections. A partial description of these topics has been presented in previous chapters; the following provides a more focused discussion that can be useful in model development.

6.2.1 Heat Transfer

Heat transfer during continuous flow of a fluid product containing particulates involves several factors, including (1) particulate size and shape, (2) particulate size distribution, (3) residence time distribution of particulates and liquid component of the food in the heat exchanger and the holding tube, (4) convective heat transfer at the heat exchanger surface and at the particulate/liquid interface, and (5) the type of heat exchanger used for heating and cooling. Ultimately, the design involves establishment of the holding tube length.

> *a. Heat Transfer in Fluids Flowing in a Heat Exchanger or a Holding Tube*

Normal heat transfer in the heating, holding, and cooling sections may be calculated by conducting energy balances on the fluid (or fluid containing particulates) over incremental areas of a heat exchanger or a holding tube. In a tubular heat exchanger the moving fluid gains thermal energy from steam condensing on the outside of the tube, and the fluid loses energy to the particulates. In addition, there may be viscous dissipation of energy if a scraped-surface heat exchanger is being used. Assuming that viscous dissipation of energy is negligible and there is perfect mixing of fluid in the radial direction, Sastry (1986) and Chandarana and Gavin (1989) have presented the following equations for heat transfer in the heating, holding, and cooling sections for an incremental length Δx.

Heating

$$m_f c_{pf}\left(T_f^{n+1} - T_f^n\right) = U_{hx} A_{hx}(T_{st} - T_{fm}) + h_{fp} A_p n'_{hx}(T_{ps} - T_{fm}) \quad (6.1)$$

where

$$T_{fm} = \left(T_f^{n+1} + T_f^n\right)/2$$

$$T_{ps} = \left(T_s^{n+1} + T_s^n\right)/2$$

$$A_{hx} = \pi d_{hx} \Delta x_{hx}$$

$$T_p(x, y, z, t) \le T_f(t)$$

Holding Tube

$$m_f c_{pf}\left(T_f^{n+1} - T_f^n\right) = U_{ht} A_{ht}(T_{fm} - T_a) + h_{fp} A_p n'_{ht}(T_{fm} - T_{ps}) \quad (6.2)$$

where

$$A_{ht} = \pi d_{ht} \Delta x_{ht}$$

Cooling

$$m_f c_{pf}\left(T_f^{n+1} - T_f^n\right) = U_{ct} A_{ct}(T_{fm} - T_w) + h_{fp} A_p n'_{ct}(T_{fm} - T_{ps}) \quad (6.3)$$

where

$$T_p = T_p(x, y, z, t)$$

$$T_f = T_f(t)$$

$$A_{ct} = \pi d_{ct} \Delta x_{ct}$$

b. Heat Transfer in Particulates

Heating or cooling of particulates occurs by conduction. The following transient heat conduction equation can be used to describe heat transfer in a particulate in Cartesian coordinates.

$$\rho c_p \frac{\partial T}{\partial t} = k\left[\frac{\partial^2 T}{\partial x^2} + \frac{\partial^2 T}{\partial y^2} + \frac{\partial^2 T}{\partial z^2}\right] \quad (6.4)$$

Subject to the boundary condition

$$-k\frac{\partial T}{\partial x} = h_{\text{fp}}\left(T_{\text{ps}} - T_{\text{fm}}(t)\right) \tag{6.5}$$

The boundary condition is shown for the x direction; similar equations can be written for the y and z directions. Equations (6.2, 6.3, 6.4) are solved simultaneously using numerical methods. Sastry (1986) and Chandarana and Gavin (1989) have used the above equations to solve for temperature history in solid particles and the surrounding liquid. The solution requires knowledge of the magnitude of convective heat transfer coefficient (h_{fp}) at the fluid/particle interface. Although limited information is presently available, the following empirical equations have been used to examine certain limiting case.

Fluid-to-Particulate Convective Heat Transfer Coefficient   For fluid flow over a sphere, a correlation developed by Ranz and Marshall (1952) can be used.

$$N_{\text{Nu}} = 2.0 + 0.6 N_{\text{Re}}^{0.5} N_{\text{Pr}}^{0.33} \tag{6.6}$$

If one assumes that particle and fluid are traveling at identical velocities, the Reynolds number is reduced to zero, and

$$N_{\text{Nu}} = 2.0 \tag{6.7}$$

Equation (6.7) gives the most conservative estimate of the convective heat transfer coefficient between the fluid and the particulate. Recent studies that measure the heat transfer coefficients include Heppell (1985), Zuritz et al. (1987), Sastry et al. (1989) and Chandarana et al. (1989). These studies emphasize that the magnitude of the convective heat transfer coefficient at the particle/liquid interface is finite and small. It should be noted that while assuming an infinite convective heat transfer coefficient for the particle/liquid interface simplifies the solution (deRuyter and Brunet, 1973; Manson and Cullen, 1974), this assumption can predict significantly higher particle temperatures and underestimate lethality.

The expressions found by Chandarana et al. (1990) were

$$N_{\text{Nu}} = 2 + 2.82 \times 10^{-3} N_{\text{Re}}^{1.16} N_{\text{Pr}}^{0.89} \tag{6.8}$$

$$1.23 < N_{\text{Re}} < 27.38$$

$$9.47 < N_{\text{Pr}} < 376.18$$

for starch solutions, and

$$N_{\text{Nu}} = 2 + 1.33 \times 10^{-3} N_{\text{Re}}^{1.08} \tag{6.9}$$

$$287.29 < N_{\text{Re}} < 880.76$$

for water. The expressions apply to convective heat transfer coefficients between 55.63 and 89.5 W/m^2 °C for starch solutions and between 64.67 and 107.11 W/m^2 °C for water.

Holding Tube Wall-to-Fluid Convective Heat Transfer Coefficient   If the holding tube is horizontal, the following relationship may be used to determine the convective heat transfer coefficient between tube-wall and the fluid.

$$N_{Nu} = 0.023 N_{Re}^{0.8} N_{Pr}^{0.4} \qquad (6.10)$$

Scraped-Surface Heat Exchanger Wall-to-Fluid Convective Heat Transfer Coefficient   The wall-to-fluid convective heat transfer coefficient for a scraped-surface heat exchanger may be estimated from the relationship suggested by Weisser (1972).

$$N_{Nu} = 1.2 N_{Re}^{0.5} N_{Pr}^{0.33} N_{m}^{0.26} \qquad (6.11)$$

where N_m is the number of mutator blades.

6.2.2   Residence Time Distribution

Danckwerts (1953) has studied the problem of residence time distribution of fluid flowing in a pipe. Some specific approaches related to aseptic processing of foods are presented in this section.

a. Residence Time of Liquid Foods in a Holding Tube

For laminar flow conditions and a Newtonian fluid flowing in a circular pipe, the velocity profile is parabolic. The ratio between the mean velocity $\bar{u}$ and maximum velocity u_{max} is

$$\frac{\bar{u}}{u_{max}} = 0.5 \qquad (6.12)$$

The velocity ratio for turbulent flow of Newtonian fluid is

$$\frac{\bar{u}}{u_{max}} = 0.82 \qquad (6.13)$$

For liquids with non-Newtonian flow characteristics, the velocity ratio is

$$\frac{\bar{u}}{u_{max}} = \frac{n + 1}{3n + 1} \qquad (6.14)$$

where n is the flow behavior index.

Figure (6.2) provides a relationship between the velocity ratio and the generalized Reynolds number.

b. Residence Time of Liquid Foods in Heating / Cooling Section

The temperature effects on the viscous properties of the liquid must be considered when calculating residence time distribution in the heating and

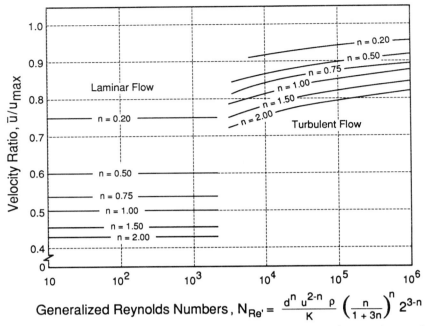

Generalized Reynolds Numbers, $N_{Re'} = \dfrac{d^n \, u^{2-n} \, \rho}{K} \left(\dfrac{n}{1+3n}\right)^n 2^{3-n}$

Fig. 6.2 Plot of velocity ratio versus generalized Reynolds numbers. [From Palmer and Jones (1976).]

cooling sections. This fact complicates the prediction of temperature profiles in the heating and cooling sections. This is one of the reasons that the FDA (in the United States) does not allow consideration of lethality accumulated by the product in the heating section.

c. Residence Time Distribution of Foods Containing Particulates

Specific studies done with aseptic systems show that in a scraped-surface heat exchanger, as the mutator speed is increased, the residence time of the particulate also increases. With an increasing flow rate, the mean residence time of the particles decreases. There is experimental evidence that particle residence time depends on particulate size, viscosity of fluid, and holding tube configuration (McCoy *et al.*, 1987).

EXAMPLE 6.1

An aseptic processing system is being designed for a vegetable soup in which the largest particulate is a 15-mm spherical potato. The carrier liquid is a starch solution that achieves the temperature of 140°C at the exit of the scraped-surface heating portion of the system and entrance to the holding tube. The particulates enter the holding tube at a uniform temperature of 80°C. The product flow rate is 1.5 m^3/hr with laminar flow in the holding tube, where the inside diameter is 4.75 cm. The relative velocity between particulate and solution is 0.005 m/s. The thermal process must achieve a 12-log reduction in microbial population at the center of the particulates. The microorganism has a decimal reduction time (D) at 121°C of 1.665 s and a thermal resistance factor (z) of 10°C. The starch solution has a specific heat of 4 kJ/kg °C, thermal conductivity of 0.6 W/m °C, density of 1000 kg/m^3, and viscosity of 1.5×10^{-2} Pa · s. Determine the length of holding tube required to complete the desired thermal process.

APPROACH

The holding tube length will be based on residence time for largest particulate.

SOLUTION

(1) To compute lethality at the particulate center, the temperature history must be estimated. Figure 4.46 (Time–Temperature chart in Chapter 4) can be used for this purpose.

(2) Use of Fig. 4.46 requires the following information:

- Thermal conductivity of potato (Table A.2.2)

$$k = 0.554 \text{ W/m K}$$

- Thermal diffusivity of potato

$$\alpha = \frac{k}{\rho c_p} = \frac{0.554}{(950)(3634.0)} = 1.6 \times 10^{-7} \text{ m}^2/\text{s}$$

where density is estimated from water and specific heats are obtained from Table A.2.1.

Particulate radius $R = 0.0075$ m
Initial particulate temperature $T_i = 80°C$
Medium temperature $T_a = 140°C$

(3) The convective heat transfer coefficient h requires use of Eq. (6.8).

$$N_{Nu} = 2 + 2.82 \times 10^{-3} N_{Re}^{1.16} N_{Pr}^{0.89}$$

where

$$N_{Re} = \frac{\rho \, du}{\mu} = \frac{(1000)(0.015)(0.005)}{1.5 \times 10^{-2}} = 5$$

$$N_{Pr} = \frac{c_p \mu}{k} = \frac{(4000)(1.5 \times 10^{-2})}{0.6} = 100$$

and all properties are for starch solution. Then

$$N_{Nu} = \frac{hd}{k} = 2 + 2.82 \times 10^{-3}(5)^{1.16}(100)^{0.89} = 3.099$$

and

$$h = \frac{3.099 \times 0.6}{0.015} = 123.96 \text{ W/m}^2 °C$$

(4) For use in Fig. 4.46:

$$\frac{k}{hR} = \frac{0.554}{(123.96)(0.0075)} = 0.6$$

Then particulate center temperatures become

Time, t (s)	$\alpha t/R^2$	$\dfrac{T_a - T}{T_a - T_i}$	T (°C)
0	0	1.0	80
60	0.171	0.9	86
80	0.228	0.69	98.6
100	0.284	0.58	105.2
120	0.341	0.47	111.8
140	0.398	0.40	116.0
160	0.455	0.35	119.0

(5) The evaluation of temperature history on lethality within the particulate is determined by computation of lethality (F) as a function of time.

- The total lethality requirement is

$$F_{121} = 12D_{121} = 12(1.665) = 19.98 \text{ s}$$

- For temperature history within the particulate:

Time (s)	Temp, T (°C)	Lethality, F (s)	Accumulated lethality (s)
0	80	—	—
60	86	0.0063	0.0063
80	98.6	0.1151	0.1214
100	105.2	0.5261	0.6475
120	111.8	2.4045	3.0520
140	116.0	6.3246	9.3766
160	119.0	12.6191	21.9957

- The accumulated lethality computations illustrate that 160 seconds of particulate residence time in the holding tube exceeds the lethality requirement of 19.98 seconds.
- By assuming linear lethality accumulations within each minute of residence time, 10.6 seconds of lethality would be required for residence time beyond 140 seconds. An additional 16.8 seconds of residence time would be sufficient to provide the additional lethality. The total residence time in the holding tube becomes 2.61 minutes.

(6) To determine holding-tube length, product flow rate must be considered.

- Based on volumetric flow rate of 1.5 m^3/hr and the pipe diameter of 0.0475 m,

$$\bar{u} = \frac{1.5}{\pi(0.02375)^2} = 846 \text{ m/hr} = 14.1 \text{ m/minute}$$

- Since laminar flow in the holding tube is 0.5,

$$\frac{\bar{u}}{u_{max}} = 0.5$$

$$u_{max} = 28.2 \text{ m/minute}.$$

- Using the residence time of 2.61 minutes,

$$\text{Holding-tube length} = (28.2)(2.61) = 73.6 \text{ m}$$

Problems

6.1 Estimate the convective heat transfer coefficient at the surface of a 10 mm diameter spherical piece of apple carried in fluid through the holding tube of an aseptic processing system. The relative velocity between the particle and the fluid is 0.002 m/s. The carrier fluid has a density of 1050 kg/m^3, specific heat of 3.9 kJ/kg K, thermal conductivity of 0.57 W/m K and viscosity of 1.6×10^{-2} Pa · s.

6.2 A non-Newtonian carrier fluid for a vegetable soup has a flow behavior index of 0.65. Estimate the velocity ratio under laminar flow conditions and under turbulent flow in a 5 cm inside diameter pipe. The mean velocity required for turbulent flow is 0.3 m/s. The carrier fluid has a density of 950 kg/m^3, specific heat of 4.1 kJ/kg K, and thermal conductivity of 0.62 W/m K. The mean velocity providing a generalized Reynolds number of 10^3 is 0.2 m/s.

6.3 An aseptic packaging machine is being sterilized using saturated steam at 130°C. The most thermally resistant microorganism is a spore with $D_{121} = 5$ min and $z = 10$°C. Determine the time and pressure for the equipment sterilization process if a $12D$ reduction in spore population is needed. Estimate the initial spore population resulting in product spoilage rates of greater than 1 container per 10,000.

6.4 Compare the length of a holding tube required for a $12D_{121}$ sterilization of a high viscosity liquid ($\mu = 0.03$ Pa · s) under laminar and turbulent flow conditions. The holding tube diameter is 4 cm and the liquid density is 1050 kg/m^3. The D-value for the spoilage microorganism at 121°C is 0.02 min.

6.5 An aseptic processing system has a 100 m holding tube with 5 cm inside diameter. The system will be used to provide a thermal process for a new product, a starch solution carrier for 10 mm diameter spherical particles with the properties of lean beef. The carrier solution enters the holding tube at 135°C and the particles are at a uniform temperature of 65°C. The product flow rate is 40 kg/min and the relative velocity between carrier fluid and particles is 1 m/min. The spoilage microorganism has a decimal reduction time D of 5 min at 121°C and a z of 7°C. The starch solution has the following properties: viscosity = 0.02 Pa · s, thermal conductivity = 0.75 W/m K, density = 950 kg/m³, and specific heat = 3.8 kJ/kg K. Estimate the spoilage rate for the product processed in the system when the initial population of spoilage microorganism is 10^5 per container.

6.6 Using the equations presented by Palmer and Jones (1976), develop a spreadsheet to determine the velocity ratios if the generalized Reynolds number is 100,000 and the n values are (a) 0.2; (b) 0.75; (c) 1.00; (d) 1.25; (e) 1.75. *Note*: An iterative calculation process will be necessary to determine the friction factor f such that equation (3) in the original paper is satisfied.

List of Symbols

A_{ct} incremental surface area for cooling tube (m²)
A_{ht} incremental surface area for holding tube (m²)
A_{hx} incremental surface area for heat exchanger (m²)
A_p surface area of particle (m²)
α thermal diffusivity (m²/s)
c_p specific heat (kJ/kg K)
D decimal reduction time (s)
d diameter (m)
F thermal death time (s)
h convective heat transfer coefficient (W/m² K)
K consistency coefficient (Pa · s^n)
k thermal conductivity (W/m K)
m mass flow rate (kg/s)
μ viscosity (Pa · s)

N_m number of mutator blades
N_{Nu} Nusselt number
N_{Pr} Prandtl number
N_{Re} Reynolds number
N_{GRe} Generalized Reynolds number
n flow behavior index in Eq. (6.14)
n' number of particles in incremental volume
R radius (m)
ρ density (kg/m³)
t time (s)
T temperature (°C)
U overall heat transfer coefficient (W/m² K)
$\bar{u}$ mean velocity (m/s)
u_{max} maximum velocity
Δx incremental distance (m)
z thermal resistance factor (°C)

Subscripts: a, ambient; ct, cooling tube; f, fluid; fp, fluid-particle; fm, mean fluid; hx, heat exchanger; ht, holding tube; i, initial; p, particle; ps, mean particle surface; s, particle surface; st, steam; T, temperature; w, cooling water.

Superscripts: $n, n + 1$, time reference.

Bibliography

Ball, C. O. (1936). Apparatus for a method of canning. U.S. Patent 2,020,303.

Ball, C. O., and Olson, F. C. W. (1957). "Sterilization in Food Technology." McGraw-Hill, New York.

Chandarana, D., and Gavin, A. III (1989). Establishing thermal processes for heterogenous foods to be processed aseptically: A theoretical comparison of process development methods. *J. Food Sci.* **54**(1), 198–204.

Chandarana, D., Gavin, A. III, and Wheaton, F. W. (1989). Simulation of parameters for modeling aseptic processing of foods containing particulates. *Food Technol.* **43**(3), 137–143.

Chandarana, D. I., Gavin, A. III, and Wheaton, F. W. (1990). Particle/fluid interface heat transfer under UHT conditions at low particle/fluid relative velocities. *J. Food Process Eng.* **13**, 191–206.

Danckwerts, P. V. (1953). Continuous flow systems. *Chem. Eng. Sci.* **2**(1).

de Ruyter, P. W., and Burnet, R. (1973). Estimation of process conditions for continuous sterilization of food containing particulates. *Food Technol.* **27**(7), 44.

Dignan, D. M., Barry, M. R., Pflug, I. J., and Gardine, T. D. (1989). Safety considerations in establishing aseptic processes for low-acid foods containing particulates. *Food Technol.* **43**(3), 118–121.

Dixon, M. S., Warshall, R. B., and Crerar, J. B. (1963). Food processing method and apparatus. U.S. Patent No. 3,096,161.

Heppell, N. J. (1985). Measurement of the liquid–solid heat transfer coefficient during continuous sterilization of foodstuffs containing particles. Proceedings of Symposium on Aseptic Processing and Packing of Foods. Tylosand, Sweden, Sept. 9–12.

Lopez, A. (1969). "A Complete Course in Canning," 9th ed. The Canning Trade, Baltimore, Maryland.

Manson, J. E., and Cullen, J. F. (1974). Thermal process simulation for aseptic processing of foods containing discrete particulate matter. *J. Food Sci.* **39**, 1084.

Martin, W. M. (1948). Flash process, aseptic fill, are used in new canning unit. *Food Ind.* **20**, 832–836.

McCoy, S. C., Zuritz, C. A., and Sastry, S. K. (1987). Residence time distribution of simulated food particles in a holding tube. ASAE Paper No. 87-6536. American Society of Agricultural Engineers, St. Joseph, Michigan.

Mitchell, E. L. (1989). A review of aseptic processing. *Adv. Food Res.* **32**, 1–37.

NFPA (1980). "Laboratory Manual for Food Canners and Processors." AVI Publishing Co., Westport, Connecticut.

Palmer, J., and Jones, V. (1976). Prediction of holding times for continuous thermal processing of power law fluids. *J. Food Sci.* **41**(5), 1233.

Ranz, W. E., and Marshall, W. R. Jr. (1952). Evaporation from drops. *Chem. Eng. Prog.* **48**, 141–180.

Sastry, S. (1986). Mathematical evaluation of process schedules for aseptic processing of low-acid foods containing discrete particulates. *J. Food Sci.* **51**, 1323.

Sastry, S. K., Heskitt, B. F., and Blaisdell, J. L. (1989). Experimental and modeling studies on convective heat transfer at the particle–liquid interface in aseptic processing systems. *Food Technol.* **43**(3), 132–136.

Sizer, C. (1982). Aseptic system and European experience. *Proc. Annu. Short Course Food Ind.*, *22nd*, pp. 93–100. University of Florida, Gainesville.

Stumbo, C. R. (1973). "Thermobacteriology in Food Processing." Academic Press, New York.

Weisser, H. (1972). Untersuchungen zum Warmeubergang im Kratzkuhler. Ph.D. thesis, Karlsruhe Universitat, Germany.

Zuritz, C. A., McCoy, S., and Sastry, S. K. (1987). Convective heat transfer coefficients for non-Newtonian flow past food-shaped particulates. ASAE Paper No. 87-6538. American Society of Agricultural Engineers, St. Joseph, Michigan.

CHAPTER 7

Refrigeration

7.1 Introduction

Temperature plays an important role in maintaining the quality of stored food products. Lowering the temperature retards the rates of reactions that cause quality deterioration. It is generally agreed that the reaction rate is reduced by half by lowering the temperature by 10°C.

In earlier days, a lower temperature was obtained by the use of ice. Ice was allowed to melt in an insulated chamber that contained food products (Fig. 7.1). During melting, ice requires latent heat (333 kJ/kg) to be converted from the solid phase to liquid water. This heat was extracted from the product that was kept next to ice in an insulated chamber.

Today, the cooling process is achieved by the use of a mechanical refrigeration system. Refrigeration systems allow transfer of heat from the cooling chamber to a location where the heat can be easily discarded. The transfer of heat is accomplished by using a refrigerant, which like water changes state—from liquid to vapor. Unlike water, a refrigerant has a much lower boiling point. For example, ammonia, a commonly used refrigerant in industrial plants, has a boiling point of −33.3°C. This is a much lower temperature compared with 100°C, the boiling point of water at atmospheric pressure. Similar to water, ammonia needs latent heat to change its phase from liquid to gas at its boiling point. The boiling point of a refrigerant can be varied by changing the pressure. Thus, to increase the boiling point of ammonia to 0°C, its pressure must be raised to 430.43 kPa.

A very simple refrigeration system that utilizes a refrigerant is shown in Fig. 7.2. The only drawback in this illustration is the one-time use of the refrigerant. Because refrigerants are expensive, they must be reused. Thus, the system must be modified to allow collection of the refrigerant vapors and their conversion to liquid state so that the same refrigerant can be used repetitively. This is accomplished with the use of a mechanical vapor-compression system.

Before we discuss a mechanical vapor-compression system, it is necessary to examine the properties of refrigerants. The selection of a refrig-

Fig. 7.1   An ice box.

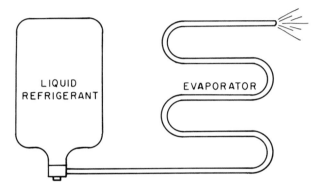

Fig. 7.2   Use of liquid refrigerant to accomplish refrigeration.

erant is based on suitable properties at a desired temperature. After examining the properties of refrigerants, we will consider various components of a mechanical vapor-compression system. We will use a thermodynamic chart for a refrigerant to examine a mechanical vapor-compression refrigeration system. The concluding section in this chapter will include several application problems where mathematical expressions will be used to design simple refrigeration systems.

7.2   Selection of a Refrigerant

A wide variety of refrigerants are commercially available for use in vapor-compression systems. Selection of a refrigerant is based on several performance characteristics that assist in determining the refrigerant's suitability for a given system. The following is a list of important characteristics that are usually considered:

(1) *Latent heat of vaporization*. A high latent heat of vaporization is preferred. For a given capacity, a high value of latent heat of vaporization indicates that a smaller amount of refrigerant will be circulated per unit of time.

(2) *Condensing pressure*. Excessively high condensing pressure requires considerable expenditure on heavy construction of condenser and piping.

(3) *Freezing temperature*. The freezing temperature of the refrigerant should be below the evaporator temperature.

(4) *Critical temperature*. The refrigerant should have sufficiently high critical temperature. At temperatures above the critical temperature, the refrigerant vapor cannot be liquefied. Particularly in the case of air-cooled condensers, the critical temperature should be above the highest ambient temperature expected.

(5) *Toxicity*. In many applications, including airconditioning systems, the refrigerant must be nontoxic.

(6) *Flammability*. The refrigerant should be nonflammable.

(7) *Corrosiveness*. The refrigerant should not be corrosive to the materials used in the construction of the refrigeration system.

(8) *Chemical stability*. The refrigerant must be chemically stable.

(9) *Detection of leaks*. If a leak develops in the refrigeration system, the detection of such a leak should be easy.

(10) *Cost*. Low-cost refrigerant is preferred in industrial applications.

(11) *Environmental impact*. The refrigerant released from the refrigeration systems due to leaks should not cause environmental damage.

Table 7.1 includes properties and performance characteristics of some commonly used refrigerants. The performance characteristics are given at −15°C (5°F) and 30°C (86°F), the evaporator and condenser temperatures, respectively. These temperatures are used as standard conditions to make comparisons of refrigerants by the American Society of Heating, Refrigeration, and Air Conditioning Engineers (ASHRAE).

Ammonia offers an exceptionally high latent heat of vaporization among all other refrigerants. It is noncorrosive to iron and steel but corrodes copper, brass, and bronze. It is irritating to mucous membranes and eyes. It can be toxic at concentrations of 0.5% by volume in air. A leak in the refrigeration system that uses ammonia as a refrigerant can be easily detected either by smell or by burning sulfur candles and noting white smoke created by the ammonia vapors.

Standard designations for refrigerants are based on ANSI/ASHRAE Standard 34-1978. Some of the commonly used refrigerants and their standard designations are listed in Table 7.2.

A number of refrigerants used in commercial practice are halocarbons. For example, Refrigerant-12, also called Freon 12, is commonly used in comfort-conditioning systems. Freon is a trade name; the refrigerant, manufactured by DuPont, is dichlorodifluoromethane. The latent heat of

TABLE 7.1

**Comparison between Commonly Used Refrigerants
(Performance Based on − 15°C Evaporator Temperature
and 30°C Condenser Temperature)**

Chemical formula	Freon 12 (dichloro-difluoro-methane, CCl_2F_2)	Freon 22 (monochloro-difluoro-methane, $CHClF_2$)	Methyl chloride (CH_3Cl)	Ammonia (NH_3)
Molecular weight	120.9	86.5	50.5	17.0
Boiling point (°C) at 101.3 kPa	− 29.8	− 40.8	− 23.8	− 33.3
Evaporator pressure at − 15°C (kPa)	182.7	296.4	145.5	236.5
Condensing pressure at 30°C (kPa)	744.6	1203.0	652.9	1166.5
Freezing point (°C) at 101.3 kPa	− 157.8	− 160.0	− 97.8	− 77.8
Critical temperature (°C)	112.2	96.1	142.8	132.8
Critical pressure (kPa)	4115.7	4936.1	6680.3	11423.4
Compressor discharge temperature (°C)	37.8	55.0	77.8	98.9
Compression ratio (30°C/ − 15°C)	4.07	5.06	4.48	4.94
Latent heat of vaporization at − 15°C (kJ/kg)	161.7	217.7	420.3	1314.2
Horsepower/ton refrigerant, ideal	1.002	1.011	0.962	0.989
Refrigerant circulated/ ton refrigeration (kg/s), ideal	2.8×10^{-2}	2.1×10^{-2}	0.97×10^{-2}	0.31×10^{-2}
Compressor displacement/ ton refrigeration (m^3/s)	2.7×10^{-4}	1.7×10^{-4}	2.8×10^{-4}	1.6×10^{-4}
Stability (toxic decomposition products)	Yes	Yes	Yes	No
Flammability	None	None	Yes	Yes
Odor	Ethereal	Ethereal	Ethereal	Acrid
Evaporator temperature range (°C)	− 73 to 10	− 87 to 10	− 62 to 10	− 68 to − 7

TABLE 7.2
Standard Designations of Refrigerants

Refrigerant number	Chemical name	Chemical formula
Halocarbons		
12	Dichlorodifluoromethane	CCl_2F_2
22	Chlorodifluoromethane	$CHCLF_2$
30	Methylene Chloride	CH_2Cl_2
114	Dichlorotetrafluoroethane	$CClF_2CClF_2$
134a	1,1,1,2-tertrafluoroethane	CF_3CH_2F
Azeotropes		
502	R-22/R-115	$CHClF_2/CClF_2CF_3$
Inorganic compound		
717	Ammonia	NH_3

vaporization of Freon (R-12) is low compared to ammonia (R-717); therefore, considerably more weight of refrigerant must be circulated to achieve the same refrigeration capacity.

Refrigerant-22 (monochlorodifluoromethane) is particularly useful with low-temperature applications (-40 to $-87°C$). Use of Refrigerant-22, which has a low specific volume, can result in greater heat removal than with Refrigerant-12 for a compressor with the same size piston.

During the mid 1970s, it was first postulated that chlorofluorocarbons (CFCs), because of their extremely stable characteristics, have a long life in the lower atmosphere and they migrate to the upper atmosphere over a period of time. In the upper atmosphere, the chlorine portion of the CFC molecule is split off due to the sun's ultraviolet radiation, and it reacts with ozone, resulting in the depletion of ozone concentration. Ozone depletion in the upper atmosphere permits more of the sun's harmful ultraviolet radiation to reach the earth's surface. In the early 1990s, increasing concern was directed at the role of CFCs in damaging the protective ozone layer surrounding the planet. Many of the commonly used refrigerants are fully halogenated chlorofluorocarbons (CFCs) containing chlorine. Alternatives to the CFCs that are being actively considered at the time of writing of this edition are hydrofluorocarbons (HFCs) and hydrochlorofluorocarbons (HCFCs). Hydrogen-containing fluorocarbons have weak carbon–hydrogen bonds, which are more susceptible to cleavage; thus they are postulated to have shorter lifetimes.

The selection of refrigerants as alternatives to CFCs has been a topic of major interest in the scientific community. A new refrigerant that shows considerable promise is HFC 134a. Table 7.3 includes some important thermodynamic properties of HFC 134a. The vapor pressure of HFC 134a can be determined using the following equation:

$$\ln(p/p_c) = a_1\tau/(1-\tau) + a_2\tau + a_3\tau^{1.89} + a_4\tau^3 \qquad (7.1)$$

TABLE 7.3
Thermodynamic Properties of HFC 134a

Molecular mass	102.03 g mol^{-1}
Triple point	172 K
Normal boiling point	247 K
Freezing temperature	172 K
Liquid density	1375 kg m^{-3}
Critical point	374.21 K
	4056 kPa
	515 kg/m^{-3}
Vapor pressure[a]	$a_1 = -8.798572$
	$a_2 = 1.379055$
	$a_3 = 3.587903$
	$a_4 = -2.390161$

Source: McLinden (1990)
[a]Coefficients for Eq. (7.1)

where $\tau = (1 - T/T_c)$; T_c, p_c are temperature and pressure at the critical point, respectively. The coefficients a_1, a_2, a_3, and a_4 are given in Table 7.3.

Despite the efforts to reduce the use of CFCs, they are still the leading refrigerants in commercial use; therefore, this chapter includes several examples on design and performance analysis of refrigeration systems that use these refrigerants. Use of other refrigerants such as ammonia is also presented.

7.3 Components of a Refrigeration System

Major components of a simple mechanical vapor compression refrigeration system are shown in Fig. 7.3. As the refrigerant flows through these components its phase changes from liquid to gas and then back to liquid. The flow of refrigerant can be examined by tracing the path of the refrigerant in Fig. 7.3.

At location d on Fig. 7.3, just prior to the entrance to the expansion valve, the refrigerant is in a saturated liquid state. It is at or below its condensation temperature. The expansion valve separates the high-pressure region from the low-pressure region. After passing through the expansion valve, the refrigerant experiences a drop in pressure accompanied by a drop in temperature. Due to the drop in pressure, some of the liquid refrigerant changes to gas. The liquid/gas mixture leaving the expansion valve is termed "flash gas."

The liquid/gas mixture enters the evaporator coils at location e. In the evaporator, the refrigerant completely vaporizes to gas by accepting heat from the media surrounding the evaporator coils. The saturated vapors may reach a superheated stage due to gain of additional heat from the surroundings.

The saturated or superheated vapors enter the compressor, where the refrigerant is compressed to a high pressure. This high pressure must be below the critical pressure of the refrigerant and high enough to allow condensation of the refrigerant at a temperature slightly higher than that

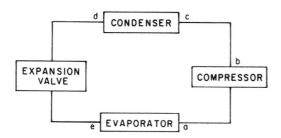

Fig. 7.3 A mechanical vapor-compression refrigeration system.

of commonly available heat sinks, such as ambient air or well water. Inside the compressor, the compression process of the vapors occurs at constant entropy (called an isentropic process). As the pressure of the refrigerant increases, the temperature increases, and the refrigerant becomes super-heated.

The superheated vapors are then conveyed to a condenser. Using either an air-cooled or a water-cooled condenser, the refrigerant discharges heat to the surrounding media. The refrigerant condenses back to the liquid state in the condenser. After the entire amount of refrigerant has been converted to saturated liquid, the temperature of the refrigerant may decrease below that of its condensation temperature due to additional heat discharged to the surrounding media; in other words, it may be subcooled. The subcooled or saturated liquid then enters the expansion valve and the cycle continues.

7.3.1 Evaporator

Inside the evaporator, the liquid refrigerant vaporizes to gaseous state. The change of state requires latent heat, which is extracted from the surroundings.

Based on their use, evaporators can be classified into two categories. *Direct-expansion* evaporators allow the refrigerant to vaporize inside the evaporator coils; the coils are in direct contact with the object or fluid being refrigerated. *Indirect-expansion* evaporators involve the use of a carrier medium, such as water or brine, which is cooled by the refrigerant vaporizing in the evaporator coils. The cooled carrier medium is then pumped to the object that is being refrigerated. The indirect-expansion evaporators require additional equipment. They are useful when cooling is desired at several locations in the system. Water may be used as a carrier medium if the temperature stays above freezing. For lower temperatures, brine (a proper concentration of $CaCl_2$) or glycols, such as ethylene or propylene glycol, are commonly used.

The evaporators are either bare-pipe, finned-tube, or plate type, as shown in Fig. 7.4. Bare-pipe evaporators are most simple, easy to defrost and clean. The fins added to the finned-tube evaporators allow increase in surface area, thus increasing the rate of heat transfer. The plate evaporators allow an indirect contact between the product (e.g., a liquid food) to be cooled and the refrigerant.

Evaporators can also be classified as direct-expansion and flooded types. In the direct-expansion type of evaporators, there is no recirculation of the refrigerant within the evaporator. The liquid refrigerant changes to gas as it is conveyed through a continuous tube. In contrast, the flooded evaporator allows recirculation of liquid refrigerant. The liquid refrigerant, after going through the metering device, enters a surge chamber. As shown in Fig. 7.5, the liquid refrigerant boils in the evaporator coil and extracts

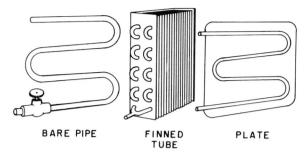

BARE PIPE   **FINNED**   **PLATE**
                      TUBE

Fig. 7.4   Different types of evaporator coils. (Courtesy of Carrier Co.)

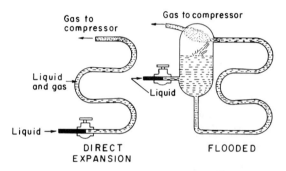

DIRECT   **FLOODED**
EXPANSION

Fig. 7.5   A direct-expansion evaporator and a flooded-type evaporator. (Courtesy of Carrier Co.)

heat from the surroundings. The liquid refrigerant is recirculated through the surge tank and the evaporator coil. The refrigerant gas leaves the surge tank for the compressor.

7.3.2   Compressor

The refrigerant enters the compressor in vapor state at low pressure and temperature. The compressor raises the pressure and temperature of the refrigerant. It is due to this action of the compressor that heat can be discharged by the refrigerant in the condenser. The compression processes raise the temperature of the refrigerant sufficiently above the temperature of the ambient surrounding the condenser, so that the temperature gradient between the refrigerant and the ambient promotes the heat flow from the refrigerant to the ambient.

The three common types of compressors are reciprocating, centrifugal, and rotary. As is evident from the name, the reciprocating compressor

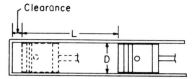

FIG. 5.6. Operation of a cylinder.

contains a piston that travels back and forth in a cylinder (as shown in Fig. 7.6). Reciprocating compressors are most commonly used and vary in capacity from a fraction of a ton to 100 tons of refrigeration per unit (for definition of ton of refrigeration, see Section 7.5.1). The centrifugal compressor contains an impeller with several blades that turn at high speed. The rotary compressor involves a vane that rotates inside a cylinder.

The compressor may be operated with an electric motor or an internal combustion engine. Figure 7.7 shows a typical installation of a reciprocating compressor operated with an electric motor.

An important parameter that influences the performance of a compressor is the compressor capacity. The compressor capacity is affected by several factors. Factors that are inherent to the design of equipment include (a) piston displacement, (b) clearance between the piston head and the end of the cylinder when the piston is at the top of its stroke, and (c) size of the suction and discharge valves. Other factors that influence the compressor capacity are associated with the operating conditions. These factors include (a) revolutions per minute, (b) type of refrigerant, (c) suction pressure, and (d) discharge pressure.

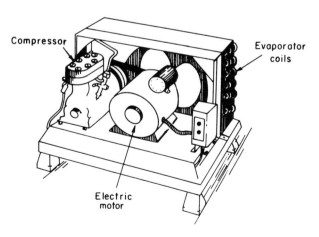

Fig. 7.7 A typical compression refrigeration system of two-cylinder, air-cooled condenser driven by an electric motor.

The piston displacement can be computed from the following equation:

$$\text{Piston displacement} = \frac{\pi D^2 L N}{4}$$

where D is the diameter of cylinder bore (cm), L is the length of stroke (cm), and N is the number of cylinders.

The compressor displacement can be computed from the following equation:

$$\text{Compressor displacement} = (\text{piston displacement})(\text{revolutions per minute})$$

The piston displacement can be examined by considering Fig. 7.8. Point A refers to the cylinder volume of 100% with the vapors at the suction pressure. The vapors are compressed to about 15% of cylinder volume, shown by point B. During the compression cycle, both the suction valve and discharge valve remain closed. During the discharge cycle BC, the discharge valve opens and the gas is released. The cylinder volume is decreased to 5%. This value represents the volume between the head of the piston and the end of the cylinder. As the piston starts traveling in the opposite direction, during the expansion cycle CD, the high-pressure gas remaining in the clearance expands. Attempts are always made to keep the clearance as small as practically possible, since the clearance space represents a loss in capacity. Process DA represents suction; the suction valve remains open during this process and the vapors are admitted to the cylinder. The piston retracts to the location indicated by point A. The cycle is then repeated.

In actual practice, the suction and discharge pressure lines (BC and DA) are not straight lines, due to the pressure drop across the valves. The

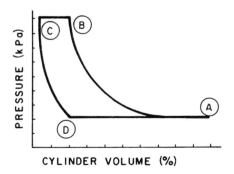

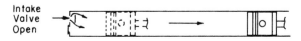

Fig. 7.8   A complete cycle of a reciprocating compressor. (Courtesy of Carrier Co.)

discharge line lies above, and the suction line lies below the theoretical straight lines indicated in Fig. 7.8. This difference can be explained by the fact that at the beginning of discharge, the cylinder pressure must be higher than the discharge pressure to force the valve open against the spring pressure. Similarly, at the beginning of the suction process, the pressure must be lower than the suction pressure to open the suction valve.

It is often necessary to control the compressor capacity, since the refrigeration loads are seldom constant. Thus, the compressor is mostly operated at partial loads compared to the refrigeration load used in the design of a compressor. The compressor capacity can be controlled by (a) controlling the speed (revolutions per minute), (b) bypassing gas from the high-pressure side to the low-pressure side of the compressor, and (c) internal bypassing of gas in a compressor, by keeping the suction valve open.

The speed can be controlled by the use of a variable-speed electric motor.

Bypassing gas is the most commonly used method of capacity control. In one bypass system, the discharge side of the compressor is connected to the suction side. A solenoid valve is used to bypass the discharge gas directly to the suction side of the compressor. Thus, the refrigerant delivered from a bypassed cylinder of the compressor is stopped, and the compressor capacity is reduced. The bypass system described here does not result in any significant savings in power requirement.

A more desirable bypass system involves keeping the suction valve open, allowing the gas to simply surge back and forth in the cylinder. Thus, the bypassed cylinder delivers no refrigerant. Hermetically sealed solenoids are used to control the opening of the suction valves. In multicylinder compressors, it is possible to inactivate desired cylinders when the load is low. For a four-cylinder compressor with three cylinders inoperative, the compressor capacity can be reduced by as much as 75%.

7.3.3 Condenser

The function of the condenser in a refrigeration system is to transfer heat from the refrigerant to another medium, such as air and/or water. By rejecting heat, the gaseous refrigerant condenses to liquid inside the condenser.

The major types of condensers used are (1) water-cooled, (2) air-cooled, and (3) evaporative. In evaporative condensers, both air and water are used.

Three common types of water-cooled condensers are (1) double pipe, (2) shell and tube (as shown in Fig. 7.9), and (3) shell and coil.

In a double-pipe condenser, water is pumped in the inner pipe and the refrigerant flows in the outer pipe. Counter-current flows are maintained to

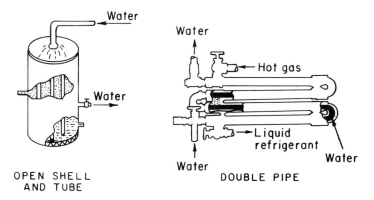

Fig. 7.9 An open shell-and-tube condenser and double-pipe condenser. (Courtesy of Carrier Co.)

obtain high heat-transfer efficiencies. Although double-pipe condensers have been commonly used in the past, the large number of gaskets and flanges used in these heat exchangers leads to maintenance problems.

In a shell-and-tube condenser, water is pumped through the pipes while refrigerant flows in the shell. Installation of fins in pipes allows better heat transfer. The shell-and-tube condensers are generally low in cost and easy to maintain.

In a shell-and-coil condenser, a welded shell contains a coil of finned water tubing. It is generally most compact and low in cost.

Air-cooled condensers can be either tube-and-fin type or plate type, as shown in Fig. 7.10. Fins on tubes allow a large heat transfer area in a compact case. The plate condensers have no fins, so they require considerably larger surface area. However, they are cheaper to construct and

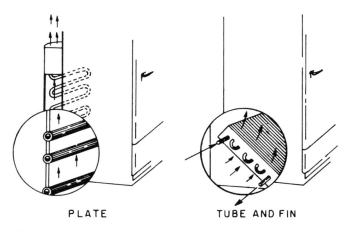

Fig. 7.10 A plate and tube-and-fin condenser. (Courtesy of Carrier Co.)

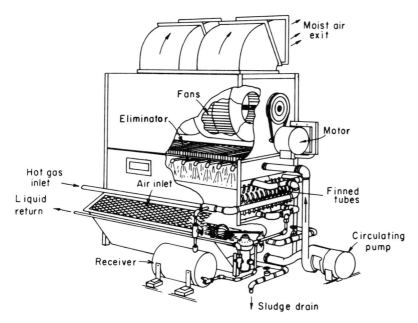

Fig. 7.11 An evaporative condenser. [From Jennings (1970). Copyright©1939, 1944, 1949, 1956, 1958, 1970 by Harper and Row, Publishers, Inc. Reprinted with permission of the publisher.]

require little maintenance. Both these types of condensers can be found in household refrigerators.

Air-cooled condensers can also employ artificial movement of air by using a fan. The fan helps in obtaining higher convective heat-transfer coefficients at the surface of the condenser.

In evaporative condensers, a circulating water pump draws water from a pan at the base of the condenser and sprays the water onto the coils. In addition, a large amount of air is drawn over the condenser coils. Evaporation of water requires latent heat, which is extracted from the refrigerant. Figure 7.11 shows an evaporative condenser. These units can be quite large.

7.3.4 Expansion Valve

An expansion valve is essentially a metering device that controls the flow of liquid refrigerant to an evaporator. The valve can be operated either manually or by sensing pressure or temperature at another desired location in the refrigeration system.

The common types of metering devices used in the refrigeration system include (1) manually operated expansion valve, (2) automatic low-side float

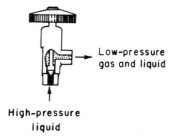

Fig. 7.12 A manually controlled expansion valve. (Courtesy of Carrier Co.)

valve, (3) automatic high-side float valve, (4) automatic expansion valve, and (5) thermostatic expansion valve.

A simple, manually operated expansion valve is shown in Fig. 7.12. The valve, manually adjusted, allows a desired amount of flow of refrigerant from the high-pressure liquid side to the low-pressure gas/liquid side. The refrigerant cools as it passes through the valve. The heat given up by the liquid refrigerant is absorbed to convert some of the liquid into vapor. This partial conversion of the liquid refrigerant to gas as it passes through the expansion valve is called "flashing."

The automatic low-pressure float valve is used in a flooded evaporator. The float ball is located on the low-pressure side of system, as shown in Fig. 7.13. As more liquid is boiled away in the evaporator, the float ball drops and opens the orifice to admit more liquid from the high-pressure side. The orifice closes as the float rises. This type of expansion valve is simple, almost trouble-free, and provides excellent control.

In an automatic high-pressure float valve, the float is immersed in high-pressure liquid (Fig. 7.14). As the heated gas is condensed in the condenser, the liquid-refrigerant level rises inside the chamber. The float

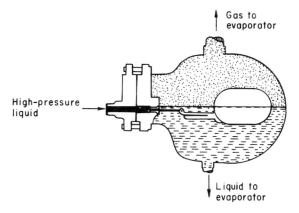

Fig. 7.13 A low-pressure float valve. (Courtesy of Carrier Co.)

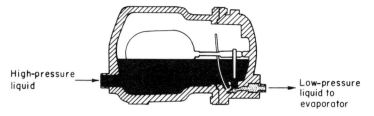

Fig. 7.14 A high-pressure float valve. (Courtesy of Carrier Co.)

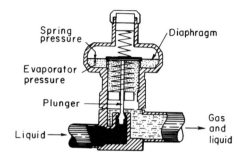

Fig. 7.15 An automatic expansion valve. (Courtesy of Carrier Co.)

consequently rises and opens the orifice, allowing the refrigerant to flow to the evaporator.

The automatic expansion valve maintains a constant pressure in the evaporator. As shown in Fig. 7.15, an increase in evaporator pressure causes the diaphragm to rise against the spring pressure, which results in the valve closing. The valve opens when the evaporator pressure decreases. This valve is used in applications that require a constant refrigeration load and constant evaporator temperature—for example, in a household refrigerator.

Thermal expansion valves contain a thermostatic bulb clamped to the side of the suction pipe to the compressor (Fig. 7.16). The thermostatic

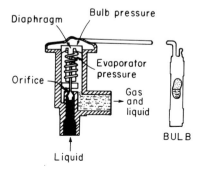

Fig. 7.16 A thermostatic expansion valve. (Courtesy of Carrier Co.)

bulb senses the temperature of the superheated gas leaving the evaporator. The relatively high temperature of the thermostatic bulb causes the fluid in the bulb (usually the same refrigerant) to increase in pressure. The increased pressure is transmitted via the thermostatic tube to the bellows and the diaphragm chamber. The valve consequently opens to allow more liquid refrigerant to flow through. Thermostatic valves are the most widely used of all metering devices in the refrigeration industry.

7.4   Pressure–Enthalpy Charts

Both pressure and enthalpy of the refrigerant change as the refrigerant is conveyed through various components of a refrigeration system. In both the evaporator and the condenser, the enthalpy of the refrigerant changes and the pressure remains constant. During the compression step, work is done by the compressor, resulting in an increase in the enthalpy of the refrigerant along with an increase in pressure. The expansion valve is a constant-enthalpy process that allows the liquid refrigerant under high pressure to pass at a controlled rate into the low-pressure section of the refrigeration system.

Charts or diagrams have been used extensively in the literature to present thermodynamic properties of refrigerants. These charts are particularly useful during the early, conceptual stages of refrigeration system design. Looking at a chart, one can easily comprehend a standard process, as well as any deviations from the standard. Most commonly used charts depict pressure and enthalpy values on the x and y axes, respectively. Another type of chart involves pressure and entropy values plotted along x and y axes, respectively. The entire refrigeration cycle comprising evaporator, compressor, condenser, and expansion valve can be conveniently depicted on the pressure–enthalpy charts. Figure A.6.1 (see Appendix) is a pressure–enthalpy chart for Freon R-12 refrigerant. In this chart, which conforms to the specifications of the International Institute of Refrigeration (IIR), the value of the enthalpy of saturated liquid is assumed to be 200 kJ/kg at a chosen datum temperature of 0°C. Similar charts can be obtained for other refrigerants from their manufacturers. Charts conforming to the specifications of the American Society of Heating and Refrigerating and Air Conditioning Engineers (ASHRAE) use different reference enthalpy values (ASHRAE, 1981).

A skeleton description of the pressure–enthalpy chart is given in Fig. 7.17. Pressure (kPa) is plotted on a logarithmic scale on the vertical axis. The horizontal axis gives enthalpy (kJ/kg).

The pressure–enthalpy chart may be divided into different regions, based on saturated liquid and saturated vapor curves. In the sketch shown in Fig. 7.17, the area enclosed by the bell-shaped curve represents a

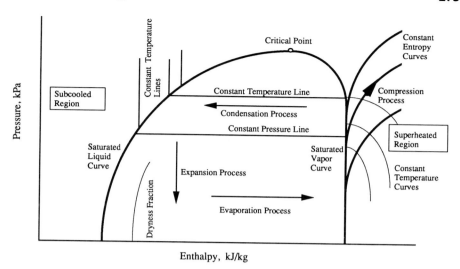

Fig. 7.17 A pressure–enthalpy diagram.

two-phase region containing a mixture of both liquid and vapor refrigerant. The horizontal lines extending across the chart are constant-pressure lines. The temperature lines are horizontal within the bell-shaped area, vertical in subcooled liquid region, and skewed downward in the superheated region. The area on the left-hand side of the saturated liquid curve denotes subcooled liquid refrigerant with temperatures below the saturation temperature for a corresponding pressure. The area to the right-hand side of the dry saturated vapor curve depicts the region where the refrigerant vapors are at superheated temperatures above the saturation temperature of vapor at the corresponding pressure. Within the bell-shaped curve, the dryness fraction curves are useful in determining the liquid and vapor content of the refrigerant.

Let us consider a simple vapor-compression refrigeration system, where the refrigerant enters the expansion valve as saturated liquid and leaves the evaporator as saturated vapor. Such a system is shown on a pressure–enthalpy diagram in Fig. 7.18.

As dry saturated vapors enter the compressor, the condition of refrigerant is represented by location a. The refrigerant vapors are at pressure P_1 and enthalpy H_2. During the compression stroke, the vapors are compressed isentropically (or at constant entropy) to pressure P_2. Location b is in the superheated vapor region. The enthalpy of the refrigerant increases from H_2 to H_3 during the compression process. In the condenser, first the superheat is removed in the de-superheater section of the condenser, and then the latent heat of condensation is removed from c to d. The saturated liquid enters the expansion valve at location d, and the pressure drops to P_1 while the enthalpy remains constant at H_1. Some

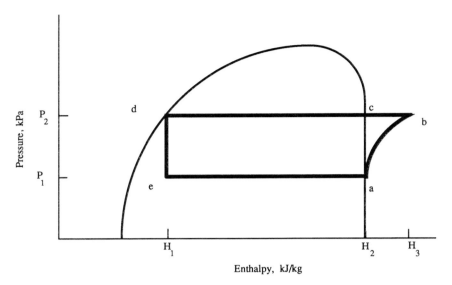

Fig. 7.18 A pressure–enthalpy chart for a vapor-compression refrigeration cycle under saturated conditions.

flashing of the refrigerant occurs within the expansion valve; as a result, location e indicates refrigerant containing liquid as well as vapor. The liquid–vapor mix of refrigerant accepts heat in the evaporator and converts completely to the vapor phase. The evaporator section is represented by the horizontal line from location e to a; the enthalpy of the refrigerant increases from H_1 to H_2.

In actual practice, deviations from the cycle discussed above may be observed. For example, it is common to encounter a refrigeration cycle as shown in Fig. 7.19. To prevent a refrigerant in liquid state from entering the compressor, the refrigerant is allowed to convert completely into the saturated vapor state inside the evaporator coils before reaching the exit location. Once the refrigerant is converted into vapors, and if those vapors are still inside the evaporator coils, the refrigerant will gain additional heat from its surroundings due to the temperature gradient. Thus, by the time the refrigerant vapors enter the compressor suction, they are superheated, as shown by location a'.

Another deviation from the ideal cycle involves subcooled refrigerant. The refrigerant may be subcooled in a receiver tank between the condenser and the expansion valve. Another factor causing subcooling is the heat loss from the refrigerant that is completely converted to saturated liquid but still inside the condenser coils. The subcooled refrigerant is represented by location d' on the pressure–enthalpy chart.

These pressure–enthalpy charts, such as shown in Fig. A.6.1, are useful in obtaining values of H_1, H_2, and H_3. Since the superheated region is

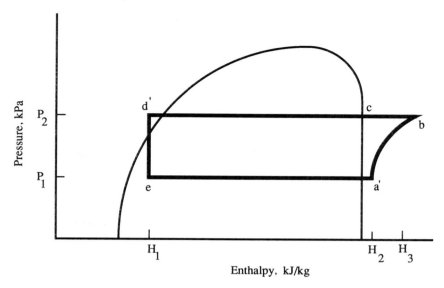

Fig. 7.19 A pressure–enthalpy chart for a vapor-compression refrigeration cycle with deviations.

crowded with a number of curves, an expanded portion for that region is more convenient to use to draw process a to b, and obtain a value for H_3 (Figs. A.6.2 for R-12 and A.6.3 for R-717).

As noted previously, temperature–entropy charts can also be used to represent the refrigeration cycle. In Fig. 7.20 a refrigeration cycle is drawn on temperature–entropy coordinates. The processes a to b (compression

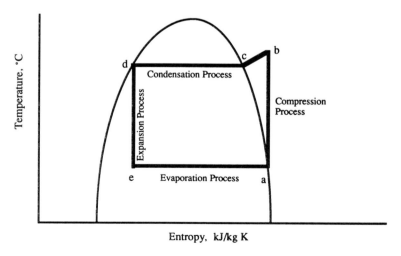

Fig. 7.20 A temperature–entropy diagram.

process) and d to e (expansion process) are isoentropic processes represented by vertical lines. Processes c to d and e to a are isothermal processes represented by horizontal lines. The temperature of the superheated vapors leaving the compressor is denoted by location b.

7.4.1 Pressure – Enthalpy Tables

More precise values for enthalpy and other thermodynamic properties of refrigerants may be obtained from tables such as Tables A.6.1 for R-12 and A.6.2 for R-717.

The following approach is used to determine the enthalpy values. Before using the tables, it is always useful to first draw a sketch of pressure–enthalpy diagram and a refrigeration cycle. For example, in Fig. 7.21 a refrigeration cycle depicting an evaporator temperature of $-20°C$ and a condenser temperature of $+30°C$ is shown. Assume that the refrigerant being used is ammonia. Since location a represents saturated vapor conditions, from Table A.6.2 we can find at $-20°C$ the enthalpy of the refrigerant in saturated vapor state is 1437.23 kJ/kg. Thus, H_2 is 1437.23 kJ/kg. At location d, the refrigerant is in saturated liquid state at the condenser temperature. Thus, from Table A.6.2, at 30°C, the enthalpy of ammonia refrigerant under saturated liquid conditions is 341.76 kJ/kg. Thus, H_1 is 341.76 kJ/kg. To determine the enthalpy value H_3, although tables for superheated properties at various conditions are available, they

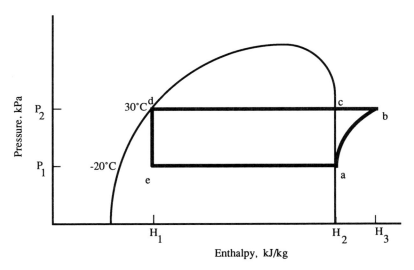

Fig. 7.21 A pressure–enthalpy diagram for evaporator temperature of $-20°C$ and condenser temperature of 30°C.

are more cumbersome to use as they require several interpolations. It is more convenient to use the expanded chart for the superheated region; for example, Fig. A.6.3 is useful to determine the value for H_3 as 1710 kJ/kg.

7.4.2 Use of Computer - Aided Procedures to Determine Thermodynamic Properties of Refrigerants

Another approach to determine the thermodynamic properties of refrigerants is to use computer-aided methods with empirical correlations. Cleland (1986) has provided such empirical correlations for several commonly used refrigerants. Some selected empirical equations and their coefficients for refrigerants R-12, R-22, and R-717 follow:

Vapor pressure

$$P_{sat} = \exp(a_1 + a_2/(T_{sat} + a_3)) \tag{7.2}$$

where P_{sat} is saturation pressure and T_{sat} is saturation temperature.

Saturation temperature

$$T_{sat} = a_2/[\ln(P_{sat}) - a_1] - a_3 \tag{7.3}$$

Liquid enthalpy

$$\Delta T_b = T_{sat} - T_L \tag{7.4}$$

$$H_L = a_4 + a_5 T_L + a_6 T_L^2 + a_7 T_L^3 \tag{7.5}$$

where T_b is the temperature of subcooled liquid, T_L is the temperature of liquid refrigerant, and H_L is the enthalpy of liquid refrigerant.

Saturated vapor enthalpy

$$H_{i1} = a_8 + a_9 T_{sat} + a_{10} T_{sat}^2 + a_{11} T_{sat}^3 \tag{7.6}$$

$$H_v = H_{i1} + a_{12} \tag{7.7}$$

where H_{i1} is an intermediate enthalpy value and H_v is the enthalpy of saturated vapor.

Superheated vapor enthalpy

$$\Delta T_s = T_s - T_{sat} \tag{7.8}$$

$$\begin{aligned} H_{i2} = H_{i1}\big(1 + a_{13}\,\Delta T_s + a_{14}(\Delta T_s)^2 + a_{15}(\Delta T_s)(T_{sat}) \\ + a_{16}(\Delta T_s)^2(T_{sat}) + a_{17}(\Delta T_s)(T_{sat})^2 \\ + a_{18}(\Delta T_s)^2(T_{sat})^2\big) \end{aligned} \tag{7.9}$$

$$H_s = H_{i2} + a_{12} \tag{7.10}$$

where T_s is the temperature of superheated vapors, H_{i2} is an intermediate enthalpy value, and H_s is the enthalpy of superheated vapors.

Saturated vapor specific volume

$$v_v = \exp\left[a_{19} + a_{20}/(T_{sat} + 273.15)\right]\left(a_{21} + a_{22}T_{sat} + a_{23}T_{sat}^2 + a_{24}T_{sat}^3\right)$$

$$(7.11)$$

where v_v is the specific volume of saturated vapors.

TABLE 7.4
Coefficients for Empirical Equations to Calculate
Thermodynamic Properties of Refrigerants

Coefficient	R-12	R-22	R-717
a_1	20.82963	21.25384	22.11874
a_2	−2033.5646	−2025.4518	−2233.8226
a_3	248.3	248.94	244.2
a_4	200000	200000	200000
a_5	923.88	1170.36	4751.63
a_6	0.83716	1.68674	2.04493
$a_7 \ (\times 10^{-3})$	5.3772	5.2703	−37.875
a_8	187565	250027	1441467
a_9	428.992	367.265	920.154
a_{10}	−0.75152	−1.84133	−10.20556
$a_{11} \ (\times 10^{-3})$	5.6695	−11.4556	−26.5126
a_{12}	163994	155482	15689
$a_{13} \ (\times 10^{-3})$	3.43263	2.85446	1.68973
$a_{14} \ (\times 10^{-7})$	7.27473	4.0129	−3.47675
$a_{15} \ (\times 10^{-6})$	7.27759	13.3612	8.55525
$a_{16} \ (\times 10^{-8})$	−6.63650	−8.11617	−3.04755
$a_{17} \ (\times 10^{-8})$	6.95693	14.1194	9.79201
$a_{18} \ (\times 10^{-10})$	−4.17264	−9.53294	−3.62549
a_{19}	−11.58643	−11.82344	−11.09867
a_{20}	2372.495	2390.321	2691.680
a_{21}	1.00755	1.01859	0.99675
$a_{22} \ (\times 10^{-4})$	4.94025	5.09433	4.02288
$a_{23} \ (\times 10^{-6})$	−6.04777	−14.8464	2.64170
$a_{24} \ (\times 10^{-7})$	−2.29472	−2.49547	−1.75152
$a_{25} \ (\times 10^{-3})$	4.99659	5.23275	4.77321
$a_{26} \ (\times 10^{-6})$	−5.11093	−5.59394	−3.11142
$a_{27} \ (\times 10^{-5})$	2.04917	3.45555	1.58632
$a_{28} \ (\times 10^{-7})$	−1.51970	−2.31649	−0.91676
$a_{29} \ (\times 10^{-7})$	3.64536	5.80303	2.97255
$a_{30} \ (\times 10^{-9})$	−1.67593	−3.20189	−0.86668
a_{31}	1.086089	1.137423	1.325798
$a_{32} \ (\times 10^{-3})$	−1.81486	−1.50914	0.24520
$a_{33} \ (\times 10^{-6})$	−14.8704	−5.59643	3.10683
$a_{34} \ (\times 10^{-6})$	2.20685	−8.74677	−11.3335
$a_{35} \ (\times 10^{-7})$	1.97069	−1.49547	−1.42736
$a_{36} \ (\times 10^{-8})$	−7.86500	5.97029	6.35817
$a_{37} \ (\times 10^{-9})$	−1.96889	1.41458	0.95979
$a_{38} \ (\times 10^{-4})$	−5.62656	−4.52580	−3.82295

Superheated vapor specific volume

$$v_s = v_v\left(1.0 + a_{25}(\Delta T_s) + a_{26}(\Delta T_s)^2 + a_{27}(\Delta T_s)(T_{sat})\right.$$

$$\left. + a_{28}(\Delta T_s)^2(T_{sat}) + a_{29}(\Delta T_s)(T_{sat})^2 + a_{30}(\Delta T_s)^2(T_{sat})^2\right)$$

$$(7.12)$$

where v_s is the specific volume of superheated vapors.

Enthalpy change in isentropic compression with no vapor superheat at suction

$$\Delta h = \frac{c}{c-1}P_1 v_1\left(\left(\frac{P_2}{P_1}\right)^{(c-1)/c} - 1\right) \qquad (7.13)$$

where c is an empirical coefficient, P is absolute pressure, v is specific volume, and subscripts 1 and 2 represent conditions at suction and discharge of the compressor.

$$\Delta T_c = T_{sat2} - T_{sat1} \qquad (7.14)$$

where ΔT_c is the change in saturation temperature due to compression.

$$c_{i1} = a_{31} + a_{32}(T_{sat1}) + a_{33}(T_{sat1})^2 + a_{34}(T_{sat1})(\Delta T_c)$$

$$+ a_{35}(T_{sat1})^2(\Delta T_c) + a_{36}(T_{sat1})(\Delta T_c)^2$$

$$+ a_{37}(T_{sat1})^2(\Delta T_c) + a_{38}(\Delta T_c) \qquad (7.15)$$

$$c = c_{i1} \qquad (7.16)$$

The coefficients for the above equations are given in Table 7.4. More details about the applicable range and accuracy of these equations are given in Cleland (1986).

7.5 Mathematical Expressions Useful in Analysis of Vapor-Compression Refrigeration

7.5.1 Cooling Load

The cooling load is the rate of heat energy removal from a given space (or object) in order to lower the temperature of that space (or object) to a desired level. Before the era of mechanical refrigeration, ice was the cooling medium most widely used. Cooling capacity was often related to melting of ice. A typical unit for cooling load still commonly used in commercial practice is *"ton of refrigeration."* One ton of refrigeration is equivalent to the latent heat of fusion of one ton of ice (2000 pounds × 144 Btu/pound)/24 hr = 288,000 Btu/24 hr = 303,852 kJ/24 hr = 3.5168 kW. Thus, a mechanical refrigeration system that has the capacity to absorb heat from the refrigerated space at the rate of 3.5168 kW is rated at *one ton of refrigeration*.

Several factors should be considered in calculating the cooling load from a given space. If the product stored in the space is a fresh fruit or vegetable, it gives out heat due to respiration. This heat of respiration must be removed to keep the product and the space at a low temperature. Heat of respiration of fresh fruits and vegetables are tabulated in Table A.2.6. Other factors affecting the cooling load calculations include heat infiltration through walls, floor, and ceiling; heat gain through doors; heat given by lights, people, and use of fork lifts for material handling.

EXAMPLE 7.1

Calculate the cooling load present in a walk-in chamber, caused by the heat evolution of 2000 kg of cabbage stored at 5°C.

GIVEN

Amount of cabbage stored = 2000 kg
Storage temperature = 5°C

APPROACH

We will use Table A.2.6 to obtain the value of heat evolution (due to respiration) of cabbage.

SOLUTION

(1) From Table A.2.6, heat evolution for cabbage stored at 5°C is 28–63 W/mg.

(2) Choose the larger value of 63 W/Mg for design purposes.

(3) Total heat evolution for 2000 kg of cabbage is

$$(2000 \text{ kg})(63 \text{ W/Mg}) \times \left(\frac{1 \text{ Mg}}{1000 \text{ kg}} \right) = 126 \text{ W}$$

(4) The cooling load rate due to 2000 kg of cabbage stored at 5°C is 126 W.

7.5.2 Compressor

The work done on the refrigerant during the isoentropic compression step can be calculated from the enthalpy rise of the refrigerant and the refrigerant flow rate,

$$q_w = \dot{m}(H_3 - H_2) \qquad (7.17)$$

where $\dot{m}$ is refrigerant mass flow rate (kg/s), H_3 is enthalpy of refrigerant at the end of compression stroke (kJ/kg refrigerant), H_2 is enthalpy of refrigerant at the beginning of compression stroke (kJ/kg refrigerant), and q_w is rate of work done on the refrigerant (kW).

7.5.3 Condenser

Within the condenser, the refrigerant is cooled at constant pressure. The heat rejected to the environment can be expressed as

$$q_c = \dot{m}(H_3 - H_1) \qquad (7.18)$$

where q_c is rate of heat exchanged in the condenser (kW) and H_1 is enthalpy of refrigerant at exit from the condenser (kJ/kg refrigerant).

7.5.4 Evaporator

Within the evaporator the refrigerant changes phase from liquid to vapor and accepts heat from the surroundings at a constant pressure. The enthalpy difference of the refrigerant between the inlet and the outlet locations of an evaporator is called the *refrigeration effect*. The rate of heat accepted by the refrigerant as it undergoes evaporation process in the evaporator is given by

$$q_e = \dot{m}(H_2 - H_1) \qquad (7.19)$$

where q_e is the rate of heat exchanged in the evaporator (kW), and the refrigeration effect is $H_2 - H_1$.

7.5.5 Coefficient of Performance

The purpose of a mechanical refrigeration system is to transfer heat from a low-temperature environment to one that is at a higher temperature. The refrigeration effect or the amount of heat absorbed from the low-temperature environment is much greater than the heat equivalence of the work required to produce this effect. Therefore, the performance of a refrigeration system is measured, like that of an engine, by the ratio of the useful refrigeration effect obtained from the system to the work expended on it to produce that effect. This ratio is called the coefficient of performance. It is used to indicate the efficiency of the system.

The coefficient of performance (C.O.P.) is defined as a ratio between the heat absorbed by the refrigerant as it flows through the evaporator to the heat equivalence of the energy supplied to the compressor.

$$\text{C.O.P.} = \frac{H_2 - H_1}{H_3 - H_2} \qquad (7.20)$$

7.5.6 Refrigerant Flow Rate

The refrigerant flow rate depends on the total cooling load imposed on the system and the refrigeration effect. The total cooling load on the system is computed from the heat to be removed from the space or object that is intended to be refrigerated (see Section 7.5.1). The following expression is used to determine the refrigerant flow rate:

$$\dot{m} = \frac{q}{(H_2 - H_1)} \qquad (7.21)$$

where $\dot{m}$ is the refrigerant flow rate (kg/s), and q is the total cooling load rate (kW).

EXAMPLE 7.2

A cold storage room is being maintained at 2°C using a vapor-compression refrigeration system that uses Freon R-12. The evaporator and condenser temperatures are −5 and 40°C, respectively. The refrigeration load is 20 tons. Calculate the mass flow rate of refrigerant, the compressor power requirement, and the C.O.P. Assume the unit operates under saturated conditions and the compressor efficiency is 85%.

GIVEN

Room temperature = 2°C
Evaporator temperature = −5°C
Condenser temperature = 40°C
Refrigeration load = 20 tons
Compressor efficiency = 85%

APPROACH

We will draw the refrigeration cycle on a pressure–enthalpy diagram for Freon R-12. From the diagram we will obtain the required enthalpy values for use in Eqs. (7.17)–(7.21).

SOLUTION

(1) On a pressure–enthalpy chart for Freon R-12, draw lines *fa* and *dc*, representing the evaporator and condenser conditions, as shown in Fig. 7.22. Follow the constant-entropy curve (may require interpolation) from *a* to intersect horizontal line *dc* extended to *b*. From point *d*, draw a vertical line to intersect line *fa* at point *e*. Thus, *abcde* represents the refrigeration cycle under saturated conditions for the given data.

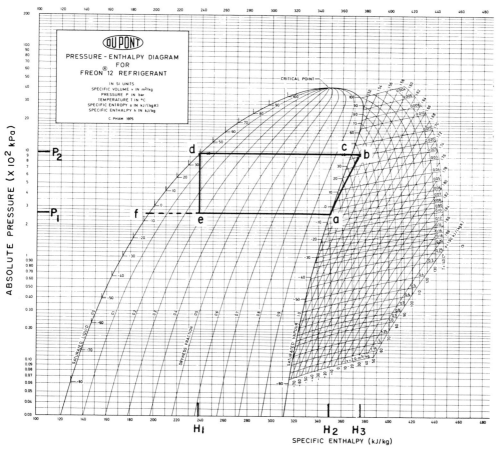

Fig. 7.22 A pressure–enthalpy chart for a vapor-compression refrigeration cycle for conditions given in Example 7.2.

(2) From the chart, read the following:

Evaporator pressure = 260 kPa
Condenser pressure = 950 kPa

$$H_1 = 238 \text{ kJ/kg}$$

$$H_2 = 350 \text{ kJ/kg}$$

$$H_3 = 375 \text{ kJ/kg}$$

(3) From Eq. (7.21), mass flow of refrigerant (noting that 1 ton of refrigeration = 303,852 kJ/24 hr) is

$$\dot{m} = \frac{(20 \text{ tons})(303852 \text{ kJ/ton})}{(24 \text{ hr})(3600 \text{ s/hr})(350 \text{ kJ/kg} - 238 \text{ kJ/kg})}$$

$$= 0.628 \text{ kg/s}$$

(4) From Eq. (7.17), compressor power requirement, assuming compressor efficiency of 85%, is

$$q_w = \frac{(0.628 \text{ kg/s})(375 \text{ kJ/kg} - 350 \text{ kJ/kg})}{0.85}$$

$$= 18.47 \text{ kW}$$

(5) From Eq. (7.20), coefficient of performance is

$$\text{C.O.P.} = \frac{(350 \text{ kJ/kg} - 238 \text{ kJ/kg})}{(375 \text{ kJ/kg} - 350 \text{ kJ/kg})} = 4.48$$

EXAMPLE 7.3

Redo Example 7.2 using pressure–enthalpy tables.

GIVEN

Room temperature = 2°C
Evaporator temperature = −5°C
Condenser temperature = 40°C
Refrigeration load = 20 tons
Compressor efficiency = 85%

APPROACH

We will use pressure–enthalpy Table A.6.1 for Freon (R-12) given in the Appendix. In addition, we will use Fig. A.6.2 for the expanded portion of the superheated gas region.

SOLUTION

(1) It is convenient to draw a skeleton pressure–enthalpy diagram (similar to Fig. 7.18) and represent values determined from the tables.
(2) In using pressure–enthalpy tables, it is important to know the condition of the refrigerant at locations a, b, d, and e. We know that at a the refrigerant exists as saturated vapor, and at d it exists as saturated liquid. The temperature of the refrigerant at a is −5°C, and at d it is 40°C.
(3) At −5°C, the enthalpy for saturated vapor is 349.3 kJ/kg. Therefore, $H_2 = 349.3$ kJ/kg.
(4) At 40°C, the enthalpy for saturated liquid is 238.5 kJ/kg. Therefore, $H_1 = 238.5$ kJ/kg.
(5) The superheated portion of the cycle is drawn on Fig. A.6.2, and H_3 is obtained as 372 kJ/kg.
(6) The remaining calculations are done in the same manner as in Example 7.2.

EXAMPLE 7.4

Repeat Example 7.2 assuming that the vapors leaving the evaporator have a 10°C superheat, and the liquid refrigerant discharging from the condenser is subcooled an additional 15°C.

GIVEN

See Example 7.2.
Superheat = 10°C
Subcooling = 15°C

APPROACH

On a pressure–enthalpy chart we will account for the superheating and sub-cooling of the refrigerant.

SOLUTION

(1) Since the additional superheat is 10°C, the temperature of vapors entering compressor is 5°C, and the temperature of liquid leaving the condenser is 25°C.

(2) Draw line fa, representing the evaporator temperature of −5°C.

(3) Extend line fa, on Fig. 7.23, to fa_1. Point a_1 is found by following the 5°C isotherm in the superheated region.

(4) Draw a_1b, by following a constant-entropy curve originating from a_1.

(5) Draw bd, corresponding to a condenser temperature of 40°C.

(6) Extend bd to bd_1, where point d_1 is located by drawing a vertical line from the point representing 25°C on the saturated liquid curve.

(7) Draw d_1e, a vertical line for the adiabatic process in the expansion valve.

(8) From the refrigeration cycle ea_1bcd_1, determine the following enthalpy values:

$$H_1 = 225 \text{ kJ/kg}$$

$$H_2 = 355 \text{ kJ/kg}$$

$$H_3 = 380 \text{ kJ/kg}$$

(9) Thus,

$$\text{Mass flow rate of refrigerant} = \frac{(20 \text{ ton})(303852 \text{ kJ/ton})}{(24 \text{ hr})(3600 \text{ s/hr})(355 \text{ kJ/kg} - 225 \text{ kJ/kg})}$$

$$= 0.54 \text{ kg/s}$$

(10) From Eq. (7.17), compressor power requirement, assuming compressor efficiency of 85%, is

$$q_w = \frac{(0.54 \text{ kg/s})(380 - 355 \text{ kJ/kg})}{0.85}$$

$$= 15.9 \text{ kW}$$

(11) From Eq. (7.20), coefficient of performance is

$$\text{C.O.P.} = \frac{(355 \text{ kJ/kg} - 225 \text{ kJ/kg})}{(380 \text{ kJ/kg} - 355 \text{ kJ/kg})}$$

$$= 5.2$$

(12) The example shows the influence of superheating and subcooling on the refrigerant flow rate and the compressor horsepower.

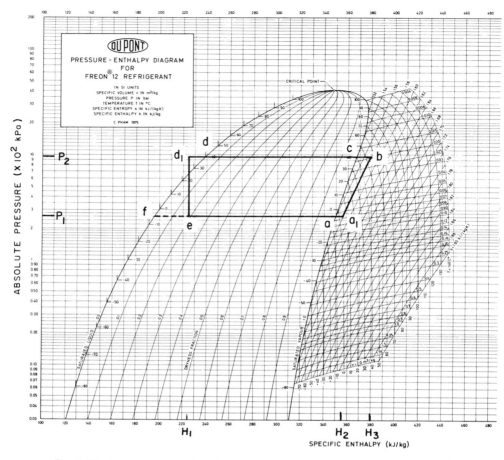

Fig. 7.23 A pressure-enthalpy chart for a vapor-compression refrigeration cycle for conditions given in Example 7.4.

EXAMPLE 7.5

Redo Example 7.2, using ammonia as a refrigerant instead of Freon R-12.

GIVEN

Same as in Example 7.2

APPROACH

We will use pressure–enthalpy Table A.6.2, and the expanded diagram in Fig. A.6.3 for ammonia.

SOLUTION

(1) Draw a skeleton pressure–enthalpy diagram and identify points a, b, c, d, and e (similar to Fig. 7.18).

(2) At a, the refrigerant is in saturated vapor state. From Table A.6.2, the enthalpy of saturated vapor at $-5°C$ is 1456.15 kJ/kg. Thus, $H_2 = 1456.15$ kJ/kg.

(3) At d, the refrigerant is in saturated liquid state. From Table A.6.2, the enthalpy of saturated liquid at $40°C$ is 390.59 kJ/kg. Therefore, $H_1 = 390.59$ kJ/kg.

(4) From Fig. A.6.3, point b is identified and H_3 is obtained as 1680 kJ/kg.

(5) The mass flow rate of refrigerant, from Eq. (7.21) is

$$\dot{m} = \frac{(20 \text{ tons})(303852 \text{ kJ/ton})}{(24 \text{ hr})(3600 \text{ s/hr})(1456.15 \text{ kJ/kg} - 390.59 \text{ kJ/kg})}$$

$$= 0.066 \text{ kg/s}$$

(6) From Eq. (7.17), compressor power requirement, assuming compressor efficiency of 85%, is

$$q_w = \frac{(0.066 \text{ kg/s})(1680 \text{ kJ/kg} - 1456.15 \text{ kJ/kg})}{0.85}$$

$$= 17.38 \text{ kW}$$

(7) From Eq. (7.20), coefficient of performance is

$$C.O.P. = \frac{(1456.15 \text{ kJ/kg} - 390.59 \text{ kJ/kg})}{(1680 \text{ kJ/kg} - 1456.15 \text{ kJ/kg})}$$

$$= 4.76$$

(8) In contrast to Freon R-12, the use of ammonia reduces the refrigerant flow rate by 84%.

EXAMPLE 7.6

Using a spreadsheet, develop a computer-aided procedure to determine the following refrigerant properties for R-12 and R-717.

(a) Enthalpy of saturated liquid at condenser temperature.
(b) Enthalpy of saturated vapor at evaporator temperature.
(c) Specific volume of saturated vapors at evaporator temperature.
(d) Determine the enthalpy values H_1, H_2, and H_3 for Example 7.2 using the spreadsheets for both R-12 and R-717.

GIVEN

Same as in Example 7.2.

APPROACH

We will use the empirical correlations given by Cleland (1986) for developing a spreadsheet using EXCEL™. The spreadsheets will be developed both for R-12 and R-717.

SOLUTION

(1) Using empirical relations given by Cleland (1986), the following spreadsheets are prepared (Figs. 7.24 and 7.25). All empirical correlations are presented in D6:H11.

(2) The following input parameters may be used: Temperature at suction (saturated vapor); temperature of saturated liquid (at the entrance to expansion valve).

	A	B	C	D	E	F	G	H
1	T_evaporator	-5	C					
2	T_condenser	40	C					
3	Tcondenser-Tevaporat	45	C					
4					Coefficients from Cleland(1986)			
5								
6				20.82963	-2033.5646	248.3	200000	923.88
7				0.83716	5.38E-03	187565	428.992	-0.75152
8				-5.67E-03	163994	-11.58643	2372.495	1.00755
9				4.94E-04	-6.05E-06	-2.29E-07	1.086089	-1.81E-03
10				-1.49E-05	2.21E-06	1.97E-07	-7.87E-08	-1.97E-09
11				-5.63E-04				
12				=EXP(D6+E6/(B1+F6))/1000				
13	P_suction	260.76		=EXP(D6+E6/(B2+F6))/1000				
14	P_discharge	961.2495656						
15				=(G6+H6*B2+D7*B2^2+E7*B2^3)/1000				
16	H_1	238.6387968		=(F7+G7*B1+H7*B1^2+D8*B1^3+E8)/1000				
17	H_2	349.3959607		=EXP(F8+G8/(B1+273.15))*(H8+D9*B1+E9*B1^2+F9*B1^3)				
18	v_saturated	0.064969092						
19	c_constant	1.069991298		=G9+H9*B1+D10*B1^2+E10*B1*B3+F10*B1^2*B3+G10*B1*B3^2+H10*				
20	delta_H (kJ/kg)	23.07282178		B1^2*B3+D11*B3				
21	H_3 (kJ/kg)	372.4687825		=(B19/(B19-1))*B13*B18*((B14/B13)^((B19-1)/B19)-1)				
22				=B17+B20				
23								

Fig. 7.24 Spreadsheet for determining various refrigerant properties of Freon (R-12).

	A	B	C	D	E	F	G	H
1	T_evaporator	-5	C					
2	T_condenser	40	C					
3	Tcondenser-Tevaporatc	45	C					
4					Coefficients from Cleland(1986)			
5								
6				22.11874	-2233.8226	244.2	200000	4751.63
7				2.04493	-0.037875	1441467	920.154	-10.20556
8				-0.0265126	15689	-11.09867	2691.68	0.99675
9				0.000402288	2.6417E-06	-1.752E-07	1.325798	0.0002452
10				3.10683E-06	1.13335E-05	-1.427E-07	6.358E-08	9.5979E-10
11				-0.000382295				
12				=EXP(D6+E6/(B1+F6))/1000				
13	P_suction	355.05		=EXP(D6+E6/(B2+F6))/1000				
14	P_discharge	1557.671603						
15				=(G6+H6*B2+D7*B2^2+E7*B2^3)/1000				
16	H_1	390.913088		=(F7+G7*B1+H7*B1^2+D8*B1^3+E8)/1000				
17	H_2	1452.303405		=EXP(F8+G8/(B1+273.15))*(H8+D9*B1+E9*B1^2+F9*B1^3)				
18	v_saturated	0.344420114						
19	c	1.304093095		=G9+H9*B1+D10*B1^2+E10*B1*B3+F10*B1^2*B3+G10*B1*B3^2+H10*				
20	delta_H (kJ/kg)	215.9126031		B1^2*B3+D11*B3				
21	H_3 (kJ/kg)	1668.216008		=(B19/(B19-1))*B13*B18*((B14/B13)^((B19-1)/B19)-1)				
22				=B17+B20				
23								

Fig. 7.25 Spreadsheet for determining various refrigerant properties of ammonia (R-717).

(3) The calculations include the following:

   (a) Pressure (saturated) calculated at the suction temperature of compressor.
   (b) Pressure (saturated) calculated for the temperature of refrigerant in the condenser.
   (c) H_1.
   (d) H_2.
   (e) Specific volume of saturated vapors at inlet to the compressor suction.
   (f) An interim constant "c" (see Cleland, 1986).
   (g) For an isoentropic compression process, for Example 7.2, the value of ΔH can be calculated and then added to H_2 to determine H_3.
   (h) Tables 7.5 and 7.6 provide a listing of the pressure–enthalpy spreadsheets for Freon R-12 and ammonia R-717, respectively.

(4) For conditions given in Example 7.2,

$$T_{evaporator} = -5°C$$
$$T_{condenser} = 40°C$$

From the spreadsheet for R-12,

$$H_1 = 238.64 \text{ kJ/kg}$$
$$H_2 = 349.4 \text{ kJ/kg}$$
$$H_3 = 372.46 \text{ kJ/kg}$$

From the spreadsheet for R-717,

$$H_1 = 390.91 \text{ kJ/kg}$$
$$H_2 = 1452.30 \text{ kJ/kg}$$
$$H_3 = 1668.21 \text{ kJ/kg}$$

7.6   Use of Multistage Systems

Multistage systems involve using more than one compressor, often with an objective of reducing the total power requirements. Although adding additional compressors requires an increase in capital spending, the total operating costs must be reduced for the multistage systems to be justifiable. The following discussion involves a commonly used approach for using a dual-stage refrigeration system—a flash gas removal system.

7.6.1   Flash Gas Removal System

As seen previously in Fig. 7.18, a refrigerant leaves the condenser in a saturated liquid state, and in the expansion valve there is a pressure drop from a high condenser pressure to the low evaporator pressure. The drop in pressure of the refrigerant with a partial conversion to vapor state, commonly called "flashing," is accompanied by the conversion of some of the refrigerant from liquid to vapor state. If one considers the state of the refrigerant at some intermediate pressure between P_1 and P_2, such as at location k on Fig. 7.26, the refrigerant is existing partially as a vapor, but mostly in liquid state. The refrigerant already converted to vapors in the expansion valve can no longer provide any useful purpose in the evaporator. It therefore may be desirable to take the vapors at that intermediate pressure in the expansion valve, and compress them with another small compressor to the condensing pressure.

The liquid refrigerant, with only a small fraction of vapors (due to further flashings that occur with lowering the pressure to the evaporator pressure), then enters the evaporator.

A schematic of the flash-gas removal system is shown in Fig. 7.27. The refrigerant leaving the condenser in liquid state is allowed to go through a throttling valve that is controlled by the liquid level in a flash tank. The separation of the vapors from the liquid is done in the flash tank. The liquid refrigerant is then conveyed to an expansion valve prior to entering the evaporator, while the vapors are conveyed to a secondary compressor. The use of the flash-gas system results in an overall decrease in power requirements.

The reduction in power requirements becomes significant when the temperature difference between the condenser and the evaporator is large; in other words, this system is most useful for low-temperature chilling or freezing applications. The secondary compressor required for compressing the flash-gas is usually small, and the primary compressor is also smaller than in a standard system that does not remove flash gas. Since most of the flash gas is removed, and gas has significantly larger volume than liquid, the piping used for intake and exit of the refrigerant from the evaporator

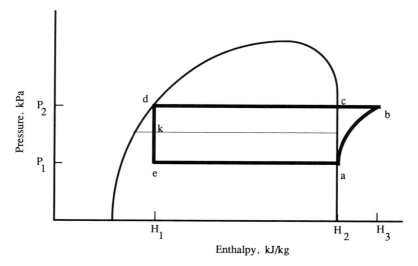

Fig. 7.26 A pressure–enthalpy diagram for a flash-gas removal system.

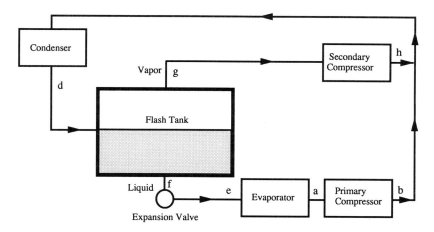

Fig. 7.27 A flash-gas removal system.

can be smaller. The additional costs of the flash-gas system include the need for a secondary compressor (although small), flash-gas tank, and associated valves, piping, and fittings. The use of the flash-gas removal system is illustrated with the following example.

EXAMPLE 7.7

An ammonia refrigeration system involves an evaporator operating at $-20°C$ and the condenser temperature set at $40°C$. Determine the reduction in power requirements per ton of refrigeration with the use of a flash-gas removal system at an intermediate pressure of 519 kPa. (See Fig. 7.27.)

GIVEN

Evaporator temperature $= -20°C$
Condenser temperature $= 40°C$
Intermediate pressure for the flash-gas removal system $= 519$ kPa

APPROACH

We will determine the enthalpy values for ammonia for the ideal cycle as well as when a flash-gas removal system is considered. These values will be obtained using the spreadsheet developed in Example 7.6.

SOLUTION

(1) Using the spreadsheet program for ammonia, the enthalpy values for the ideal and modified system are as follows (see Fig. 7.28):

Ideal System
$$H_1 = 391 \text{ kJ/kg}$$
$$H_2 = 1435 \text{ kJ/kg}$$
$$H_3 = 1750 \text{ kJ/kg}$$

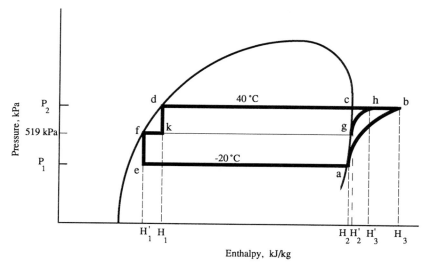

Fig. 7.28 A pressure–enthalpy diagram for a flash-gas removal system as described in Example 7.7.

Modified System
$$H_{1'} = 200 \text{ kJ/kg}$$
$$H_{2'} = 1457 \text{ kJ/kg}$$
$$H_{3'} = 1642 \text{ kJ/kg}$$

IDEAL SYSTEM

(2) The refrigerant flow rate may be calculated per ton of refrigeration load (noting that one ton of refrigeration is equivalent to 3.517 kW) as

$$\dot{m} = \frac{3.517 \text{ kJ/s}}{1435 \text{ kJ/kg} - 391 \text{ kJ/kg}}$$
$$= 0.00337 \text{ kg/s}$$

(3) Then compressor power

$$q_w = (0.00337 \text{ kg/s})(1750 \text{ kJ/kg} - 1435 \text{ kJ/kg})$$
$$= 1.062 \text{ kW/ton of refrigeration}$$

MODIFIED SYSTEM

(4) To determine the power requirements of the compressor for the modified system, it is necessary to determine the refrigerant flow rates. The refrigerant flow rate through the evaporator and the primary compressor is

$$\dot{m}_a = \dot{m}_b = \dot{m}_f = \dot{m}_e = \frac{3.517 \text{ kJ/s}}{1435 \text{ kJ/kg} - 200 \text{ kJ/kg}}$$
$$= 0.00285 \text{ kg/s}$$

(5) To determine the power requirement of the secondary compressor in the modified system, it is necessary to calculate the refrigerant flow rate through it. This can be obtained by conducting a mass and energy balance on the flash-gas tank. Thus,

$$\dot{m}_d = \dot{m}_e + \dot{m}_g$$
$$\dot{m}_d = 0.00285 + \dot{m}_g$$

(6) The energy balance gives
$$(\dot{m}_d)(H_1) = (0.00285)(H_1') + (\dot{m}_g)(H_2')$$
$$(0.00285 + \dot{m}_g)(391) = (0.00285 \times 200) + (\dot{m}_g)(1457)$$
(7) Solving the mass and energy balances we get
$$\dot{m}_g = 0.000511 \text{ kg/s}$$
(8) Then the power required by the primary compressor is
$$q_{w_1} = 0.00285(1750 - 1435)$$
$$= 0.8977 \text{ kW}$$
and the power required by the secondary compressor is
$$q_{w_2} = 0.000511(1642 - 1457)$$
$$= 0.0945 \text{ kW}$$
(9) Then the total power required by the flash-gas removal system is
$$q_w = 0.8977 + 0.0945$$
$$= 0.992 \text{ kW}$$
(10) Thus the use of the flash-gas removal system results in a 7% reduction in power requirements.

Problems

7.1 Determine the C.O.P. of a simple saturated ammonia (R-717) compression refrigeration cycle. The evaporation temperature is $-20°C$ and the condenser temperature is $30°C$.

7.2 For a 10-ton-capacity refrigeration system, the pressure of refrigerant in the evaporator is 210 kPa, whereas in the condenser it is 750 kPa. If ammonia (R-717) is used under saturated conditions, calculate the theoretical power required to operate the compressor.

7.3 A food storage chamber requires a refrigeration system of 15-ton capacity operating at an evaporator temperature of $-8°C$ and a condenser temperature of $30°C$. Refrigerant ammonia (R-717) is used and the system operates under saturated conditions. Determine:

(a) C.O.P.
(b) Refrigerant flow rate.
(c) Rate of heat removed by condenser.

***7.4** Repeat problem 7.3, with the refrigerant subcooled by 5°C before entering the expansion valve and vapor superheated by 6°C.

***7.5** A vapor-compression refrigeration system, using ammonia (R-717) as refrigerant, is operating with an evaporator temperature of $-5°C$

---

*Indicates an advanced level of difficulty in solving.

and condenser temperature of 40°C. It is desired to determine the influence of raising the evaporator temperature to 5°C while holding condenser temperature at 40°C. Calculate the percent changes in

(a) Refrigeration effect per kg refrigerant flow rate.
(b) C.O.P.
(c) Heat of compression.
(d) Theoretical power requirements.
(e) Rate of heat rejected at the condenser, anticipated due to raising the evaporator temperature.

7.6 A vapor-compression refrigeration system, using ammonia (R-717) as refrigerant, is operating with an evaporator temperature of $-25°C$ and condenser temperature of 40°C. It is desired to determine the influence of raising the condenser temperature to 50°C. Calculate the percent changes in

(a) Refrigeration effect per kg of refrigerant flow rate.
(b) C.O.P.
(c) Heat of compression.
(d) Theoretical power requirement.
(e) Rate of heat rejected at the condenser, anticipated due to raising the condenser temperature.

7.7 A refrigerated room, used for product cooling, is being maintained at the desired temperature using an evaporator temperature of 0°C and condenser pressure of 900 kPa with an ammonia (R-717) vapor-compression refrigeration system. The condenser is a countercurrent tubular heat exchanger with water entering at 25°C and leaving at 35°C. Evaluate the following for a refrigeration load of 5 tons:

(a) The rate of heat exchange at the condenser.
(b) The compressor power requirement at 80% efficiency.
(c) The coefficient of performance for the system.
(d) The heat transfer surface area in the condenser when the overall heat transfer coefficient is 500 $W/m^2 \cdot °C$.
(e) The flow rate of water through the condenser.

7.8 An ammonia (R-717) vapor-compression refrigeration system is operating under saturated conditions. The following data were obtained: condenser pressure, 900 kPa; state of vapors entering the evaporator, 70% liquid. This refrigeration system is being used to maintain a controlled-temperature chamber at $-5°C$. The walls of the chamber provide an overall resistance to conductive heat transfer equivalent to 0.5 $m^2 \cdot °C/W$. The convective heat-transfer coefficient on the outside wall/ceiling is 2 $W/m^2 \cdot °C$ and on the inside wall/ceiling is 10 $W/m^2 \cdot °C$. The outside ambient temperature is

38°C. The total wall and ceiling area is 100 m². Ignore any heat gain from the floor.

    (a) Calculate the flow rate of refrigerant for the above system.
    (b) Calculate the power requirements (in kW) of the compressor operating to maintain above conditions.

7.9 A vapor compression refrigeration system, using Freon, is operating under ideal conditions. The system is being used to provide cold air for a walk-in freezer. The evaporator temperature is $-35°C$ and the condenser temperature is 40°C. You hire a consultant to find different ways to conserve energy. The consultant suggests that the work done by the compressor can be reduced by half if the condenser temperature is lowered to 0°C. Check the consultant's numerical results. Prepare a reply to either accept or deny the consultant's conclusions and justify your opinion.

7.10 A mass of 100 kg of a liquid food contained in a large vessel is to be cooled from 40°C to 5°C in 10 min. The specific heat of the liquid food is 3600 J/kg °C. Cooling is done by immersing an evaporator coil inside the liquid. The evaporator coil temperature is 1°C, and condenser temperature is 41°C. The refrigerant being used is Freon 12. Draw the refrigeration cycle on a pressure–enthalpy diagram and use the refrigerant property tables to solve the following parts of this problem:

    (a) Show the refrigeration cycle on a pressure–enthalpy diagram for Freon 12.
    (b) Determine the flow rate of Freon 12.
    (c) Determine the C.O.P. of the system.
    (d) If the condenser is a countercurrent tubular heat exchanger, and water is used as a cooling medium, and the temperature of water increases from 10°C to 30°C, determine the length of the heat exchanger pipe needed for the condenser. The overall heat transfer coefficient is $U_0 = 1000$ W/m² °C; for the inner pipe, the outside diameter is 2.2 cm and the inner diameter is 2 cm.

List of Symbols

c	empirical coefficient in Eq. (7.13)		isoentropic compression (kJ/kg)
c_{i1}	empirical coefficient in Eq. (7.15)	H_1	enthalpy of refrigerant at the exit from the condenser (kJ/kg refrigerant)
D	diameter of cylinder bore (cm)		
Δh	enthalpy change in	H_2	enthalpy of refrigerant at

the beginning of compression stroke (kJ/kg refrigerant)

H_3 enthalpy of refrigerant at the end of compression stroke (kJ/kg refrigerant)

H_{i1}, H_{i2} intermediate enthalpy values in Eqs. (7.6) and (7.9)

H_L enthalpy of liquid refrigerant (same as H_1) (kJ/kg refrigerant)

H_s enthalpy of superheated vapor (same as H_3) (kJ/kg refrigerant)

H_v enthalpy of saturated vapor (same as H_2) (kJ/kg refrigerant)

L length of stroke (cm)

$\dot{m}$ refrigerant mass flow rate (kg/s)

N number of cylinders

P pressure (kPa)

p vapor pressure (kPa)

p_c vapor pressure at critical point (kPa)

p_{sat} saturation pressure (kPa)

q rate of cooling load (kW)

q_c rate of heat exchanged in the condenser (kw)

q_e rate of heat absorbed by the evaporators (kW)

q_w rate of work done on the refrigerant (kW)

τ constant in Eq. (7.1)

T_b temperature of subcooled liquid (°C)

T_c temperature at critical point (°C)

T_L temperature of liquid refrigerant (°C)

T_s temperature of superheated vapor (°C)

T_{sat} saturation temperature (°C)

U overall heat transfer coefficient (W/m² · K)

v specific volume (m³/kg)

v_s specific volume of superheated vapor (m³/kg)

v_v specific volume of saturated vapor (m³/kg)

Bibliography

American Society of Heating, Refrigerating and Air Conditioning Engineers, Inc. (1981). "ASHRAE Handbook of 1981 Fundamentals." ASHRAE, Atlanta, Georgia.

Cleland, A. C. (1986). Computer subroutines for rapid evaluation of refrigerant thermodynamic properties. *Int. J. Refrigeration* **9** (Nov.), 346–351.

Jennings, B. H. (1970). "Environmental Engineering, Analysis and Practice." International Textbook Company, New York.

McLinden, M. O. (1990). Thermodynamic properties of CFC alternatives: A survey of the available data. *Int. J. Refrigeration*, **13**(3), 149–162.

Stoecker, W. F., and Jones, J. W. (1982). "Refrigeration and Air Conditioning." McGraw-Hill, New York.

CHAPTER 8

Food Freezing

The preservation of food by freezing has become a major industry in the United States as well as in other parts of the world. As of 1975 (Williams, 1976), per capita consumption of frozen foods in the United States was 37–38 kg. Although the increase in frozen-food consumption is quite modest, this preservation process represents a very significant industry.

Preservation of a food by freezing occurs by several mechanisms. The reduction of the product temperature to levels below 0°C causes a significant reduction in growth rates for microorganisms and the corresponding deterioration of the product due to microbial activity. The same temperature influence will apply to most other reactions that might normally occur in the product, such as enzymatic and oxidation reactions. In addition, the formation of ice crystals within the product changes the availability of water to participate in reactions. As the temperature is reduced and more water is converted to the solid state, less water is available to support deterioration reactions.

Although freezing as a preservation process generally results in a high-quality product for consumption, the quality is influenced by the freezing process and frozen-storage conditions. The freezing rate or time allowed for the product temperature to be reduced from above to below the initial freezing temperature will influence product quality, but in a different manner depending on the food commodity. For some products, rapid freezing (short freezing time) is required in order to ensure small ice crystals within the product structure and the corresponding minimal damage to the product texture. Other products are not influenced by structural changes and do not justify the added costs associated with rapid freezing. Still other products have geometric configurations and sizes that do not allow rapid freezing. The storage-temperature conditions influence frozen-food quality in a significant manner. Any elevation in storage temperature tends to reduce the quality preservation of the process, and fluctuations in storage temperature tend to be even more detrimental to product quality.

From these brief introductory comments, it is obvious that the optimum freezing process will be dependent on the product characteristics.

299

Consequently, numerous freezing systems are available, each designed to achieve the product freezing in the most efficient manner and with the maximum product quality. The importance of residence time in the freezing system must be emphasized, as well as the need for accurate freezing time prediction.

8.1 Freezing Systems

To achieve freezing of a food product, the product must be exposed to a low-temperature medium for sufficient time to remove sensible heat and latent heat of fusion from the product. The removal of the sensible and latent heat results in a reduction in the product temperature as well as a conversion of the water from a liquid to a solid state (ice). In most cases, approximately 20% of the water remains in the liquid state at the storage temperature of the frozen food. To accomplish the freezing process in desired short times, the low-temperature medium is much lower than the desired final temperature of the product and large convective heat-transfer coefficients are created.

The freezing process can be accomplished using either indirect or direct contact systems. Most often, the type of system used will depend on the product characteristics, both before and after freezing is completed. There are a variety of circumstances where direct contact between the product and refrigerant is not possible.

8.1.1 Indirect Contact Systems

In numerous food-product freezing systems the product and refrigerant are separated by a barrier throughout the freezing process. This type of system is illustrated schematically in Fig. 8.1. Although many systems use a nonpermeable barrier between product and refrigerant, indirect freezing

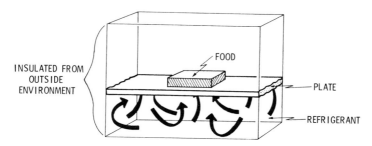

Fig. 8.1 Schematic diagram of an indirect-contact freezing system.

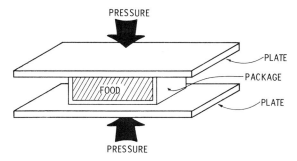

Fig. 8.2 Schematic illustration of a plate freezing system.

systems include any system without direct contact, including those where the package material becomes the barrier.

a. Plate Freezers

The most easily recognized type of indirect freezing system is the plate freezer, illustrated in Fig. 8.2. As indicated, the product is frozen while held between two refrigerated plates. In most cases, the barrier between product and refrigerant will include both the plate and package material. The heat transfer through the barrier (plate and package) can be enhanced by using pressure as illustrated (Fig. 8.2) to reduce resistance to heat transfer across the barrier. In some cases, plate systems may use single plates in contact with the product and accomplish freezing with heat transfer across a single package surface. As would be expected, these systems are less efficient, but they are less costly to acquire and operate.

Plate-freezing systems can be operated as a batch system with the product placed on the plates for a specified residence time before being removed. In this situation, the freezing time is the residence time and represents the total time required to reduce the product from the initial temperature to some desired final temperature. In general, the batch plate-freezing system has significant flexibility in terms of handling diverse product types and product sizes.

The plate-freezing system operates in a continuous mode by moving the plates holding the product through an enclosure in some prescribed manner. In Fig. 8.3, the product is held between two refrigerated plates throughout the freezing process. The movement of plates (and product) occurs as the plates index upward or across within the compartment. At the entrance and exit to the freezing system, the plates are opened to allow the product to be conveyed to or from the system. In a continuous plate-freezing system, the freezing time is the total time required for the product to move from entrance to exit. During the residence time, the desired amounts of sensible and latent heat are removed to achieve the desired frozen product temperature.

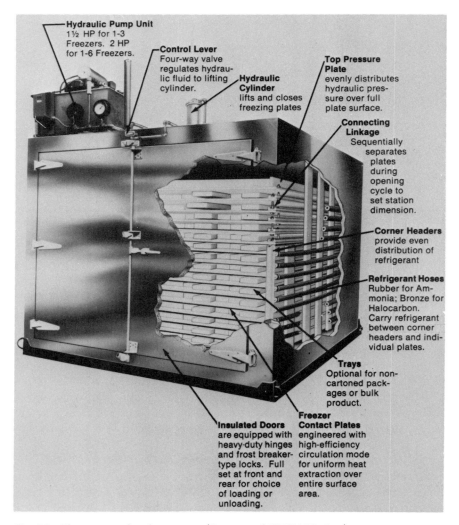

Hydraulic Pump Unit
1½ HP for 1-3
Freezers. 2 HP
for 1-6 Freezers.

Control Lever
Four-way valve
regulates hydrau-
lic fluid to lifting
cylinder.

**Hydraulic
Cylinder**
lifts and closes
freezing plates

**Top Pressure
Plate**
evenly distributes
hydraulic pres-
sure over full
plate surface.

**Connecting
Linkage**
Sequentially
separates
plates
during
opening
cycle to
set station
dimension.

Corner Headers
provide even
distribution of
refrigerant

Refrigerant Hoses
Rubber for Am-
monia; Bronze for
Halocarbon.
Carry refrigerant
between corner
headers and indi-
vidual plates.

Trays
Optional for non-
cartoned pack-
ages or bulk
product.

Insulated Doors
are equipped with
heavy-duty hinges
and frost breaker-
type locks. Full
set at front and
rear for choice
of loading or
unloading.

**Freezer
Contact Plates**
engineered with
high-efficiency
circulation mode
for uniform heat
extraction over
entire surface
area.

Fig. 8.3 Plate contact freezing system. (Courtesy of CREPACO, Inc.)

b. Air-Blast Freezers

In many situations, the product size and/or shape may not accommodate plate freezing. For these situations, the air-blast freezing systems
become the best alternative. In some cases, the package film becomes the
barrier for indirect freezing, with cold air becoming the source of refrigeration.

Air-blast freezers can be a simple design, as in the case of a refrigerated room. In this situation, the product is placed in the room and the
low-temperature air is allowed to circulate around the product for the
desired residence or freezing time. This approach represents a batch mode,

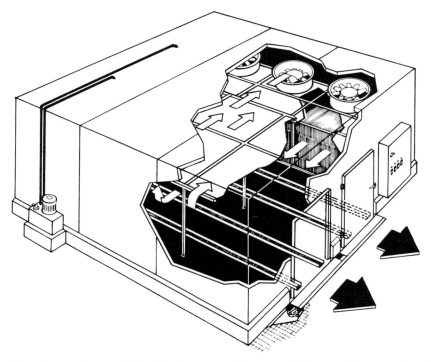

Fig. 8.4 Continuous air-blast freezing system. (Courtesy of Frigoscandia Contracting, Inc.)

and the refrigerated room may act as a storage space in addition to the freezing compartment. In most cases, freezing times will be long due to lower air speeds over the product, inability to achieve intimate contact between product and cold air, and the smaller temperature gradients between product and air.

Most air-blast freezers are continuous, such as illustrated in Fig. 8.4. In these systems, the product is carried on a conveyor that moves through a stream of high-velocity air. The length and speed of the conveyor establish the residence or freezing time. These times can be relatively small based on the use of very low-temperature air, high air velocities, and good contact between individual product packages and the cold air.

Continuous air-blast freezing systems use a variety of different conveying arrangements for movement of product through the refrigerated air. Alternate arrangements to Fig. 8.4 include tray conveyors, spiral conveyors, and roller conveyors. Most often, the system utilized will depend on product characteristics.

c. Freezers for Liquid Foods

The third general type of indirect freezing systems includes those designed primarily for liquid foods. In most situations, the most efficient removal of thermal energy from a liquid food can be accomplished before the product is placed in a package. Although any indirect heat exchanger designed for a liquid food would be acceptable, the most used type is a scraped-surface system, as described in Section 4.1.3. The heat exchangers for freezing liquid foods are designed specifically for freezing, with the heat-exchange shell surrounding the product compartment becoming an evaporator for a vapor-compression refrigeration system. This approach provides precise control of the heat-exchange surface by adjustment of pressure on the low-pressure side of the refrigeration system.

For freezing liquid foods, the residence time in the freezing compartment is sufficient to decrease the product temperature by several degrees below the temperature of initial ice-crystal formation. At these temperatures, from 60 to 80% of the latent heat has been removed from the product, and the product is in the form of a frozen slurry. In this condition, the product flows quite readily and can be placed in a package for final freezing in a low-temperature refrigerated space. The scraped-surface heat exchanger assures efficient heat exchange between the slurry and the cold surface.

Freezing systems for liquid foods can be batch or continuous. The batch system places a given amount of unfrozen liquid in the compartment and allows the freezing process to continue until the desired final temperature is reached. The product compartment is a scraped-surface heat exchanger, but operated as a batch system. In the case of ice cream freezing, the system is designed with facility for injection of air into the frozen slurry to achieve the desired product consistency.

A continuous freezing system for liquid foods is illustrated in Fig. 8.5. As indicated, the basic system is a scraped-surface heat exchanger using refrigerant during phase change as the cooling medium. The rotor acts as a mixing device, and the scraper blades enhance heat transfer at the heat-exchange surface. For these systems, the residence time for product in the compartment will be sufficient to reduce the product temperature by the desired amount and to provide time for any other changes in the product before it is placed in the package for final freezing.

8.1.2 Direct Contact Systems

Several freezing systems for food operate with direct contact between the refrigerant and the product, as illustrated in Fig. 8.6. In most situations, these systems will operate more efficiently since there are no barriers to heat transfer between the refrigerant and the product. The refrigerants used in these systems may be low-temperature air at high speeds or liquid refrigerants with phase change while in contact with the product surface. In all cases, the systems are designed to achieve rapid freezing, and the term *individual quick freezing* (IQF) will apply.

Fig. 8.5   Continuous freezing system for liquid foods. (Courtesy of Cherry-Burrell Corporation.)

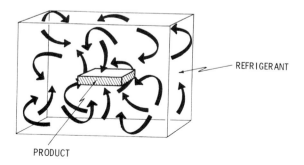

Fig. 8.6   Schematic diagram of a direct-contact freezing system.

a. Air Blast

The use of low-temperature air at high speeds in direct contact with small product objects is a form of IQF. The combination of low-temperature air, high convective heat-transfer coefficient (high air speed), and small product shape leads to short freezing time or rapid freezing. In these systems, the product is moved through the high-speed-air region on a conveyor in a manner that controls the residence time. The types of product that can be frozen in these systems are limited to those that have the appropriate geometries and that require rapid freezing for maximum quality.

A modification of the regular air-blast IQF system is the fluidized-bed IQF freezing system, as illustrated in Fig. 8.7. In these systems, the high-speed air is directed vertically upward through the mesh conveyor carrying product through the system. By careful adjustment of the air speed in relation to the product size, the product is lifted from the conveyor surface and remains suspended in the low temperature air. Although the air flow is not sufficient to maintain the product in suspension at all times, the fluidized action results in the highest possible convective heat-transfer coefficients for the freezing process. This type of freezing

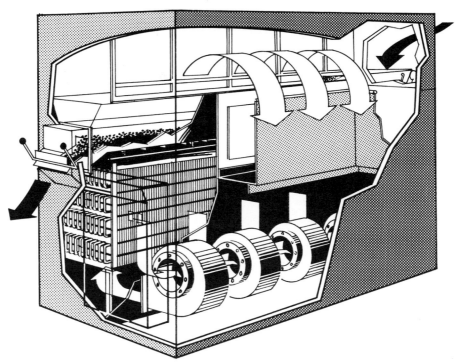

Fig. 8.7 A fluidized-bed freezing system. (Courtesy of Frigoscandia Contracting, Inc.)

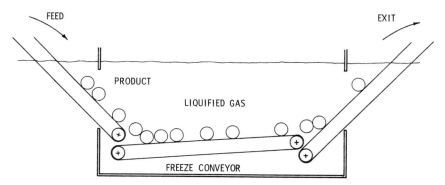

Fig. 8.8 Schematic illustration of an immersion freezing system.

process results in rapid freezing of product shapes and sizes that can be fluidized in the manner described. The use of the process is limited by the size of product that can be fluidized at air speeds of reasonable magnitude.

b. Immersion

By immersion of the food product in liquid refrigerant, the product surface is reduced to a very low temperature. Assuming the product objects are relatively small, the freezing process is accomplished very rapidly or under IQF conditions. For typical products, the freezing time is shorter than for the air blast or fluidized bed systems. As illustrated in Fig. 8.8, the

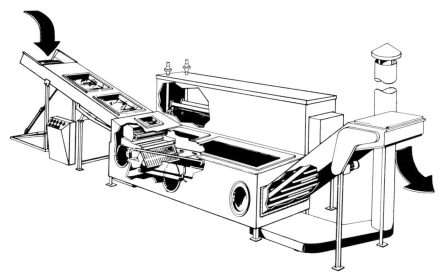

Fig. 8.9 Individual quick freezing (IQF) using liquid refrigerant. (Courtesy of Frigoscandia Contracting, Inc.)

product is carried into a bath of liquid refrigerant and is conveyed through the liquid while the refrigerant changes from liquid to vapor and absorbs heat from the product. The most common refrigerants for this purpose are nitrogen, carbon dioxide, and Freon.

A commercial version of the immersion IQF freezing system is shown in Fig. 8.9. In this illustration, the product freezing compartment is filled with refrigerant vapors while the product is conveyed through the system. In addition, the product is exposed to a spray of liquid refrigerant, which absorbs thermal energy from the product while changing phase from liquid to vapor. One of the major disadvantages of immersion-type freezing systems is the cost of the refrigerant. Since the refrigerant changes from liquid to vapor while the products freezes, it becomes difficult to recover the vapors leaving the freezing compartment. These refrigerants are expensive, and the overall efficiency of the freezing system is a function of the ability to recover and reuse the vapors produced in the freezing compartments.

8.2   Frozen-Food Properties

The freezing process has a dramatic influence on the thermal properties of the food product. Due to the significant amount of water in most foods and the influence of phase change on properties of water, the properties of the

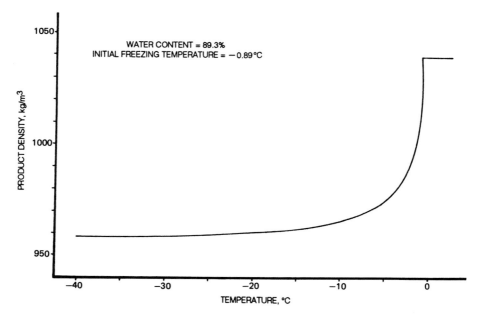

Fig. 8.10   Influence of freezing on the predicted density of strawberries. [From Heldman and Lund (1992).]

food product change in a proportional manner. As the water within the product changes from liquid to solid, the density, thermal conductivity, heat content (enthalpy), and the apparent specific heat of the product change gradually as the temperature decreases below the initial freezing point for water in the food.

8.2.1 Density

The density of solid water (ice) is less than the density of liquid water. The density of a frozen food will be less than the unfrozen product, with the influence of temperature on density as illustrated in Fig. 8.10. The gradual change in density is due to the gradual change in the proportion of water frozen as a function of temperature. The magnitude of change in density is proportional to the moisture content of the product.

8.2.2 Thermal Conductivity

The thermal conductivity of ice is approximately a factor of four larger than the thermal conductivity of liquid water. This relationship has a similar influence on the thermal conductivity of a frozen food. Since the change of phase for water in the product is gradual as temperature decreases, the thermal conductivity of the product changes in a manner illustrated in Fig. 8.11. The majority of the thermal conductivity increase

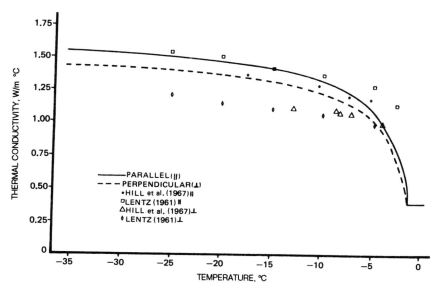

Fig. 8.11 Thermal conductivity of frozen lean beef as a function of temperature. [From Heldman and Lund (1992).]

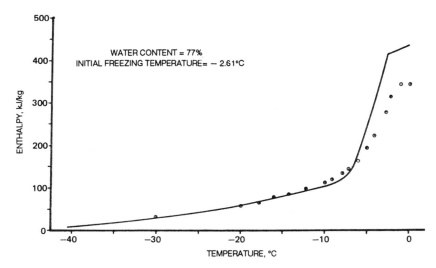

Fig. 8.12   Enthalpy of sweet cherries as a function of temperature. [From Heldman and Lund (1992).]

occurs within 10°C below the initial freezing temperature for the product. If the product happens to contain a fibrous structure, the thermal conductivity will be less when measured in a direction perpendicular to the fibers.

8.2.3   Enthalpy

The heat content or enthalpy of a frozen food is an important property in computations of refrigeration requirements for freezing the product. The heat content is normally zero at −40°C and increases with increasing temperature in a manner illustrated in Fig. 8.12. Significant changes in enthalpy occur in 10°C just below the initial freezing temperature when most of the phase change in product water occurs.

8.2.4   Apparent Specific Heat

Based on the thermodynamic definition of specific heat, the profile of apparent specific heat for a food product as a function of temperature would appear as in Fig. 8.13. This illustration reveals that the specific heat of a frozen food at a temperature greater than 20°C below the initial freezing point is not significantly different than specific heat of the unfrozen product. The apparent specific heat profile clearly illustrates the range of temperature where most of the phase changes for water in the product occur.

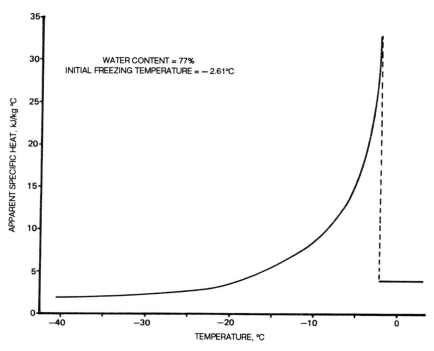

Fig. 8.13   Predicted apparent specific heat of frozen sweet cherries as a function of tempera-ture. [From Heldman and Lund (1992).]

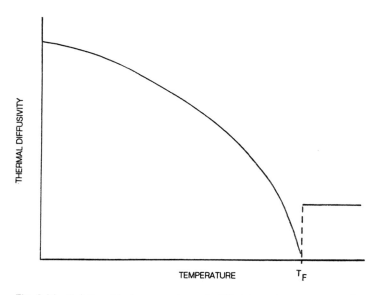

Fig. 8.14   Relationship between thermal diffusivity and temperature during freezing of food product as predicted from initial freezing temperature assumption. [From Heldman and Lund (1992).]

8.2.5   Apparent Thermal Diffusivity

When the density, thermal conductivity, and apparent specific heat of a frozen food are combined to compute apparent thermal diffusivity, the profile in Fig. 8.14 is obtained. The relationship illustrates that apparent thermal diffusivity increases gradually as the temperature decreases below the initial freezing point. The magnitudes of the property for the frozen product are significantly larger than for the unfrozen food.

8.3   Freezing Time

As indicated earlier in this chapter, freezing time is the most critical factor associated with selection of a freezing system to ensure optimum product quality. Freezing-time requirements establish system capacity, while the same parameter has a direct influence on product quality. To ensure efficient selection of freezing systems, methods for prediction of freezing times are very important.

8.3.1   Plank's Equation

The first and most popular equation for prediction of freezing time was proposed by Plank (1913) and adapted to foods by Ede (1949). The equation is as follows:

$$t_F = \frac{\rho H_L}{T_F - T_\infty}\left(\frac{P'a}{h_c} + \frac{R'a^2}{k}\right) \tag{8.1}$$

where it is obvious that the freezing time t_F will increase with increasing density ρ, latent heat of fusion H_L, and increasing size a. With an increase in the temperature gradient, the convective heat-transfer coefficient h_c, and the thermal conductivity k or frozen product, the freezing time will decrease. The constants P and R are used to account for the influence of product shape, with $P = \frac{1}{2}$, $R = \frac{1}{8}$ for infinite plate; $P = \frac{1}{4}$, $R = \frac{1}{16}$ for infinite cylinder; and $P = \frac{1}{6}$, $R = \frac{1}{24}$ for sphere. The dimension a is product thickness for an infinite slab, diameter for an infinite cylinder, and diameter for a sphere.

EXAMPLE 8.1

A spherical food product is being frozen in an air-blast wind tunnel. The initial product temperature is 10°C and the cold air −15°C. The product has a 7-cm diameter with density of 1000 kg/m³ · K, the initial freezing temperature is −1.25°C, and the latent heat of fusion is 250 kJ/kg. Compute the freezing time.

GIVEN

Initial product temperature $T_i = 10°C$
Air temperature $T_\infty = -15°C$
Initial freezing temperature $T_F = -1.25°C$
Product diameter $a = 7$ cm $= 0.07$ m
Product density $\rho = 1000$ kg/m³
Thermal conductivity of frozen product $k = 1.2$ W/m · K
Latent heat $H_L = 250$ kJ/kg
Shape constants for spheres:

$$P' = \tfrac{1}{6}$$

$$R' = \tfrac{1}{24}$$

Convective heat-transfer coefficient $h_c = 50$ W/m² · K

APPROACH

Use Plank's equation [Eq. (8.1)] and insert parameters as given to compute freezing time.

SOLUTION

(1) Using Eq. (8.1),

$$t_F = \frac{(1000 \text{ kg/m}^3)(250 \text{ kJ/kg})}{[-1.25°C - (-15°C)]}\left[\frac{0.07 \text{ m}}{6(50 \text{ W/m}^2 \cdot \text{K})} + \frac{(0.07 \text{ m})^2}{24(1.2 \text{ W/m} \cdot \text{K})}\right]$$

$$= (18.182 \times 10^3 \text{ kJ/m}^3 \cdot °C)\left(2.33 \times 10^{-4} \frac{\text{m}^3 \cdot \text{K}}{\text{W}}\right.$$

$$\left. + 1.7014 \times 10^{-4} \frac{\text{m}^3 \cdot \text{K}}{\text{W}}\right)$$

$$= 7.335 \text{ kJ/W}$$

(2) Since 1000 J $= 1$ kJ and 1 W $= 1$ J/s,

$$t_F = 7.335 \times 10^3 \text{ s}$$

$$= 2.04 \text{ hr}$$

The limitations to Plank's equation are primarily related to assignment of quantitative values to the components of the equation. Density values for frozen foods are difficult to locate or measure. Most often, latent heats of fusion are the product of the latent heat for water and the water content for the product. Although the initial freezing temperature is tabulated for many foods, the initial and final product temperatures are not accounted for in the equation for computation of freezing time. The thermal conductivity k should be for the frozen product, and accurate values are not readily available for most foods.

Even with these limitations, the ease of using Plank's equation results in it being the most popular method for freezing time prediction. Most other available analytical methods are modifications of Plank's equation with emphasis on developments to overcome limitations to the original equation.

8.3.2 Other Freezing-Time Prediction Methods

Numerous attempts have been made to improve freezing-time capabilities using analytical equations. These equations or approaches include those of Nagaoka *et al.* (1955), Charm and Slavin (1962), Tao (1967), Joshi and Tao (1974), Tien and Geiger (1967, 1968), Tien and Koumo (1968, 1969), and Mott (1964). In general, all of these approaches have been satisfactory for conditions closely related to defined experimental conditions. In addition to analytical methods, numerical procedures have been developed to predict freezing times as reviewed by Cleland (1990) and Singh and Mannapperuma (1990). An approach to predict freezing/thawing times of foods using a numerical method based on enthalpy formulation of heat conduction with gradual phase change was found to provide good agreement with experimental results (Mannapperuma and Singh, 1989).

Cleland (1990) has described a new method for prediction of food freezing and thawing times. This method can be used for finite-size objects of any shape by approximating them to be similar to an ellipsoid. Another advantage of this method is that it is easy to use yet it provides answers with reasonable accuracy. In the following sections, we will use this method first to determine the freezing time for a one-dimensional infinite slab, and then consider objects of other shapes. The following assumptions are used in developing this method:

- Constant environmental conditions.
- Uniform initial temperature T_i.
- A fixed value for the final temperature T_f.
- The convective heat transfer at the surface of an object is described by Newton's law of cooling.

a. One-Dimensional Infinite Slab

The procedure to determine the temperature for freezing a one-dimensional slab involves using the following equation to determine the time for freezing:

$$t_{slab} = \frac{R}{h}\left[\frac{\Delta H_1}{\Delta T_1} + \frac{\Delta H_2}{\Delta T_2}\right]\left(1 + \frac{N_{Bi}}{2}\right) \tag{8.2}$$

where

$$\Delta H_1 = C_u(T_i - T_3) \tag{8.3}$$

$$\Delta H_2 = L + C_f(T_3 - T_f) \tag{8.4}$$

$$\Delta T_1 = \frac{(T_i + T_3)}{2} - T_a \tag{8.5}$$

$$\Delta T_2 = T_3 - T_a \tag{8.6}$$

$$T_3 = 1.8 + 0.263 T_f + 0.105 T_a \tag{8.7}$$

The above expressions are valid within the following ranges:

$$0.02 < N_{Bi} < 11, \qquad 0.11 < N_{Ste} < 0.36, \qquad 0.03 < N_{Pk} < 0.61$$

where

$$\text{Stefan number, } N_{Ste} = \frac{C_f(T_F - T_\infty)}{\Delta H} \tag{8.8}$$

$$\text{Plank number, } N_{Pk} = \frac{C_u(T_i - T_F)}{\Delta H} \tag{8.9}$$

For thawing purposes the following expression is recommended:

$$t_{slab} = 5.7164 \frac{C_u R^2}{k_u} \left[\frac{0.25}{N_{Bi} N_{Ste}} + \frac{0.125}{N_{Ste}} \right]^{1.0248} N_{Ste}^{0.2712} N_{Pk}^{0.061} \tag{8.10}$$

applicable for thawing to $T_f = 0°C$. This expression is valid for the following ranges for appropriately modified Stefan and Plank's numbers:

$$0.3 < N_{Bi} < 41, \qquad 0.08 < N_{Ste} < 0.77, \qquad 0.06 < N_{Pk} < 0.27$$

b. Ellipsoid Shapes

Studies done by Cleland et al. (1987) show that in actual practice the effect of shape is relatively independent of conditions other than Biot number and the physical geometry. Using this observation they have suggested determining a shape factor E for a given object and then calculating the freezing or thawing time using the following expression to determine the time for freezing:

$$t_{ellipsoid} = \frac{t_{slab}}{E} \tag{8.11}$$

where t_{slab} is obtained by using Eq. (8.2). The shape factor for an ellipsoid with its three axes R, $\beta_1 R$ and $\beta_2 R$ (as shown in Fig. 8.15) is given by the following equation

$$E = 1 + \frac{\left(1 + \dfrac{2}{N_{Bi}}\right)}{\left(\beta_1^2 + \dfrac{2\beta_1}{N_{Bi}}\right)} + \frac{\left(1 + \dfrac{2}{N_{Bi}}\right)}{\left(\beta_2^2 + \dfrac{2\beta_2}{N_{Bi}}\right)} \tag{8.12}$$

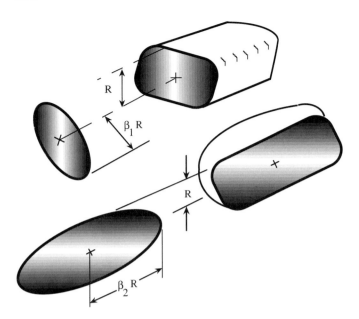

Fig. 8.15 An ellipsoid.

Note that for an infinite slab the shape factor $E = 1$ (since β_1 = infinity and β_2 = infinity); for an infinite cylinder the shape factor $E = 2$ (since $\beta_1 = 1$ and β_2 = infinity); and for a sphere the shape factor $E = 3$ (since $\beta_1 = 1$ and $\beta_2 = 1$).

c. Shapes Other Than Ellipsoids

For shapes other than ellipsoids, such as a rectangular brick shape or a finite cylinder, the shape factor E can be calculated by defining a model ellipsoid. The model ellipsoid is considered to have the following similarities with the actual shape of a given object:

- Same characteristic dimension R; that is, the shortest distance from the thermal center to the surface of the object
- Same smallest orthogonal cross-sectional area A; that is, the smallest cross-section that incorporates R.
- Same volume V.

Thus, parameters β_1 and β_2 are obtained from the following:

$$\beta_1 = \frac{A}{\pi R^2} \tag{8.13}$$

$$\beta_2 = \frac{V}{\beta_1\left(\frac{4}{3}\pi R^3\right)} \tag{8.14}$$

EXAMPLE 8.2

Lean beef with 74.5% moisture content and 1 m length, 0.6 m width, and 0.25 m thickness is being frozen in an air-blast freezer with $h_c = 30$ W/m$^2 \cdot$ K and air temperature of $-30°$C. If the initial product temperature is 5°C, estimate the time required to reduce the product temperature to $-10°$C. An initial freezing temperature of 1.75°C has been measured for the product. The thermal conductivity of frozen beef is 1.5 W/m $\cdot$ K, and the specific heat of unfrozen beef is 3.5 kJ/kg $\cdot$ K. A product density of 1050 kg/m^3 can be assumed, and a specific heat of 1.8 kJ/kg $\cdot$ K for frozen beef can be estimated from properties of ice.

GIVEN

Product length $d_2 = 1$ m
Product width $d_1 = 0.6$ m
Product thickness $a = 0.25$ m
Convective heat-transfer coefficient $h_c = 30$ W/m$^2 \cdot$ K
Air temperature $T_\infty = -30°$C
Initial product temperature $T_i = 5°$C
Initial freezing temperature $T_F = -1.75°$C
Product density $\rho = 1050$ kg/m^3
Enthalpy change $(\Delta H) = 0.745(333.22$ kJ/kg$) = 248.25$ kJ/kg
  (estimated for moisture content of product)
Thermal conductivity k of frozen product $= 1.5$ W/m $\cdot$ K
Specific heat of product $(c_{pu}) = 3.5$ kJ/kg $\cdot$ K
Specific heat of frozen product $(c_{pf}) = 1.8$ kJ/kg $\cdot$ K

APPROACH

The freezing time can be computed using Eq. (8.2) after computation of appropriate dimensionless numbers and determining parameters from Eqs. (8.3) through (8.9).

SOLUTION

(1) To determine the shape factor, we first calculate β_1 and β_2.

$$\beta_1 = \frac{0.25 \times 0.6}{\pi(0.125)^2} = 3.056$$

$$\beta_2 = \frac{0.25 \times 0.6 \times 1}{3.056 \times \frac{4}{3}\pi(0.125)^3} = 5.999$$

(2) The Biot number is

$$N_{Bi} = \frac{h_c R}{k} = \frac{30 \times 0.125}{1.5}$$

$$= 2.5$$

(3) From Eq. (8.12) we obtain E as follows:

$$E = 1 + \frac{\left(1 + \frac{2}{2.5}\right)}{\left(3.056^2 + \frac{2 \times 3.056}{2.5}\right)} + \frac{\left(1 + \frac{2}{2.5}\right)}{\left(5.999^2 + \frac{2 \times 5.999}{2.5}\right)}$$

$$= 1.19688$$

(4) From Eq. (8.7),

$$T_3 = 1.8 + 0.263(-10) + 0.105(-30)$$

$$= -3.98$$

(5) From Eqs. (8.3 and 8.4),

$$\Delta H_1 = (3500 \text{ J/kg} \cdot \text{K}) \times (1050 \text{ kg/m}^3) \times [5°\text{C} - (-3.98°\text{C})]$$

$$= 33,001,500 \text{ J/m}^3$$

$$\Delta H_2 = (333.22 \text{ kJ/kg}) \times (0.745) \times (1050 \text{ kg/m}^3) \times (1000 \text{ J/kJ})$$

$$+ (1800 \text{ J/kg} \cdot \text{K}) \times (1050 \text{ kg/m}^3) \times (-3.98°\text{C} - (-10°\text{C}))$$

$$= 272,039,145 \text{ J/m}^3$$

Note: In the preceding calculation for ΔH_2 the latent heat of water is multiplied with the moisture content of beef to obtain a value of latent heat for beef.

(6) Next ΔT_1 and ΔT_2 are obtained.

$$\Delta T_1 = \frac{5 - 3.98}{2} - (-30)$$

$$= 30.51°\text{C}$$

$$\Delta T_2 = -3.98 + 30$$

$$= 26.02°\text{C}$$

(7) Use Eq. (8.2)

$$t_{\text{slab}} = \frac{0.125}{30}\left[\frac{33001500}{30.51} + \frac{272039145}{26.02}\right]\left(1 + \frac{2.5}{2}\right)$$

$$= 108,156 \text{ s}$$

(8) Using Eq. (8.11) we obtain

$$t = t_{\text{slab}}/E$$

$$= 90,364 \text{ s}$$

$$= 25.1 \text{ h}$$

Thus the large block of lean beef (1 m × 0.6 m × 0.25 m) will require 25.1 hours to freeze.

8.3.3 Experimental Measurement

The evaluation of situations where freezing times are to be verified or products where predictions are difficult requires use of experimental methods. These methods are designed to simulate the actual conditions as closely as possible and should provide for measurement of temperature history at a minimum of one location as the freezing process is completed. If only one location is utilized, the temperature sensor should be located at the slowest cooling point in the product or at a well-defined location near the slowest cooling point. The boundary conditions should be identical to the actual conditions, in terms of medium temperature and the factors influencing the magnitude of the convective heat-transfer coefficient. Under some conditions, the temperature history required to evaluate freezing time should be measured for different variables influencing the magnitude of freezing time.

8.3.4 Factors Influencing Freezing Time

As indicated by Plank's equation, several parameters influence freezing time and will influence the design of equipment used for food freezing. One of the first factors is the freezing-medium temperature, where lower magnitudes will decrease freezing time in a significant manner. According to Plank's equation, product size will influence freezing time directly, but this factor may not be used to influence freezing time since product shape may dictate dimensions.

The parameter with the most significant influence on freezing time is the convective heat-transfer coefficient h_c. This parameter can be used to influence freezing time through equipment design and should be analyzed carefully. At low magnitudes of the convective heat-transfer coefficient, small changes will influence the freezing time in a significant manner. The initial product temperature and final product temperature will influence freezing times slightly, but are not accounted for in the original Plank's equation. Product properties (T_F, ρ, k) will influence freezing-time predictions, as indicated in Plank's equation. Although these parameters are not variables to be used in equipment design, the selection of appropriate values is important in accurate freezing-time prediction. A detailed analysis of all factors influencing freezing-time prediction has been presented by Heldman (1983).

8.3.5 Freezing Rate

The freezing rate (°C/hr) for a product or a package is defined as the difference between the initial and the final temperature divided by the freezing time (IIR, 1986). Since the temperature at different locations of a product may vary during freezing, a *local freezing rate* is defined for a given location in a product as the difference between the initial temperature and the desired temperature divided by the time elapsed until the moment at which the latter temperature is achieved at that location.

8.4 Frozen-Food Storage

Although the efficiency of food freezing is influenced most directly by the freezing process, the quality of the frozen food is influenced significantly by the storage conditions. Since the influence of factors causing quality loss is reduced at lower temperatures, the storage temperature for the frozen food is very important. Major consideration must be given to using the lowest storage temperatures feasible in terms of extending storage life without using refrigeration energy inefficiently.

The most detrimental factor influencing frozen food quality is fluctuation in storage temperature. If frozen foods are exposed to temperature cycles resulting in changes in product temperatures, the storage life is reduced significantly. The quantitative aspects of frozen-food storage life have been investigated by Schwimmer *et al.* (1955), Van Arsdel and Guadagni (1959), and summarized by Van Arsdel *et al.* (1969). More recently, Singh and Wang (1977) and Heldman and Lai (1983) have described numerical and computer prediction of frozen-food storage time.

Based on experimental data for storage of frozen foods, recommendations on frozen food storage have been developed (IIR, 1986).

8.4.1 Quality Changes in Foods during Frozen Storage

A commonly used descriptor of storage life of frozen foods is the practical storage life (PSL). The practical storage life of a product is the period of frozen storage after freezing during which the product retains is characteristic properties and remains suitable for consumption or other intended process (IIR, 1986).

In Table 8.1, the practical storage life of a variety of frozen foods is given. The shelf life of frozen fish is considerably less than most other commodities. The typical temperature used for storing frozen foods in the commercial food chain is −18°C. However, for seafoods, use of a lower storage temperature may be more desirable to retain the quality.

Another term used to describe the storage life of frozen foods is the high quality life (HQL). As defined by IIR (1986), the high quality life is the time elapsed from freezing of an initially high quality product and the moment when, by sensory assessment, a statistically significant difference ($P < 0.01$) from the initial high quality (immediately after freezing) can be established. The observed difference is termed the just noticeable difference (JND). When a triangular test is used for sensory assessment of the quality, a just noticeable difference can be postulated when 70% of experienced panelists successfully distinguish the product from the control sample stored under such conditions as have been proven to produce no detectable degradation during the time period under consideration (IIR, 1986). A typical temperature used for control experiments is −35°C.

TABLE 8.1
The Practical Storage Life (PSL) of Frozen Foods
at Several Storage Temperatures

Product	Storage time (months)		
	− 12°C	− 18°C	− 24°C
Fruits			
Raspberries/Strawberries (raw)	5	24	> 24
Raspberries/Strawberries in sugar	3	24	> 24
Peaches, Apricots, Cherries (raw)	4	18	> 24
Peaches, Apricots, Cherries in sugar	3	18	> 24
Fruit juice concentrate	—	24	> 24
Vegetables			
Asparagus (with green spears)	3	12	> 24
Beans, green	4	15	> 24
Beans, lima	—	18	> 24
Broccoli	—	15	24
Brussels sprouts	6	15	> 24
Carrots	10	18	> 24
Cauliflower	4	12	24
Corn-on-the-cob	—	12	18
Cut corn	4	15	> 24
Mushrooms (cultivated)	2	8	> 24
Peas, green	6	24	> 24
Peppers, red and green	—	6	12
Potatoes, French fried	9	24	> 24
Spinach (chopped)	4	18	> 24
Onions	—	10	15
Leeks (blanched)	—	18	—
Meats and poultry			
Beef carcass (unpackaged)[a]	8	15	24
Beef steaks/cuts	8	18	24
Ground beef	6	10	15
Veal carcass (unpackaged)[a]	6	12	15
Veal steaks/cuts	6	12	15
Lamb carcass, Grass fed (unpackaged)[a]	18	24	> 24
Lamb steaks	12	18	24
Pork carcass (unpackaged)[a]	6	10	15
Pork steaks/cuts	6	10	15
Sliced bacon (vacuum packed)	12	12	12
Chicken, Whole	9	18	> 24
Chicken, parts/cuts	9	18	> 24
Turkey, Whole	8	15	> 24
Ducks, Geese, Whole	6	12	18
Liver	4	12	18
Seafood			
Fatty fish, Glazed	3	5	> 9
Lean fish[b]	4	9	> 12
Lobster, Crab, Shrimps in shell (cooked)	4	6	> 12
Clams and Oysters	4	6	> 9
Shrimps (cooked/peeled)	2	5	> 9
Eggs			
Whole egg magma	—	12	> 24

(continues)

TABLE 8.1 (*Continued*)

	Storage time (months)		
Product	− 12°C	− 18°C	− 24°C
Milk and milk products			
Butter, Lactic, unsalted pH 4.7	15	18	20
Butter, Lactic, salted pH 4.7	8	12	14
Butter, Sweet-cream, unsalted pH 6.6	—	> 24	> 24
Butter, Sweet-cream, salt (2%) pH 6.6	20	> 24	> 24
Cream	—	12	15
Ice cream	1	6	24
Bakery and confectionery products			
Cakes (cheese, sponge, chocolate, fruit etc.)	—	15	24
Breads	—	3	—
Raw dough	—	12	18

Source: IIR (1986).
[a]Carcass may be wrapped in stockinette.
[b] The PSL for single fillets of lean fish would be 6, 9, and 12 months at − 18°C, − 24°C, and − 30°C, respectively.

The quality loss in frozen foods can be predicted using the experimentally obtained data on acceptable time for storage. Singh and Wang (1977) and Heldman and Lai (1983) have described numerical and computer predictions of storage time based on a kinetic analysis of changes occurring in foods during frozen storage.

Jul (1984) has provided values for typical exposure times that a product may encounter in different components of the frozen food chain. In Fig. 8.16, data on acceptable time for storage of frozen strawberries is presented (Jul, 1984). The acceptable shelf life in this figure is based on experimental data. In column 1 of Table 8.2, a frozen food chain is described, starting with the producer's warehouse and finishing at the consumer's freezer. In Table 8.2, columns 2 and 3 denote the expected time and temperature at various locations in the chain. Column 4 is the acceptable days corresponding to the temperatures as obtained from Fig. 8.16. Values in column 5 are the inverse of those in column 4 and multiplied by 100 to obtain percent loss per day. Column 6 gives the calculated values of loss obtained by multiplying values in column 2 with those in column 5. Thus in the example shown in Table 8.2, the frozen strawberries have lost 77.3% of their acceptable quality after 344.1 days in the frozen food chain. This analysis assists in identifying those components of the chain where major losses are occurring. For the example shown in Table 8.2, major losses in quality occur in the producer's and the retailer's warehouse. Reduction of either storage temperature or time in the identified components can help reduce quality loss for a given food.

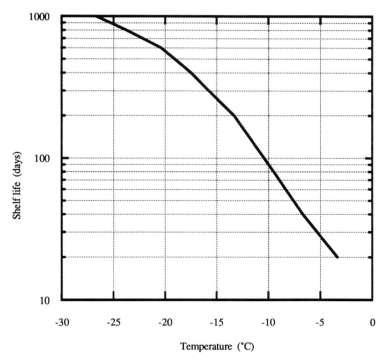

Fig. 8.16 Semilogarithmic plot of shelf life versus temperature for frozen strawberries.

TABLE 8.2
An Example of the Conditions of Storage and Quality Loss in Strawberries in Different Stages in a Frozen Food Chain

Stage	Time (days)	Temperature (°C)	Acceptability (days)	Loss per day (percent/day)	Loss percent
Producer	250	−22	660	0.15152	37.88
Transport	2	−14	220	0.45455	0.91
Wholesale	50	−23	710	0.14085	7.04
Transport	1	−12	140	0.71429	0.71
Retail	21	−11	110	0.90909	19.09
Transport	0.1	−3	18	5.55556	0.56
Home freezer	20	−13	180	0.55556	11.11
Total storage (days) = 344.1			Total quality loss (percent) = 77.30		

Source: Jul (1984).

Problems

8.1 Estimate the latent heat of fusion for a food product with 68% moisture content.

8.2 A food product with 82% moisture content is being frozen. Estimate the specific heat of the product at −10°C when 80% of the water is in a frozen state. The specific heat of dry product solid is 2.0 kJ/kg · °C. Assume specific heat of water at −10°C is similar to specific heat of water at 0°C.

8.3 A 5-cm-thick beef steak is being frozen in a −30°C room. The product has 73% moisture content, density of 970 kg/m³, and thermal conductivity (frozen) of 1.1 W/m · K. Estimate the freezing time using Plank's equation. The product has an initial freezing temperature of −1.75°C, and the movement of air in the freezing room provides a convective heat-transfer coefficient of 5 W/m² · K.

*8.4 Partially frozen ice cream is being placed in a package before completion of the freezing process. The package has dimensions of 8 cm by 10 cm by 20 cm and is placed in air-blast freezing with convective heat coefficient of 50 W/m² · K for freezing. The product temperature is −5°C when placed in the package, and the air temperature is −25°C. The product density is 700 kg/m³, the thermal conductivity (frozen) is 1.2 W/m · K, and the specific heat of the frozen product is 1.9 kJ/kg · K. If the latent heat to be removed during blast freezing is 100 kJ/kg, estimate the freezing time.

*8.5 A food product with 80% moisture content is being frozen in a 6-cm-diameter can. The product density is 1000 kg/m³, the thermal conductivity is 1.0 W/m · K, and the initial freezing temperature is −2°C. After 10 hr in the −15°C freezing medium, the product temperature is −10°C. Estimate the convective heat-transfer coefficient for the freezing medium. Assume the can has infinite height.

8.6 Develop a spreadsheet to solve Example 8.2. Determine time for freezing for the following h_c values: 30, 50, 80, and 100 W/m² °C.

8.7 Using the spreadsheet developed in Problem 8.6, determine the time for freezing if the shape of lean beef is assumed to be

> (a) a finite cylinder, with a diameter of 0.5 m and 1 m long.
> (b) an infinite cylinder with a diameter of 0.5 m.
> (c) a sphere of diameter 0.5 m.

List of Symbols

A	area (m²)	C_u	volumetric specific heat
a	thickness or diameter of product (m)		capacity, unfrozen, J/m³ · K
β_1, β_2	coefficients in Eq. (8.12)	C_f	volumetric specific heat

---

*Indicates an advanced level of difficulty in solving.

capacity, frozen,
$J/m^3 \cdot K$

c_{pf} specific heat of frozen product $(kJ/kg \cdot K)$

c_{pu} specific heat of unfrozen product $(kJ/kg \cdot K)$

D characteristic dimension (m)

d_1 width of product (m)

d_2 length of product (m)

ΔH change in enthalpy for freezing (kJ/kg)

E shape factor in Eq. (8.11)

H enthalpy (kJ/kg)

h_c convective heat-transfer coefficient $(W/m^2 \cdot K)$

H_L latent heat of fusion (kJ/kg)

k thermal conductivity $(W/m \cdot K)$

k_u thermal conductivity of unfrozen medium $(W/m \cdot K)$

N_{Bi} Biot number

N_{Pk} Plank's number, defined in Eq. (8.9)

N_{Ste} Stefan number, defined in Eq. (8.8)

P' constant in Plank's equation

R' constant in Plank's equation

R characteristic dimension shown in Fig. 8.15

ρ product density (kg/m^3)

T temperature (°C)

t time(s)

$t_{ellipsoid}$ time to freeze an ellipsoid (s)

T_F initial freezing point (°C)

T_f final temperature (°C)

t_F freezing time(s)

T_i initial product temperature (°C)

t_{slab} time to freeze an infinite slab (s)

T_∞ freezing-medium temperature (°C)

V volume (m^3)

Bibliography

Charm, S. E., and Slavin, J. (1962). A method for calculating freezing time of rectangular packages of food. *Annexe. Bull. Inst. Int. Froid.* 567–578.

Cleland, A. C. (1990). "Food Refrigeration Processes, Analysis, Design and Simulation." Elsevier Applied Science, New York.

Cleland, A. C., and Earle, R. L. (1976). A new method for prediction of surface heat-transfer coefficients in freezing. *Annexe. Bull. Inst. Int. Froid.* **1**, 361.

Cleland, A. C., and Earle, R. L. (1977). A comparison of analytical and numerical methods of predicting the freezing times of foods. *J. Food Sci.* **42**, 1390–1395.

Cleland, A. C., and Earle, R. L. (1979a). A comparison of methods for predicting the freezing times of cylindrical and spherical foodstuffs. *J. Food Sci.* **44**, 958–963.

Cleland, A. C., and Earle, R. L. (1979b). Prediction of freezing times for foods in rectangular packages. *J. Food Sci.* **44**, 964–970.

Cleland D. J., (1991). A generally applicable simple method for prediction of food freezing and thawing times. Paper presented at the 18th International Congress of Refrigeration. Montreal, Quebec.

Cleland, D. J., Cleland, A. C., and Earle, R. L. (1987). Prediction of freezing and thawing times for multi-dimensional shapes by simple formulae: I—Regular shapes. *Int. J. Refrig.* **10**, 156–164.

Ede, A. J. (1949). The calculation of the freezing and thawing of foodstuffs. *Mod. Refrig.* **52**, 52.

Heldman, D. R. (1983). Factors influencing food freezing rates. *Food Technol.* **37**(4), 103–109.

Heldman, D. R., and Gorby, D. P. (1975). Prediction of thermal conductivity of frozen foods. *Trans. ASAE* **18**, 740.

Heldman, D. R., and Lund, D. B. (1992). "Handbook of Food Engineering." Marcel Dekker, New York.

Heldman, D. R., and Lai, D. J. (1983). A model for prediction of shell-life for frozen foods. *Proc. Int. Congr. Refrig., 16th Commission* C2, 427–433.

Hill, J. E., Litman, J. E., and Sutherland, J. E. (1967). Thermal conductivity of various meats. *Food Technol.* **21**, 1143.

IIR (1986). "Recommendations for the Processing and Handling of Frozen Foods," 3rd ed. International Institute of Refrigeration, Paris, France.

Joshi, C., and Tao, L. C. (1974). A numerical method of simulating the axisymmetrical freezing of food systems. *J. Food Sci.* **39**, 623.

Jul, M. (1984). "The Quality of Frozen Foods." Academic Press, Orlando.

Lentz, C. P. (1961). Thermal conductivity of meats, fats, gelatin gels and ice. *Food Technol.* **15**, 243.

Mannapperuma, J. D., and Singh, R. P. (1989). A computer-aided method for the prediction of properties and freezing/thawing times of foods. *J. Food Eng.* **9**, 275–304.

Mott, L. F. (1964). The prediction of product freezing time. *Aust. Refrig., Air Cond. Heat.* **18**, 16.

Nagaoka, J., Takagi, S., and Hotani, S. (1955). Experiments on the freezing of fish in an air-blast freezer. *Proc. Int. Congr. Refrig., 9th*, Vol. 2, p. 4.

Plank, R. Z. (1913). *Z. Gesamte Kalte-Ind.* **20**, 109 (cited by Ede, 1949).

Schwimmer, S., Ingraham, L. L., and Highes, H. M. (1955). Temperature tolerance in frozen food processing. *Ind. Eng. Chem.* **47**(6), 1149–1151.

Singh, R. P., and Mannapperuma, J. D. (1990). Developments in food freezing. *In* "Biotechnology and Food Process Engineering" (H. Schwartzberg and A. Rao, Eds.). Marcel Dekker, New York.

Singh, R. P., and Wang, C. Y. (1977). Quality of frozen foods—A review, *J. Food Process Eng.* **1**(2), 97.

Tao, L. C. (1967). Generalized numerical solutions of freezing a saturated liquid in cylinders and spheres. *AIChE J.* **13**, 165.

Tien, R. H., and Geiger, G. E. (1967). A heat transfer analysis of the solidification of a binary eutectic system. *J. Heat Transfer* **9**, 230.

Tien, R. H., and Geiger, G. E. (1968). The unidimensional solidification of a binary eutectic system with a time-dependent surface temperature. *J. Heat Transfer.* **9C**(1), 27.

Tien, R. H., and Koumo, V. (1968). Unidimensional solidification of a slabvariable surface temperature. *Trans. Metal Soc. AIME* **242**, 283.

Tien, R. H., and Koumo, V. (1969). Effect of density change on the solidification of alloys. *Am. Soc. Mech. Eng.* [Pap.] **69-HT-45**.

Van Arsdel, W. B., and Guadagni, D. G. (1959). Time–temperature tolerance of frozen foods. XV. Method of using temperature histories to estimate changes in frozen food quality. *Food Technol.* **13**(1), 14–19.

Van Arsdel, W. B., Copley, M. J., and Olson, R. D. (1969). "Quality and Stability of Frozen Foods." Wiley, New York.

Williams, E. W. (1976). Frozen foods in America. *Quick Frozen Foods* **17**(5), 16–40.

CHAPTER 9

Evaporation

9.1 Introduction

Evaporation is an important unit operation commonly employed to remove water from dilute liquid foods to obtain concentrated liquid products. Removal of water from foods provides microbiological stability and assists in reducing transportation and storage costs. A typical example of the evaporation process is in the manufacture of tomato paste, usually around 35–37% total solids, obtained by evaporating water from tomato juice, which has an initial concentration of 5–6% total solids. Evaporation differs from dehydration, since the final product of evaporation process remains in liquid state. It also differs from distillation, since the vapors produced in the evaporator are not further divided into fractions as in distillation.

In Fig. 9.1 a simplified schematic of an evaporator is shown. Essentially, an evaporator consists of a heat exchanger enclosed in a large chamber; a noncontact heat exchanger provides the means to transfer heat from low-pressure steam to the product. The product inside the evaporation chamber is kept under vacuum. The presence of vacuum causes the temperature difference between steam and product to increase and the product boils at relatively low temperatures, thus minimizing heat damage. The vapors produced are conveyed through a condenser to a vacuum system. The steam condenses inside the heat exchanger and the condensate is discarded.

In the evaporator shown in Fig. 9.1, the vapors produced are discarded without further utilizing their inherent heat, therefore this type of evaporator is called a single-effect evaporator, since the vapors produced are discarded. If the vapors are reused as the heating medium in another evaporator chamber, as shown in Fig. 9.2, the evaporator system is called a multiple-effect evaporator. More specifically, the evaporator shown in Fig. 9.2 is a triple-effect evaporator, as vapors produced from first and second effects (or evaporation chambers) are used again as the heating medium in second and third effects, respectively.

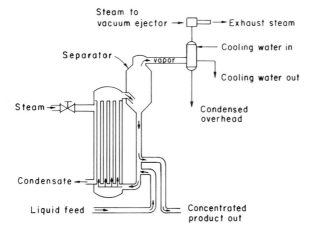

Fig. 9.1 Schematic of a single-effect evaporator.

Note that in a multi-effect evaporator, steam is used only in the first effect. The use of vapors as a heating medium in additional effects results in obtaining higher energy-use efficiency from the system. The partially concentrated product leaving the first effect is introduced as feed into the second effect. After additional concentration, product from the second effect becomes feed for the third effect. The product from the third effect leaves at the desired concentration. This particular arrangement is called a forward feed system. Other flow arrangements used in the industrial practice include backward feed system, and parallel feed system.

The characteristics of the liquid food have a profound effect on the performance of the evaporation process. As water is removed, the liquid becomes increasingly concentrated, resulting in reduced heat transfer. The boiling point rises as the liquid concentrates, resulting in a smaller differ-

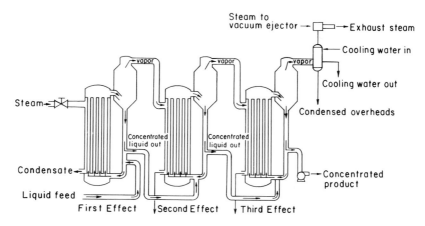

Fig. 9.2 Schematic of a triple-effect evaporator.

ential of temperature between the heating medium and the product. This causes reduced rate of heat transfer.

Food products are noted for their heat sensitivity. Evaporation processes must involve reducing temperature for boiling as well as time of heating to avoid excessive product degradation.

In addition, fouling of the heat-exchange surface can seriously reduce the rate of heat transfer. Frequent cleaning of heat-exchange surfaces requires shutdown of the equipment, thus decreasing the processing capacity. Liquid foods that foam during vaporization cause product losses due to escape through vapor outlets. In designing evaporation systems, it is important to keep in perspective the preceding unique characteristics of liquid food.

In this chapter we will consider the boiling-point elevation in liquid foods during concentration, describe various types of evaporators based on the method of heat exchange from steam to product, and then we will design single- and multiple-effect evaporators.

9.2 Boiling-Point Elevation

Boiling-point elevation of a solution (liquid food) is defined as the increase in boiling point over that of pure water, at a given pressure.

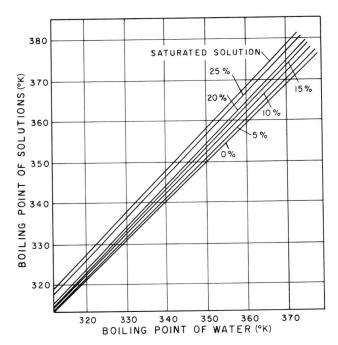

Fig. 9.3 Dühring lines illustrating the influence of solute concentrations of boiling-point elevation of NaCl. [From Coulson and Richardson (1978).]

A simple method to estimate boiling-point elevation is the use of Dühring's rule. The Dühring rule states that a linear relationship exists between the boiling-point temperature of the solution and the boiling-point temperature of water at the same pressure. The linear relationship does not hold over a wide range of temperatures, but over moderate temperature ranges, it is quite acceptable. Dühring lines for a sodium chloride–water system are shown in Fig. 9.3. The following example illustrates the use of the figure to estimate boiling-point elevation.

EXAMPLE 9.1

Use Dühring's chart to determine the initial and final boiling point of a liquid food with a composition that exerts vapor pressure similar to that of sodium chloride solution. The pressure in the evaporator is 20 kPa. The product is being concentrated from 5% to 25% total solids concentration.

GIVEN

Initial concentration = 5% total solids
Final concentration = 25% total solids
Pressure = 20 kPa

APPROACH

To use Dühring's chart, given in Fig. 9.3, we need the boiling point of water. This value is obtained from the steam tables. The boiling point of the liquid food can then be read directly from Fig. 9.3.

PROCEDURE

(1) From a steam table (Appendix A.4.2) at 20 kPa, the boiling point of water is 60°C or 333 K.
(2) From Fig. 9.3,

Boiling point at initial concentration of 5% total solids is 333 K = 60°C
Boiling point at final concentration of 25% total solids is 337 K = 64°C

The boiling-point elevation merits consideration since the temperature difference between steam and product decreases as the boiling point of the liquid increases due to concentration. The reduced temperature differential causes a reduction in rate of heat transfer between steam and product.

9.3 Types of Evaporators

Several types of evaporators are used in the food industry. In this section, a brief discussion of the more common types is given.

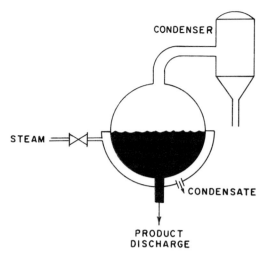

Fig. 9.4 A batch-type pan evaporator. (Courtesy of APV Equipment, Inc.)

9.3.1 Batch-Type Pan Evaporator

One of the simplest and perhaps oldest types of evaporators used in the food industry is the batch-type pan evaporator, shown in Fig. 9.4. The product is heated in a steam-jacketed spherical vessel. The heating vessel may be open to the atmosphere or connected to a condenser and vacuum. Vacuum permits boiling the product at temperatures lower than the boiling point at atmospheric pressure, thus reducing the thermal damage to heat-sensitive products.

The heat-transfer area per unit volume in a pan evaporator is small. Thus, the residence time of the product is usually very long, up to several hours. Heating of the product occurs mainly due to natural convection, resulting in smaller convective heat-transfer coefficients. The poor heat-transfer characteristics substantially reduce the processing capacities of the batch-type pan evaporators.

9.3.2 Natural Circulation Evaporators

In natural circulation evaporators, short vertical tubes, typically 1–2 m long and 50–100 mm in diameter, are arranged inside the steam chest. The whole calandria (tubes and steam chest) is located in the bottom of the vessel. The product when heated rises through these tubes by natural circulation while steam condenses outside the tubes. Evaporation takes place inside the tubes and the product is concentrated. The concentrated liquid falls back to the base of the vessel through a central annular section.

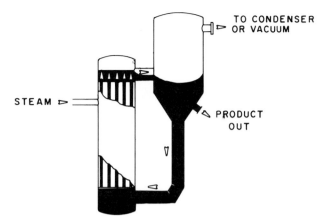

Fig. 9.5 A natural-circulation evaporator. (Courtesy of APV Equipment, Inc.)

A natural-circulation evaporator is shown in Fig. 9.5. A shell-and-tube heat exchanger can be provided outside the main evaporation vessel to preheat the liquid feed.

9.3.3 Rising-Film Evaporator

In a rising-film evaporator (Fig. 9.6), a low-viscosity liquid food is allowed to boil inside 10–15 m-long vertical tubes. The tubes are heated from the outside with steam. The liquid rises inside these tubes by vapors formed near the bottom of the heating tubes. The upward movement of vapors

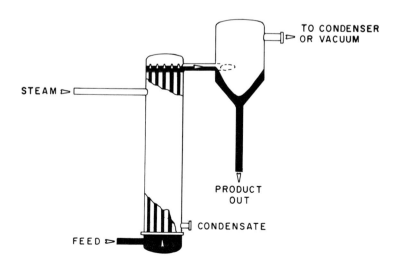

Fig. 9.6 A rising-film evaporator. (Courtesy of APV Equipment, Inc.)

causes a thin liquid film to move rapidly upward. A temperature differential of at least 14°C between the product and the heating medium is necessary to obtain a well-developed film. High convective heat-transfer coefficients are achieved in these evaporators. Although the operation is mostly once-through, liquid can be recirculated if necessary to obtain the required solid concentration.

9.3.4 Falling-Film Evaporator

In contrast to the rising-film evaporator, the falling-film evaporator has a thin liquid film moving downward under gravity on the inside of the vertical tubes (Fig. 9.7). The design of such evaporators is complicated by the fact that distribution of liquid in a uniform film flowing downward in a tube is more difficult to obtain than an upward-flow system such as in a rising-film evaporator. This is accomplished by the use of specially designed distributors or spray nozzles.

The falling-film evaporator allows a greater number of effects than the rising-film evaporator. For example, if steam is available at 110°C and the boiling temperature in the last effect is 50°C, then the total available temperature differential is 60°C. Since rising-film evaporators require 14°C temperature differential across the heating surface, only four effects are

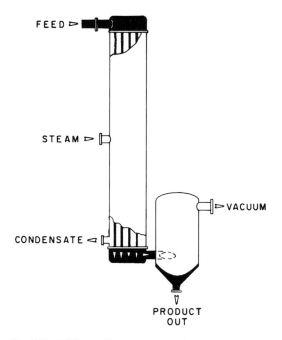

Fig. 9.7 A falling-film evaporator. (Courtesy of APV Equipment, Inc.)

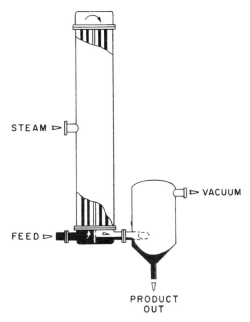

STEAM ▷

▷ VACUUM

FEED ▷

PRODUCT
OUT

Fig. 9.8   A rising/falling-film evaporator. (Courtesy of APV Equipment, Inc.)

feasible. However, as many as 10 or more effects may be possible using a falling-film evaporator. The falling-film evaporator can handle more viscous liquids than the rising-film type. This type of evaporator is best suited for highly heat-sensitive products such as orange juice. Typical residence time in a falling-film evaporator is 20–30 seconds, compared with a residence time of 3–4 minutes in a rising-film evaporator.

9.3.5   Rising/Falling-Film Evaporator

In the rising/falling-film evaporator, the product is concentrated by circulation through a rising-film section followed by a falling-film section of the evaporator. As shown in Fig. 9.8, the product is first concentrated as it ascends through a rising tube section, followed by the preconcentrated product descending through a falling-film section; there it attains its final concentration.

9.3.6   Forced-Circulation Evaporator

The forced-circulation evaporator involves a noncontact heat exchanger where liquid food is circulated at high rates (Fig. 9.9). A hydrostatic head, above the top of the tubes, eliminates any boiling of the liquid. Inside the

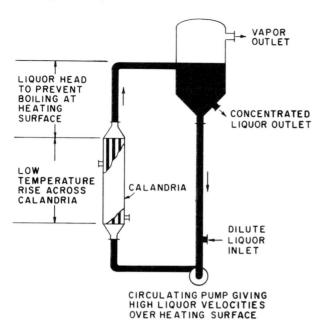

VAPOR
OUTLET

LIQUOR HEAD
TO PREVENT
BOILING AT
HEATING
SURFACE

CONCENTRATED
LIQUOR OUTLET

LOW
TEMPERATURE
RISE ACROSS
CALANDRIA

CALANDRIA

DILUTE
LIQUOR
INLET

CIRCULATING PUMP GIVING
HIGH LIQUOR VELOCITIES
OVER HEATING SURFACE

Fig. 9.9 A forced-circulation evaporator. (Courtesy of APV Equipment, Inc.)

separator, absolute pressure is kept slightly lower than that in the tube bundle. Thus, the liquid entering the separator flashes to form a vapor. The temperature difference across the heating surface in the heat exchanger is usually 3–5°C. Axial flow pumps are generally used to maintain high circulation rates with linear velocities of 2–6 m/s, compared with a linear velocity of 0.3–1 m/s in natural-circulation evaporators. Both capital and operating costs of these evaporators are very low in comparison to other types of evaporators.

9.3.7 Agitated Thin-Film Evaporator

For very viscous fluid foods, feed is spread on the inside of the cylindrical heating surface by wiper blades, as shown in Fig. 9.10. Due to high agitation, considerably higher rates of heat transfer are obtained. The cylindrical configuration results in low heat-transfer area per unit volume of the product. High-pressure steam is used as the heating medium to obtain high wall temperatures for reasonable evaporation rates. The major disadvantages are the high capital and maintenance costs and low processing capacity.

In addition to the tubular shape, plate evaporators are also used in the industry. Plate evaporators use the principles of rising/falling-film,

TABLE 9.1
Types of Evaporators Employed in Concentrating Liquid Foods[a]

Evaporator type	Tube depth	Circulation	Viscosity capability $(Pa \cdot s \times 10^3)$	Able to handle suspended solids	Applicable to multiple effects
Vertical tubular	Long	Natural	Up to 50	Yes	Yes
Vertical tubular	Long	Assisted	Up to 150	Yes	Yes
Vertical tubular	Short	Natural	Up to 20	Yes	Yes
Vertical tubular	Short	Assisted	Utp to 2000	Yes	No
Vertical tubular	Long	Forced— suppressed boiling	Up to 500	Yes	Limited
Plate heat exchanger	N/A	Forced— suppressed boiling	Up to 500	Limited	Yes
Vertical tubular rising film	Long	None or limited	Up to 1000	Not desirable	Yes
Vertical tubular rising/ falling film	Medium	None or limited	Up to 2000	Not desirable	Yes
Plate rising/ falling film	N/A	None or limited	Up to 2000	Very limited	Yes
Vertical tubular falling film	Long	None or limited	Up to 3000	Not desirable	Yes
Vertical tubular falling film	Long	Medium	Up to 1000	Yes	Yes
Plate falling film	N/A	None or limited	Up to 3000	No	Yes
Swept surface	N/A	None	Up to 10,000	Yes	No

[a] Courtesy of APV Equipment, Inc.

TABLE 9.1
(*Continued*)

Applicable to mechanical vapor recompression	Heat transfer rate	Residence time	Capital cost	Remarks
No	Medium	High	Low	
No	Good	High	Low–medium	
No	Medium	High	HIgh	Calandria usually internal to separator
No	Low	Very high	High	Calandria usually internal to separator
No	Medium	Very high	Very high	Used on scaling duties
No	Good	Medium	Medium	Used on scaling duties
No	Good	Low	Medium	
No	Good	Low	Medium	
No	Good	Low	Low–medium	
Yes	Excellent	Very low	Medium	Used on heat-sensitive products
Yes	Good	Low	Medium	
Yes	Excellent	Very low	Medium	Used on heat-sensitive products
No	Excellent	Low	Very high	

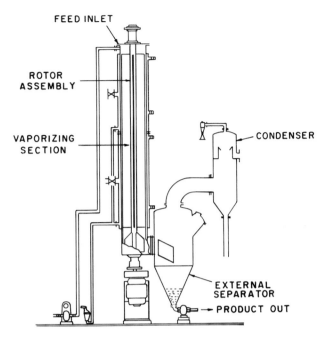

FEED INLET

ROTOR
ASSEMBLY

VAPORIZING
SECTION

CONDENSER

EXTERNAL
SEPARATOR
PRODUCT OUT

Fig. 9.10   An agitated thin-film evaporator. (Courtesy of APV Equipment, Inc.)

falling-film, wiped-film, and forced-circulation evaporators. The plate configuration often provides features that make it more acceptable. A
rising/falling-film plate evaporator is more compact, thus requiring less
floor area than a tubular unit. The heat-transfer areas can easily be
inspected. A falling-film plate evaporator with a capacitor of 25,000 to
30,000 kg water removed per hour is not uncommon.

Table 9.1 summarizes the various comparative features of different
types of evaporators used in concentrating liquid foods. The characteristics
are presented in a general way. Custom-designed modifications of these
types can significantly alter the specific duties.

9.4   Design of a Single-Effect Evaporator

In a single-effect evaporator, as shown in Fig. 9.11, dilute liquid feed is
pumped into the heating chamber, where it is heated indirectly with steam.
Steam is introduced into the heat exchanger, where it condenses to give up
its heat of vaporization to the feed, and exits the system as condensate.

The temperature of evaporation T_1 is controlled by maintaining vacuum inside the heating chamber. The vapors leaving the product are
conveyed through a condenser to a vacuum system, usually a steam ejector
or a vacuum pump. In a batch system, the feed is heated until the desired

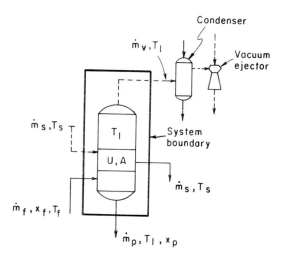

Fig. 9.11 Schematic of a single-effect evaporator.

concentration is obtained. The concentrated product is then pumped out of the evaporator system.

Heat and mass balances conducted on the evaporator system allow determination of various design and operating variables. Such variables may include mass flow rates, final concentration of product, and heat-exchanger area.

The following expressions can be obtained by conducting a mass balance on flow streams and product solids, respectively.

$$\dot{m}_f = \dot{m}_v + \dot{m}_p \tag{9.1}$$

where $\dot{m}_f$ is the mass flow rate of dilute liquid feed (kg/s), $\dot{m}_v$ is the mass flow rate of vapor (kg/s), and $\dot{m}_p$ is the mass flow rate of concentrated product (kg/s),

$$x_f \dot{m}_f = x_p \dot{m}_p \tag{9.2}$$

where x_f is the solid fraction in feed stream (dimensionless) and x_p is the solid fraction in product stream (dimensionless).

An enthalpy balance conducted on the evaporator system gives the following expression:

$$\dot{m}_f H_f(T_f, x_f) + \dot{m}_s H_v(T_s) = \dot{m}_v H_v(T_1) + \dot{m}_p H_p(T_1, x_p) + \dot{m}_s H_c(T_s) \tag{9.3}$$

where $\dot{m}_s$ is the mass flow rate of steam (kg/s); $H_f(T_f, x_f)$ is enthalpy of dilute liquid feed (kJ/kg); $H_p(T_1, x_p)$ is enthalpy of concentrated product (kJ/kg); $H_v(T_s)$ is enthalpy of saturated vapor at temperature T_s (kJ/kg); $H_v(T_1)$ is enthalpy of saturated vapor at temperature T_1 (kJ/kg); $H_c(T_s)$ is enthalpy of condensate (kJ/kg); T_s is temperature of steam (°C); T_1 is the boiling temperature maintained inside the evaporator chamber (°C); and T_f is the temperature of dilute liquid feed (°C).

The first term in Eq. (9.3), $\dot{m}_f H_f(T_f, x_f)$, represents the total enthalpy associated with the incoming dilute liquid feed, where $H_f(T_f, x_f)$ means that enthalpy H_f is a function of T_f and x_f. The enthalpy content $H_f(T_f, x_f)$ can be computed from

$$H_f(T_f, x_f) = c_{pf}(T_f - 0°C) \qquad (9.4)$$

The specific heat may be obtained either from Table A.2.1 or by using Eq. (4.2) or Eq. (4.3).

The second term, $\dot{m}_s H_v(T_s)$, gives the total heat content of steam. It is assumed that saturated steam is being used. The enthalpy, $H_v(T_s)$, is obtained from the steam table (Table A.4.2) as enthalpy of saturated vapors evaluated at the steam temperature T_s.

On the right-hand side of Eq. (9.3), the first term, $\dot{m}_v H_v(T_1)$, represents total enthalpy content of the vapors leaving the system. The enthalpy $H_v(T_1)$ is obtained from the steam table (Table A.4.2) as the enthalpy of saturated vapors evaluated at temperature T_1.

The second term, $\dot{m}_p H_p(T_1, x_p)$, is the total enthalpy associated with the concentrated product stream leaving the evaporator. The enthalpy content $H_p(T_1, x_p)$ is obtained using the following equation:

$$H_p(T_1, x_p) = c_{pp}(T_1 - 0°C) \qquad (9.5)$$

where c_{pp} is the specific heat content of concentrated product (kJ/kg · °C).

Again, c_{pp} is obtained from Table A.2.1 or by using Eq.(4.2) or Eq. (4.3).

The last term, $\dot{m}_s H_c(T_s)$, represents the total enthalpy associated with the condensate leaving the evaporator. Since an indirect type of heat exchanger is used in evaporator systems, the rate of mass flow of incoming steam is the same as the rate of mass flow of condensate leaving the evaporator. The enthalpy $H_c(T_s)$ is obtained from the steam table (Table A.4.2) as enthalpy of saturated liquid evaluated at temperature T_s. If the condensate leaves at a temperature lower than T_s, then the lower temperature should be used to determine the enthalpy of the saturated liquid.

In addition to the mass and enthalpy balances given above, the following two equations are also used in computing design and operating variables of an evaporator system.

For the heat exchanger, the following expression gives the rate of heat transfer:

$$q = UA(T_s - T_1) = \dot{m}_s H_v(T_s) - \dot{m}_s H_c(T_s) \qquad (9.6)$$

where q is the rate of heat transfer (W), U is the overall heat transfer coefficient (W/m^2 · K), and A is the area of the heat exchanger (m^2).

The overall heat-transfer coefficient decreases as product becomes concentrated, due to increased resistance of heat transfer on the product side of the heat exchanger. In addition, the boiling point of the product rises as the product becomes concentrated. In Eq. (9.6), a constant value of the overall heat-transfer coefficient is used and would result in some "overdesign" of the equipment.

Steam economy is a term often used in expressing the operating performance of an evaporator system. This term is a ratio of rate of mass of water vapor produced from the liquid feed per unit rate of steam consumed.

$$\text{Steam economy} = \dot{m}_v / \dot{m}_s \qquad (9.7)$$

A typical value for steam economy of a single-effect evaporator system is close to 1.

EXAMPLE 9.2

Apple juice is being concentrated in a natural-circulation single-effect evaporator. At steady-state conditions, dilute juice is the feed introduced at a rate of 0.67 kg/s. The concentration of the dilute juice is 11% total solids. The juice is concentrated to 75% total solids. The specific heats of dilute apple juice and concentrate are 3.9 and 2.3 kJ/kg ·°C, respectively. The steam pressure is measured to be 304.42 kPa. The inlet feed temperature is 43.3°C. The product inside the evaporator boils at 62.2°C. The overall heat-transfer coefficient is assumed to be 943 W/m² ·°C. Assume negligible boiling-point elevation. Calculate the mass flow rate of concentrated product, steam requirements, steam economy, and the heat-transfer area.

GIVEN

Mass flow rate of feed $\dot{m}_f = 0.67$ kg/s
Concentration of food $x_f = 0.11$
Concentration of product $x_p = 0.75$
Steam pressure = 304.42 kPa
Feed temperature $T_f = 43.3°C$
Boiling temperature T_1 in evaporator = 62.2°C
Overall heat transfer coefficient $U = 943$ W/m² · K
Specific heat of dilute feed $c_{pf} = 3.9$ kJ/kg ·°C
Specific heat of concentrated product $c_{pp} = 2.3$ kJ/kg ·°C

SYSTEM DIAGRAM

See Fig. 9.12.

APPROACH

We will use the heat and mass balances given in Eqs. (9.1), (9.2), and (9.3) to determine the unknowns. Appropriate values of enthalpy for steam and vapors will be obtained from steam tables.

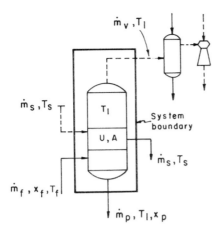

Fig. 9.12 Schematic of a single-effect evaporator.

SOLUTION

(1) From Eq. (9.2),

$$(0.11)(0.67 \text{ kg/s}) = (0.75)\dot{m}_p$$

$$\dot{m}_p = 0.098 \text{ kg/s}$$

Thus, mass flow rate of concentrated product is 0.098 kg/s.

(2) From Eq. (9.1),

$$\dot{m}_v = (0.67 \text{ kg/s}) - (0.098 \text{ kg/s})$$

$$\dot{m}_v = 0.57 \text{ kg/s}$$

Thus, mass flow rate of vapors is 0.57 kg/s.

(3) To use the enthalpy balance of Eq. (9.3), the following quantities are first determined:

From Eq. (9.4),

$$H_f(T_f, X_f) = (3.9 \text{ kJ/kg} \cdot {}^\circ\text{C})(43.3^\circ\text{C} - 0^\circ\text{C}) = 168.9 \text{ kJ/kg}$$

From Eq. (9.5),

$$H_p(T_1, X_p) = (2.3 \text{ kJ/kg} \cdot {}^\circ\text{C})(62.2^\circ\text{C} - 0^\circ\text{C}) = 143.1 \text{ kJ/kg}$$

From the steam table (Table A.4.2),

Temperature of steam at 304.42 kPa $= 134^\circ\text{C}$

Enthalpy for saturated vapor H_v ($T_s = 134^\circ\text{C}$) $= 2725.9$ kJ/kg

Enthalpy for saturated liquid H_c ($T_s = 134^\circ\text{C}$) $= 563.41$ kJ/kg

Enthalpy for saturated vapor H_v ($T_1 = 62.2^\circ\text{C}$) $= 2613.4$ kJ/kg

$$(0.67 \text{ kg/s})(168.9 \text{ kJ/kg}) + (\dot{m}_s \text{ kg/s})(2725.9 \text{ kJ/kg})$$

$$= (0.57 \text{ kg/s})(2613.4 \text{ kJ / kg}) + (0.098 \text{ kg/s})(143.1 \text{ kJ / kg})$$

$$+ (\dot{m}_s \text{ kg/s})(563.41 \text{ kJ / kg})$$

$$2162.49 \dot{m}_s = 1390.5$$

$$\dot{m}_s = 0.64 \text{ kg/s}$$

(4) To calculate steam economy, we use Eq. (9.7).

$$\text{Steam economy} = \frac{\dot{m}_v}{\dot{m}_s} = \frac{0.57}{0.64} = 0.89 \text{ kg water evaporated/kg steam}$$

(5) To compute area of heat transfer, we use Eq. (9.6).

$$A(943 \text{ W/m}^2 \cdot {}^\circ\text{C})(134^\circ\text{C} - 62.2^\circ\text{C})$$

$$= (0.64 \text{ kg/s})(2725.9 - 563.14 \text{ kJ / kg})(1000 \text{ J/kJ})$$

$$A = 20.4 \text{ m}^2$$

9.5 Design of a Multiple-Effect Evaporator

In a triple-effect evaporator, shown in Fig. 9.13, dilute liquid feed is pumped into the evaporator chamber of the first effect. Steam enters the heat exchanger and condenses, thus discharging its heat to the product. The condensate is discarded. The vapors produced from the first effect are used as the heating medium in the second effect, where the feed is the partially concentrated product from the first effect. The vapors produced from the second effect are used in the third effect as heating medium, and the final product with the desired final concentration is pumped out of the evaporator chamber of the third effect. The vapors produced in the third effect are conveyed to a condenser and a vacuum system. In the forward feed system shown, partially concentrated product from the first effect is fed to the second effect. After additional concentration, product leaving the

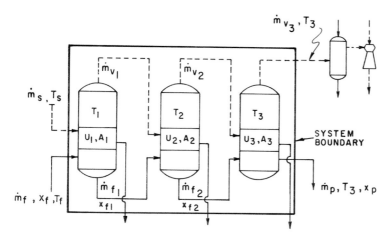

Fig. 9.13 Schematic of a triple-effect evaporator.

second effect is introduced into the third effect. Finally, product with the desired concentration leaves the third effect.

Design expressions for multiple-effect evaporators can be obtained in the same manner as for a single-effect evaporator, discussed in Section 9.4.

Conducting mass balance analysis on the flow streams,

$$\dot{m}_f = \dot{m}_{v1} + \dot{m}_{v2} + \dot{m}_{v3} + \dot{m}_p \tag{9.8}$$

where $\dot{m}_f$ is the mass flow rate of dilute liquid feed to the first effect (kg/s); $\dot{m}_{v1}$, $\dot{m}_{v2}$, and $\dot{m}_{v3}$ are the mass flow rates of vapor from the first, second, and third effect, respectively (kg/s); and $\dot{m}_p$ is the mass flow rate of concentrated product from the third effect (kg/s).

Using mass balance on the solids fraction in the flow streams,

$$x_f \dot{m}_f = x_p \dot{m}_p \tag{9.9}$$

where x_f is the solid fraction in feed stream to the first effect (dimensionless) and x_p is the solid fraction in product stream from the third effect (dimensionless).

We write enthalpy balances around each effect separately.

$$\dot{m}_f H_f(T_f, x_f) + \dot{m}_s H_v(T_s)$$
$$= \dot{m}_{v1} H_v(T_1) + \dot{m}_{f1} H_{f1}(T_1, x_{f1}) + \dot{m}_s H_c(T_s) \tag{9.10}$$

$$\dot{m}_{f1} H_{f1}(T_1, x_{f1}) + \dot{m}_{v1} H_v(T_1)$$
$$= \dot{m}_{v2} H_v(T_2) + \dot{m}_{f2} H_{f2}(T_2, x_{f2}) + \dot{m}_{v1} H_c(T_1) \tag{9.11}$$

$$\dot{m}_{f2} H_{f2}(T_2, x_{f2}) + \dot{m}_{v2} H_v(T_2)$$
$$= \dot{m}_{v3} H_v(T_3) + \dot{m}_p H_p(T_3, x_p) + \dot{m}_{v2} H_c(T_2) \tag{9.12}$$

where the subscripts 1, 2, and 3 refer to the first, second, and third effect, respectively. The other symbols are the same as defined previously for a single-effect evaporator.

The heat transfer across heat exchangers of various effects can be expressed by the following three expressions:

$$q_1 = U_1 A_1(T_s - T_1) = \dot{m}_s H_v(T_s) - \dot{m}_s H_c(T_s) \tag{9.13}$$

$$q_2 = U_2 A_2(T_1 - T_2) = \dot{m}_{v1} H_v(T_1) - \dot{m}_{v1} H_c(T_1) \tag{9.14}$$

$$q_3 = U_3 A_3(T_2 - T_3) = \dot{m}_{v2} H_v(T_2) - \dot{m}_{v2} H_c(T_2) \tag{9.15}$$

The steam economy for a triple-effect evaporator as shown in Fig. 9.13 is given by

$$\text{Steam economy} = \frac{\dot{m}_{v1} + \dot{m}_{v2} + \dot{m}_{v3}}{\dot{m}_s} \tag{9.16}$$

The following example illustrates the use of these expressions in evaluating the performance of multiple-effect evaporators.

EXAMPLE 9.3

Calculate the steam requirements of a double-effect forward-feed evaporator (see Fig. 9.14) to concentrate a liquid food from 11% total solids to 50% total solids concentrate. The feed rate is 10,000 kg/hr at 20°C. The boiling of liquid inside the second effect takes place under vacuum at 70°C. The steam is being supplied to the first effect at 198.5 kPa. The condensate from the first effect is discarded at 95°C and from the second effect at 70°C. The overall heat-transfer coefficient in the first effect is 1000 W/m² · °C; in the second effect it is 800 W/m² · °C. The specific heats of the liquid food are 3.8, 3.0, and 2.5 kJ/kg · °C at initial, intermediate, and final concentrations. Assume the areas and temperature gradients are equal in each effect.

GIVEN

Mass flow rate of feed $\dot{m}_f$ = 10,000 kg/hr = 2.78 kg/s
Concentration of feed x_f = 0.11
Concentration of product x_p = 0.5
Steam pressure = 198.5 kPa
Feed temperature = 20°C
Boiling temperature T_2 in second effect = 70°C
Overall heat-transfer coefficient U_1 in first effect = 1000 W/m² · °C
Overall heat-transfer coefficient U_2 in second effect = 800 W/m² · °C
Specific heat of dilute feed c_{pf} = 3.8 kJ/kg · °C
Specific heat of feed at intermediate concentration c'_{pf} = 3.0 kJ/kg · °C
Specific heat of concentrated food product c_{pp} = 2.5 kJ/kg · °C

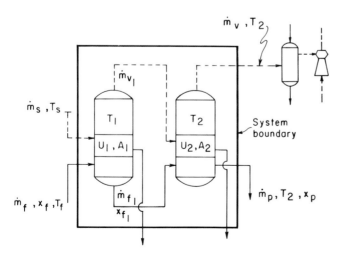

Fig. 9.14 Schematic of a double-effect evaporator.

APPROACH

Since this is a double-effect evaporator, we will use modified forms of Eqs. (9.8), (9.9), (9.10), (9.11), (9.13), and (9.14). Enthalpy values of steam and vapors will be obtained from steam tables.

(1) From Eq. (9.9),

$$(0.11)(2.78 \text{ kg/s}) = (0.5)\dot{m}_p$$

$$\dot{m}_p = 0.61 \text{ kg/s}$$

(2) From Eq. (9.8),

$$2.78 = \dot{m}_{v1} + \dot{m}_{v2} + 0.61$$

Thus, the total amount of water evaporating is

$$\dot{m}_{v1} + \dot{m}_{v2} = 2.17 \text{ kg/s}$$

(3) Steam is being supplied at 198.5 kPa or 120°C, the temperature in the second effect is 70°C, and thus the total temperature gradient is 50°C.

$$\Delta T_1 + \Delta T_2 = 50°C$$

Assuming equal temperature gradient in each evaporator effect,

$$\Delta T_1 = \Delta T_2 = 25°C$$

(4) The area of heat transfer in the first and second effects are the same. Thus, from Eqs. (9.13) and (9.14),

$$\frac{q_1}{U_1(T_s - T_1)} = \frac{q_2}{U_2(T_1 - T_2)}$$

or

$$\frac{\dot{m}_s H_v(T_s) - \dot{m}_s H_c(T_s)}{U_1(T_s - T_1)} = \frac{\dot{m}_{v1} H_v(T_1) - \dot{m}_{v1} H_c(T_1)}{U_2(T_1 - T_2)}$$

(5) To use Eqs. (9.10) and (9.11), we need values for enthalpy of product.

$$H_f(T_f, x_f) = c_{pf}(T_f - 0)$$

$$= (3.8 \text{ kJ} / \text{kg} \cdot °C)(20°C - 0°C) = 76 \text{ kJ} / \text{kg}$$

$$H_{f1}(T_1, x_{f1}) = c'_{pf}(T_1 - 0)$$

$$= (3.0 \text{ kJ} / \text{kg} \cdot °C)(95°C - 0°C) = 285 \text{ kJ} / \text{kg}$$

$$H_{f2}(T_2, x_{f2}) = c_{pp}(T_2 - 0)$$

$$= (2.5 \text{ kJ} / \text{kg} \cdot °C)(70°C - 0°C) = 175 \text{ kJ} / \text{kg}$$

In addition, from steam tables,

$$\text{At } T_s = 120°C \qquad H_v(T_s) = 2706.3 \text{ kJ} / \text{kg}$$

$$H_c(T_s) = 503.71 \text{ kJ} / \text{kg}$$

$$\text{At } T_1 = 95°C \qquad H_v(T_1) = 2668.1 \text{ kJ} / \text{kg}$$

$$H_c(T_1) = 397.96 \text{ kJ} / \text{kg}$$

$$\text{At } T_2 = 70°C \qquad H_v(T_2) = 2626.8 \text{ kJ} / \text{kg}$$

$$H_c(T_2) = 292.98 \text{ kJ} / \text{kg}$$

(6) Thus, substituting enthalpy values from step (5) in the equation given in step (4),

$$\frac{[(\dot{m}_s \text{ kg}/\text{s})(2706.3 \text{ kJ}/\text{kg}) - (\dot{m}_s \text{ kg}/\text{s})(503.71 \text{ kJ}/\text{kg})](1000 \text{ J}/\text{kJ})}{(1000 \text{ W}/\text{m}^2 \cdot {}^\circ\text{C})(120{}^\circ\text{C} - 95{}^\circ\text{C})}$$

$$= \frac{[(\dot{m}_{v1} \text{ kg}/\text{s})(2668.1 \text{ kJ}/\text{kg}) - (\dot{m}_{v1} \text{ kg}/\text{s})(397.96 \text{ kJ}/\text{kg})](1000 \text{ J}/\text{kJ})}{(800 \text{ W}/\text{m}^2 \cdot {}^\circ\text{C})(95{}^\circ\text{C} - 70{}^\circ\text{C})}$$

or

$$\frac{2202.59\dot{m}_s}{25,000} = \frac{2270.14\dot{m}_{v1}}{20,000}$$

(7) Using Eqs. (9.10) and (9.11),

$$(2.78)(76) + (\dot{m}_s)(2706.3)$$
$$= (\dot{m}_{v1})(2668.1) + (\dot{m}_{f1})(285) + (\dot{m}_s)(503.71)$$
$$(\dot{m}_{f1})(285) + (\dot{m}_{v1})(2668.1)$$
$$= (\dot{m}_{v2})(2626.8) + (\dot{m}_p)(175) + (\dot{m}_{v1})(397.96)$$

(8) Let us assemble all equations representing mass flow rates of product, feed, vapor, and steam.

From step (1): $\dot{m}_p = 0.61$
From step (2): $\dot{m}_{v1} + \dot{m}_{v2} = 2.17$
From step (6): $0.088\dot{m}_s = 0.114\dot{m}_{v1}$
From step (7):

$$2202.59\dot{m}_s = 2668.1\dot{m}_{v1} + 285\dot{m}_{f1} - 211.28$$

$$2270.14\dot{m}_{v1} = 2626.8\dot{m}_{v2} + 175\dot{m}_p - 285\dot{m}_{f1}$$

(9) In step (8), we have five equations with five unknowns, namely, $\dot{m}_p$, $\dot{m}_{v1}$, $\dot{m}_{v2}$, $\dot{m}_s$, and $\dot{m}_{f1}$. We will solve these equations using a spreadsheet procedure to solve simultaneous equations. The method described in the following was executed on EXCEL^{TM} on a Macintosh computer.

(10) The simultaneous equations are rewritten so that all unknown variables are collected on the right-hand side. The equations are rewritten so that the coefficients can be easily arranged in a matrix. The spreadsheet method will use a matrix inversion process to solve the simultaneous equations.

$$\dot{m}_p + 0\dot{m}_s + 0\dot{m}_{v1} + 0\dot{m}_{v2} + 0\dot{m}_{f1} = 0.61$$

$$0\dot{m}_p + 0\dot{m}_s + \dot{m}_{v1} + \dot{m}_{v2} + 0\dot{m}_{f1} = 2.17$$

$$0\dot{m}_p + 0.088\dot{m}_s - 0.114\dot{m}_{v1} + 0\dot{m}_{v2} + 0\dot{m}_{f1} = 0$$

$$0\dot{m}_p + 2202.59\dot{m}_s - 2668.1\dot{m}_{v1} + 0\dot{m}_{v2} - 285\dot{m}_{f1} = -211.28$$

$$- 175\dot{m}_p + 0\dot{m}_s + 2270.14\dot{m}_{v1} - 2626.8\dot{m}_{v2} + 285\dot{m}_{f1} = 0$$

(11) As shown in Fig. 9.15, enter the coefficients of the left-hand side of the above equations in array B2:F6; enter the right-hand side coefficients in a column vector H2:H6.

	A	B	C	D	E	F	G	H
1								
2		1.00	0.00	0.00	0.00	0.00		0.61
3		0.00	0.00	1.00	1.00	0.00		2.17
4		0.00	0.09	-0.11	0.00	0.00		0.00
5		0.00	2202.59	-2668.10	0.00	-285.00		-211.28
6		-175.00	0.00	2270.14	-2626.80	285.00		0.00
7	+MINVERSE(B2:F6)						+MMULT(B9:F13, H2:H6)	
8								
9		1.00	0.00	0.00	0.00	0.00		0.61
10		0.04	0.67	4.98	0.00	0.00		1.43
11		0.03	0.52	-4.92	0.00	0.00		1.10
12		-0.03	0.48	4.92	0.00	0.00		1.07
13		0.02	0.34	84.62	0.00	0.00		1.46
14								

Fig. 9.15   A spreadsheet to solve simultaneous equations.

(12) Select another array B9:F13 (by dragging the curser starting from cell B9). Type + MINVERSE(B2:F6) in cell B9 and press command and return key together. This procedure will invert the matrix B2:F6 and give the coefficients of the inverted matrix in array B9:F13.

(13) Highlight cells H9:H13 by dragging the cursor starting from cell H9. Type + MMULT(B9:F13,H2:H6) into cell H9; press command and return keys together. The answers are displayed in the column vector H9:H13. Thus,

$$\dot{m}_p = 0.61 \text{ kg / s}$$

$$\dot{m}_s = 1.43 \text{ kg / s}$$

$$\dot{m}_{v1} = 1.10 \text{ kg / s}$$

$$\dot{m}_{v2} = 1.07 \text{ kg / s}$$

$$\dot{m}_{f1} = 1.46 \text{ kg / s}$$

(14) The steam requirements are computed to be 1.43 kg / s.

(15) The steam economy can be computed as

$$\frac{\dot{m}_{v1} + \dot{m}_{v2}}{\dot{m}_s} = \frac{1.10 + 1.07}{1.43} = 1.5 \text{ kg water vapor/kg steam}$$

9.6   Vapor Recompression Systems

The preceding discussion on multiple-effect evaporators has shown how energy requirements of the total system are decreased by using exit vapors as heating medium in subsequent effects. Two additional systems that employ vapor recompression assist in reduction of energy requirements.

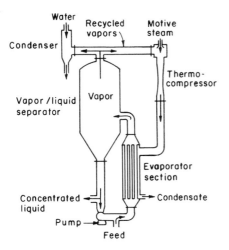

Fig. 9.16 Schematic of a thermal recompression system.

These systems are thermal recompression and mechanical vapor recompression. A brief introduction to these two systems follows.

9.6.1 Thermal Recompression

Thermal recompression involves the use of a steam-jet booster to recompress part of the exit vapors, as shown in Fig. 9.16. Through recompression, the pressure and temperature of exit vapors are increased. These systems are usually applied to single-effect evaporators or to the first effect of multiple-effect evaporators. Application of this system requires that steam be available at high pressure, and low-pressure steam is needed for the evaporation process.

9.6.2 Mechanical Vapor Recompression

Mechanical vapor recompression involves compression of all vapors leaving the evaporator, as shown in Fig. 9.17. Vapor compression is accomplished mechanically, using a compressor driven by an electric motor, a steam turbine, or a gas engine. A steam-turbine-driven compressor is most suitable for mechanical recompression if high-pressure steam is available. Availability of electricity at low cost would favor the use of an electric motor.

Mechanical vapor recompression systems are very effective in reducing energy demands. Under optimum conditions, these systems can lower the

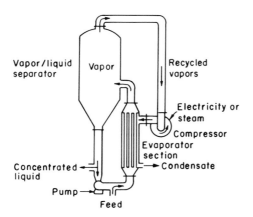

Vapor/liquid separator

Vapor

Recycled vapors

Electricity or steam

Compressor

Evaporator section

Concentrated liquid

Condensate

Pump

Feed

Fig. 9.17 Schematic of a mechanical vapor recompression system.

energy requirements by an amount equivalent to adding 15 effects. These systems can be very noisy to operate due to the use of large compressors.

Mathematical procedures useful in designing vapor recompression systems are beyond the scope of this text. Students could consult Heldman and Singh (1981) for more information on these procedures.

Problems

9.1 A fruit juice at 20°C with 5% total solids is being concentrated in a single-effect evaporator. The evaporator is being operated at a sufficient vacuum to allow the product moisture to evaporate at 80°C, while steam with 85% quality is being supplied at 169.06 kPa. The desired concentration of the final product is 40% total solids. The concentrated product exits the evaporator at a rate of 3000 kg/hr. Calculate the (a) steam requirements and (b) steam economy for the process, when condensate is released at 90°C. The specific heat of liquid feed is 4.05 kJ / kg · °C, and of concentrated product is 3.175 kJ / kg · °C.

9.2 A single-effect evaporator is being used to concentrate tomato juice from 5% total solids to 30% total solids. The juice enters the evaporator at 15°C. The evaporator is operated with steam (80% quality) at 143.27 kPa. The vacuum inside the evaporator allows the juice to boil at 75°C. Calculate (a) the steam requirements and (b) steam economy for the process. Assume the condensate is discharged at 75°C. The overall heat transfer coefficient is 4000 W/m² · °C, and the heat transfer area is 20 m². The specific heat of the liquid feed is 4.1 kJ/kg · °C and the concentrated product is 3.1 kJ / kg · °C.

*9.3 A four-effect evaporator is being considered for concentrating a fruit juice that has no appreciable boiling-point elevation. Steam is available at 143.27 kPa, and the boiling point of the product in the fourth effect is 45°C. The overall heat-transfer coefficients are 3000 W/m^2 ·°C in the first effect, 2500 W/m^2 ·°C in the second effect, 2100 W/m^2 ·°C in the third effect, and 1800 W/m ·°C in the fourth effect. Calculate the boiling-point temperatures of the product in the first, second, and third effects. Assume the heating areas in all the effects are equal to 50 m^2 each. The mass flow rate of steam to the first effect is 2400 kg/hr, the feed rate to the first effect of 5% total solids fluid is 15,000 kg/hr, the concentrated product from the first effect leaves at 6.25% total solids, and the concentration of product leaving the second effect is 8.82% total solids.

*9.4 A double-effect evaporator is being used to concentrate fruit juice at 25,000 kg/hr. The juice is 10% total solid at 80°C. The juice must be concentrated to 50% total solids. Saturated steam at 1.668 atm is available. The condensing temperature of the vapor in the second effect is 40°C. The overall heat-transfer coefficient in the first effect is 1000 W/m^2 ·°C, and in the second effect it is 800 W/m^2 · C. Calculate the steam economy and area required in each effect, assuming the areas are equal in each effect. (Hint: Assume $(\Delta T)_2 = 1.3 \times (\Delta T)_1$.)

*9.5 A double-effect evaporator is being used to concentrate a liquid food from 5 to 35% total solids. The concentrated product leaves the second effect at a rate of 1000 kg/hr. The juice enters the first effect at 60°C. Saturated steam at 169.06 kPa is available. Assume the areas in each effect are equal and the evaporation temperature inside the second effect is 40°C. The overall heat-transfer coefficients inside the first effect is 850 W/m^2 ·°C and inside the second effect is 600 W/m^2 ·°C. Calculate the steam economy and the area required in each effect. [Hint: Assume $(\Delta T)_{1st\ effect} = (\Delta T)_{2nd\ effect}$ and do at least one iteration.)

List of Symbols

A	area of heat exchanger (m^2)		concentrated product (kJ / kg ·°C)
c_{pf}	specific heat content of dilute liquid feed (kJ/kg ·°C)	ΔT	temperature gradient inside an evaporator; temperature of steam −
c_{pp}	specific heat content of		temperature of boiling

*Indicates an advanced level of difficulty in solving.

liquid inside the evaporator
chamber (°C)

$H_c(T_s)$ enthalpy of condensate at
temperature T_s (kJ / kg)

H_f enthalpy of liquid feed
(kJ / kg)

H_p enthalpy of concentrated
product (kJ / kg)

$H_v(T_1)$ enthalpy of saturated vapor
at temperature T_1 (kJ / kg)

$H_v(T_s)$ enthalpy of saturated vapor
at temperature T_s (kJ / kg)

$\dot{m}_f$ mass flow rate of dilute
liquid feed (kg / s)

$\dot{m}_p$ mass flow rate of concentrated product (kg / s)

$\dot{m}_s$ mass flow rate of steam or

condensate (kg / s)

$\dot{m}_v$ mass flow rate of vapor
(kg / s)

q rate of heat transfer (W)

T_1 boiling temperature
maintained inside the
evaporator chamber (°C)

T_f temperature of dilute
liquid feed (°C)

T_s temperature of steam (°C)

T temperature (°C)

U overall heat transfer
coefficient (W/m^2 · K)

x_f solid fraction in feed
stream, dimensionless

x_p solid fraction in product
stream, dimensionless

Bibliography

Anonymous (1977). "Upgrading Existing Evaporators to Reduce Energy Consumption."
Technical Information Center, Department of Energy, Oak Ridge, Tennessee.

Blakebrough, N. (1968). "Biochemical and Biological Engineering Science." Academic Press,
New York.

Charm, S. E. (1978). "The Fundamentals of Food Engineering." 3rd ed. AVI Publ. Co.,
Westport, Connecticut.

Coulson, J. M., and Richardson, J. F. (1978). "Chemical Engineering," Vol. II, 3rd ed.
Pergamon Press, New York.

Geankoplis, C. J. (1978), "Transport Processes and Unit Operations," Allyn & Bacon, Boston,
Massachusetts.

Heldman, D. R., and Singh, R. P. (1981). "Food Process Engineering," 2nd ed. AVI Publ. Co.,
Westport, Connecticut.

Kern, D. W. (1950). "Process Heat Transfer." McGraw-Hill, New York.

McCabe, W. L., Smith, J. C., and Harriott, P. (1985). "Unit Operations of Chemical Engineering," 4th ed. McGraw-Hill, New York.

CHAPTER 10

Psychrometrics

10.1 Introduction

The subject of psychrometrics involves determination of thermodynamic properties of gas-vapor mixtures. The most common applications are associated with the air–water vapor system.

An understanding of the procedures used in computations involving psychrometric properties is useful in design and analysis of various food processing and storage systems. Knowledge of properties of air–water vapor mixture is imperative in design of systems such as airconditioning equipment for storage of fresh produce, dryers for drying cereal grains, and cooling towers in food processing plants.

In this chapter, important thermodynamic properties used in psychrometric computations are defined. Psychrometric charts useful in determining such properties are presented. In addition, procedures to evaluate certain airconditioning processes are discussed.

10.2 Properties of Dry Air

10.2.1 Composition of Air

Air is a mixture of several constituent gases. The composition of air varies slightly depending on the geographical location and altitude. For scientific purposes, the commonly accepted composition is referred to as standard air. The composition of standard air is given in Table 10.1.

The apparent molecular weight of standard dry air is 28.9645. The gas constant for dry air R_a is computed as

$$\frac{8314.41}{28.9645} = 287.055 \text{ m}^3 \cdot \text{Pa/kg} \cdot \text{K}$$

TABLE 10.1
Composition of Standard Air

Constituent	Percentage by volume
Nitrogen	78.084000
Oxygen	20.947600
Argon	0.934000
Carbon dioxide	0.031400
Neon	0.001818
Helium	0.000524
Other gases (traces of methane, sulfur dioxide, hydrogen, krypton, and xenon)	0.000658
	100.0000000

10.2.2 Specific Volume of Dry Air

Ideal gas laws can be used to determine the specific volume of dry air. Therefore,

$$V_a' = \frac{R_a T_A}{p_a} \tag{10.1}$$

where V_a' is the specific volume of dry air (m^3/kg); T_A is the absolute temperature (K); p_a is partial pressure of dry air (kPa); and R_a is the gas constant ($m^3 \cdot Pa/kg \cdot K$).

10.2.3 Specific Heat of Dry Air

At 1 atm (101.325 kPa), the specific heat of dry air c_{pa} in a temperature range of -40 to $60°C$ varying from 0.997 kJ/kg · K to 1.022 kJ/kg · K can be used. For most calculations, an average value of 1.005 kJ/kg · K may be used.

10.2.4 Enthalpy of Dry Air

Enthalpy, the heat content of dry air, is a relative term and requires selection of a reference point. In psychrometric calculations the reference pressure is selected as the atmospheric pressure and the reference temperature is 0°C. Use of atmospheric pressure as the reference allows the use of the following equation to determine the specific enthalpy:

$$H_a = 1.005(T_a - T_0) \tag{10.2}$$

where H_a is enthalpy of dry air (kJ/kg); T_a is the dry bulb temperature (°C); and T_0 is the reference temperature, usually selected as 0°C.

10.2.5   Dry Bulb Temperature

Dry bulb temperature is the temperature indicated by an unmodified temperature sensor. This is in contrast to the wet bulb temperature (described in Section 10.4.8) where the sensor is kept covered with a layer of water. Whenever the term temperature is used without any prefix in this book, dry bulb temperature is implied.

10.3   Properties of Water Vapor

In Section 10.2, constituents of standard dry air were given. However, atmospheric air always contains some moisture. Moist air is a binary mixture of dry air and vapor. The vapor in the air is essentially superheated steam at low partial pressure and temperature. Air containing superheated vapor is clear; however, under certain conditions the air may contain suspended water droplets leading to the condition commonly referred to as "foggy."

The molecular weight of water is 18.01534. The gas constant for water vapor can be determined as

$$R_w = \frac{8314.41}{18.01534} = 461.52 \text{ m}^3 \cdot \text{Pa/kg} \cdot \text{K}$$

10.3.1   Specific Volume of Water Vapor

Below temperatures of 66°C, the saturated or superheated vapor follows ideal gas laws. Thus, the characteristic state equation can be used to determine its properties.

$$V_w' = \frac{R_w T_A}{p_w} \tag{10.3}$$

where p_w is the partial pressure of water vapor (kPa); V_w' is the specific volume of water vapor (m^3/kg); R_w is the gas constant for water vapor (m^3 · Pa/kg K); and T_A is the absolute temperature (K).

10.3.2   Specific Heat of Water Vapor

Experiments indicate that within a temperature range of -71 to 124°C, the specific heat of both saturated and superheated vapor changes only slightly. For convenience, a specific-heat value of 1.88 kJ/kg · K can be selected.

10.3.3 Enthalpy of Water Vapor

The following expression can be used to determine the enthalpy of water vapor:

$$H_w = 2501.4 + 1.88(T_a - T_0) \qquad (10.4)$$

where H_w is enthalpy of saturated or superheated water vapor (kJ/kg); T_a is the dry bulb temperature (°C); and T_0 is the reference temperature (°C).

10.4 Properties of Air–Vapor Mixtures

Similar to gas molecules, the water molecules present in an air–vapor mixture exert pressure on the surroundings. Air–vapor mixtures do not exactly follow the perfect gas laws, but for total pressures up to about 3 atm these laws can be used with sufficient accuracy.

10.4.1 Gibbs – Dalton Law

In atmospheric air–steam mixtures, the Gibbs–Dalton law is closely followed. Thus, the total pressure exerted by a mixture of perfect gases is the same as that exerted by the constituent gases independently. Atmospheric air exists at a total pressure equal to the barometric pressure. From the Gibbs–Dalton law,

$$p_B = p_a + p_w \qquad (10.5)$$

where p_B is the barometric or total pressure of moist air (kPa); p_a is the partial pressure exerted by dry air (kPa); and p_w is the partial pressure exerted by water vapor (kPa).

10.4.2 Dew - Point Temperature

Water vapors present in the air can be considered steam at low pressure. The water vapor in the air will be saturated when air is at a temperature equal to the saturation temperature corresponding to the partial pressure exerted by the water vapor. This temperature of air is called the dew-point temperature. The dew-point temperature can be obtained from the steam table; for example, if the partial pressure of water vapor is 2.064 kPa, then the dew-point temperature can be directly obtained as the corresponding saturation temperature, 18°C.

A conceptual description of the dew-point temperature is as follows: When an air–vapor mixture is cooled at constant pressure and constant humidity ratio, a temperature is reached when the mixture becomes saturated. Further lowering of temperature results in condensation of moisture. The temperature at which this condensation process begins is called the dew-point temperature.

10.4.3 Humidity Ratio (or Moisture Content)

The humidity ratio W (sometimes called moisture content or specific humidity) is defined as the mass of water vapor per unit mass of dry air. The common unit for the humidity ratio is kg water/kg dry air. Thus,

$$W = \frac{m_w}{m_a} \tag{10.6}$$

or

$$W = \left(\frac{18.01534}{28.9645} \right) \frac{x_w}{x_a} = 0.622 \frac{x_w}{x_a} \tag{10.7}$$

where x_w is the mole fraction for water vapor and x_a is the mole fraction for dry air.

The mole fractions x_w and x_a can be expressed in terms of partial pressure as follows. From the perfect gas equations for dry air, water vapor, and mixture, respectively,

$$p_a V = n_a RT \tag{10.8}$$

$$p_w V = n_w RT \tag{10.9}$$

$$pV = nRT \tag{10.10}$$

Equation (10.10) can be written as

$$(p_a + p_w)V = (n_a + n_w)RT \tag{10.11}$$

Dividing Eq. (10.8) by Eq. (10.11),

$$\frac{p_a}{p_a + p_w} = \frac{n_a}{n_a + n_w} = x_a \tag{10.12}$$

and, dividing Eq. (10.9) by Eq. (10.11),

$$\frac{p_w}{p_a + p_w} = \frac{n_w}{n_a + n_w} = x_w \tag{10.13}$$

Thus, from Eqs. (10.7), (10.12), and (10.13),

$$W = 0.622 \frac{p_w}{p_a}$$

Since $p_a = p_B - p_w$,

$$W = 0.622 \frac{p_w}{p_B - p_w} \tag{10.14}$$

10.4.4 Relative Humidity

Relative humidity ϕ is the ratio of mole fraction of water vapor in a given moist air sample to the mole fraction in an air sample saturated at the same temperature and pressure. Thus,

$$\phi = \frac{x_w}{x_{ws}} \times 100 \tag{10.15}$$

From Eq. (10.13),

$$\phi = \frac{p_w}{p_{ws}} \times 100$$

where p_{ws} is the saturation pressure of water vapor.

For conditions where the perfect gas laws hold, the relative humidity can also be expressed as a ratio of the density of water vapor in the air to the density of saturated water vapor at the dry bulb temperature of air. Thus,

$$\phi = \frac{\rho_w}{\rho_s} \times 100 \tag{10.16}$$

where ρ_w is the density of water vapor in the air (kg/m^3) and ρ_s is the density of saturated water vapor at the dry bulb temperature of air (kg/m^3). As the name suggests, relative humidity is not a measure of the absolute amount of moisture in the air. Instead, it provides a measure of the amount of moisture in the air relative to the maximum amount of moisture in air saturated at the dry bulb temperature. Since the maximum amount of moisture in the air increases as the temperature increases, it is important to express the temperature of the air whenever relative humidity is expressed.

10.4.5 Humid Heat of an Air – Water Vapor Mixture

The humid heat c_s is defined as the amount of heat (kJ) required to raise the temperature of 1 kg dry air plus the water vapor present by 1 K. Since the specific heat of dry air is 1.005 kJ/kg dry air $\cdot$ K and 1.88 kJ/kg water $\cdot$ K for water, humid heat of the air–vapor mixture is given by

$$c_s = 1.005 + 1.88 W \tag{10.17}$$

where c_s is the humid heat of moist air (kJ/kg dry air $\cdot$ K) and W is the humidity ratio (kg water/kg dry air).

10.4.6 Specific Volume

The volume of 1 kg dry air plus the water vapor in the air is called specific volume. The commonly used units are cubic meter per kilogram (m^3/kg)

of dry air.

$$V'_m = \left(\frac{22.4 \text{ m}^3}{1 \text{ kg} \cdot \text{mol}}\right)\left(\frac{1 \text{ kg} \cdot \text{mol air}}{29 \text{ kg air}}\right)\left(\frac{T_a + 273}{0 + 273}\right)$$
$$+ \left(\frac{22.4 \text{ m}^3}{1 \text{ kg} \cdot \text{mol}}\right)\left(\frac{1 \text{ kg} \cdot \text{mol water}}{18 \text{ kg water}}\right)\left(\frac{T_a + 273}{0 + 273}\right)\frac{W \text{ kg water}}{\text{kg air}}$$

(10.18)

$$V'_m = (0.082 T_a + 22.4)\left(\frac{1}{29} + \frac{W}{18}\right)$$

(10.19)

EXAMPLE 10.1

Calculate the specific volume of air at 92°C and a humidity ratio of 0.01 kg water/kg dry air.

GIVEN

Dry bulb temperature = 92°C
Humidity ratio = 0.01 kg water/kg dry air

SOLUTION

Using Eq. (10.19),

$$V'_m = (0.082 \times 92 + 22.4)\left(\frac{1}{29} + \frac{0.01}{18}\right)$$

$$= 1{,}049 \text{ m}^3/\text{kg dry air}$$

10.4.7 Adiabatic Saturation of Air

The phenomenon of adiabatic saturation of air is applicable to the convective drying of food materials.

The adiabatic saturation process can be visualized by the following experiment. In a well-insulated chamber as shown in Fig. 10.1, air is allowed to contact a large surface area of water. The insulated chamber assures no gain or loss of heat to the surroundings (adiabatic conditions). In this process, part of the sensible heat of entering air is transformed into latent heat.

For the conditions described above, the process of evaporating water into the air results in saturation by converting part of the sensible heat of the entering air into latent heat and is defined as adiabatic saturation.

The equation for adiabatic saturation is

$$T_{a1} = H_L \frac{(W_2 - W_1)}{(1.005 + 1.88 W_1)} + T_{a2}$$

(10.20)

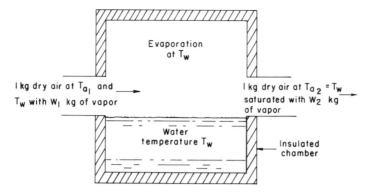

Fig. 10.1 Adiabatic saturation of air in an insulated chamber. [From Jennings (1970). Copyright©1970 by Harper and Row, Publishers. Reprinted with permission of the publisher.]

Equation (10.20) can be written as

$$\frac{W_2 - W_1}{T_{a1} - T_{a2}} = \frac{\bar{c}_s}{H_L} \qquad (10.21)$$

where $\bar{c}_s = 1.005 + 1.88(W_1 + W_2)/2$.

EXAMPLE 10.2

Air at 60°C dry bulb temperature and 27.5°C wet bulb temperature, and a humidity ratio of 0.01 kg water/kg dry air is mixed with water adiabatically and is cooled and humidified to a humidity ratio of 0.02 kg water/kg dry air. What is the final temperature of the conditioned air?

GIVEN

Inlet: dry bulb temperature = 60°C
        wet bulb temperature = 27.5°C
Initial humidity ratio W_1 = 0.01 kg water/kg dry air
Final humidity ratio W_2 = 0.02 kg water/kg dry air

SOLUTION

(1) From Table A.4.2, Latent heat of vaporization at 27.5°C = 2436.37 kJ/kg
(2) Using Eq. (10.20),

$$T_{\text{exit}} = 60 - \frac{2436.37(0.02 - 0.01)}{[1.005 + (1.88)(0.015)]}$$

$$= 36.4°C$$

10.4.8 Wet Bulb Temperature

In describing air–vapor mixtures, two wet bulb temperatures are commonly used: the psychrometric wet bulb temperature and the thermodynamic wet bulb temperature. For moist air, the numerical values of these two temperatures are approximately the same. However, in other gas–vapor systems, the difference between the two temperatures can be substantial.

The psychrometric wet bulb temperature is obtained when the bulb of a mercury thermometer is covered with a wet wick and exposed to unsaturated air flowing past the bulb at high velocity (about 5 m/s). Alternatively, the bulb covered with a wet wick can be moved through unsaturated air. When the wick is exposed to unsaturated air, moisture evaporates due to the vapor pressure of saturated wet wick being higher than that of the unsaturated air.

The evaporation process requires latent heat from the wick and causes the temperature of the covered bulb to decrease. As the temperature of the wick decreases below the dry bulb temperature of air, the sensible heat flows from the air to the wick and tends to raise its temperature. A steady state is achieved when the heat flow from air to wick is equal to the latent heat of vaporization required to evaporate the moisture from the wick. This equilibrium temperature indicated by a wet bulb thermometer or similarly modified temperature sensor is called the wet bulb temperature.

As mentioned previously, the movement of air past the wet wick is essential, otherwise the wick will attain an equilibrium temperature between T_a and T_w.

In contrast to the psychrometric wet bulb temperature, the thermodynamic wet bulb temperature is reached by moist air when it is adiabatically saturated by the evaporating water. The thermodynamic wet bulb temperature is nearly equal to the psychrometric wet bulb temperature for moist air.

A mathematical equation that relates partial pressures and temperatures of air–vapor mixtures, developed by Carrier, has been widely used in calculations to determine psychrometric properties. The equation is

$$p_w = p_{wb} - \frac{(p_B - p_{wb})(T_a - T_w)}{1555.56 - 0.722 T_w} \qquad (10.22)$$

where p_w is the partial pressure of water vapor at dew-point temperature (kPa); p_B is the barometric pressure (kPa); p_{wb} is the saturation pressure of water vapor at the wet bulb temperature (kPa); T_a is the dry bulb temperature (°C); and T_w is the wet bulb temperature (°C).

EXAMPLE 10.3

Find the dew-point temperature, humidity ratio, humid volume, and relative humidity of air having a dry bulb temperature of 40°C and a wet bulb temperature of 30°C.

GIVEN

Dry bulb temperature = 40°C
Wet bulb temperature = 30°C

SOLUTION

(1) From Table A.4.2,
Vapor pressure at 40°C = 7.384 kPa
Vapor pressure at 30°C = 4.246 kPa
(2) From Eq. (10.22),

$$p_w = 4.246 - \frac{(101.325 - 4.246)(40 - 30)}{1555.56 - (0.722 \times 30)}$$

$$= 3.613 \text{ kPa}$$

From Table A.4.2, the corresponding temperature for 3.613 kPa vapor pressure is 27.2°C. Thus, the dew-point temperature = 27.2°C.

(3) Humidity ratio, from Eq. (10.14),

$$W = \frac{(0.622)(3.613)}{(101.325 - 3.613)} = 0.023 \text{ kg H}_2\text{O/kg dry air}$$

(4) Humid volume, from Eq. (10.19),

$$V'_m = (0.082 \times 40 + 22.4)\left(\frac{1}{29} + \frac{0.023}{18}\right)$$

$$= 0.918 \text{ m}^3/\text{kg dry air}$$

(5) Relative humidity: Based on Eq. (10.15), the relative humidity is the ratio of the partial pressure of water vapor in the air (3.613 kPa) to the vapor pressure at dry bulb temperature (7.384 kPa), or

$$\phi = \frac{3.613}{7.384} \times 100 = 48.9\%$$

EXAMPLE 10.4

Develop a spreadsheet, that can be used to determine psychrometric properties such as dew-point temperature, humidity ratio, humid volume, and relative humidity for air with a dry bulb temperature of 35°C and a wet bulb temperature of 25°C.

GIVEN

Dry bulb temperature = 35°C
Wet bulb temperature = 25°C

SOLUTION

(1) The spreadsheet is developed using EXCEL™. To determine, under saturation conditions, temperature when pressure is known or pressure when

	A	B	C	D	E
1	Dry bulb temperature	35	C	7.46908269	-7.50675994E-03
2	Wet bulb temperature	25	C	-4.62032290E-09	-1.2154701110E-03
3	x1	-610.398			
4	x2	-628.398			35.15789
5	vapor pressure (at dbt)	5.622	kPa		24.592588
6	vapor pressure (at wbt)	3.167	kPa		2.1182069
7	pw (SI units)	2.529	kPa		-0.3414474
8	pw (English units)	0.367	psia		0.15741642
9	pw_inter	1.299			-0.031329585
10	Dew Point Temperature	21.3	C		0.003865828
11	Humidity Ratio	0.016	kg water/kg dry air		-0.000249018
12	Specific Volume	0.904	cubic meter/kg dry air		6.8401559E-06
13	Relative Humidity	44.98	%		
14					

Cell	Formula
B3	=(B1*1.8+32)-705.398
B4	=(B2*1.8+32)-705.398
B5	=6.895*EXP(8.0728362+(B3*(D1+E1*B3+D2*B3^3))/((1+E2*B3)*((B1*1.8+32)+459.688))))
B6	=6.895*EXP(8.0728362+(B4*(D1+E1*B4+D2*B4^3))/((1+E2*B4)*((B2*1.8+32)+459.688))))
B7	B6-((101.325-B6)*(B1-B2)/(1555.56-(0.722*B2)))
B8	=B7/6.895
B9	=LN(10*B8)
B10	=((E4+E5*B9+E6*(B9)^2+E7*(B9)^3+E8*(B9)^4+E9*(B9)^5+E10*(B9)^6+E11*(B9)^7+E12*(B9)^8)-32)/1.8
B11	=0.622*B7/(101.325-B7)
B12	=(0.082*B1+22.4)*(1/29+0.023/18)
B13	=B7/B5*100

Steps:
1) Enter equations for cells B3 to B13 as shown
2) Enter coefficients in cells D1, D2, E1, E2, E4 to E12 as shown above. These coefficients are obtained from Martin (1961)
3) Enter temperature values in cells B1 and B2, results are calculated in B10 to B13

Fig. 10.2   Calculation of psychrometric properties for Example 10.3.

temperature is known, empirical expressions developed for steam table by Martin (1961) and Steltz et al. (1958) are used. The equations used for this spreadsheet are valid between 10 and 93°C, and .029 and 65.26 kPa.

(2) The spreadsheet formulas and results are shown in Fig. 10.2. The procedure for calculation of psychrometric properties is the same as used in Example 10.3.

(3) Enter empirical coefficients in cells D1:E2 and E4:E12; these coefficients are obtained from Martin (1961) and Steltz et al. (1958).

(4) Enter mathematical expressions for calculating various psychrometric properties in cells B3:B13.

(5) Enter 35 in cell B1 and 25 in cell B2. The results are calculated in the spreadsheet.

10.5 The Psychrometric Chart

10.5.1 Construction of the Chart

From the preceding sections, it should be clear that the various properties of air–vapor mixtures are interrelated, and such properties can be computed using appropriate mathematical expressions. Another method to determine such properties is the use of a psychrometric chart drawn for a given barometric pressure. If two independent property values are known, the chart allows rapid determination of all psychrometric properties.

The construction of a psychrometric chart can be understood from Fig. 10.3. The basic coordinates of the chart are dry bulb temperature plotted as the abscissa and humidity ratio (or specific humidity) as the ordinate. The wet bulb and dew-point temperatures are plotted on the curve that swings upward to the right. The constant wet bulb temperature lines drawn obliquely are shown on Fig. 10.3. The constant enthalpy lines coincide with the wet bulb temperature lines. The relative humidity curves also swing upward to the right. Note that the saturation curve represents 100% relative humidity. The constant specific volume lines are drawn obliquely; however, they have a different slope than the wet bulb temperature lines.

The psychrometric chart with all the thermodynamic data is shown in Appendix A.5. To use this chart, any two independent psychrometric properties are required. This allows location of a point on the psychrometric chart. The remaining property values can then be read from the chart. As an example, in Fig. 10.4, a point A is located for known dry bulb and wet bulb temperatures. The various property values such as relative humidity, humidity ratio, specific volume, and enthalpy can then be read from the

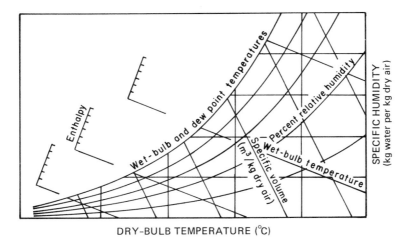

DRY-BULB TEMPERATURE (°C)

Fig. 10.3 A skeleton psychrometric chart.

chart. It may be necessary to interpolate a property value, depending on the location of the point.

It should be noted that the psychrometric chart given in Appendix A.5 is for a barometric pressure of 101.325 kPa. All example problems discussed in this book assume a barometric pressure of 101.325 kPa. For other pressure values, charts drawn specifically for those pressures would be required.

EXAMPLE 10.5

An air-vapor mixture is at 60°C dry bulb temperature and 35°C wet bulb temperature. Using the psychrometric chart (Appendix A.5), determine the relative humidity, humidity ratio, specific volume, enthalpy, and dew-point temperature.

SOLUTION

(1) From the two given independent property values, identify a point on the psychrometric chart. As shown in the skeleton chart (Fig. 10.4), the following steps illustrate the procedure.

(2) Location of point A: Move up on the 60°C dry bulb line until it intersects with the 35°C wet bulb temperature line.

(3) Relative humidity: Read the relative humidity curve passing through A; $\phi = 20\%$.

(4) Specific humidity: Move horizontally to the right to the ordinate to read $W = 0.026$ kg water/kg dry air.

(5) Enthalpy: Move left on the oblique line for constant enthalpy (same as constant wet bulb temperature) to read $H_w = 129$ kJ/kg dry air.

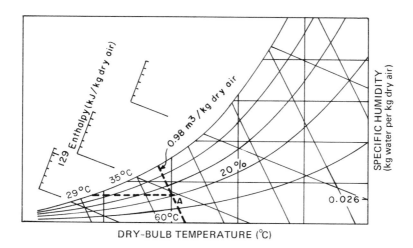

Fig. 10.4 A psychrometric chart with conditions of air given in Example 10.5.

(6) Specific volume: By interpolation between specific volume lines, read $V'_m = 0.98$ m³/kg dry air.

(7) Dew-point temperature: Move horizontally to the left to intersect the 100% relative humidity (saturation curve). The temperature at the intersection is the dew-point temperature, or 29°C.

10.5.2 Use of Psychrometric Chart to Evaluate Complex Air-Conditioning Processes

Several air-conditioning processes can be evaluated using the psychrometric chart. Usually, it is possible to describe an entire process by locating certain points as well as drawing lines on the chart that describe the psychrometric changes occurring during the given process. The value of such analysis is in relatively quick estimation of information useful in the design of equipment used in several food storage and processing plants, including air-conditioning, heating, drying, evaporative cooling, and humidification, as well as dehumidification of air. The following are some processes with important applications to food processing.

a. Heating (or Cooling) of Air

Heating (or cooling) of air is accomplished without addition or removal of moisture. Thus, the humidity ratio remains constant. Consequently, a straight horizontal line on the psychrometric chart exhibits a heating (or cooling) process.

As shown in Fig. 10.5, the process identified by line AB indicates a heating/cooling process. It should be obvious that if the air–vapor mixture

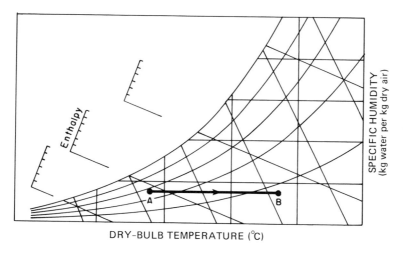

DRY-BULB TEMPERATURE (°C)

Fig. 10.5 A heating process A–B shown on a psychrometric chart.

is heated, the dry bulb temperature would increase; thus the process conditions will change from A to B. Conversely, the cooling process will change from B to A.

To calculate the amount of thermal energy necessary to heat moist air from state A to state B, the following equation can be used:

$$q = \dot{m}(H_B - H_A) \tag{10.23}$$

where H_B and H_A are enthalpy values read from the chart.

EXAMPLE 10.6

Calculate the rate of thermal energy required to heat 10 m^3/s of outside air at 30°C dry bulb temperature and 80% relative humidity to a dry bulb temperature of 80°C.

SOLUTION

(1) Using the psychrometric chart, we find at 30°C dry bulb temperature and 80% relative humidity, the enthalpy $H_1 = 85.2$ kJ/kg dry air, humidity ratio $W_1 = 0.0215$ kg water/kg dry air, and specific volume $V_1' = 0.89$ m^3/kg dry air. At the end of the heating process, the dry bulb temperature is 80°C with a humidity ratio of 0.0215 kg water/kg dry air. The remaining values are read from the chart as follows: enthalpy $H_2 = 140$ kJ/kg dry air; relative humidity $\phi_2 = 7\%$.

(2) Using Eq. (10.23),

$$q = \frac{10}{0.89}(140 - 85.2)$$

$$= 615.7 \text{ kJ/s}$$

$$= 615.7 \text{ kW}$$

(3) The rate of heat required to accomplish the given process is 615.7 kW.

(4) In these calculations, it is assumed that during the heating process there is no gain of moisture. This will not be true if a directly fired gas or oil combustion system is used, since in such processes small amounts of water are produced as part of the combustion reaction (see Section 3.3.3).

b. Mixing of Air

It is often necessary to mix two streams of air of different psychrometric properties. Again, the psychrometric chart can be easily used to determine the state of the mixed air.

The procedure involves first locating the conditions of the two air masses on the chart, as shown in Fig. 10.6, points A and B. Next, the two points are joined with a straight line. This straight line is then divided in inverse proportion to the weights of the individual air quantities. If the two

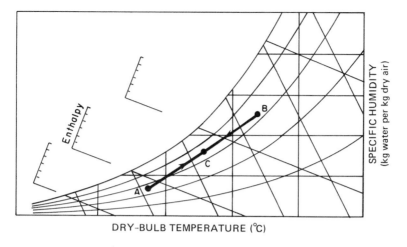

Fig. 10.6 Mixing of air in equal parts shown on a psychrometric chart.

air quantities are equal in weight, the air mixture will be denoted by point C (midpoint of line AB), as shown in Fig. 10.6.

EXAMPLE 10.7

In efforts to conserve energy, a food dryer is being modified to reuse part of the exhaust air along with ambient air. The exhaust airflow of 10 m^3/s at 70°C and 30% relative humidity is mixed with 20 m^3/s of ambient air at 30°C and

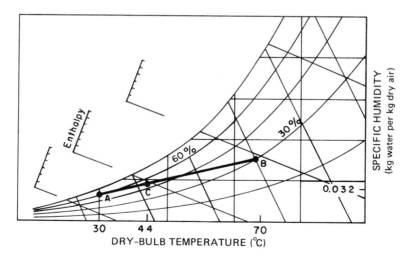

Fig. 10.7 Mixing of air in unequal parts for data given in Example 10.7.

60% relative humidity. Using the psychrometric chart (Appendix A.5), determine the dry bulb temperature and humidity ratio of the mixed air.

SOLUTION

(1) From the given data, locate the state points A and B, identifying the exit and ambient air as shown on the skeleton chart (Fig. 10.7).

(2) Join points A and B with a straight line.

(3) The division of line AB is done according to the relative influence of the particular air mass. Since the mixed air contains 2 parts ambient air and 1 part exhaust air, line AB is divided in 1 : 2 proportion to locate point C. Thus, the shorter length of line AC corresponds to larger air mass.

(4) The mixed air, represented by point C, will have a dry bulb temperature of 44°C and a humidity ratio of 0.032 kg water/kg dry air.

c. Drying

When heated air is forced through a bed of moist granular food, the drying process can be described on the psychrometric chart as an adiabatic saturation process. The heat of evaporation required to dry the product is supplied only by the drying air; no transfer of heat occurs due to conduction or radiation from the surroundings. As air passes through the granular mass, a major part of the sensible heat of air is converted to latent heat, as more water is held in the air in vapor state.

As shown in Fig. 10.8, during the adiabatic saturation process the dry bulb temperature decreases and the enthalpy remains constant, which also implies a practically constant wet bulb temperature. As air gains moisture from the product, the humidity ratio increases.

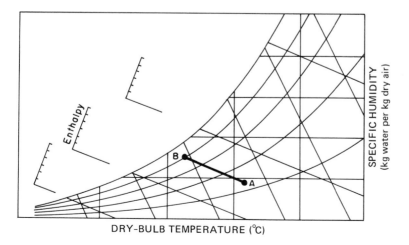

Fig. 10.8 Drying (or adiabatic saturation) process shown on a psychrometric chart.

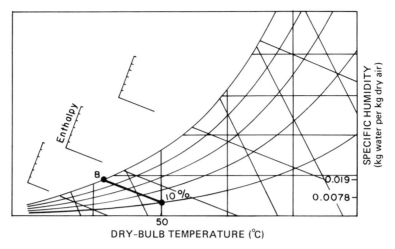

Fig. 10.9 Drying process for conditions given in Example 10.8.

EXAMPLE 10.8

Heated air at 50°C and 10% relative humidity is used to dry rice in a bin dryer. The air exits the bin under saturated conditions. Determine the amount of water removed per kg of dry air.

SOLUTION

(1) Locate point A on the psychrometric chart, as shown on Fig. 10.9. Read humidity ratio = 0.0078 kg water/kg dry air.

(2) Follow constant enthalpy line to the saturation curve, point B.

(3) At point B, read humidity ratio = 0.019 kg water/kg dry air.

(4) The amount of moisture removed from rice = 0.019 − 0.0078 = 0.0112 kg water/kg dry air.

Problems

10.1 The barometer for atmospheric air reads 750 mm Hg; the dry bulb temperature is 30°C; wet bulb temperature is 20°C. Determine (a) the relative humidity, (b) the humidity ratio, and (c) the dew-point temperature.

10.2 The humidity ratio of moist air at atmospheric pressure and at 27°C is 0.015 kg water/kg dry air. Determine (a) the partial pressure of water vapor, (b) relative humidity, and (c) the dew-point temperature.

10.3 Calculate (a) specific volume, (b) enthalpy, and (c) humidity ratio for moist air at 21°C and relative humidity of 30%, at a barometric pressure of 755 mm Hg.

*__**10.4**__ Atmospheric air at 750 mm Hg has an 11°C wet bulb depression from 36°C dry bulb temperature, during an adiabatic saturation process. Determine:

> (a) Humidity ratio from adiabatic saturation equation.
> (b) Vapor pressure and relative humidity at 36°C.
> (c) Dew-point temperature.

10.5 Atmospheric air at 760 mm Hg is at 22°C dry bulb temperature and 20°C wet bulb temperature. Using the psychrometric chart, determine (a) relative humidity, (b) humidity ratio, (c) dew-point temperature, (d) enthalpy of air per kg dry air, and (e) volume of moist air/kg dry air.

10.6 Moist air flowing at 2 kg/s and a dry bulb temperature of 46°C and wet bulb temperature of 20°C mixes with another stream of moist air flowing at 3 kg/s at 25°C and relative humidity of 60%. Using a psychrometric chart, determine the (a) humidity ratio, (b) enthalpy, and (c) dry bulb temperature of the two streams mixed together.

*__**10.7**__ Air at a dry bulb temperature of 20°C and relative humidity of 80% is to be heated and humidified to 40°C and 40% relative humidity. The following options are available for this objective: (a) by passing air through heated water-spray air washer; (b) by preheating sensibly, and then passing through water-spray washer with recirculated water until relative humidity rises to 95% and then again heating sensibly to final required state. Determine for (a) and (b) the total heating required, the make-up water required in water-spray air washer, and the humidifying efficiency of the recirculated spray water.

10.8 Moist air at 35°C and 55% relative humidity is heated using a common furnace to 70°C. From the psychrometric chart, determine how much heat is added per m^3 initial moist air and what the final dew-point temperature is.

*__**10.9**__ A water-cooling tower is to be designed with a blower capacity of 75 m^3/s. The moist air enters at 25°C and wet bulb temperature of 20°C. The exit air leaves at 30°C and relative humidity of 80%. Determine the flow rate of water, in kg/s, that can be cooled if the cooled water is not recycled. The water enters the tower at 40°C and leaves the tower at 25°C.

---

*Indicates an advanced level of difficulty in solving.

*10.10   Ambient air with a dew point of 1°C and a relative humidity of 60%
         is conveyed at a rate of 1.5 m³/s through an electric heater. The
         air is heated to a dry bulb temperature of 50°C. The heated air is
         then allowed to pass through a tray drier that contains 200 kg of
         apple slices with an initial moisture content of 80% wet basis. The
         air exits the dryer with a dew-point temperature of 21.2°C.

         (a) If the electrical energy costs 5¢/kW·hr, calculate the elec-
             trical costs for heating the air per hour of operation.
         (b) Calculate the amount of water removed by air from apple
             slices per hour of operation.
         (c) If the dryer is operated for 2 hr, what will be the final
             moisture content of the apple slices (wet basis)?

List of Symbols

c_{pa}	specific heat of dry air (kJ/kg · K)	p_{wb}	partial pressure of water vapor at wet bulb temperature (kPa)
c_{pw}	specific heat of water vapor (kJ/kg · K)	p_{ws}	saturation pressure of water vapor (kPa)
c_s	humid heat of moist air (kJ/kg dry air · K)	ϕ	relative humidity (%)
H_a	enthalpy of dry air (kJ/kg)	q	rate of heat transfer (kW)
H_L	latent heat of vaporization (kJ/kg)	R	gas constant (m³ · Pa/kg · K)
H_w	enthalpy of saturated or superheated water vapor (kJ/kg)	R_a	gas constant dry air (m³ · Pa/kg · K)
m_a	mass of dry air (kg)	R_0	universal gas constant (8314.41 m³ · Pa/kg · K)
$\dot{m}$	mass flow rate of moist air (kg/s)	R_w	gas constant water vapor (m³ · Pa/kg · K)
M_w	molecular weight of water	ρ_s	density of saturated water vapor at the dry bulb temperature (kg/m³)
m_w	mass of water vapor (kg)	ρ_w	density of water vapor in the air (kg/m³)
n	number of moles	T	temperature (°C)
n_a	number of moles of air	T_A	absolute temperature (K)
n_w	number of moles of water vapor	T_a	dry bulb temperature (°C)
p	partial pressure (kPa)	T_0	reference temperature (°C)
p_a	partial pressure of dry air (kPa)	T_w	wet bulb temperature (°C)
p_B	barometric or total pressure of moist air (kPa)	V	volume (m³)
		V'_a	specific volume of dry air (m³/kg dry air)
p_w	partial pressure of water vapor (kPa)	V'_m	specific volume of moist air (m³/kg)

V_w' specific volume of water vapor x_a mole fraction for dry air
    (m^3/kg) x_w mole fraction for water vapor

W humidity ratio (kg water/kg x_{ws} mole fraction for saturated air
    dry air)

Bibliography

American Society of Heating, Refrigerating and Air-Conditioning Engineers, Inc. (1981). "ASHRAE Handbook of 1981 Fundamentals." ASHRAE, Atlanta, Georgia.

Geankoplis, C. J. (1978). "Transport Processes and Unit Operations." Allyn & Bacon, Boston, Massachusetts.

Jennings, B. H. (1970). "Environmental Engineering, Analysis and Practice." International Textbook Company, New York.

Martin, T. W. (1961). Improved computer oriented methods for calculation of steam properties. *J. Heat Transfer*, 515–516.

Steltz, W. G., and Silvestri, G. J. (1958). The formulation of steam properties for digital computer application. *Trans. ASME* **80**, 967–973.

CHAPTER 11

Mass Transfer

11.1 Introduction

In food processing, we often create conditions that allow selected chemical reactions to occur and produce desirable products in a most efficient manner. Frequently, in addition to desirable products, several byproducts may be produced. These secondary products must then be separated from the primary product of interest. The by-products may be undesirable from the process standpoint, but may be of considerable economic value. In designing separation processes, an understanding of the mass transfer processes becomes important.

Mass transfer plays a key role in the creation of favorable conditions for reactants to physically come together, allowing a particular reaction to occur. Once the reactants are in proximity at a particular site, the reaction can then proceed at a rapid rate. Under these circumstances, we find that the given reaction is limited by the movement of the reactants to the reaction site or movement of products away from the reaction site; in other words, the reaction is mass-transfer limited, instead of being limited by the kinetics of the reaction.

To study operations that depend on mass transfer processes, it is important that we understand the term mass transfer (as used in this textbook). In situations where we have a bulk flow of a fluid from one location to another, although there is a movement of the fluid (of a certain mass), the process is *not* mass transfer, according to our context. Our use of the term mass transfer, is restricted to the migration of a constituent of a fluid or a component of a mixture. The migration occurs because of changes in the physical equilibrium of the system that is caused by the concentration differences. Such transfer may occur within one phase or may involve a transfer from one phase to another.

Let us consider an example. If we carefully let fall a droplet of ink into a stagnant pool of water, the ink will start migrating in various directions. Initially the concentration of ink in the droplet is very high and the concentration of ink in the water is zero, thus setting up a concentration gradient. The process of ink migration will continue, and the concentration gradient will decrease. Once the ink has been fully dissipated in the water, the concentration gradient will become zero, and the mass transfer process will cease. The concentration gradient is considered the "driving force" for the movement of a given component. For example, in a room, if one opens a bottle of highly volatile material such as nail polish remover, the component, acetone, will flow to various parts of the room because of the concentration gradient with respect to acetone. If the air is stationary, the transfer occurs as a result of random motion of the acetone molecules. If a fan or any other external means are used to cause turbulence, eddy currents will enhance the transfer of acetone molecules to distant regions in the room.

As we will find in this chapter, there are a number of similarities between mass transfer and heat transfer. In mass transfer, we will encounter similar terms that are important in heat transfer, for example, flux, gradient, resistance, transfer coefficient, and boundary layer.

From Chapter 1, according to the second law of thermodynamics, systems that are not in equilibrium tend to move toward equilibrium with time. In the case of chemical reactions, any difference between the chemical potential of a species from one region of a space to another is a departure from the equilibrium state; over time there will be a shift toward equilibrium, such that the chemical potential of that species is the same throughout the region. These differences in chemical potential may occur due to the different concentration of the species from one point to another, difference in temperature and/or pressure, or differences caused by other external fields, such as gravitational force.

11.2   The Diffusion Process

Mass transfer involves both mass diffusion occurring at a molecular scale and bulk transport of mass due to convection flow. The diffusion process can be described mathematically using Fick's law of diffusion, which states that the mass flux per unit area of a component is proportional to its concentration gradient. Thus, for a component B,

$$\frac{\dot{m}_B}{A} = -D\frac{\partial c}{\partial x} \qquad (11.1)$$

where $\dot{m}_B$ is mass flow rate of component B, kg/hr; c is the concentration of component B, mass per unit volume or moles per unit volume, kg/m^3 or kg-mole/m^3; D is diffusion coefficient, m^2/s; and A is area, m^2.

We note that the Fick's law is similar to Fourier's law of heat conduction

$$\frac{q}{A} = -k\frac{\partial T}{\partial x}$$

and Newton's equation for shear stress–strain relationship

$$\sigma = -\mu \frac{\partial u}{\partial y}$$

The above similarities between the three transport equations suggest additional analogies between mass transfer and heat and momentum transfer. We will examine these similarities later in Section 11.2.2.

   Consider two gases B and E in a chamber, initially separated by a partition (Fig. 11.1a). At some instant, the partition is removed; then, due to concentration gradients, B and E will diffuse through the container. The following derivation is developed to express the mass diffusion of gas B into gas E, and gas E into gas B. Figure 11.1b shows the gas concentrations at some time after the partition is removed. Concentration is expressed in molecules per unit volume. In our simplistic diagram, circles represent molecules of a gas, and the concentration of a gas is expressed as molecules per unit volume. The molecules move in random directions. However, since initially the concentration of gas B is high on the right-hand side of the partition, there is a greater likelihood of molecules of B crossing the partition from right to left, indicating a net transport of B from right to left. Similarly there is a net transport of E from left to right.

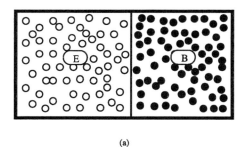

(a)

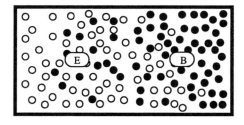

(b)

Fig. 11.1   Diffusion of gases in an enclosed chamber.

From the perfect gas equation,

$$p_B = \rho_B R_B T \qquad (11.2)$$

where p_B is the partial pressure of the gas B, kPa; R_B is the gas constant of gas B; T is temperature, K; and ρ_B is mass concentration of B, kg/m^3.

The gas constant R_B for gas B can be written in terms of the universal gas constant R_u as follows:

$$R_B = \frac{R_u}{M_B} \qquad (11.3)$$

where R_u is universal gas constant 8314.41 m$^3 \cdot$ Pa/mole $\cdot$ K, and M_B is molecular weight of the gas.

Thus, from Eq. (11.2)

$$\rho_B = \frac{p_B}{R_B T} \qquad (11.4)$$

or

$$\rho_B = \frac{p_B M_B}{R_u T} \qquad (11.5)$$

Since ρ_B is mass concentration, same as c_B, we can substitute c in Eq. (11.1) with Eq. (11.5). Thus,

$$\frac{\dot{m}_B}{A} = -D_{BE} \frac{d}{dx}\left(\frac{p_B M_B}{R_u T}\right) \qquad (11.6)$$

or

$$\frac{\dot{m}_B}{A} = -\frac{D_{BE} M_B}{R_u T} \frac{dp_B}{dx} \qquad (11.7)$$

Diffusivity D_{BE} refers to diffusivity of gas B in gas E.

Equation (11.7) expresses mass diffusion of gas B into E. Similarly, we can obtain Eq. (11.8) to express mass diffusion of gas E into B.

$$\frac{\dot{m}_E}{A} = -\frac{D_{EB} M_E}{R_u T} \frac{\partial p_E}{\partial x} \qquad (11.8)$$

Diffusivities in solids **are** less than that in liquids, and the diffusivity in liquids is less than that in gases. This is due to the mobility of molecules. Diffusivity values are expressed as centimeters squared per second (cm^2/s). In solids, the diffusion coefficients range from 10^{-9} to 10^{-1} cm^2/s; in liquids the range of diffusion coefficients is from 10^{-6} to 10^{-5} cm^2/s; and in the case of gases the range is from 5×10^{-1} to 10^{-1} cm^2/s. The diffusivity value is a function of temperature and concentration; in the case of gases the diffusivity is substantially influenced by pressure.

Some representative values of the diffusion coefficient of gases in air and in water are presented in Tables 11.1a and 11.1b.

TABLE 11.1a
Diffusion Coefficients of Selected
Gases in Water at 20°C

Gas	$D \times 10^9$ (m^2/s)
Ammonia	1.8
Carbon dioxide	1.8
Chlorine	1.6
Hydrogen	5.3
Nitrogen	1.9
Oxygen	2.1

For other temperatures $D_T = D_{20}[1 + 0.02(T - 20)]$

TABLE 11.1b
Diffusion Coefficients of Selected
Gases and Vapors in Air (under Standard Conditions)

Gas	$D \times 10^6$ (m^2/s)
Ammonia	17.0
Benzene	7.7
Carbon dioxide	13.8
Ethyl alcohol	10.2
Hydrogen	61.1
Methyl alcohol	13.3
Nitrogen	13.2
Oxygen	17.8
Sulfur dioxide	10.3
Sulfur trioxide	9.4
Water vapor	21.9

11.2.1   Steady-State Diffusion of Gases (and Liquids) through Solids

Assuming the diffusion coefficient is independent of concentration, from Eq. (11.1) we obtain

$$\frac{\dot{m}_A}{A} = -D_{AB}\frac{dc_A}{dx} \qquad (11.9)$$

where D_{AB} is diffusivity of a gas A (or liquid A) in a solid B. Subscript A for $\dot{m}$ and c represents a gas or liquid diffusing through a solid.

Separating variables and integrating Eq. (11.9)

$$\frac{\dot{m}_A}{A} \int_{x_1}^{x_2} dx = -D_{AB} \int_{c_{A1}}^{c_{A2}} dc_A \qquad (11.10)$$

$$\frac{\dot{m}_A}{A} = \frac{D_{AB}(c_{A1} - c_{A2})}{(x_2 - x_1)} \qquad (11.11)$$

Equation (11.11) is used for rectangular coordinates. Similarly, for a cylindrical shape in radial coordinates, we can obtain

$$\dot{m}_A = \frac{D_{AB} 2\pi L(c_{A1} - c_{A2})}{\ln(r_2/r_1)} \qquad (11.12)$$

11.2.2 Mass Transfer Coefficients

Mass transfer coefficient k_m is defined as the rate of mass transfer per unit area per unit concentration difference. Thus,

$$k_m = \frac{\dot{m}_A}{A(c_{A1} - c_{A2})} \qquad (11.13)$$

where $\dot{m}_A$ is the mass flow rate, kg/s; c is concentration of component A, either mass per unit volume or molar mass per unit volume, kg/m^3 or kmol/m^3; A is area, m^2. The units of k_m are m^3/m$^2 \cdot$ s^{-1} or m/s.

Mass transfer coefficients can be calculated using dimensional analysis, analogous to the methods used in Chapter 4 for heat transfer coefficients. In this section, we will consider some of the important dimensionless numbers involved in mass transfer.

In situations that involve molecular diffusion and mass transfer due to forced convection, the following variables are important: diffusivity D_{AB}, the velocity of the fluid u, the mass density of the fluid ρ, the viscosity of the fluid μ, the characteristic dimension d, and the mass transfer coefficient k_m. In the case of natural convection additional important variables include the acceleration due to gravity g and the mass density difference $\Delta\rho$. These variables are grouped in the following dimensionless numbers:

$$\text{Sherwood number, } N_{Sh} = \frac{k_m d}{D_{AB}} \qquad (11.14)$$

$$\text{Schmidt number, } N_{Sc} = \frac{\mu}{\rho D_{AB}} \qquad (11.15)$$

$$\text{Reynolds number, } N_{Re} = \frac{\rho u d}{\mu} \qquad (11.16)$$

$$\text{Lewis number, } N_{Le} = \frac{k}{\rho c_p D_{AB}} \qquad (11.17)$$

Consider a fluid flowing over a flat plate as shown in Fig. 11.2. For the boundary layer from the leading edge of the plate, we can write the

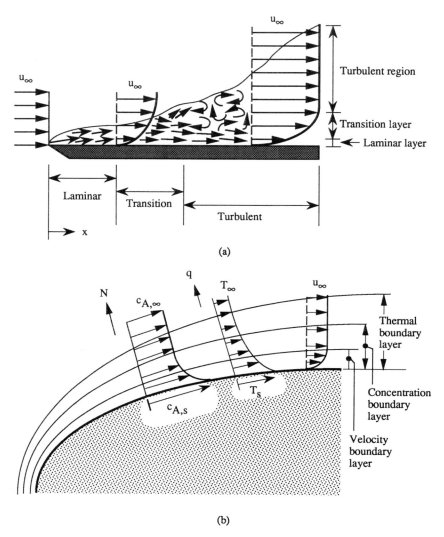

Fig. 11.2 (a) The development of a boundary layer on a flat plate. (b) The development of the thermal, concentration, and velocity boundary layers on a surface. [From Incropera, F. P., and Dewitt, D. P. (1985). "Fundamentals of Heat and Mass Transfer." Wiley, New York. Copyright © 1985 by John Wiley & Sons.]

following equation for momentum, energy, and concentration, respectively.

$$u\frac{\partial u}{\partial x} + v\frac{\partial u}{\partial y} = \nu\frac{\partial^2 u}{\partial y^2} \tag{11.18}$$

$$u\frac{\partial T}{\partial x} + v\frac{\partial T}{\partial y} = \alpha\frac{\partial^2 T}{\partial y} \tag{11.19}$$

$$u\frac{\partial c_A}{\partial x} + v\frac{\partial c_A}{\partial y} = D_{AB}\frac{\partial^2 c_A}{\partial y^2} \tag{11.20}$$

In Eq. (11.20), c_A represents concentration of component A that diffuses through the boundary layer. Velocity, v, is in the y direction.

Note that

$$\frac{\nu}{\alpha} = \frac{\mu c_p}{k} = N_{Pr} = \text{Prandtl number} \qquad (11.21)$$

Thus, the Prandtl number provides the link between velocity and temperature profiles. Note that ν represents kinematic viscosity, m^2/s.

From Eqs. (11.18) and (11.20), if

$$\frac{\nu}{D_{AB}} = 1 \qquad (11.22)$$

then velocity and concentration profiles have the same shape. The ratio

$$\frac{\nu}{D_{AB}} = \frac{\mu}{\rho D_{AB}} = N_{Sc} = \text{Schmidt number} \qquad (11.23)$$

The concentration and temperature profiles will have the same shape if

$$\frac{\alpha}{D_{AB}} = 1 \qquad (11.24)$$

The ratio

$$\frac{\alpha}{D_{AB}} = N_{Le} = \text{Lewis number} \qquad (11.25)$$

The functional relationships that correlate these dimensional numbers for forced convection are

$$N_{Sh} = f(N_{Re}, N_{Sc}) \qquad (11.26)$$

If we compare these correlations with those obtained for heat transfer in Chapter 3, and assume that the dimensionless profiles of velocity, temperature, and concentration are similar, then the Nusselt number and the Prandtl number in heat transfer are replaced in mass transfer by the Sherwood number and the Schmidt number, respectively. Thus, it may be deduced that

$$N_{Sh} = \frac{\text{total mass transferred}}{\text{total mass transferred by molecular diffusion}} \qquad (11.27)$$

$$N_{Sc} = \frac{\text{molecular diffusion of momentum}}{\text{molecular diffusion of mass}} \qquad (11.28)$$

Next, we will consider a number of dimensionless correlations that are useful in evaluating the mass transfer coefficient. These correlations are based on the following assumptions.

- constant physical properties
- no chemical reactions in the fluid
- small bulk flow at the interface
- no viscous dissipation
- no interchange of radiant energy
- no pressure, thermal, or forced diffusion.

11.2.3 Laminar Flow Past a Flat Plate

Laminar flow conditions over a flat plate are obtained if $N_{Re} < 5 \times 10^5$.

$$N_{Sh_x} = \frac{k_{m,x} x}{D_{AB}} = 0.332 N_{Re_L}^{1/2} N_{Sc}^{1/3} \qquad N_{Sc} \geq 0.6 \qquad (11.29)$$

In Eq. (11.29), the mass transfer coefficient $k_{m,x}$ used in the Sherwood number is at a fixed point, therefore the $N_{Sh,x}$ is termed the local Sherwood number. The characteristic dimension used in the Sherwood and Reynolds numbers is the distance from the leading edge of the plate.

If the flow is laminar over the entire surface of the plate, an average Sherwood number is obtained using the following relationship:

$$N_{Sh_L} = \frac{k_{m,L} x}{D_{AB}} = 0.664 N_{Re_L}^{1/2} N_{Sc}^{1/3} \qquad N_{Sc} \geq 0.6 \qquad (11.30)$$

In Eq. (11.30) the characteristic dimension is the total length of the plate, L; and mass transfer coefficient $k_{m,L}$, obtained from the Sherwood number, is an average value.

EXAMPLE II.I

Determine the rate of water evaporated from a tray full of water. Air at a velocity of 2 m/s is flowing over the tray. The temperature of water and air is 25°C. The width of the tray is 45 cm and its length along the direction of air flow is 20 cm. The diffusivity of water vapor in air is $D = 0.26 \times 10^{-4}$ m^2/s.

GIVEN

Velocity = 2 m/s
Temperature of water and air = 25°C
Width of the tray = 45 cm
Length of the tray = 20 cm
Diffusivity = 0.26×10^{-4} m^2/s
Kinematic viscosity of air at 25°C = 16.14×10^{-6} m^2/s

APPROACH

We will first determine the Reynolds number and then use an appropriate dimensionless correlation to obtain the mass transfer coefficient and the water evaporation rate.

SOLUTION

(1) Reynolds number for the 20 cm long tray is

$$N_{Re} = \frac{2 \times 0.2}{16.14 \times 10^{-6}} = 24,783$$

Since $N_{Re} < 5 \times 10^5$, the flow is laminar.

(2) We use Eq. (11.30).

$$N_{Sh} = \frac{k_m L}{D_{AB}} = 0.664(N_{Re})^{1/2}(N_{Sc})^{1/3}$$

where

$$N_{Sc} = \frac{\nu}{D_{AB}} = \frac{16.14 \times 10^{-6}}{0.26 \times 10^{-4}} = 0.62$$

(3) Thus,

$$\frac{k_m \times 0.2}{0.26 \times 10^{-4}} = 0.664(24783)^{1/2}(0.62)^{1/3}$$

$$k_m = 1.1587 \times 10^{-2} \text{ m/s}$$

(4) The evaporation rate for the tank is

$$\dot{m}_A = k_m A (c_{A,s} - c_{A,\infty})$$

where $c_{A,s}$ is the concentration under saturated conditions,

$$c_{A,s} = \rho_{A,s} = 0.02298 \text{ kg/m}^3$$

and $c_{A,\infty}$ is the concentration of water in the free stream, since relative humidity is 50%; then

$$\rho_{A,\infty} = (0.5)(0.02298) = 0.01149 \text{ kg/m}^3$$

(5) Therefore,

$$\dot{m}_A = (1.1587 \times 10^{-2} \text{ m/s}) \times (0.45 \text{ m} \times 0.2 \text{ m})$$

$$\times (0.02298 \text{ kg/m}^3 - 0.01149 \text{ kg/m}^3)$$

$$\dot{m}_A = 1.1982 \times 10^{-5} \text{ kg/s}$$

(6) The water evaporation rate from the tray is 0.043 kg/hr.

11.2.4 Turbulent Flow Past a Flat Plate

The dimensionless relationship between dimensionless groups for turbulent flow ($N_{Re} > 5 \times 10^5$) past a flat plate is expressed by the following:

$$N_{Sh_x} = \frac{k_{m,x} x}{D_{AB}} = 0.0296 N_{Re_x}^{4/5} N_{Sc}^{1/3} \qquad 0.6 < N_{Sc} < 3000 \quad (11.31)$$

In Eq. (11.31) the characteristic dimension is the distance from the leading edge of the plate.

11.2.5 Laminar Flow in a Pipe

For laminar flow in a pipe, the following equation is suggested:

$$\overline{N}_{Sh_d} = \frac{k_m d}{D_{AB}} = 1.86\left(\frac{N_{Re_d}N_{Sc}}{L/d}\right)^{1/3} \qquad N_{Re} < 10,000 \qquad (11.32)$$

where d is the diameter of the pipe.

11.2.6 Turbulent Flow in a Pipe

For turbulent flow in a pipe,

$$\overline{N}_{Sh_d} = \frac{k_m d}{D_{AB}} = 0.023 N_{Re_d}^{0.8} N_{Sc}^{1/3} \qquad N_{Re} > 10,000 \qquad (11.33)$$

where d is the diameter of the pipe.

11.2.7 Mass Transfer for Flow over Spherical Objects

Mass transfer to or from a spherical object is obtained from an expression similar to the Froessling correlation obtained in Eq. (4.42) for heat transfer

$$\overline{N}_{Sh_d} = 2.0 + \left(0.4 N_{Re_d}^{1/2} + 0.06 N_{Re_d}^{2/3}\right) N_{Sc}^{0.4} \qquad (11.34)$$

For mass transfer from freely falling liquid droplets, the following expression is recommended.

$$\overline{N}_{Sh_d} = 2.0 + 0.6 N_{Re_d}^{1/2} N_{Sc}^{1/3} \qquad (11.35)$$

EXAMPLE 11.2

A 0.3175-cm sphere of glucose is placed in a water stream flowing at a rate of 0.15 m/s. The temperature of water is 25°C. The diffusivity of glucose in water is 0.69×10^{-5} cm^2/s. Determine the mass transfer of coefficient.

GIVEN

Diameter of sphere = 0.3175 cm = 0.003175 m
Velocity of water = 0.15 m/s
Temperature of water = 25°C
Diffusivity of glucose in water = 0.69×10^{-5} cm^2/s

From Table A.4.1 @ 25°C

$$\text{Density} = 997.1 \text{ kg/m}^3$$

$$\text{Viscosity} = 880.637 \times 10^{-6} \text{ Pa} \cdot \text{s}$$

APPROACH

We will first determine the Reynolds number and Schmidt number. Since the glucose sphere is submerged in a stream of water, we will use Eq. (11.35) to determine the Sherwood number. The mass transfer coefficient will be obtained from the Sherwood number.

SOLUTION

(1) The Reynolds number is

$$N_{Re} = \frac{997.1 \text{ kg/m}^3 \times 0.15 \text{ m/s} \times 0.003175 \text{ m}}{880.637 \times 10^{-6} \text{ Pa} \cdot \text{s}}$$

$$= 539$$

(2) The Schmidt number is

$$N_{Sc} = \frac{880.637 \times 10^{-6} \text{ Pa} \cdot \text{s} \times 10000 \text{ cm}^2/\text{m}^2}{997.1 \text{ kg/m}^3 \times 0.69 \times 10^{-5} \text{ cm}^2/\text{s}}$$

$$= 1279$$

(3) The Sherwood number can be obtained from Eq. (11.35).

$$N_{Sh} = 2.0 + 0.6(1279)^{1/3} \times (539)^{1/2}$$

$$= 153$$

(4) The mass transfer coefficient

$$k_m = \frac{153 \times 0.69 \times 10^{-5} \text{ cm}^2/\text{s}}{0.003175 \text{ m} \times 10000 \text{ cm}^2/\text{m}^2}$$

$$= 3.32 \times 10^{-5} \text{ m/s}$$

(5) The mass transfer coefficient will be 3.32×10^{-5} m/s, assuming that by dissolving glucose in water we will not alter the physical properties of water to any significant magnitude.

11.3 Membrane Separation Systems

Membrane separation systems have been used extensively in the chemical process industry. Their use in the food industry is now becoming more common. Some of the typical food-related applications include purification of water, concentration and clarification of fruit juices, milk products, alcoholic beverages, and waste waters.

An extensively used method to concentrate liquid foods is the evaporation process. As we observed in Chapter 9, to evaporate water, a sufficient amount of heat, equivalent to the latent heat of vaporization, must be added for the water to change its phase from liquid to vapor. In an evaporator, the latent heat of vaporization represents a substantial part of

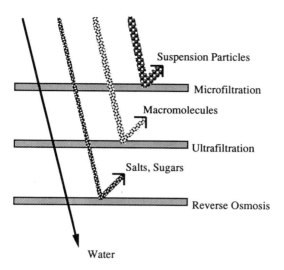

Fig. 11.3 Use of membrane systems to separate substances of different sized molecules. [From Cheryan, M. (1989). Membrane separations: mechanisms and models. *In* "Food Properties and Computer-Aided Engineering of Food Processing Systems" (R. P. Singh and A. Medina, eds.). Kluwer Academic Publishers, Amsterdam.]

the energy requirements or operating costs. In contrast, membrane separation systems allow separating water from a solution without a phase change.

In a membrane separation system, a fluid containing two or more components is allowed to come into contact with a membrane that permits selected components (for example, water in the fluid) to permeate more readily than other components. The physical and chemical nature of the membrane—for example, pore size and pore size distribution—affects the separation of liquid streams. As seen in Fig. 11.3, in a reverse osmosis system, the membranes allow water to permeate while salts and sugars are rejected. Ultrafiltration membranes are useful in fractionating components by rejecting macromolecules. In microfiltration, the membranes separate suspended particulates. The application of each of the membranes for separating different matter is seen in Fig. 11.4.

The permeation of the selected component(s) is the result of a "driving force." In the case of dialysis, the concentration difference across the membrane is the driving force, whereas, in the case of reverse osmosis, ultrafiltration, and microfiltration systems, hydrostatic pressure is the key driving force. The microfiltration membrane systems require the least amount of hydraulic pressure, about 1–2 bars (or 15–30 psig). In the case of ultrafiltration membrane systems, higher pressures, in the order of 1–7 bars (or 15–100 psig), are required to overcome the hydraulic resistance caused by a macromolecular layer next to the membrane (explained later in Section 11.3.5). In a reverse osmosis system, considerably higher hydraulic pressures, in the range of 20–50 bars (300–750 psig), are necessary to overcome the osmotic pressures.

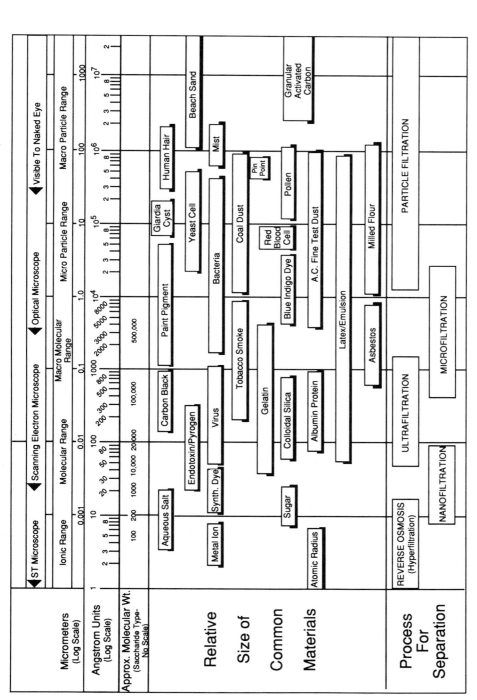

Fig. 11.4 A separation spectrum. (Courtesy of Osmonics.)

Fig. 11.5   The structure of an ultrafiltration membrane. [From Lacey (1972).]

The process of selective permeation is best understood by examining the structure of a membrane. Figure 11.5 is a visualization of a membrane represented as a composite material consisting of polymeric chains interconnected by cross linking. Any material being transported through a membrane must move through the interstitial spaces. When the interstitial openings are small, the transporting material makes its way through a membrane by pushing aside the neighboring polymeric chains. The resistance to the movement of a given material through a membrane depends on how "tight" or "loose" a membrane is. A polymeric membrane with a considerable degree of cross-linkages and crystallinity is considered "tight" and it will offer considerable resistance to the permeation of a transporting material.

In this chapter, we will consider three types of membrane systems, namely, electrodialysis, reverse osmosis, and ultrafiltration.

11.3.1   Electrodialysis Systems

Electrodialysis systems are based on the selective movement of ions in solution. These systems derive their selectivity from the ions (whether anions or cations) that they allow to permeate through them. Selected ions are removed from water as they pass through the semipermeable membranes. These membranes do not permit permeation of water.

If a polymeric chain in a membrane has a fixed negative charge, it will repulse any anion that tries to enter the membrane. This is shown schematically in Fig. 11.6. For example, a negatively charged chain attracts cations and allows them to move through it. In this type of membrane, the distance

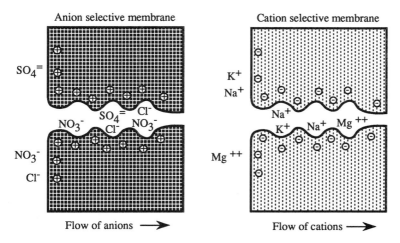

Fig. 11.6   The movement of ions in ion-selective membranes. [From Applegate (1984).]

between the cross linkages of the polymeric chain should be large enough to minimize the resistance offered to the transporting ion. At the same time, the distance between the cross linkages must not be too large, or the repulsive forces will be insufficient to provide the desired selectivity. This functional property of an ion membrane system is used in the electrodialysis system as shown in Fig. 11.7.

The electrodialysis system, as shown in Fig. 11.7, uses an electric current to transfer ions through a membrane. The membranes have fixed

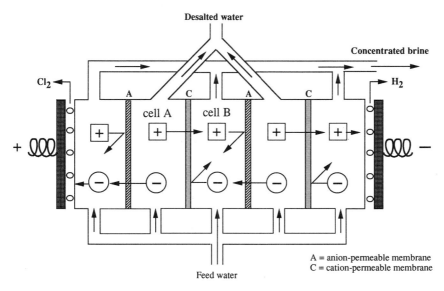

Fig. 11.7   Desalting of water with an electrodialysis system. [From Lacey (1972).]

ionic groups that are chemically bound to the structure of the membrane. As seen in Fig. 11.7, the electrodialysis system involves an array of membranes, alternating between anion-exchange and cation-exchange membranes. In between the membranes are small compartments (0.5 mm to 1.0 mm thick) that contain the solution. On either side of this membrane assembly, electric charge is applied by electrodes. Depending on the fixed charge of the polymer chain in the membrane, only the compatible ions are able to move through a given membrane. Thus cations will readily move through cation-exchange membranes; however, they will be repulsed by anion exchange membranes.

Let us follow the path of cations (such as Na^+ in a salt solution) shown in Fig. 11.7. The cations in cell A are attracted toward the anode, and they readily move through the cation-exchange membrane. However, the anions are repulsed back into the solution. After the cations move to cell B, they cannot move farther to the right because they are repulsed toward left by the anion-exchange membrane. Thus, either ion-concentrated or ion-depleted solution streams are obtained from alternating chambers.

Electrodialysis has been extensively used in desalting processes employing membranes that are permeable to ions but impervious to water. Water leaving from the ion-depleted cells is the desalted product, while brine is obtained from the ion-concentrated cells. For the desalting applications, anion-selective membranes are made from cross-linked polystyrene with quaternary ammonia groups; cation-selective membranes are made from cross-linked polystyrene that is sulfonated, such that sulfonate groups are attached to the polymer. The sulfonate (SO_4) and ammonia (NH_3) groups provide the electronegative and electropositive charge, respectively. The ions of opposite charge attach with electric charges on the membrane and easily migrate from one charge to another. The migration of ions causes the flow of electric current. The pores in these membranes are too small to allow water to transport through them. The electrodialysis process does not remove colloidal material, bacteria, or un-ionized matter.

The energy consumption for the electrodialysis process is given by

$$E = I^2 nRt \tag{11.36}$$

where E is energy consumption; I is electric current through the stack, ampere; n is number of cells in the stack; R is resistance of the cell, ohm; and t is time, s.

The electric current I can be calculated from the following equation:

$$I = \frac{zF\dot{m}\,\Delta c}{U} \tag{11.37}$$

where z is electrochemical valence; F is Faraday's constant, 96,500 ampere/second equivalent; $\dot{m}$ is feed solution flow rate, L/s; Δc is concentration difference between feed and product; U is current utilization factor, and I is direct current, ampere.

TABLE 11.2
Total Dissolved Solids Content of Saline Water

Term	Total dissolved solids ppm
Fresh	< 1000
Brackish	
Mildly brackish	1000–5000
Moderately brackish	5,000–15,000
Heavily brackish	15,000–35,000
Sea water	35,000 (approximately)

From Eqs. (11.36) and (11.37),

$$E = (nRt)\left(\frac{zF\dot{m}\,\Delta c}{U}\right)^2 \qquad (11.38)$$

For applications involving desalination of water, it is evident from Eq. (11.38) that the energy required to desalt water is directly proportional to the concentration of salt in the feed. When the salt concentration is very high, the energy consumption will be correspondingly high. Economics of the electrodialysis process usually limits its application to feedwater of less than 10,000 ppm total dissolved solids. Typically, for commercial applications, the most favorable economic installation of electrodialysis requires a feed with a total dissolved solids content (TDS) of 1000 to 5000 mg/L to obtain a product with a TDS content of 500 mg/L. The United States Public Health Service Drinking Water Standards require that potable water should not contain more than 500 ppm of total dissolved solids, (although up to 1000 ppm may be considered acceptable). Table 11.2 lists terms used to express the solids content of different levels of saline water.

In Japan, the electrodialysis process has been used extensively to obtain table salt from sea water. Other food applications of the electrodialysis process include removing salts from whey and orange juice.

11.3.2 Reverse Osmosis Membrane Systems

It is well known that when a plant or an animal membrane is used to separate two solutions of different solute concentrations, pure water passes through the membrane. The movement of water occurs from a solution with high concentration of water to a solution with low concentration of water, thus tending to equalize the water concentration on the two sides of the membrane. This movement of water is generally referred to as *osmosis*. Plant root hairs absorb water from the soil according to this phenomenon. The water is usually present in high concentration in soil surrounding the root hairs, whereas, inside the root cells, due to dissolved sugars, salts and

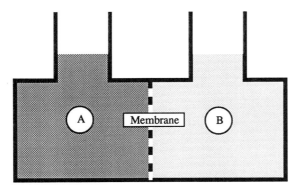

(a) Solute concentration same in cells A and B

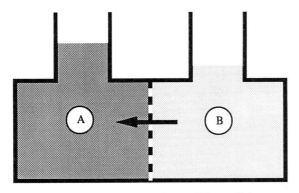

(b) Water movement from cell B to cell A

Fig. 11.8 The reverse osmosis process. (*Figure continues.*)

other substances, the water concentration is low. Water moves from the soil into the root hairs due to osmotic diffusion.

Let us consider a solution of water containing a solute. In Fig. 11.8a, a semipermeable membrane separates the solution of the same solute concentration contained in chambers A and B. Since the chemical potential of the solvent (water) is the same on both sides of the membrane, no net flow of water occurs through the membrane. In Fig. 11.8b, chamber A contains a solution with a higher solute concentration than chamber B; that is, chamber A has a lower water concentration than in chamber B. This also means that the chemical potential of the solvent (water) in chamber A will be lower in comparison to that of chamber B. As a result, water will flow from chamber B to chamber A. As seen in Fig. 11.8c, this movement of water will cause an increase in the volume of water in chamber A. Once equilibrium is reached, the increased volume represents a change in head, or pressure, which will be equal to the *osmotic pressure*. If an external

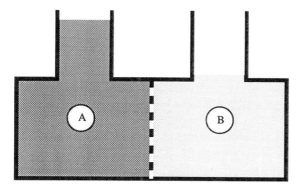

(c) Osmosis equilibrium

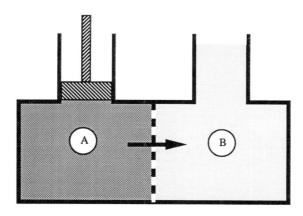

(d) Reverse osmosis, water movement from cell A to cell B

Fig. 11.8 *Continued.*

pressure greater than the osmotic pressure is then applied to chamber A, as shown in Fig. 11.8d, the chemical potential of water in chamber A will increase, resulting in water flow from chamber A to chamber B. The reversal in the direction of water flow, obtained by the application of external pressure that exceeds the osmotic pressure, is termed *reverse osmosis*.

A reverse osmosis membrane system is used to remove water from a water–solute mixture by the application of external pressure. In contrast to electrodialysis, the membrane used in the reverse osmosis system must be permeable to water.

In the 1950s, it was discovered that cellulose acetate, a highly organized polymer, has groups that can hydrogen-bond with water (as well as with other solvents such as ammonia or alcohol). Figure 11.9 shows the chemical structure of cellulose acetate polymer. The hydrogen in the water

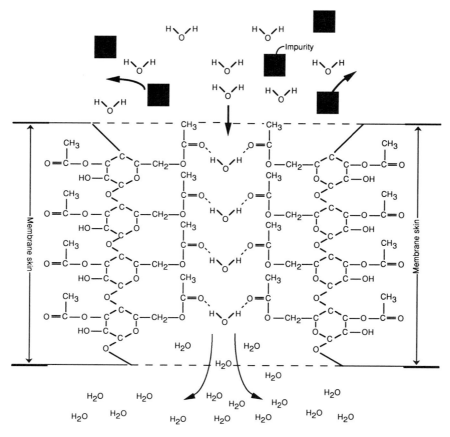

Fig. 11.9 The movement of water through a cellulose acetate membrane. [From Lacey (1972).]

molecule bonds to the carbonyl group of cellulose acetate. The water molecules hydrogen-bond on one side of the membrane, then move through the membrane by bonding to neighboring carbonyl groups. This process continues as water permeates the membrane to the other side. As illustrated in Figure 11.9 the polymer must be highly organized with carbonyl groups occurring at fixed locations or water molecules will be unable to permeate the membrane. The driving force for the water molecules to move from one set of hydrogen-bonding sites to the next is the pressure difference across the membrane.

Structurally, a polymeric membrane can be viewed as strands of the polymer and interstitial spaces. Since the polymer used in reverse osmosis membrane is a highly organized polymer, its structure must be tight, meaning the interstitial spaces should be small.

To obtain high flux rates through the membrane, the thickness of the membrane must be small. Loeb and Sourirajan, in the late 1950s, invented a method to fabricate extremely thin films of anisotropic cellulose acetate attached to a supporting matrix with an open structure. Since their initial discovery, many developments have taken place in the selection of the membrane materials.

In a reverse osmosis system, water is the permeating material referred to as "permeate," and the remaining solution concentrated with the solutes is called "retentate."

The osmotic pressures Π of a dilute solution can be obtained by Van't Hoff's equation that uses colligative properties of dilute solutions.

$$\Pi = cRT/M \qquad (11.39)$$

where Π is osmotic pressure, Pa; c is solute concentration, g/L of solution; T is temperature, absolute; R is gas constant; and M is molecular weight.

From Eq. (11.39), we observe that the presence of small molecules in a solution results in a high osmotic pressure. Another equation found to be more accurate over a wider range of solute concentrations utilizes Gibb's relationship, given as

$$\Pi = -\frac{RT \ln X_A}{V_m} \qquad (11.40)$$

where V_m is the molar volume of pure liquid, and X_A is mole fraction of pure liquid.

Osmotic pressures of some food materials are given in Table 11.3. Foods with smaller molecular-weight constituents have higher osmotic pressure. Data on osmotic pressures of foods or food components is very limited. These data are important in membrane processing. For example, in a reverse osmosis membrane, to obtain any flow through the membrane, the pressure applied to the feed solution must exceed the osmotic pressure.

TABLE 11.3
Osmotic Pressure of Foods and Food Constituents at Room Temperature

Food	Concentration	Osmotic pressure (kPa)
Milk	9% solids-not-fat	690
Whey	6% total solids	690
Orange juice	11% total solids	1587
Apple juice	15% total solids	2070
Grape juice	16% total solids	2070
Coffee extract	28% total solids	3450
Lactose	5% w/v	380
Sodium chloride	1% w/v	862
Lactic acid	1% w/v	552

Source: Cheryan (1986).

EXAMPLE I 1.3

Determine the osmotic pressure of a 0.1-m solution of sucrose in water at 20°C.

GIVEN

Concentration of sucrose solution = 0.1 m
Temperature = 20°C

APPROACH

We will determine the osmotic pressure using Eq. (11.39)

SOLUTION

(1) The molar concentration of a 0.1-m solution of sucrose is 0.098 mol/dm^3

(2) From Eq. (11.39)

$$\Pi = 0.000098 \, (\text{mol} \cdot \text{cm}^{-3}) \times 82.0575 \, (\text{cm}^3 \cdot \text{atm} \cdot \text{K}^{-1} \cdot \text{mol}^{-1})$$

$$\times 293 \, (\text{K}) \times 101.325 \, (\text{kPa/atm})$$

$$= 238.74 \, \text{kPa}$$

(3) The osmotic pressure is 238.74 kPa

The Hagen–Poiseuille law is useful in developing a relationship between the flux through a membrane and the pressure differential across it. Thus,

$$N = K_p(\Delta P - \Delta \Pi) \tag{11.41}$$

where N is rate of flux of solvent permeation; K_p is the permeability coefficient of the membrane; ΔP is the difference in transmembrane hydrostatic pressure; and $\Delta \Pi$ is the difference in the osmotic pressure between the feed solution and the permeate.

In Eq. (11.41), the permeability coefficient K_p is a function of membrane properties such as porosity, pore size distribution, and membrane thickness. In addition, the viscosity of the solvent has an influence on K_p. For membranes that provide high rejection—that is, if they do not allow most of the impurities in water to pass through—the osmotic pressure of the permeate is negligible.

EXAMPLE I 1.4

In a reverse osmosis system being used for a feed solution of 1% NaCl, determine the flux if a transmembrane pressure of 1400 kPa is applied. The permeability coefficient of the membrane is 0.014 L/m^2 · hr · kPa.

GIVEN

Concentration of salt solution = 1%
Transmembrane pressure = 1400 kPa
Permeability coefficient = 0.014 L/m^2 · hr · kPa

APPROACH

We will determine the osmotic pressure of the feed solution, namely 1% NaCl. The transmembrane pressure must be greater than the osmotic pressure. We will then calculate the flux rate using Eq. (11.41).

SOLUTION

(1) From Table 11.2, for NaCl, the osmotic pressure = 862 kPa.
(2) From Eq. (11.41),

$$N = 0.014 \left(\text{L/m}^2 \cdot \text{hr} \cdot \text{kPa} \right) \times \left[1400 \, (\text{kPa}) - 862 \, (\text{kPa}) \right]$$

$$= 7.53 \, \text{L/m}^2 \, \text{hr}$$

(3) The flux of water through the membrane will be 7.53 L/m^2 hr.

The osmotic pressure of a liquid feed is useful in selecting membranes, since the membrane must be able to physically withstand transmembrane pressures higher than the osmotic pressure.

11.3.3 Membrane Performance

The flow of water through a membrane is described by

$$\dot{m}_w = \frac{K_w A (\Delta P - \Delta \Pi)}{t} \tag{11.42}$$

where $\dot{m}_w$ is water flow rate, kg/s; ΔP is hydraulic pressure differential across the membrane, kPa; $\Delta \Pi$ is osmotic pressure difference across the membrane, kPa; t is time, s; A is area, m^2; K_w is coefficient of water permeability through the membrane, kg/m^2 · kPa.

The flow of a solute through a membrane is given by

$$\dot{m}_s = \frac{K_s A \, \Delta c}{t} \tag{11.43}$$

where $\dot{m}_s$ is solute flow rate; Δc is differential of solute concentration across membrane, kg/m^3; K_s is coefficient of solute permeability through the membrane, L/m.

From Eqs. (11.42) and (11.43), increasing the hydraulic pressure gradient across the membrane increases the water flow rate; however, it has no effect on the solute flow rate. The solute flow is influenced by the concentration gradient across the membrane.

The performance of a membrane system is often described by the "retention factor," R_f.

$$R_f = \frac{(c_f - c_p)}{c_f} \tag{11.44}$$

where c_f is concentration of a solute in the feed stream, kg/m^3; and c_p is concentration of a solute in permeate stream, kg/m^3.

Another factor, used to describe the performance of a membrane system is "rejection factor," R_j.

$$R_j = \frac{(c_f - c_p)}{c_p} \tag{11.45}$$

Membrane performance is also expressed as "molecular weight cutoff." It is the molecular weight below which a species can pass through the membrane.

Another term used to denote membrane performance is conversion percentage, Z.

$$Z = \frac{\dot{m}_p \times 100}{\dot{m}_f} \tag{11.46}$$

where $\dot{m}_p$ is product flow rate and $\dot{m}_f$ is feed flow rate.

Thus, operating a membrane at a conversion percentage of 70% means that a feed of 100 liter/hour will yield 70 liter/hour of product (permeate) and 30 liter/hour of retentate.

11.3.4 Ultrafiltration Membrane Systems

Ultrafiltration membranes have pore sizes much larger than the reverse osmosis membrane. Mostly ultrafiltration membranes are used for fractionating purposes, that is, to separate high molecular weight solutes from those with low molecular weight. Since the ultrafiltration membranes have larger pore sizes, the hydraulic pressures required as a driving force are much smaller when compared with the reverse osmosis membrane systems. Typically, for ultrafiltration membrane systems, pressures in the range of 70 to 700 kPa are needed. As shown in Fig. 11.4, the pore size of ultrafiltration membranes ranges from 0.001 to 0.02 m, with a molecular weight cutoffs from 1000 to 80,000.

The flow rate through an ultrafiltration membrane can be obtained from the following equation:

$$\dot{m}_w = \frac{\Delta P K A}{t} \tag{11.47}$$

where ΔP is pressure difference across the membrane; K is a constant expressing membrane permeability; A is area, m^2; and t is time, s.

11.3.5 *Concentration Polarization*

In membrane separation processes, when a liquid solution containing salts and particulates is brought next to a semi-permeable membrane, some of the molecules accumulate in the boundary layer next to the membrane surface (Fig. 11.10). Thus, the concentration of a retained species will be higher in the boundary layer adjacent to the membrane than in the bulk. This phenomenon is called concentration polarization, and it has a major effect on the performance of a membrane system.

Both in the reverse osmosis and ultrafiltration system, the causes leading to concentration polarization are the same; however, the consequences are different. In reverse osmosis, as the low molecular weight material is retained on the membrane surface, the increase in the solute concentration increases the osmotic pressure [Eq. (11.39)]. For a given transmembrane pressure, increasing the osmotic pressure will decrease the flux through the membrane [Eq. (11.41)]. In ultrafiltration membranes, since larger molecules are retained on the membrane surface, their influence on the osmotic pressure is small. But these retained molecules can lead to precipitation and formation of a solid layer at the membrane surface, this phenomenon of gel formation will be elaborated later in this section.

The concentration profiles of a solute adjacent to the membrane surface can be described using Fig. 11.11. As permeation of a solute proceeds through the membrane, the solute concentration at the membrane surface, c_w, increases in comparison to the solute concentration in the bulk fluid, c_b. This is due to convective transport of the solute toward the membrane. Due to the increased concentration of the solute at the membrane surface there will be a concentration gradient set up between the concentration at the wall and the concentration in the bulk, resulting in back diffusion of the solute. At steady state, the back diffusion must equal the convective flux. The rate of convective transport of the solute can be

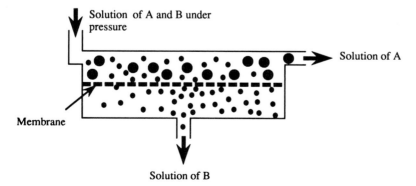

Fig. 11.10 Separation process in a pressure-driven membrane system. [From Lacey (1972).]

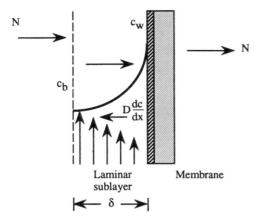

Fig. 11.11 A profile of solute concentration during ultrafiltration showing concentration polarization. [From Schweitzer, P. A. (1979). "Handbook of Separation Processes." McGraw-Hill, New York.]

written as

$$\text{Convective transport of a solute} = N \cdot c \qquad (11.48)$$

where N is the permeate flux rate, m^3/m^2 per second; c is the concentration of a solute, kg/m^3.

The solute rejected at the wall moves back into the bulk liquid. The rate of flux back-transport of the solute is expressed as

$$\text{Flux rate of a solute due to back transport} = D\frac{dc}{dx} \qquad (11.49)$$

where D is the diffusion coefficient of the solute, m^2/s.

Under steady-state conditions, the convective transport of a solute equals the back transport due to concentration gradient; thus,

$$D\frac{dc}{dx} = Nc \qquad (11.50)$$

Separating the variables and integrating with boundary conditions, $c = c_w$ at $x = 0$ and $c = c_b$ at $x = \delta$, we obtain

$$\frac{N\delta}{D} = \ln\frac{c_w}{c_b} \qquad (11.51)$$

$$N = \frac{D}{\delta}\ln\frac{c_w}{c_b} \qquad (11.52)$$

The preceding equation may be rearranged as

$$\frac{c_w}{c_b} = \exp\left(\frac{N\delta}{D}\right) \qquad (11.53)$$

According to Eq. (11.53), c_w/c_b, also referred to as concentration modulus, increases exponentially with transmembrane flux and with the thickness of

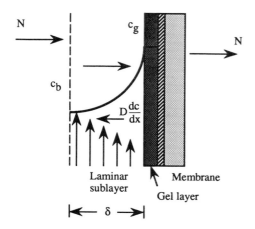

Fig. 11.12 A concentration profile showing the formation of a gel layer on an ultrafiltration membrane. [From Schweitzer, P. A. (1979). "Handbook of Separation Processes." McGraw-Hill, New York.]

the boundary layer, and it decreases exponentially with the increasing values of solute diffusivity. Thus, the influence of concentration polarization is particularly severe with membranes that have high permeability, such as ultrafiltration membranes, and solutes that have high molecular weights. The thickness of the boundary layer is the result of the flow conditions next to the membrane surface.

The above derivation is valid for both reverse osmosis and ultrafiltration membranes. In the case of ultrafiltration membranes, as observed in the preceding paragraph, the solute concentration will increase rapidly and the solute may precipitate, forming a gel layer (Fig. 11.12). The resistance to permeation by this gel layer may become more prominent than the membrane resistance. Under these conditions, the solute concentration at the surface of the gel layer, referred to as c_g, becomes a constant and it is no longer influenced by the solute concentration in the bulk, the membrane characteristics, operating pressures, or the fluid flow conditions.

For situations when the pressure has no more influence on the flux, we can rewrite Eq. (11.52) as

$$N = k_m \ln\left(\frac{c_w}{c_b}\right) \tag{11.54}$$

where k_m is mass transfer coefficient $L/m^2 \cdot hr$.

Equation (11.54) indicates that the ultrafiltration rate N is influenced mainly by the solute concentration in the bulk, c_b, and the mass transfer coefficient, k_m.

The mass transfer coefficient can be evaluated using dimensional analysis.

$$N_{Sh} = B(N_{Re})^a (N_{Sc})^b \tag{11.55}$$

where

$$\text{Sherwood number, } N_{Sh} = \frac{k_m d_h}{D}$$

$$\text{Reynolds number, } N_{Re} = \frac{\rho u d_h}{\mu}$$

$$\text{Schmidt number, } N_{Sc} = \frac{\mu}{\rho D}$$

$$d_h = 4 \left(\frac{\begin{array}{c} \text{cross section} \\ \text{available for flow} \end{array}}{\text{wetted perimeter}} \right)$$

For turbulent flow,

$$N_{Sh} = 0.023 (N_{Re})^{0.8} (N_{Sc})^{0.33} \qquad (11.56)$$

Example 11.5 illustrates the use of the dimensional analysis to determine mass transfer coefficient (Cheryan, 1986).

EXAMPLE 11.5

Determine the flux rate expected in a tubular ultrafiltration system being used to concentrate milk. The following conditions apply: density of milk = 1.03 g/cm^3, viscosity = 0.8 cp, diffusivity = 7 × 10^{-7} cm^2/s, c_B = 3.1% weight per unit volume, and c_g = 22% weight per unit volume. Diameter of tube = 1.1 cm, length = 220 cm, number of tubes = 15, and fluid velocity = 1.5 m/s.

GIVEN

   Density of milk = 1.03 g/cm^3
   Viscosity = 0.8 cp
   Diffusivity = 7 × 10^{-7} cm^2/s
   Concentration in bulk, c_B = 3.1% weight per unit volume
   Concentration in gel layer, c_g = 22% weight per unit volume
   Diameter of tube = 1.1 cm
   Length of tube = 220 cm
   Number of tubes = 15
   Fluid velocity = 1.5 m/s
   Pressure drop = 2 kg/cm^2

APPROACH

We will first determine the mass transfer coefficient from dimensional analysis. Then, using Eq. (11.54), we will calculate the flux rate.

SOLUTION

(1) Reynolds number,

$$N_{Re} = \frac{\rho u d}{\mu}$$

$$= \frac{1.03 \text{ g/cm}^3 \times 150 \text{ cm/s} \times 1.1 \text{cm}}{0.008 \text{ poise}}$$

$$= 21243$$

(2) Schmidt number,

$$N_{Sc} = \frac{0.008 \text{ poise}}{1.03 \text{ g/cm}^3 \times 7 \times 10^{-7} \text{ m}^2/\text{s}}$$

$$= 1.11 \times 10^4$$

(3) Sherwood number,

$$N_{Sh} = 0.023(21243)^{0.8}(1.11 \times 10^4)^{0.33}$$

$$= 1440$$

$$\frac{k_m d}{D} = 1440$$

$$k_m = \frac{1440 \times 7 \times 10^{-7}}{1.10} = 0.92 \times 10^{-3} \text{ cm/s}$$

$$= 0.92 \times 10^{-3} \text{ cm}^3/\text{m}^2 \text{ s}$$

$$= 33 \text{ L/m}^2 \text{ hr}$$

(4) From Eq. (11.54)

$$N = 33 \times \ln \frac{22}{3.1}$$

$$= 64.67 \text{ L/m}^2 \text{ hr}$$

(5) The flux rate through the membrane is 64.67 L/m² hr.

Typical materials used in ultrafiltration membranes include cellulose acetate, polyvinyl chloride, polysulfones, polycarbonates, and polyacrylonitriles.

11.3.6 Types of Reverse Osmosis and Ultrafiltration Systems

Four major types of membrane devices are used for reverse osmosis and ultrafiltration systems: plate and frame, tubular, spiral-wound, and hollow fiber. Table 11.4 provides a general comparison among these four types. A brief description of each type of membrane module is given in the following.

a. Plate and Frame

The plate and frame membrane systems involve a large number of flat membranes that are sandwiched together with the use of spacers. As shown in Fig. 11.13, the spacers provide the channels for flow. The membranes (usually 50 to 500 μm thick) are bonded on a porous, inert matrix that offers little resistance to the fluid flow. The flow of feed and retentate occur

TABLE 11.4
**Comparison of Process-Related Characteristics
for Membrane Module Configurations**

Characteristic	Module type			
	Plate-and-frame	Spiral-wound	Tube-in-shell	Hollow-fiber
Packing density [m^2/m^3]	200–400	300–900	150–300	9,000–30,000
Permeate flux [m^3/m^2 day]	0.3–1.0	0.3–1.0	0.3–1.0	0.004–0.08
Flux density [m^3/m^3 day]	60–400	90–900	45–300	36–2400
Feed channel diameter (mm)	5	1.3	13	0.1
Method of replacement	As sheets	As module assembly	As tubes	As entire module
Replacement labor	High	Medium	High	Medium
Pressure drop				
Product side	Medium	Medium	Low	High
Feed side	Medium	Medium	High	Low
Concentration polarization	High	Medium	High	Low
Suspended solids buildup	Low/medium	Medium/high	Low	High

in alternate channels. This arrangement of membranes is very similar to
the plate heat exchangers described in Chapter 4.

b. Tubular

The tubular design was the first commercial design of a reverse osmosis
system. It consists of a porous tube coated with the membrane material
such as cellulose acetate. Typically, feed solution is pumped into the tube
through one end and forced in the radial direction through the porous

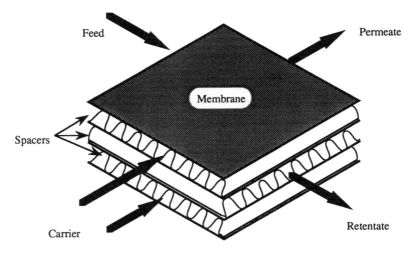

Fig. 11.13　A module used in a plate-and-frame membrane system.

Feed Solution

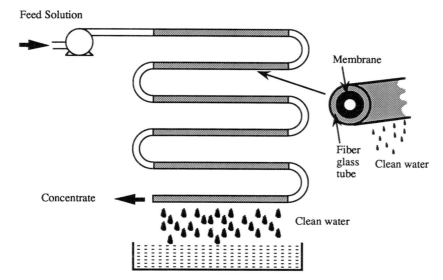

Fig. 11.14 A tubular membrane system. [From Applegate (1984).]

pipe and the membrane (Fig. 11.14). Water drips from the outer surface of the membrane while the concentrated stream "retentate" leaves through the outer end of the tube. This type of reverse osmosis device is expensive to use for high volumetric flow rates since the membrane area is relatively small.

c. Spiral-Wound

To increase the membrane surface area per unit volume, a spiral-wound configuration was a key commercial development following the tubular design. This design, shown in Fig. 11.15, can be visualized as a composite of multilayers. The two layers of membrane are separated by a plastic mesh, and on either side of the membrane is a porous sheet. These five layers are then spirally wound around a perforated tube. The ends of the rolled layers are sealed to prevent mixing of feed and product streams. The whole spiral assembly is housed in a tubular metal jacket that can withstand applied pressures. Feed is pumped through the perforated tube on one side of the spiral-wound roll. Feed enters inside the plastic mesh, which aids in creating turbulence and minimizing fouling. The feed then permeates the membrane in a radial direction and exits the membrane into the porous layers. The permeate (water) transports through the porous sheet in a spiral manner and leaves the assembly through the exit tube, whereas the retentate leaves through the other end of the spiral-wound roll. Typical dimensions of spiral cartridges are diameter 11 cm, length 84 cm, mem-

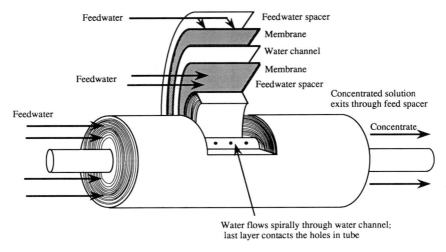

Feedwater — Feedwater spacer
Membrane
Water channel
Membrane
Feedwater — Feedwater spacer
Concentrated solution exits through feed spacer
Feedwater
Concentrate

Water flows spirally through water channel; last layer contacts the holes in tube

Fig. 11.15 A spiral-wound membrane system with a cross-sectional view showing the water flow patterns.

brane spacing 0.7 mm, and area 5 m^2. The spiral wound systems are similar for both reverse osmosis and ultrafiltration applications.

d. Hollow Fiber

A hollow fiber, made out of aramid, was first introduced by DuPont in 1970. Hollow fibers, finer than human hair, have an internal diameter of about 40 μm, and an external diameter of about 85 μ, respectively. A large number of hollow fibers (several millions) are arranged in a bundle around a perforated distributor tube (Fig. 11.16). In the reverse osmosis system, the fibers are glued with epoxy to either end. These fibers provide extremely large surface areas; thus, hollow fiber membrane systems can be made very compact. Feed water is introduced through the distributor pipe; the permeate flows through the annular space of the fibers into the hollow bore of the fibers, and moves to the tube sheet end, discharging from the exit port. The retentate or brine stays on the outside of the fibers and leaves the device from the brine port. Hollow fibers are mainly used to purify water. Liquid foods are difficult to handle in hollow fiber systems because of problems associated with fouling of the fibers.

The hollow fibers used for ultrafiltration membranes are quite different than those used for reverse osmosis systems. For ultrafiltration applications, hollow fibers are made from acrylic copolymers.

Most membrane systems in the food industry have been in dairy and fruit juice applications. Other commercial applications include processing of coffee, tea, alcohol, gelatins, eggs, and blood, and corn refining and soybean processing.

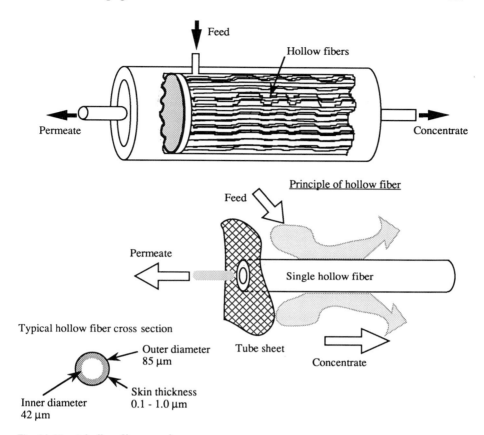

Fig. 11.16 A hollow fiber membrane system.

11.4 Food Packaging

11.4.1 Mass Transfer in Packaging Materials

An important requirement in selecting packaging systems for foods is the barrier property of the packaging material. To keep a food product crisp and fresh, the package must provide a barrier to moisture. The rancidity of a food can be minimized by keeping it protected from light. To reduce oxidation of food constituents, the packaging material must be a good barrier to oxygen. The original aroma and flavor of a food can be maintained by using a packaging material that offers a barrier to a particular aroma. Thus, properly selected packaging materials are beneficial in extending the shelf life of foods. The barrier properties of a packaging material can be expressed in terms of permeability.

Permeability of a packaging material provides a measure of how well a certain gas or vapor can penetrate the packaging material. In quantitative

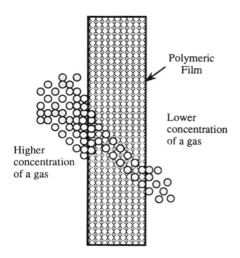

Higher concentration of a gas

Polymeric Film

Lower concentration of a gas

Fig. 11.17 Mass transfer of a gas through a polymeric material.

terms, permeability is the mass of gas or vapor transferred per unit of time, area, and a "driving force." In the case of diffusional mass transfer, the driving force is a difference in concentrations or in partial pressures. If the driving force is a difference in total pressure, the mass transfer occurs due to bulk flow of a gas or vapor. A polymeric membrane may be thought of as an aggregate of wriggling worms. The worms represent the long chains of polymers. The space between the worms is like the interstitial space through which a species passes. The wriggling of worms is representative of thermal motion of the polymeric chains.

The mass transport through polymeric materials can be described as a step process. Referring to Fig. 11.17, in step I, the gas vapor or liquid molecules dissolve in the polymeric material on the side of the film exposed to the higher concentration. In step II, the gas or vapor molecules diffuse through the polymeric material moving toward the side of the film exposed to the lower concentration. The movement of molecules depends on the availability of "holes" in the polymeric material. The "holes" are formed as large chain segments of the polymer slide over each other due to thermal agitation. The last step III involves the desorption of the gas or vapor molecules and evaporation from the surface of the film.

We can again use Fick's law of diffusion to develop an expression for the transport process of a gas through a polymeric material. From Eq. (11.11)

$$\frac{\dot{m}_B}{A} = \frac{D_B(c_{B1} - c_{B2})}{(x_2 - x_1)}$$

This equation would be sufficient to determine the rate of flux, $\dot{m}_B/A$, but the concentrations of a gas at the film surfaces are more difficult to

TABLE 11.5
Conversion Factors for Various Units of Permeability Coefficient

	$\dfrac{cm^3 \cdot cm}{s \cdot cm^2 \,(cm\,Hg)}$	$\dfrac{cm^3 \cdot cm}{s \cdot cm^2 \,(Pa)}$	$\dfrac{cm^3 \cdot cm}{day \cdot m^2 \,(atm)}$
$\dfrac{cm^3 \cdot cm}{s \cdot cm^2 \,(cm\,Hg)}$	1	7.5×10^{-4}	6.57×10^{10}
$\dfrac{cm^3 \cdot mm}{s \cdot cm^2 \,(cm\,Hg)}$	10^{-1}	7.5×10^{-5}	6.57×10^{9}
$\dfrac{cm^3 \cdot cm}{s \cdot cm^2 \,(atm)}$	1.32×10^{-2}	9.9×10^{-6}	8.64×10^{8}
$\dfrac{cm^3 \cdot mil}{day \cdot m^2 \,(atm)}$	3.87×10^{-14}	2.9×10^{-17}	2.54×10^{-3}
$\dfrac{in^3 \cdot mil}{day \cdot 100\,in^2 \,(atm)}$	9.82×10^{-12}	7.37×10^{-15}	6.46×10^{-1}
$\dfrac{cm^3 \cdot cm}{day \cdot m^2 \,(atm)}$	1.52×10^{-11}	1.14×10^{-14}	1

Source: Yasuda and Stannett (1989).

measure than partial pressures. The concentrations can be converted to partial pressures by using Henry's law.

$$c = Sp \qquad (11.57)$$

where S is solubility (moles/cm^3 atm) and p is partial pressure of gas (atm). Thus, we have

$$\dot{m}_B = \frac{D_B SA(p_{B1} - p_{B2})}{(x_2 - x_1)} \qquad (11.58)$$

The quantity $D_B S$ is known as the permeability coefficient P_B.

$$P_B = \frac{(\text{amount of gas or vapor})(\text{thickness of film})}{(\text{area})(\text{time})(\text{pressure difference across the film})} \qquad (11.59)$$

A wide variety of units are used to report the permeability coefficient (Table 11.5).

Another parameter used by some authors is *permeance*, which is not corrected to a unit thickness. Sometimes permeance to water vapor is reported in units that are neither corrected to unit thickness nor to unit pressure, but this value always must be reported with specified thickness, humidity, and temperature. For example, water vapor permeability is defined as grams of water per day per 100 cm^2 of package surface for a specified thickness and temperature and/or a relative humidity on one side of approximately 0% and on the other side of 95%.

11.4.2 Permeability of Packaging Material to "Fixed" Gases

Gases such as oxygen, nitrogen, hydrogen, and carbon dioxide, which have low boiling points, are known as "fixed gases." They show similar ideal behavior with respect to permeability through packaging materials. The permeability of O_2, CO_2, and N_2, for several polymeric materials is shown in Table 11.6. It is evident that for any given gas there exist materials with widely differing permeabilities. For example, Saran is 100,000 times less permeable to oxygen than is silicone rubber. And there are certain regularities in transmission of different gases through the same material. For example, carbon dioxide permeates four to six times faster than oxygen, and oxygen four to six times faster than nitrogen. Since carbon dioxide is the largest of the three gas molecules, one expects its diffusion coefficient to be low, and it is. Its permeability coefficient is high because its solubility S in polymers is much greater than that for other gases.

"Fixed" gases also show ideal behaviors.

(1) Permeabilities can be considered independent of concentration.

(2) The permeabilities change with temperature in accordance with the following relation:

$$P = P_0 e^{-E_p/RT} \qquad (11.60)$$

where E_p is the activation energy for permeability (kcal/mole).

For some materials there is a break in the permeability temperature curve, and above a critical temperature the material is much more permeable. For polyvinyl acetate around 30°C and polystyrene around 80°C,

TABLE 11.6
Permeability Coefficients, Diffusion Constants, and Solubility Coefficients of Polymers[a]

Polymer	Permeant	T [°C]	$P \times 10^{10}$	$D \times 10^6$	$S \times 10^2$
Poly(ethylene) (density 0.914)	O_2	25	2.88	0.46	4.78
	CO_2	25	12.6	0.37	25.8
	N_2	25	0.969	0.32	2.31
	H_2O	25	90		
Poly(ethylene) (density 0.964)	O_2	25	0.403	0.170	1.81
	CO_2	25	1.69	0.116	11.1
	CO	25	0.193	0.096	1.53
	N_2	25	0.143	0.093	1.17
	H_2O	25	12.0		
Poly(propylene)	H_2	20	41	2.12	
	N_2	30	0.44		
	O_2	30	2.3		
	CO_2	30	9.2		
	H_2O	25	51		

TABLE 11.6 (*Continued*)

Polymer	Permeant	T [°C]	$P \times 10^{10}$	$D \times 10^6$	$S \times 10^2$
Poly(oxyethyleneoxyterephthaloyl) (Poly(ethylene terephthalate))					
crystalline	O_2	25	0.035	0.0035	7.5
	N_2	25	0.0065	0.0014	5.0
	CO_2	25	0.17	0.0006	200
	H_2O	25	130		
Cellulose acetate	N_2	30	0.28		
	O_2	30	0.78		
	CO_2	30	22.7		
	H_2O	25	5,500		
Cellulose (Cellophane)	N_2	25	0.0032		
	O_2	25	0.0021		
	CO_2	25	0.0047		
	H_2O	25	1,900		
Poly(vinyl acetate)	O_2	30	0.50	0.055	6.3
Poly(vinyl alcohol)	H_2	25	0.009		
	N_2	14^b	< 0.001		
		14^c	0.33	0.045	5.32
	O_2	25	0.0089		
	CO_2	25	0.012		
		23^b	0.001		
		23^d	11.9	0.0476	190
	ethylene oxide	0	0.002		
Poly(vinyl chloride)	H_2	25	1.70	0.500	2.58
	N_2	25	0.0118	0.00378	2.37
	O_2	25	0.0453	0.0118	2.92
	CO_2	25	0.157	0.00250	47.7
	H_2O	25	275	0.0238	8780.0
Poly(vinylidene chloride) (Saran)					
	N_2	30	0.00094		
	O_2	30	0.0053		
	CO_2	30	0.03		
	H_2O	25	0.5		
Poly(imino(1-oxohexamethylene) (Nylon 6)					
	N_2	30	0.0095		
	O_2	30	0.038		
	CO_2	20	0.088		
		30^b	0.10		
		30^e	0.29		
	H_2O	25	177		
Poly(imino(1-oxoundecamethylene) (Nylon 11)					
	CO_2	40	1.00	0.019	40

Source: Yasuda and Stannett (1989).
[a] Units used are as follows: P in [cm^3 (STP) cm cm^{-2} s^{-1} (cm Hg)$^{-1}$], D in [cm^2 s^{-1}], and S in [cm^3 (STP) cm^{-3} atm^{-1}]. To obtain corresponding coefficients in suggested new international units, the following factors should be used: $P \times 7.5 \times 10^{-4}$ = [cm^3 (STP) cm cm^{-2} s^{-1} Pa^{-1}] $S \times 0.987 \times 10^{-5}$ = [cm^3 (STP) cm^{-3} Pa^{-1}]
[b] Relative humidity 0%.
[c] Relative humidity 90%.
[d] Relative humidity 94%.
[e] Relative humidity 95%.

breaks are due to a glass transition temperature T'_g. Below T'_g the material is glassy, and above it is rubbery.

EXAMPLE 11.6

The permeability coefficient for a 0.1 mm polyethylene film is being measured by maintaining a moisture vapor gradient across the film in a sealed test apparatus. The high moisture vapor side of the film is maintained at 90% RH and a salt ($ZnCl \cdot 1/2\ H_2O$) maintains the opposite side at 10% RH. The area of film exposed to vapor transfer is 10 cm by 10 cm. When the test is conducted at 30°C, a weight gain of 50 g in the dessicant salt is recorded after 24 hr. From these given data, calculate the permeability coefficient of the film.

GIVEN

Film thickness = 0.1 mm = 1×10^{-4} m
High relative humidity = 90%
Low relative humidity = 10%
Temperature = 30°C
Film area = 10 cm × 10 cm = 100 cm² = 0.01 m²
Moisture rate of flow = 50 g/24 hr = 5.787×10^{-4} g water/s

APPROACH

We will use Eq. (11.58) to calculate the permeability coefficient (P_B) after vapor pressures are expressed in terms of moisture contents of air.

SOLUTION

(1) By using Eq. (10.16) modified with vapor pressures,

$$\phi = \frac{p_w}{p_{ws}} \times 100$$

(2) From Table A.4.2

$$p_{ws} = 4.246 \text{ kPa at } 30°C$$

(3) From steps 1 and 2, at 10% relative humidity;

$$p_w = 4.246 \times 10/100$$
$$= 0.4246 \text{ kPa}$$

At 90% relative humidity

$$p_w = 4.246 \times 90/100$$
$$= 3.821 \text{ kPa}$$

Using Eq. (11.58) and solving for permeability coefficient:

$$P_B = \frac{(5.787 \times 10^{-4} \text{ g water/s})(1 \times 10^{-4} \text{ m})}{(0.01 \text{ m}^2)(3.821 \text{ kPa} - 0.4246 \text{ kPa})(1000 \text{ Pa/kPa})}$$

$$P_B = 1.7 \times 10^{-9} \text{ g water} \cdot \text{m/m}^2 \cdot \text{Pa} \cdot \text{s}$$

(4) The permeability coefficient of the film is calculated to be 1.7×10^{-9} g water $\cdot$ m/m^2 $\cdot$ Pa $\cdot$ s; the units may be converted to any other form desired using Table 11.5.

Problems

11.1 An ultrafiltration system is being used to concentrate gelatin. The following data were obtained: A flux rate was 1630 L/m^2 per day at 5% solids by weight concentration, and a flux rate was 700 L/m^2 per day at 10% solids by weight. Determine the concentration of the gel layer and the flux rate at 7% solids.

11.2 A droplet of water is falling through 20°C air at the terminal velocity. The relative humidity of the air is 10% and the droplet is at the wet bulb temperature. The diffusivity of water vapor in air is 0.2×10^{-4} m^2/s. Estimate the convective mass transfer coefficient for a 100 μm diameter droplet.

11.3 Estimate the osmotic pressure of a 20% sucrose solution at a temperature of 10°C.

11.4 Determine the transmembrane pressure required to maintain a flux of 220 kg/m^2 hr in a reverse osmosis system when the feed solution is 6% total solids whey. The permeability coefficient of the membrane is 0.02 kg/m^2 hr kPa.

11.5 An ultrafiltration system is being used to concentrate orange juice at 30°C from an initial solids content of 10% to 35% total solids. The ultrafiltration system contains six tubes with 1.5 cm diameter. The product properties include density of 1100 kg/m^3, viscosity of 1.3×10^{-3} Pa s, and solute diffusivity of 2×10^{-8} m^2/s. The concentration of solute at the membrane surface is 25%. Estimate the length of ultrafiltration tubes required to achieve the desired concentration increase.

11.6 A dry food product is contained in a 1 cm $\times$ 4 cm $\times$ 3 cm box using a polymer film to protect the oxygen sensitivity of the product. The concentration gradient across the film is defined by the oxygen concentration in air and 1% within the package. The oxygen diffusivity for the polymer film is 3×10^{-16}. Estimate the film thickness needed to ensure a product shelf life of 10 months. The shelf life of the product is established as the time when oxidation reactions within the product have used 0.5 moles of oxygen.

List of Symbols

A area (m^2)

B constant in Eq. (11.55)

c concentration of component A, either mass per unit volume or molar mass per unit volume $(kg/m^3$ or $kmol/m^3)$

D diffusion coefficient, or diffusivity (m^2/s)

d characteristic dimension (m)

D_{AB} diffusivity of a gas A (or liquid A) in a solid B (m^2/s)

d_h 4(cross-sectional area/wetted perimeter) (m)

ΔP the difference in transmembrane hydrostatic pressure (Pa)

$\Delta\Pi$ the difference in the osmotic pressure between the feed solution and the permeate (Pa)

E energy consumption

E_p the activation energy for permeability $(kJ/mole \cdot k)$

F Faraday's constant; 96,500 ampere second/equivalent

I electric current through the stack (ampere)

k_m mass transfer coefficient $(m^3/m^2 \cdot s$ or m/s or $L/m^2 \cdot hr)$

K coefficient of water

   permeability through the membrane $(kg/m^2 \cdot kPa)$

M molecular weight

$\dot{m}$ the mass flow rate (kg/s)

μ viscosity $(Pa \cdot s)$

N permeate flux rate $(m^3/m^2 \cdot s^{-1})$

n number of cells in the stack

N_{Re} Reynolds number $(\rho u d/\mu)$

N_{Sc} Schmidt number $(\mu/\rho D)$

N_{Sh} Sherwood number $(k_m d/D)$

ν kinematic viscosity (m^2/s)

Ω resistance of the cell (ohm)

p partial pressure of gas (kPa)

P permeability coefficient of the membrane

P_0 constant in Eq. (11.60)

Π osmotic pressure (bar)

R gas constant $(m^3 \cdot Pa/kg\ K)$

ρ mass concentration of B (kg/m^3)

S solubility $(moles/cm^3\ atm)$

T temperature (K)

t time (s)

U current utilization factor

u velocity of fluid (m/s)

V molar volume of pure liquid

X mole fraction of pure liquid

z electrochemical valence

Subscripts: A, component A; B, component B; f, feed; p, product (or permeate); s, solute; u, universal; w, water.

Bibliography

Applegate L. (1984). Membrane separation processes. *Chem. Eng.* (June 11), pp. 64–89.

Cheryan, M. (1986). "Ultrafiltration Handbook." Technomic Publishing Co., Lancaster, Pennsylvania.

Lacey, R. E. (1972). Membrane separation processes. *Chem. Eng.* (Sept. 4), pp. 56–74.

McCabe, W. L., Smith, J. C., and Harriott, P. (1985). "Unit Operations of Chemical Engineering." McGraw Hill, New York.

Yasuda, H., and Stannett, V. (1989). Permeability coefficients. *In* "Polymer Handbook" 3rd ed. (J. Brandrup and E. H. Immergut, eds.). Wiley, New York.

CHAPTER 12

Food Dehydration

The removal of moisture from a food product is one of the oldest preservation methods. By reduction of the water content of a food product to very low levels, the opportunity for microbial deterioration is eliminated and the rates of other deterioration reactions are reduced significantly. In addition to preservation, dehydration reduces product weight and volume by significant amounts and improves the efficiency of product transportation and storage. Often, the dehydration of a food product results in a product that is more convenient for consumer use.

The preservation of fruits and vegetables by dehydration offers a unique challenge. Due to the structural configuration of these products, the removal of moisture must be accomplished in a manner that will be least detrimental to the product quality. This requires that the process produce a dry product that can be returned to approximately the original quality after rehydration. To achieve the desired results for dehydrated fruits and vegetables, the process must provide the optimum heat and mass transfer within the product. The design of these processes requires careful analysis of the heat and mass transfer occurring within the product structure. Only through analysis and understanding of these processes can the maximum efficiency and optimum quality be achieved.

12.1 Basic Drying Processes

To achieve moisture removal from a food product in the most efficient manner, the design of the dehydration system must account for the various processes and mechanism occurring within the product. These processes and mechanisms are of particular importance for fruits and vegetables when product structure will influence the movement of moisture from the product.

12.1.1 Water Activity

One of the most important parameters in food dehydration is the equilibrium condition that establishes a limit to the process. Although this value represents an important part of the gradient for moisture movement, water activity has become important in analysis of storage stability for a dry food.

By definition, water activity is the equilibrium relative humidity of the product divided by 100. For most food products, the relationship between moisture content and water activity is as illustrated in Fig. 12.1. The sygmoid isotherm is typical for dry foods as is the difference between the adsorption and desorption isotherms for the same product. In addition to the water activity values establishing the storage stability of the product against various deterioration reactions (Fig. 12.2), the equilibrium moisture contents are the lower limit of the gradient for moisture removal from the product. As might be expected, higher temperatures result in lower equilibrium moisture content and a large moisture gradient for moisture movement.

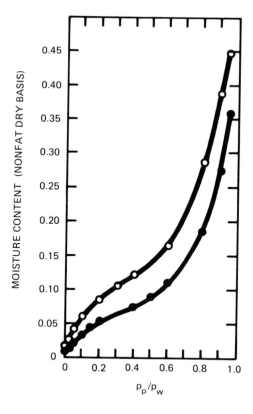

Fig. 12.1 Equilibrium moisture content isotherm for a freeze-dried food product, illustrating hysteresis. ○, Desorption; ●, adsorption; [Adapted from Heldman and Singh (1981).]

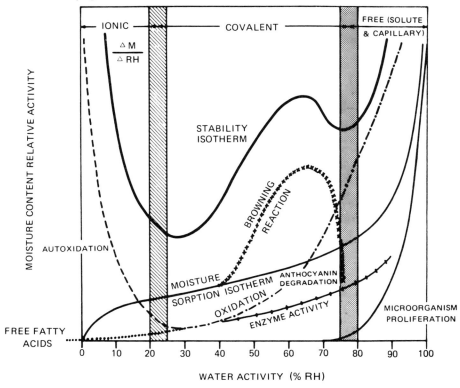

Fig. 12.2   Influence of water activity on rates of various deterioration reactions in foods. [From Rockland and Nishi (1980). Copyright © by Institute of Food Technologists. Reprinted with permission of *Food Technology*.]

One of the most widely used models to fit data obtained on water activity is the GAB model (named after Guggenheim–Anderson–DeBoer). This model is used to fit and draw the sorption data obtained for a given food. The GAB model is expressed as follows:

$$\frac{w}{w_m} = \frac{Cka_w}{(1 - ka_w)(1 - ka_w + Cka_w)} \tag{12.1}$$

where w is the equilibrium moisture content, fraction dry basis; w_m is the monolayer moisture content, fraction dry basis; C is the Guggenheim constant, $C' \exp(H_1 - H_m)/RT$; H_1 is heat of condensation of pure water vapor; H_m is total heat of sorption of the first layer on primary sites; k is a factor correcting properties of multilayer with respect to the bulk liquid, $k' \exp(H_1 - H_q)/RT$; and H_q is total heat of sorption of the multilayers.

The GAB model can be used to a maximum water activity of 0.9. The following procedure is suggested by Bizot (1983) to fit data on water activities and equilibrium moisture content.

Equation (12.1) can be transformed as follows:

$$\frac{a_w}{w} = \alpha a_w^2 + \beta a_w + \gamma \tag{12.2}$$

where

$$\alpha = \frac{k}{w_m}\left[\frac{1}{C} - 1\right]$$

$$\beta = \frac{1}{w_m}\left[1 - \frac{2}{C}\right]$$

$$\gamma = \frac{1}{w_m Ck}$$

Equation (12.2) indicates that GAB equation is a three-parameter model. The water activity and equilibrium moisture content data are regressed using Eq. (12.2), and values of three coefficients α, β, and γ are obtained. From these coefficients, the values of k, w_m, and C can be obtained.

EXAMPLE 12.1

A dry food product has been exposed to a 30% relative-humidity environment at 15°C for 5 hr without a weight change. The moisture content has been measured and is at 7.5% (wet basis). The product is moved to a 50% relative-humidity environment, and a weight increase of 0.1 kg/kg product occurs before equilibrium is achieved.

(a) Determine the water activity of the product in the first and second environments.

(b) Compute the moisture contents of the product on a dry basis in both environments.

GIVEN

Equilibrium relative humidity = 30% in first environment
Product moisture content = 7.5% wet basis in first environment
For 30% relative-humidity environment, moisture content will be 0.075 kg H₂O/kg product.

APPROACH

Water activities of product are determined by dividing equilibrium relative humidity by 100. Dry-basis moisture contents for product are computed by expressing mass of water in product on a per unit dry solids basis.

SOLUTION

(1) The water activity of the food product is equilibrium relative humidity divided by 100; the water activities are 0.3 in the first environment and 0.5 in the second.

(2) The dry basis moisture content of the product at equilibrium in 30% RH is

$$7.5\% = \frac{7.5 \text{ kg H}_2\text{O}}{100 \text{ kg product}} = 0.075 \text{ kg H}_2\text{O/kg product}$$

or

$$\frac{0.075 \text{ kg H}_2\text{O/product}}{0.925 \text{ kg solids/kg product}} = 0.08108 \text{ kg H}_2\text{O/kg solids}$$

$$= 8.11\% \text{ MC (dry basis)}$$

(3) Based on weight gain at 50% RH,

$$0.075 \text{ kg H}_2\text{O/kg product} + 0.1 \text{ kg H}_2\text{O/kg product}$$

$$= 0.175 \text{ kg H}_2\text{O/kg product} = 17.5\% \text{ MC (wet basis)}$$

or

$$0.175 \text{ kg H}_2\text{O/kg product} = 0.212 \frac{\text{kg H}_2\text{O}}{\text{kg solids}} = 21.2\% \text{ MC (dry basis)}$$

12.1.2 Moisture Diffusion

Significant amounts of moisture removal from a food product will occur due to diffusion of liquid and/or water vapor through the product structure. This stage of moisture movement will follow the evaporation of water at some location within the product, and rates of diffusion can be estimated by mechanisms used to describe molecular diffusion. The mass flux for moisture movement becomes a function of the vapor pressure gradient as well as diffusivity for water vapor in air, distance of movement, and temperature. Since heat is required for moisture evaporation, the process becomes simultaneous heat and mass transfer.

The moisture removal from the product will depend, in part, on convective mass transfer at the product surface. Although this transport process may not be rate-limiting, the importance of maintaining the optimum boundary conditions for moisture transport cannot be overlooked.

12.1.3 Drying-Rate Curves

The removal of moisture from a typical food product will follow a series of drying rates, as illustrated in Fig. 12.3. The initial removal of moisture (AB) occurs as the product and the water within the product experience a slight temperature increase. Following the initial stages of drying, significant reductions in moisture content will occur at a constant rate (BC) and at a constant temperature. This stage of drying occurs with the product at the wet bulb temperature of the air. In most situations, the constant-rate drying period will stop at the critical moisture content, and one or more falling-rate

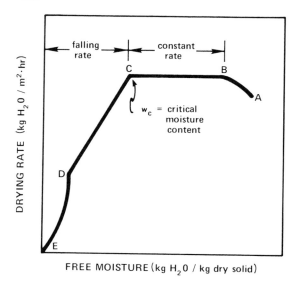

Fig. 12.3 Illustration of constant-rate and falling-rate drying periods. [Adapted from Heldman and Singh (1981).]

drying periods (CD) will follow. The critical moisture content should be well defined due to the abrupt change in the mode of moisture removal.

12.1.4 Heat and Mass Transfer

As indicated previously, the removal of moisture from a food product involves simultaneous heat and mass transfer. Heat transfer occurs within the product structure and is related to the temperature gradient between the product surface and the water surface at some location within the product. As sufficient thermal energy is added to the water to cause evaporation, the vapors are transported from the water surface within the product to the product surface. The gradient causing moisture-vapor diffusion is vapor pressure at the water surface, compared to vapor pressure of air at the product surface. The heat and the mass transfer within the product structure occurs at the molecular level, with heat transfer being limited by thermal conductivity of the product structure, while mass transfer is proportional to the molecular diffusion of water vapor in air.

At the product surface, simultaneous heat and mass transfer occurs but is controlled by convective processes. The transport of vapor from the product surface to the air and the transfer of heat from the air to the product surface is a function of the existing vapor pressure and temperature gradients, respectively.

Since the drying rate is directly proportional to the slowest of the four processes, it is important to account for all processes. In most products, the heat and mass transfer within the product structure will be the rate-limiting processes.

EXAMPLE 12.2

The initial moisture content of a food product is 77% (wet basis), and the critical moisture content is 30% (wet basis). If the constant drying rate is 0.1 kg $H_2O/m^2 \cdot s$, compute the time required for the product to begin the falling-rate drying period. The product has a cube shape with 5-cm sides, and the initial product density is 950 kg/m^3.

GIVEN

Initial moisture content = 77% wet basis
Critical moisture content = 30% wet basis
Drying rate for constant rate period = 0.1 kg $H_2O/m^2 \cdot s$
Product size = cube with 5-cm sides
Initial product density = 950 kg/m^3

APPROACH

The time for constant-rate drying will depend on mass of water removed and the rate of water removal. Mass of water removed must be expressed on dry basis, and rate of water removal must account for product surface area.

SOLUTION

(1) The initial moisture content is

$$0.77 \text{ kg } H_2O/\text{kg product} = 3.35 \text{ kg } H_2O/\text{kg solids}$$

(2) The critical moisture content is

$$0.3 \text{ kg } H_2O/\text{kg product} = 0.43 \text{ kg } H_2O/\text{kg solids}$$

(3) The amount of moisture to be removed from product during constant-rate drying will be

$$3.35 - 0.43 = 2.92 \text{ kg } H_2O/\text{kg solids}$$

(4) The surface area of the product during drying will be

$$0.05 \text{ m} \times 0.05 \text{ m} = 2.5 \times 10^{-3} \text{ m}^2/\text{side}$$

$$2.5 \times 10^{-3} \times 6 \text{ sides} = 0.015 \text{ m}^2$$

(5) The drying rate becomes

$$0.1 \text{ kg } H_2O/m^2 \cdot s \times 0.015 \text{ m}^2 = 1.5 \times 10^{-3} \text{ kg } H_2O/s$$

(6) Using the product density, the initial product mass can be established.

$$950 \text{ kg/m}^3 \times (0.05)^3 \text{ m}^3 = 0.11875 \text{ kg product}$$

$$0.11875 \text{ kg product} \times 0.23 \text{ kg solid/kg product} = 0.0273 \text{ kg solid}$$

(7) The total amount of water to be removed becomes

2.92 kg H_2O/kg solids $\times$ 0.0273 kg solids = 0.07975 kg H_2O

(8) Using the drying rate, the time for constant-rate drying becomes

$$\frac{0.07975 \text{ kg } H_2O}{1.5 \times 10^{-3} \text{ kg } H_2O/s} = 53.2 \text{ s}$$

12.2 Dehydration Systems

Based on the analysis of heat and mass transfer, the most efficient dehydration systems will maintain the maximum vapor-pressure gradient and maximum temperature gradient between the air and the interior parts of the product. These conditions along with high convective coefficents at the product surface can be maintained in several different designs of dehydration systems. The systems to be described are representative of the systems used for dehydration of foods.

12.2.1 Tray or Cabinet Dryers

These types of drying systems utilize trays or similar product holders to expose the product to heated air in an enclosed space. The trays holding the product inside a cabinet or similar enclosure (Fig. 12.4) are exposed to heated air so that the dehydration will proceed. Air movement over the

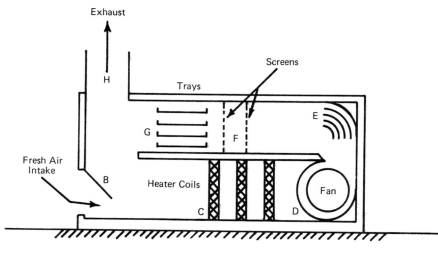

Fig. 12.4 Schematic of a cabinet-type tray dryer. [From Van Arsdel *et al.* (1973).]

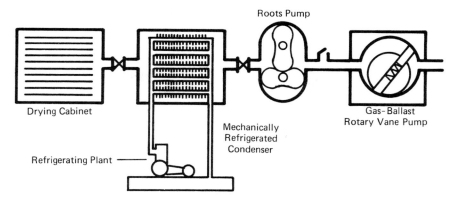

Fig. 12.5 Cabinet dryer with vacuum. [From Potter (1978).]

product surface is at relatively high velocities to ensure that heat and mass transfer will proceed in an efficient manner.

A slight variation of the cabinet dryer incorporates a vacuum within the chamber (Fig. 12.5). This type of dehydration system uses a vacuum to maintain the lowest possible vapor pressure in the space around the product. The reduction in pressure also reduces the temperature at which product moisture evaporates, resulting in improvements in product quality.

In most cases, cabinet dryers are operated as batch systems and have the disadvantages of nonuniform drying of a product at different locations within the system. Normally, rotation of the product trays is required, to improve uniformity of drying.

12.2.2 Tunnel Dryers

The dehydration system illustrated in Figs. 12.6 and 12.7 are examples of tunnel drying. As is evident, the heated drying air is introduced at one end of the tunnel and moves at an established velocity through trays of products

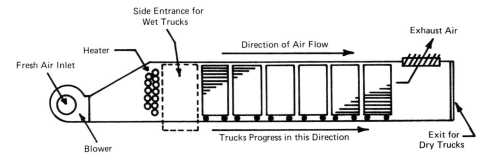

Fig. 12.6 Schematic of a concurrent-flow tunnel dryer. [From Van Arsdel (1951).]

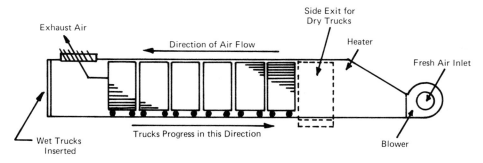

Fig. 12.7 Schematic of a counter current-flow tunnel dryer. [From Van Arsdel (1951).]

being carried on trucks. The product trucks are moved through the tunnel at a rate required to maintain the residence time needed for dehydration. The product can be moved in the same direction as the air flow to provide concurrent dehydration (Fig. 12.6), or the tunnel can be operated in a countercurrent manner (Fig. 12.7) with product moving in the direction opposite to air flow. The arrangement utilized will depend on the product and the sensitivity of quality characteristics to temperature.

With concurrent systems, high-moisture product is exposed to high-temperature air and evaporation assists in maintaining lower product temperature. At locations near the tunnel exit, the lower-moisture product is exposed to lower temperature air. In countercurrent systems, lower-moisture product is exposed to high-temperature air and a smaller temperature gradient exists near the product entrance to the tunnel. Although the overall efficiency of the countercurrent system may be higher than the concurrent, product quality considerations may not allow its use. The concept of air recirculation is utilized whenever possible to conserve energy.

12.2.3 Puff Drying

A relatively new process that has been applied successfully to several different fruits and vegetables is explosion puff-drying. The process is accomplished by exposing a relatively small piece of product to high pressure and high temperature for a short time. After the short time period, the product is moved to atmospheric pressure, resulting in flash evaporation of water and escape of the vapors from interior parts of the product. The product produced by puff-drying has very high porosity with rapid rehydration characteristics. Puff-drying is particularly effective for products with significant falling-rate drying periods. The rapid moisture evaporation and resulting product porosity contribute to rapid moisture removal during the final stages of drying.

The puff-drying process is accomplished most efficiently by using three-quarter-inch cube shapes. These pieces will dry rapidly and uniformly

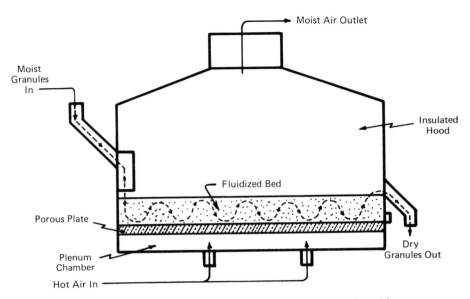

Fig. 12.8 Schematic illustration of a fluidized-bed dryer. [From Joslyn (1963).]

and will rehydrate within 15 minutes. Although the process may not have applications for all foods, the superior quality encourages additional investigation of the process.

12.2.4 Fluidized - Bed Drying

A second relatively new design for drying solid-particle foods incorporates the concept of the fluidized bed. In this system, the product pieces are suspended in the heated air throughout the time required for drying. As illustrated in Fig. 12.8, the movement of product through the system is enhanced by the change in mass of individual particles as moisture is evaporated. The movement of the product created by fluidized particles results in equal drying from all product surfaces. The primary limitation to the fluidized-bed process is the size of particles that will allow efficient drying. As would be expected, smaller particles can be maintained in suspensions with lower air velocities and will dry more rapidly. Although these are desirable characteristics, not all products can be adapted to the process.

12.2.5 Spray Drying

The drying of liquid food products is often accomplished in a spray dryer. Moisture removal from a liquid food occurs after the liquid is atomized or sprayed into heated air within a drying chamber. Although various config-

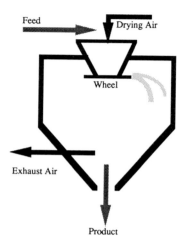

Feed

Drying Air

Wheel

Exhaust Air

Product

Fig. 12.9   Schematic illustration of a spray drying system.

urations of the chamber are utilized, the arrangement shown in Fig. 12.9 illustrates the introduction of liquid droplets into a heated air stream.

While the liquid food droplets are moving with the heated air, the water evaporates and is carried away by the air. Much of the drying occurs during a constant-rate period and is limited by mass transfer at the droplet surface. After reaching the critical moisture content, the dry food particle structure influences the falling-rate drying period. During this portion of the process, moisture diffusion within the particle becomes the rate-limiting parameter.

After the dry food particles leave the drying chamber, the product is separated from air in a cyclone separator. The dried product is then placed in a sealed container at moisture contents that are usually below 5%. Product quality is considered excellent due to the protection of product solids by evaporative cooling in the spray dryer. The small particle size of dried solids promotes easy reconstitution when mixed with water.

12.2.6   Freeze Drying

By reduction of the product temperature so that most of the product moisture is in a solid state and by decreasing the pressure around the product, sublimation of ice can be achieved. Freeze drying of many foods is utilized, especially when the quality achieved by using the process is important to consumer acceptance.

The heat- and mass-transfer processes during freeze drying are unique. Depending on the configuration of the drying system (Fig. 12.10), heat transfer can occur through a frozen product layer or through a dry product

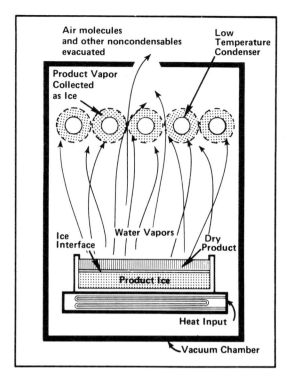

Fig. 12.10 Schematic of a freeze-drying system. (Courtesy of The Vitris Company, Inc.)

layer. Obviously, heat transfer through the frozen layer will be rapid and not rate-limiting. Heat transfer through the dry product layer will be at a slow rate due to the low thermal conductivity of the highly porous structure in a vacuum. In both situations, the mass transfer will occur in the dry product layer. The diffusion of water vapor would be expected to be the rate-limiting process due to the low rates of molecular diffusion in a vacuum.

The advantages of the freeze-drying process are superior product quality due to low temperature during sublimation and the maintenance of product structure. These advantages are balanced against the energy-intensive aspects of the product freezing and vacuum requirements.

12.3   Dehydration System Design

The design of dehydration systems involves several considerations. The parameters that have a direct influence on capacity of a system include the quantity and characteristics of air available for drying, along with the

Fig. 12.11   Mass and energy balance for dehydration process.

drying time required for individual pieces of the product being dried. These parameters require somewhat different approaches to analysis.

12.3.1   Mass and Energy Balance

By application of mass and energy balance analysis to an entire dehydration system, as illustrated in Fig. 12.11, several parameters influencing design are accounted for. Although the analysis being conducted is for a countercurrent system, a similar approach could be applied to a concurrent system or a batch system.

An overall moisture balance on the system gives

$$\dot{m}_a W_2 + \dot{m}_p w_1 = \dot{m}_a W_1 + \dot{m}_p w_2 \qquad (12.3)$$

where $\dot{m}_a$ is air flow rate (kg dry air/hr);
$\quad\quad \dot{m}_p$ is product flow rate (kg dry solids/hr);
$\quad\quad W$ is absolute humidity (kg water/kg dry air);
$\quad\quad$ and w is product moisture content (kg water/kg dry solids).

EXAMPLE 12.3

A cabinet dryer is being used to dry a food product from 68% moisture content (wet basis) to 5.5% moisture content (wet basis). The drying air enters the system at 54°C and 10% RH and leaves at 30°C and 70% RH. The product temperature is 25°C throughout drying. Compute the quantity of air required for drying on the basis of 1 kg of product solids.

GIVEN

Initial product moisture content $w_1 = 0.68/0.32 = 2.125$ kg H_2O/kg solids
Final product moisture content $w_2 = 0.055/0.945 = 0.0582$ kg H_2O/kg solids
Air entering dryer = 54°C and 10% RH
Air leaving dryer = 30°C and 70% RH
Product temperature = 25°C
Computations based on 1 kg product solids

APPROACH

The air requirements for drying can be determined by using Eq. (12.3) with the following modification:

$$(\dot{m}_a/\dot{m}_p)W_2 + w_1 = (\dot{m}_a/\dot{m}_p)W_1 + w_2$$

SOLUTION

(1) Using Appendix A.5

$W_1 = 0.0186$ kg H_2O/kg dry air (using 30°C and 70% RH)

$W_2 = 0.0094$ kg H_2O/kg dry air (using 54°C and 10% RH)

(2) Using the modification of Eq. (12.3),

$\dot{m}_a/\dot{m}_p(0.0094$ kg H_2O/kg dry air$) + 2.125$ kg H_2O/kg solids

$= \dot{m}_a/\dot{m}_p(0.0186$ kg H_2O/kg dry air$) + 0.0582$ kg H_2O/kg solids

$0.0092\dot{m}_a/\dot{m}_p = 2.067$

$\dot{m}_a/\dot{m}_p = 224.65$ kg dry air/kg solids

An energy balance for the dehydration system leads to the relationship

$$\dot{m}_a H_{a2} + \dot{m}_p H_{p1} = \dot{m}_a H_{a1} + \dot{m}_p H_{p2} + q \qquad (12.4)$$

where q is heat loss from the dehydration system;
H_a is the heat content of air (kJ/kg dry air);
and H_p is the heat content of product (kJ/kg dry solids).
Expressions for heat content of air and product are as follows:

$$H_a = c_s(T_a - T_0) + WH_L \qquad (12.5)$$

where c_s is humid heat (kJ/kg dry air · K) = $1.005 + 1.88W$;
T_a is air temperature (°C);
T_0 is the reference temperature (0°C);
H_L is latent heat of vaporization for water (kJ/kg water); and

$$H_p = c_{pp}(T_p - T_0) + wc_{pw}(T_p - T_0) \qquad (12.6)$$

where c_{pp} is specific heat of product solids (kJ/kg · K);
T_p is product temperature (°C);
and c_{pw} is specific heat of water.
Using these equations, the quantity of air required for drying an established amount of product over a known inlet condition of air, the moisture characteristics of air at the system outlet can be established.

EXAMPLE 12.4

A fluidized-bed dryer is being used to dry diced carrots. The product enters the dryer with 60% moisture content (wet basis) at 25°C. The air used for drying enters the dryer at 120°C after being heated from ambient air with 60% RH at 20°C. Estimate the production rate when air is entering the dryer at 700 kg dry air/hr and product leaving the dryer is at 10% moisture content (wet basis). Assume product leaves the dryer at the wet bulb temperature of air and the specific heat of product solid is 2.0 kJ/kg $\cdot$ °C. Air leaves the dryer 10°C above the product temperature.

GIVEN

Initial product moisture content $w_1 = 0.6/0.4 = 1.5$ kg H_2O/kg solids
Initial air condition = 20°C and 60% RH ($W_2 = 0.009$ kg H_2O/kg dry air)
Air temperature entering dryer = 120°C
Air flow rate $\dot{m}_a = 700$ kg dry air/hr
Final product moisture content (w_2) $= 0.1/0.9 = 0.111$ kg H_2O/kg solids
Specific heat of product solids (c_{pp}) = 2.0 kJ/kg $\cdot$ K
Final product temperature = wet bulb temperature of air
Final air temperature (T_{a1}) $= T_{p2} + 10°C$

APPROACH

The product production rate will be determined using the material balance, Eq. (12.3), and the energy balance, Eq. (12.4), along with parameters obtained from the psychrometric chart (Appendix A.5).

SOLUTION

(1) Using Eq. (12.3):

(700 kg dry air/hr)(0.009 kg water/kg dry air) $+ \dot{m}_p$ (1.5 kg water/kg solids)

$\quad = $ (700 kg dry air/hr) $W_1 + \dot{m}_p$ (0.111 kg water/kg solids)

(2) To use Eq. (12.4), the following computations are required from Eqs. (12.5) and (12.6):

For the air:

$$H_{a2} = c_{s2}(120 - 0) + 0.009 H_{L2}$$

where

$$c_{s2} = 1.005 + 1.88(0.009) = 1.0219 \text{ kJ/kg dry air} \cdot \text{K}$$

$$H_{L2} = 2202.59 \text{ kJ/kg water at } 120°C \text{ (from Table A.4.2)}$$

Therefore,

$$H_{a2} = (1.0219 \text{ kJ/kg dry air} \cdot \text{K}) (120°C)$$

$$+ (0.009 \text{ kg water/kg dry air})(2202.59 \text{ kJ/kg water})$$

$$H_{a2} = 142.45 \text{ kJ/kg dry air}$$

since $T_{p2} = 38°C$ [wet bulb temperature of air (Appendix A.5)]

$$T_{a1} = 38 + 10 = 48°C$$

Then,

$$H_{a1} = c_{s1}(T_{a1} - 0) + W_1(H_{L1})$$

where

$$c_{s1} = 1.005 + 1.88W_1$$

and

$$H_{L1} = 2387.56 \text{ kJ/kg water at } 48°C \text{ (from Table A.4.2)}$$

Therefore,

$$H_{a1} = (1.005 + 1.88\ W_1)(48°C) + W_1(2387.56 \text{ kJ/kg water})$$

For the product:

$$H_{p1} = (2.0 \text{ kJ/kg solids} \cdot \text{K})(25°C - 0)$$
$$+ (1.5 \text{ kg water/kg solids})(4.178 \text{ kJ/kg water} \cdot \text{K})(25°C - 0)$$

Then $H_{p1} = 206.75$ kJ/kg solids

$$H_{p2} = (2.0 \text{ kJ/kg solids} \cdot \text{K})(T_{p2}°C - 0)$$
$$+ (0.111 \text{ kg water/kg solids})(4.175 \text{ kJ/kg water} \cdot \text{K})(T_{p2}°C - 0)$$

Then from Eq. (12.4)

$$(700 \text{ kg dry air/hr})(142.45 \text{ kJ/kg dry air}) + \dot{m}_p(206.75 \text{ kJ/kg solids})$$
$$= (700 \text{ kg dry air/hr})[(1.005 + 1.88W_1)(48°C)$$
$$+ W_1(2387.56 \text{ kJ/kg water})]$$
$$+ \dot{m}_p[(2.0 \text{ kJ/kg solids} \cdot \text{K})(38°C)$$
$$+ (0.111 \text{ kg water/kg solids})(4.175 \text{ kJ/kg water} \cdot \text{K})(38°C)] + 0$$

where $q = 0$, indicating negligible heat loss from surface of dryer.

(3) The material-balance (step 2) and energy-balance (step 3) equations can be solved simultaneously:

(a) $700(0.009) + 1.5\dot{m}_p = 700W_1 + 0.111\dot{m}_p$
(b) $700(142.45) + \dot{m}_p(206.75) = 700[(1.005 + 1.88W_1)(48) + 2387.56W_1] + \dot{m}_p[(2.0)(38) + (0.111)(4.175)(38)]$
(a) $6.3 + 1.5\dot{m}_p = 700W_1 + 0.111\dot{m}_p$
(b) $99715 + 206.75\dot{m}_p = 700(48.24 + 2477.8W_1) + 93.61\dot{m}_p$
(a) $W_1 = (1.389\dot{m}_p + 6.3)/700$
(b) $65947 + 113.14\dot{m}_p = 1734460W_1$

Then

$$65947 + 113.14\dot{m}_p = 1734460(1.389\dot{m}_p + 6.3)/700$$
$$\dot{m}_p = 15.12 \text{ kg solids/hr}$$

(4) The absolute humidity of air leaving the dryer is

$$W_1 = (1.389 \times 15.12 + 6.3)/700$$
$$= 0.039 \text{ kg water/kg dry air}$$

indicating that air leaving the dryer will be 48°C and 55% RH.

12.3.2 Drying-Time Prediction

To determine the time required to achieve the desired reduction in product moisture content, the rate of moisture removal from the product must be predicted. For the constant-rate drying period, the following general expression would apply:

$$R_c = \frac{dw}{dt} = \frac{w_0 - w_c}{t_c} \tag{12.7}$$

where w_c is critical moisture content (kg water/kg dry solids) and t_c is time for constant-rate drying.

During falling-rate drying, the following analysis would exist:

$$-\frac{dw}{dt} = \frac{R_c}{w_c}(w) \tag{12.8}$$

or

$$-\frac{w_c}{R_c}\int_{w_c}^{w}\frac{dw}{w} = \int_{t_c}^{t} dt \tag{12.9}$$

where the limits of integration are between the critical moisture content w_c or end of constant-rate drying t_c and some desired final moisture content w. Integration of Eq. (12.9) leads to

$$t - t_c = \frac{w_c}{R_c}\ln\left(\frac{w_c}{w}\right) \tag{12.10}$$

or the time for falling-rate drying becomes

$$t_F = \frac{w_c}{R_c}\ln\left(\frac{w_c}{w}\right) \tag{12.11}$$

and the total drying time becomes

$$t = \frac{w_0 - w_c}{R_c} + \frac{w_c}{R_c}\ln\left(\frac{w_c}{w}\right) \tag{12.12}$$

Equation (12.12) indicates that the time for complete drying from some initial moisture content w_0 to a desired final moisture content w depends on knowledge of the critical moisture content w_c, the time for constant-rate drying t_c, and the rate for constant-rate drying R_c. Since most foods exhibit more than one falling-rate drying period, Eq. (12.12) will not describe the entire dehydration process, and additional experimental information will be required for accurate prediction of drying times.

EXAMPLE 12.5

A tunnel dryer is being designed for drying apple halves from an initial moisture content of 70% (wet basis) to a final moisture content of 5% (wet basis). An experimental drying curve for the product indicates that the critical moisture content is 25% (wet basis) and the time for constant-rate drying is 5 minutes. Based on information provided, estimate the total drying time for the product. Assume 1 kg of product as the basis.

GIVEN

Initial product moisture content $w_0 = 0.7/0.3 = 2.33$ kg H_2O/kg solids
Critical moisture content $w_c = 0.25/0.75 = 0.333$ kg H_2O/kg solids
Final moisture content $w = 0.05/0.95 = 0.0526$ kg H_2O/kg solids
Time for constant rate drying $t_c = 5$ minutes

APPROACH

The total drying time will be the time for constant-rate drying plus time for the falling-rate drying. By using Eq. (12.7) and Eq. (12.11), the required parameters can be determined.

SOLUTION

(1) Using Eq. (12.7),

$$R_c = \frac{(2.33 \text{ kg } H_2O/\text{kg solids} - 0.33 \text{ kg } H_2O/\text{kg solids})}{(5 \text{ minutes})}$$

$$= 0.4 \text{ kg } H_2O/\text{kg solids minute}$$

(2) Using Eq. (12.11),

$$t_F = \frac{(0.333 \text{ kg } H_2O/\text{kg solids})}{(0.4 \text{ kg } H_2O/\text{kg solids} \cdot \text{min})} \ln\left(\frac{0.333 \text{ kg } H_2O/\text{kg solids}}{0.0526 \text{ kg } H_2O/\text{kg solids}}\right)$$

$$= 1.54 \text{ minutes}$$

(3) Total drying time becomes

$$t = 5 + 1.54 = 6.54 \text{ minutes}$$

Expressions for predicting constant-rate drying are a function of several parameters and may be rate-limited by heat transfer or mass transfer. Often, this phase of drying is described by evaporation from a free water surface, and rates are a function of convective heat-transfer coefficients or convective mass-transfer coefficients at the surface of the product.

An example of a drying process where the rate is limited by the evaporation from a free water surface is spray drying. Within the drying chamber, the droplets of liquid food are moving through heated air, causing water at the droplet surface to change to vapor. The water vapor is carried away from the droplet surface by heated air. The constant rate drying of the droplet is limited by heat and mass transfer at the droplet surface.

During the constant-rate period of drying, a spray drying process may be limited by heat transfer from the heated air to the droplet surface or by mass transfer from the droplet surface to the heated air. If the process is limited by heat transfer, the convective heat transfer coefficient may be estimated by Eq. (4.42). For situations controlled by mass transfer, the mass transfer coefficient is estimated by Eq. (11.35). The similarity between the expressions used to estimate the surface coefficients should be noted.

During the falling-rate drying periods, the rate of spray drying is controlled by heat and mass transfer within the product particle structure. For a heat transfer limited process, the heat transfer is by conduction through the product and will be a function of thermal conductivity of the product solids. Alternatively, mass transfer occurs by diffusion of water vapor through the porous structure of the product particle.

The heat transfer can be described by expressions given in Section 4.5.3, while mass transfer would be estimated by an equation similar to Eq. (11.9). Expressions to estimate rate of spray drying have been derived by Ranz and Marshall (1952) and they are based on equations presented previously. The most useable equation is

$$t = \frac{\rho_L H_L d_0^2}{8 k_a (T_a - T_w)} + \frac{\rho_P d_c^2 H_L (w_c - w_e)}{12 k_a \Delta T_{ave}} \qquad (12.13)$$

where ρ_L is the density of the liquid (kg/m^3); H_L is latent heat of vaporization (kJ/kg water); d_0 is the initial diameter of the droplet (m); k_a is the thermal conductivity of air (W/m K); T_a is the air temperature (°C); T_w is the wet bulb temperature (°C); ρ_P is the density of product solids (kg/m^3); d_c is the droplet diameter at critical moisture content (m); w_c is the critical moisture content (kg water/kg dry solids); w_e is the final moisture content (kg water/kg solids); and ΔT_{ave} is the average temperature difference between air and product (°C).

In Eq. (12.13) the first term on the right side of the equation is the time for the constant-rate drying period. The second term represents the time for falling rate drying. One of the critical parameters in Eq. (12.13) is the droplet diameter (d_c) at the critical moisture content (w_c). Although these two parameters are most often established through experimental measurements, most other inputs required for Eq. (12.13) can be obtained from handbooks or tables of properties.

EXAMPLE 12.6

A concentrated dairy product is being spray dried to a final moisture content of 4% using 120°C heated air with 7% RH. The density of the concentrated liquid is 1000 kg/m^3 and the density of the dry product is 1250 kg/m^3. Separate measurements have indicated that the critical moisture content for the product is 0.45 kg water/kg product and the particle diameter at the critical moisture content is 45 μm. The latent heat of vaporization during the constant rate period of the drying is 2150 kJ/kg and it is 2375 kJ/kg during the falling rate period. Estimate the drying time for the product based on the largest droplet diameter of 120 μm.

GIVEN

Liquid density = 1000 kg/m^3
Latent heat of vaporization = 2150 kJ/kg (constant rate)
Initial droplet diameter = 120 μm = 120 $\times$ 10^{-6} m
Thermal conductivity of air = 0.032 W/m K (from Table A.4.4)
Air temperature = 120°C
Product density = 1250 kg/m^3
Critical droplet diameter = 45 μm = 45 $\times$ 10^{-6} m
Latent heat of vaporization = 2375 kJ/kg (falling rate period)
Critical moisture content = 0.45 kg water/kg product
                = 0.818 kg water/kg solids
Final moisture content = 0.04 kg water/kg product
                = 0.042 kg water/kg solids

APPROACH

We will estimate the drying time for the product using Eq. (12.13)

SOLUTION

(1) In order to use Eq. (12.13), the temperature at the droplet surface must be estimated. During the constant rate drying period, this temperature will become the wet bulb temperature of the heated air. Using the psychrometric chart (Appendix A.5), the wet bulb temperature is obtained as 57.1°C, using the dry bulb temperature of 120°C and relative humidity of 7%.

(2) During the falling rate drying period, the average temperature difference between the air and product is determined by using the temperature difference at the critical moisture content (120 − 57.1) and the temperature difference at the end of drying (0°C).

$$\Delta T_{ave} = \frac{(120 - 57.1) + 0}{2} = 31.45°C$$

(3) Using Eq. (12.13)

$$t = \frac{(1000 \text{ kg/m}^3)(2150 \text{ kJ/kg})(120 \times 10^{-6} \text{ m})^2(1000 \text{ J/kJ})}{8(0.032 \text{ W/m K})(120 - 57.1)\text{K}}$$

$$+ \left[\frac{(1250 \text{ kg/m}^3)(45 \times 10^{-6} \text{ m})^2(2375 \text{ kJ/kg})(1000 \text{ J/kJ})}{12(0.032 \text{ W/m K})(31.45 \text{ K})} \right]$$

$$\times [0.818 \text{ kg water/kg solids} - 0.042 \text{ kg water/kg solids}]$$

$$t = 1.92 + 0.39 = 2.31 \text{ s}$$

(4) The result indicates that the total time for spray drying is 2.31 s, with 1.92 s for the constant rate period and 0.39 s for the falling rate portion of drying.

(5) The design of the spray drying chamber must account for the time required for drying of the largest droplet produced by the atomizing system.

A more accurate description of falling-rate drying requires better definition of the processes occurring within the product structure. Estimates have involved use of diffusion coefficients for liquid and/or vapor within a porous material. Most of these procedures require knowledge of the equilibrium moisture content or the limiting condition for moisture removal from the product in air with known humidity characteristics.

A drying process that illustrates the type of drying when the drying rate is limited by internal mass transfer is freeze drying. An analysis of the heat and mass transfer for the system in Fig. 12.10 is simplified, since heat transfer occurs from the hot plate to the drying front through the frozen product layer. The moisture produced at the drying front diffuses through the layer of dry product, and moisture diffusion becomes the rate limiting process.

The heat and mass transfer during freeze drying as illustrated in Fig. 12.10 has been analyzed by King (1970, 1973). His analysis provided an equation for estimating the drying time as follows:

$$t = \frac{RT_A L^2}{8DMV_W(p_I - p_a)}\left(1 + \frac{4D}{k_m L}\right) \qquad (12.14)$$

where L is the thickness of product layer (m); T_A is the absolute temperature (K); M is the molecular weight (kg/kg mole); V_W is the specific volume of water (m^3/kg water); P_I is the vapor pressure of ice (Pa); P_a is the vapor pressure of air at the condenser surface (Pa); k_m is the mass transfer coefficient (kg mole/s m^2 Pa); R is universal gas constant (8314.41 m^3 Pa/kg mole K); and D is the diffusion coefficient (m^2/s).

Equation (12.14) is limited to situations where the drying time is based on a process whose rate is limited by moisture diffusion within the structure of the dry product layer. The calculation of drying time requires knowledge of the moisture diffusivity (D) and the mass transfer coefficient (k_m), and the magnitude of both are likely to be product dependent. Often, these property values must be measured for individual situations.

EXAMPLE 12.7

A concentrated liquid coffee is being freeze dried by placing a 2 cm thick frozen layer of the product over a heated platen. The product is frozen to $-75°C$ initially and before placing over the 30°C platen. The freeze drying is accomplished in a chamber at a pressure of 38.11 Pa with a condenser temperature of $-65°C$. Properties needed to describe the process have been measured in an experimental system; mass diffusivity $= 2 \times 10^{-3}$ m^2/s and mass transfer coefficient $= 1.5$ kg mole/s m^2 Pa. The initial moisture content of the concentrate is 40% and the density of dry product solids is 1400 kg/m^3. Compute the drying time for the product.

GIVEN

Thickness of product layer = 2 cm = 0.02 m
Mass diffusivity $= 2 \times 10^{-3}$ m^2/s
Mass transfer coefficient = 1.5 kg mole/s m^2 Pa

APPROACH

We will compute the drying time for the coffee concentrate by using Eq. (12.14)

SOLUTION

(1) To use Eq. (12.14), several parameters must be determined from the thermodynamic tables.

Universal gas constant = 8314.41 m^3 Pa/kg mole K
Absolute temperature (T_A) = 243 K (based on ice temperature at pressure 38.11 Pa)
Vapor pressure of ice (P_I) = 38.11 Pa
Vapor pressure of condenser surface (P_a) = 0.5 Pa
Molecular weight of water (M_w) = 18

(2) The specific volume of water is computed from initial moisture content of product and density of product solids.

Moisture content (dry basis) = 0.4/0.6 = 0.667 kg water/kg solids

Then,

$$V_w = \frac{1}{(0.667)(1400)} = 0.00107 \frac{m^3 \text{ solid}}{kg \text{ water}}$$

(3) Using Eq. (12.14)

$$t = \frac{(8314.41)(243)(0.02)^2}{8(2 \times 10^{-3})(18)(0.00107)(38.11 - 0.5)}\left(1 + \frac{4(2 \times 10^{-3})}{(1.5)(0.02)}\right)$$

$$t = 88324 \text{ s} = 1472 \text{ min} = 24.5 \text{ hr}$$

The dehydration process for foods results in products with reduced mass and possible reductions in volume. These reductions provide for increased efficiency in transportation and storage, in addition to effective preservation. The selection of the most appropriate process for a given food product will depend on two primary considerations: cost of drying and product quality.

Of the processes discussed in this chapter, air drying by cabinet or tunnel would have the lowest cost when expressed as cost per unit of water removed. The use of vacuum increases the cost of water removal somewhat, and the value would be comparable to fluidized-bed drying. The explosion puff-drying process would be more costly than previously mentioned processes, but appears to be more efficient than freeze-drying.

The product quality resulting from the various processes will be opposite to the cost comparisons. The freeze-drying process produces the highest quality product and can be utilized for products where the quality characteristics allow product pricing at a level to recover the extra drying cost. Based on available literature, the puff-drying process produces quality that is comparable to freeze-drying with somewhat lower cost. The product quality resulting from fluidized-bed drying and vacuum drying should be somewhat similar to but lower than puff-drying and freeze-drying processes. The lowest quality dehydrated products are produced by the lowest cost processes—tunnel and cabinet drying using heated air. Although these comparisons suggest a direct trade-off between dehydration cost and dry product quality, it must be recognized that process selection will depend on adaptability of product to a given process. The physical characteristics of the product before and/or after drying may dictate the process utilized for dehydration.

Problems

12.1 The following equilibrium moisture-content data have been collected for a dry food:

Water activity	Equilibrium Moisture content (g H_2O/g product)
0.1	0.060
0.2	0.085
0.3	0.110
0.4	0.122
0.5	0.125
0.6	0.148
0.7	0.173
0.8	0.232

Develop a plot of the equilibrium moisture isotherm for moisture content on a dry weight basis.

12.2 A 50-μm-diameter droplet of a liquid food is being dried in a spray dryer. Experiments have indicated that the constant-rate drying period for this type of situation requires 2 s. If the product entering the spray dryer has 10% total solids and the critical moisture content is 35% (wet basis), determine the moisture removal rate during constant-rate drying. Assume droplet size does not change during the constant-rate period and the product density is 1050 kg/m³.

12.3 A product enters a tunnel dryer with 56% moisture content (wet basis) at a rate of 10 kg/hr. The tunnel is supplied with 1500 kg dry air/hr at 50°C and 10% RH, and the air leaves at 25°C in equilibrium with the product at 50% RH. Determine the moisture content of product leaving the dryer and the final water activity.

*__12.4__ A countercurrent tunnel dryer is being used to dry apple slices from an initial moisture content (wet basis) of 70% to 5%. The heated air

---

*Indicates an advanced level of difficulty in solving.

enters at 100°C with 1% RH and leaves at 50°C. If the product temperature is 20°C throughout the dryer and the specific heat of product solids is 2.2 kJ/kg · °C, determine the quantity of heated air required for drying the product at a rate of 100 kg/hr. Determine the relative humidity of outlet air.

12.5 A cabinet dryer is to be used for drying of a new food product. The product has an initial moisture content of 75% (wet basis) and requires 10 minutes to reduce the moisture content to a critical level of 30% (wet basis). Determine the final moisture of the product if a total drying time of 15 minutes is used.

12.6 The following data were obtained by Labuza *et al.* (1985) on fish flour at 25°C. Determine the GAB model for these data and the values of k, w_m, and C.

a_w	g water/100 g solids
0.115	2.12
0.234	3.83
0.329	5.53
0.443	6.82
0.536	7.65
0.654	10.29
0.765	13.40
0.848	17.50

12.7 Pistachios are to be dried using a countercurrent dryer operating at steady state. The nuts are dried from 80% (wet basis) to 12% (wet basis) at 25°C. Air enters the heater at 25°C (dry bulb temperature) and 80% relative humidity. The heater supplies 84 kJ/kg dry air. The air exits the dryer at 90% relative humidity. For this given information solve the following parts:

(a) What is the relative humidity of the air leaving the heater section of the dryer?
(b) What is the temperature (dry bulb temperature) of air leaving the dryer?
(c) What is the flow rate (m^3/s) of air required to dry 50 kg/hr of pistachio nuts?

12.8 It is desired to rehydrate 10 kg of dried apples (3% dry basis) to a moisture content of 70% wet basis.

(a) How much water must be added?
(b) What is the weight of the rehydrated apples?

12.9 A sample of a food material weighing 20 kg is initially at 450% moisture content dry basis. It is dried to 25% moisture content wet basis. How much water is removed from the sample per kg of dry solids?

12.10   Air enters a counter-flow drier at 60°C dry bulb temperature and
25°C dew point temperature. Air leaves the drier at 40°C and 60%
relative humidity. The initial moisture content of the product is
72% (wet basis). The amount of air moving through the drier is 200
kg of dry air/hr. The mass flow rate of the product is 1000 kg dry
solid per hour. What is the final moisture content of the dried
product (in wet basis)?

List of Symbols

a_w	water activity, dimensionless	k_a	thermal conductivity of air (W/m K)
α	constant in Eq. (12.2)		
β	constant in Eq. (12.2)	k_m	mass transfer coefficient (kg mole/s m^2 Pa)
C	Guggenheim constant		
c_p	specific heat (kJ/kg · K)	L	thickness of product layer (m)
c_{pp}	specific heat of product solids (kJ/kg · K)	M	molecular weight (kg/kg mole)
c_{pw}	specific heat of water (kJ/kg · K)	$\dot{m}$	flow rate (kg/s)
c_s	humid heat of air (kJ/kg · K)	p	vapor pressure (Pa)
		p_a	vapor pressure of air at the condenser surface (Pa)
D	diffusion coefficient (m^2/s)		
d_c	droplet diameter at critical moisture content (m)	p_I	vapor pressure of ice (Pa)
		q	heat loss (kJ/s)
d_0	initial diameter of the droplet (m)	R	universal gas constant (8314.41 m^3 Pa/ kg mole K)
ΔT_{ave}	average temperature difference between air and product (°C)		
		R_c	drying rate during constant period (kg H$_2$O/ kg solids · s)
g	constant in Eq. (12.2)		
H	heat content (kJ/kg)	ρ_L	density of the liquid (kg/m^3)
H_1	heat of condensation of pure water vapor (kJ)	ρ_P	density of product solids (kg/m^3)
H_L	latent heat of vaporization (kJ/kg water)	T	temperature (°C)
		t	time (s)
H_m	total heat of sorption of the first layer on the primary sites (kJ)	T_A	absolute temperature (K)
		T_a	air temperature (°C)
		T_w	wet bulb temperature (°C)
H_q	total heat of sorption of the multilayers (kJ)	V_W	specific volume of water (m^3/kg water)
k	correction factor in Eq. (12.1)	W	absolute humidity (kg H$_2$O/kg dry air)

w	moisture content	w_e	equilibrium moisture
	(kg H_2O/kg solids)		content (kg water/kg solids)
w_c	critical moisture content	w_m	monolayer moisture content
	(kg water/kg dry solids)		(kg water/kg solid)

Subscripts: a, air; c, constant rate or critical; p, product; w, water; 0, initial or reference; 1, entrance; and 2, exit.

Bibliography

Bizot, H. (1983). Using the GAB model to construct sorption isotherms. *In* "Physical Properties of Foods" (R. Jowitt, F. Escher, B. Hallstrom, H. Th. Meffert, W. E. L. Spiess, and G. Vos, eds.), pp. 43–54. Applied Science Publishers, London.

Charm, S. E. (1978). "The Fundamentals of Food Engineering," 3rd ed. AVI Publ. Co., Westport, Connecticut.

Eisenhardt, N. H., Cording, J., Jr., Eskew, R. K., and Sullivan, J. F. (1962). Quick-cooking dehydrated vegetable pieces. *Food Technol.* **16**(5), 143–146.

Fish, B. P. (1958). Diffusion and thermodynamics of water in potato starch gel. *In* "Fundamental Aspects of Dehydration of Foodstuffs," pp. 143–157. MacMillan, New York.

Flink, J. M. (1977). Energy analysis in dehydration processes. *Food Technol.* **31**(3), 77.

Forrest, J. C. (1968). Drying processes. *In* "Biochemical and Biological Engineering Science" (N. Blakebrough, ed.), pp. 97–135. Academic Press, New York.

Gorling, P. (1958). Physical phenomena during the drying of foodstuffs. *In* "Fundamental Aspects of the Dehydration of Foodstuffs," pp. 42–53. Macmillan, New York.

Heldman, D. R., and Hohner, G. A. (1974). Atmospheric freeze-drying processes of food. *J. Food Sci.* **39**, 147.

Jason, A. C. (1958). A study of evaporation and diffusion processes in the drying of fish muscle. *In* "Fundamental Aspects of the Dehydration of Foodstuffs," pp. 103–135. Macmillan, New York.

Joslyn, M. A. (1963). Food processing by drying and dehydration. *In* "Food Processing Operations": (M. A. Joslyn and J. L. Heid, eds.), Vol. 2, pp. 545–584. AVI Publ. Co., Westport, Connecticut.

King, C. J. (1970). Freeze-drying of foodstuffs. *CRC Crit. Rev. Food Technol.* **1**, 379.

King, C. J. (1973). Freeze-drying. *In* "Food Dehydration" (W. B. Van Arsdel, M. J. Copley, and A. I. Morgan, Jr., eds.), 2nd ed., Vol. 1, 161–200. AVI Publ. Co., Westport, Connecticut.

Labuza, T. P. (1968). Sorption phenomena in foods. *CRC Crit. Rev. Food Technol.* **2**, 355.

Labuza, T. P., Kaanane, A., and Chen, J. Y. (1985). Effect of temperature on the moisture sorption isotherms and water activity shift of two dehydrated foods. *J. Food Sci.* **50**, 385.

Potter, N. N. (1978). "Food Science," 3rd ed. AVI Publ. Co., Westport, Connecticut.

Ranz, W. E., and Marshall, W. R., Jr. (1952). Evaporation from drops. *Chem. Eng. Prog.* **48**, 141–180.

Rockland, L. B., and Nishi, S. K. (1980). Influence of water activity on food product quality and stability. *Food Technol.* **34**(4), 42–51.

Sherwood, T. K. (1929). Drying of solids. *Ind. Eng. Chem.* **21**, 12.

Sherwood, T. K. (1931). Application of theoretical diffusion equations to the drying of solids. *Trans. Am. Inst. Chem. Eng.* **27**, 190.

Van Arsdel, W. B. (1951). Tunnel-and-truck dehydrators, as used for dehydrating vegetables. *USDA Agric. Res. Admin. Pub.* **AIC-308**. Washington, D.C.

Van Arsdel, W. B., Copley, M. J., and Morgan, A. I., Jr., eds. (1973). "Food Dehydration," 2nd ed., Vol. 1 AVI Publ. Co., Westport, Connecticut.

Appendices

A.1 SI System of Units and Conversion Factors

A.1.1 *Rules for Using SI Units*

The following rules for SI usage are based on recommendations from several international conferences, the International Organization for Standardization, and the American Society of Agricultural Engineers.

SI Prefixes

The prefixes along with the SI symbols are given in Table A.1.1. The prefix symbols are printed in roman (upright) type without spacing between the prefix symbol and the unit symbol. The prefixes provide an order of magnitude, thus eliminating insignificant digits and decimals. For example,

$$19{,}200 \text{ m or } 19.2 \times 10^3 \text{ m} \quad \text{becomes} \quad 19.2 \text{ km}$$

An exponent attached to a symbol containing a prefix indicates that the multiple or submultiple of the unit is raised to the power expressed by the exponent. For example,

$$1 \text{ mm}^3 = \left(10^{-3} \text{ m}\right)^3 = 10^{-9} \text{ m}^3$$

$$1 \text{ cm}^{-1} = \left(10^{-2} \text{ m}\right)^{-1} = 10^2 \text{ m}^{-1}$$

Compound prefixes, formed by the juxtaposition of two or more SI prefixes, are not to be used. For example,

$$1 \text{ nm} \quad \text{but not} \quad 1 \text{ m}\mu\text{m}$$

TABLE A.1.1
SI Prefixes

Factor	Prefix	Symbol	Factor	Prefix	Symbol
10^{18}	exa	E	10^{-1}	deci	d
10^{15}	peta	P	10^{-2}	centi	c
10^{12}	tera	T	10^{-3}	milli	m
10^{9}	giga	G	10^{-6}	micro	μ
10^{6}	mega	M	10^{-9}	nano	n
10^{3}	kilo	k	10^{-12}	pico	p
10^{2}	hecto	h	10^{-15}	femto	f
10^{1}	deka	da	10^{-18}	atto	a

Among the base units, the unit of mass is the only one whose name, for historical reasons, contains a prefix. To obtain names of decimal multiples and submultiples of the unit mass, attach prefixes to the word "gram."

Attach prefixes to the numerator of compound units, except when using "kilogram" in the denominator. For example, use

$$550 \text{ J/kg} \quad \text{not} \quad 5.5 \text{ dJ/g}$$
$$2.5 \text{ kJ/s} \quad \text{not} \quad 2.5 \text{ J/ks}$$

In selecting prefixes, a prefix should be chosen so that the numerical value preferably lies between 0.1 and 1000. However, double prefixes and hyphenated prefixes should not be used. For example, use

$$\text{GJ} \quad \text{not} \quad \text{kMJ}$$

Capitalization

The general principle governing the writing of unit symbols is as follows: roman (upright) type, in general lower case, is used for symbols of units; however, if the symbols are derived from proper names, capital roman type is used (for the first letter), for example, K, N. These symbols are not followed by a full stop (period).

If the units are written in an unabbreviated form, the first letter is not capitalized (even for those derived from proper nouns): for example, kelvin, newton. The numerical prefixes are not capitalized except for symbols E (exa), P (peta), T (tera), G (giga), and M (mega).

Plurals

The unit symbols remain the same in the plural form. In unabbreviated form the plural units are written in the usual manner. For example:

$$45 \text{ newtons} \quad \text{or} \quad 45 \text{ N}$$
$$22 \text{ centimeters} \quad \text{or} \quad 25 \text{ cm}$$

Punctuation

For a numerical value less than one, a zero should precede the decimal point. The SI symbols should not be followed by a period, except at the end of a sentence. English-speaking countries use a centered dot for a decimal point; others use a comma. Large numbers should be grouped into threes (thousands) by using spaces instead of commas. For example,

$$3\ 456\ 789.291\ 22$$

not

$$3, 456, 789.291, 22$$

Derived Units

The product of two or more units may be written in either of the following ways:

$$N \cdot m \qquad N\,m$$

A solidus (oblique stroke, /), a horizontal line, or negative powers may be used to express a derived unit formed from two others by division. For example:

$$m/s \qquad \frac{m}{s} \qquad m \cdot s^{-1}$$

A solidus must not be repeated on the same line. In complicated cases, parentheses or negative powers should be used. For example:

$$m/s^2 \text{ or } m \cdot s^{-2} \qquad \text{but not} \qquad m/s/s$$

$$J/(s \cdot m \cdot K)^{-1} \qquad \text{or} \qquad J \cdot s^{-1} \cdot m^{-1} \cdot K^{-1} \qquad \text{but not} \qquad J/s/m/K$$

TABLE A.1.2
Useful Conversion Factors

Acceleration of gravity
$g = 9.80665 \text{ m/s}^2$
$g = 980.665 \text{ cm/s}^2$
$g = 32.174 \text{ ft/s}^2$
$1 \text{ ft/s}^2 = 0.304799 \text{ m/s}^2$

Area
$1 \text{ acre} = 4.046856 \times 10^3 \text{ m}^2$
$1 \text{ ft}^2 = 0.0929 \text{ m}^2$
$1 \text{ in}^2 = 6.4516 \times 10^{-4} \text{ m}^2$

Density
$1 \text{ lb}_m/\text{ft}^3 = 16.0185 \text{ kg/m}^3$
$1 \text{ lb}_m/\text{gal} = 1.198264 \times 10^2 \text{ kg/m}^3$
Density of dry air at 0°C, 760 mm Hg = 1.2929 g/liter
1 kg mol ideal gas at 0°C, 760 mm Hg = 22.414 m^3

Diffusivity
$1 \text{ ft}^2/\text{hr} = 2.581 \times 10^{-5} \text{ m}^2/\text{s}$

Energy
$1 \text{ Btu} = 1055 \text{ J} = 1.055 \text{ kJ}$
$1 \text{ Btu} = 252.16 \text{ cal}$
$1 \text{ kcal} = 4.184 \text{ kJ}$
$1 \text{ J} = 1 \text{ N} \cdot \text{m} = 1 \text{ kg} \cdot \text{m}^2/\text{s}^2$
$1 \text{ kW} \cdot \text{h} = 3.6 \times 10^3 \text{ kJ}$

Enthalpy
$1 \text{ Btu/lb}_m = 2.3258 \text{ kJ/kg}$

Force
$1 \text{ lb}_f = 4.4482 \text{ N}$
$1 \text{ N} = 1 \text{ kg} \cdot \text{m/s}^2$
$1 \text{ dyne} = 1 \text{ g} \cdot \text{cm/s}^2 = 10^{-5} \text{ kg} \cdot \text{m/s}^2$

Heat flow
$1 \text{ Btu/hr} = 0.29307 \text{ W}$
$1 \text{ Btu/min} = 17.58 \text{ W}$
$1 \text{ kJ/hr} = 2.778 \times 10^{-4} \text{ kW}$
$1 \text{ J/s} = 1 \text{ W}$

Heat flux
$1 \text{ Btu/hr} \cdot \text{ft}^2 = 3.1546 \text{ W/m}^2$

Heat transfer coefficient
$1 \text{ Btu/hr} \cdot \text{ft}^2 \cdot °\text{F} = 5.6783 \text{ W/m}^2 \cdot \text{K}$
$1 \text{ Btu/hr} \cdot \text{ft}^2 \cdot °\text{F} = 1.3571 \times 10^{-4} \text{ cal/s} \cdot \text{cm}^2 \cdot °\text{C}$

Length
$1 \text{ ft} = 0.3048 \text{ m}$
$1 \text{ micron} = 10^{-6} \text{ m} = 1 \text{ } \mu\text{m}$
$1 \text{ Å} = 10^{-10} \text{ m}$
$1 \text{ in} = 2.54 \times 10^{-2} \text{ m}$
$1 \text{ mile} = 1.609344 \times 10^3 \text{ m}$

Mass
$1 \text{ carat} = 2 \times 10^{-4} \text{ kg}$
$1 \text{ lb}_m = 0.45359 \text{ kg}$
$1 \text{ lb}_m = 16 \text{ oz} = 7000 \text{ grains}$
1 ton (metric) = 1000 kg8c05

(*continues*)

TABLE A.I.2 (*Continued*)

Mass transfer coefficient
  1 lb mole/hr · ft^2 · mol fraction = 1.3562×10^{-3} kg mol/s · m^2 · mol fraction
Power
  1 hp = 0.7457 kW
  1 W = 14.34 cal/min
  1 hp = 550 ft · lb$_f$/s
  1 Btu/hr = 0.29307 W
  1 hp = 0.7068 Btu/s
  1 J/s = 1 W
Pressure
  1 psia = 6.895 kPa
  1 psia = 6.895×10^3 N/m^2
  1 bar = 1×10^5 Pa = 1×10^5 N/m^2
  1 Pa = 1 N/m^2
  1 mm Hg (0°C) = 1.333224×10^2 N/m^2
  1 atm = 29.921 in. Hg at 0°C
  1 atm = 33.90 ft H$_2$O at 4°C
  1 atm = 14.696 psia = 1.01325×10^5 N/m^2
  1 atm = 1.01325 bars
  1 atm = 760 mm Hg at 0°C = 1.01325×10^5 Pa
  1 lb$_f$/ft^2 = 4.788×10^2 dyne/cm^2 = 47.88 N/m^2
Specific heat
  1 Btu/lb$_m$ · °F = 4.1865 J/g · K
  1 Btu/lb$_m$ · °F = 1 cal/g · °C
Temperature
  $T_{°F} = T_{°C} \times 1.8 + 32$
  $T_{°C} = (T_{°F} - 32)/1.8$
Thermal conductivity
  1 Btu/hr · ft · °F = 1.731 W/m · K
  1 Btu · in./ft^2 · hr · °F = 1.442279×10^{-2} W/m · K
Viscosity
  1 lb$_m$/ft · hr = 0.4134 cp
  1 lb$_m$/ft · s = 1488.16 cp
  1 cp = 10^{-2} g/cm · s = 10^{-2} poise
  1 cp = 10^{-3} Pa · s = 10^{-3} kg/m · s = 10^{-3} N · s/m^2
  1 lb$_f$ s/ft^2 = 4.7879×10^4 cp
  1 N · s/m^2 = 1 Pa · s
  1 kg/m · s = 1 Pa · s
Volume
  1 ft^3 = 0.02832 m^3
  1 U.S. gal = 3.785×10^{-3} m^3
  1 liter = 1000 cm^3
  1 m^3 = 1000 liter
  1 U.S. gal = 4 qt
  1 ft^3 = 7.481 U.S. gal
  1 British gal = 1.20094 U.S. gal
Work
  1 hp · hr = 0.7457 kW · hr
  1 hp · hr = 2544.5 Btu
  1 ft · lb$_f$ = 1.35582 J

TABLE A.1.3
Conversion Factors for Pressure

	$lb_f/in.^2$	kPa	kg_f/cm^2	in. Hg (at 21°C)	mm Hg (at 21°C)	in. H_2O (at 21°C)	atm
1 $lb_f/in.^2$ =	1	689.473×10^{-2}	0.07031	2.036	51.715	27.71	0.06805
1 kPa =	0.1450383	1	101.972×10^{-4}	0.2952997	7.5003	4.0188	986.923×10^{-5}
1 kg_f/cm^2 =	14.2234	980.665×10^{-1}	1	28.959	735.550	394.0918	967.841×10^{-3}
1 in. Hg (21°C) =	0.4912	338.64×10^{-2}	0.03452	1	25.40	13.608	0.03342
1 mm Hg (21°C) =	0.01934	0.1333273	1.359×10^{-3}	0.03937	1	0.5398	1.315×10^{-3}
1 in. H_2O (21°C) =	0.03609	24.883×10^{-2}	2.537×10^{-3}	0.0735	1.8665	1	2.458×10^{-3}
1 atm =	14.6959	101.3251	1.03323	29.9212	760	406	1

A.2 Physical Properties of Foods

TABLE A.2.1
Specific Heats of Foods

Produce	Water	Protein	Carbohydrate	Fat	Ash	Eq. (4.2) (kJ/kg · K)	Eq. (4.3) (kJ/kg · K)	Experimental[a] (kJ/kg · K)
Beef (hamburger)	68.3	20.7	0.0	10.0	1.0	3.39	3.35	3.52
Fish, canned	70.0	27.1	0.0	0.3	2.6	3.43	3.35	
Starch	12.0	0.5	87.0	0.2	0.3	1.976	1.754	
Orange juice	87.5	0.8	11.1	0.2	0.4	3.873	3.822	
Liver, raw beef	74.9	15.0	0.9	9.1	1.1	3.554	3.525	
Dry milk, nonfat	3.5	35.6	52.0	1.0	7.9	1.763	1.520	
Butter	15.5	0.6	0.4	81.0	2.5	2.064	2.043	2.051–2.135
Milk, whole pasteurized	87.0	3.5	4.9	3.9	0.7	3.860	3.831	3.852
Blueberries, syrup pack	73.0	0.4	23.6	0.4	2.6	3.508	3.445	
Cod, raw	82.6	15.0	0.0	0.4	2.0	3.751	3.697	
Skim milk	90.5	3.5	5.1	0.1	0.8	3.948	3.935	3.977–4.019
Tomato soup, concentrate	81.4	1.8	14.6	1.8	0.4	3.718	3.676	
Beef, lean	77.0	22.0	—	—	1.0	3.559	3.579	
Egg yolk	49.0	13.0	—	11.0	1.0	2.905	2.449	2.810
Fish, fresh	76.0	19.0	—	—	1.4	3.617	3.500	3.600
Beef, lean	71.7	21.6	0.0	5.7	1.0	3.458	3.437	3.433
Potato	79.8	2.1	17.1	0.1	0.9	3.680	3.634	3.517
Apple, raw	84.4	0.2	14.5	0.6	0.3	3.793	3.759	3.726–4.019
Bacon	49.9	27.6	0.3	17.5	4.7	2.926	2.851	2.01
Cucumber	96.1	0.5	1.9	0.1	1.4	4.090	4.061	4.103
Blackberry, syrup pack	76.0	0.7	22.9	0.2	0.2	3.588	3.521	
Potato	75.0	0.0	23.0	0.0	2.0	3.559	3.483	3.517
Veal	68.0	21.0	0.0	10.0	1.0	3.383	3.349	3.223
Fish	80.0	15.0	4.0	0.3	0.7	3.684	3.651	3.60
Cheese, cottage	65.0	25.0	1.0	2.0	7.0	3.307	3.215	3.265
Shrimp	66.2	26.8	0.0	1.4	0.0	3.337	3.404	3.014
Sardines	57.4	25.7	1.2	11.0	0.0	3.115	3.002	3.014
Beef, roast	60.0	25.0	0.0	13.0	0.0	3.081	3.115	3.056
Carrot, fresh	88.2	1.2	9.3	0.3	1.1	3.889	3.864	3.81–3.935

Source: Adapted from Heldman and Singh (1981).
[a] Experimental specific heat values from Reidy (1968).

TABLE A.2.2
Thermal Conductivity of Selected Food Products

Product	Moisture content (%)	Temperature (°C)	Thermal conductivity (W/m · K)
Apple	85.6	2–36	0.393
Applesauce	78.8	2–36	0.516
Beef, freeze dried			
1000 mm Hg pressure	—	0	0.065
0.001 mm Hg pressure	—	0	0.037
Beef, lean			
Perpendicular to fibers	78.9	7	0.476
Perpendicular to fibers	78.9	62	0.485
Parallel to fibers	78.7	8	0.431
Parallel to fibers	78.7	61	0.447
Beef fat	—	24–38	0.19
Butter	15	46	0.197
Cod	83	2.8	0.544
Corn, yellow dust	0.91	8–52	0.141
	30.2	8–52	0.172
Egg, frozen whole	—	−10 to −6	0.97
Egg, white	—	36	0.577
Egg, yolk	—	33	0.338
Fish muscle	—	0–10	0.557
Grapefruit, whole	—	30	0.45
Honey	12.6	2	0.502
	80	2	0.344
	14.8	69	0.623
	80	69	0.415
Juice, apple	87.4	20	0.559
	87.4	80	0.632
	36.0	20	0.389
	36.0	80	0.436
Lamb			
Perpendicular to fiber	71.8	5	0.45
		61	0.478
Parallel to fiber	71.0	5	0.415
		61	0.422
Milk	—	37	0.530
Milk, condensed	90	24	0.571
	—	78	0.641
	50	26	0.329
	—	78	0.364

(*continues*)

TABLE A.2.2 (*Continued*)

Product	Moisture content (%)	Temperature (°C)	Thermal conductivity (W/m · K)
Milk, skimmed	—	1.5	0.538
	—	80	0.635
Milk, nonfat dry	4.2	39	0.419
Olive oil	—	15	0.189
	—	100	0.163
Oranges, combined	—	30	0.431
Peas, black-eyed	—	3–17	0.312
Pork			
Perpendicular to fibers	75.1	6	0.488
		60	0.54
Parallel to fibers	75.9	4	0.443
		61	0.489
Pork fat	—	25	0.152
Potato, raw flesh	81.5	1–32	0.554
Potato, starch gel	—	1–67	0.04
Poultry, broiler muscle	69.1–74.9	4–27	0.412
Salmon			
Perpendicular	73	4	0.502
Salt	—	87	0.247
Sausage mixture	65.72	24	0.407
Soybean oil meal	13.2	7–10	0.069
Strawberries	—	14 to 25	0.675
Sugars	—	29–62	0.087–0.22
Turkey, breast			
Perpendicular to fibers	74	3	0.502
Parallel to fibers	74	3	0.523
Veal			
Perpendicular to fibers	75	6	0.476
		62	0.489
Parallel to fibers	75	5	0.441
		60	0.452
Vegetable and animal oils	—	4–187	0.169
Wheat flour	8.8	43	0.45
		65.5	0.689
		1.7	0.542
Whey		80	0.641

Source: Reidy (1968).

TABLE A.2.3
Thermal Diffusivity of Some Foodstuffs

Product	Water content (% wt.)	Temperature[a] (°C)	Thermal diffusivity ($\times 10^{-7}$ m^2/s)
Fruits, vegetables, and by-products			
Apple, whole, Red Delicious	85	0–30	1.37
Applesauce	37	5	1.05
	37	65	1.12
	80	5	1.22
	80	65	1.40
	—	26–129	1.67
Avocado, flesh	—	24, 0	1.24
Seed	—	24, 0	1.29
Whole	—	41, 0	1.54
Banana, flesh	76	5	1.18
	76	65	1.42
Beans, baked	—	4–122	1.68
Cherries, tart, flesh	—	30, 0	1.32
Grapefruit, Marsh, flesh	88.8	—	1.27
Grapefruit, Marsh, albedo	72.2	—	1.09
Lemon, whole	—	40, 0	1.07
Lima bean, pureed	—	26–122	1.80
Pea, pureed	—	26–128	1.82
Peach, whole	—	27, 4	1.39
Potato, flesh	—	25	1.70
Potato, mashed, cooked	78	5	1.23
	78	65	1.45
Rutabaga	—	48, 0	1.34
Squash, whole	—	47, 0	1.71
Strawberry, flesh	92	5	1.27
Sugarbeet	—	14, 60	1.26
Sweet potato, whole	—	35	1.06
	—	55	1.39
	—	70	1.91
Tomato, pulp	—	4, 26	1.48
Fish and meat products			
Codfish	81	5	1.22
	81	65	1.42
Corned beef	65	5	1.32
	65	65	1.18
Beef, chuck[b]	66	40–65	1.23
Beef, round[b]	71	40–65	1.33
Beef, tongue[b]	68	40–65	1.32
Halibut	76	40–65	1.47
Ham, smoked	64	5	1.18
Ham, smoked	64	40–65	1.38
Water	—	30	1.48
	—	65	1.60
Ice	—	0	11.82

Source: Singh (1982). Reprinted from *Food Technology* **36**(2), 87–91. Copyright © by Institute of Food Technologists.
[a]Where two temperatures separated by a comma are given, the first is the initial temperature of the sample, and the second is that of the surroundings.
[b]Data are applicable only where juices that exuded during heating remain in the food samples.

TABLE A.2.4
Viscosity of Liquid Foods

Product	Composition	Temperature (°C)	Viscosity (Pa · s)
Cream	10% fat	40	0.00148
	10% fat	60	0.00107
	10% fat	80	0.00083
Cream	20% fat	60	0.00171
	30% fat	60	0.00289
	40% fat	60	0.00510
Homogenized milk	—	20	0.0020
	—	40	0.0015
	—	60	0.000775
	—	80	0.0006
Raw milk	—	0	0.00344
	—	10	0.00264
	—	20	0.00199
	—	30	0.00149
	—	40	0.00123
Corn oil	—	25	0.0565
	—	38	0.0317
Cottonseed oil	—	20	0.0704
	—	38	0.0306
Peanut oil	—	25	0.0656
	—	38	0.0251
Safflower oil	—	25	0.0522
	—	38	0.0286
Soybean oil	—	30	0.04
Honey, buckwheat	18.6% T.S.	24.8	3.86
sage	18.6% T.S.	25.9	8.88
white clover	18.2% T.S.	25.0	4.80
Apple juice	20° Brix	27	0.0021
	60° Brix	27	0.03
Grape juice	20° Brix	27	0.0025
	60° Brix	27	0.11
Corn syrup	48.4% T.S.	27	0.053

Source: Steffe (1983).

TABLE A.2.5
Properties of Ice as a Function of Temperature

Temperature (°C)	Thermal conductivity (W/m · K)	Specific heat (kJ/kg · K)	Density (kg/m³)
− 101	3.50	1.382	925.8
− 73	3.08	1.587	924.2
− 45.5	2.72	1.783	922.6
− 23	2.41	1.922	919.4
− 18	2.37	1.955	919.4
− 12	2.32	1.989	919.4
− 7	2.27	2.022	917.8
0	2.22	2.050	916.2

Source: Adapted from Dickerson (1969).

TABLE A.2.6
Approximate Heat Evolution Rates of Fresh Fruits and Vegetables
When Stored at Temperatures Shown

Commodity	Watts per megagram (W/Mg)[a]			
	0°C	5°C	10°C	15°C
Apples	10–12	15–21	41–61	41–92
Apricots	15–17	19–27	33–56	63–101
Artichokes, globe	67–133	94–177	161–291	229–429
Asparagus	81–237	161–403	269–902	471–970
Avocados	—	59–89	—	183–464
Bananas, ripening	—	—	65–116	87–164
Beans, green or snap	—	101–103	161–172	251–276
Beans, lima (unshelled)	31–89	58–106	—	296–369
Beets, red (roots)	16–21	27–28	35–40	50–69
Blackberries	46–68	85–135	154–280	208–431
Blueberries	7–31	27–36	69–104	101–183
Broccoli, sprouting	55–63	102–474	—	514–1000
Brussels sprouts	46–71	95–143	186–250	282–316
Cabbage	12–40	28–63	36–86	66–169
Cantaloupes	15–17	26–30	46	100–114
Carrots, topped	46	58	93	117
Cauliflower	53–71	61–81	100–144	136–242
Celery	21	32	58–81	110
Cherries, sour	17–39	38–39	—	81–148
Cherries, sweet	12–16	28–42	—	74–133
Corn, sweet	125	230	331	482
Cranberries	—	12–14	—	—
Cucumbers	—	—	68–86	71–98
Figs, Mission	—	32–39	65–58	145–187
Garlic	9–32	17–29	27–29	32–81
Gooseberries	20–26	36–40	—	64–95
Grapefruit	—	—	20–27	35–38
Grapes, American	8	16	23	47
Grapes, European	4–7	9–17	24	30–35
Honeydew melons	—	9–15	24	35–47
Horseradish	24	32	78	97
Kohlrabi	30	48	93	145
Leeks	28–48	58–86	158–201	245–346
Lemons	9	15	33	47
Lettuce, head	27–50	39–59	64–118	114–121
Lettuce, leaf	68	87	116	186
Mushrooms	83–129	210	297	—
Nuts, kind not specified	2	5	10	10
Okra	—	163	258	431

(*continues*)

TABLE A.2.6 (*Continued*)

Commodity	Watts per megagram (W/Mg)[a]			
	0°C	5°C	10°C	15°C
Onions	7–9	10–20	21	33
Onions, green	31–66	51–201	107–174	195–288
Olives	—	—	—	64–115
Oranges	9	14–19	35–40	38–67
Peaches	11–19	19–27	46	98–125
Pears	8–20	15–46	23–63	45–159
Peas, green (in pod)	90–138	163–226	—	529–599
Peppers, sweet	—	—	43	68
Plums, Wickson	6–9	12–27	27–34	35–37
Potatoes, immature	—	35	42–62	42–92
Potatoes, mature	—	17–20	20–30	20–35
Radishes, with tops	43–51	57–62	92–108	207–230
Radishes, topped	16–17	23–24	45–47	82–97
Raspberries	52–74	92–114	82–164	243–300
Rhubarb, topped	24–39	32–54	—	92–134
Spinach	—	136	327	529
Squash, yellow	35–38	42–55	103–108	222–269
Strawberries	36–52	48–98	145–280	210–273
Sweet potatoes	—	—	39–95	47–85
Tomatoes, mature green	—	21	45	61
Tomatoes, ripening	—	—	42	79
Turnips, roots	26	28–30	—	63–71
Watermelons	—	9–12	22	—

[a]Conversion factor: (watts per megagram) × 74.12898 = Btu per ton per 24 hr. From American Society of Heating, Refrigerating and Air-Conditioning Engineers; with permission of the American Society of Heating, Refrigerating, and Air-Conditioning Engineers, Atlanta, Georgia (1978).

TABLE A.2.7
Enthalpy of Frozen Foods

Temperature (°C)	Beef (kJ/kg)	Lamb (kJ/kg)	Poultry (kJ/kg)	Fish (kJ/kg)	Beans (kJ/kg)	Broccoli (kJ/kg)	Peas (kJ/kg)	Mashed potatoes (kJ/kg)	Cooked rice (kJ/kg)
−28.9	14.7	19.3	11.2	9.1	4.4	4.2	11.2	9.1	18.1
−23.3	27.7	31.4	23.5	21.6	16.5	16.3	23.5	21.6	31.9
−17.8	42.6	45.4	37.7	35.6	29.3	28.8	37.7	35.6	47.7
−12.2	62.8	67.2	55.6	52.1	43.7	42.8	55.6	52.1	70.0
−9.4	77.7	84.2	68.1	63.9	52.1	51.2	68.1	63.9	87.5
−6.7	101.2	112.6	87.5	80.7	63.3	62.1	87.5	80.7	115.1
−5.6	115.8	130.9	99.1	91.2	69.8	67.9	99.1	91.2	133.0
−4.4	136.9	157.7	104.4	105.1	77.9	75.6	104.4	105.1	158.9
−3.9	151.6	176.8	126.8	115.1	83.0	80.7	126.8	115.1	176.9
−3.3	170.9	201.6	141.6	128.2	90.2	87.2	141.6	128.2	177.9
−2.8	197.2	228.2	142.3	145.1	99.1	95.6	142.3	145.1	233.5
−2.2	236.5	229.8	191.7	170.7	112.1	107.7	191.7	170.7	242.3
−1.7	278.2	231.2	240.9	212.1	132.8	126.9	240.9	212.1	243.9
−1.1	280.0	232.8	295.4	295.1	173.7	165.1	295.4	295.1	245.6
1.7	288.4	240.7	304.5	317.7	361.9	366.8	304.5	317.7	254.9
4.4	297.9	248.4	313.8	327.2	372.6	377.5	313.8	327.2	261.4
7.2	306.8	256.3	323.1	336.5	383.3	388.2	323.1	336.5	269.3
10.0	315.8	263.9	332.1	346.3	393.8	398.9	332.1	346.3	277.2
15.6	333.5	279.6	350.5	365.4	414.7	420.3	350.5	365.4	292.8

Source: Mott (1964), by permission of H. G. Goldstein, editor of *Aust. Refrig. Air Cond. Heat.*

A.3   Physical Properties of Nonfood Materials

TABLE A.3.1
Physical Properties of Metals

Metal	Properties at 20°C			
	ρ (kg/m^3)	c_p $(kJ/kg \cdot °C)$	k $(W/m \cdot °C)$	α $(\times 10^{-5} \ m^2/s)$
Aluminum				
Pure	2,707	0.896	204	8.418
Al–Cu (Duralumin, 94–96% Al, 3–5% Cu, trace Mg)	2,787	0.883	164	6.676
Al–Si (Silumin, copper-bearing: 86.5% Al, 1% Cu)	2,659	0.867	137	5.933
Al–Si (Alusil, 78–80% Al, 20–22% Si)	2,627	0.854	161	7.172
Al–Mg–Si, 97% Al, 1% Mg, 1% Si, 1% Mn	2,707	0.892	177	7.311
Lead	11,373	0.130	35	2.343
Iron				
Pure	7,897	0.452	73	2.034
Steel				
(C max ≈ 1.5%):				
Carbon steel				
C ≈ 0.5%	7,833	0.465	54	1.474
1.0%	7,801	0.473	43	1.172
1.5%	7,753	0.486	36	0.970
Nickel steel				
Ni ≈ 0%	7,897	0.452	73	2.026
20%	7,933	0.46	19	0.526
40%	8,169	0.46	10	0.279
80%	8,618	0.46	35	0.872
Invar 36% Ni	8,137	0.46	10.7	0.286
Chrome steel				
Cr = 0%	7,897	0.452	73	2.026
1%	7,865	0.46	61	1.665
5%	7,833	0.46	40	1.110
20%	7,689	0.46	22	0.635
Cr–Ni (chrome–nickel)				
15% Cr, 10% Ni	7,865	0.46	19	0.526
18% Cr, 8% Ni (V2A)	7,817	0.46	16.3	0.444
20% Cr, 15% Ni	7,833	0.46	15.1	0.415
25% Cr, 20% Ni	7,865	0.46	12.8	0.361

(continues)

TABLE A.3.1 (*Continued*)

Metal	ρ (kg/m^3)	c_p (kJ/kg $\cdot$ °C)	k (W/m $\cdot$ °C)	α ($\times 10^{-5}$ m^2/s)
Tungsten steel				
W = 0%	7,897	0.452	73	2.026
W = 1%	7,913	0.448	66	1.858
W = 5%	8,073	0.435	54	1.525
W = 10%	8,314	0.419	48	1.391
Copper				
Pure	8,954	0.3831	386	11.234
Aluminum bronze (95% Cu, 5% Al)	8,666	0.410	83	2.330
Bronze (75% Cu, 25% Sn)	8,666	0.343	26	0.859
Red brass (85% Cu, 9% Sn, 6% Zn)	8,714	0.385	61	1.804
Brass (70% Cu, 30% Zn)	8,522	0.385	111	3.412
German silver (62% Cu, 15% Ni, 22% Zn)	8,618	0.394	24.9	0.733
Constantan (60% Cu, 40% Ni)	8,922	0.410	22.7	0.612
Magnesium				
Pure	1,746	1.013	171	9.708
Mg–Al (electrolytic), 6–8% Al, 1–2% Zn	1,810	1.00	66	3.605
Molybdenum	10,220	0.251	123	4,790
Nickel				
Pure (99.9%)	8,906	0.4459	90	2.266
Ni–Cr (90% Ni, 10% Cr)	8,666	0.444	17	0.444
80% Ni, 20% Cr	8,314	0.444	12.6	0.343
Silver				
Purest	10,524	0.2340	419	17.004
Pure (99.9%)	10,524	0.2340	407	16.563
Tin, pure	7,304	0.2265	64	3.884
Tungsten	19,350	0.1344	163	6.271
Zinc, pure	7,144	0.3843	112.2	4.106

Source: Adapted from Holman (1990). Reproduced with permission of the publisher.

TABLE A.3.2
Physical Properties of Nonmetals

Substance	Temperature (°C)	k (W/m · °C)	ρ (kg/m³)	c (kJ/kg · °C)	α ($\times 10^{-7}$ m²/s)
Asphalt	20–55	0.74–0.76			
Brick					
Building brick, common	20	0.69	1600	0.84	5.2
Fireclay brick, burnt 133°C	500	1.04	2000	0.96	5.4
	800	1.07			
	1100	1.09			
Cement, Portland		0.29	1500		
Mortar	23	1.16			
Concrete, cinder	23	0.76			
Glass, window	20	0.78 (avg)	2700	0.84	3.4
Plaster, gypsum	20	0.48	1440	0.84	4.0
Metal lath	20	0.47			
Wood lath	20	0.28			
Stone					
Granite		1.73–3.98	2640	0.82	8–18
Limestone	100–300	1.26–1.33	2500	0.90	5.6–5.9
Marble		2.07–2.94	2500–2700	0.80	10–13.6
Sandstone	40	1.83	2160–2300	0.71	11.2–11.9
Wood (across the grain)					
Cypress	30	0.097	460		
Fir	23	0.11	420	2.72	0.96
Maple or oak	30	0.166	540	2.4	1.28
Yellow pine	23	0.147	640	2.8	0.82
White pine	30	0.112	430		
Asbestos					
Loosely packed	−45	0.149			
	0	0.154	470–570	0.816	3.3–4
	100	0.161			
Sheets	51	0.166			
Cardboard, corrugated	—	0.064			
Corkboard, 160 kg/m³	30	0.043	160		
Cork, regranulated	32	0.045	45–120	1.88	2–5.3
Ground	32	0.043	150		
Diatomaceous earth (Sil-o-cel)	0	0.061	320		
Fiber, insulating board	20	0.048	240		
Glass wool, 24 kg/m³	23	0.038	24	0.7	22.6
Magnesia, 85%	38	0.067	270		
	93	0.071			
	150	0.074			
	204	0.080			
Rock wool, 24 kg/m³	32	0.040	160		
Loosely packed	150	0.067	64		
	260	0.087			
Sawdust	23	0.059			
Wood shavings	23	0.059			

Source: Adapted from Holman (1990). Reproduced with permission of the publisher.

A.4 Physical Properties of Water and Air

TABLE A.4.1
Physical Properties of Water at the Saturation Pressure

Temperature		Density ρ	Coefficient of volumetric thermal expansion β	Specific heat c_p	Thermal conductivity k	Thermal diffusivity α	Absolute viscosity μ	Kinematic viscosity ν	Prandtl number Pr
t (°C)	T (K)	(kg/m^3)	$(\times 10^{-4}\ K^{-1})$	$(kJ/kg \cdot K)$	$(W/m \cdot K)$	$(\times 10^{-6}\ m^2/s)$	$(\times 10^{-6}\ Pa \cdot s)$	$(\times 10^{-6}\ m^2/s)$	
0	273.15	999.9	−0.7	4.226	0.558	0.131	1793.636	1.789	13.7
5	278.15	1000.0	—	4.206	0.568	0.135	1534.741	1.535	11.4
10	283.15	999.7	0.95	4.195	0.577	0.137	1296.439	1.300	9.5
15	288.15	999.1	—	4.187	0.587	0.141	1135.610	1.146	8.1
20	293.15	998.2	2.1	4.182	0.597	0.143	993.414	1.006	7.0
25	298.15	997.1	—	4.178	0.606	0.146	880.637	0.884	6.1
30	303.15	995.7	3.0	4.176	0.615	0.149	792.377	0.805	5.4
35	308.15	994.1	—	4.175	0.624	0.150	719.808	0.725	4.8
40	313.15	992.2	3.9	4.175	0.633	0.151	658.026	0.658	4.3
45	318.15	990.2	—	4.176	0.640	0.155	605.070	0.611	3.9
50	323.15	988.1	4.6	4.178	0.647	0.157	555.056	0.556	3.55
55	328.15	985.7	—	4.179	0.652	0.158	509.946	0.517	3.27
60	333.15	983.2	5.3	4.181	0.658	0.159	471.650	0.478	3.00
65	338.15	980.6	—	4.184	0.663	0.161	435.415	0.444	2.76
70	343.15	977.8	5.8	4.187	0.668	0.163	404.034	0.415	2.55

75	348.15	974.9	—	4.190	0.671	0.164	376.575	0.366	2.23
80	353.15	971.8	6.3	4.194	0.673	0.165	352.059	0.364	2.25
85	358.15	968.7	—	4.198	0.676	0.166	328.523	0.339	2.04
90	363.15	965.3	7.0	4.202	0.678	0.167	308.909	0.326	1.95
95	368.15	961.9	—	4.206	0.680	0.168	292.238	0.310	1.84
100	373.15	958.4	7.5	4.211	0.682	0.169	277.528	0.294	1.75
110	383.15	951.0	8.0	4.224	0.684	0.170	254.973	0.268	1.57
120	393.15	943.5	8.5	4.232	0.685	0.171	235.360	0.244	1.43
130	403.15	934.8	9.1	4.250	0.686	0.172	211.824	0.226	1.32
140	413.15	926.3	9.7	4.257	0.684	0.172	201.036	0.212	1.23
150	423.15	916.9	10.3	4.270	0.684	0.173	185.346	0.201	1.17
160	433.15	907.6	10.8	4.285	0.680	0.173	171.616	0.191	1.10
170	443.15	897.3	11.5	4.396	0.679	0.172	162.290	0.181	1.05
180	453.15	886.6	12.1	4.396	0.673	0.172	152.003	0.173	1.01
190	463.15	876.0	12.8	4.480	0.670	0.171	145.138	0.166	0.97
200	473.15	862.8	13.5	4.501	0.665	0.170	139.254	0.160	0.95
210	483.15	852.8	14.3	4.560	0.655	0.168	131.409	0.154	0.92
220	493.15	837.0	15.2	4.605	0.652	0.167	124.544	0.149	0.90
230	503.15	827.3	16.2	4.690	0.637	0.164	119.641	0.145	0.88
240	513.15	809.0	17.2	4.731	0.634	0.162	113.757	0.141	0.86
250	523.15	799.2	18.6	4.857	0.618	0.160	109.834	0.137	0.86

Source: Adapted from Raznjevic (1978).

TABLE A.4.2
Properties of Saturated Steam

Temperature (°C)	Vapor pressure (kPa)	Specific volume (m³/kg) Liquid	Specific volume (m³/kg) Saturated vapor	Enthalpy (kJ/kg) Liquid (H_c)	Enthalpy (kJ/kg) Saturated vapor (H_v)	Entropy (kJ/kg · K) Liquid	Entropy (kJ/kg · K) Saturated vapor
0.01	0.6113	0.0010002	206.136	0.00	2501.4	0.0000	9.1562
3	0.7577	0.0010001	168.132	12.57	2506.9	0.0457	9.0773
6	0.9349	0.0010001	137.734	25.20	2512.4	0.0912	9.0003
9	1.1477	0.0010003	113.386	37.80	2517.9	0.1362	8.9253
12	1.4022	0.0010005	93.784	50.41	2523.4	0.1806	8.8524
15	1.7051	0.0010009	77.926	62.99	2528.9	0.2245	8.7814
18	2.0640	0.0010014	65.038	75.58	2534.4	0.2679	8.7123
21	2.487	0.0010020	54.514	88.14	2539.9	0.3109	8.6450
24	2.985	0.0010027	45.883	100.70	2545.4	0.3534	8.5794
27	3.567	0.0010035	38.774	113.25	2550.8	0.3954	8.5156
30	4.246	0.0010043	32.894	125.79	2556.3	0.4369	8.4533
33	5.034	0.0010053	28.011	138.33	2561.7	0.4781	8.3927
36	5.947	0.0010063	23.940	150.86	2567.1	0.5188	8.3336
40	7.384	0.0010078	19.523	167.57	2574.3	0.5725	8.2570
45	9.593	0.0010099	15.258	188.45	2583.2	0.6387	8.1648
50	12.349	0.0010121	12.032	209.33	2592.1	0.7038	8.0763
55	15.758	0.0010146	9.568	230.23	2600.9	0.7679	7.9913
60	19.940	0.0010172	7.671	251.13	2609.6	0.8312	7.9096
65	25.03	0.0010199	6.197	272.06	2618.3	0.8935	7.8310
70	31.19	0.0010228	5.042	292.98	2626.8	0.9549	7.7553
75	38.58	0.0010259	4.131	313.93	2635.3	1.0155	7.6824
80	47.39	0.0010291	3.407	334.91	2643.7	1.0753	7.6122
85	57.83	0.0010325	2.828	355.90	2651.9	1.1343	7.5445
90	70.14	0.0010360	2.361	376.92	2660.1	1.1925	7.4791
95	84.55	0.0010397	1.9819	397.96	2668.1	1.2500	7.4159
100	101.35	0.0010435	1.6729	419.04	2676.1	1.3069	7.3549
105	120.82	0.0010475	1.4194	440.15	2683.8	1.3630	7.2958
110	143.27	0.0010516	1.2102	461.30	2691.5	1.4185	7.2387
115	169.06	0.0010559	1.0366	482.48	2699.0	1.4734	7.1833
120	198.53	0.0010603	0.8919	503.71	2706.3	1.5276	7.1296
125	232.1	0.0010649	0.7706	524.99	2713.5	1.5813	7.0775
130	270.1	0.0010697	0.6685	546.31	2720.5	1.6344	7.0269
135	313.0	0.0010746	0.5822	567.69	2727.3	1.6870	6.9777
140	316.3	0.0010797	0.5089	589.13	2733.9	1.7391	6.9299
145	415.4	0.0010850	0.4463	610.63	2740.3	1.7907	6.8833
150	475.8	0.0010905	0.3928	632.20	2746.5	1.8418	6.8379
155	543.1	0.0010961	0.3468	653.84	2752.4	1.8925	6.7935
160	617.8	0.0011020	0.3071	675.55	2758.1	1.9427	6.7502
165	700.5	0.0011080	0.2727	697.34	2763.5	1.9925	6.7078
170	791.7	0.0011143	0.2428	719.21	2768.7	2.0419	6.6663
175	892.0	0.0011207	0.2168	741.17	2773.6	2.0909	6.6256
180	1002.1	0.0011274	0.19405	763.22	2778.2	2.1396	6.5857
190	1254.4	0.0011414	0.15654	807.62	2786.4	2.2359	6.5079
200	1553.8	0.0011565	0.12736	852.45	2793.2	2.3309	6.4323
225	2548	0.0011992	0.07849	966.78	2803.3	2.5639	6.2503
250	3973	0.0012512	0.05013	1085.36	2801.5	2.7927	6.0730
275	5942	0.0013168	0.03279	1210.07	2785.0	3.0208	5.8938
300	8581	0.0010436	0.02167	1344.0	2749.0	3.2534	5.7045

Source: Abridged from Keenan *et al.* (1969). Copyright © 1969 by John Wiley and Sons. Reprinted by permission of John Wiley and Sons, Inc.

TABLE A.4.3
Properties of Superheated Steam (Steam Table)

Absolute pressure [in kPa, with sat. temp., °C][a]		Temperature (°C)							
		100	150	200	250	300	360	420	500
10 (45.81)	V	17.196	19.512	21.825	24.136	26.445	29.216	31.986	35.679
	H	2687.5	2783.0	2879.5	2977.3	3076.5	3197.6	3320.9	3489.1
	s	8.4479	8.6882	8.9038	9.1002	9.2813	9.4821	9.6682	9.8978
50 (81.33)	V	3.418	3.889	4.356	4.820	5.284	5.839	6.394	7.134
	H	2682.5	2780.1	2877.7	2976.0	3075.5	3196.8	3320.4	3488.7
	s	7.6947	7.9401	8.1580	8.3556	8.5373	8.7385	8.9249	9.1546
75	V	2.270	2.587	2.900	3.211	3.520	3.891	4.262	4.755
(91.78)	H	2679.4	2778.2	2876.5	2975.2	3074.9	3196.4	3320.0	3488.4
	s	7.5009	7.7496	7.9690	8.1673	8.3493	8.5508	8.7374	8.9672
100	V	1.6958	1.9364	2.172	2.406	2.639	2.917	3.195	3.565
(99.63)	H	2676.2	2776.4	2875.3	2974.3	3074.3	3195.9	3319.6	3488.1
	s	7.3614	7.6134	7.8343	8.0333	8.2158	8.4175	8.6042	8.8342
150	V		1.2853	1.4443	1.6012	1.7570	1.9432	2.129	2.376
(111.37)	H		2772.6	2872.9	2972.7	3073.1	3195.0	3318.9	3487.6
	s		7.4193	7.6433	7.8438	8.0720	8.2293	8.4163	8.6466
400	V		0.4708	0.5342	0.5951	0.6458	0.7257	0.7960	0.8893
(143.63)	H		2752.8	2860.5	2964.2	3066.8	3190.3	3315.3	3484.9
	s		6.9299	7.1706	7.3789	7.5662	7.7712	7.9598	8.1913
700	V			0.2999	0.3363	0.3714	0.4126	0.4533	0.5070
(164.97)	H			2844.8	2953.6	3059.1	3184.7	3310.9	3481.7
	s			6.8865	7.1053	7.2979	7.5063	7.6968	7.9299

(*continues*)

TABLE A.4.3 (*Continued*)

Absolute pressure [in kPa, with sat. temp., °C][a]		100	150	200	250	300	360	420	500
						Temperature (°C)			
1000 (179.91)	V			0.2060	0.2327	0.2579	0.2873	0.3162	0.3541
	H			2827.9	2942.6	3051.2	3178.9	3306.5	3478.5
	s			6.6940	6.9247	7.1229	7.3349	7.5275	7.7622
1500 (198.32)	V			0.13248	0.15195	0.16966	0.18988	0.2095	0.2352
	H			2796.8	2923.3	3037.6	3.1692	3299.1	3473.1
	s			6.4546	6.7090	6.9179	7.1363	7.3323	7.5698
2000 (212.42)	V				0.11144	0.12547	0.14113	0.15616	0.17568
	H				2902.5	3023.5	3159.3	3291.6	3467.6
	s				6.5453	6.7664	6.9917	7.1915	7.4317
2500 (223.99)	V				0.08700	0.09890	0.11186	0.12414	0.13998
	H				2880.1	3008.8	3149.1	3284.0	3462.1
	s				6.4085	6.6438	6.8767	7.0803	7.3234
3000 (233.90)	V				0.07058	0.08114	0.09233	0.10279	0.11619
	H				2855.8	2993.5	3138.7	3276.3	3456.5
	s				6.2872	6.5390	6.7801	6.9878	7.2338

Source: Abridged from Keenan *et al.* (1969). Copyright © 1969 by John Wiley and Sons. Reprinted by permission of John Wiley and Sons, Inc.

[a]V, Specific volume, m^3/kg; H, enthalpy, kJ/kg; s, entropy, $kJ/kg \cdot K$.

TABLE A.4.4
Physical Properties of Dry Air at Atmospheric Pressure

Temperature t (°C)	T (K)	Density (ρ) (kg/m³)	Volumetric coefficient of expansion (β) ($\times 10^{-3}$ K⁻¹)	Specific heat (c_p) (kJ/kg·K)	Thermal conductivity (k) (W/m·K)	Thermal diffusivity (α) ($\times 10^{-6}$ m²/s)	Viscosity (μ) ($\times 10^{-6}$ N·s/m²)	Kinematic viscosity (ν) ($\times 10^{-6}$ m²/s)	Prandtl number (Pr)
−20	253.15	1.365	3.97	1.005	0.0226	16.8	16.279	12.0	0.71
0	273.15	1.252	3.65	1.011	0.0237	19.2	17.456	13.9	0.71
10	283.15	1.206	3.53	1.010	0.0244	20.7	17.848	14.66	0.71
20	293.15	1.164	3.41	1.012	0.0251	22.0	18.240	15.7	0.71
30	303.15	1.127	3.30	1.013	0.0258	23.4	18.682	16.58	0.71
40	313.15	1.092	3.20	1.014	0.0265	24.8	19.123	17.6	0.71
50	323.15	1.057	3.10	1.016	0.0272	26.2	19.515	18.58	0.71
60	333.15	1.025	3.00	1.017	0.0279	27.6	19.907	19.4	0.71
70	343.15	0.996	2.91	1.018	0.0286	29.2	20.398	20.65	0.71
80	353.15	0.968	2.83	1.019	0.0293	30.6	20.790	21.5	0.71
90	363.15	0.942	2.76	1.021	0.0300	32.2	21.231	22.82	0.71
100	373.15	0.916	2.69	1.022	0.0307	33.6	21.673	23.6	0.71
120	393.15	0.870	2.55	1.025	0.0320	37.0	22.555	25.9	0.71
140	413.15	0.827	2.43	1.027	0.0333	40.0	23.340	28.2	0.71
150	423.15	0.810	2.37	1.028	0.0336	41.2	23.732	29.4	0.71
160	433.15	0.789	2.31	1.030	0.0344	43.3	24.124	30.6	0.71
180	453.15	0.755	2.20	1.032	0.0357	47.0	24.909	33.0	0.71
200	473.15	0.723	2.11	1.035	0.0370	49.7	25.693	35.5	0.71
250	523.15	0.653	1.89	1.043	0.0400	60.0	27.557	42.2	0.71

Source: Adapted from Raznjevic (1978).

A.5   A Psychrometric Chart

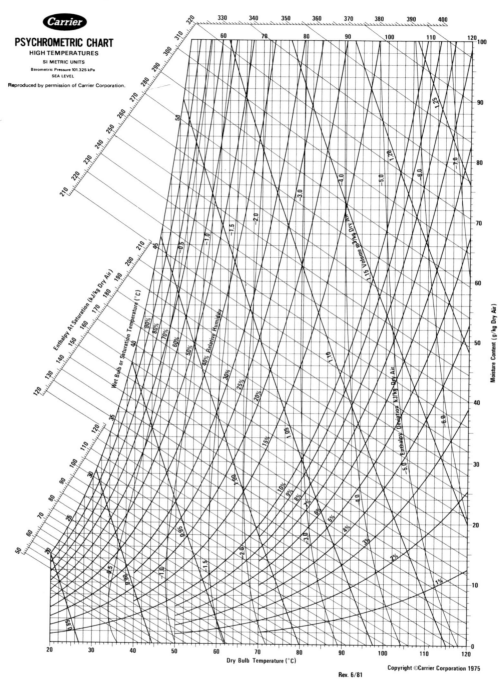

Reproduced with permission of Carrier Corporation. (Full-sized copies of this chart, suitable for tracing, may be obtained from Carrier Corporation, P.O. Box 4808, Carrier Parkway, Syracuse, New York 13221.)

A.6   Pressure–Enthalpy Data

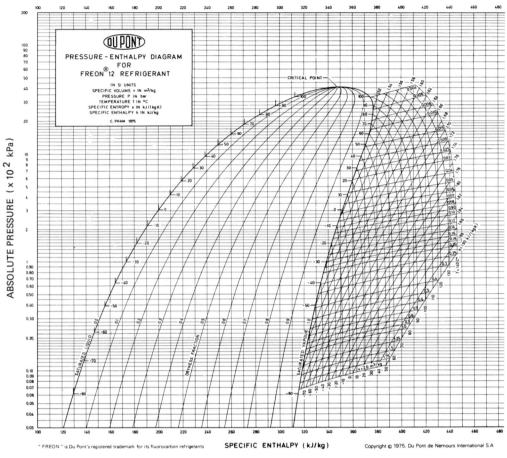

Fig. A.6.1 Pressure–enthalpy diagram for Refrigerant 12. [Reproduced by permission of Du Pont de Nemours International S.A. (Full-sized copies of diagrams for Freon 12 and other refrigerants, suitable for tracing, may be obtained from Du Pont de Nemours International S.A., 9, Route des Jeunes, CH-1211 Geneva 24, Switzerland.)]

TABLE A.6.1
Properties of Saturated Liquid and Vapor R-12^a

t (°C)	P (kPa)	Enthalpy (kJ/kg)		Entropy (kJ/kg · K)		Specific volume (L/kg)	
		h_f	h_g	s_f	s_g	v_f	v_g
− 60	22.62	146.463	324.236	0.77977	1.61373	0.63689	637.911
− 55	29.98	150.808	326.567	0.79990	1.60552	0.64226	491.000
− 50	39.15	155.169	328.897	0.81964	1.59810	0.64782	383.105
− 45	50.44	159.549	331.223	0.83901	1.59142	0.65355	302.683
− 40	64.17	163.948	333.541	0.85805	1.58539	0.65949	241.910
− 35	80.71	168.369	335.849	0.86776	1.57996	0.66563	195.398
− 30	100.41	172.810	338.143	0.89516	1.57507	0.67200	159.375
− 28	109.27	174.593	339.057	0.90244	1.57326	0.67461	147.275
− 26	118.72	176.380	339.968	0.90967	1.57152	0.67726	136.284
− 24	128.80	178.171	340.876	0.91686	1.56985	0.67996	126.282
− 22	139.53	179.965	341.780	0.92400	1.56825	0.68269	117.167
− 20	150.93	181.764	342.682	0.93110	1.56672	0.68547	108.847
− 18	163.04	183.567	343.580	0.93816	1.56526	0.68829	101.242
− 16	175.89	185.374	344.474	0.94518	1.56385	0.69115	94.2788
− 14	189.50	187.185	345.365	0.95216	1.56250	0.69407	87.8951
− 12	203.90	189.001	346.252	0.95910	1.56121	0.69703	82.0344
− 10	219.12	190.822	347.134	0.96601	1.55997	0.70004	76.6464
− 9	227.04	191.734	347.574	0.96945	1.55938	0.70157	74.1155
− 8	235.19	192.647	348.012	0.97287	1.55897	0.70310	71.6864
− 7	243.55	193.562	348.450	0.97629	1.55822	0.70465	69.3543
− 6	252.14	194.477	348.886	0.97971	1.55765	0.70622	67.1146
− 5	260.96	195.395	349.321	0.98311	1.55710	0.70780	64.9629
− 4	270.01	196.313	349.755	0.98650	1.55657	0.70939	62.8952
− 3	279.30	197.233	350.187	0.98989	1.55604	0.71099	60.9075
− 2	288.82	198.154	350.619	0.99327	1.55552	0.71261	58.9963
− 1	298.59	199.076	351.049	0.99664	1.55502	0.71425	57.1579
0	308.61	200.000	351.477	1.00000	1.55452	0.71590	55.3892
1	318.88	200.925	351.905	1.00335	1.55404	0.71756	53.6869
2	329.40	201.852	352.331	1.00670	1.55356	0.71324	52.0481
3	340.19	202.780	352.755	1.01004	1.55310	0.72094	50.4700
4	351.24	203.710	353.179	1.01337	1.55264	0.72265	48.9499
5	363.55	204.642	353.600	1.01670	1.55220	0.72438	47.4853
6	374.14	205.575	354.020	1.02001	1.55176	0.72612	46.0737
7	386.01	206.509	354.439	1.02333	1.55133	0.72788	44.7129
8	398.15	207.445	354.856	1.02663	1.55091	0.72966	43.4006
9	410.58	208.383	355.272	1.02993	1.55050	0.73146	42.1349
10	423.30	209.323	355.686	1.03322	1.55010	0.73326	40.9137
11	436.31	210.264	356.098	1.03650	1.54970	0.73510	39.7352
12	449.62	211.207	356.509	1.03978	1.54931	0.73695	38.5975
13	463.23	212.152	356.918	1.04305	1.54893	0.73882	37.4991
14	477.14	213.099	357.325	1.04632	1.54856	0.74071	36.4382
15	491.37	214.048	357.730	1.04958	1.54819	0.74262	35.4133
16	505.91	214.998	358.134	1.05284	1.54783	0.74455	34.4230
17	520.76	215.951	358.535	1.05609	1.54748	0.74649	33.4658
18	535.94	216.906	358.935	1.05933	1.54713	0.74846	32.5405
19	551.45	217.863	359.333	1.06258	1.54679	0.75045	31.6457
20	567.29	218.821	359.729	1.06581	1.54645	0.75246	30.7802

(continues)

TABLE A.6.1 (*Continued*)

t (°C)	P (kPa)	Enthalpy (kJ/kg) h_f	Enthalpy (kJ/kg) h_g	Entropy (kJ/kg · K) s_f	Entropy (kJ/kg · K) s_g	Specific volume (L/kg) v_f	Specific volume (L/kg) v_g
21	583.47	219.783	360.122	1.06904	1.54612	0.75449	29.9429
22	599.98	220.746	360.514	1.07227	1.54579	0.75655	29.1327
23	616.84	221.712	360.904	1.07549	1.54547	0.75863	28.3485
24	634.05	222.680	361.291	1.07871	1.54515	0.76073	27.5894
25	651.62	223.650	361.676	1.08193	1.54484	0.76286	26.8542
26	669.54	224.623	362.059	1.08514	1.54453	0.76501	26.1442
27	687.82	225.598	362.439	1.08835	1.54423	0.76718	25.4524
28	706.47	226.576	362.817	1.09155	1.54393	0.76938	24.7840
29	725.50	227.557	363.193	1.09475	1.54363	0.77161	24.1362
30	744.90	228.540	363.566	1.09795	1.54334	0.77386	23.5082
31	764.68	229.526	363.937	1.10115	1.54305	0.77614	22.8993
32	784.85	230.515	364.305	1.10434	1.54276	0.77845	22.3088
33	805.41	231.506	364.670	1.10753	1.54247	0.78079	21.7359
34	826.36	232.501	365.033	1.11072	1.54219	0.78316	21.1802
35	847.72	233.498	365.392	1.11391	1.54191	0.78556	20.6408
36	869.48	234.499	365.749	1.11710	1.54163	0.78799	20.1173
37	891.64	235.503	366.103	1.12028	1.54135	0.79045	19.6091
38	914.23	236.510	366.454	1.12347	1.54107	0.79294	19.1156
39	937.23	237.521	366.802	1.12665	1.54079	0.79546	18.6362
40	960.65	238.535	367.146	1.12984	1.54051	0.79802	18.1706
41	984.51	239.552	267.487	1.13302	1.54024	0.80062	17.7182
42	1008.8	240.574	367.825	1.13620	1.53996	0.80325	17.2785
43	1033.5	241.598	368.160	1.13938	1.53968	0.80592	16.8511
44	1058.7	242.627	368.491	1.14257	1.53941	0.80863	16.4356
45	1084.3	243.659	368.818	1.14575	1.53913	0.81137	16.0316
46	1110.4	244.696	369.141	1.14894	1.53885	0.81416	15.6386
47	1136.9	245.736	369.461	1.15213	1.53856	0.81698	15.2563
48	1163.9	246.781	369.777	1.15532	1.53828	0.81985	14.8844
49	1191.4	247.830	370.088	1.15851	1.53799	0.82277	14.5224
50	1219.3	248.884	370.396	1.16170	1.53770	0.82573	14.1701
52	1276.6	251.004	370.997	1.16810	1.53712	0.83179	13.4931
54	1335.9	253.144	371.581	1.17451	1.53651	0.83804	12.8509
56	1397.2	255.304	372.145	1.18093	1.53589	0.84451	12.2412
58	1460.5	257.486	372.688	1.18738	1.53524	0.85121	11.6620
60	1525.9	259.690	373.210	1.19384	1.53457	0.85814	11.1113
62	1593.5	261.918	373.707	1.20034	1.53387	0.86534	10.5872
64	1663.2	264.172	374.180	1.20686	1.53313	0.87282	10.0881
66	1735.1	266.452	374.625	1.21342	1.53235	0.88059	9.61234
68	1809.3	268.762	375.042	1.22001	1.53153	0.88870	9.15844
70	1885.8	271.102	375.427	1.22665	1.53066	0.89716	8.72502
75	2087.5	277.100	376.234	1.24347	1.52821	0.92009	7.72258
80	2304.6	283.341	376.777	1.26069	1.52526	0.94612	6.82143
85	2538.0	289.879	376.985	1.27845	1.52164	0.97621	6.00494
90	2788.5	296.788	376.748	1.29691	1.51708	1.01190	5.25759
95	3056.9	304.181	375.887	1.31637	1.51113	1.05581	4.56341
100	3344.1	312.261	374.070	1.33732	1.50296	1.11311	3.90280

Source: Stoecker (1988).
[a]Subscripts: f = liquid, g = gas.

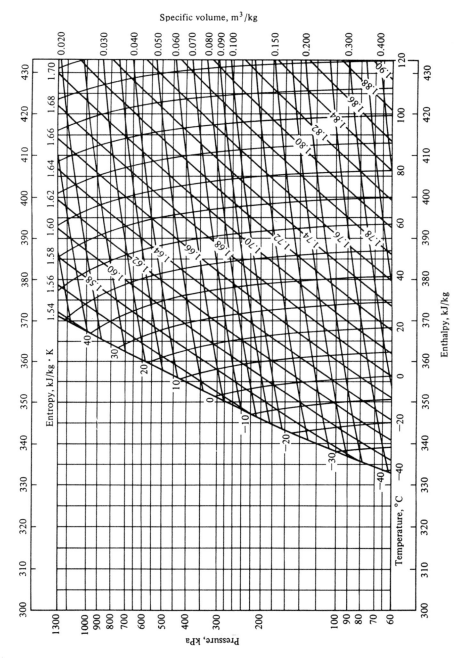

Fig. A.6.2 Pressure–enthalpy diagram of superheated R-12 vapor. (Courtesy, Technical University of Denmark).

TABLE A.6.2
Properties of Saturated Liquid and Vapor R-717 (Ammonia)[a]

t (°C)	P (kPa)	Enthalpy (kJ/kg)		Entropy (kJ/kg · K)		Specific volume (L/kg)	
		h_f	h_g	s_f	s_g	v_f	v_g
− 60	21.99	− 69.5330	1373.19	− 0.10909	6.6592	1.4010	4685.08
− 55	30.29	− 47.5062	1382.01	− 0.00717	6.5454	1.4126	3474.22
− 50	41.03	− 25.4342	1390.64	− 0.09264	6.4382	1.4245	2616.51
− 45	54.74	− 3.3020	1399.07	− 0.19049	6.3369	1.4367	1998.91
− 40	72.01	18.9024	1407.26	0.28651	6.2410	1.4493	1547.36
− 35	93.49	41.1883	1415.20	0.38082	6.1501	1.4623	1212.49
− 30	119.90	63.5629	1422.86	0.47351	6.0636	1.4757	960.867
− 28	132.02	72.5387	1425.84	0.51015	6.0302	1.4811	878.100
− 26	145.11	81.5300	1428.76	0.54655	5.9974	1.4867	803.761
− 24	159.22	90.5370	1431.64	0.58272	5.9652	1.4923	736.868
− 22	174.41	99.5600	1434.46	0.61865	5.9336	1.4980	676.570
− 20	190.74	108.599	1437.23	0.65436	5.9025	1.5037	622.122
− 18	208.26	117.656	1439.94	0.68984	5.8720	1.5096	572.875
− 16	227.04	126.729	1442.60	0.72511	5.8420	1.5155	528.257
− 14	247.14	135.820	1445.20	0.76016	5.8125	1.5215	487.769
− 12	268.63	144.929	1447.74	0.79501	5.7835	1.5276	450.971
− 10	291.57	154.056	1450.22	0.82965	5.7550	1.5338	417.477
− 9	303.60	158.628	1451.44	0.84690	5.7409	1.5369	401.860
− 8	316.02	163.204	1452.64	0.86410	5.7269	1.5400	386.944
− 7	328.84	167.785	1453.83	0.88125	5.7131	1.5432	372.692
− 6	342.07	172.371	1455.00	0.89835	5.6993	1.5464	359.071
− 5	355.71	176.962	1456.15	0.91541	5.6856	1.5496	346.046
− 4	369.77	181.559	1457.29	0.93242	5.6721	1.5528	333.589
− 3	384.26	186.161	1458.42	0.94938	5.6586	1.5561	321.670
− 2	399.20	190.768	1459.53	0.96630	5.6453	1.5594	310.263
− 1	414.58	195.381	1460.62	0.98317	5.6320	1.5627	299.340
0	430.43	200.000	1461.70	1.00000	5.6189	1.5660	288.880
1	446.74	204.625	1462.76	1.01679	5.6058	1.5694	278.858
2	463.53	209.256	1463.80	1.03354	5.5929	1.5727	269.253
3	480.81	213.892	1464.83	1.05024	5.5800	1.5762	260.046
4	498.59	218.535	1465.84	1.06691	5.5672	1.5796	251.216
5	516.87	223.185	1466.84	1.08353	5.5545	1.5831	242.745
6	535.67	227.841	1467.82	1.10012	5.5419	1.5866	234.618
7	555.00	232.503	1468.78	1.11667	5.5294	1.5901	226.817
8	574.87	237.172	1469.72	1.13317	5.5170	1.5936	219.326
9	595.28	241.848	1470.64	1.14964	5.5046	1.5972	212.132
10	616.25	246.531	1471.57	1.16607	5.4924	1.6008	205.221
11	637.78	251.221	1472.46	1.18246	5.4802	1.6045	198.580
12	659.89	255.918	1473.34	1.19882	5.4681	1.6081	192.196
13	682.59	260.622	1474.20	1.21515	5.4561	1.6118	186.058
14	705.88	265.334	1475.05	1.23144	5.4441	1.6156	180.154

(*continues*)

TABLE A.6.2 (*Continued*)

t (°C)	P (kPa)	Enthalpy (kJ/kg)		Entropy (kJ/kg · K)		Specific volume (L/kg)	
		h_f	h_g	s_f	s_g	v_f	v_g
15	729.29	270.053	1475.88	1.24769	5.4322	1.6193	174.475
16	754.31	274.779	1476.69	1.26391	5.4204	1.6231	169.009
17	779.46	279.513	1477.48	1.28010	5.4087	1.6269	163.748
18	805.25	284.255	1478.25	1.29626	5.3971	1.6308	158.683
19	831.69	289.005	1479.01	1.31238	5.3855	1.6347	153.804
20	858.79	293.762	1479.75	1.32847	5.3740	1.6386	149.106
21	886.57	298.527	1480.48	1.34452	5.3626	1.6426	144.578
22	915.03	303.300	1481.18	1.36055	5.3512	1.6466	140.214
23	944.18	308.081	1481.87	1.37654	5.3399	1.6507	136.006
24	974.03	312.870	1482.53	1.39250	5.3286	1.6547	131.950
25	1004.6	316.667	1483.18	1.40843	5.3175	1.6588	128.037
26	1035.9	322.471	1483.81	1.42433	4.3063	1.6630	124.261
27	1068.0	327.284	1484.42	1.44020	5.2953	1.6672	120.619
28	1100.7	332.104	1485.01	1.45064	5.2843	1.6714	117.103
29	1134.3	336.933	1485.59	1.47185	5.2733	1.6757	113.708
30	1168.6	341.769	1486.14	1.48762	5.2624	1.6800	110.430
31	1203.7	346.614	1486.67	1.50337	5.2516	1.6844	107.263
32	1239.6	351.466	1487.18	1.51908	5.2408	1.6888	104.205
33	1276.3	356.326	1487.66	1.53477	5.2300	1.6932	101.248
34	1313.9	361.195	1488.13	1.55042	5.2193	1.6977	98.3913
35	1352.2	366.072	1488.57	1.56605	5.2086	1.7023	95.6290
36	1391.5	370.957	1488.99	1.58165	5.1980	1.7069	92.9579
37	1431.5	375.851	1489.39	1.59722	5.1874	1.7115	90.3743
38	1472.4	380.754	1489.76	1.61276	5.1768	1.7162	87.8748
39	1514.3	385.666	1490.10	1.62828	5.1663	1.7209	85.4561
40	1557.0	390.587	1490.42	1.64377	5.1558	1.7257	83.1150
41	1600.6	395.519	1490.71	1.65924	5.1453	1.7305	80.8484
42	1645.1	400.462	1490.98	1.67470	5.1349	1.7354	78.6536
43	1690.6	405.416	1491.21	1.69013	5.1244	1.7404	76.5276
44	1737.0	410.382	1491.41	1.70554	5.1140	1.7454	74.4678
45	1784.3	415.362	1491.58	1.72095	5.1036	1.7504	72.4716
46	1832.6	420.358	1491.72	1.73635	5.0932	1.7555	70.5365
47	1881.9	425.369	1491.83	1.75174	5.0827	1.7607	68.6602
48	1932.2	430.399	1491.88	1.76714	5.0723	1.7659	66.8403
49	1983.5	435.450	1491.91	1.78255	5.0618	1.7712	65.0746
50	2035.9	440.523	1491.89	1.79798	5.0514	1.7766	63.3608
51	2089.2	445.623	1491.83	1.81343	5.0409	1.7820	61.6971
52	2143.6	450.751	1491.73	1.82891	5.0303	1.7875	60.0813
53	2199.1	455.913	1491.58	1.84445	5.0198	1.7931	58.5114
54	2255.6	461.112	1491.38	1.86004	5.0092	1.7987	56.9855
55	2313.2	466.353	1491.12	1.87571	4.9985	1.8044	55.5019

Source: Stoecker (1988).
[a]Subscripts: f = liquid, g = gas.

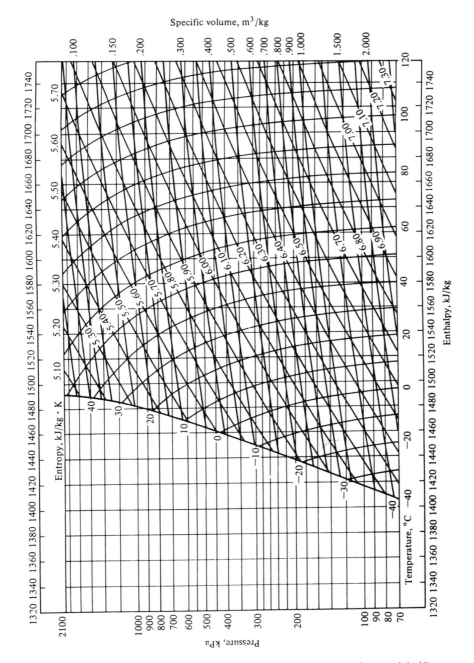

Fig. A.6.3   Pressure–enthalpy diagram of superheated R-717 vapor (ammonia). (Courtesy, Technical University of Denmark).

A.7 Symbols for Use in Drawing Food Engineering Process Equipment (Adapted from British and American Standards)

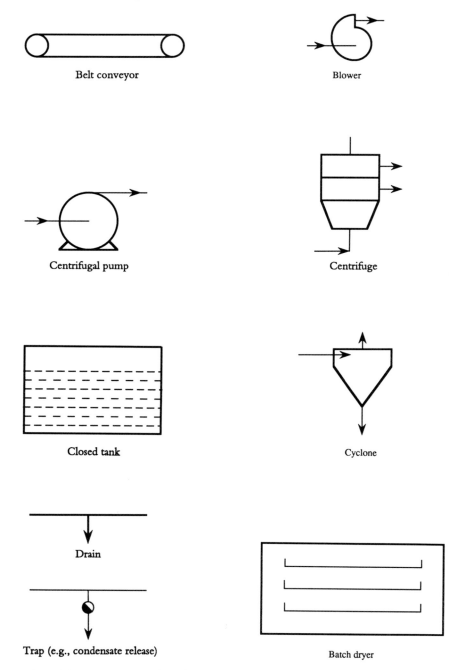

Belt conveyor

Blower

Centrifugal pump

Centrifuge

Closed tank

Cyclone

Drain

Trap (e.g., condensate release)

Batch dryer

Adapted from D. G. Austin (1979). "Chemical Engineering Drawing Symbols." John Wiley & Sons Inc., New York.

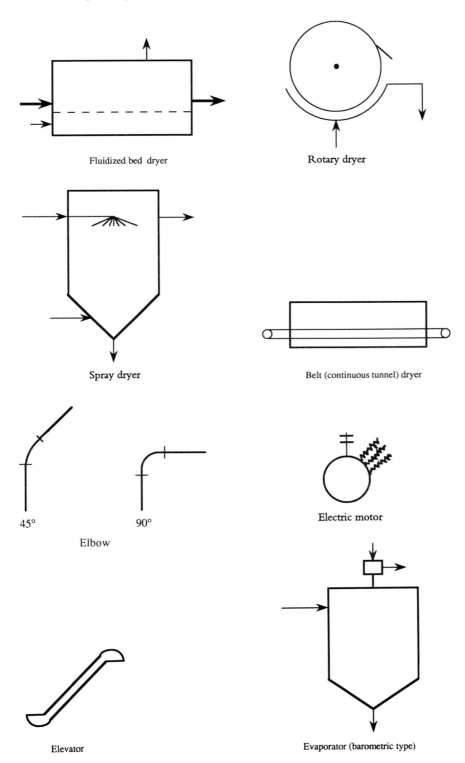

Fluidized bed dryer

Rotary dryer

Spray dryer

Belt (continuous tunnel) dryer

45°   90°

Elbow

Electric motor

Elevator

Evaporator (barometric type)

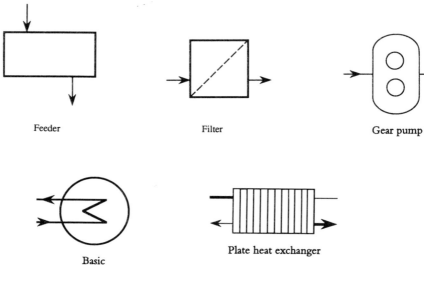

Feeder

Filter

Gear pump

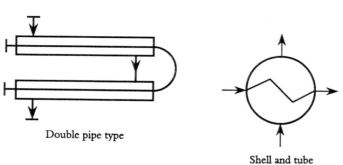

Basic

Plate heat exchanger

Double pipe type

Shell and tube

Heat exchangers

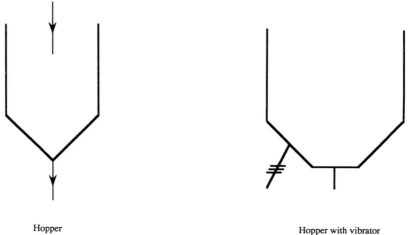

Hopper

Hopper with vibrator

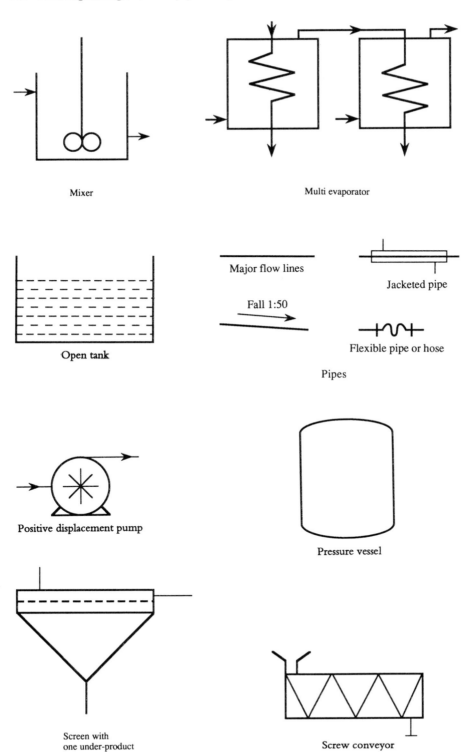

Mixer

Multi evaporator

Open tank

Major flow lines

Fall 1:50

Pipes

Jacketed pipe

Flexible pipe or hose

Positive displacement pump

Pressure vessel

Screen with
one under-product

Screw conveyor

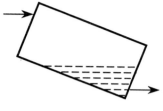

Settling tank

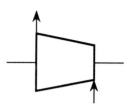

Turbine

In-line valve

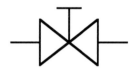

Screw down valve

Globe valve

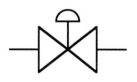

Diaphragm valve

Valves

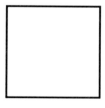

Vessel

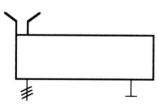

Vibrator feeder

Bibliography

American Society of Agricultural Engineers (1982). "Agricultural Engineers Yearbook," ASAE, St. Joseph, Michigan.

American Society of Heating, Refrigerating and Air Conditioning Engineers, Inc. (1978). "Handbook and Product Directory. 1978 Applications." ASHRAE, Atlanta, Georgia.

Dickerson, R. W., Jr. (1969). Thermal properties of foods. *In* "The Freezing Preservation of Foods, 4th ed.," Vol. 2. (D. K. Tressler, W. B. Van Arsdel, and M. J. Copley, eds.) pp. 26–51. AVI Publ. Co., Westport, Connecticut.

Heldman, D. R., and Singh, R. P. (1981). "Food Process Engineering," 2nd ed. AVI Publ. Co., Westport, Connecticut.

Holman, J. P. (1990). "Heat Transfer," 7th ed. McGraw-Hill, New York.

Keenan, J. H., Keyes, F. G., Hill, P. G., and Moore, J. G. (1969). "Steam Tables—Metric Units." Wiley, New York.

Ranznevic, K. (1978). "Handbook of Thermodynamic Tables and Charts." Hemisphere Publ. Corp., Washington, D.C.

Reidy, G. A. (1968). Thermal properties of foods and methods of their determination. M.S. Thesis, Food Science Department, Michigan State University, East Lansing.

Singh, R. P. (1982). Thermal diffusivity in food processing. *Food Technol.* **36**(2), 87–91.

Steffe, J. F. (1983). Rheological properties of liquid foods. ASAE Paper No. 83-6512. ASAE, St. Joseph, Michigan.

Stoecker, W. F. (1988). "Industrial Refrigeration." Business News Publishing Company, Troy, Michigan.

Index

Examples and problems solved in the text can be found under the entry "Applications."

FOOD SCIENCE AND TECHNOLOGY

International Series

Maynard A. Amerine, Rose Marie Pangborn, and Edward B. Roessler, *Principles of Sensory Evaluation of Food*. 1965.

Martin Glicksman, *Gum Technology in the Food Industry*. 1970.

C. R. Stumbo, *Thermobacteriology in Food Processing*, second edition. 1973.

Aaron M. Altschul (ed.), *New Protein Foods*: Volume 1, Technology, Part A—1974. Volume 2, Technology, Part B—1976. Volume 3, Animal Protein Supplies, Part A—1978. Volume 4, Animal Protein Supplies, Part B—1981. Volume 5, Seed Storage Proteins—1985.

S. A. Goldblith, L. Rey, and W. W. Rothmayr, *Freeze Drying and Advanced Food Technology*. 1975.

R. B. Duckworth (ed.), *Water Relations of Food*. 1975.

John A. Troller and J. H. B. Christian, *Water Activity and Food*. 1978.

A. E. Bender, *Food Processing and Nutrition*. 1978.

D. S. Osborne and P. Voogt, *The Analysis of Nutrients in Foods*. 1978.

Marcel Loncin and R. L. Merson, *Food Engineering: Principles and Selected Applications*. 1979.

J. G. Vaughan (ed.), *Food Microscopy*. 1979.

J. R. A. Pollock (ed.), *Brewing Science*, Volume 1—1979. Volume 2—1980. Volume 3—1987.

J. Christopher Bauernfeind (ed.), *Carotenoids as Colorants and Vitamin A Precursors: Technological and Nutritional Applications*. 1981.

Pericles Markakis (ed.), *Anthocyanins as Food Colors*. 1982.

George F. Stewart and Maynard A. Amerine (eds.), *Introduction to Food Science and Technology*, second edition. 1982.

Malcolm C. Bourne, *Food Texture and Viscosity: Concept and Measurement*. 1982.

Héctor A. Iglesias and Jorge Chirife, *Handbook of Food Isotherms: Water Sorption Parameters for Food and Food Components*. 1982.

Colin Dennis (ed.), *Post-Harvest Pathology of Fruits and Vegetables*. 1983.

P. J. Barnes (ed.), *Lipids in Cereal Technology*. 1983.

David Pimentel and Carl W. Hall (eds.), *Food and Energy Resources*. 1984.

Joe M. Regenstein and Carrie E. Regenstein, *Food Protein Chemistry: An Introduction for Food Scientists*. 1984.

Maximo C. Gacula, Jr., and Jagbir Singh, *Statistical Methods in Food and Consumer Research*. 1984.

Fergus M. Clydesdale and Kathryn L. Wiemer (eds.), *Iron Fortification of Foods*. 1985.

Robert V. Decareau, *Microwaves in the Food Processing Industry*. 1985.

S. M. Herschdoerfer (ed.), *Quality Control in the Food Industry*, second edition. Volume 1—1985. Volume 2—1985. Volume 3—1986. Volume 4—1987.

Walter M. Urbain, *Food Irradiation*. 1986.

Peter J. Bechtel (ed.), *Muscle as Food*. 1986.

H. W.-S. Chan (ed.), *Autoxidation of Unsaturated Lipids*. 1986.

F. E. Cunningham and N. A. Cox (eds.), *Microbiology of Poultry Meat Products*. 1987.

Chester O. McCorkle, Jr. (ed.), *Economics of Food Processing in the United States*. 1987.

J. Solms, D. A. Booth, R. M. Dangborn, and O. Raunhardt (eds.), *Food Acceptance and Nutrition*. 1987.

Jethro Jagtiani, Harvey T. Chan, Jr., and Williams S. Sakai (eds.), *Tropical Fruit Processing*, 1988.

R. Macrae (ed.), *HPLC in Food Analysis*, second edition. 1988.

A. M. Pearson and R. B. Young, *Muscle and Meat Biochemistry*. 1989.

Dean O. Cliver (ed.), *Foodborne Diseases*. 1990.

Majorie P. Penfield and Ada Marie Campbell, *Experimental Food Science*, third edition. 1990.

Leroy C. Blankenship (ed.), *Colonization Control of Human Bacterial Enteropathogens in Poultry*. 1991.

Yeshajahu Pomeranz, *Functional Properties of Food Components*, second edition. 1991.

Reginald H. Walter (ed.), *The Chemistry and Technology of Pectin*. 1991.

Herbert Stone and Joel L. Sidel, *Sensory Evaluation Practices*, second edition. 1993.

Robert L. Shewfelt and Stanley E. Prussia (eds.), *Postharvest Handling: A Systems Approach*. 1993.

R. Paul Singh and Dennis R. Heldman, *Introduction to Food Engineering*, second edition. 1993.

Tilak Nagodawithana and Gerald Reed (eds.), *Enzymes in Food Processing*, third edition. 1993.

Takayaki Shibamoto and Leonard Bjeldanes, *Introduction to Food Toxicology*. 1993.

Dallas G. Hoover and Larry R. Steenson (eds.), *Bacteriocins of Lactic Acid Bacteria*. 1993.

John A. Troller, *Sanitation in Food Processing*, second edition. 1993.

Ronald S. Jackson, *Wine Science: Principles and Applications*. In Preparation.

Robert G. Jensen, and Marvin P. Thompson (eds.), *Handbook of Milk Composition*. In Preparation

Tom Brody, *Nutritional Biochemistry*. In Preparation.